Microeconomics with Calculus

Begleitbuch zur Vorlesung Mikroökonomie
an den Universitäten Basel und Rostock

PEARSON

We work with leading authors to develop the strongest learning experiences, bringing cutting-edge thinking and best learning practice to a global market. We craft our print and digital resources to do more to help learners not only understand their content, but to see it in action and apply what they learn, whether studying or at work.

Pearson is the world's leading learning company. Our portfolio includes Penguin, Dorling Kindersley, the Financial Times and our educational business, Pearson International. We are also a leading provider of electronic learning programmes and of test development, processing and scoring services to educational institutions, corporations and professional bodies around the world.

Pearson Custom Publishing enables our customers to access a wide and expanding range of market-leading content from world-renowned authors and develop their own tailor-made book. You choose the content that meets your needs and Pearson Custom Publishing produces a high-quality printed book.

Every day our work helps learning flourish, and wherever learning flourishes, so do people.

To learn more please visit us at: www.pearsoncustom.co.uk

PEARSON CUSTOM PUBLISHING

Microeconomics with Calculus

Begleitbuch zur Vorlesung Mikroökonomie
an den Universitäten Basel und Rostock

Second Edition
Jeffrey M. Perloff

Zusammengestellt von
Georg Nöldeke, Universität Basel und
Philipp C. Wichardt, Universität Rostock

PEARSON

Harlow, England • London • New York • Boston • San Francisco • Toronto • Sydney • Auckland • Singapore • Hong Kong
Tokyo • Seoul • Taipei • New Delhi • Cape Town • Sao Paulo • Mexico City • Madrid • Amsterdam • Munich • Paris • Milan

Pearson Education Limited
Edinburgh Gate
Harlow
Essex CM20 2JE

And associated companies throughout the world

Visit us on the World Wide Web at:
www.pearsoned.co.uk

This Custom Book Edition © Pearson Education Limited 2013

Compiled from:

Microeconomics with Calculus
Second Edition
Jeffrey M. Perloff
ISBN 978 0 13 800847 5
© Pearson Education Limited 2011

All rights reserved. No part of this publication may be reproduced, stored in a retrieval system, or transmitted in any form or by any means, electronic, mechanical, photocopying, recording or otherwise, without either the prior written permission of the publisher or a licence permitting restricted copying in the United Kingdom issued by the Licensing Agency Ltd, Saffron House, 6–10 Kirby Street, London EC1N 8TS.

ISBN 978 1 78273 646 2

Printed and bound in Great Britain by Clays Ltd, Bungay, Suffolk.

Contents

Chapter 1 Introduction 1

1.1 **Microeconomics: The Allocation of Scarce Resources** 1
 Trade-Offs 2
 Who Makes the Decisions 2
 APPLICATION Flu Vaccine Shortage 2
 How Prices Determine Allocations 3
 APPLICATION Twinkie Tax 3

1.2 **Models** 3
 APPLICATION Income Threshold Model and China 4
 Simplifications by Assumption 4
 Testing Theories 5
 Maximizing Subject to Constraints 5
 Positive Versus Normative 6

1.3 **Uses of Microeconomic Models** 7
 Summary 8

Chapter 2 Supply and Demand 9

2.1 **Demand** 10
 The Demand Function 11
 Summing Demand Functions 15
 APPLICATION Aggregating the Demand for Broadband Service 15

2.2 **Supply** 16
 The Supply Function 16
 Summing Supply Functions 18
 How Government Import Policies Affect Supply Curves 19

2.3 **Market Equilibrium** 20
 Finding the Market Equilibrium 20
 Forces That Drive a Market to Equilibrium 21

2.4 **Shocking the Equilibrium: Comparative Statics** 22
 Comparative Statics with Discrete (Relatively Large) Changes 23
 APPLICATION Occupational Licensing 24
 Comparative Statics with Small Changes 24
 SOLVED PROBLEM 2.1 26
 Why the Shapes of Demand and Supply Curves Matter 27

2.5 **Elasticities** 28
 Demand Elasticity 28
 SOLVED PROBLEM 2.2 32
 APPLICATION Substitution May Save Endangered Species 33
 Supply Elasticity 34
 Long Run Versus Short Run 35
 APPLICATION Oil Drilling in the Arctic National Wildlife Refuge 36
 SOLVED PROBLEM 2.3 37

2.6 **Effects of a Sales Tax** 38
 Two Types of Sales Taxes 38
 Equilibrium Effects of a Specific Tax 39
 How Specific Tax Effects Depend on Elasticities 40
 SOLVED PROBLEM 2.4 41
 APPLICATION Gas Taxes and the Environment 42
 The Same Equilibrium No Matter Who Is Taxed 43
 The Similar Effects of Ad Valorem and Specific Taxes 44

2.7 **Quantity Supplied Need Not Equal Quantity Demanded** 44
 Price Ceiling 45
 APPLICATION Price Controls Kill 47
 Price Floor 48

2.8 **When to Use the Supply-and-Demand Model** 49
 Summary 51
 Questions 51
 Problems 54

Chapter 3 Consumer Theory 57

3.1 **Preferences** 58
 Properties of Consumer Preferences 59

APPLICATION Income Buys Happiness 60
Preference Maps 60
Indifference Curves 62
SOLVED PROBLEM 3.1 64

3.2 **Utility** 64
Utility Function 64
Ordinal Preferences 65
Utility and Indifference Curves 66
Willingness to Substitute Between Goods 67
SOLVED PROBLEM 3.2 69
APPLICATION *MRS* Between Recorded Tracks and Live Music 69
Curvature of Indifference Curves 70
SOLVED PROBLEM 3.3 72
APPLICATION Indifference Curves Between Food and Clothing 73

3.3 **Budget Constraint** 74

3.4 **Constrained Consumer Choice** 75
The Consumer's Optimal Bundle 76
APPLICATION Buying an SUV in the United States Versus Europe 78
SOLVED PROBLEM 3.4 79
Maximizing Utility Subject to a Constraint Using Calculus 81
SOLVED PROBLEM 3.5 83
SOLVED PROBLEM 3.6 85
SOLVED PROBLEM 3.7 85
APPLICATION Utility Maximization for Recorded Tracks and Live Music 86
Minimizing Expenditure 87
SOLVED PROBLEM 3.8 88

3.5 **Behavioral Economics** 89
Tests of Transitivity 89
Endowment Effect 90
APPLICATION How You Ask the Question Matters 91
Salience 91

Summary 92
Questions 93
Problems 95

Chapter 4 Demand 97

4.1 **Deriving Demand Curves** 98
System of Demand Equations 98
Graphical Interpretation 100
APPLICATION Calling It Quits on Smoking 103

4.2 **Effects of an Increase in Income** 103
How Income Changes Shift Demand Curves 103
SOLVED PROBLEM 4.1 105
Consumer Theory and Income Elasticities 106
SOLVED PROBLEM 4.2 110

4.3 **Effects of a Price Increase** 111
Income and Substitution Effects with a Normal Good 112
Income and Substitution Effects with an Inferior Good 113
Compensated Demand Curve 114
Slutsky Equation 116
SOLVED PROBLEM 4.3 117
SOLVED PROBLEM 4.4 119
APPLICATION Shipping the Good Stuff Away 120

4.4 **Cost-of-Living Adjustment** 120
Inflation Indexes 120
Effects of Inflation Adjustments 122
SOLVED PROBLEM 4.5 125
APPLICATION Paying Workers to Relocate 126
APPLICATION Fixing the CPI Substitution Bias 127

4.5 **Revealed Preference** 128
Recovering Preferences 128
Substitution Effect 129

Summary 130
Questions 130
Problems 132

Chapter 5 Consumer Welfare and Policy Analysis 134

5.1 **Consumer Welfare** 134
Willingness to Pay 135
APPLICATION Willingness to Pay and Consumer Surplus on eBay 137
SOLVED PROBLEM 5.1 139

5.2 **Expenditure Function and Consumer Welfare** 140
Indifference Curve Analysis 141
APPLICATION Compensating Variation for Television 142
Comparing the Three Welfare Measures 142
SOLVED PROBLEM 5.2 145

5.3 **Market Consumer Surplus** 146
Loss of Market Consumer Surplus from a Higher Price 146
Markets in Which Consumer Surplus Losses Are Large 146
SOLVED PROBLEM 5.3 148

5.4 **Effects of Government Policies on Consumer Welfare** 149
Quotas 149
APPLICATION Water Quota 150
Food Stamps 151
APPLICATION Benefiting from Food Stamps 152
APPLICATION Child Care Subsidies 155

5.5 Deriving Labor Supply Curves 156
  Labor-Leisure Choice 156
  SOLVED PROBLEM 5.4 159
  Income and Substitution Effects 159
  SOLVED PROBLEM 5.5 160
  Shape of the Labor Supply Curve 161
  APPLICATION Working After Winning the Lottery 162
  Income Tax Rates and the Labor Supply Curve 163
  APPLICATION Maximizing Income Tax Revenue 166
Summary 167
Questions 168
Problems 170

Chapter 6 Firms and Production 172

6.1 The Ownership and Management of Firms 173
  Private, Public, and Nonprofit Firms 173
  The Ownership of For-Profit Firms 174
  The Management of Firms 175
  What Owners Want 175

6.2 Production 176
  Production Functions 176
  Time and the Variability of Inputs 177

6.3 Short-Run Production: One Variable and One Fixed Input 177
  SOLVED PROBLEM 6.1 178
  Interpretation of Graphs 180
  SOLVED PROBLEM 6.2 181
  Law of Diminishing Marginal Returns 182
  APPLICATION Malthus and the Green Revolution 182

6.4 Long-Run Production: Two Variable Inputs 184
  Isoquants 184
  APPLICATION A Semiconductor Integrated Circuit Isoquant 187
  Substituting Inputs 189
  SOLVED PROBLEM 6.3 189
  Diminishing Marginal Rates of Technical Substitution 190
  The Elasticity of Substitution 191
  SOLVED PROBLEM 6.4 192

6.5 Returns to Scale 193
  Constant, Increasing, and Decreasing Returns to Scale 193
  SOLVED PROBLEM 6.5 194
  APPLICATION Returns to Scale in U.S. Manufacturing 194
  Varying Returns to Scale 196

6.6 Productivity and Technical Change 196
  Relative Productivity 197
  APPLICATION U.S. Electric Generation Efficiency 198
  Innovations 198
  APPLICATION Tata Nano's Technical and Organizational Innovations 200
Summary 200
Questions 201
Problems 203

Chapter 7 Costs 205

7.1 Measuring Costs 206
  Opportunity Costs 206
  APPLICATION The Opportunity Cost of an MBA 207
  SOLVED PROBLEM 7.1 207
  Capital Costs 207
  APPLICATION Swarthmore College's Cost of Capital 208
  Sunk Costs 209

7.2 Short-Run Costs 209
  Short-Run Cost Measures 210
  SOLVED PROBLEM 7.2 211
  Short-Run Cost Curves 212
  Production Functions and the Shape of Cost Curves 213
  APPLICATION Short-Run Cost Curves for a Furniture Manufacturer 215
  Effects of Taxes on Costs 216
  Short-Run Cost Summary 217

7.3 Long-Run Costs 218
  Input Choice 218
  APPLICATION Semiconductor Outsourcing 225
  SOLVED PROBLEM 7.3 225
  How Long-Run Cost Varies with Output 226
  SOLVED PROBLEM 7.4 226
  SOLVED PROBLEM 7.5 228
  The Shape of Long-Run Cost Curves 229
  APPLICATION Innovations and Economies of Scale 230
  Estimating Cost Curves Versus Introspection 230

7.4 Lower Costs in the Long Run 231
  Long-Run Average Cost as the Envelope of Short-Run Average Cost Curves 231
  APPLICATION Choosing an Inkjet or Laser Printer 233
  Short-Run and Long-Run Expansion Paths 233
  How Learning by Doing Lowers Costs 234
  APPLICATION Learning by Drilling 236

7.5 **Cost of Producing Multiple Goods** 237
   APPLICATION Economies of Scope 238
Summary 238
Questions 239
Problems 241

Chapter 8 Competitive Firms and Markets 243

8.1 **Perfect Competition** 244
   Price Taking 244
   Why a Firm's Demand Curve Is Horizontal 244
   Deviations from Perfect Competition 245
   Derivation of a Competitive Firm's Demand Curve 246
   Why Perfect Competition Is Important 248

8.2 **Profit Maximization** 248
   Profit 248
   APPLICATION Breaking Even on Christmas Trees 249
   Two Steps to Maximizing Profit 250

8.3 **Competition in the Short Run** 253
   Short-Run Competitive Profit Maximization 253
   SOLVED PROBLEM 8.1 256
   APPLICATION Oil, Oil Sands, and Oil Shale Shutdowns 259
   Short-Run Firm Supply Curve 260
   SOLVED PROBLEM 8.2 260
   Short-Run Market Supply Curve 262
   Short-Run Competitive Equilibrium 264
   SOLVED PROBLEM 8.3 265

8.4 **Competition in the Long Run** 266
   Long-Run Competitive Profit Maximization 266
   Long-Run Firm Supply Curve 267
   Long-Run Market Supply Curve 268
   APPLICATION Upward-Sloping Long-Run Supply Curve for Cotton 271
   APPLICATION Reformulated Gasoline Supply Curves 275
   SOLVED PROBLEM 8.4 276
   Long-Run Competitive Equilibrium 276
   SOLVED PROBLEM 8.5 278
Summary 279
Questions 280
Problems 283

Chapter 9 Applications of the Competitive Model 285

9.1 **Zero Profit for Competitive Firms in the Long Run** 286
   Zero Long-Run Profit with Free Entry 286
   Zero Long-Run Profit When Entry Is Limited 286
   APPLICATION Tiger Woods' Rents 288
   The Need to Maximize Profit 289

9.2 **Producer Welfare** 289
   Measuring Producer Surplus Using a Supply Curve 289
   Using Producer Surplus 291
   SOLVED PROBLEM 9.1 291

9.3 **How Competition Maximizes Welfare** 293
   Why Producing Less Than the Competitive Output Lowers Welfare 293
   Why Producing More Than the Competitive Output Lowers Welfare 295
   APPLICATION Deadweight Loss of Christmas Presents 296

9.4 **Policies That Shift Supply Curves** 297
   Restricting the Number of Firms 297
   APPLICATION Licensing Cabs 299
   Raising Entry and Exit Costs 300

9.5 **Policies That Create a Wedge Between Supply and Demand Curves** 301
   Welfare Effects of a Sales Tax 301
   Welfare Effects of a Price Floor 303
   SOLVED PROBLEM 9.2 305
   APPLICATION Giving Money to Farmers 307
   Welfare Effects of a Price Ceiling 307
   SOLVED PROBLEM 9.3 308
   APPLICATION The Social Cost of a Natural Gas Price Ceiling 309

9.6 **Comparing Both Types of Policies: Trade** 309
   Free Trade Versus a Ban on Imports 310
   SOLVED PROBLEM 9.4 311
   Free Trade Versus a Tariff 312
   SOLVED PROBLEM 9.5 314
   Free Trade Versus a Quota 315
   Rent Seeking 316
Summary 317
Questions 318
Problems 321

Chapter 11 Monopoly 358

11.1 **Monopoly Profit Maximization** 359
   The Necessary Condition for Profit Maximization 359
   Marginal Revenue and the Demand Curves 360
   SOLVED PROBLEM 11.1 361
   Marginal Revenue Curve and the Price Elasticity of Demand 362
   An Example of Monopoly Profit Maximization 363
   APPLICATION Cable Cars and Profit Maximization 365

Choosing Price or Quantity 366
Effects of a Shift of the Demand Curve 366

11.2 Market Power 367
Market Power and the Shape of the Demand Curve 367
Lerner Index 369
APPLICATION Apple's iPod 369
SOLVED PROBLEM 11.2 369
Sources of Market Power 371

11.3 Welfare Effects of Monopoly 372

11.4 Taxes and Monopoly 373
Effects of a Specific Tax 373
SOLVED PROBLEM 11.3 374
Welfare Effects of Ad Valorem Versus Specific Taxes 376

11.5 Cost Advantages That Create Monopolies 377
Sources of Cost Advantages 377
APPLICATION China's New Monopolies 378
Natural Monopoly 378
SOLVED PROBLEM 11.4 380

11.6 Government Actions That Create Monopolies 380
Barriers to Entry 380
Patents 381
APPLICATION Botox Patent Monopoly 381
APPLICATION Property Rights and Piracy 383

11.7 Government Actions That Reduce Market Power 384
Regulating Monopolies 384
SOLVED PROBLEM 11.5 386
APPLICATION Natural Gas Regulation 388
Increasing Competition 389

11.8 Monopoly Decisions over Time and Behavioral Economics 389
Network Externalities 390
APPLICATION Critical Mass and eBay 391
A Two-Period Monopoly Model 392

Summary 392
Questions 393
Problems 395

Chapter 12 Pricing and Advertising 398

12.1 Why and How Firms Price Discriminate 399
Why Price Discrimination Pays 400
Who Can Price Discriminate 400
Preventing Resales 400
APPLICATION Disneyland Pricing 400
APPLICATION Preventing Resale of Designer Bags 402
Not All Price Differences Are Price Discrimination 402
Types of Price Discrimination 402

12.2 Perfect Price Discrimination 403
How a Firm Perfectly Price Discriminates 403
APPLICATION Google Uses Bidding for Ads to Price Discriminate 406
Perfect Price Discrimination: Efficient but Harmful to Consumers 406
APPLICATION Botox Revisited 407
Transaction Costs and Perfect Price Discrimination 408
SOLVED PROBLEM 12.1 409
APPLICATION Unions That Set Wages and Hours 409

12.3 Quantity Discrimination 410

12.4 Multimarket Price Discrimination 411
Multimarket Price Discrimination with Two Groups 412
APPLICATION Smuggling Prescription Drugs into the United States 414
SOLVED PROBLEM 12.2 415
Identifying Groups 417
APPLICATION Buying Discounts 418
SOLVED PROBLEM 12.3 419
Welfare Effects of Multimarket Price Discrimination 420

12.5 Two-Part Tariffs 420
A Two-Part Tariff with Identical Consumers 421
A Two-Part Tariff with Nonidentical Consumers 422

12.6 Tie-In Sales 423
Requirement Tie-In Sales 424
APPLICATION IBM 424
Bundling 424
APPLICATION Available for a Song 426

12.7 Advertising 427
The Decision Whether to Advertise 427
How Much to Advertise 428
APPLICATION Advertising Subsidizes Subscriptions 429
SOLVED PROBLEM 12.4 430

Summary 431
Questions 432
Problems 434

Chapter 14 Oligopoly 474

14.1 Market Structures 475

14.2 Cartels 477
Why Cartels Succeed or Fail 477
APPLICATION Catwalk Cartel 480
Maintaining Cartels 481
APPLICATION Hospital Mergers: Market Power Versus Efficiency 482

14.3 Noncooperative Oligopoly 483

14.4 Cournot Oligopoly Model 483
Cournot Model of an Airline Market 484
The Cournot Equilibrium with Two or More Firms 488
SOLVED PROBLEM 14.1 490
APPLICATION Incidence of a Cigarette Tax 490
The Cournot Model with Nonidentical Firms 492
SOLVED PROBLEM 14.2 492
APPLICATION Air Ticket Prices and Rivalry 494
SOLVED PROBLEM 14.3 495
APPLICATION Bottled Water 496

14.5 Stackelberg Oligopoly Model 497
Calculus Solution 497
Graphical Solution 498
Why Moving Sequentially Is Essential 498
Strategic Trade Policy: An Application of the Stackelberg Model 500
APPLICATION Government Aircraft Subsidies 503
SOLVED PROBLEM 14.4 504

14.6 Comparison of Collusive, Cournot, Stackelberg, and Competitive Equilibria 505
APPLICATION Deadweight Losses in the Food and Tobacco Industries 508

14.7 Bertrand Oligopoly Model 508
Bertrand Equilibrium with Identical Products 508
Nash-Bertrand Equilibrium with Differentiated Products 510
APPLICATION Welfare Gain from Greater Toilet Paper Variety 514

14.8 Monopolistic Competition 514
Monopolistically Competitive Equilibrium 515
Fixed Costs and the Number of Firms 516
SOLVED PROBLEM 14.5 517
APPLICATION Zoning Laws as a Barrier to Entry by Hotel Chains 518

Summary 518
Questions 519
Problems 520

Calculus Appendix A-1

A.1 Functions A-1
Functions of a Single Variable A-1
Functions of Several Variables A-2

A.2 Properties of Functions A-2
Monotonicity A-3
Continuity A-3
Concavity and Convexity A-3
Homogeneous Functions A-5
Special Properties of Logarithmic Functions A-5

A.3 Derivatives A-6
Rules for Calculating Derivatives A-7
Higher-Order Derivatives A-9
Partial Derivatives A-9
Euler's Homogeneous Function Theorem A-11

A.4 Maximum and Minimum A-11
Local Extrema A-11
Global Extrema A-12
Existence of Extrema A-12
Uniqueness of Extrema A-14
Interior Extrema A-14

A.5 Finding the Extrema of a Function A-14
Examples A-16
Indirect Objective Functions and the Envelope Theorem A-17

A.6 Maximizing with Equality Constraints A-19
Substitution Method A-19
Lagrange's Method A-20

Definitions D-1

Index I-1

Introduction

I've often wondered what goes into a hot dog. Now I know and I wish I didn't. —William Zinsser

If each of us could get all the food, clothing, and toys we want without working, no one would study economics. Unfortunately, most of the good things in life are scarce—we can't all have as much as we want. Thus, scarcity is the mother of economics.

Microeconomics is the study of how individuals and firms make themselves as well off as possible in a world of scarcity, and the consequences of those individual decisions for markets and the entire economy. In studying microeconomics, we examine how individual consumers and firms make decisions and how the interaction of many individual decisions affects markets.

Microeconomics is often called *price theory* to emphasize the important role that prices play in determining market outcomes. Microeconomics explains how the actions of all buyers and sellers determine prices and how prices influence the decisions and actions of individual buyers and sellers.

In this chapter, we discuss three main topics

1. **Microeconomics: The Allocation of Scarce Resources.** Microeconomics is the study of the allocation of scarce resources.
2. **Models.** Economists use models to make testable predictions.
3. **Uses of Microeconomic Models.** Individuals, governments, and firms use microeconomic models and predictions in decision making.

1.1 Microeconomics: The Allocation of Scarce Resources

Individuals and firms allocate their limited resources to make themselves as well off as possible. Consumers select the mix of goods and services that makes them as happy as possible given their limited wealth. Firms decide which goods to produce, where to produce them, how much to produce to maximize their profits, and how to produce those levels of output at the lowest cost by using more or less of various inputs such as labor, capital, materials, and energy. The owners of a depletable natural resource such as oil decide when to use it.

Government decision makers decide which goods and services the government will produce and whether to subsidize, tax, or regulate industries and consumers so as to benefit consumers, firms, or government employees.

Trade-Offs

People make trade-offs because they can't have everything. A society faces three key trade-offs:

1. **Which goods and services to produce:** If a society produces more cars, it must produce fewer of other goods and services, because there are only so many *resources*—workers, raw materials, capital, and energy—available to produce goods.
2. **How to produce:** To produce a given level of output, a firm must use more of one input if it uses less of another input. Cracker and cookie manufacturers switch between palm oil and coconut oil, depending on which is less expensive.
3. **Who gets the goods and services:** The more of society's goods and services you get, the less someone else gets.

Who Makes the Decisions

These three allocation decisions may be made explicitly by the government, or they may reflect the interaction of independent decisions by many individual consumers and firms. In the former Soviet Union, the government told manufacturers how many cars of each type to make and which inputs to use to make them. The government also decided which consumers would get cars.

In most other countries, how many cars of each type are produced and who gets them are determined by how much it costs to make cars of a particular quality in the least expensive way and how much consumers are willing to pay for them. More consumers would own a handcrafted Rolls-Royce and fewer would buy a mass-produced Ford Taurus if a Rolls were not 21 times more expensive than a Taurus.

APPLICATION

Flu Vaccine Shortage

In 2004, the U.S. government expected a record 100 million flu vaccine doses to be available, but one vaccine maker, Chiron, could not ship 46 million doses because of contamination.[1] As a consequence, the government expected a shortage at the traditional price.

In response, government and public health officials urged young, healthy people to forgo getting shots until the sick, the elderly, and other high-risk populations, such as health care providers and pregnant women, were inoculated. Public spirit failed to dissuade enough healthy people. Perversely, the high-priority adult population was the group most likely to show self-control and not ask for a shot (de Janvry et al., 2008). Consequently, federal, state, and local governments restricted access to the shots to high-risk populations. Again, in 2009 and 2010, when faced with shortages of the H1N1 "swine flu" vaccine, most government agencies restricted access to the highest risk groups.

In most non-health-related goods markets, prices adjust to prevent shortages. In contrast, during the flu shot shortage, governments didn't increase the price to reduce demand, but relied on exhortation and formal allocation schemes.

---

[1] Sources for applications appear at the end of the book.

How Prices Determine Allocations

An Economist's Theory of Reincarnation: If you're good, you come back on a higher level. Cats come back as dogs, dogs come back as horses, and people—if they've been real good like George Washington—come back as money.

Prices link the decisions about *which goods and services to produce, how to produce them,* and *who gets them.* Prices influence the decisions of individual consumers and firms, and the interactions of these decisions by consumers, firms, and the government determine price.

Interactions between consumers and firms take place in a **market**, which is an exchange mechanism that allows buyers to trade with sellers. A market may be a town square where people go to trade food and clothing, or it may be an international telecommunications network over which people buy and sell financial securities. Typically, when we talk about a single market, we are referring to trade in a single good or a group of goods that are closely related, such as soft drinks, movies, novels, or automobiles.

Most of this book concerns how prices are determined within a market. We show that the organization of the market, especially the number of buyers and sellers in the market and the amount of information they have, helps determine whether the price equals the cost of production. We also show that if there is no market—and hence no market price—serious problems, such as high levels of pollution, result.

APPLICATION

Twinkie Tax

Many American, Australian, British, Canadian, New Zealand, and Taiwanese jurisdictions are proposing a "Twinkie tax" on unhealthful fatty and sweet foods to reduce obesity and cholesterol problems, particularly among children. One survey found that 45% of adults would support a 1¢ tax per pound of soft drinks, chips, and butter, with the revenues used to fund health education programs. In 2009, the U.S. Senate debated adding a nearly $2 per six-pack tax on beer, as well as taxes on other alcoholic beverages and sugary drinks to fund an expansion of health insurance for uninsured Americans.

Many proponents and opponents of these proposed laws seem unaware that at least 25 states and 3 cities differentially tax soft drinks, candy, chewing gum, and snack foods such as potato chips. Today, many school districts throughout the United States ban soft drink vending machines. This ban discourages consumption, as would an extremely high tax. In 2008, Britain's largest life insurance firm started charging more for life insurance policies for the obese.

New taxes will affect *which foods are produced*, as firms offer new low-fat and low-sugar programs, and *how fast-foods are produced*, as manufacturers reformulate their products to lower their tax burden. These taxes will also influence *who gets these goods* as consumers, especially children, replace them with less expensive, untaxed products.

1.2 Models

Everything should be made as simple as possible, but not simpler. —Albert Einstein

To *explain* how individuals and firms allocate resources and how market prices are determined, economists use a **model**: a description of the relationship between two or more economic variables. Economists also use models to *predict* how a change in one variable will affect another variable.

APPLICATION

Income Threshold Model and China

According to an *income threshold model*, no one who has an income level below a threshold buys a particular consumer durable, which is a good that can be used for long periods of time, such as a refrigerator or car. The theory also holds that almost everyone whose income is above the threshold does buy the durable.

If this theory is correct, we predict that, as most people's incomes rise above that threshold in less-developed countries, consumer durable purchases will go from near zero to large numbers virtually overnight. This prediction is consistent with evidence from Malaysia, where the income threshold for buying a car is about $4,000.

Incomes are rising rapidly in China and are exceeding the threshold levels for many types of durable goods. As a result, many experts predicted that the greatest consumer durable goods sales boom in history would take place there over the next decade. Anticipating this boom, many companies greatly increased their investments in durable goods manufacturing plants in China. Annual foreign direct investments went from $916 million a year in 1983 to $82.7 billion in 2007. In expectation of this growth potential, even traditional political opponents of the People's Republic—Taiwan, South Korea, and Russia—invested in China.

Li Rifu, a 46-year-old Chinese farmer and watch repairman, thought that buying a car would improve the odds that his 22- and 24-year-old sons would find girlfriends, marry, and produce grandchildren. After Mr. Li purchased his Geely King Kong for the equivalent of $9,000, both sons soon found girlfriends, and his older son quickly married. Four-fifths of all new cars sold in China are bought by first-time customers. An influx of first-time buyers was responsible for China's more than eightfold increase in car sales from 2000 to 2008.

Simplifications by Assumption

We stated the income threshold model verbally, but we could have presented it using graphs or mathematics. Regardless of how the model is described, an economic model is a simplification of reality that contains only reality's most important features. Without simplifications, it is difficult to make predictions because the real world is too complex to analyze fully.

By analogy, if the owner's manual accompanying a new DVD recorder had a diagram showing the relationships among all the parts in the DVD, the diagram would be overwhelming and useless. But a diagram that includes a photo of the buttons on the front of the machine, with labels describing the purpose of each, is useful and informative.

Economists make many *assumptions* to simplify their models.[2] When using the income threshold model to explain car-purchasing behavior in Malaysia, we assume that factors other than income, such as the color of cars, are irrelevant to the decision to buy cars. Therefore, we ignore the color of cars that are sold in Malaysia when we describe the relationship between average income and the number of cars that consumers want. If this assumption is correct, by ignoring color we make our analysis of the auto market simpler without losing important details. If we're wrong and these ignored issues are important, our predictions may be inaccurate.

---

[2]An economist, an engineer, and a physicist are stranded on a deserted island with a can of beans but no can opener. How should they open the can? The engineer proposes hitting the can with a rock. The physicist suggests building a fire under the can to build up pressure and burst it open. The economist thinks for a while and then says, "Assume that we have a can opener...."

Throughout this book, we start with strong assumptions to simplify our models. Later, we add complexities. For example, in most of the book, we assume that consumers know the price each firm charges for a product. In many markets, such as the New York Stock Exchange, this assumption is realistic. However, it is not realistic in other markets, such as the market for used automobiles, in which consumers do not know the prices that each firm charges. To devise an accurate model for markets in which consumers have limited information, in Chapter 18, we add consumer uncertainty about price into the model.

Testing Theories

Given a choice between two theories, take the one which is funnier. —Blore's Razor

Economic *theory* is the development and use of a model to test *hypotheses*, which are predictions about cause and effect. We are interested in models that make clear, testable predictions, such as "If the price rises, the quantity demanded falls." A theory stating that "People's behaviors depend on their tastes, and their tastes change randomly at random intervals" is not very useful because it does not lead to testable predictions.

Economists test theories by checking whether predictions are correct. If a prediction does not come true, economists may reject the theory.[3] Economists use a model until it is refuted by evidence or until a better model is developed.

A good model makes sharp, clear predictions that are consistent with reality. Some very simple models make sharp predictions that are incorrect, and other, more complex models make ambiguous predictions—in which any outcome is possible—that are untestable. The skill in model building is to chart a middle ground.

The purpose of this book is to teach you how to think like an economist, in the sense that you can build testable theories using economic models or apply existing models to new situations. Although economists think alike, in that they develop and use testable models, they often disagree. One may present a logically consistent argument that prices will go up in the next quarter. Another economist, using a different but equally logical theory, may contend that prices will fall in that quarter. If the economists are reasonable, they agree that pure logic alone cannot resolve their dispute. Indeed, they agree that they'll have to use empirical evidence—facts about the real world—to find out which prediction is correct.

Maximizing Subject to Constraints

Although one economist's model may differ from another's, a key assumption in most microeconomic models is that individuals allocate their scarce resources so as to make themselves as well off as possible. Of all the affordable combinations of goods, consumers pick the bundle of goods that gives them the most possible enjoyment. Firms try to maximize their profits given limited resources and existing technology. That resources are limited plays a crucial role in these models. Were it not for scarcity, people could consume unlimited amounts of goods and services, and sellers could become rich beyond limit.

---

[3]We can use evidence of whether a theory's predictions are correct to refute the theory but not to prove it. If a model's prediction is inconsistent with what actually happened, the model must be wrong, so we reject it. Even if the model's prediction is consistent with reality, however, the model's prediction may be correct for the wrong reason. Hence, we cannot prove that the model is correct—we can only fail to reject it.

As we show throughout this book, the maximizing behavior of individuals and firms determines society's three main allocation decisions: which goods are produced, how they are produced, and who gets them. For example, diamond-studded pocket combs will be sold only if firms find it profitable to sell them. The firms will make and sell these combs only if consumers value the combs at least as much as it costs the firm to produce them. Consumers will buy the combs only if they get more pleasure from the combs than they would from the other goods they could buy with the same resources.

Many of the models that we examine are based on maximizing an objective that is subject to a constraint. Consumers maximize their well-being subject to a budget constraint, which says that their resources limit how many goods they can buy. Firms maximize profits subject to technological and other constraints. Governments may try to maximize the welfare of consumers or firms subject to constraints imposed by limited resources and the behavior of consumers and firms. We cover the formal economic analysis of maximizing behavior in the following chapters and review the underlying mathematics in the Calculus Appendix at the end of the book.

Positive Versus Normative

Those are my principles. If you don't like them I have others. —Groucho Marx

The use of models of maximizing behavior sometimes leads to predictions that seem harsh or heartless. For instance, a World Bank economist predicted that if an African government used price controls to keep the price of food low during a drought, food shortages would occur and people would starve. The predicted outcome is awful, but the economist was not heartless. The economist was only making a scientific prediction about the relationship between cause and effect: Price controls (cause) lead to food shortages and starvation (effect).

Such a scientific prediction is known as a **positive statement**: a testable hypothesis about cause and effect. "Positive" does not mean that we are certain about the truth of our statement—it indicates only that we can test the truth of our statement.

If the World Bank economist is correct, should the government control prices? If government policymakers believe the economist's predictions, they'll know that the low prices will help consumers who are lucky enough to be able to buy as much food as they want but hurt both the firms that sell food and the people who cannot buy as much food as they want, some of whom may die. As a result, the government's decision of whether to use price controls turns on whether the government cares more about the winners or the losers. In other words, to decide on its policy, the government makes a value judgment.

Instead of first making a prediction and testing it and then making a value judgment to decide whether to use price controls, government policymakers could make a value judgment directly. The value judgment could be based on the belief that "because people *should* have prepared for the drought, the government should not try to help them by keeping food prices low." Alternatively, the judgment could be based on the view that "people should be protected against price gouging during a drought, so the government should use price controls."

These two statements are *not* scientific predictions. Each is a value judgment or **normative statement**: a conclusion as to whether something is good or bad. A normative statement cannot be tested because a value judgment cannot be refuted by evidence. It is a prescription rather than a prediction. A normative statement concerns what somebody believes should happen; a positive statement concerns what will happen.

Although a normative conclusion can be drawn without first conducting a positive analysis, a policy debate will be more informed if positive analyses are conducted first.[4] Suppose your normative belief is that the government should help the poor. Should you vote for a candidate who advocates a higher minimum wage (a law that requires firms to pay wages at or above a specified level); a European-style welfare system (guaranteeing health care, housing, and other basic goods and services); an end to our current welfare system; a negative income tax (in which the less income a person receives, the more the government gives to that person); or job training programs? Positive economic analysis can be used to predict whether these programs will benefit poor people but *not* whether these programs are good or bad. Using these predictions and your value judgment, you decide for whom to vote.

Economists' emphasis on positive analysis has implications for what they study and even their use of language. For example, many economists stress that they study people's *wants* rather than their needs. Although people need certain minimum levels of food, shelter, and clothing to survive, most people in developed economies have enough money to buy goods well in excess of the minimum levels necessary to maintain life. Consequently, calling something a "need" in a wealthy country is often a value judgment. You almost certainly have been told by some elder that "you need a college education." That person was probably making a value judgment—"you should go to college"—rather than a scientific prediction that you will suffer terrible economic deprivation if you do not go to college. We can't test such value judgments, but we can test a hypothesis such as "One-third of the college-age population wants to go to college at current prices."

1.3 Uses of Microeconomic Models

Have you ever imagined a world without hypothetical situations? —Steven Wright

Because microeconomic models *explain* why economic decisions are made and allow us to make *predictions*, they can be very useful for individuals, governments, and firms in making decisions. Throughout this book, we consider examples of how microeconomics aids in actual decision making. Here, we briefly look at some uses by individuals and governments.

Individuals use microeconomics to make purchasing and other decisions (Chapters 3 through 5). For example, we examine how inflation and adjustments for inflation affect individuals in Chapter 5. In Chapter 15, we explore how to determine whether it pays financially to go to college. How to invest in stocks, bonds, and other financial instruments, and whether to buy insurance is covered in Chapter 17. Individuals have to decide whether a used car is a lemon or worth buying (Chapter 18). Whether potential employers regard your college degree as proof of your abilities depends on the fraction of people who have advanced degrees and whether education provides useful training (Chapter 18). Whether you should hire a lawyer by the hour or offer the lawyer a percentage of any winnings depends on the type of case (Chapter 19).

Another use of microeconomics is to help citizens make voting decisions on the basis of candidates' views on economic issues. Your government's elected and

---

[4]Some economists draw the normative conclusion that, as social scientists, we economists should restrict ourselves to positive analyses. Others argue that we shouldn't give up our right to make value judgments just like the next person (who happens to be biased, prejudiced, and pigheaded, unlike us).

appointed officials use (or could use) economic models in many ways. Recent administrations have placed increased emphasis on economic analysis. Today, economic and environmental impact studies are required before many projects can commence. The President's Council of Economic Advisers and other federal economists analyze and advise national government agencies on the likely economic effects of all major policies.

Indeed, a major use of microeconomic models by governments is to predict the probable impact of a policy. In Chapter 2, we show how to predict the likely impact of a tax on the prices consumers pay and on the tax revenues raised. In Chapter 9, we analyze the effects on markets of various international trade policies, such as tariffs and quotas. Chapter 11 considers how San Francisco should set the price for cable car rides and the effects of government regulations on electric utilities. Governments also use economics to decide how best to prevent pollution and global warming (Chapter 16).

Decisions by firms reflect microeconomic analysis. Firms price discriminate or bundle goods to increase their profits (Chapter 12). Many strategic decisions concerning pricing, setting quantities, advertising, or entry into a market can be predicted using game theory (Chapter 13). In particular, oligopolistic and monopolistically competitive markets, such as American and United Airlines competition on the Chicago–Los Angeles route, can be analyzed and predicted using game theory (Chapter 14). When the phone company should replace telephone poles or a mining company should extract ore depends on interest rates (Chapter 15). Firms decide whether to offer employees deferred payments to ensure hard work (Chapter 19).

SUMMARY

1. **Microeconomics: The Allocation of Scarce Resources.** Microeconomics is the study of the allocation of scarce resources. Consumers, firms, and governments must make allocation decisions. A society faces three key trade-offs: which goods and services to produce, how to produce them, and who gets them. These decisions are interrelated and depend on the prices that consumers and firms face and on government actions. Market prices affect the decisions of individual consumers and firms, and the interaction of the decisions of individual consumers and firms determines market prices. The organization of the market, especially the number of firms in the market and the information consumers and firms have, plays an important role in determining whether the market price is equal to or higher than the cost of producing an additional unit of output.

2. **Models.** Models based on economic theories are used to predict the future or to answer questions about how some change, such as a tax increase, will affect various sectors of the economy. A good theory is simple to use and makes clear, testable predictions that are not refuted by evidence. Most microeconomic models are based on maximizing behavior. Economists use models to construct *positive* hypotheses concerning how a cause leads to an effect. These positive questions can be tested. In contrast, *normative* statements, which are value judgments, cannot be tested.

3. **Uses of Microeconomic Models.** Individuals, governments, and firms use microeconomic models and predictions to make decisions. For example, to maximize its profits, a firm needs to know consumers' decision-making criteria, the trade-offs between various ways of producing and marketing its product, government regulations, and other factors. For a large company, beliefs about how its rivals will react to its actions play a critical role in how the company forms its business strategies.

Supply and Demand

Talk is cheap because supply exceeds demand.

When asked "What is the most important thing you know about economics?" many people reply, "Supply equals demand." This statement is a shorthand description of one of the simplest yet most powerful models of economics. The supply-and-demand model describes how consumers and suppliers interact to determine the quantity of a good or service sold in a market and the price at which it is sold. To use the model, you need to determine three things: buyers' behavior, sellers' behavior, and how buyers' and sellers' actions affect price and quantity. After reading this chapter, you should be able to use the supply-and-demand model to analyze some of the most important policy questions facing your country today, such as those concerning international trade, minimum wages, and price controls on health care.

After reading that grandiose claim, you might ask, "Is that all there is to economics? Can I become an expert economist that fast?" The answer to both questions, of course, is no. In addition, you need to learn the limits of this model and which other models to use when this one does not apply. (You must also learn the economists' secret handshake.)

Even with its limitations, the supply-and-demand model is the most widely used economic model. It provides a good description of how markets function, and it works particularly well in markets that have many buyers and many sellers, such as most agriculture and labor markets. Like all good theories, the supply-and-demand model can be tested—and possibly shown to be false. But in markets where it is applicable, it allows us to make accurate predictions easily.

In this chapter, we examine eight main topics

1. **Demand.** The quantity of a good or service that consumers demand depends on price and other factors such as consumers' incomes and the prices of related goods.

2. **Supply.** The quantity of a good or service that firms supply depends on price and other factors such as the cost of inputs that firms use to produce the good or service.

3. **Market Equilibrium.** The interaction between consumers' demand curve and firms' supply curve determines the market price and quantity of a good or service that is bought and sold.

4. **Shocking the Equilibrium: Comparative Statics.** Changes in a factor that affect demand (such as consumers' incomes), supply (such as a rise in the price of inputs), or a new government policy (such as a new tax), alter the market price and quantity of a good.

5. **Elasticities.** Given estimates of summary statistics called elasticities, economists can forecast the effects of changes in taxes and other factors on market price and quantity.

6. **Effects of a Sales Tax.** How a sales tax increase affects the equilibrium price and the quantity of a good, and whether the tax falls more heavily on consumers or on suppliers, depend on the supply and demand curves.

7. **Quantity Supplied Need Not Equal Quantity Demanded.** If the government regulates the prices in a market, the quantity supplied might not equal the quantity demanded.

8. **When to Use the Supply-and-Demand Model.** The supply-and-demand model applies only to competitive markets.

2.1 Demand

The amount of a good that consumers are willing to buy at a given price during a specified time period (such as a day or a year), holding constant the other factors that influence purchases, is the **quantity demanded**. The quantity demanded of a good or service can exceed the quantity actually sold. For example, as a promotion, a local store might sell DVDs for $1 each today only. At that low price, you might want to buy 25 DVDs, but because the store has run out of stock, you can buy only 10 DVDs. The quantity you demand is 25—it's the amount you want—even though the amount you actually buy is only 10.

Potential consumers decide how much of a good or service to buy on the basis of its price, which is expressed as an amount of money per unit of the good (for example, dollars per pound), and many other factors, including consumers' own tastes, information, and income; prices of other goods; and government actions. Before concentrating on the role price plays in determining demand, let's look briefly at some of the other factors.

Consumers make purchases based on their *tastes*. Consumers do not purchase foods they dislike, works of art they hate, or clothes they view as unfashionable or uncomfortable. However, advertising can influence people's tastes.

Similarly, *information* (or misinformation) about the uses of a good affects consumers' decisions. A few years ago, when many consumers were convinced that oatmeal could lower their cholesterol level, they rushed to grocery stores and bought large quantities of oatmeal. (They even ate some of it until they remembered that they couldn't stand how it tastes.)

The *prices of other goods* also affect consumers' purchase decisions. Before deciding to buy Levi's jeans, you might check the prices of other brands. If the price of a close *substitute*—a product that you view as similar or identical to the one you are considering purchasing—is much lower than the price of Levi's jeans, you might buy that other brand instead. Similarly, the price of a *complement*—a good that you like to consume at the same time as the product you are considering buying—could affect your decision. If you only eat pie with ice cream, the higher the price of ice cream, the less likely you are to buy pie.

People's incomes play a major role in determining what and how much of a good or service they purchase. A person who suddenly inherits great wealth might purchase a Mercedes or other luxury items, and may be less likely to buy do-it-yourself repair kits.

Government rules and regulations affect people's purchase decisions. Sales taxes increase the price that a consumer must spend on a good, and government-imposed limits on the use of a good can affect demand. For example, if a city's government bans the use of skateboards on its streets, skateboard sales fall.[1]

Other factors can also affect the demand for specific goods. Some people are more likely to buy $200 pairs of shoes if their friends do too. The demand for small, dying evergreen trees is substantially higher in December than in other months.

Although many factors influence demand, economists usually concentrate on how a product's price affects the quantity of it demanded. To determine how a change in price affects the quantity demanded, economists must hold constant other factors, such as income and tastes, that affect the quantity demand.

The Demand Function

The **demand function** shows the correspondence between the quantity demanded, price, and other factors that influence purchases. For example, the demand function might be

$$Q = D(p, p_s, p_c, Y), \tag{2.1}$$

where Q is the quantity demanded of a particular good in a given time period, p is its price per unit of the good, p_s is the price per unit of a substitute good (a good that might be consumed instead of this good), p_c is the price per unit of a complementary good (a good that might be consumed jointly with this good, such as cream with coffee), and Y is consumers' income.

An example is the estimated demand function for processed pork in Canada,[2]

$$Q = 171 - 20p + 20p_b + 3p_c + 2Y, \tag{2.2}$$

where Q is the quantity of pork demanded in million kilograms (kg) of dressed cold pork carcass weight per year, p is the price of pork in Canadian dollars per kilogram, p_b is the price of beef (a substitute good) in dollars per kilogram, p_c is the price of chicken (another substitute good) in dollars per kilogram, and Y is the income of consumers in dollars per year. Any other factors that are not explicitly listed in the demand function are assumed to be irrelevant (such as the price of llamas in Peru) or held constant (such as the price of fish).

Usually we're primarily interested in the relationship between the quantity demanded and the price of the good. That is, we want to know the relationship between the quantity demanded and price, holding all other factors constant. For

---

[1] When a Mississippi woman attempted to sell her granddaughter for $2,000 and a car, state legislators were horrified to discover that they had no law on the books prohibiting the sale of children and quickly passed such a law. (Gordon, Mac "Legislators Make Child-Selling Illegal," *Jackson Free Press*, March 16, 2009.)

[2] Because prices, quantities, and other factors change simultaneously over time, economists use statistical techniques to hold constant the effects of factors other than the price of the good so that they can determine how price affects the quantity demanded. (See the Regression Appendix at the end of the book.) Moschini and Meilke (1992) used such techniques to estimate the pork demand curve. In Equation 2.2, I've rounded the number slightly for simplicity. As with any estimate, their estimates are probably more accurate in the observed range of pork prices ($1 to $6 per kg) than at very high or very low prices.

example, we could set p_b, p_c, and Y at their averages over the period studied: $p_b = \$4$ per kg, $p_c = \$3\frac{1}{3}$ per kg, and $Y = \$12.5$ thousand. If we substitute these values for p_b, p_c, and Y in Equation 2.2, we can rewrite the quantity demanded as a function of only the price of pork:

$$\begin{aligned} Q &= 171 - 20p + 20p_b + 3p_c + 2Y \\ &= 171 - 20p + (20 \times 4) + (3 \times 3\tfrac{1}{3}) + (2 \times 12.5) \\ &= 286 - 20p = D(p). \end{aligned} \quad (2.3)$$

We can graphically show this relationship, $Q = D(p) = 286 - 20p$, between the quantity demanded and price. A **demand curve** is a plot of the demand function that shows the quantity demanded at each possible price, holding constant the other factors that influence purchases. Figure 2.1 shows the estimated demand curve, D^1, for processed pork in Canada. (Although this demand curve is a straight line, demand curves can be smooth curves or wavy lines.) By convention, the vertical axis of the graph measures the price, p, per unit of the good, which in our pork example is dollars per kilogram (kg). The horizontal axis measures the quantity, Q, of the good, per physical measure of the good per time period, which in this case is million kg of dressed cold pork carcasses per year.

The demand curve, D^1, hits the price (vertical) axis at $\$14.30$, indicating that no quantity is demanded when the price is $\$14.30$ per kg or higher. Using Equation 2.3, if we set $Q = 286 - 20p = 0$, we find that the demand curve hits the price axis at $p = 286/20 = \$14.30$. The demand curve hits the horizontal quantity axis at 286 million kg—the amount of pork that consumers want if the price is zero. If we set the price equal to zero in Equation 2.3, we find that the quantity demanded is $Q = 286 - (20 \times 0) = 286$.[3] By plugging the particular values for p in the figure into

Figure 2.1 A Demand Curve

The estimated demand curve, D^1, for processed pork in Canada (Moschini and Meilke, 1992) shows the relationship between the quantity demanded per year and the price per kg. The downward slope of the demand curve shows that, holding other factors that influence demand constant, consumers demand less of a good when its price is high and more when the price is low. A change in price causes a *movement along the demand curve*.

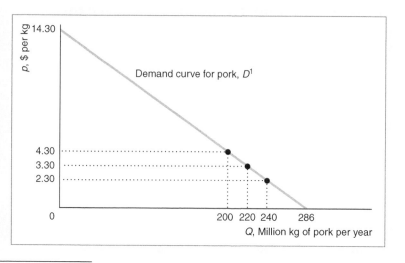

---

[3] Economists typically do not state the relevant physical and time period measures unless these measures are particularly useful in context. I'll generally follow this convention and refer to the price as, say, $3.30 (with the "per kg" understood) and the quantity as 220 (with the "million kg per year" understood).

[4] In Chapter 4, we show that the Law of Demand need not hold theoretically; however, available empirical evidence strongly supports the Law of Demand.

the demand equation, we can determine the corresponding quantities. For example, if $p = \$3.30$, then $Q = 286 - (20 \times 3.30) = 220$.

A Change in a Product's Price Causes a Movement Along the Demand Curve. The demand curve in Figure 2.1 shows that if the price increases from $3.30 to $4.30, the quantity consumers demand decreases by 20 units, from 220 to 200. These changes in the quantity demanded in response to changes in price are *movements along the demand curve*. The demand curve is a concise summary of the answers to the question "What happens to the quantity demanded as the price changes, when all other factors are held constant?"

One of the most important empirical findings in economics is the **Law of Demand**: Consumers demand more of a good the lower its price, holding constant tastes, the prices of other goods, and other factors that influence the amount they consume.[4] One way to state the Law of Demand is that the demand curve slopes downward, as in Figure 2.1.

Because the derivative of the demand function with respect to price shows the *movement along the demand curve as we vary price*, another way to state the Law of Demand is that this derivative is negative: A higher price results in a lower quantity demanded. If the demand function is $Q = D(p)$, then the Law of Demand says that $dQ/dp < 0$, where dQ/dp is the derivative of the D function with respect to p. (Unless we state otherwise, we assume that all demand and other functions are continuous and differentiable everywhere.) The derivative of the quantity of pork demanded with respect to its price in Equation 2.3 is

$$\frac{dQ}{dp} = -20,$$

which is negative, so the Law of Demand holds.[5] Given $dQ/dp = -20$, a small change in the price (measured in dollars per kg) causes a 20-times-larger fall in the quantity demanded (measured in million kg per year).

This derivative gives the change in the quantity demanded in response to an infinitesimal change in the price. In general, if we look at a discrete, relatively large increase in the price, the change in the quantity might not be proportional to the change for a small increase in the price. However, here the derivative is a constant that does not vary with the price, so the same derivative holds for large as well as for small price changes.

For example, let the price increase from $p_1 = \$3.30$ to $p_2 = \$4.30$. That is, the change in the price $\Delta p = p_2 - p_1 = \$4.30 - \$3.30 = \$1$. (The Δ symbol, the Greek letter capital delta, means "change in" the following variable, so Δp means "change in price.") As Figure 2.1 shows, the corresponding quantities are $Q_1 = 220$ and $Q_2 = 200$. Thus, if $\Delta p = \$1$, the change in the quantity demanded is $\Delta Q = Q_2 - Q_1 = 200 - 220 = -20$, or 20 times the change in price.

Because we put price on the vertical axis and quantity on the horizontal axis, the slope of the demand curve is the reciprocal of the derivative of the demand function: slope $= dp/dQ = 1/(dQ/dp)$. In our example, the slope of demand curve D^1 in Figure 2.1 is $dp/dQ = 1/(dQ/dp) = 1/(-20) = -0.05$. We can also calculate the

---

[5]We can show the same result using the more general demand function in Equation 2.2, where the demand function has several arguments: price, prices of two substitutes, and income. With several arguments, we need to use a partial derivative with respect to price because we are interested in determining how the quantity demanded changes as the price changes, holding other relevant factors constant. The partial derivative with respect to price is $\partial Q/\partial p = -20 < 0$. Thus, using either approach, we find that the quantity demanded falls by 20 times as much as the price rises.

slope in Figure 2.1 using the rise-over-run formula and the numbers we just calculated (because the slope is the same for small and for large changes):

$$\text{slope} = \frac{\text{rise}}{\text{run}} = \frac{\Delta p}{\Delta Q} = \frac{\$1 \text{ per kg}}{-20 \text{ million kg per year}} = -\$0.05 \text{ per million kg per year.}$$

This slope tells us that to sell one more unit (million kg per year) of pork, the price (per kg) must fall by 5¢.

A Change in Other Prices Causes the Demand Curve to Shift. If a demand curve measures the effects of price changes when all other factors that affect demand are held constant, how can we use demand curves to show the effects of a change in one of these other factors, such as the price of beef? One solution is to draw the demand curve in a three-dimensional diagram with the price of pork on one axis, the price of beef on a second axis, and the quantity of pork on the third axis. But just thinking about drawing such a diagram probably makes your head hurt.

Economists use a simpler approach to show how a change in a factor other than the price of a good affects its demand. A change in any factor other than the price of the good itself causes a *shift of the demand curve* rather than a *movement along the demand curve*.

If the price of beef rises while the price of pork remains constant, some people will switch from buying beef to buying pork. Suppose that the price of beef rises by 60¢ from $4.00 per kg to $4.60 per kg, but that the price of chicken and income remain at their average levels. Using the demand function in Equation 2.2, we can calculate the new pork demand function relating the quantity demanded to only the price:[6]

$$Q = 298 - 20\,p. \tag{2.4}$$

Figure 2.2 shows that the higher price of beef causes the entire pork demand curve to shift 12 units to the right from D^1 (corresponding to the demand function in Equation 2.3) to D^2 (corresponding to the demand function in Equation 2.4). (In the figure, the quantity axis starts at 176 instead of 0 to emphasize the relevant portion of the demand curve.)

Why does the demand function shift by 12 units? Using the demand function Equation 2.2, we find that the partial derivative of the quantity of pork demanded with respect to the price of beef is $\partial Q/\partial p_b = 20$. Thus, if the price of beef increases by 60¢, the quantity of pork demanded rises by $20 \times 0.6 = 12$ units, holding all other factors constant.

To properly analyze the effects of a change in some variable on the quantity demanded, we must distinguish between a *movement along a demand curve* and a *shift of a demand curve*. A change in the *price of a good* causes a *movement along its demand curve*. A change in *any other factor besides the price of the good* causes a *shift of the demand curve*.

---

[6]Substituting $p_b = \$4.60$ into Equation 2.2 and using the same values as before for p_c and Y, we find that

$$Q = 171 - 20p + 20p_b + 3p_c + 2Y = 171 - 20p + (20 \times 4.60) + (3 \times 3\tfrac{1}{3}) + (2 \times 12.5)$$
$$= 298 - 20p.$$

Figure 2.2 A Shift of the Demand Curve

The demand curve for processed pork shifts to the right from D^1 to D^2 as the price of beef rises from \$4 to \$4.60. As a result of the increase in beef prices, more pork is demanded at any given price.

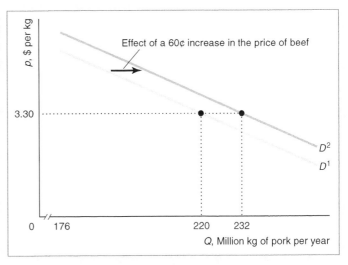

Summing Demand Functions

If we know the demand curve for each of two consumers, how do we determine the total demand for the two consumers combined? The total quantity demanded at a given price is the sum of the quantity each consumer demands at that price.

We can use the demand functions to determine the total demand of several consumers. Suppose the demand function for Consumer 1 is

$$Q_1 = D^1(p),$$

and the demand function for Consumer 2 is

$$Q_2 = D^2(p).$$

At price p, Consumer 1 demands Q_1 units, Consumer 2 demands Q_2 units, and the total demand of both consumers is the sum of the quantities each demands separately:

$$Q = Q_1 + Q_2 = D^1(p) + D^2(p).$$

We can generalize this approach to look at the total demand for three or more consumers.

APPLICATION

Aggregating the Demand for Broadband Service

We illustrate how to combine individual demand curves to get a total demand curve graphically using estimated demand curves for broadband (high-speed) Internet service (Duffy-Deno, 2003). The following figure shows the demand curve for small firms (1 to 19 employees), the demand curve for larger firms, and the total demand curve for all firms, which is the horizontal sum of the other two demand curves.

When the price per kilobyte per second (Kbps) of data transmitted is 40¢, the quantity demanded by small firms is $Q_s = 10$ (in millions of Kbps), and the quantity demanded by larger firms is $Q_l = 11.5$. Thus, the total quantity demanded at that price is $Q = Q_s + Q_l = 10 + 11.5 = 21.5$.

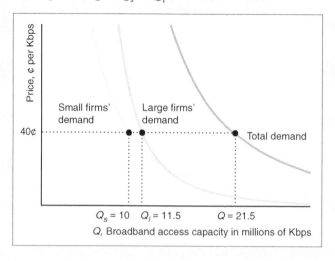

2.2 Supply

To determine the market price and quantity sold of a product, knowing how much consumers want of it is not enough. We also need to know how much firms want to supply at any given price.

The **quantity supplied** is the amount of a good that firms *want* to sell during a given time period at a given price, holding constant other factors that influence firms' supply decisions, such as costs and government actions. Firms determine how much of a good to supply on the basis of the price of that good and other factors, including the costs of production and government rules and regulations. Usually, we expect firms to supply more at a higher price. Before concentrating on the role price plays in determining supply, we'll briefly consider the role of some of the other factors.

Production cost affects how much of a good firms want to sell. As a firm's cost rises, it is willing to supply less of the good, all else the same. In the extreme case where the firm's cost exceeds what it can earn from selling the good, the firm sells nothing. Thus, factors that affect cost also affect supply. For example, a technological advance that allows a firm to produce a good at a lower cost causes the firm to supply more of that good, all else the same.

Government rules and regulations affect how much firms want to sell or are allowed to sell. Taxes and many government regulations—such as those designed to prevent pollution, improve sanitation, and provide health insurance to workers—increase the costs of production and therefore lower the amount of products firms want to supply to the marketplace. Other regulations affect when and how products can be sold. For instance, the sale of cigarettes and liquor to children is prohibited. Also, most major cities around the world restrict the number of taxicabs.

The Supply Function

The **supply function** shows the correspondence between the quantity supplied, price, and other factors that influence the number of units offered for sale. Written generally (without specifying the functional form), the processed pork supply function is

$$Q = S(p, p_h), \quad (2.5)$$

where Q is the quantity of processed pork supplied per year, p is the price of processed pork per kg, and p_h is the price of hogs (the major input used to produce processed pork). The supply function, Equation 2.5, may be a function of other factors such as wages as well. By leaving out these other factors, we are implicitly holding them constant. Based on Moschini and Meilke (1992), the linear pork supply function in Canada is

$$Q = 178 + 40p - 60p_h, \quad (2.6)$$

where the quantity is in millions of kg of processed pork per year, and the prices are in Canadian dollars per kg of processed pork.

If we hold the price of hogs fixed at its typical value of $1.50 per kg, we can rewrite the supply function in Equation 2.6 as[7]

$$Q = 88 + 40p. \quad (2.7)$$

Because we hold fixed other variables that may affect the quantity supplied, such as costs and government rules, this supply function concisely answers the question "What happens to the quantity supplied as the price changes, holding all other factors constant?"

Corresponding to the supply function is a **supply curve**, which shows the quantity supplied at each possible price, holding constant the other factors that influence firms' supply decisions. Figure 2.3 shows the supply curve, S^1, for processed pork that corresponds to the supply function, Equation 2.7. Because the supply function is linear, the corresponding supply curve is a straight line. As the price of processed pork increases from $3.30 to $5.30, holding other factors (the price of hogs) constant, the quantity of pork supplied increases from 220 to 300 million kg per year, which is a *movement along the supply curve*.

Figure 2.3 A Supply Curve

The estimated supply curve, S^1, for processed pork in Canada (Moschini and Meilke, 1992) shows the relationship between the quantity supplied per year and the price per kg, holding input prices and other factors that influence supply constant. The upward slope of this supply curve indicates that firms supply more of this good when its price is high and less when the price is low. An increase in the price of pork causes a *movement along the supply curve*, resulting in a larger quantity of pork supplied.

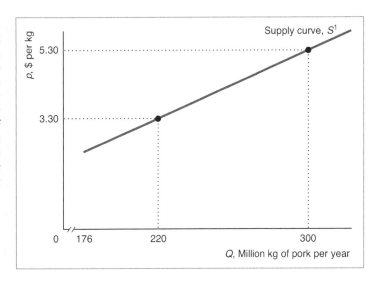

---

[7]If $p_h = \$1.50$, then Equation 2.6 is $Q = 178 + 40p - 60p_h = 178 + 40p - (60 \times 1.50) = 88 + 40p$.

How much does an increase in the price affect the quantity supplied? By differentiating the supply function, Equation 2.7, with respect to price, we find that $dQ/dp = 40$. As this derivative is not a function of p, it holds for all price changes, both small and large. It shows that the quantity supplied increases by 40 units for each \$1 increase in price.

Because the derivative is positive, the supply curve S^1 slopes upward in Figure 2.3. Although the Law of Demand requires that the demand curve slope downward, there is *no* "Law of Supply" that requires the market supply curve to have a particular slope. The market supply curve can be upward sloping, vertical, horizontal, or downward sloping.

A change in a factor other than a product's price causes a *shift of the supply curve*. If the price of hogs increases by 25¢, the supply function becomes

$$Q = 73 + 40p. \tag{2.8}$$

By comparing this supply function to the original one in Equation 2.7, $Q = 88 + 40p$, we see that the supply curve, S^1, shifts 15 units to the left, to S^2 in Figure 2.4.

Alternatively, we can determine how far the supply curve shifts by partially differentiating the supply function Equation 2.6 with respect to the price of hogs: $\partial Q/\partial p_h = -60$. This partial derivative holds for all values of p_h and hence for both small and large changes in p_h. Thus, a 25¢ increase in the price of hogs causes a $-60 \times 0.25 = -15$ units change in the quantity of pork supplied at any price of pork.

Again, it is important to distinguish between a *movement along a supply curve* and a *shift of the supply curve*. When the price of pork changes, the change in the quantity supplied reflects a *movement along the supply curve*. When costs, government rules, or other variables that affect supply change, the entire *supply curve shifts*.

Summing Supply Functions

The total supply curve shows the total quantity of a product produced by all suppliers at each possible price. For example, the total supply curve of rice in Japan is the sum of the domestic and the foreign supply curves of rice.

Figure 2.4 A Shift of a Supply Curve

An increase in the price of hogs from \$1.50 to \$1.75 per kg causes a *shift of the supply curve* from S^1 to S^2. At the price of processed pork of \$3.30, the quantity supplied falls from 220 on S^1 to 205 on S^2.

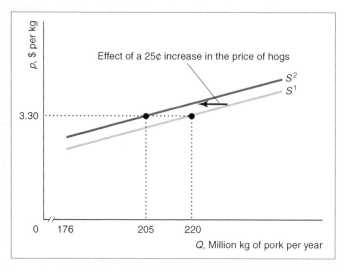

Figure 2.5 shows the domestic supply curve, panel a, and foreign supply curve, panel b, of rice in Japan. The total supply curve, S in panel c, is the horizontal sum of the Japanese *domestic* supply curve, S^d, and the *foreign* supply curve, S^f. In the figure, the Japanese and foreign supplies are zero at any price equal to or less than $\underline{p}$, so the total supply is zero. At prices above $\underline{p}$, the Japanese and foreign supplies are positive, so the total supply is positive. For example, when the price is p^*, the quantity supplied by Japanese firms is Q_d^* panel a, the quantity supplied by foreign firms is Q_f^*, panel b, and the total quantity supplied is $Q^* = Q_d^* + Q_f^*$ panel c. Because the total supply curve is the horizontal sum of the domestic and foreign supply curves, the total supply curve is flatter than either of the other two supply curves.

How Government Import Policies Affect Supply Curves

We can use this approach for deriving the total supply curve to analyze the effect of government policies on the total supply curve. Traditionally, the Japanese government has banned the importation of foreign rice. We want to determine how much less rice is supplied at any given price to the Japanese market because of this ban.

Without a ban, the foreign supply curve is S^f in panel b of Figure 2.5. A ban on imports eliminates the foreign supply, so the foreign supply curve after the ban is imposed, $\bar{S}^f$ is a vertical line at $Q_f = 0$. The import ban has no effect on the domestic supply curve, S^d, so the supply curve is the same as in panel a.

Because the foreign supply with a ban, $\bar{S}^f$ in panel b, is zero at every price, the total supply with a ban, $\bar{S}$ in panel c, is the same as the Japanese domestic supply, S^d, at any given price. The total supply curve under the ban lies to the left of the total supply curve without a ban, S. Thus, the effect of the import ban is to rotate the total supply curve toward the vertical axis.

Figure 2.5 Total Supply: The Sum of Domestic and Foreign Supply

If foreigners are allowed to sell their rice in Japan, the total Japanese supply of rice, S, is the horizontal sum of the domestic Japanese supply, S^d, and the imported foreign supply, S^f. With a ban on foreign imports, the foreign supply curve, $\bar{S}^f$, is zero at every price, so the total supply curve, $\bar{S}$, is the same as the domestic supply curve, S^d.

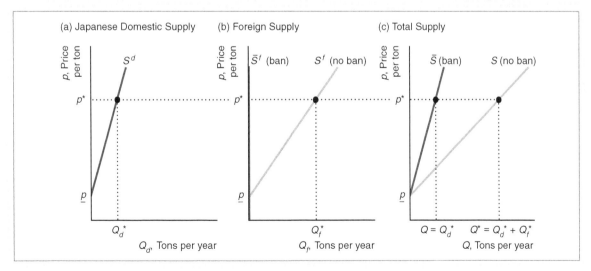

A limit that a government sets on the quantity of a foreign-produced good that may be imported is called a **quota**. By absolutely banning the importation of rice, the Japanese government sets quota of zero on rice imports. Sometimes governments set positive quotas, $\bar{Q} > 0$. The foreign firms may supply as much as they want, Q_f, as long as they supply no more than the quota: $Q_f \leq \bar{Q}$.

2.3 Market Equilibrium

The supply and demand curves jointly determine the price and quantity at which goods and services are bought and sold. The demand curve shows the quantities that consumers want to buy at various prices, and the supply curve shows the quantities that firms want to sell at various prices. Unless the price is set so that consumers want to buy exactly the same amount that suppliers want to sell, either some buyers cannot buy as much as they want or some sellers cannot sell as much as they want.

When all traders are able to buy or sell as much as they want, we say that the market is in **equilibrium**: a situation in which no participant wants to change its behavior. A price at which consumers can buy as much as they want and sellers can sell as much as they want is called an *equilibrium price*. The quantity that is bought and sold at the equilibrium price is called the *equilibrium quantity*.

Finding the Market Equilibrium

This little piggy went to market....

To illustrate how supply and demand curves determine the equilibrium price and quantity, we use our old friend, the processed pork example. Figure 2.6 shows the supply, S, and the demand, D, curves for pork. The supply and demand curves intersect at point e, the market equilibrium, where the equilibrium price is $3.30 and the equilibrium quantity is 220 million kg per year, which is the quantity that firms want to sell and the quantity that consumers want to buy at the equilibrium price.

Figure 2.6 Market Equilibrium

The intersection of the supply curve, S, and the demand curve, D, for processed pork determines the market equilibrium point, e, where $p = \$3.30$ per kg and $Q = 220$ million kg per year. At the lower price of $p = \$2.65$, the quantity supplied is only 194, whereas the quantity demanded is 233, so there is excess demand of 39. At $p = \$3.95$, a price higher than the equilibrium price, there is an excess supply of 39 because the quantity demanded, 207, is less than the quantity supplied, 246. When there is excess demand or supply, market forces drive the price back to the equilibrium price of $3.30.

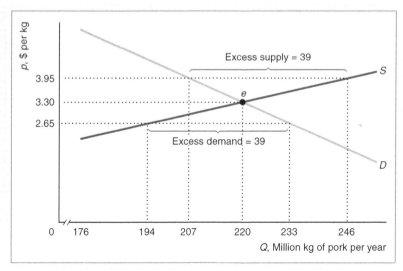

We can determine the market equilibrium for processed pork mathematically using the demand and supply functions, Equations 2.3 and 2.7. We use these two functions to solve for the equilibrium price at which the quantity demanded equals the quantity supplied (the equilibrium quantity).

The demand function in Equation 2.3 shows the relationship between the quantity of processed pork demanded, Q_d, and the price:

$$Q_d = 286 - 20p.$$

The supply function in Equation 2.7 describes the relationship between the quantity of processed pork supplied, Q_s, and the price:

$$Q_s = 88 + 40p.$$

We want to find the price at which $Q_d = Q_s = Q$, the equilibrium quantity. Because the left-hand sides of the two equations are equal in equilibrium, $Q_s = Q_d$, the right-hand sides of the two equations must be equal as well:

$$286 - 20p = 88 + 40p.$$

Adding $20p$ to both sides of this expression and subtracting 88 from both sides, we find that $198 = 60p$. Dividing both sides of this last expression by 60, we learn that the equilibrium price is $p = \$3.30$. We can determine the equilibrium quantity by substituting this equilibrium price, $p = \$3.30$, into either the supply or the demand equation:

$$Q_d = Q_s$$
$$286 - (20 \times 3.30) = 88 + (40 \times 3.30)$$
$$220 = 220.$$

Thus, the equilibrium quantity is 220 million kg.

Forces That Drive a Market to Equilibrium

A market equilibrium is not just an abstract concept or a theoretical possibility: We observe markets in equilibrium. The ability to buy as much as you want of a good at the market price is indirect evidence that a market is in equilibrium. You can almost always buy as much as you want of milk, ballpoint pens, and many other goods.

Amazingly, a market equilibrium occurs without any explicit coordination between consumers and firms. In a competitive market such as that for agricultural goods, millions of consumers and thousands of firms make their buying and selling decisions independently. Yet, each firm can sell as much as it wants, and each consumer can buy as much as he or she wants. It is as though an unseen market force, like an *invisible hand*, directs people to coordinate their activities to achieve market equilibrium.

What really causes the market to be in equilibrium? If the price were not at the equilibrium level, consumers or firms would have an incentive to change their behavior in a way that would drive the price to the equilibrium level.[8]

If the price were initially lower than the equilibrium price, consumers would want to buy more than suppliers would want to sell. If the price of pork were $2.65 in Figure 2.6, firms would be willing to supply 194 million kg per year, but

---

[8]Our model of competitive market equilibrium, which occurs at a point in time, does not formally explain how dynamic adjustments occur. The following explanation, though plausible, is just one of a number of possible dynamic adjustment stories that economists have modeled.

consumers would demand 233 million kg. At this price, the market would be in *disequilibrium*, meaning that the quantity demanded would not equal the quantity supplied. There would be **excess demand**—the amount by which the quantity demanded exceeds the quantity supplied at a specified price—of 39 (= 233 − 194) million kg per year at a price of $2.65.

Some consumers would be lucky enough to be able to buy the pork at $2.65. Other consumers would not find anyone willing to sell them pork at that price. What could they do? Some frustrated consumers might offer to pay suppliers more than $2.65. Alternatively, suppliers, noticing these disappointed consumers, might raise their prices. Such actions by consumers and producers would cause the market price to rise. At higher prices, the quantity that firms want to supply increases and the quantity that consumers want to buy decreases. The upward pressure on the price would continue until it reached the equilibrium price, $3.30, where there is no excess demand.

If, instead, the price were initially above the equilibrium level, suppliers would want to sell more than consumers would want to buy. For example, at a price of pork of $3.95, suppliers would want to sell 246 million kg per year but consumers would want to buy only 207 million, as the figure shows. At $3.95, the market would be in disequilibrium. There would be an **excess supply**—the amount by which the quantity supplied is greater than the quantity demanded at a specified price—of 39 (= 246 − 207) at a price of $3.95. Not all firms could sell as much as they wanted. Rather than incur storage costs (and possibly have their unsold pork spoil), firms would lower the price to attract additional customers. As long as the price remained above the equilibrium price, some firms would have unsold pork and would want to lower the price further. The price would fall until it reached the equilibrium level, $3.30, where there is no excess supply and hence no more pressure to lower the price further.[9]

In summary, at any price other than the equilibrium price, either consumers or suppliers would be unable to trade as much as they want. These disappointed people would act to change the price, driving the price to the equilibrium level. The equilibrium price is called the *market clearing price* because it removes from the market all frustrated buyers and sellers: There is no excess demand or excess supply at the market clearing price.

2.4 Shocking the Equilibrium: Comparative Statics

If the variables we hold constant in the demand and supply functions do not change, an equilibrium would persist indefinitely because none of the participants in the market would apply pressure to change the price. However, the equilibrium changes if a shock occurs so that one of the variables we were holding constant changes, causing a shift in either the demand curve or the supply curve.

Comparative statics is the method economists use to analyze how variables controlled by consumers and firms—here, price and quantity—react to a change in

---

[9]Not all markets reach equilibrium through the independent actions of many buyers or sellers. In institutionalized or formal markets, such as the Chicago Mercantile Exchange—where agricultural commodities, financial instruments, energy, and metals are traded—buyers and sellers meet at a single location (or on a single Web site). In these markets, certain individuals or firms, sometimes referred to as *market makers*, act to adjust the price and bring the market into equilibrium very quickly.

2.4 Shocking the Equilibrium: Comparative Statics

environmental variables (also called *exogenous variables*) that they do not control. Such environmental variables include the prices of substitutes, the prices of substitutes and complements, the income level of consumers, and the prices of inputs. The term *comparative statics* literally refers to comparing a *static* equilibrium—an equilibrium at a point in time from before the change—to a static equilibrium after the change. (In contrast, economists may examine a dynamic model, in which the dynamic equilibrium adjusts over time.)

Comparative Statics with Discrete (Relatively Large) Changes

We can determine the comparative statics properties of an equilibrium by examining the effects of a discrete (relatively large) change in one environmental variable. We can do so by solving for the before- and after-equilibria and comparing them using mathematics or a graph. We illustrate this approach using our beloved pork example. Suppose all the environmental variables remain constant except the price of hogs, which increases by 25¢. It is now more expensive to produce pork because the price of a major input, hogs, has increased.

Because the price of hogs is not an argument to the demand function—a change in the price of an input does not affect consumers' desires—the demand curve does not shift. However, as we saw in Figure 2.4, the increase in the price of hogs causes the supply curve for pork to shift 15 units to the left from S^1 to S^2 at every possible price of pork.

Figure 2.7 reproduces this shift of the supply curve and adds the original demand curve. At the original equilibrium price of pork, $3.30, consumers still want to buy 220 million kg, but suppliers are now willing to supply only 205 million kg at that price, so there is excess demand of 15. Market pressure then forces the price of pork upward until it reaches the new equilibrium, e_2. At e_2, the new equilibrium price is $3.55, and the new equilibrium quantity is 215 million kg. Thus, the increase in the price of hogs causes the equilibrium price of processed pork to rise by 25¢ per kg, but the equilibrium quantity to fall by 15 million kg. Here the increase in the price

Figure 2.7 The Equilibrium Effect of a Shift of the Supply Curve

A 25¢ increase in the price of hogs causes the supply curve for processed pork to shift to the left from S^1 to S^2, driving the market equilibrium from e_1 to e_2, and the market equilibrium price from $3.30 to $3.55.

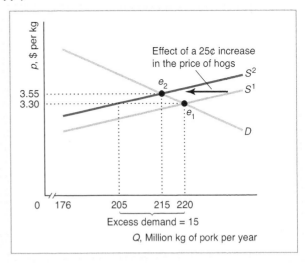

of a factor causes a *shift of the supply curve* and a *movement along the demand curve*.

We can derive the same result by using equations to solve for the equilibrium before the change and after the discrete change in the price of hogs and by comparing the two equations. We have already solved for the original equilibrium, e_1, by setting the quantity in the demand function Equation 2.3 equal to the quantity in the supply function Equation 2.7. We obtain the new equilibrium, e_2, by equating the quantity in the demand function Equation 2.3 to that of the new supply function, with a 25¢ higher price of hogs, Equation 2.8:

$$286 - 20p = 73 + 40p.$$

Simplifying this expression, we find that the new equilibrium price is $p_2 = \$3.55$. Substituting that price into either the demand or the supply function, we learn that the new equilibrium quantity is $Q_2 = 215$, as Figure 2.7 shows. Thus, both methods show that an increase in the price of hogs causes the equilibrium price to rise and the equilibrium quantity to fall.

APPLICATION

Occupational Licensing

To work in many occupations in the United States, you must have a license. More than 800 occupations require licenses issued by local, state, or federal government agencies, including animal trainers, dietitians and nutritionists, doctors, electricians, embalmers, funeral directors, hairdressers, librarians, nurses, psychologists, real estate brokers, respiratory therapists, salespeople, teachers, and tree trimmers (but not economists).

During the early 1950s, fewer than 5% of U.S. workers were in occupations covered by licensing laws at the state level. Since then, the share of licensed workers has grown, reaching nearly 18% by the 1980s, at least 20% in 2000, and 29% in 2008. Licensing is more common in occupations that require extensive education: more than 40% of workers with a post-college education are required to have a license, compared to only 15% of those with less than a high school education.

To obtain a license in some occupations, you must pass a test, which is frequently designed by licensed members of the occupation. By making exams difficult, current members of the occupation can limit entry by new workers. For example, only 37.1% of people taking the California State Bar Examination in February 2010 passed it, although all of them had law degrees. (The national rate for lawyers passing state bar exams in 2009 was higher, but still only 53%.)

To the degree that testing is objective, licensing may raise the average quality of the workforce. However, too often its primary effect is to restrict the number of workers in an occupation. To analyze the effects of licensing, we can use a graph similar to Figure 2.7, where the wage is on the vertical axis and the number of workers per year is on the horizontal axis. Licensing shifts the occupational supply curve to the left, which reduces the equilibrium quantity of workers and raises the equilibrium wage. Kleiner and Kruger (2010) find that licensing raises occupational wages by 15% on average.

Comparative Statics with Small Changes

Alternatively, we can use calculus to determine the effect of a small change (as opposed to the discrete change we just used) in one environmental variable, holding the other such variables constant. Until now, we have used calculus to examine how an argument of a demand function affects the quantity demanded or how an argument of a supply function affects the quantity supplied. Now, however, we want to know how an environmental variable affects the equilibrium price and quantity that are determined by the intersection of the supply and demand curves.

Our first step is to characterize the equilibrium values as functions of the relevant environmental variables. Suppose that we hold constant all the environmental variables that affect demand so that the demand function is

$$Q = D(p). \tag{2.9}$$

One environmental variable, a, in the supply function changes, which causes the supply curve to shift. We write the supply function as

$$Q = S(p, a). \tag{2.10}$$

As before, we determine the equilibrium price by equating the quantities, Q, in Equations 2.9 and 2.10:

$$D(p) = S(p, a). \tag{2.11}$$

Equation 2.11 is an example of an *identity*. As a changes, p changes so that this equation continues to hold—the market remains in equilibrium. Thus, based on this equation, we can write the equilibrium price as an implicit function of the environmental variable: $p = p(a)$. That is, we can write the equilibrium condition in Equation 2.11 as

$$D(p(a)) = S(p(a), a). \tag{2.12}$$

We can characterize how the equilibrium price changes with a by differentiating the equilibrium condition Equation 2.12 with respect to a using the chain rule at the original equilibrium,[10]

$$\frac{\mathrm{d}D(p(a))}{\mathrm{d}p}\frac{\mathrm{d}p}{\mathrm{d}a} = \frac{\partial S(p(a), a)}{\partial p}\frac{\mathrm{d}p}{\mathrm{d}a} + \frac{\partial S(p(a), a)}{\partial a}. \tag{2.13}$$

Using algebra, we can rearrange Equation 2.13 as

$$\frac{\mathrm{d}p}{\mathrm{d}a} = \frac{\frac{\partial S}{\partial a}}{\frac{\mathrm{d}D}{\mathrm{d}p} - \frac{\partial S}{\partial p}}, \tag{2.14}$$

where we suppress the arguments of the functions for notational simplicity. Equation 2.14 shows the derivative of $p(a)$ with respect to a.

We know that $\mathrm{d}D/\mathrm{d}p < 0$ because of the Law of Demand. If the supply curve is upward sloping, then $\partial S/\partial p$ is positive, so the denominator of Equation 2.14, $\mathrm{d}D/\mathrm{d}p - \partial S/\partial p$, is negative. Thus, $\mathrm{d}p/\mathrm{d}a$ has the opposite sign as the numerator of Equation 2.14. If $\partial S/\partial a$ is negative, then $\mathrm{d}p/\mathrm{d}a$ is positive: As a increases, the equilibrium price rises. If $\partial S/\partial a$ is positive, an increase in a causes the equilibrium price to fall.

By using either the demand function or the supply function, we can use this result concerning the effect of a on the equilibrium price to determine the effect of a on the equilibrium quantity. For example, we can rewrite the demand function Equation 2.9 as

$$Q = D(p(a)). \tag{2.15}$$

---

[10]The chain rule is a formula for the derivative of the composite of two functions, such as $f(g(x))$. According to this rule, $\mathrm{d}f/\mathrm{d}x = (\mathrm{d}f/\mathrm{d}g)(\mathrm{d}g/\mathrm{d}x)$. See the Calculus Appendix at the end of the book.

Differentiating the demand function Equation 2.15 with respect to a using the chain rule, we find that

$$\frac{dQ}{da} = \frac{dD}{dp}\frac{dp}{da}. \quad (2.16)$$

Because $\partial D/\partial p < 0$ by the Law of Demand, the sign of dQ/da is the opposite of that of dp/da. That is, as a increases, the equilibrium price moves in the opposite direction of the equilibrium quantity. In Solved Problem 2.1, we use the pork example to illustrate this type of analysis.

SOLVED PROBLEM 2.1

How do the equilibrium price and quantity of pork vary as the price of hogs changes if the variables that affect demand are held constant at their typical values? Answer this comparative statics question using calculus. (*Hint*: This problem is of the same form as the more general one we just analyzed. In the pork market, the environmental variable that shifts supply, a, is p_h.)

Answer

1. *Solve for the equilibrium price of processed pork in terms of the price of hogs.* To obtain an expression for the equilibrium similar to Equation 2.14, we equate the right-hand sides of the demand function in Equation 2.3 and the supply function Equation 2.6 to obtain

$$286 - 20p = 178 + 40p - 60p_h, \text{ or}$$

$$p = 1.8 + p_h. \quad (2.17)$$

   (As a check, when p_h equals its typical value, \$1.50, the equilibrium price of pork is $p = \$3.30$ according to Equation 2.17, which is consistent with our earlier calculations.)

2. *Use this equilibrium price equation to show how the equilibrium price changes as the price of hogs changes.* Differentiating the equilibrium price Equation 2.17 with respect to p_h gives an expression of the form of Equation 2.16:

$$\frac{dp}{dp_h} = 1. \quad (2.18)$$

   That is, as the price of hogs increases by 1¢, the equilibrium price of pork increases by 1¢. Because this condition holds for any value of p_h, it also holds for larger changes in the price of hogs. Thus, a 25¢ increase in the price of hogs causes a 25¢ increase in the equilibrium price of pork.

3. *Write the pork demand function as in Equation 2.15, and then differentiate it with respect to the price of hogs to show how the equilibrium quantity of pork varies with the price of hogs.* From the pork demand function, Equation 2.3, we can write the quantity demanded as

$$Q = D(p(p_h)) = 286 - 20\, p(p_h).$$

   Differentiating this expression with respect to p_h using the chain rule, we obtain an expression in the form of Equation 2.16 with respect to p_h:

$$\frac{dQ}{dp_h} = \frac{dD}{dp}\frac{dp}{dp_h} = -20 \times 1 = -20. \quad (2.19)$$

   That is, as the price of hogs increases by \$1, the equilibrium quantity of processed pork falls by 20 units.

Why the Shapes of Demand and Supply Curves Matter

The shapes and positions of the demand and supply curves determine by how much a shock affects the equilibrium price and quantity. We illustrate the importance of the shape of the demand curve by showing how our comparative statics results would change if the processed pork demand curve had a different shape. We continue to use the estimated supply curve of pork and examine what happens if the price of hogs increases by 25¢, causing the supply curve of pork to shift to the left from S^1 to S^2 in panel a of Figure 2.8. In the actual market, the shift of the supply curve causes a movement along the downward-sloping demand curve, D^1, so the equilibrium quantity falls from 220 to 215 million kg per year, and the equilibrium price rises from $3.30 to $3.55 per kg. The supply shock—an increase in the price of hogs—hurts consumers by increasing the equilibrium price of processed pork by 25¢ per kg. Consequently, customers buy less of it: 215 million kg instead of 220 million kg.

A supply shock would have different effects if the demand curve had a different shape. Suppose that the quantity demanded were not sensitive to a change in the price, so the same amount is demanded no matter what the price is, as the vertical demand curve D^2 in panel b shows. A 25¢ increase in the price of hogs again shifts the supply curve from S^1 to S^2. The equilibrium quantity does not change, but the price consumers pay rises by 37.5¢ to $3.675. Thus, the amount consumers spend rises by more when the demand curve is vertical instead of downward sloping.

Now suppose that consumers are very sensitive to price changes, as the horizontal demand curve, D^3, in panel c shows. Consumers will buy virtually unlimited quantities of pork at $3.30 per kg (or less). However, if the price rises even slightly, they will stop buying pork altogether. With a horizontal demand curve, an increase in the price of hogs has *no* effect on the price consumers pay; however, the equilibrium quantity drops substantially to 205 million kg per year. Thus, how much the equilibrium quantity falls and how much the equilibrium price of processed pork rises when the price of hogs increases depend on the shape of the demand curve.

Figure 2.8 **The Effect of a Shift of the Supply Curve, Depending on the Shape of the Demand Curve**

A 25¢ increase in the price of hogs causes the supply curve for processed pork to shift to the left from S^1 to S^2. (a) Given the actual downward-sloping linear demand curve, the equilibrium price rises from $3.30 to $3.55, and the equilibrium quantity falls from 220 to 215. (b) If the demand curve were vertical, the supply shock would cause the price to rise to $3.675 while the quantity would remain unchanged. (c) If the demand curve were horizontal, the supply shock would not affect price but would cause quantity to fall to 205.

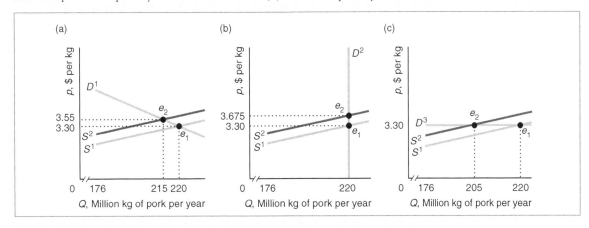

2.5 Elasticities

It is convenient to be able to summarize the responsiveness of one variable to a change in another variable using a summary statistic. In our last example, we wanted to know whether an increase in the price of a product causes a large or a small change in the quantity demanded (that is, whether the demand curve is relatively vertical or relatively horizontal at the current price). We can use summary statistics of the responsiveness of the quantity demanded and the quantity supplied to determine comparative statics properties of the equilibrium. Often, we have reasonable estimates of these summary statistics and can use them to predict what will happen to the equilibrium in a market—that is, to make comparative statistics predictions. Later in this chapter, we will examine how the government can use these summary measures to predict how a tax on a product will affect the equilibrium price and quantity, and hence firms' revenues and the government's tax receipts.

Suppose that a variable z (for example, the quantity demanded or the quantity supplied) is a function of a variable x (say, the price of z) and possibly other variables such as y: $z = f(x, y)$. For example, f could be the demand function, where z is the quantity demanded, x is the price, and y is income. We want a summary statistic that describes how much z changes as x changes, holding y constant. An **elasticity** is the percentage change in one variable (here, z) in response to a given percentage change in another variable (here, y), holding other relevant variables (here, y) constant. The elasticity, E, of z with respect to x is

$$E = \frac{\text{percentage change in } z}{\text{percentage change in } x} = \frac{\Delta z / z}{\Delta x / x} = \frac{\partial z}{\partial x} \frac{x}{z}, \quad (2.20)$$

where Δz is the change in z, so $\Delta z/z$ is the percentage change in z. If z changes by 3% when x changes by 1%, then the elasticity E is 3. Thus, the elasticity is a pure number (it has no units of measure).[11] As Δx goes to zero, $\Delta z/\Delta x$ goes to the partial derivative $\partial z/\partial x$. Economists usually calculate elasticities at this limit—that is, for infinitesimal changes in x.

Demand Elasticity

The **price elasticity of demand** (or simply the *demand elasticity* or *elasticity of demand*) is the percentage change in the quantity demanded, Q, in response to a given percentage change in the price, p, at a particular point on the demand curve. The price elasticity of demand (represented by ε, the Greek letter epsilon) is

$$\varepsilon = \frac{\text{percentage change in quantity demanded}}{\text{percentage change in price}} = \frac{\Delta Q / Q}{\Delta p / p} = \frac{\partial Q}{\partial p} \frac{p}{Q}, \quad (2.21)$$

where $\partial Q/\partial p$ is the partial derivative of the demand function with respect to p (that is, holding constant other variables that affect the quantity demanded). For example, if $\varepsilon = -2$, then a 1% increase in the price results in a 2% decrease in the quantity demanded.

---

[11]Economists use the elasticity rather than the slope, $\partial z/\partial x$, as a summary statistic because the elasticity is a pure number, whereas the slope depends on the units of measurement. For example, if x is a price measured in pennies and we switch to measuring price using dollars, the slope changes, but the elasticity remains unchanged.

We can use Equation 2.21 to calculate the elasticity of demand for a linear demand function that holds fixed other variables that affect demand:

$$Q = a - bp,$$

where a is the quantity demanded when the price is zero, $Q = a - (b \times 0) = a$, and $-b$ is the ratio of the fall in the quantity relative to the rise in price: the derivative dQ/dp. The elasticity of demand is

$$\varepsilon = \frac{dQ}{dp}\frac{p}{Q} = -b\frac{p}{Q}. \tag{2.22}$$

For the linear demand function for pork, $Q = a - bp = 286 - 20p$, at the initial equilibrium where $p = \$3.30$ and $Q = 220$, the elasticity of demand is

$$\varepsilon = b\frac{p}{Q} = -20 \times \frac{3.30}{220} = -0.3.$$

The negative sign on the elasticity of demand of pork illustrates the Law of Demand: Less quantity is demanded as the price rises.

The elasticity of demand concisely answers the question "How much does the quantity demanded of a product fall in response to a 1% increase in its price?" A 1% increase in price leads to an ε% change in the quantity demanded. For example, at the equilibrium, a 1% increase in the price of pork leads to a -0.3% fall in the quantity of pork demanded. Thus, a price increase causes a less than proportionate fall in the quantity of pork demanded.

Elasticities Along the Demand Curve. The elasticity of demand varies along most demand curves. On downward-sloping linear demand curves that are neither vertical nor horizontal, the higher the price, the more negative the elasticity of demand. Consequently, even though the slope of the linear demand curve is constant, the elasticity varies along the curve. A 1% increase in the price causes a larger percentage fall in the quantity demanded near the top (left) of the demand curve than near the bottom (right).

Where a linear demand curve hits the quantity axis ($p = 0$ and $Q = a$), the elasticity of demand is $\varepsilon = -b \times (0/a) = 0$, according to Equation 2.22. The linear pork demand curve in Figure 2.9 illustrates this pattern. Where the price is zero, a 1% increase in price does not raise the price, so quantity demanded does not change. At a point where the elasticity of demand is zero, the demand curve is said to be *perfectly inelastic*. As a physical analogy, if you try to stretch an inelastic steel rod, the length does not change. The change in the price is the force pulling at demand; if the quantity demanded does not change in response to this force, the demand curve is perfectly inelastic.

For quantities between the midpoint of the linear demand curve and the lower end, where $Q = a$, the demand elasticity lies between 0 and -1: $0 > \varepsilon > -1$. A point along the demand curve where the elasticity is between 0 and -1 is *inelastic* (but not perfectly inelastic): A 1% increase in price leads to a fall in quantity of less than 1%. For example, at the original pork equilibrium, $\varepsilon = -0.3$, so a 1% increase in price causes quantity to fall by -0.3%.

At the midpoint of the linear demand curve, $p = a/(2b)$ and $Q = a/2$, so $\varepsilon = -bp/Q = -b[a/(2b)]/(a/2) = -1$.[12] Such an elasticity of demand is called a *unitary elasticity*.

---

[12]The linear demand curve hits the price axis at $p = a/b$ and the quantity axis at $p = 0$. The midpoint occurs at $p = (a/b - 0)/2 = a/(2b)$. The corresponding quantity is $Q = a - b[a/(2b)] = a/2$.

Figure 2.9 The Demand Elasticity Varies Along a Linear Demand Curve

On a linear demand curve, such as the pork demand curve, the higher the price, the more elastic the demand curve (ε is larger in absolute value—a larger negative number). The demand curve is perfectly inelastic ($\varepsilon = 0$) where the demand curve hits the horizontal axis, is perfectly elastic where the demand curve hits the vertical axis, and has unitary elasticity ($\varepsilon = -1$) at the midpoint of the demand curve.

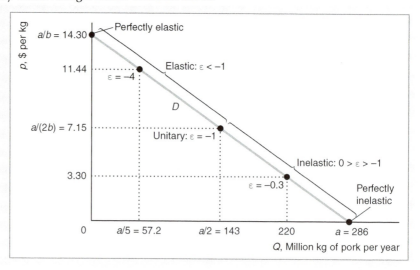

At prices higher than at the midpoint of the demand curve, the elasticity of demand is less than negative one, $\varepsilon < -1$. In this range, the demand curve is called *elastic*: A 1% increase in price causes more than a 1% fall in quantity. A physical analogy is a rubber band that stretches substantially when you pull on it. In the figure where $Q = a/5$, the elasticity is -4, so a 1% increase in price causes a 4% drop in quantity.

As the price rises, the elasticity gets more and more negative, approaching negative infinity. Where the demand curve hits the price axis, it is *perfectly elastic*.[13] At the price a/b where $Q = 0$, a 1% decrease in p causes the quantity demanded to become positive, which is an infinite increase in quantity.

The elasticity of demand varies along most demand curves, not just downward-sloping linear ones. However, along a special type of demand curve, called a *constant-elasticity demand curve*, the elasticity is the same at every point along the curve. Constant-elasticity demand curves all have the exponential form

$$Q = Ap^\varepsilon, \qquad (2.23)$$

where A is a positive constant and ε, a negative constant, is the elasticity at every point along this demand curve. By taking natural logarithms of both sides of Equation 2.23, we can rewrite this exponential demand curve as a log-linear demand curve:

$$\ln Q = \ln A + \varepsilon \ln p. \qquad (2.24)$$

For example, in the application "Aggregating the Demand for Broadband Service," the estimated demand function for broadband services by large firms is $Q = 16p^{-0.296}$. Here $A = 16$, and $\varepsilon = -0.296$ is the constant elasticity of demand. That is, the demand for broadband services by large firms is inelastic: $0 > \varepsilon > -1$. We

---

[13]The linear demand curve hits the price axis at $p = a/b$ and $Q = 0$, so the elasticity of demand is $-bp/0$. As the price approaches a/b, the elasticity approaches negative infinity. An intuition for this convention is provided by looking at a sequence where -1 divided by $1/10$ is -10, -1 divided by $1/100$ is -100, and so on. The smaller the number we divide by, the more negative the result, which goes to $-\infty$ (negative infinity) in the limit.

Figure 2.10 Constant-Elasticity Demand Curves

These constant elasticity demand curves, $Q = Ap$, vary with respect to their elasticities. Curves with negative, finite elasticities are convex to the origin. The vertical, constant-elasticity demand curve is perfectly inelastic, while the horizontal curve is perfectly elastic.

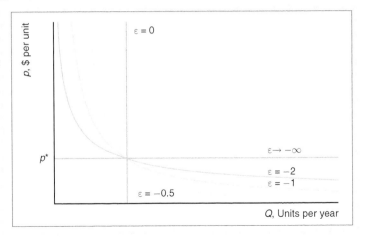

can equivalently write this demand function as $\ln Q = \ln 16 - 0.296 \ln p \approx 2.773 - 0.296 \ln p$.

Figure 2.10 shows several constant-elasticity demand curves with different elasticities. Except for the vertical and the horizontal demand curves, the curves are convex to the origin (bend away from the origin). The two extreme cases of these constant-elasticity demand curves are the vertical and the horizontal demand curves. Along the demand curve that is horizontal at p^* in Figure 2.10, the elasticity is infinite everywhere. It is also a special case of a linear demand curve with a zero slope ($b = 0$). Along this demand curve, people are willing to buy as much as firms sell at any price less than or equal to p^*. If the price increases even slightly above p^*, however, demand falls to zero. Thus, a small increase in price causes an infinite drop in the quantity demanded, which means that the demand curve is perfectly elastic.

Why would a demand curve be horizontal? One reason is that consumers view one good as identical to another good and do not care which one they buy. Suppose that consumers view Washington State apples and Oregon apples as identical. They won't buy Washington apples if these apples sell for more than Oregon apples. Similarly, they won't buy Oregon apples if their price is higher than that of Washington apples. If the two prices are equal, consumers do not care which type of apple they buy. Thus, the demand curve for Oregon apples is horizontal at the price of Washington apples.

The other extreme case is the vertical demand curve, which is perfectly inelastic everywhere. Such a demand curve is also an extreme case of the linear demand curve with an infinite (vertical) slope. If the price goes up, the quantity demanded is unchanged, $dQ/dp = 0$, so the elasticity of demand must be zero: $\varepsilon = (dQ/dp)(p/Q) = 0 \times (p/Q) = 0$.

A demand curve is vertical for *essential goods*—goods that people feel they must have and will pay anything to get. Because Sydney is a diabetic, his demand curve for insulin could be vertical at a day's dose, Q^*.[14]

---

[14]More realistically, he may have a maximum price, p^*, that he can afford to pay. Thus, his demand curve is vertical at Q^* up to p^* and horizontal at p^* to the left of Q^*.

SOLVED PROBLEM 2.2

Show that the price elasticity of demand is a constant ε if the demand function is exponential, $Q = Ap^\varepsilon$, or, equivalently, log-linear, $\ln Q = \ln A + \varepsilon \ln p$.

Answer

1. *Differentiate the exponential demand curve with respect to price to determine* dQ/dp, *and substitute that expression into the definition of the elasticity of demand.* Differentiating the demand curve $Q = Ap^\varepsilon$, we find that $dQ/dp = \varepsilon A p^{\varepsilon-1}$. Substituting that expression into the elasticity definition, we learn that the elasticity is

$$\frac{dQ}{dp}\frac{p}{Q} = \varepsilon A p^{\varepsilon-1}\frac{p}{Q} = \varepsilon A p^{\varepsilon-1}\frac{p}{Ap^\varepsilon} = \varepsilon.$$

Because the elasticity is a constant that does not depend on the particular value of p, it is the same at every point along the demand curve.

2. *Differentiate the log-linear demand curve to determine* dQ/dp, *and substitute that expression into the definition of the elasticity of demand.* Differentiating the log-linear demand curve, $\ln Q = \ln A + \varepsilon \ln p$, with respect to p, we find that $d(\ln Q)/dp = (dQ/dp)/Q = \varepsilon/p$. Multiplying this equation by p, we again discover that the elasticity is constant:

$$\frac{dQ}{dp}\frac{p}{Q} = \varepsilon \frac{Q}{p}\frac{p}{Q} = \varepsilon.$$

Other Demand Elasticities. We refer to the price elasticity of demand as *the* elasticity of demand. However, there are other demand elasticities that show how the quantity demanded changes in response to changes in variables other than price that affect the quantity demanded. Two such demand elasticities are the income elasticity of demand and the cross-price elasticity of demand.

As people's incomes increase, their demand curves for products shift. If a demand curve shifts to the right, a larger quantity is demanded at any given price. If instead the demand curve shifts to the left, a smaller quantity is demanded at any given price.

We can measure how sensitive the quantity demanded at a given price is to income by using the **income elasticity of demand** (or *income elasticity*), which is the percentage change in the quantity demanded in response to a given percentage change in income, Y. The income elasticity of demand is

$$\xi = \frac{\text{percentage change in quantity demanded}}{\text{percentage change in income}} = \frac{\Delta Q/Q}{\Delta Y/Y} = \frac{\partial Q}{\partial Y}\frac{Y}{Q},$$

where ξ is the Greek letter xi. If the quantity demanded increases as income rises, the income elasticity of demand is positive. If the quantity demanded does not change as income rises, the income elasticity is zero. Finally, if the quantity demanded falls as income rises, the income elasticity is negative.

By partially differentiating the pork demand function, Equation 2.2, $Q = 171 - 20p + 20p_b + 3p_c + 2Y$, with respect to Y, we find that $\partial Q/\partial Y = 2$, so the income elasticity of demand for pork is $\xi = 2Y/Q$. At our original equilibrium, quantity $Q = 220$ and income $Y = 12.5$, so the income elasticity is $\xi = 2 \times (12.5/220) \approx 0.114$, or about one-ninth. The positive income elasticity shows that an increase in income causes the pork demand curve to shift to the right.

Income elasticities play an important role in our analysis of consumer behavior in Chapter 5. Typically, goods that consumers view as necessities, such as food, have income elasticities near zero. Goods that they consider to be luxuries generally have income elasticities greater than one.

The **cross-price elasticity of demand** is the percentage change in the quantity demanded in response to a given percentage change in the price of another good, p_o. The cross-price elasticity may be calculated as

$$\frac{\text{percentage change in quantity demanded}}{\text{percentage change in price of another good}} = \frac{\Delta Q/Q}{\Delta p_o/p_o} = \frac{\partial Q}{\partial p_o}\frac{p_o}{Q}.$$

When the cross-price elasticity is negative, the goods are complements. If the cross-price elasticity is negative, people buy less of one good when the price of the other, second good increases: The demand curve for the first good shifts to the left. For example, if people like cream in their coffee, as the price of cream rises, they consume less coffee, so the cross-price elasticity of the quantity of coffee with respect to the price of cream is negative.

If the cross-price elasticity is positive, the goods are substitutes.[15] As the price of the second good increases, people buy more of the first good. For example, the quantity demanded of pork increases when the price of beef, p_b, rises. By partially differentiating the pork demand function, Equation 2.2, $Q = 171 - 20p + 20p_b + 3p_c + 2Y$, with respect to the price of beef, we find that $\partial Q/\partial p_b = 20$. As a result, the cross-price elasticity between the price of beef and the quantity of pork is $20p_b/Q$. At the original equilibrium where $Q = 220$ million kg per year, and $p_b = \$4$ per kg, the cross-price elasticity is $20 \times (4/220) \approx 0.364$. As the price of beef rises by 1%, the quantity of pork demanded rises by a little more than one-third of 1%.

APPLICATION

Substitution May Save Endangered Species

One reason that many species—including tigers, rhinoceroses, green turtles, geckos, sea horses, pipefish, and sea cucumbers—are endangered, threatened, or vulnerable to extinction is that certain of their body parts are used as aphrodisiacs in traditional Chinese medicine. Is it possible that consumers will switch from such potions to Viagra, a less expensive and almost certainly more effective alternative treatment, and thereby help save these endangered species?

We cannot directly calculate the cross-price elasticity of demand between Viagra and the price of body parts of endangered species because their trade is illicit and not reported. However, harp seal and hooded seal genitalia, which are used as aphrodisiacs in Asia, may be legally traded. Before 1998, Viagra was unavailable (effectively, it had an infinite price—one could not pay a high enough price to obtain it). When it became available at about $15 to $20 Canadian per pill, the demand for seal sex organs fell, and the demand curve shifted substantially to the left. According to von Hippel and von Hippel (2002, 2004), 30,000 to 50,000 seal organs were sold in the years just before 1998. In 1998, only 20,000 organs were sold. By 1999–2000 (and thereafter), virtually none were sold. A survey of older Chinese males confirms that, after the introduction of Viagra, they were much more likely to use a Western medicine than traditional Chinese medicines for erectile dysfunction, but not for other medical problems (von Hippel et al., 2005).

This evidence suggests a strong willingness to substitute Viagra for seal organs at current prices, and consequently that the cross-price elasticity between the price of seal organs and Viagra is positive. Thus, Viagra can perhaps save more than marriages.

---

[15]*Jargon alert*: Graduate-level textbooks generally call these goods *gross substitutes* (and the goods in the previous example would be called *gross complements*).

Supply Elasticity

Just as we can use the elasticity of demand to summarize information about the responsiveness of the quantity demanded to price or other variables, we can use the elasticity of supply to summarize how responsive the quantity supplied of a product is to price changes or other variables. The **price elasticity of supply** (or *supply elasticity*) is the percentage change in the quantity supplied in response to a given percentage change in the price. The price elasticity of supply (η, the Greek letter eta) is

$$\eta = \frac{\text{percentage change in quantity supplied}}{\text{percentage change in price}} = \frac{\Delta Q/Q}{\Delta p/p} = \frac{\partial Q}{\partial p}\frac{p}{Q}, \quad (2.25)$$

where Q is the *quantity supplied*. If $\eta = 2$, a 1% increase in price leads to a 2% increase in the quantity supplied.

The definition of the price elasticity of supply, Equation 2.25, is very similar to the definition of the price elasticity of demand, Equation 2.21. The key distinction is that the elasticity of supply describes the movement along the *supply* curve as price changes, whereas the elasticity of demand describes the movement along the *demand* curve as price changes. That is, in the numerator, supply elasticity depends on the percentage change in the *quantity supplied*, whereas demand elasticity depends on the percentage change in the *quantity demanded*.

If the supply curve is upward sloping, $\partial p/\partial Q > 0$, the supply elasticity is positive: $\eta > 0$. If the supply curve slopes downward, the supply elasticity is negative: $\eta < 0$. For the pork supply function Equation 2.7, $Q = 88 + 40p$, the supply elasticity of pork at the original equilibrium, where $p = \$3.30$ and $Q = 220$, is

$$\eta = \frac{dQ}{dp}\frac{p}{Q} = 40 \times \frac{3.30}{220} = 0.6.$$

As the price of pork increases by 1%, the quantity supplied rises by slightly less than two-thirds of 1%.

The elasticity of supply varies along an upward-sloping supply curve. For example, because the elasticity of supply for the pork is $\eta = 40p/Q$, as the ratio p/Q rises, the supply elasticity rises.

At a point on a supply curve where the elasticity of supply is $\eta = 0$, we say that the supply curve is *perfectly inelastic*: The supply does not change as the price rises. If $0 < \eta < 1$, the supply curve is *inelastic* (but not perfectly inelastic): A 1% increase in the price causes a less than 1% rise in the quantity supplied. If $\eta > 1$, the supply curve is *elastic*. If η is infinite, the supply curve is *perfectly elastic*.

The supply elasticity does not vary along constant-elasticity supply functions, which are exponential or (equivalently) log-linear: $Q = Bp^\eta$ or $\ln Q = \ln B + \eta \ln p$. If η is a positive, finite number, the constant-elasticity supply curve starts at the origin, as Figure 2.11 shows. Two extreme examples of both constant-elasticity of supply curves and linear supply curves are the vertical supply curve and the horizontal supply curve.

A supply curve that is vertical at a quantity, Q^*, is perfectly inelastic. No matter what the price is, firms supply Q^*. An example of inelastic supply is a perishable item such as already-picked fresh fruit. If the perishable good is not sold, it quickly becomes worthless. Thus, the seller will accept any market price for the good.

A supply curve that is horizontal at a price, p^*, is perfectly elastic. Firms supply as much as the market wants—a potentially unlimited amount—if the price is p^* or above. Firms supply nothing at a price below p^*, which does not cover their cost of production.

Figure 2.11 Constant Elasticity Supply Curves

Constant elasticity supply curves, $Q = Bp^\eta$, with positive, finite elasticities start at the origin. They are concave to the horizontal axis if $1 < \eta < \infty$ and convex if $0 < \eta < 1$. The unitary elasticity supply curve is a straight line through the origin. The vertical constant elasticity supply curve is perfectly inelastic, while the horizontal curve is perfectly elastic.

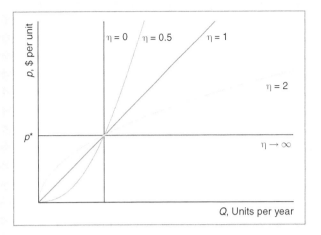

Long Run Versus Short Run

Typically, short-run demand or supply elasticities differ substantially from long-run elasticities. The duration of the short run depends on the planning horizon—how long it takes consumers or firms to adjust for a particular good.

Demand Elasticities over Time. Two factors that determine whether short-run demand elasticities are larger or smaller than long-run elasticities are the ease of substitution and storage opportunities. Often one can substitute between products in the long run but not in the short run.

For example, when oil prices rose rapidly in the 1970s and 1980s because the Organization of Petroleum Exporting Countries (OPEC) limited the supply of crude oil, most Western consumers could not greatly alter the amount of gasoline they demanded in the short run. Someone who drove 27 miles to and from work every day in a 1969 Chevy couldn't dramatically reduce the amount of gasoline he or she purchased right away. However in the long run, this person could buy a smaller car, get a job closer to home, join a carpool, or in other ways reduce the amount of gasoline purchased.

A survey of hundreds of estimates of gasoline demand elasticities across many countries (Espey, 1998), found that the average estimate of the short-run elasticity for gasoline was −0.26, and the long-run elasticity was −0.58. Thus, a 1% increase in price lowers the quantity demanded by only 0.26% in the short run but by more than twice as much, 0.58%, in the long run. Li et al. (2009) examined the effects of gasoline prices on fleets of autos, and found that high gasoline prices cause fleet owners to buy more fuel-efficient vehicles and get rid of older, less fuel-efficient used vehicles more quickly. As a result, they estimate that a 10% increase in gasoline prices causes a negligible 0.22% increase in fleet fuel economy in the short run, but a 2.04% increase in the long run.

Similarly, Grossman and Chaloupka (1998) estimated that a rise in the street price of cocaine has a larger long-run effect than its short-run effect on cocaine consumption by young adults (aged 17 to 29). The long-run demand elasticity is −1.35, whereas the short-run elasticity is −0.96.

In contrast, the short-run demand elasticity for goods that can be stored easily may be more elastic than the long-run ones. Prince (2008) found that the demand for computers was more elastic in the short run (−2.74) than in the long run (−2.17). His explanation was that consumers are concerned about getting locked-in with an older technology in the short run so that they were more sensitive to price in the short run.

Supply Elasticities over Time. Short-run supply curve elasticities may differ from long-run elasticities. If a manufacturing firm wants to increase production in the short run, it can do so by hiring workers to use its machines around the clock. However, how much it can expand its output is limited by the fixed size of its manufacturing plant and the number of machines it has. In the long run, however, the firm can build another plant and buy or build more equipment. Thus, we would expect a firm's long-run supply elasticity to be greater than it is in the short run.

Adelaja (1991) found that the short-run supply elasticity of milk is 0.36, whereas the long-run supply elasticity is 0.51. Thus, the long-run quantity response to a 1% increase in price is about 42% [= (0.51 − 0.36)/0.36] more than it is in the short run.

APPLICATION

Oil Drilling in the Arctic National Wildlife Refuge

We can use information about demand and supply elasticities to answer an important public policy question: Would selling oil from the Arctic National Wildlife Refuge (ANWR) substantially affect the price of oil? Established in 1980, the ANWR covers 20 million acres and is the largest of Alaska's 16 national wildlife refuges. It is believed to contain massive deposits of petroleum (about the amount consumed annually in the United States). For decades, a debate has raged over whether the ANWR's owners—the citizens of the United States—should keep it undeveloped or permit oil drilling.[16]

In the simplest form of this complex debate, President Obama has sided with environmentalists who stress that drilling would harm the wildlife refuge and pollute the environment, whereas former President George W. Bush and other drilling proponents argue that extracting this oil would substantially reduce the price of petroleum (as well as decrease U.S. dependence on foreign oil and bring in large royalties). Recent spurts in the price of gasoline and the war in Iraq have heightened this intense debate.

The effect of the sale of ANWR oil on the world price of oil is a key element in this debate. We can combine oil production information with supply and demand elasticities to make a "back of the envelope" estimate of the price effects.

A number of studies estimate that the long-run elasticity of demand, ε, for oil is about −0.4 and the long-run supply elasticity, η, is about 0.3. Analysts agree less about how much ANWR oil will be produced. The Department of Energy's Energy Information Service (EIS) predicts that production from the ANWR would average about 800,000 barrels per day. That production would be about 1% of the worldwide oil production, which averaged about 84 million barrels per day from 2007 through early 2010.

A report of the U.S. Department of Energy predicted that ANWR drilling could lower the price of oil by about 1%. Severin Borenstein, the director of the

---

[16]I am grateful to Robert Whaples, who wrote an earlier version of this analysis. In the following discussion, we assume for simplicity that the oil market is competitive, and we use current values for the prices and quantities of oil, even though drilling in the ANWR will not take place for at least a decade.

University of California Energy Institute, concluded that the ANWR might reduce oil prices by up to a few percentage points but that "drilling in ANWR will never noticeably affect gasoline prices."

In the following solved problem, we make our own calculation of the price effect of drilling in the ANWR. Here and in many of the solved problems in this book, you are asked to determine how a change in a variable or policy (such as permitting drilling in the ANWR) affects one or more variables (such as the world equilibrium price of oil).

SOLVED PROBLEM 2.3

What would be the effect of ANWR production on the world equilibrium price of oil given that $\varepsilon = -0.4$, $\eta = 0.3$, the pre-ANWR daily world production of oil is $Q_1 = 82$ million barrels per day, the pre-ANWR world price is $p_1 = \$50$ per barrel, and daily ANWR production is 0.8 million barrels per day?[17] We assume that the supply and demand curves are linear and that the introduction of ANWR oil would cause a parallel shift in the world supply curve to the right by 0.8 million barrels per day.

Answer

1. *Determine the long-run linear demand function that is consistent with pre-ANWR world output and price.* At the original equilibrium, e_1 in the figure, $p_1 = \$50$ and $Q_1 = 82$, and the elasticity of demand is $\varepsilon = (dQ/dp)(p_1/Q_1) = (dQ/dp)(50/82) = -0.4$. Using algebra, we find that dQ/dp equals $-0.4(82/50) = -0.656$, which is the inverse of the slope of the demand curve, D, in the figure. Knowing this slope and that demand equals 82 at $50 per barrel, we can solve for the intercept because the quantity demanded rises by 0.656 for each dollar by which the price falls. The demand when the price is zero is $82 + (0.656 \times 50) = 114.8$. Thus, the equation for the demand curve is $Q = 114.8 - 0.656p$.

2. *Determine the long-run linear supply function that is consistent with pre-ANWR world output and price.* Where S^1 intercepts D at the original equilibrium, e_1, the elasticity of supply is $\eta = (dQ/dp)(p_1/Q_1) = (dQ/dp)(50/82) = 0.3$. Solving, we find that $dQ/dp = 0.3(82/50) = 0.492$. Because the quantity supplied falls by 0.492 for each dollar by which the price drops, the quantity supplied when the price is zero is $82 - (0.492 \times 50) = 57.4$. Thus, the equation for the pre-ANWR supply curve, S^1, in the figure, is $Q = 57.4 + 0.492p$.

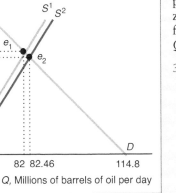

3. *Determine the post-ANWR long-run linear supply function.* The oil pumped from the ANWR would cause a parallel shift in the supply curve, moving S^1 to the right by 0.8 to S^2. That is, the slope remains the same, but the intercept on the quantity axis increases by 0.8. Thus, the supply function for S^2 is $Q = 58.2 + 0.492p$.

---

[17]From 2007 through early 2010, the price of a barrel of oil fluctuated between about $30 and $140. The calculated percentage change in the price in this Solved Problem is not sensitive to the choice of the initial price of oil.

4. *Use the demand curve and the post-ANWR supply function to calculate the new equilibrium price and quantity.* The new equilibrium, e_2, occurs where S^2 intersects D. Setting the right-hand sides of the demand function and the post-ANWR supply function equal, we obtain an expression in the new price, p_2:

$$58.2 + 0.492p_2 = 114.8 - 0.656p_2.$$

We can solve this expression for the new equilibrium price: $p_2 \approx \$49.30$. That is, the price drops about 70¢, or approximately 1.4%. If we substitute this new price into either the demand curve or the post-ANWR supply curve, we find that the new equilibrium quantity is 82.46 million barrels per day. That is, equilibrium output rises by 0.46 million barrels per day (0.56%), which is only a little more than half of the predicted daily ANWR supply, because other suppliers will decrease their output slightly in response to the lower price.

Comment: Our estimate of a small drop in the world oil price if ANWR oil is sold would not change substantially if our estimates of the elasticities of supply and demand were moderately larger or smaller or if the equilibrium price of oil were higher or lower. The main reason for this result is that the ANWR output would be a very small portion of worldwide supply—the new supply curve would be only slightly to the right of the initial supply curve. Thus, drilling in the ANWR cannot insulate the American market from international events that roil the oil market. In contrast, a new war in the Persian Gulf could shift the worldwide supply curve to the left by 3 million barrels a day or more (nearly four times the ANWR production). Such a shock would cause the price of oil to soar whether we drill in the ANWR or not.

2.6 Effects of a Sales Tax

How much a tax affects the equilibrium price and quantity and how much of the tax falls on consumers depends on the elasticities of demand and supply. Knowing only the elasticities of demand and supply, we can make accurate predictions about the effects of a new tax and determine how much of the tax falls on consumers.

In this section, we examine three questions about the effects of a sales tax:

1. What effect does a sales tax have on a product's equilibrium price and quantity?
2. Is it true, as many people claim, that taxes assessed on producers are *passed along* to consumers? That is, do consumers pay for the entire tax, or do producers pay part of it?
3. Do the equilibrium price and quantity depend on whether the tax is assessed on consumers or on producers?

Two Types of Sales Taxes

Governments use two types of sales taxes. The most common sales tax is called an *ad valorem* tax by economists and the sales tax by real people. For every dollar that a consumer spends, the government keeps a fraction, α, which is the ad valorem tax rate. Japan's national sales tax is $\alpha = 5\%$. If a consumer in Japan buys a Nintendo

Wii for ¥20,000,[18] the government collects $\alpha \times$ ¥20,000 $= 5\% \times$ ¥20,000 $=$ ¥1,000 in taxes, and the seller receives $(1-\alpha) \times$ ¥20,000 $=$ ¥19,000.[19]

The other type of sales tax is a *specific* or *unit* tax, where a specified dollar amount, τ, is collected per unit of output. For example, the federal government collects $\tau = 18.4$¢ on each gallon of gas sold in the United States.

Equilibrium Effects of a Specific Tax

To answer the three questions listed at the beginning of this section, we must extend the standard supply-and-demand analysis to take taxes into account. Let's start by assuming that the specific tax is assessed on firms at the time of sale. If the consumer pays p for a good, the government takes τ and the seller receives $p - \tau$.

Suppose that the government collects a specific tax of $\tau = \$1.05$ per kg of processed pork from pork producers. Because of the tax, suppliers keep only $p - \tau$ of price p that consumers pay. Thus, at every possible price paid by consumers, firms are willing to supply less than when they received the full amount consumers paid. Before the tax, firms were willing to supply 206 million kg per year at a price of \$2.95 as the pretax supply curve S^1 in Figure 2.12 shows. After the tax, firms receive only \$1.90 if consumers pay \$2.95, so they are no longer willing to supply a quantity of 206. For firms to be willing to supply a quantity of 206, they must receive \$2.95 after the tax, so consumers must pay \$4. By this reasoning, the after-tax

Figure 2.12 The Effect of a \$1.05 Specific Tax on the Pork Market Collected from Producers

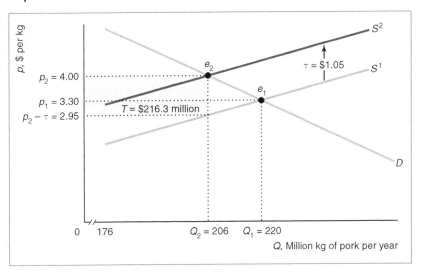

The specific tax of $\tau = \$1.05$ per kg collected from producers shifts the pretax pork supply curve from S^1 to the post-tax supply curve, S^2. The tax causes the equilibrium to shift from e_1 (determined by the intersection of S^1 and D) to e_2 (intersection of S^2 with D). The equilibrium price increases from \$3.30 to \$4. Two-thirds of the incidence of the tax falls on consumers, who spend 70¢ more per unit. Producers receive 35¢ less per unit after the tax. The government collects tax revenues of $T = \tau Q_2 = \$216.3$ million per year.

---

[18] The symbol for Japan's currency, the yen, is ¥. Roughly, ¥100 $=$ \$1.

[19] For specificity, we assume that the price firms receive is $p = (1 - \alpha)p^*$, where p^* is the price consumers pay, and α is the ad valorem tax rate on the price consumers pay. However, many governments (including the U.S. and Japanese governments) set the ad valorem sales tax, β, as an amount added to the price sellers charge, so consumers pay $p^* = (1 + \beta)p$. By setting α and β appropriately, the taxes are equivalent. Here, $p = p^*/(1 + \beta)$, so $(1 - \alpha) = 1/(1 + \beta)$. For example, if $\beta = \frac{1}{3}$ then $\alpha = \frac{1}{4}$.

supply curve, S^2, is $\tau = \$1.05$ above the original supply curve S^1 at every quantity, as the figure shows.

We can use this figure to illustrate the answer to our first question concerning the effects of the tax on the pork market equilibrium. *The specific tax causes the equilibrium price consumers pay to rise, and the equilibrium quantity to fall.*

The intersection of the pretax pork supply curve S^1 and the pork demand curve D in Figure 2.12 determines the pretax equilibrium, e_1. The equilibrium price is $p_1 = \$3.30$, and the equilibrium quantity is $Q_1 = 220$. The tax shifts the supply curve to S^2, so the after-tax equilibrium is e_2. At e_2 consumers pay $p_2 = \$4$, firms receive $p_2 - \$1.05 = \$2.95$, and $Q_2 = 206$. Thus, the tax causes the price that consumers pay to increase, $\Delta p = p_2 - p_1 = \$4 - \$3.30 = 70¢$, and the quantity to fall, $\Delta Q = Q_2 - Q_1 = 206 - 220 = -14$.

Although consumers and producers are worse off because of the tax, the government acquires new tax revenue of $T = \tau Q = \$1.05$ per kg × 206 million kg per year = \$216.3 million per year. The length of the shaded rectangle in the figure is $Q_2 = 206$ million kg per year, and its height is $\tau = \$1.05$ per kg, so the area of the rectangle equals the tax revenue. (The figure shows only part of the length of the rectangle because the horizontal axis starts at 176.)

How Specific Tax Effects Depend on Elasticities

We now turn to our second question: Who is hurt by the tax? To answer this comparative static question, we want to determine how the price that consumers pay and firms receive changes after the tax is imposed.

Because the government collects a specific or unit tax, τ, from sellers, sellers receive $p - \tau$ when consumers pay p. We can use this information to determine the effect of the tax on the equilibrium. In the new equilibrium, the price that consumers pay is determined by the equality between the demand function and the after-tax supply function,

$$D(p) = S(p - \tau).$$

Thus, the equilibrium price is an implicit function of the specific tax: $p = p(\tau)$. Consequently, the equilibrium condition is

$$D(p(\tau)) = S(p(\tau) - \tau). \tag{2.26}$$

We determine the effect a small tax has on the price by differentiating Equation 2.26 with respect to τ:

$$\frac{dD}{dp}\frac{dp}{d\tau} = \frac{dS}{dp}\frac{d(p(\tau) - \tau)}{d\tau} = \frac{dS}{dp}\left(\frac{dp}{d\tau} - 1\right).$$

Rearranging the terms, it follows that the change in the price that consumers pay with respect to the change in the tax is

$$\frac{dp}{d\tau} = \frac{\dfrac{dS}{dp}}{\dfrac{dS}{dp} - \dfrac{dD}{dp}}. \tag{2.27}$$

We know that $dD/dp < 0$ from the Law of Demand. If the supply curve slopes upward so that $dS/dp > 0$, then $dp/d\tau > 0$, as Figure 2.12 illustrates. The higher the tax, the greater the price consumers pay. If $dS/dp < 0$, the direction of change is ambiguous: It depends on the relative slopes of the supply and demand curves (the denominator).

By multiplying both the numerator and denominator of the right-hand side of Equation 2.27 by p/Q, we can express this derivative in terms of elasticities,

$$\frac{dp}{d\tau} = \frac{\dfrac{dS}{dp}\dfrac{p}{Q}}{\dfrac{dS}{dp}\dfrac{p}{Q} - \dfrac{dD}{dp}\dfrac{p}{Q}} = \frac{\eta}{\eta - \varepsilon}, \qquad (2.28)$$

where the last equality follows because dS/dp and dD/dp are the changes in the quantities supplied and demanded as price changes, and the consumer and producer prices are identical when $\tau = 0$.[20] This expression holds for any size change in τ if both the demand and supply curves are linear. For most other shaped curves, the expression holds only for small changes.

We can now answer our second question: Who is hurt by the tax? The **incidence of a tax on consumers** is the share of the tax that falls on consumers. The incidence of the tax that falls on consumers is $dp/d\tau$, the amount by which the price to consumers rises as a fraction of the amount the tax increases. Firms receive $p - \tau$, so the change in the price that firms receive as the tax changes is $d(p - \tau)/d\tau = dp/d\tau - 1$. The *incidence of the tax on firms* is the amount by which the price paid to firms falls: $1 - dp/d\tau$. The sum of the incidence of the tax to consumers and firms is $dp/d\tau + 1 - dp/d\tau = 1$. That is, the increase in the price consumers pay plus the drop in the price paid to firms equals the tax.

In the pork example, $\varepsilon = -0.3$ and $\eta = 0.6$, so the incidence of a specific tax on consumers is $dp/d\tau = \eta/(\eta - \varepsilon) = 0.6/[0.6 - (-0.3)] = 0.6/0.9 = \frac{2}{3}$, and the incidence of the tax on firms is $1 - \frac{2}{3} = \frac{1}{3}$.

Thus, a discrete change in the tax of $\Delta\tau = \tau - 0 = \$1.05$ causes the price that consumers pay to rise by $\Delta p = p_2 - p_1 = \$4.00 - \$3.30 = [\eta/(\eta - \varepsilon)]\Delta\tau = \frac{2}{3} \times \$1.05 = 70¢$, and the price to firms to fall by $\frac{1}{3} \times \$1.05 = 35¢$, as Figure 2.12 shows. The sum of the increase to consumers plus the loss to firms is $70¢ + 35¢ = \$1.05 = \tau$.

Equation 2.28 shows that, for a given supply elasticity, the more elastic the demand, the less the equilibrium price rises when a tax is imposed. Similarly, for a given demand elasticity, the smaller the supply elasticity, the smaller the increase in the equilibrium price that consumers pay when a tax is imposed. In the pork example, if the supply elasticity were $\eta = 0$ (a perfectly inelastic vertical supply curve), $dp/d\tau = 0/[0 - (-0.3)] = 0$, so that none of the incidence of the tax falls on consumers, and the entire incidence of the tax falls on firms.[21]

SOLVED PROBLEM 2.4

If a product's demand curve is perfectly inelastic, and its supply curve is linear and upward sloping, what effect does a $1 specific tax collected from producers have on the product's equilibrium price and quantity? What effect does the tax have on consumers? Why?

---

[20]To determine the effect on quantity, we can combine the price result from Equation 2.28 with information from either the demand or the supply function. Differentiating the demand function with respect to τ, we know that

$$\frac{dD}{dp}\frac{dp}{d\tau} = \frac{dD}{dp}\frac{\eta}{\eta - \varepsilon},$$

which is negative if the supply curve is upward sloping so that $\eta > 0$.

[21]For another application, see "Incidence of a Tax on Restaurant Meals" in the Supplemental Material to Chapter 2 in **MyEconLab**'s textbook resources.

Answer

1. *Determine the equilibrium in the absence of a tax.* Before the tax, the supply curve S^1 in the figure intersects the perfectly inelastic, vertical demand curve D at e_1, where the price is p_1 and the quantity is Q.

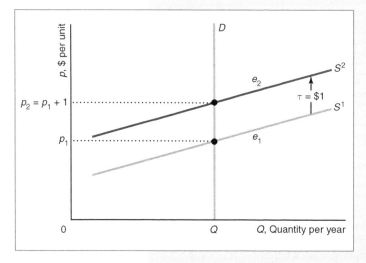

2. *Show how the tax shifts the supply curve and determine the new equilibrium.* A specific tax of $1 shifts the pretax supply curve S^1 upward by $1 to S^2. The intersection of D and S^2 determines the after-tax equilibrium e^2, where the price consumers pay is $p_2 = p_1 + 1$ and quantity is Q.

3. *Compare the before- and after-tax equilibria.* The specific tax does not affect the equilibrium quantity, which remains at Q. The price rises by a dollar from p_1 to $p_2 = p_1 + 1$. Thus, the entire incidence of the tax falls on consumers:

$$\frac{\Delta p}{\Delta \tau} = \frac{p_2 - p_1}{\$1} = \frac{\$1}{\$1} = 1.$$

We get the same incidence by setting the demand elasticity equal to zero (because the demand curve is perfectly inelastic) in Equation 2.28: $dp/d\tau = \eta/(\eta - \varepsilon) = \eta/(\eta - 0) = \eta/\eta = 1$.

4. *Explain why.* Because the demand curve is perfectly inelastic or vertical, consumers continue to buy the same quantity even if the after-tax price rises. For suppliers to continue to provide the same quantity as before the tax, the price they receive must rise by the full amount of the tax. Effectively, the reason why consumers must absorb the entire tax is that consumers will "pay anything" for this good.

APPLICATION

Gas Taxes and the Environment

Burning fossil fuels such as gasoline, coal, and heating oil releases "greenhouse gases" containing carbon into the atmosphere, which contributes to global warming and other associated climate changes. To reduce this problem, many environmentalists and political leaders propose levying a carbon tax on the carbon content in fossil fuels. Because one-third of U.S. carbon dioxide emissions come from the transportation sector, knowing how buyers will respond to the tax is crucial to determining how effective the tax will be.

Davis and Kilian (2010) estimate that in the short run (up to one year), the price elasticity of demand for fossil fuels is –0.46, which is inelastic. All else the same, the less elastic a demand curve is, the smaller the effect a tax will have on the equilibrium quantity. As Solved Problem 2.4 shows, for a completely inelastic demand curve, the tax has no effect on the equilibrium quantity, and consumers absorb the full price increase.

A commonly proposed tax of $10 per ton of carbon dioxide would increase gasoline taxes by about 9¢ (roughly half of the current federal specific gas tax of 18.4¢ per gallon). Bento et al. (2009) estimate that a 25¢ gasoline tax would increase the average household's cost by about $30 a year (in 2001 dollars). Given their elasticity estimate, Davis and Kilian calculate that adding a 10¢ gas tax would reduce gasoline consumption and carbon emissions from vehicles in the United States by only about 1.4%, thereby reducing U.S. carbon emissions by 0.5% and worldwide carbon emissions by just 0.1%. Because total U.S. carbon dioxide emissions increased by 1.1% annually between 1990 and 2007, the tax would roughly offset half a year of growth in total U.S. emissions. That is, such a tax would not have a substantial effect on carbon emissions in the short run. Unfortunately, Bento et al. (2009) do not find that a tax on gasoline consumption will have a much larger effect in the long run.

The Same Equilibrium No Matter Who Is Taxed

Our third question is, "Does the equilibrium or the incidence of the tax depend on whether the tax is collected from producers or consumers?" Surprisingly, in the supply-and-demand model, the equilibrium and the incidence of the tax are the same regardless of whether the government collects the tax from producers or from consumers.

We've already seen that firms are able to pass on some or all of the tax collected from them to consumers. We now show that, if the tax is collected from consumers, they can pass the producers' share back to the firms.

Suppose the specific tax $\tau = \$1.05$ on pork is collected from consumers rather than from producers. Because the government takes τ from each p that consumers spend, producers receive only $p - \tau$. Thus, the demand curve as seen by firms shifts downward by $\$1.05$ from D to D^s in Figure 2.13.

The intersection of D^2 and S determines the after-tax equilibrium, where the equilibrium quantity is Q_2 and the price received by producers is $p_2 - \tau$. The price paid

Figure 2.13 The Effects of a Specific Tax and an Ad Valorem Tax on Consumers

Without a tax, the demand curve is D and the supply curve is S. A specific tax of $\tau = \$1.05$ per kg collected from consumers shifts the demand curve to D^s, which is parallel to D. The new equilibrium is e_2 on the original demand curve D. If instead an ad valorem tax of $\alpha = 26.25\%$ is imposed, the demand curve facing firms is D^a. The gap between D and D^a, the per-unit tax, is larger at higher prices. The after-tax equilibrium is the same with both of these taxes.

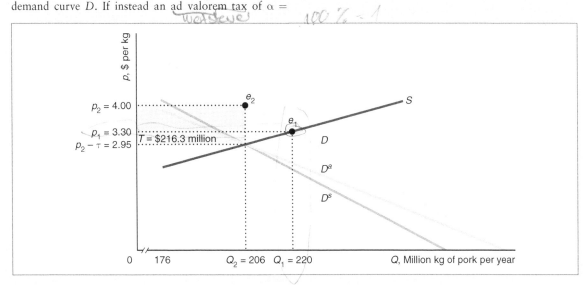

by consumers, p_2 (on the original demand curve D at Q_2), is τ above the price received by producers. We place the after-tax equilibrium, e_2, bullet on the market demand D in Figure 2.13 to show that it is the same as the e_2 in Figure 2.12.

Comparing Figure 2.13 to Figure 2.12, we see that the after-tax equilibrium is the same regardless of whether the tax is imposed on consumers or producers. The price to consumers rises by the same amount, $\Delta p = 70¢$, and the incidence of the tax, $\Delta p/\Delta t = \frac{2}{3}$, is the same.

A specific tax, regardless of whether the tax is collected from consumers or producers, creates a *wedge* equal to the per-unit tax of τ between the price consumers pay, p, and the price producers receive, $p - \tau$. In short, regardless of whether firms or consumers pay the tax to the government, you can solve tax problems by shifting the supply curve, shifting the demand curve, or inserting a wedge between the supply and demand curves. All three approaches give the same answer.

The Similar Effects of Ad Valorem and Specific Taxes

In contrast to specific sales taxes, which are applied to relatively few goods, governments levy ad valorem taxes on a wide variety of goods. Most states apply ad valorem sales taxes to most goods and services, exempting only a few staples such as food and medicine. There are 6,400 different ad valorem sales tax rates across the United States (Besley and Rosen, 1999), some of which are as high as 10.75% (in some areas of California).

Suppose that the government imposes an ad valorem tax of α, instead of a specific tax, on the price that consumers pay for processed pork. We already know that the equilibrium price is \$4 with a specific tax of \$1.05 per kg. At that price, an ad valorem tax of $\alpha = \$1.05/\$4 = 26.25\%$ raises the same amount of tax per unit as a \$1.05 specific tax.

It is usually easiest to analyze the effects of an ad valorem tax by shifting the demand curve. Figure 2.13 shows how an ad valorem tax shifts the processed pork demand curve to D^a. At any given price p, the gap between D and D^a is αp, which is greater at high prices than at low prices. The gap is \$1.05 ($= 0.2625 \times \$4$) per unit when the price is \$4, and \$2.10 when the price is \$8.

Imposing an ad valorem tax causes the after-tax equilibrium quantity, Q_2, to fall below the original quantity, Q_1, and the after-tax price, p_2, to rise above the original price, p_1. The tax collected per unit of output is $\tau = \alpha p_2$. The incidence of the tax that falls on consumers is the change in price, $\Delta p = (p_2 - p_1)$, divided by the change in the per-unit tax, $\Delta \tau = \alpha p_2 - 0$, that is collected, $\Delta p/(\alpha p_2)$. The incidence of an ad valorem tax is generally shared between consumers and producers. Because the ad valorem tax of $\alpha = 26.25\%$ has exactly the same impact on the equilibrium pork price and raises the same amount of tax per unit as the $\tau = \$1.05$ specific tax, the incidence is the same for both types of taxes. (As with specific taxes, the incidence of the ad valorem tax depends on the elasticities of supply and demand, but we'll spare your having to go through that in detail.)

2.7 Quantity Supplied Need Not Equal Quantity Demanded

In a supply-and-demand model, the quantity supplied does not necessarily equal the quantity demanded because of the way we defined these two concepts. We defined the quantity supplied as the amount firms want to sell at a given price, holding constant other factors that affect supply, such as the price of inputs. We defined the quantity demanded as the quantity that consumers want to buy at a given price, if other factors that affect demand are held constant. The quantity that firms want to sell and the quantity that consumers want to buy at a given price need not equal the actual quantity that is bought and sold.

We could have defined the quantity supplied and the quantity demanded so that they must be equal. If we had defined the quantity supplied as the amount firms *actually* sell at a given price and the quantity demanded as the amount consumers *actually* buy, supply would have to equal demand in all markets because we *defined* the quantity demanded and the quantity supplied as the same quantity.

It is worth emphasizing this distinction because politicians, pundits, and the press are so often confused on this point. Someone insisting that "demand *must* equal supply" must be defining demand and supply as the *actual* quantities sold. Because we define the quantities supplied and demanded in terms of people's *wants* and not *actual* quantities bought and sold, the statement that "supply equals demand" is a theory, not merely a definition.

According to our theory, the quantity supplied equals the quantity demanded at the intersection of the supply and demand curves if the government does not intervene. However, not all government interventions prevent markets from *clearing*: equilibrating the quantity supplied and the quantity demanded. For example, as we've seen, a government tax affects the equilibrium by shifting the supply curve or demand curve of a good but does not cause a gap between the quantity demanded and the quantity supplied. However, some government policies do more than merely shift the supply curve or demand curve.

For example, governments may directly control the prices of some products. For example, New York City limits the price or rent that landlords can charge for an apartment. If the price a government sets for a product differs from its market clearing price, either excess supply or excess demand results. We illustrate this result with two types of price control programs. The government may set a *price ceiling* at $\bar{p}$ so that the price at which goods are sold may be no higher than $\bar{p}$. When the government sets a *price floor* at $\bar{p}$, the price at which goods are sold may not fall below $\bar{p}$.

We can study the effects of such regulations using the supply-and-demand model. Despite the lack of equality between the quantity supplied and the quantity demanded, the supply-and-demand model is useful for analyzing price controls because it predicts the excess demand or excess supply that is observed.

Price Ceiling

A price ceiling legally limits the amount that can be charged for a product. The ceiling does not affect market outcomes if it is set above the equilibrium price that would be charged in the absence of the price control. For example, if the government says firms can charge no more than $\bar{p} = \$5$ per gallon of gas and firms are actually charging $p = \$3$, the government's price control policy is irrelevant. However, if the equilibrium price would have been $6 per gallon, the price ceiling would limit the price in that market to only $5.

The U.S. government imposed price controls on gasoline several times. In the 1970s, OPEC reduced supplies of oil—which is converted into gasoline—to Western countries. As a result, the total supply curve for gasoline in the United States—the horizontal sum of domestic and OPEC supply curves—shifted to the left from S^1 to S^2 in Figure 2.14. Because of this shift, the equilibrium price of gasoline would have risen substantially, from p_1 to p_2. In an attempt to protect consumers by keeping gasoline prices from rising, the U.S. government set price ceilings on gasoline in 1973 and 1979.

Figure 2.14 The Effects of a Gasoline Price Ceiling

Supply shifts from S^1 to S^2. Under the government's price control program, gasoline stations may not charge a price above the price ceiling $\bar{p} = p_1$. At that price, producers are willing to supply only Q_s, which is less than the amount $Q_1 = Q_d$ that consumers want to buy. The result is excessive demand, or a shortage of $Q_d - Q_s$.

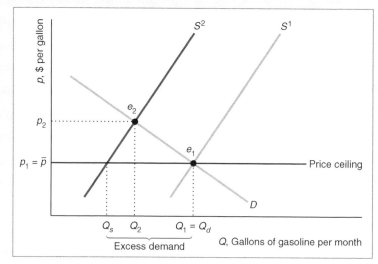

The government told gas stations that they could charge no more than $\bar{p} = p_1$. Figure 2.14 shows the price ceiling as a solid horizontal line extending from the price axis at $\bar{p}$. The price control is binding because $p_2 > \bar{p}$. The observed price is the price ceiling. At $\bar{p}$, consumers *want* to buy $Q_d = Q_1$ gallons of gasoline, which is the equilibrium quantity they bought before OPEC acted. However, because of the price control, firms are willing to supply only Q_s gallons, which is determined by the intersection of the price control line with S^2. As a result of the binding price control, there is excess demand of $Q_d - Q_s$.

Were it not for the price controls, market forces would drive up the market price to p_2, where the excess demand would be eliminated. The government's price ceiling prevents this adjustment from occurring, which causes a **shortage**, or persistent excess demand.

At the time the controls were implemented, some government officials falsely contended that the shortages were caused by OPEC's cutting off its supply of oil to the United States. Without the price controls, the new equilibrium would be e_2, where the equilibrium price, p_2, is greater than p_1, and the equilibrium, Q_2, is greater than the quantity sold under the control program, Q_s. However, there would have been no shortage.

The supply-and-demand model predicts that a binding price control results in equilibrium *with a shortage*. In this equilibrium, the quantity demanded does not equal the quantity supplied. The reason that we call this situation an equilibrium even though a shortage exists is that no consumers or firms want to act differently, *given the law*. Without a price control, consumers facing a shortage would try to get more output by offering to pay more, or firms would raise their prices. With an enforced price control, they know that they can't drive up the price, so they live with the shortage.

So what happens when there is a price shortage? Lucky consumers get to buy Q_s units at the low price of $\bar{p}$. Other potential customers are disappointed: They would like to buy at that price, but they cannot find anyone willing to sell gas to them. With enforced price controls, sellers use criteria other than price to allocate the scarce commodity. They may supply the commodity to their friends, long-term customers, or people of a certain race, gender, age, or religion. They may sell their goods on a first-come, first-served basis. Or they may limit everyone to only a few gallons.

Another possibility is for firms and customers to evade the price controls. A consumer could go to a gas station owner and say, "Let's not tell anyone, but I'll pay you twice the price the government sets if you'll sell me as much gas as I want." If enough customers and gas station owners behaved that way, no shortage would occur. A study of 92 major U.S. cities during the 1973 gasoline price control found no gasoline lines in 52 of the cities, where apparently the law was not enforced. However, in cities where the law was effective such as Chicago, Hartford, New York, Portland, and Tucson, potential customers waited in line at the pump for an hour or more.[22] Deacon and Sonstelie (1989) calculated that for every dollar consumers saved during the 1980 gasoline price controls, they lost $1.16 in waiting time and other factors.[23]

This experience dissuaded most U.S. jurisdictions from imposing gasoline price controls even when gasoline prices spiked following Hurricane Katrina in the summer of 2008. The one exception was Hawaii, which imposed price controls on the wholesale price of gasoline starting in September 2005, but suspended the controls indefinitely in early 2006 due to the public's unhappiness with the law.

APPLICATION

Price Controls Kill

Robert G. Mugabe, who has ruled Zimbabwe with an iron fist for nearly three decades, has used price controls to try to stay in power by currying favor among the poor.[24] In 2001, he imposed price controls on many basic commodities, including food, soap, and cement, leading to shortages of these goods and the development of a thriving *black*, or *parallel*, *market* in which price controls were ignored. Prices on the black market were two or three times higher than the controlled prices.

He imposed more extreme controls in 2007. A government edict cut the prices of 26 essential items by up to 70%, and a subsequent edict imposed price controls on a much wider range of goods. Gangs of price inspectors patrolled shops and factories, imposing arbitrary price reductions. State-run newspapers exhorted citizens to turn in store owners whose prices exceeded the limits.

The Zimbabwean police reported that they arrested at least 4,000 businesspeople for not complying with the price controls. The government took over the nation's slaughter-

---

[22]See "Gas Lines," in the Supplemental Material to Chapter 2 in **MyEconLab**'s textbook resources for a more detailed discussion of the effects of the 1973 and 1979 gasoline price controls.

[23]Some economists interpret this market as being in an equilibrium in which the effective price that consumers face is the actual price plus the value of the waiting time. Thus, the quantity demanded at the effective price equals the quantity supplied.

[24]Mr. Mugabe justified price controls as a means to deal with profiteering businesses that he said were part of a Western conspiracy to reimpose colonial rule. Actually, they were a vain attempt to slow the hyperinflation that resulted from his printing Zimbabwean money rapidly. Prices increased several billion times in 2008, and the government printed currency with a face value of 100 trillion Zimbabwe dollars.

houses after meat disappeared from stores, but in a typical week, butchers killed and dressed only 32 cows for the entire city of Bulawayo, which consists of 676,000 people.

Ordinary citizens initially greeted the price cuts with euphoria because they had been unable to buy even basic necessities because of hyperinflation and past price controls. Yet most ordinary citizens were unable to obtain much food because most of the cut-rate merchandise was snapped up by the police, soldiers, and members of Mr. Mugabe's governing party, who were tipped off prior to the price inspectors' rounds.

Manufacturing slowed to a crawl because firms could not buy raw materials and because the prices firms received were less than their costs of production. Businesses laid off workers or reduced their hours, impoverishing the 15% or 20% of adult Zimbabweans who still had jobs. The 2007 price controls on manufacturing crippled this sector, forcing manufacturers to sell goods at roughly half of what it cost to produce them. By mid-2008, the output by Zimbabwe's manufacturing sector had fallen 27% compared to the previous year. As a consequence, Zimbabweans died from starvation. Although we have no exact figures, according to the World Food Program, over 5 million Zimbabweans faced starvation in 2008.

Aid shipped into the country from international relief agencies and the two million Zimbabweans who have fled abroad have helped keep some people alive. In 2008, the World Food Program made an urgent appeal for $140 million in donations to feed Zimbabweans, stating that drought and political upheaval would soon exhaust the organization's stockpiles. Thankfully, the price controls were lifted in 2009.

Price Floor

Governments also commonly impose price floors. One of the most important examples of a price floor is the minimum wage in labor markets.

The minimum wage law forbids employers from paying less than a minimum wage, $\underline{w}$. Minimum wage laws date from 1894 in New Zealand, 1909 in the United Kingdom, and 1912 in Massachusetts. The Fair Labor Standards Act of 1938 set a federal U.S. minimum wage of 25¢. Today, the federal minimum wage is $7.25 an hour. The statutory monthly minimum wage ranges from the equivalent of 19€ in the Russian Federation to 375€ in Portugal, 1,154€ in France, and 1,466€ in Luxembourg. If the minimum wage binds—exceeds the equilibrium wage, w^*—the minimum wage causes *unemployment*, which is a persistent excess supply of labor.[25]

For simplicity, suppose that there is a single labor market in which everyone is paid the same wage. Figure 2.15 shows the supply and demand curves for labor services (hours worked). Firms buy hours of labor service—they hire workers. The quantity measure on the horizontal axis is hours worked per year, and the price measure on the vertical axis is the wage per hour.

---

[25]The U.S. Department of Labor maintains at its Web site (**www.dol.gov**) an extensive history of the federal minimum wage law, labor markets, state minimum wage laws, and other information. For European minimum wages, see **www.fedee.com/minwage.html**. Where the minimum wage applies to only some labor markets (Chapter 10) or where only a single firm hires all the workers in a market (Chapter 15), a minimum wage might not cause unemployment. Card and Krueger (1995) provide evidence that recent rises in the minimum wage had negligible (at most) effects on employment in certain low-skill labor markets.

Figure 2.15 The Effects of a Minimum Wage

In the absence of a minimum wage, the equilibrium wage is w^*, and the equilibrium number of hours worked is L^*. A minimum wage, $\underline{w}$, set above w^*, leads to unemployment—persistent excess supply—because the quantity demanded, L_d, is less than the quantity supplied, L_s.

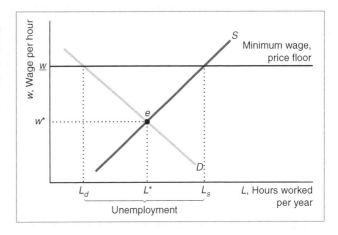

With no government intervention, the market equilibrium is e, where the wage is w^* and the number of hours worked is L^*. The minimum wage creates a price floor, a horizontal line, at $\underline{w}$. At that wage, the quantity demanded falls to L_d and the quantity supplied rises to L_s. As a result, there is an excess supply or unemployment of $L_s - L_d$. The minimum wage prevents market forces from eliminating the excess supply, so it leads to an equilibrium with unemployment. The original 1938 U.S. minimum wage law caused massive unemployment in the U.S. territory of Puerto Rico.[26]

It is ironic that a law designed to help workers by raising their wages harms some of them by causing them to become unemployed. Minimum wage laws benefit only people who manage to remain employed.[27]

2.8 When to Use the Supply-and-Demand Model

As we've seen, the supply-and-demand model can help us to understand and predict real-world events in many markets. Through Chapter 10, we discuss *perfectly competitive* markets in which the supply-and-demand model is a powerful tool for predicting what will happen to market equilibrium if underlying conditions—tastes, incomes, and prices of inputs—change. A perfectly competitive market (Chapter 8) is one in which all firms and consumers are *price takers*: no market participant can affect the market price.

Perfectly competitive markets have five characteristics that result in price taking behavior:

1. There are a large number of buyers and sellers.
2. All firms produce identical products.
3. All market participants have full information about prices and product characteristics.

---

[26]See "Minimum Wage Law in Puerto Rico" in the Supplemental Material to Chapter 2 in **MyEconLab**'s textbook resources.

[27]The minimum wage could raise the wage enough that total wage payments, wL, rise despite the fall in demand for labor services (see Problem 40 at the end of the chapter). If so, workers could share the unemployment (all working fewer than the number of hours they desire), and all workers could benefit from the minimum wage.

4. Transaction costs are negligible.
5. Firms can easily enter and exit the market.

When there are many firms and consumers in a market, no single firm or consumer is a large enough part of the market to affect the price. If you stop buying bread or if one of the many thousands of wheat farmers stops selling the wheat used to make the bread, the price of bread will not change.

In contrast, if there is only one seller of a good or service—a *monopoly* (Chapter 11)—that seller is a *price setter* and can affect the market price. Because demand curves slope downward, a monopoly can increase the price it receives by reducing the amount of a good it supplies. Firms are also price setters in an *oligopoly*—a market with only a small number of firms—or in markets in which they sell differentiated products, and consumers prefer one product to another (Chapter 14). In markets with price setters, the market price is usually higher than that predicted by the supply-and-demand model. That doesn't make the supply-and-demand model generally wrong. It means only that the supply-and-demand model does not apply to markets with a small number of sellers or buyers. In such markets, we use other models.

If consumers believe all firms produce identical products, consumers do not prefer one firm's good to another's. Thus, if one firm raised its price, consumers would all buy from the other firm. In contrast, if some consumers prefer Coke to Pepsi, Coke can charge more than Pepsi and not lose all its customers.

If consumers know the prices all firms charge and one firm raises its price, that firm's customers will buy from other firms. If consumers have less information about a product's quality than the firm that produces it, the firm can take advantage of consumers by selling them inferior-quality goods or by charging a much higher price than that charged by other firms. In such a market, the observed price may be higher than that predicted by the supply-and-demand model, the market may not exist at all (consumers and firms cannot reach agreements), or different firms may charge different prices for the same good (Chapter 18).

If it is cheap and easy for a buyer to find a seller and make a trade and if one firm raises its price, consumers can easily arrange to buy from another firm. That is, perfectly competitive markets typically have very low **transaction costs**: the expenses, over and above the price of the product, of finding a trading partner and making a trade for the product. These costs include the time and money spent gathering information about a product's quality and finding someone with whom to trade. Other transaction costs include the costs of writing and enforcing a contract, such as the cost of a lawyer's time. If transaction costs are very high, no trades at all might occur. In less extreme cases, individual trades may occur, but at a variety of prices.

The ability of firms to enter and exit a market freely leads to a large number of firms in a market and promotes price taking. Suppose a firm could raise its price and make a higher profit. If other firms could not enter the market, this firm would not be a price taker. However, if other firms can quickly and easily enter the market, the higher profit will encourage entry until the price is driven back to its original level.

Thus, the supply-and-demand model is not appropriate in markets in which there are only one or a few sellers (such as the market for local water and sewage services), firms produce differentiated products (such as music CDs), consumers know less than sellers about the quality of products (such as used cars) or their prices, there are high transaction costs (such as nuclear turbine engines), or high entry and exit costs (such as aircraft manufacturing). Markets in which the supply-and-demand model has proved useful include agriculture, finance, labor, construction, services, wholesale, and retail—markets with many firms and consumers and where firms sell identical products.

SUMMARY

1. **Demand.** The quantity of a good or service demanded by consumers depends on their tastes, the price of a good, the price of goods that are substitutes and complements, consumers' income, information, government regulations, and other factors. The *Law of Demand*—which is based on observation—says that *demand curves slope downward*. The higher the price, the less quantity is demanded, holding constant other factors that affect demand. A change in price causes a *movement along the demand curve*. A change in income, tastes, or another factor that affects demand other than price causes a *shift of the demand curve*. To derive a total demand curve, we horizontally sum the demand curves of individuals or types of consumers or countries. That is, we add the quantities demanded by each individual at a given price to determine the total quantity demanded.

2. **Supply.** The quantity of a good or service supplied by firms depends on the price, the firm's costs, government regulations, and other factors. The market supply curve need not slope upward but usually does. A change in price causes a *movement along the supply curve*. A change in the price of an input or government regulation causes a *shift of the supply curve*. The total supply curve is the horizontal sum of the supply curves for individual firms.

3. **Market Equilibrium.** The intersection of the demand curve and the supply curve determines the equilibrium price and quantity in a market. Market forces—actions of consumers and firms—drive the price and quantity to the equilibrium levels if they are initially too low or too high.

4. **Shocking the Equilibrium: Comparative Statics.** A change in an underlying factor other than price causes a shift of the supply curve or the demand curve, which alters the equilibrium. Comparative statics is the method that economists use to analyze how variables controlled by consumers and firms—such as price and quantity—react to a change in *environmental variables* such as prices of substitutes and complements, income, and prices of inputs.

5. **Elasticities.** An elasticity is the percentage change in a variable in response to a given percentage change in another variable, holding all other relevant variables constant. The price elasticity of demand, ε, is the percentage change in the quantity demanded in response to a given percentage change in price: a 1% increase in price causes the quantity demanded to fall by ε%. Because demand curves slope downward according to the Law of Demand, the elasticity of demand is always negative. The price elasticity of supply, η, is the percentage change in the quantity supplied in response to a given percentage change in price. Given estimated elasticities, we can forecast the comparative statics effects of a change in taxes or other variables that affect the equilibrium.

6. **Effects of a Sales Tax.** The two common types of sales taxes are ad valorem taxes, by which the government collects a fixed percentage of the price paid per unit, and specific taxes, by which the government collects a fixed amount of money per unit sold. Both types of sales taxes typically raise the equilibrium price and lower the equilibrium quantity. Both usually also raise the price consumers pay and lower the price suppliers receive, so consumers do not bear the full burden or incidence of the tax. The effects on quantity, price, and the incidence of the tax that falls on consumers depend on the demand and supply elasticities. In competitive markets, the impact of a tax on equilibrium quantities, prices, and the incidence of the tax is unaffected by whether the tax is collected from consumers or producers.

7. **Quantity Supplied Need Not Equal Quantity Demanded.** The quantity supplied equals the quantity demanded in a competitive market if the government does not intervene. However, some government policies—such as price floors or ceilings—cause the quantity supplied to be greater or less than the quantity demanded, leading to persistent excesses or shortages.

8. **When to Use the Supply-and-Demand Model.** The supply-and-demand model is a powerful tool to explain what happens in a market or to make predictions about what will happen if an underlying factor in a market changes. However, this model is applicable only in competitive markets, which are markets with many buyers and sellers, firms sell identical goods, participants have full information, transaction costs are low, and firms can easily enter and exit.

QUESTIONS

If you ask me anything I don't know, I'm not going to answer. —Yogi Berra

■ = exercise is available on **MyEconLab**; * = answer appears at the back of this book; V = video answer by James Dearden is available online.

*1. Use a supply-and-demand diagram to explain the statement "Talk is cheap because supply exceeds demand." At what price is this comparison being made?

2. The 9/11 terrorist attacks caused the U.S. airline travel demand curve to shift left by an estimated 30%

(Ito and Lee, 2005). Use a supply-and-demand diagram to show the likely effect on price and quantity (assuming that the market is competitive). Indicate the magnitude of the likely equilibrium price and quantity effects—for example, would you expect equilibrium quantity to change by about 30%? Show how the answer depends on the shape and location of the supply and demand curves.

3. When he was the top American administrator in Iraq, L. Paul Bremer III set a rule that upheld Iraqi law: anyone 25 years and older with a "good reputation and character" could own one firearm, including an AK-47 assault rifle. Iraqi citizens quickly began arming themselves. Akram Abdulzahra has a revolver handy at his job in an Internet cafe. Haidar Hussein, a Baghdad bookseller, has a new fully automatic assault rifle. After the bombing of a sacred Shiite shrine in Samarra at the end of February 2006 and the subsequent rise in sectarian violence, the demand for guns increased, resulting in higher prices. The average price of a legal, Russian-made Kalashnikov AK-47 assault rifle jumped from $112 to $290 from February to March 2006. The price of bullets shot up from 24¢ to 33¢ each. (Jeffrey Gettleman, "Sectarian Suspicion in Baghdad Fuels a Seller's Market for Guns," *New York Times*, April 3, 2006.) The increase occurred despite the hundreds of thousands of firearms and millions of rounds of ammunition that American troops had been providing to Iraqi security forces, some of which eventually ended up in the hands of private citizens. Use a graph to illustrate why prices rose.

4. The Federation of Vegetable Farmers Association of Malaysia reported that a lack of workers caused a 25% drop in production that drove up vegetable prices by 50% to 100% in 2005 ("Vegetable Price Control Sought," **thestar.com.my**, June 6, 2005). Consumers called for price controls on vegetables. Show why the price increased and predict the effects of a binding price control. V

*5. Soon after the United States revealed the discovery of a single mad cow in December 2003, more than 40 countries slapped an embargo on U.S. beef. In addition, some U.S. consumers stopped eating beef. In the three weeks after the discovery, the quantity sold increased by 43% during the last week of October 2003, and the U.S. price in January 2004 fell by about 15%. Use supply-and-demand diagrams to explain why these events occurred.

6. Ethanol, a fuel, is made from corn. Ethanol production increased 5.5 times from 2000 to 2008 (**www.ethanolrfa.org**). What effect did this increased use of corn for producing ethanol have on the price of corn and the consumption of corn as food?

7. The prices received by soybean farmers in Brazil, the world's second-largest soybean producer and exporter, tumbled 30%, in part because of China's decision to cut back on imports, and in part because of a bumper soybean crop in the United States, the world's leading exporter (Todd Benson, "A Harvest at Peril," *New York Times*, January 6, 2005, C6). In addition, Asian soy rust, a deadly crop fungus, is destroying large quantities of the Brazilian crops.

   a. Use a supply-and-demand diagram to illustrate why Brazilian farmers are receiving lower prices.

   b. If you knew only the *direction* of the shifts in both the supply and the demand curves, could you predict that prices would fall? Why or why not? V

8. On January 1, 2005, a three-decades-old system of global quotas that had limited how much China and other countries could ship to the United States and other wealthy nations ended. Over the next four months, U.S. imports of Chinese-made cotton trousers rose by more than 1,505% and their price fell 21% in the first quarter of the year (Tracie Rozhon, "A Tangle in Textiles," *New York Times*, April 21, 2005, C1). The U.S. textile industry demanded quick action, saying that 18 U.S. plants had already been forced to close that year and that 16,600 textile and apparel jobs had been lost. The Bush administration reacted to the industry pressure. The United States (and Europe, which faced similar large increases in imports) pressed China to cut back its textile exports, threatening to restore quotas on Chinese exports or to take other actions. Illustrate what happened, and show how the U.S. quota reimposed in May 2005 affected the equilibrium price and quantity in the United States.

9. After Hurricane Katrina damaged a substantial portion of the nation's oil-refining capacity in 2005, the price of gasoline shot up around the country. In 2006, many state and federal elected officials called for price controls. Had they been imposed, what effect would price controls have had? Who would have benefited, and who would have been harmed by the controls? Use a supply-and-demand diagram to illustrate your answers.

10. Argentines love a sizzling steak, consuming twice as much per capita as U.S. citizens. Thus, when the price of beef started to shoot up, Argentina's President Néstor Kirchner took dramatic action to force down beef prices. (Larry Rohter, "For Argentina's Sizzling Economy, a Cap on Steak Prices," *New York Times*, April 3, 2006.) He ordered government ministries to cease their purchases, prohibited the export of most cuts of beef, and urged consumers to boycott beef. But beef-loving Argentines, benefiting from higher

wages due to a growing economy, largely ignored his call. When these actions failed to lower prices substantially, he turned to "voluntary" price controls ("encouraging" grocery chains and others not to raise prices for extended periods of time). Use graphs to illustrate this sequence of events.

*11. Between 1971 and 2006, the United States from time to time imposed quotas or other restrictions on importing steel. Suppose both the domestic supply curve of steel, S^d, and the foreign supply curve of steel for sale in the United States, S^f, are upward-sloping straight lines. How did a quota set by the United States on foreign steel imports of $\bar{Q} > 0$ affect the total American supply curve for steel (domestic and foreign supply combined)?

*12. Given the answer to Question 11, what effect does a U.S. quota on steel of $\bar{Q} > 0$ have on the equilibrium in the U.S. steel market? (*Hint*: The answer depends on whether the quota binds—is low enough to affect the equilibrium.)

13. Will Mexico stop producing tequila? Because of record-low industry prices for the agave azul plant, from which tequila is distilled, farmers in Jalisco and other Mexican states are switching to more lucrative plants like corn, which is used for the now-trendy ethanol fuel alternative. (Kyle Arnold, "No Mas Tequila," *The Monitor*, September 17, 2007.) Planting of agave rose substantially from 2000 through 2004, and then started to plummet as the price of inexpensive tequila fell. The number of agave planted went from 60 million in 2000, to 93 million in 2002, to 12.8 million in 2006, and the downward trend continued in 2007. It takes seven years for an agave plant to be ready for harvesting. The price of inexpensive tequila has dropped 35% to 40% in recent years, but the price of high-end tequilas, which has been growing in popularity, has remained stable. Discuss the relative sizes of the short-run and long-run supply elasticities of tequila. What do you think the supply elasticity of high-quality tequila is? Why? If the demand curve for inexpensive tequila has remained relatively unchanged, is the demand curve relatively elastic or inelastic at the equilibrium? Why?

14. For years, Anthony Gallis, his wife, and their four children traveled from Dallas, Pennsylvania to South Bend, Indiana, where they rented a house for $1,200 a weekend so that they could attend Notre Dame football games. On the weekend of the 2006 home opener against Penn State, someone else arranged to rent his house months earlier, and another house recommended to him at $3,000 was also taken. A parking pass sold for $500, and a pair of tickets with face prices of $59 went for $3,200 for the Penn State game on eBay. Hotel prices and the cost of restaurant meals are also much higher on football weekends than during the other 341 days of the year—particularly in years when Notre Dame is expected to have a winning season. (Ilan Brat, "Why Fans Pay Through the Nose to See Notre Dame," *Wall Street Journal*, September 7, 2006.) Use a supply-and-demand diagram to illustrate why, when the demand curve shifts to the right, the prices of hotel rooms and rental apartments shoot up. (*Hint*: Carefully explain the shape of the supply curve, taking into account what happens when capacity is reached, such as when all hotel rooms are filled.)

15. The application "Substitution May Save Endangered Species" describes how the equilibrium changed in the market for seal genitalia (used as an aphrodisiac in Asia) when Viagra was introduced. Use a supply-and-demand diagram to illustrate what happened. Show whether the following is possible: A positive quantity is demanded at various prices, yet nothing is sold in the market.

16. According to Borjas (2003), immigration to the United States increased the labor supply of working men by 11.0% from 1980 to 2000, and reduced the wage of the average native worker by 3.2%. From these results, can we make any inferences about the elasticity of supply or demand? Which curve (or curves) changed, and why? Draw a supply-and-demand diagram and label the axes to illustrate what happened.

17. The U.S. Bureau of Labor Statistics reports that the average salary for postsecondary economics teachers in the Raleigh-Durham-Chapel Hill metropolitan area, which has many top universities, rose to $105,200 (based on a 52-week work year) in 2003. According to the *Wall Street Journal* (Timothy Aeppel, "Economists Gain Star Power," February 22, 2005, A2), the salary increase resulted from an outward shift in the demand curve for academic economists due to the increased popularity of the economics major, while the supply curve of Ph.D. economists did not shift and the quantity supplied did not change.

   a. If this explanation is correct, what is the short-run price elasticity of supply of academic economists?

   b. If these salaries are expected to remain high, will more people enter doctoral programs in economics? How would such entry affect the long-run price elasticity of supply? V

18. What effect does a $1 specific tax have on equilibrium price and quantity, and what is the incidence on consumers, if the following is true:

   a. The demand curve is perfectly inelastic.

   b. The demand curve is perfectly elastic.

c. The supply curve is perfectly inelastic.

d. The supply curve is perfectly elastic.

e. The demand curve is perfectly elastic and the supply curve is perfectly inelastic.

Use graphs and math to explain your answers.

19. On July 1, 1965, the federal ad valorem taxes on many goods and services were eliminated. Comparing prices before and after this change, we can determine how much the price fell in response to the tax's elimination. When the tax was in place, the tax per unit on a good that sold for p was αp. If the price fell by αp when the tax was eliminated, consumers must have been bearing the full incidence of the tax. Consequently, consumers got the full benefit of removing the tax from those goods. The entire amount of the tax cut was passed on to consumers for all commodities and services that were studied for which the taxes were collected at the retail level (except admissions and club dues) and for most commodities for which excise taxes were imposed at the manufacturer level, including face powder, sterling silverware, wristwatches, and handbags (Brownlee and Perry, 1967). List the conditions (in terms of the elasticities or shapes of supply or demand curves) that are consistent with 100% pass-through of the taxes. Use graphs to illustrate your answer.

20. Essentially none of the savings from removing the federal ad valorem tax were passed on to consumers for motion picture admissions and club dues (Brownlee and Perry, 1967; see Question 19). List the conditions (in terms of the elasticities or shapes of supply or demand curves) that are consistent with 0% pass-through of the taxes. Use graphs to illustrate your answer.

*21. Do you care whether a 15¢ tax per gallon of milk is collected from milk producers or from consumers at the store? Why or why not?

*22. Usury laws place a ceiling on interest rates that lenders such as banks can charge borrowers. Low-income households in states with usury laws have significantly lower levels of consumer credit (loans) than comparable households in states without usury laws (Villegas, 1989). Why? (*Hint*: The interest rate is the price of a loan, and the amount of the loan is the quantity.)

PROBLEMS

*23. Using the estimated demand function for processed pork in Canada, Equation 2.2, show how the quantity demanded, Q, at a given price changes as per capita income, Y, increases slightly (that is, calculate the partial derivative of the quantity demanded with respect to income). How much does Q change if income rises by $100 a year?

*24. Suppose that the inverse demand function (where the demand curve is rearranged so that price is a function of quantity) for movies is $p = 120 - Q_1$ for college students and $p = 120 - 2Q_2$ for other town residents. What is the town's total demand function ($Q = Q_1 + Q_2$ as a function of p)? Use a diagram to illustrate your answer.

25. The demand function for movies is $Q_1 = 120 - p$ for college students and $Q_2 = 120 - 2p$ for other town residents. What is the total demand function? Use a diagram to illustrate your answer. (*Hint*: By looking at your diagram, you'll see that some care must be used in writing the demand function.)

26. In the application "Aggregating the Demand for Broadband Service" (based on Duffy-Deno, 2003), the demand function is $Q_s = 5.97p^{-0.563}$ for small firms and $Q_l = 8.77p^{-0.296}$ for larger firms, where price is in cents per kilobyte per second and quantity is in millions of kilobytes per second (Kbps). What is the total demand function for all firms? If the supply curve for broadband service is horizontal at 40¢ per Kbps (firms will supply as much service as desired at that price), what is the equilibrium quantity demanded by small firms, large firms, and all firms?

27. In the application "Aggregating the Demand for Broadband Service" (based on Duffy-Deno, 2003), the demand function is $Q_s = 5.97p^{-0.563}$ for small firms and $Q_l = 8.77p^{-0.296}$ for larger ones. As the graph in the application shows, the two demand functions cross. What are the elasticities of demand for small and large firms where they cross? Explain. [*Hint*: This problem can be answered without doing any calculations.]

*28. Green, Howitt, and Russo (2005) estimate the supply and demand curves for California processing tomatoes. The supply function is $\ln Q = 0.2 + 0.55 \ln p$, where Q is the quantity of processing tomatoes in millions of tons per year and p is the price in dollars per ton. The demand function is $\ln Q = 2.6 - 0.2 \ln p + 0.15 \ln p_t$, where p_t is the price of tomato paste (which is what processing tomatoes are used to produce) in dollars per ton. In 2002, $p_t = 110$. What is the demand function for processing tomatoes, where the quantity is solely a function of the price of processing tomatoes? Solve for the equilibrium price and the quantity of processing tomatoes (rounded to two digits after the decimal point). Draw the supply and demand curves (note that they are not straight lines), and label the equilibrium and axes appropriately.

29. The U.S. Tobacco Settlement Agreement between the major tobacco companies and 46 states caused the price of cigarettes to jump 45¢ (21%) in November 1998. Levy and Meara (2006) find only a 2.65% drop in prenatal smoking 15 months later. What is the elasticity of demand for prenatal smokers?

*30. Calculate the price and cross-price elasticities of demand for coconut oil. The coconut oil demand function (Buschena and Perloff, 1991) is $Q = 1,200 - 9.5p + 16.2p_p + 0.2Y$, where Q is the quantity of coconut oil demanded in thousands of metric tons per year, p is the price of coconut oil in cents per pound, p_p is the price of palm oil in cents per pound, and Y is the income of consumers. Assume that p is initially 45¢ per pound, p_p is 31¢ per pound, and Q is 1,275 thousand metric tons per year.

31. When the U.S. government announced that a domestic mad cow was found in December 2003, analysts estimated that domestic supplies would increase in the short run by 10.4% as many other countries barred U.S. beef. An estimate of the price elasticity of beef demand is −1.6 (Henderson, 2003). Assuming that only the domestic supply curve shifted, how much would you expect the price to change? (*Note*: The U.S. price fell by about 15% in the first month, but that probably reflected shifts in both supply and demand curves.)

32. Keeler et al. (2004) estimate that the U.S. Tobacco Settlement between major tobacco companies and 46 states caused the price of cigarettes to jump by 45¢ per pack (21%) and overall per capita cigarette consumption to fall by 8.3%. What is the elasticity of demand for cigarettes? Is cigarette demand elastic or inelastic?

33. In a commentary piece on the rising cost of health insurance ("Healthy, Wealthy, and Wise," *Wall Street Journal*, May 4, 2004, A20), economists John Cogan, Glenn Hubbard, and Daniel Kessler state, "Each percentage-point rise in health-insurance costs increases the number of uninsured by 300,000 people." Assuming that their claim is correct, demonstrate that the price elasticity of demand for health insurance depends on the number of people who are insured. What is the price elasticity if 200 million people are insured? What is the price elasticity if 220 million people are insured? V

34. Using calculus, determine the effect of an increase in the price of beef, p_b, from $4 to $4.60 on the equilibrium price and quantity in the Canadian pork example. (*Hint*: Conduct an analysis that differs from that in Solved Problem 2.1 in that the shock is to the demand curve rather than to the supply curve.) Illustrate your comparative statics analysis in a figure.

35. Solved Problem 2.3 claims that a new war in the Persian Gulf could shift the world oil supply curve to the left by 3 million barrels a day or more, causing the world price of oil to soar regardless of whether we drill in the ANWR. How accurate is that claim? Use the same type of analysis as in the solved problem to calculate how much such a shock would cause the price to rise with and without the ANWR production.

36. A subsidy is a negative tax through which the government gives people money instead of taking it from them. If the government applied a $1.05 specific subsidy instead of a specific tax in Figure 2.12, what would happen to the equilibrium price and quantity? Use the demand function and the after-subsidy supply function to solve for the new equilibrium values. What is the incidence of the subsidy on consumers?

37. Besley and Rosen (1998) found that a 10¢ increase in the federal tax on a pack of cigarettes led to an average 2.8¢ increase in state cigarette taxes. What implications does their result have for calculating the effects of an increase in the federal cigarette tax on the quantity demanded? In 2009, the U.S. federal cigarette tax was raised to $1.01 per pack, and the federal tax plus the average state tax was $1.31 per pack. Given the current federal tax and an estimated elasticity of demand for the U.S. population of −0.3, what is the effect of a 10¢ increase in the federal tax? How would your answer change if the state tax does not change?

38. Green et al. (2005) estimate that the demand elasticity is −0.47 and the long-run supply elasticity is 12.0 for almonds. The corresponding elasticities are −0.68 and 0.73 for cotton and −0.26 and 0.64 for processing tomatoes. If the government were to apply a specific tax to each of these commodities, what would be the consumer tax incidence for each of these commodities?

*39. Use calculus to show that an increase in a specific sales tax τ reduces quantity by less and tax revenue more, the less elastic the demand curve. (*Hint*: The quantity demanded depends on its price, which in turn depends on the specific tax, $Q(p(\tau))$, and tax revenue is $R = p(\tau)Q(p(\tau))$.)

*40. An increase in the minimum wage could raise the total wage payment, $W = wL(w)$, where w is the minimum wage and $L(w)$ is the demand function for labor, despite the fall in demand for labor services.

Show that whether the wage payments rise or fall depends on the elasticity of demand of labor.

41. Lewit and Coate (1982) estimated that the price elasticity of demand for cigarettes is −0.42. Suppose that the daily market demand for cigarettes in New York City is $Q = 20{,}000p^{-0.42}$ and that the inverse market supply curve of cigarettes in the city is $p = 1.5p_w$, where p_w is the wholesale price of cigarettes. (That is, the inverse market supply curve is a horizontal line at a price, p, equal to $1.5p_w$. Retailers sell cigarettes if they receive a price that is 50% higher than what they pay for the cigarettes so as to cover their other costs.)

  a. Assume that the New York retail market for cigarettes is competitive. Calculate the equilibrium price and quantity of cigarettes as a function of the wholesale price. Let Q^* represent the equilibrium quantity. Find dQ^*/dp_w.

  b. Now suppose that New York City and State each impose a $1.50 specific tax on each pack of cigarettes, for a total of $3.00 per pack on all cigarettes possessed for sale or use in New York City. The tax is paid by the retailers. Show using both math and a graph how the introduction of the tax shifts the market supply curve. How does the introduction of the tax affect the equilibrium retail price and quantity of cigarettes?

  c. With the specific tax in place, calculate the equilibrium price and quantity of cigarettes as a function of wholesale price. How does the presence of the quantity tax affect dQ^*/dp_w? V

42. Due to a recession that lowered incomes, the 2002 market prices for last-minute rentals of U.S. beachfront properties were lower than usual (June Fletcher, "Last-Minute Beach Rentals Offer Summer's Best Deals," *Wall Street Journal*, June 21, 2002, D1). Suppose that the inverse demand function for renting a beachfront property in Ocean City, New Jersey, during the first week of August is $p = 1{,}000 - Q + Y/20$, where Y is the median annual income of the people involved in this market, Q is quantity, and p is the rental price. The inverse supply function is $p = Q/2 + Y/40$.

  a. Derive the equilibrium price, p^*, and quantity, Q^*, in terms of Y.

  b. Use a supply-and-demand analysis to show the effect of decreased income on the equilibrium price of rental homes. That is, find dp^*/dY. Does a decrease in median income lead to a decrease in the equilibrium rental price? V

Consumer Theory

If this is coffee, please bring me some tea; but if this is tea, please bring me some coffee. —Abraham Lincoln

Microeconomics provides powerful insights into the myriad questions and choices facing consumers. For example, does the shift to U.S. consumers' purchasing relatively fewer SUVs and more small vehicles in the past few years reflect a change in tastes or a response to higher SUV and gas prices? How can we use information about consumers' allocations of their budgets across various goods in the past to predict how a price change will affect their demands for goods today? Are consumers better off receiving cash or a comparable amount in food stamps? Should you buy insurance or save your money? Work at home or in the marketplace? Have children? Invest in bonds or in stocks?

To answer these and other questions about how consumers allocate their income over many goods, we use a model that lets us look at an individual's decision making when faced with limited income and market-determined prices. This model allows us to derive the market demand curve that we used in our supply-and-demand model and to make a variety of predictions about consumers' responses to changes in prices and income.

Our model of consumer behavior is based on the following premises:

- Individual *tastes* or *preferences* determine the amount of pleasure people derive from the goods and services they consume.
- Consumers face *constraints*, or limits, on their choices.
- Consumers *maximize* their well-being or pleasure from consumption subject to the budget and other constraints they face.

Consumers spend their money on the bundle of products that gives them the most pleasure. If you love music and don't have much of a sweet tooth, you probably spend a lot of your money on concerts and CDs and relatively little on candy.[1] By contrast, your chocoholic friend with the tin ear might spend a great deal of money on Hershey's Kisses and very little on music.

All consumers must choose which goods to buy because their limited incomes prevent them from buying everything that catches their fancy. In addition, government rules restrict what they may buy: Young consumers cannot buy alcohol or cigarettes legally, and laws prohibit people of all ages from buying crack cocaine and other recreational drugs (although, of course, enforcement is imperfect).

---

[1]Microeconomics is the study of trade-offs: Should you save your money or buy that Superman *Action Comics* Number 1 you always wanted? Indeed, an anagram for *microeconomics* is *income or comics*.

Therefore, consumers buy the goods that give them the most pleasure, subject to the constraints that they cannot spend more money than they have and that they cannot spend it in ways that the government prevents.

When conducting economic analyses designed to explain behavior (positive analysis—see Chapter 1) rather than to judge it (normative statements), economists assume that *the consumer is the boss*. If your brother gets pleasure from smoking, economists wouldn't argue with him that it's bad for him any more than they'd tell your sister, who likes reading Stephen King, that she should read Adam Smith's *Wealth of Nations* instead.[2] Accepting each consumer's tastes is not the same as condoning how people behave. Economists want to predict behavior. They want to know, for example, whether your brother will smoke more next year if the price of cigarettes decreases 10%. The following prediction is unlikely to be correct: "He shouldn't smoke; therefore, we predict he'll stop smoking next year." A prediction based on your brother's actual tastes is more likely to be correct: "Given that he likes cigarettes, he is likely to smoke more of them next year if the price falls."

In this chapter, we examine five main topics

1. **Preferences.** We use five properties of preferences to predict which combinations, or bundle, of goods an individual prefers to other combinations.

2. **Utility.** Economists summarize a consumer's preferences using a utility function, which assigns a numerical value to each possible bundle of goods, reflecting the consumer's relative ranking of the bundles.

3. **Budget Constraint.** Prices, income, and government restrictions limit a consumer's ability to make purchases by determining the rate at which a consumer can trade one good for another.

4. **Constrained Consumer Choice.** Consumers maximize their pleasure from consuming various possible bundles of goods given their income, which limits the amount of goods they can purchase.

5. **Behavioral Economics.** Experiments indicate that people sometimes deviate from rational, utility-maximizing behavior.

3.1 Preferences

Do not do unto others as you would that they would do unto you. Their tastes may not be the same. —George Bernard Shaw

We start our analysis of consumer behavior by examining consumer preferences. Using four assumptions, we can make many predictions about people's preferences. Once we know about consumers' preferences, we can add information about the constraints that consumers face so that we can answer many questions, such as the ones posed at the beginning of the chapter, or derive demand curves, as we do in Chapter 4.

As a consumer, you choose among many goods. Should you have ice cream or cake for dessert? Should you spend most of your money on a large apartment or rent a single room and use the money you save to pay for trips and concerts? In short,

---

[2] As the ancient Romans put it: "De gustibus non est disputandum"—there is no disputing about (accounting for) tastes. Or, as it was put in the movie *Grand Hotel* (1932), "Have caviar if you like, but it tastes like herring to me."

you must allocate your money to buy a *bundle* of goods (*market basket*, or combination of goods).

How do consumers choose the bundle of goods they buy? One possibility is that consumers behave randomly and blindly choose one good or another without any thought. However, consumers appear to make systematic choices. For example, you probably buy the same specific items, more or less, each time you go to the grocery store.

To explain consumer behavior, economists *assume* that consumers have a set of tastes or preferences that they use to guide them in choosing between goods. These tastes differ substantially among individuals. Three out of four European men prefer colored underwear, while three out of four American men prefer white underwear.[3] Let's start by specifying the underlying assumptions in the economist's model of consumer behavior.

Properties of Consumer Preferences

I have forced myself to contradict myself in order to avoid conforming to my own taste. —Marcel Duchamp, Dada artist

A consumer chooses between bundles of goods by ranking them as to the pleasure the consumer gets from consuming each. We summarize a consumer's ranking using a *preference relation* $\succsim$. If the consumer likes Bundle a at least as much as Bundle b, we say that the consumer *weakly prefers* a to b, which we write as $a \succsim b$.

Given this weak preference relation, we can derive two other relations. If the consumer weakly prefers Bundle a to b, $a \succsim b$, but the consumer does not weakly prefer b to a, then we say that the consumer *strictly prefers* a to b—would definitely choose a rather than b if given a choice—which we write as $a \succ b$.

If the consumer weakly prefers a to b and weakly prefers b to a—that is $a \succsim b$ and $b \succsim a$—then we say that the consumer is *indifferent* between the bundles, or likes the two bundles equally, which we write as $a \sim b$.

We make three assumptions about the properties of consumers' preferences. For brevity, these properties are referred to as *completeness*, *transitivity*, and *more is better*.

Completeness. The completeness property holds that, when facing a choice between any two bundles of goods, Bundles a and b, a consumer can rank them so that one and only one of the following relationships is true: $a \succsim b$, $b \succsim a$, or both relationships hold so that $a \sim b$. This property rules out the possibility that the consumer cannot decide which bundle is preferable.

Transitivity. It would be very difficult to predict behavior if consumers' rankings of bundles were not logically consistent. The transitivity property eliminates the possibility of certain types of illogical behavior. According to this property, a consumer's preferences over bundles is consistent in the sense that, if the consumer *weakly prefers* a to b, $a \succsim b$, and weakly prefers b to c, $b \succsim c$, then the consumer also weakly prefers a to c, $a \succsim c$.

If your sister told you that she preferred a scoop of ice cream to a piece of cake, a piece of cake to a candy bar, and a candy bar to a scoop of ice cream, you'd probably think she'd lost her mind. At the very least, you wouldn't know which of these desserts to serve her.

---

[3]Boyd, L. M., "The Grab Bag," *San Francisco Examiner*, September 11, 1994, p. 5.

If completeness and transitivity hold, then the preference relation ≿ is said to be *rational*. That is, the consumer has well-defined preferences between any pair of alternatives.

More Is Better. The more-is-better property states that, all else the same, more of a commodity is better than less of it.[4] Indeed, economists define a **good** as a commodity for which more is preferred to less, at least at some levels of consumption. In contrast, a **bad** is something for which less is preferred to more, such as pollution. Other than in Chapter 16, we concentrate on goods.

Although the completeness and transitivity properties are crucial to the analysis that follows, the more-is-better property is included to simplify the analysis; our most important results would follow even without this property.

So why do economists assume that the more-is-better property holds? The most compelling reason is that it appears to be true for most people. A second reason is that if consumers can freely dispose of excess goods, consumers can be no worse off with extra goods. (We examine a third reason later in the chapter: We observe consumers buying goods only when this condition is met.)

APPLICATION

Income Buys Happiness

Do people become satiated? Is there an income so high that consumers can buy everything they want so that additional income does not increase their feelings of well-being?

Using recent data from as many as 131 countries, Stevenson and Wolfers (2008) find a strong positive relationship between average levels of self-reported feelings of happiness or satisfaction and income per capita within and across countries. Moreover, they find no evidence of a satiation point beyond which wealthier countries have no further increases in subjective well-being.

Less scientific, but perhaps more compelling, is a survey of wealthy U.S. citizens who were asked, "How much wealth do you need to live comfortably?" Those with a net worth of over $1 million said that they needed $2.4 million to live comfortably, those with at least $5 million in net worth said that they need $10.4 million, and those with at least $10 million wanted $18.1 million. Apparently, most people never have enough.[5]

Preference Maps

Surprisingly, with just these three properties, we can tell a lot about a consumer's preferences. One of the simplest ways to summarize information about a consumer's preferences is to create a graphical interpretation—a map—of them. For simplicity, we concentrate on choices between only two goods, but the model can be generalized to handle any number of goods.

---

[4]*Jargon alert*: Economists call this property *nonsatiation* or *monotonicity*.

[5]When teaching microeconomics to Wharton MBAs, I told them about my cousin who had just joined a commune in Oregon. His worldly possessions consisted of a tent, a Franklin stove, enough food to live on, and a few clothes. He said that he didn't need any other goods—that he was *satiated*. A few years later, one of these students bumped into me on the street and said, "Professor, I don't remember your name or much of anything you taught me in your course, but I can't stop thinking about your cousin. Is it really true that he doesn't want *anything* else? His very existence is a repudiation of my whole way of life." Actually, my cousin had given up his ascetic life and was engaged in telemarketing, but I, for noble pedagogical reasons, responded, "Of course he still lives that way—you can't expect everyone to have the tastes of an MBA."

Each semester, Lisa, who lives for fast food, decides how many pizzas and burritos to eat. The various bundles of pizzas and burritos she might consume are shown in panel a of Figure 3.1, with (individual-size) pizzas per semester, q_1, on the horizontal axis and burritos per semester, q_2, on the vertical axis.

At Bundle e, for example, Lisa consumes 25 pizzas and 15 burritos per semester. According to the more-is-better property, all the bundles that lie above and to the right (area A) are preferred to Bundle e because they contain at least as much of both pizzas and burritos as Bundle e. Thus, Bundle f (30 pizzas and 20 burritos) in that

Figure 3.1 Bundles of Pizzas and Burritos Lisa Might Consume

(a) Lisa prefers more to less, so she prefers Bundle e to any bundle in area B, including d. Similarly, she prefers any bundle in area A, such as f, to e. (b) The indifference curve, I^1, shows a set of bundles (including c, e, and a) among which she is indifferent. (c) The three indifference curves, I^1, I^2, and I^3, are part of Lisa's preference map, which summarizes her preferences.

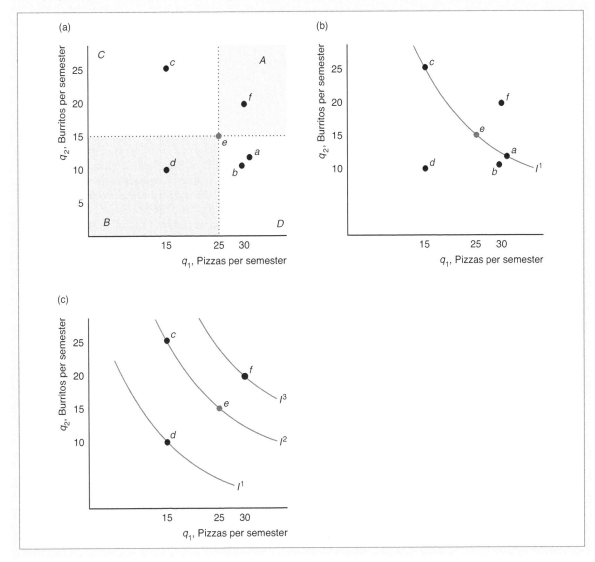

region is preferred to e. By the same reasoning, Lisa prefers e to all the bundles that lie in area B, below and to the left of e, such as Bundle d (15 pizzas and 10 burritos).

Again, because more is better, Lisa prefers e to all the bundles that lie in area B, below and to the left of e, such as Bundle d (15 pizzas and 10 burritos). All the bundles in area B contain fewer pizzas, fewer burritos, or fewer of both than does Bundle e.

From panel a, we do not know whether Lisa prefers Bundle e to bundles such as b (30 pizzas and 10 burritos) in the area D, which is the region below and to the right of e, or c (15 pizzas and 25 burritos) in area C, which is the region above and to the left of Bundle e. We can't use the more-is-better property to determine which bundle is preferred because each of these bundles contains more of one good and less of the other than e does. To be able to state with certainty whether Lisa prefers particular bundles in areas C or D to Bundle e, we have to know more about her tastes for pizza and burritos.

Indifference Curves

Suppose we asked Lisa to identify all the bundles that give her the same amount of pleasure as consuming Bundle e. In Figure 3.1 panel b, we use her answers to draw curve I^1 through all bundles she likes as much as she likes e. Curve I^1 is an **indifference curve**: the set of all bundles of goods that a consumer views as being equally desirable.

Indifference curve I^1 includes Bundles c, e, and a, so Lisa is indifferent about consuming Bundles c, e, and a. From this indifference curve, we also know that Lisa prefers e (25 pizzas and 15 burritos) to b (30 pizzas and 10 burritos). How do we know that? Bundle b lies below and to the left of Bundle a, so Bundle a is preferred to Bundle b according to the more-is-better property. Both Bundles a and e are on indifference curve I^1, so Lisa likes Bundle e as much as Bundle a. Because Lisa is indifferent between e and a, and she prefers a to b, she must prefer e to b by transitivity.

If we asked Lisa many, many questions, we could, in principle, draw an entire set of indifference curves through every possible bundle of burritos and pizzas. Lisa's preferences are summarized in an **indifference map**, or *preference map*, which is a complete set of indifference curves that summarize a consumer's tastes. It is referred to as a *map* because it uses the same principle as a topographical or contour map, in which each line shows all points with the same height or elevation. Each indifference curve in an indifference map consists of bundles of goods that provide the same utility or well-being for a consumer, but the level of well-being differs from one curve to another. Panel c of Figure 3.1 shows three of Lisa's indifference curves: I^1, I^2, and I^3. The indifference curves are parallel in the figure, but they need not be.

Given our assumptions, all indifference curve maps must have five important properties:

1. Bundles on indifference curves farther from the origin are preferred to those on indifference curves closer to the origin.
2. There is an indifference curve through every possible bundle.
3. Indifference curves cannot cross.
4. Indifference curves slope downward.
5. Indifference curves cannot be thick.

First, we show that bundles on indifference curves farther from the origin are preferred to those on indifference curves closer to the origin. Because of the more-is-better property, Lisa prefers Bundle f to Bundle e in panel c of Figure 3.1. She is indifferent among all the bundles on indifference curve I^3 and Bundle f, just as she is indifferent among all the bundles, such as Bundle c on indifference curve I^2 and Bundle e. By the transitivity property, she prefers Bundle f to Bundle e, which she likes as much as Bundle c, so she prefers Bundle f to Bundle c. Using this type of reasoning, she prefers all bundles on I^3 to all bundles on I^2.

Second, we show that there is an indifference curve through every possible bundle as a consequence of the completeness property: The consumer can compare any bundle to another bundle. Compared to a given bundle, some bundles are preferred, some are enjoyed equally, and some are inferior. Connecting the bundles that give the same pleasure produces an indifference curve that includes the given bundle.

Third, we show that indifference curves cannot cross. If two indifference curves did cross, the bundle at the point of intersection would be on both indifference curves. But a given bundle cannot be on two indifference curves. Suppose that two indifference curves crossed at Bundle e in panel a of Figure 3.2. Because Bundles e and a lie on the same indifference curve I^1, Lisa is indifferent between e and a. Similarly, she is indifferent between e and b because both are on I^2. By transitivity, if Lisa is indifferent between e and a, and she is indifferent between e and b, she must be indifferent between a and b. But that's impossible! Bundle b is above and to the right of bundle a, which means it contains more of both goods. Thus, Lisa *must* prefer b to a according to the more-is-better property. Because preferences are transitive and consumers prefer more to less, indifference curves cannot cross.

Fourth, we show that indifference curves must be downward sloping. Suppose, to the contrary, that an indifference curve sloped upward, as in panel b of Figure

Figure 3.2 Impossible Indifference Curves

(a) Suppose that the indifference curves cross at Bundle e. Lisa is indifferent between e and a on indifference curve I^0 and between e and b on I^1. If Lisa is indifferent between e and a, and she is indifferent between e and b, she must be indifferent between a and b due to transitivity. But b has more of both pizzas and burritos than a, so she *must* prefer a to b. Because of this contradiction, indifference curves cannot cross. (b) Suppose that indifference curve I slopes upward. The consumer is indifferent between b and a because they lie on I, but prefers b to a by the more-is-better assumption. Because of this contradiction, indifference curves cannot be upward sloping. (c) Suppose that indifference curve I is thick enough to contain both a and b. The consumer is indifferent between a and b because both are on I. However, the consumer prefers b to a by the more-is-better assumption because b lies above and to the right of a. Because of this contradiction, indifference curves cannot be thick.

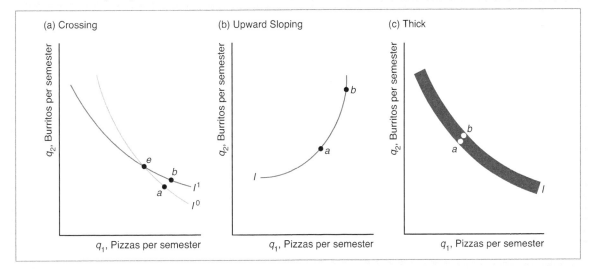

3.2. The consumer is indifferent between Bundles a and b because both lie on the same indifference curve, I. But the consumer prefers b to a by the more-is-better property: Bundle a lies strictly below and to the left of Bundle b. Because of this contradiction—the consumer cannot both be indifferent between a and b and strictly prefer b to a—indifference curves cannot be upward sloping. For example, if Lisa views pizza and burritos as goods, she cannot be indifferent between a bundle of one pizza and one burrito and another bundle with two of each.

SOLVED PROBLEM 3.1

Can indifference curves be thick?

Answer

Draw an indifference curve that is at least two bundles thick, and show that a preference property is violated. Panel c of Figure 3.2 shows a thick indifference curve, I, with two bundles, a and b, identified. Bundle b lies above and to the right of a: Bundle b has more of both burritos and pizzas. Thus, because of the more-is-better property, Bundle b must be strictly preferred to Bundle a. But the consumer must be indifferent between a and b because both bundles are on the same indifference curve. Because both relationships between a and b cannot be true, there is a contradiction. Consequently, indifference curves cannot be thick. (We illustrate this point by drawing indifference curves with very thin lines in our figures.)

3.2 Utility

Underlying our model of consumer behavior is the belief that consumers can compare various bundles of goods and decide which bundle gives them the greatest pleasure. We can summarize a consumer's preferences by assigning a numerical value to each possible bundle to reflect the consumer's relative ranking of these bundles.

Following the terminology of Jeremy Bentham, John Stuart Mill, and other nineteenth-century British utilitarian economist-philosophers, economists apply the term **utility** to this set of numerical values that reflect the relative rankings of various bundles of goods.

Utility Function

The **utility function** is the relationship between utility measures and every possible bundle of goods. If we know the utility function, we can summarize the information in indifference maps succinctly. A utility function $U(x)$ assigns a numerical value to the Bundle x, which might consist of certain numbers of pizzas and burritos. The statement that "Bonnie weakly prefers Bundle x to Bundle y," $x \succsim y$, is equivalent to the statement that "Consuming Bundle x gives Bonnie at least as much utility as consuming Bundle y," $U(x) \geq U(y)$.[6] Bonnie prefers x to y if Bundle x gives Bonnie 10 *utils*—units of utility—and Bundle y gives her 8 utils.

Suppose that the utility, U, that Lisa gets from pizzas and burritos is

$$U = \sqrt{q_1 q_2}.$$

---

[6] A utility function represents a preference relation $\succsim$ only if the preference relation is rational (which we have assumed)—that is, it is complete and transitive. A proof is based on the idea that, because the utility function over real numbers includes any possible bundle and is transitive, the preference relation must also be complete and transitive.

From this function, we know that the more Lisa consumes of either good, the greater her utility. Using this function, we can determine whether she would be happier if she had Bundle x with 16 pizzas and 9 burritos or Bundle y with 13 of each. The utility she gets from x is $U(x) = 12 \left(= \sqrt{16 \times 9}\right)$ utils. The utility she gets from y is $U(y) = 13 \left(= \sqrt{13 \times 13}\right)$ utils. Therefore, she prefers y to x.

The utility function is a concept that economists use to help them think about consumer behavior; utility functions do not exist in any fundamental sense. For example, if you asked your mother, who is trying to decide whether to go to a movie or a play, what her utility function is, she would be puzzled—unless, of course, she is an economist. But if you asked her enough questions about which goods she would choose under various circumstances, you could construct a function that accurately summarizes her preferences. For example, by questioning people about which goods they would choose, Rousseas and Hart (1951) constructed indifference curves for eggs and bacon, and MacCrimmon and Toda (1969) constructed indifference curves between French pastries and money (which can be used to buy all other goods).

Ordinal Preferences

Typically, consumers can easily answer questions about whether they prefer one bundle to another, such as "Do you prefer a bundle with one scoop of ice cream and two pieces of cake to another bundle with two scoops of ice cream and one piece of cake?" But, they have difficulty answering questions about how much more they prefer one bundle to another because they don't have a measure to describe how their pleasure from two goods or bundles differs. Therefore, we may know a consumer's rank ordering of bundles, but we are unlikely to know by how much more that consumer prefers one bundle to another.

If we know only consumers' relative rankings of bundles but not how much more they prefer one bundle to another, our measure of pleasure is an *ordinal* measure rather than a *cardinal* measure. An ordinal measure is one that tells us the relative ranking of two things but does not tell us how much more one rank is valued than another. If a professor assigns only letter grades to an exam, we know that a student who receives a grade of A did better than a student who received a B, but we can't say how much better from that ordinal scale. Nor can we tell whether the difference in performance between an A student and a B student is greater or less than the difference between a B student and a C student.

A cardinal measure is one by which absolute comparisons between ranks may be made. Money is a cardinal measure. If you have $100 and your brother has $50, we know not only that you have more money than your brother but also that you have exactly twice as much money as he does.

In most of the book, we consider only ordinal utility. However, we use cardinal utility in our analysis of uncertainty in Chapter 17, and in a couple of other cases. If we use an ordinal utility measure, we should not put any weight on the absolute differences between the utility number associated with one bundle and that associated with another. We care only about the relative utility or ranking of the two bundles.

Because preference rankings are ordinal and not cardinal, many utility functions can correspond to a particular preference map. Suppose we know that Bill prefers Bundle x to Bundle y. A utility function that assigned 5 to x and 6 to y would be consistent with Bill's preference ranking. However, if we double all the numbers in this utility function, we would obtain a different utility function that assigned 10 to x and 12 to y. Both of these utility functions are consistent with Bill's preference ordering.

In general, given a utility function that is consistent with a consumer's preference ranking, we can transform that utility function into an unlimited number of other utility functions that are consistent with that ordering. Let $U(q_1, q_2)$ be the original utility function that assigns numerical values corresponding to any given combination of q_1 and q_2. Let F be an *increasing function* (in jargon, a *positive monotonic transformation*) such that if $x > y$, then $F(x) > F(y)$. By applying this transformation to the original utility function, we obtain a new function, $V(q_1, q_2) = F(U(q_1, q_2))$, which is a utility function with the same ordinal-ranking properties as $U(q_1, q_2)$. As an example, suppose that the transformation is linear: $F(x) = a + bx$, where $b > 0$. Then, $(q_1, q_2) = a + bU(q_1, q_2)$. The rank ordering is the same for these utility functions because $V(q_1, q_2) = a + bU(q_1, q_2) > V(q_1^*, q_2^*) = a + bU(q_1^*, q_2^*)$ if and only if $U(q_1, q_2) > U(q_1^*, q_2^*)$.

Thus, when we talk about utility numbers, we need to remember that these numbers are not unique and that we assign little meaning to the absolute numbers. We care only whether one bundle's utility value is greater than that of another.

Utility and Indifference Curves

An indifference curve consists of all those bundles that correspond to a particular utility measure. If Lisa's utility function is $U(q_1, q_2)$, then the expression for one of her indifference curves is

$$\overline{U} = U(q_1, q_2). \quad (3.1)$$

This expression determines all those bundles of q_1 and q_2 that give her $\overline{U}$ utils of pleasure. For example, if her utility function is $U = \sqrt{q_1 q_2}$, then the indifference curve $4 = \overline{U} = \sqrt{q_1 q_2}$ includes any (q_1, q_2) bundles such that $q_1 q_2 = 16$, including the bundles (4, 4), (2, 8), (8, 2), (1, 16), and (16, 1).

A three-dimensional diagram, Figure 3.3, shows how Lisa's utility varies with the amounts of pizza, q_1, and burritos, q_2, that she consumes. Panel a shows this relationship from a straight-ahead view, while panel b shows the same relationship looking at it from one side. The figure measures q_1 on one axis on the "floor" of the diagram, q_2 on the other axis on the floor of the diagram, and $U(q_1, q_2)$ on the vertical axis. For example in the figure, Bundle *a* lies on the floor of the diagram and contains 2 pizzas and 2 burritos. Directly above it on the utility surface or *hill of happiness* is a point labeled $U(2, 2)$. The vertical height of this point shows how much utility Lisa gets from consuming Bundle *a*. In the figure, $U(q_1, q_2) = \sqrt{q_1 q_2}$, so this height is $U(2, 2) = \sqrt{2 \times 2} = 2$. Because she prefers more to less, her utility rises as q_1 increases, q_2 increases, or both goods increase. That is, Lisa's hill of happiness rises as she consumes more of either or both goods.

What is the relationship between Lisa's utility function and one of her indifference curves—those combinations of q_1 and q_2 that give Lisa a particular level of utility? Imagine that the hill of happiness is made of clay. If you cut the hill at a particular level of utility, the height corresponding to Bundle *a*, $U(2, 2) = 2$, you get a smaller hill above the cut. The bottom edge of this hill—the edge where you cut—is the curve I^*. Now, suppose that you lower that smaller hill straight down onto the floor and trace the outside edge of this smaller hill. The outer edge of the hill on the two-dimensional floor is indifference curve I. Making other parallel cuts in the hill of happiness, placing the smaller hills on the floor, and tracing their outside edges, you can obtain a map of indifference curves on which each indifference curve reflects a different level of utility.

Figure 3.3 The Relationship between the Utility Function and Indifference Curves

Both panels a and b show Lisa's utility, $U(q_1, q_2)$ as a function of the amount of pizza, q_1, and burritos, q_2, that she consumes. The figure measures q_1 along one axis on the floor of the diagram, and q_2 along the other axis on the floor. Utility is measured on the vertical axis. As q_1, q_2, or both increase, she has more utility: She is on a higher point on the diagram. If we take all the points, the curve I^*, that are at a given height—given level of utility—on the utility surface and project those points down onto the floor of the diagram, we obtain the indifference curve I.

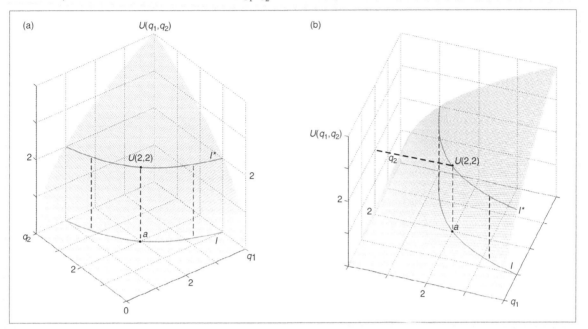

Willingness to Substitute Between Goods

"We don't have poached eggs. How about an elephant tusk?"

How willing a consumer is to trade one good for another depends on the slope of the consumer's indifference curve, dq_2/dq_1, at the consumer's initial bundle of goods. Economists call the slope at a point on an indifference curve the **marginal rate of substitution** (*MRS*), because it is the maximum amount of one good that a consumer will sacrifice (trade) to obtain one more unit of another good.

Lisa's *MRS* at Bundle e in Figure 3.4 is equal to the slope of the dashed line that is tangent to her indifference curve I at e. Because her indifference curve has a downward slope (and hence so does the line tangent to the indifference curve), her *MRS* at e is a negative number. The negative sign tells us that Lisa is willing to give up some pizza for more burritos and vice versa.

Although the *MRS* is defined as the slope at a particular bundle, we can illustrate the idea with a discrete change. If Lisa's *MRS* = -2, then she is indifferent between her current bundle and another bundle in which she gives up one unit of q_1 in exchange for two more units of q_2 (or gives up two units of q_2 for one more unit of q_1). For example, if Lisa's original bundle e has nine pizzas and three burritos, she would be indifferent between that bundle and one in which she had eight (one fewer) pizzas and five (two additional) burritos.

Figure 3.4 Marginal Rate of Substitution

Lisa's marginal rate of substitution, $MRS = dq_2/dq_1$, at her initial bundle e is the slope of indifference curve I at that point. The marginal rate of substitution at e is the same as the slope of the line that is tangent to I at e. This indifference curve illustrates a diminishing marginal rate of substitution: The slope of the indifference curve becomes flatter as we move down and to the right along the curve (from Bundle f to e to g).

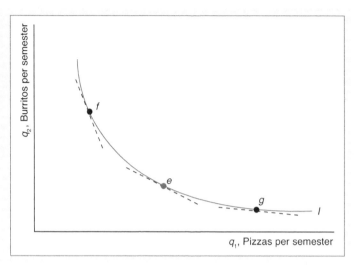

We can use calculus to determine the MRS at a point on Lisa's indifference curve in Equation 3.1. We show that the MRS depends on how much extra utility Lisa gets from a little more of each good. We call the extra utility that a consumer gets from consuming the last unit of a good the **marginal utility**. Given that Lisa's utility function is $U(q_1, q_2)$, the marginal utility she gets from a little more pizza, holding the quantity of burritos fixed, is

$$\text{marginal utility of pizza} = \frac{\partial U}{\partial q_1} = U_1.$$

Similarly, the marginal utility from more burritos is $U_2 = \partial U/\partial q_2$, where we hold the amount of pizza constant.

We determine the slope of Lisa's indifference curve, the MRS, by ascertaining the changes in q_1 and q_2 that leave her utility unchanged, keeping her on her original indifference curve: $\overline{U} = U(q_1, q_2)$. Let $q_2(q_1)$ be the implicit function that shows how much q_2 it takes to keep Lisa's utility at $\overline{U}$ given that she consumes q_1. We want to know how much q_2 must change if we increase q_1, dq_2/dq_1, given that we require her utility to remain constant. To answer this question, we differentiate $\overline{U} = U(q_1, q_2(q_1))$ with respect to q_1:

$$\frac{d\overline{U}}{dq_1} = 0 = \frac{\partial U(q_1, q_2(q_1))}{\partial q_1} + \frac{\partial U(q_1, q_2(q_1))}{\partial q_2}\frac{dq_2}{dq_1} = U_1 + U_2\frac{dq_2}{dq_1}. \quad (3.2)$$

Because $\overline{U}$ is a constant, $d\overline{U}/dq_1 = 0$.

Since Lisa derives pleasure from both goods, if we increase one of the goods, we must decrease the other to hold her utility constant and keep her on the $\overline{U}$ indifference curve. Rearranging the terms in Equation 3.2, we find that her marginal rate of substitution is

$$MRS = \frac{dq_2}{dq_1} = -\frac{\partial U/\partial q_1}{\partial U/\partial q_2} = -\frac{U_1}{U_2}. \quad (3.3)$$

Thus, the slope of her indifference curve is the negative of the ratio of her marginal utilities.

SOLVED PROBLEM 3.2

Suppose that Jackie has what economists call a *Cobb-Douglas utility function*:[7]

$$U = q_1^a q_2^{1-a}, \tag{3.4}$$

where a is a positive constant, q_1 is the number of tracks of recorded music she buys a year, and q_2 is the number of live music events she attends. What is her marginal rate of substitution?

Answer

1. *Determine the marginal utility Jackie gets from extra music tracks and the marginal utility she derives from more live music.* Her marginal utility from extra tracks is

$$U_1 = \frac{\partial U}{\partial q_1} = a q_1^{a-1} q_2^{1-a} = a \frac{U(q_1, q_2)}{q_1},$$

and her marginal utility from extra live music is

$$U_2 = (1-a) q_1^a q_2^{-a} = (1-a) \frac{U(q_1, q_2)}{q_2}.$$

2. *Express her marginal rate of substitution in terms of her marginal utilities.* Using Equation 3.3, we find that her marginal rate of substitution is

$$MRS = \frac{dq_2}{dq_1} = -\frac{U_1}{U_2} = -\frac{aU/q_1}{(1-a)U/q_2} = -\frac{a}{1-a}\frac{q_2}{q_1}. \tag{3.5}$$

APPLICATION

MRS Between Recorded Tracks and Live Music

In 2008, a typical British young person (ages 14 to 24) bought 24 music tracks, q_1, per quarter and consumed 18 units of live music, q_2, per quarter.[8] We estimate this average consumer's Cobb-Douglas utility function as

$$U = q_1^{0.4} q_2^{0.6}. \tag{3.6}$$

That is, in the general Cobb-Douglas utility function Equation 3.4, $a = 0.4$.

Using our analysis in Solved Problem 3.2, given that Jackie's Cobb-Douglas utility function is that of the typical consumer, we can determine her marginal rate of substitution by substituting $q_1 = 24$, $q_2 = 18$, and $a = 0.4$ into Equation 3.5:

$$MRS = -\frac{a}{1-a}\frac{q_2}{q_1} = -\frac{0.4}{0.6}\frac{18}{24} = -0.5.$$

---

[7]This functional form is named after its inventors, Charles W. Cobb, a mathematician, and Paul H. Douglas, an economist and U.S. senator. The Cobb-Douglas utility function can be written more generally as $U = A q_1^c q_2^d$. However, we can always transform that utility function into the simpler one in Equation 3.4 through a positive monotonic transformation: $q_1^a q_2^{1-a} = F(A q_1^c q_2^d)$, where $F(x) = x^{1/(c+d)}/A$, so that $a = c/(c+d)$.

[8]A unit of live music is the amount that can be purchased for £1 (that is, it does not correspond to a full concert or a performance in a pub). Data on total expenditures are from *The Student Experience Report*, 2007, www.unite-students.com, while budget allocations between live and recorded music are from the 2008 survey of the *Music Experience and Behaviour in Young People* produced by the British Music Rights and the University of Hertfordshire.

Curvature of Indifference Curves

Unless the indifference curve is a straight line, the marginal rate of substitution varies along the indifference curve. Because the indifference curve in Figure 3.4 is convex to the origin, as we move down and to the right along the indifference curve, the *MRS* (the slope of the indifference curve) becomes smaller in absolute value: Lisa will give up fewer burritos to obtain one pizza. This willingness to trade fewer burritos for one more pizza as we move down and to the right along the indifference curve reflects a *diminishing marginal rate of substitution*: The *MRS* approaches zero—becomes flatter or less sloped—as we move from Bundle *f* to *e* and then to *g* in the figure.

We can illustrate the diminishing marginal rate of substitution for the Cobb-Douglas utility function $U = \sqrt{q_1 q_2} = q_1^{0.5} q_2^{0.5}$, so $a = 0.5$. We know that this utility function has an $MRS = -q_2/q_1$ by setting $a = 0.5$ in Equation 3.5. On the indifference curve $4 = \overline{U} = \sqrt{q_1 q_2}$, two of the (q_1, q_2) bundles are (2, 8) and (4, 4). The *MRS* is $-8/2 = -4$ at (2, 8) and $-4/4 = -1$ at (4, 4). Thus, at (2, 8), where the consumer has a relatively large amount of q_2 compared to q_1, the consumer is willing to give up four units of q_2 to get one more unit of q_1. However at (4, 4), where the consumer has relatively less q_2, the consumer is only willing to trade a unit of q_2 for a unit of q_1.

So far, we have drawn indifference curves as convex to the origin. An indifference curve for two goods doesn't have to be convex, but casual observation suggests that most people's indifference curves are convex. When people have a lot of one good, they are willing to give up a relatively large amount of it to get a good of which they have relatively little. However, after that first trade, people are willing to give up less of the first good to get the same amount more of the second good.

It is hard to imagine that Lisa's indifference curves are *concave* to the origin. If her indifference curve were strictly concave, Lisa would be willing to give up more burritos to get one more pizza, the fewer the burritos she has. Two extreme versions of downward-sloping, convex indifference curves are plausible: straight-line or right-angle indifference curves.

Straight Line. One extreme case of an indifference curve is a straight line, which occurs when two goods are **perfect substitutes**: goods that a consumer is completely indifferent as to which to consume. Because Ben cannot taste any difference between Coca-Cola and Pepsi-Cola, he views them as perfect substitutes: He is indifferent between having one additional can of Coke and one additional can of Pepsi. His indifference curves for these two goods are straight, parallel lines with a slope of -1 everywhere along the curve, as in panel a of Figure 3.5. Thus, Ben's *MRS* is -1 at every point along these indifference curves. (His marginal utility from each good is identical, so the $MRS = -U_1/U_2 = -1$.)

The slope of indifference curves of perfect substitutes need not always be -1; it can be any constant rate. For example, Amos knows from reading the labels that Clorox bleach is twice as strong as a generic brand. As a result, Amos is indifferent between one cup of Clorox and two cups of the generic bleach. Amos' utility function over Clorox, *C*, and the generic bleach, *G*, is

$$U(C, G) = iC + jG, \tag{3.7}$$

3.2 Utility

Figure 3.5 Perfect Substitutes, Perfect Complements, Imperfect Substitutes

(a) Ben views Coke and Pepsi as perfect substitutes. His indifference curves are straight, parallel lines with a marginal rate of substitution (slope) of −1. Ben is willing to exchange one can of Coke for one can of Pepsi. (b) Maureen likes pie à la mode but does not like pie or ice cream by itself: She views ice cream and pie as perfect complements. She will not substitute between the two; she consumes them only in equal quantities. (c) Lisa views burritos and pizza as imperfect substitutes. Her indifference curve lies between the extreme cases of perfect substitutes and perfect complements.

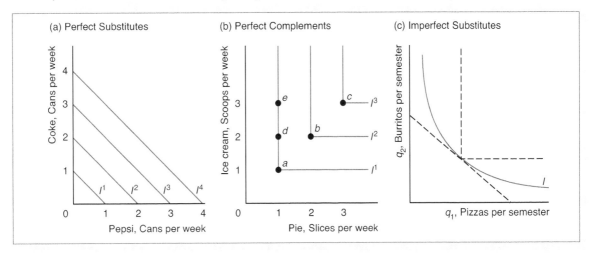

where both goods are measured in cups, $i = 2$, and $j = 1$. His indifference curves are straight lines with a slope or *MRS* of $-i/j = -2$, when the generic bleach is on the vertical axis.[9]

Right Angle. The other extreme case of an indifference curve occurs when two goods are **perfect complements**: goods that a consumer is interested in consuming only in fixed proportions. Maureen doesn't like apple pie, A, by itself or vanilla ice cream, V, by itself but loves apple pie à la mode: a slice of pie with a scoop of vanilla ice cream on top. Her utility function is

$$U(A, V) = \min(iA, jV), \quad (3.8)$$

where $i = j = 1$ and the min function says that the utility equals the smaller of the two arguments, iA or jV. Her indifference curves have right angles in panel b of Figure 3.5. If she has only one piece of pie, she gets as much pleasure from it and one scoop of ice cream, Bundle a, as from one piece and two scoops, Bundle d, or one piece and three scoops, Bundle e. The marginal utility is zero for each good, because increasing that good while holding the other one constant does not increase Maureen's utility. If she were at b, she would be unwilling to give up an extra slice of pie to get, say, two extra scoops of ice cream, as at point e. She wouldn't eat the extra scoops because she would not have pieces of pie to go with the ice cream. The only condition in which she doesn't have an excess of either good is when $iA = jV$,

---

[9]Sometimes it is difficult to guess which goods are close substitutes for other people. For example, according to *Harper's Index*, 1994, flowers, perfume, and fire extinguishers rank 1, 2, and 3 among Mother's Day gifts that Americans consider "very appropriate."

or $V/A = i/j = 1$. Because she is unwilling to substitute more of one good for less of another, she only consumes bundles like a, b, and c, where pie and ice cream are in equal proportions.

Convex Curve. The standard-shaped, convex indifference curve in panel c of Figure 3.5 lies between these two extreme examples. Convex indifference curves show that a consumer views two goods as imperfect substitutes. A consumer with a Cobb-Douglas utility function, Equation 3.4, has convex indifference curves similar to the one in panel c. That curve approaches the axes but does not hit them. One special case in which a convex indifference curve hits an axis is the *quasilinear utility function*,

$$U(q_1, q_2) = u(q_1) + q_2, \quad (3.9)$$

where $u(q_1)$ is an increasing function of q_1, $du(q_1)/dq_1 > 0$, and $d^2u(q_1)/dq_1^2 \leq 0$. We have already looked at one extreme example, the perfect substitutes utility function, $U(q_1, q_2) = q_1 + q_2$, where $u(q_1) = q_1$. Another example is $u(q_1) = \sqrt{q_1}$, which has the properties that $du(q_1)/dq_1 = 0.5 q_1^{-0.5} > 0$, and $d^2u(q_1)/dq_1^2 = -0.25 q_1^{-0.5} < 0$. This utility function is called *quasilinear* because it is linear in one argument, q_2, but not necessarily in the other, q_1.

Figure 3.6 shows three indifference curves for the quasilinear utility function $U(q_1, q_2) = \sqrt{q_1} + q_2$. Along an indifference curve in which utility is held constant at $\overline{U}$, the indifference curve is $\overline{U} = \sqrt{q_1} + q_2$. Thus, this indifference curve hits the q_2-axis at $q_2 = \overline{U}$ because $q_1 = \sqrt{q_1} = 0$ at the q_2-axis.

SOLVED PROBLEM 3.3

A consumer has a quasilinear utility function, Equation 3.9, $U = u(q_1) + q_2$, where $du(q_1)/dq_1 > 0$ and $d^2u(q_1)/dq_1^2 < 0$. Show that the consumer's indifference curves are parallel and convex.

Answer

1. *Use the formula for an indifference curve to show that the slope at any q_1 is the same for all indifference curves, and thus the indifference curves must be parallel.* At every point on an indifference curve, $\overline{U} = u(q_1) + q_2$. By rearranging this indifference curve equation, we find that the height of this indifference curve at q_1 is $q_2 = \overline{U} - u(q_1)$. By differentiating this expression with respect to q_1, we show that the slope of this indifference curve is $dq_2/dq_1 = d[\overline{U} - u(q_1)]/dq_1 = -du(q_1)/dq_1$. Because this expression is not a function of q_2, the slope for a given q_1 is independent of q_2 (the height of the indifference curve). Thus, the slope at q_1 must be the same on each indifference curve, as Figure 3.6 illustrates. Because the indifference curves have the same slopes for each given q_1 and differ only in where they hit the q_2-axis, the indifference curves are parallel.

2. *Show that the indifference curves are convex by demonstrating that the derivative of the slope of the indifference curve with respect to q_1 is positive.* We just derived that the slope of the indifference curve is $dq_2/dq_1 = -du(q_1)/dq_1$. If we differentiate it again with respect to q_1, we find that the change in the slope of the indifference curve as q_1 increases is $d^2q_2/dq_1^2 = -d^2u(q_1)/dq_1^2$. Because $d^2u(q_1)/dq_1^2 < 0$, we know that $d^2q_2/dq_1^2 \geq 0$. The negative slope of these indifference curves becomes flatter as q_1 increases, which show that an indifference curve is convex: It bends away from the origin. That is, the indifference curve has a diminishing marginal rate of substitution.

Figure 3.6 Quasilinear Preferences

The indifference curves corresponding to the quasilinear utility function $U(q_1, q_2) = \sqrt{q_1} + q_2$ are parallel. Each indifference curve has the same slope at a given q_1.

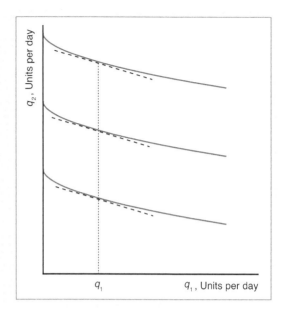

APPLICATION

Indifference Curves Between Food and Clothing

Using the estimates of Eastwood and Craven (1981), the figure shows the indifference curves of the average U.S. consumer between food consumed at home and clothing. The food and clothing measures are weighted averages of various goods. At relatively low quantities of food and clothing, the indifference curves, such as I^1, are nearly right angles: perfect complements. As we move away from the origin, the indifference curves become flatter: closer to perfect substitutes.

One interpretation of these indifference curves is that there are minimum levels of food and clothing necessary to support life. The consumer cannot trade one good for the other if it means having less than the critical level. As the consumer obtains more of both goods, however, the consumer is increasingly willing to trade between the two goods. According to Eastwood and Craven's estimates, food and clothing are perfect complements when the consumer has little of either good, and perfect substitutes when the consumer has large quantities of both goods.

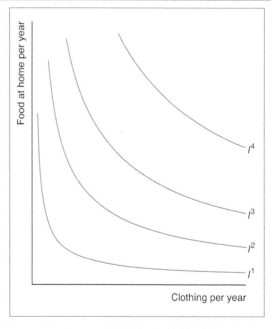

3.3 Budget Constraint

You can't have everything.... Where would you put it? —Steven Wright

Knowing an individual's preferences is only the first step in analyzing that person's consumption behavior. Consumers maximize their well-being subject to constraints. The most important constraint most of us face in deciding what to consume is our personal budget constraint.

If we cannot save and borrow, our budget is the income we receive in a given period. If we can save and borrow, we can save money early in life to consume later, such as when we retire; or we can borrow money when we are young and repay those sums later in life. Savings is, in effect, a good that consumers can buy. For simplicity, we assume that each consumer has a fixed amount of money to spend now, so we can use the terms *budget* and *income* interchangeably.

For graphical simplicity, we assume that consumers spend their money on only two goods. If Lisa spends all her budget, Y, on pizza and burritos, then

$$p_1 q_1 + p_2 q_2 = Y, \tag{3.10}$$

where $p_1 q_1$ is the amount she spends on pizza and $p_2 q_2$ is the amount she spends on burritos. Equation 3.10 is her **budget line**, or *budget constraint*: the bundles of goods that can be bought if a consumer's entire budget is spent on those goods at given prices. In Figure 3.7, we plot Lisa's budget line in pizza-burrito space, just as we did with her indifference curves. How many burritos can Lisa buy? Using algebra, we can rewrite her budget constraint, Equation 3.10, as

$$q_2 = \frac{Y - p_1 q_1}{p_2}. \tag{3.11}$$

According to Equation 3.11, she can buy more burritos with a higher income ($dq_2/dY = 1/p_2 > 0$), the purchase of fewer pizzas ($dq_2/dq_1 = -p_1/p_2 < 0$), or a lower price of burritos or pizzas [$dq_2/dp_2 = -(Y - p_1 q_1)/p_2^2 = -q_2/p_2 < 0$, $dq_2/dp_1 = -q_1/p_2 < 0$]. For example, if she has one more dollar of income (Y), she can buy $1/p_2$ more burritos.

If $p_1 = \$1$, $p_2 = \$2$, and $Y = \$50$, Equation 3.11 is

$$q_2 = \frac{\$50 - (\$1 \times q_1)}{\$2} = 25 - \frac{1}{2} q_1.$$

Figure 3.7 Budget Constraint

If $Y = \$50$, $p_1 = \$1$, and $p_2 = \$2$, Lisa can buy any bundle in the opportunity set—the shaded area—including points on the *budget line*, L, which has a slope of $-\frac{1}{2}$.

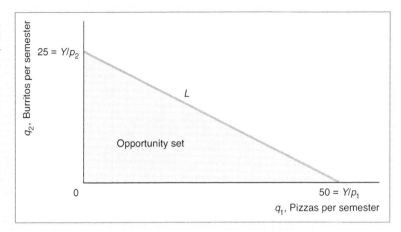

This equation is plotted in Figure 3.7. The budget line in the figure shows the combinations of burritos and pizzas that Lisa can buy if she spends all of her $50 on these two goods. As this equation shows, every two pizzas cost Lisa one burrito. How many burritos can she buy if she spends all her money on burritos? By setting $q_1 = 0$ in Equation 3.11, we find that $q_2 = Y/p_2 = \$50/\$2 = 25$. Similarly, if she spends all her money on pizzas, $q_2 = 0$ and $q_1 = Y/p_1 = \$50/\$1 = 50$.

The budget constraint in Figure 3.7 is a smooth, continuous line. The continuous line shows that Lisa can buy fractional numbers of burritos and pizzas. Is that true? Do you know of a restaurant that will sell you a quarter of a burrito? Probably not. Why, then, don't we draw the opportunity set and the budget constraint as points (bundles) of whole numbers of burritos and pizzas? The reason is that Lisa can buy a burrito at a *rate* of one-half per time period. If Lisa buys one burrito every other week, she buys an average of one-half burrito every week. Thus, it is plausible that she could purchase fractional amounts over time, and this diagram concerns her behavior over a semester.

Lisa could, of course, buy any bundle that costs less than $50. An **opportunity set** consists of all the bundles a consumer can buy, including all the bundles inside the budget constraint and on the budget constraint (all those bundles of positive q_1 and q_2 such that $p_1 q_1 + p_2 q_2 \leq Y$). Lisa's opportunity set is the shaded area in the figure. For example, she could buy 10 burritos and 15 pizzas for $35, which falls inside her budget constraint. However, she can obtain more of the two foods by spending all of her budget and picking a bundle on the budget line rather than a bundle below the line.

We call the slope of the budget line the **marginal rate of transformation** (*MRT*): the trade-off the market imposes on the consumer in terms of the amount of one good the consumer must give up to obtain more of the other good. The marginal rate of *transformation* is the rate at which Lisa is able to trade burritos for pizzas in the marketplace when the prices she pays and her income are fixed. In contrast, the marginal rate of *substitution* is the trade-off Lisa would *want* to make regardless of her income.

Holding prices and income constant and differentiating Equation 3.11 with respect to q_1, we find that the slope of the budget constraint, or the marginal rate of transformation, is

$$MRT = \frac{dq_2}{dq_1} = -\frac{p_1}{p_2}. \quad (3.12)$$

Because the price of a pizza is half that of a burrito ($p_1 = \$1$ and $p_2 = \$2$), the marginal rate of transformation that Lisa faces is

$$MRT = -\frac{p_1}{p_2} = -\frac{\$1}{\$2} = -\frac{1}{2}.$$

An extra pizza costs her half an extra burrito—or, equivalently, an extra burrito costs her two pizzas.

3.4 Constrained Consumer Choice

My problem lies in reconciling my gross habits with my net income. —Errol Flynn

Were it not for budget constraints, consumers who prefer more to less would consume unlimited amounts of at least some goods. Well, they can't have it all! Instead, consumers maximize their well-being subject to their budget constraints. To complete our analysis of consumer behavior, we have to determine the bundle of goods that maximizes an individual's well-being subject to the person's budget constraint. First, we take a graphical approach, and then we use calculus.

The Consumer's Optimal Bundle

Veni, vidi, Visa. (We came, we saw, we went shopping.) —Jan Barrett

We want to determine which bundle within the opportunity set gives the consumer the highest level of utility. That is, we are trying to solve a constrained maximization problem, where a consumer maximizes utility subject to a budget constraint.

First, we show that Lisa's optimal bundle must be on the budget line in Figure 3.8. Bundles that lie on indifference curves above the constraint, such as those on I^3, are not in her opportunity set (area $A + B$). Although Lisa prefers Bundle f on indifference curve I^3 to Bundle e on I^2, she cannot afford to purchase f. Even though Lisa could buy a bundle inside the budget line, she does not want to do so, because more is better than less: For any bundle inside the constraint (such as d on I^1), there is another bundle on the constraint with more of at least one of the two goods, and hence she prefers that bundle. Therefore, the optimal bundle must lie on the budget line.

We can also show that bundles that lie on indifference curves that cross the budget line—such as I^1, which crosses the constraint at a and c—are less desirable than certain other bundles on the constraint. Only some of the bundles on indifference curve I^1 lie within the opportunity set: Lisa can afford to purchase Bundles a and c and all the points on I^1 between them, such as d. Because I^1 crosses the budget line, the bundles between a and c on I^1 lie strictly inside the constraint, so there are affordable bundles in area B that are preferable to these bundles—that contain more of one or both good. In particular, Lisa prefers Bundle e to d because e has more of both pizza and burritos than d. Because of transitivity, e is preferred to a, c, and all the other bundles on I^1—even those, like g, that Lisa can't afford. Thus, the optimal

Figure 3.8 Interior Solution

Lisa's optimal bundle is e (10 burritos and 30 pizzas) on indifference curve I^2. Indifference curve I^2 is tangent to her budget line at e. Bundle e is the bundle on the highest indifference curve (highest utility) that she can afford. Any bundle that is preferred to e (such as points on indifference curve I^3) lies outside of her opportunity set, so she cannot afford them. Bundles inside the opportunity set, such as d, are less desirable than e because they represent less of one or both goods.

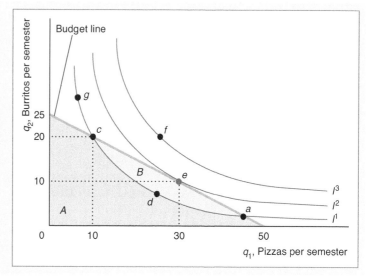

bundle—the *consumer's optimum*—must lie on the budget line and be on an indifference curve that does not cross it. If Lisa is consuming this bundle, she has no incentive to change her behavior by substituting one good for another.

There are two ways for an optimal bundle to lie on an indifference curve that touches the budget line but does not cross it. The first is an *interior solution*, in which the optimal bundle has positive quantities of both goods and lies between the ends of the budget line. The other possibility, called a *corner solution*, occurs when the optimal bundle is at one end of the budget line, where the budget line forms a corner with one of the axes.

Interior Solution. In Figure 3.8, Bundle e on indifference curve I^2 is the optimum bundle. It lies in the interior of the budget line away from the corners. Lisa prefers consuming a balanced diet, e, of 10 burritos and 30 pizzas, to eating only one type of food.

For the indifference curve I^2 to touch the budget constraint but not cross it, it must be *tangent* to the budget constraint: The budget constraint and the indifference curve have the same slope at the point e where they touch. The slope of the indifference curve is the marginal rate of substitution. It measures the rate at which Lisa is *willing* to trade burritos for pizzas: $MRS = -U_1/U_2$ (Equation 3.3). The slope of the budget line is the marginal rate of transformation. It measures the rate at which Lisa *can* trade her money for burritos or pizza in the market: $MRT = -p_1/p_2$ (Equation 3.12). Thus, Lisa's utility is maximized at the bundle where the rate at which she is willing to trade burritos for pizzas equals the rate at which she can trade in the market:

$$MRS = -\frac{U_1}{U_2} = -\frac{p_1}{p_2} = MRT. \qquad (3.13)$$

Multiplying both sides of Equation 3.13 by $-U_2/p_1$, we obtain

$$\frac{U_1}{p_1} = \frac{U_2}{p_2}. \qquad (3.14)$$

Equation 3.14 says that U_1/p_1, the marginal utility of pizzas divided by the price of a pizza—the amount of extra utility from pizza per dollar spent on pizza—equals U_2/p_2, the marginal utility of burritos divided by the price of a burrito. Thus, Lisa's utility is maximized if the last dollar she spends on pizzas gets her as much extra utility as the last dollar she spends on burritos. If the last dollar spent on pizzas gave Lisa more extra utility than the last dollar spent on burritos, Lisa could increase her happiness by spending more on pizzas and less on burritos. Her cousin Spenser is a different story.

Corner Solution. Spenser's indifference curves in Figure 3.9 are flatter than Lisa's in Figure 3.8. His optimal bundle is Bundle e, which lies on the indifference curve I^2 and touches the budget line at the upper-left corner of his opportunity set. Bundle e consists of 25 burritos and 0 pizzas. It is his optimal bundle because the indifference curve does not cross the constraint into the opportunity set. If it did, another bundle would give Spenser more pleasure.

However, Spenser's indifference curve I^2 is not tangent to his budget line. If I^2 were tangent to the budget line, it would not cross it. However, I^2 would cross the budget line if both the indifference curve and the budget line were continued into the "negative pizza" region of the diagram on the other side of the vertical, burrito axis.

Figure 3.9 Corner Solution

Spenser's indifference curves are flatter than Lisa's indifference curves in Figure 3.6. That is, he is willing to give up more pizzas for one more burrito than is Lisa. Spenser's optimal bundle occurs at a corner of the opportunity set at Bundle e: 25 burritos and 0 pizzas.

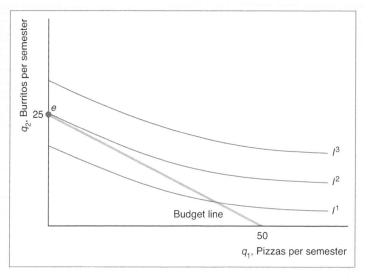

In Spenser's view, the relative price of pizza is too high, so he buys only burritos (a corner solution). At e, the extra utility from the last dollar spent on burritos, U_2/p_2, exceeds the extra utility from the last dollar spent on pizza, U_1/p_1. However, if the relative price of pizza had been lower so that the budget line was flatter, he would have bought some of both goods (an interior solution), as you are asked to show in Question 12 at the end of the chapter.

APPLICATION

Buying an SUV in the United States Versus Europe

During the 1990s and the early part of the twenty-first century, Americans had a love affair with SUVs, and Europeans saw no reason to drive a vehicle nearly the size of Luxembourg. SUVs are derided as "Chelsea tractors" in England and "Montessori wagons" in Sweden. News stories point to this difference in tastes to explain why SUVs account for less than a twentieth of total car sales in Western Europe but, until recently, a quarter of sales in the United States. The narrower European streets and Europeans' greater concern for the environment may be part of the explanation. However, differences in relative prices are probably a more important reason. Due to higher taxes in Europe, the price of owning and operating an SUV is much less in the United States than in Europe, so people with identical tastes are more likely to buy an SUV in the United States than in Europe.

Gas-guzzling SUVs are more expensive to operate in Europe than in the United States because gasoline taxes are much higher in Europe than in the United States. The average tax was 44¢ per gallon in the United States in 2008, compared to an average of $6.09 in Europe. As a consequence of higher taxes, in 2009, consumers in other countries paid substantially more for gasoline than did U.S. consumers: Germany 2.7 times more, France 2.6 times, the United Kingdom 2.4 times, Japan 1.8 times, and Canada 1.3 times more.

Many European nations subsidize efficient cars and tax polluting vehicles. In the Netherlands, a subsidy of up to €6,000 is available to purchasers of a new hybrid. France and Great Britain use a "Green Tax" system that divides cars into five categories based on the amount of carbon dioxide they produce. Consumers buying an ultra-small, efficient vehicle receive a rebate of up to €1,000 Euros (about $1,400). However, if they opt for a gas-guzzling Toyota Land Cruiser or other SUV, they're hit with a tax as high as €2,600. The annual tax on cars also is weighted by a vehicle's size and the amount of pollution it produces.

Moreover, the mayors of Paris and London have threatened to ban SUVs from their cities. London's mayor slammed SUV drivers as "complete idiots" and, in 2008, increased the daily congestion fee for the privilege of driving an SUV around the city center to £25 per day, while more fuel-efficient cars such as the Toyota Prius travel free.

In contrast, the U.S. government subsidizes SUV purchases. Under the 2003 Tax Act, people who used a vehicle that weighs more than 6,000 pounds—such as the biggest, baddest SUVs and Hummers—for their business at least 50% of the time could deduct the purchase price up to $100,000 from their taxes. They could get a state tax deduction, too. This provision of the 2003 Tax Act was intended to help self-employed ranchers, farmers, and contractors purchase a heavy pickup truck or van necessary for their businesses, but the tax loophole was quickly exploited by urban cowboys who wanted to drive massive vehicles.

When this bizarre boondoggle was reduced from $100K to $25K in October 2004, and as the price of gas rose, sales plummeted for many brands of SUVs and behemoths such as Hummers. Sales of SUVs fell significantly in 2005 and 2006 (but picked up slightly in 2007 before tanking in 2008 when gas prices shot up and the recession struck). In 2010, General Motors announced a going-out-of-business sale of Hummers. The *Boston Globe* concluded that this drop in relative SUV sales proved that U.S. consumers' "tastes are changing again." A more plausible, alternative explanation is that the drop was due to increases in the relative costs of owning and operating SUVs.[10]

SOLVED PROBLEM 3.4

Nigel, a Brit, and Bob, a Yank, run their own firms and each wants a vehicle that makes a "statement" when he arrives at a client's location. They have the same tastes, and both are indifferent between a sports utility vehicle (SUV) and a luxury sedan. Each has a budget that allows him to buy and operate one vehicle for a decade. For Nigel, the price of owning and operating an SUV is greater than for the car because of high gas prices due to high gas taxes in Britain. For Bob, an SUV is a bargain relative to the sedan because gas prices are much lower in the United States due to lower taxes and because Bob receives a tax break if he buys an SUV. Use an indifference curve–budget line analysis to explain why Nigel buys and operates a car while Bob chooses an SUV.

Answer

1. *Describe their indifference curves.* Because Nigel and Bob view the SUV and the car as perfect substitutes, each has an indifference curve for buying one

---

[10]See "Substitution Effects in Canada" in the supplemental material to Chapter 3 in **MyEconLab**'s textbook resources, which provides a similar example concerning purchases in the United States or in Canada.

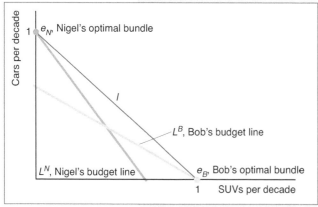

vehicle that is a straight line with a slope of -1 and that hits each axis at 1 in the figure. [*Note:* Even though each driver will own only one car at a time, a bundle such as $(0.5, 0.5)$ would correspond to owning an SUV for half of the decade and a sedan for the other half.]

2. *Describe the slopes of their budget line:* Nigel faces a budget line, L^N, that is steeper than the indifference curve because sedans are relatively less expensive than SUVs in Britain, and Bob faces one, L^B, that is flatter because SUVs are relatively less expensive than sedans in the United States.

3. *Use an indifference curve and a budget line to show why Nigel and Bob make different choices.* As the figure shows, L^N hits the indifference curve, I, at 1 on the car axis, e_N, and L^B hits I at 1 on the SUV axis, e_N. Thus, Nigel buys the relatively inexpensive car, and Bob grabs a relatively cheap SUV.

Comment: If Nigel and Bob were buying a bundle of cars and SUVs for their firms, the analysis would be similar—Bob would buy relatively more SUVs than would Nigel.

Optimal Bundles on Convex Sections of Indifference Curves. Earlier, we argued on the basis of introspection (and consistent with our assumption of strict convexity of preferences) that most indifference curves are convex to the origin. Now that we know how to determine a consumer's optimal bundle, we can give a more compelling explanation about why we assume that indifference curves are convex. We can show that if indifference curves are smooth, optimal bundles lie either on convex sections of indifference curves or at the point where the budget constraint hits an axis.

Suppose that indifference curves were strictly concave to the origin as in panel a of Figure 3.10. Indifference curve I^1 is tangent to the budget line at d, but Bundle d is not optimal. Bundle e on the corner between the budget constraint and the burrito axis is on a higher indifference curve, I^2, than d. Thus, if a consumer had strictly concave indifference curves, the consumer would buy only one good—here, burritos. Similarly, as we saw in Solved Problem 3.4, consumers with straight-line indifference curves buy only the cheapest good. Thus, if consumers are to buy more than a single good, indifference curves must have convex sections.

If indifference curves have both concave and convex sections as in panel b of Figure 3.10, the optimal bundle lies in a convex section or at a corner. Bundle d, where a concave section of indifference curve I^1 is tangent to the budget line, cannot be an optimal bundle. Here, e is the optimal bundle. It is tangent to the budget constraint in the convex portion of the higher indifference curve, I^2. If a consumer buys positive quantities of two goods, the indifference curve is convex and tangent to the budget line at the optimal bundle.

Buying Where More Is Better. A key assumption in our analysis of consumer behavior is that more is preferred to less: Consumers are not satiated. We now show that if both goods are consumed in positive quantities and their prices are positive, more of either good must be preferred to less. Suppose that the opposite were true, and that Lisa prefers fewer burritos to more. Because burritos cost her money, she

Figure 3.10 Optimal Bundles on Convex Sections of Indifference Curves

(a) If indifference curves are strictly concave to the origin, the optimal bundle is at a corner (on one of the axes, where the consumer buys only one good). Indifference curve I^1 is tangent to the budget line at Bundle d, but Bundle e is superior because it lies on a higher indifference curve, I^2. (b) If indifference curves have both concave and convex sections, a bundle such as d, which is tangent to the budget line in the concave portion of indifference curve I^1, cannot be an optimal bundle because there must be a preferable bundle, here Bundle e, in the convex portion of a higher indifference curve I^2 (or at a corner).

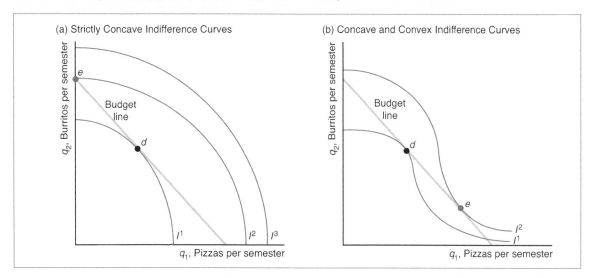

could increase her well-being by reducing the quantity of burritos she consumes until she consumes no burritos—a scenario that violates our assumption that she consumes positive quantities of both goods.[11] Although it is possible that consumers prefer less to more at some large quantities, we do not observe consumers making purchases where that occurs.

In summary, we do not observe consumers optimizing their well-being at bundles where indifference curves are concave or that consumers are satiated. Thus, we can safely assume that indifference curves are convex and that consumers prefer more to less in the ranges of goods that we actually observe.

Maximizing Utility Subject to a Constraint Using Calculus

The individual choice of garnishment of a burger can be an important point to the consumer in this day when individualism is an increasingly important thing to people. —Donald N. Smith, president of Burger King

We have just shown how to use a graphical approach to determine which affordable bundle gives a consumer the highest possible level of utility. We now express this choice problem mathematically, and use calculus to find the optimal bundle.

---
[11]Similarly, at her optimal bundle, Lisa cannot be *satiated*—indifferent between consuming more or fewer burritos. Suppose that her budget is obtained by working and that Lisa does not like working at the margin. Were it not for the goods she can buy with what she earns, she would not work as many hours as she does. Thus, if she were satiated and did not care if she consumed fewer burritos, she would reduce the number of hours she worked, thereby lowering her income, until her optimal bundle occurred at a point where more was preferred to less or where she consumed none.

Lisa's objective is to maximize her utility, $U(q_1, q_2)$, subject to (s.t.) her budget constraint:

$$\max_{q_1, q_2} U(q_1, q_2)$$
$$\text{s.t. } Y = p_1 q_1 + p_2 q_2 \qquad (3.15)$$

In this mathematical statement of her problem, 3.15, her *control variables*—those variables that she chooses—q_1 and q_2, appear under the "max" term in the equation. We assume that Lisa has no control over the prices she faces, p_1 and p_2, or her income, Y. This mathematical formulation of the problem asks what bundle or choice of q_1 and q_2 maximizes $U(q_1, q_2)$ given that this bundle lies on the budget constraint—that is, the cost of the bundle equals Y.

Because this problem is a constrained maximization (contains the "subject to" provision), we cannot use the standard unconstrained maximization approach. However, we can transform this problem into an unconstrained problem that we know how to solve. If we know that Lisa buys both goods, which means we are looking for an interior solution, there are at least two approaches we can use: substitution and the Lagrangian method.

Substitution. First, we can substitute the budget constraint into the utility function. Using algebra, we can rewrite the budget constraint as $q_1 = (Y - p_2 q_2)/p_1$. If we substitute this expression for q_1 in the utility function, $U(q_1, q_2)$, we can rewrite Lisa's problem as

$$\max_{q_2} U\left(\frac{Y - p_2 q_2}{p_1}, q_2\right). \qquad (3.16)$$

Problem 3.16 is an unconstrained problem, so we can use standard maximization techniques to solve it. The first-order condition is obtained by setting the derivative of the utility function with respect to the only remaining control variable q_2 equal to zero:

$$\frac{dU}{dq_2} = \frac{\partial U}{\partial q_1}\frac{dq_1}{dq_2} + \frac{\partial U}{\partial q_2} = \left(-\frac{p_2}{p_1}\right)\frac{\partial U}{\partial q_1} + \frac{\partial U}{\partial q_2} = \left(-\frac{p_2}{p_1}\right)U_1 + U_2 = 0, \qquad (3.17)$$

where $\partial U/\partial q_1 = U_1$ is the partial derivative of the utility function with respect to q_1 (the first argument) and dq_1/dq_2 is the derivative of $q_1 = (Y - p_2 q_2)/p_1$ with respect to q_2.

By rearranging these terms in Equation 3.17, we get the same condition for an optimum that we obtained using a graphical approach, Equation 3.13, which is that the marginal rate of substitution equals the marginal rate of transformation:[12]

$$MRS = -\frac{U_1}{U_2} = -\frac{p_1}{p_2} = MRT.$$

To be sure that we have a maximum, we need to check that the second-order conditions hold (see the Calculus Appendix). These conditions hold if the utility function is quasi-concave, which implies that the indifference curves are convex to the origin: The *MRS* is diminishing as we move down and to the right along the curve. If we combine the *MRS* = *MRT* (first-order) condition with the budget constraint, we have two equations in two unknowns, q_1 and q_2, so we can solve for the optimal q_1 and q_2 as functions of prices, p_1 and p_2, and income, Y.

---

[12]Had we substituted for q_2 instead of for q_1 (which you should do to make sure that you understand how to solve this type of problem), we would have obtained the same condition.

SOLVED PROBLEM 3.5

Michael has a constant-elasticity-of-substitution (CES) utility function, $U(q_1, q_2) = (q_1^\rho + q_2^\rho)^{\frac{1}{\rho}}$, where $0 \neq \rho \leq 1$.[13] What are his optimal values of q_1 and q_2 in terms of his income and the prices of the two goods?

Answer

1. *Substitute the income constraint into Michael's utility function to eliminate one control variable.* Michael's constrained utility maximization problem is

$$\max_{q_1, q_2} U(q_1, q_2) = (q_1^\rho + q_2^\rho)^{\frac{1}{\rho}}$$
$$\text{s.t.} \quad Y = p_1 q_1 + p_2 q_2.$$

We can rewrite Michael's budget constraint as $q_2 = (Y - p_1 q_1)/p_2$. Substituting this expression into his utility function, we can express Michael's utility maximization problem as:

$$\max_{q_1} U\left(q_1, \frac{Y - p_1 q_1}{p_2}\right) = \left(q_1^\rho + \left[\frac{Y - p_1 q_1}{p_2}\right]^\rho\right)^{1/\rho}.$$

By making this substitution, we have converted a constrained maximization problem with two control variables into an unconstrained problem with one control variable, q_1.

2. *Use the standard, unconstrained maximization approach to determine the optimal value for q_1.* Using the chain rule, we set the derivative of the utility function with respect to q_1 equal to zero (the first-order-condition):

$$\frac{1}{\rho}\left(q_1^\rho + \left[\frac{Y - p_1 q_1}{p_2}\right]^\rho\right)^{\frac{1-\rho}{\rho}} \left(\rho q_1^{\rho-1} + \rho \left[\frac{Y - p_1 q_1}{p_2}\right]^{\rho-1}\left[-\frac{p_1}{p_2}\right]\right) = 0.$$

Using algebra, we can solve this equation for Michael's optimal q_1 as a function of his income and the prices:[14]

$$q_1 = \frac{Y p_1^{z-1}}{p_1^z + p_2^z}, \quad (3.18)$$

---

[13] In Chapter 6, we discuss why this functional form has this name and that the Cobb-Douglas, perfect substitute, and perfect complement functional forms are special cases of the CES.

[14] The term at the beginning of the first-order-condition,

$$\frac{1}{\rho}\left(q_1^\rho + \left[\frac{Y - p_1 q_1}{p_2}\right]^\rho\right)^{\frac{1-\rho}{\rho}},$$

is strictly positive because Michael buys a nonnegative amount of both goods, $q_1 \geq 0$ and $q_2 = [Y - p_1 q_1]/p_2 \geq 0$, and a positive amount of at least one of them. Thus, we can divide both sides of the equation by this term, and are left with $\rho q_1^{\rho-1} + \rho \left[\frac{Y - p_1 q_1}{p_2}\right]^{\rho-1}\left[-\frac{p_1}{p_2}\right] = 0$. Next, we divide both sides of this equation by ρ, move the second term to the right-hand-side of the equation, and divide both sides by $\left[\frac{Y - p_1 q_1}{p_2}\right]^{\rho-1}$ to get $\left(\frac{p_2 q_1}{Y - p_1 q_1}\right)^{\rho-1} = \frac{p_1}{p_2}$. By exponentiating both sides by $1/[\rho - 1]$ and rearranging terms, we obtain Equation 3.18.

where $z = \rho/[\rho - 1]$. By repeating this analysis, substituting for q_1 instead of for q_2, we derive a similar expression for his optimal q_2:

$$q_2 = \frac{Y p_2^{z-1}}{p_1^z + p_2^z}. \qquad (3.19)$$

Lagrangian Method. A second approach to solving this constrained maximization problem is to use the Lagrangian method. We can write the equivalent Lagrangian problem as

$$\max_{q_1, q_2, \lambda} \mathscr{L} = U(q_1, q_2) + \lambda(Y - p_1 q_1 - p_2 q_2), \qquad (3.20)$$

where λ (the Greek letter lambda) is the Lagrange multiplier. For values of q_1 and q_2 such that the constraint holds, $Y - p_1 q_1 - p_2 q_2 = 0$, so the functions $\mathscr{L}$ and U have the same values. Thus, if we look only at values of q_1 and q_2 for which the constraint holds, finding the constrained maximum value of U is the same as finding the critical value of $\mathscr{L}$.

The conditions for a critical value of q_1, q_2, and λ—the first-order conditions—for an interior maximization are[15]

$$\frac{\partial \mathscr{L}}{\partial q_1} = \frac{\partial U}{\partial q_1} - \lambda p_1 = U_1 - \lambda p_1 = 0, \qquad (3.21)$$

$$\frac{\partial \mathscr{L}}{\partial q_2} = U_2 - \lambda p_2 = 0, \qquad (3.22)$$

$$\frac{\partial \mathscr{L}}{\partial \lambda} = Y - p_1 q_1 - p_2 q_2 = 0. \qquad (3.23)$$

Equation 3.21 shows that—at the optimal levels of q_1, q_2, and λ—the marginal utility of pizza, $U_1 = \partial U/\partial q_1$, equals its price times λ. Equation 3.22 provides an analogous condition for burritos. Equation 3.23 restates the budget constraint.

These three first-order conditions can be solved for the optimal values of q_1, q_2, and λ. Again, we should check that we have a maximum (see the Calculus Appendix at the end of the book).

What is λ? If we equate Equations 3.21 and 3.22 and rearrange terms, we find that

$$\lambda = \frac{U_1}{p_1} = \frac{U_2}{p_2}. \qquad (3.24)$$

That is, the optimal value of the Lagrangian multiplier, λ, equals the marginal utility of each good divided by its price, U_i/p_i, which is the extra utility one gets from

---

[15]To make our presentation as simple as possible, we assume that we have an interior solution, that q_1 and q_2 are infinitely divisible, and that $u(q_1, q_2)$ is continuously differentiable at least twice (so that the second-order condition is well defined). The first-order conditions determine an interior solution in which positive quantities of both goods are consumed. If these conditions do not predict that both quantities are nonnegative, the consumer is at a corner solution. One approach to solving the consumer-maximization problem allowing for a corner solution is to use a Kuhn-Tucker analysis, which is described in "Maximizing with Inequality Constraints" in the supplemental materials in **MyEconLab**'s textbook resources.

the last dollar spent on that good.[16] Equation 3.24 is the same as Equation 3.14, which we derived using a graphical argument.

SOLVED PROBLEM 3.6

If Julia has a Cobb-Douglas utility function (Equation 3.4), $U(q_1, q_2) = q_1^a q_2^{1-a}$, what are her optimal values of q_1 and q_2 in terms of income, prices, and the positive constant a? (*Note*: We can solve this problem using either substitution or the Lagrangian approach. Here, we will use the Lagrangian approach.)

Answer

1. *Show Julia's Lagrangian function and her first-order conditions.* Given that Julia's Lagrangian function is $\mathcal{L} = q_1^a q_2^{1-a} + \lambda(Y - p_1 q_1 - p_2 q_2)$, the first-order conditions for her to maximize her utility subject to the constraint are

$$\frac{\partial \mathcal{L}}{\partial q_1} = U_1 - \lambda p_1 = a q_1^{a-1} q_2^{1-a} - \lambda p_1 = a\frac{U}{q_1} - \lambda p_1 = 0, \quad (3.25)$$

$$\frac{\partial \mathcal{L}}{\partial q_2} = U_2 - \lambda p_2 = (1-a) q_1^a q_2^{-a} - \lambda p_2 = (1-a)\frac{U}{q_2} - \lambda p_2 = 0, \quad (3.26)$$

$$\frac{\partial \mathcal{L}}{\partial \lambda} = Y - p_1 q_1 - p_2 q_2 = 0. \quad (3.27)$$

2. *Solve these three first-order equations for q_1 and q_2.* By equating the right-hand sides of the first two conditions, we obtain an equation—analogous to Equation 3.24—that depends on q_1 and q_2 but not on λ:

$$(1-a) p_1 q_1 = a p_2 q_2. \quad (3.28)$$

The budget constraint, Equation 3.27, and the optimality condition, Equation 3.28, are two equations in q_1 and q_2. Rearranging the budget constraint, we know that $p_2 q_2 = Y - p_1 q_1$. By substituting for $p_2 q_2$ in Equation 3.28, we can rewrite this expression as $(1-a) p_1 q_1 = a(Y - p_1 q_1)$. Rearranging terms, we find that

$$q_1 = a\frac{Y}{p_1}. \quad (3.29)$$

Similarly, by substituting $p_1 q_1 = Y - p_2 q_2$ into Equation 3.26 and rearranging, we find that

$$q_2 = (1-a)\frac{Y}{p_2}. \quad (3.30)$$

Thus, we can use our knowledge of the form of the utility function to solve the expression for the q_1 and q_2 that maximize utility in terms of income, prices, and the utility function parameter a.

SOLVED PROBLEM 3.7

Given that Julia has a Cobb-Douglas utility function like the one in Equation 3.4, $U = q_1^a q_2^{1-a}$, what share of her budget does she spend on q_1 and q_2 in terms of her income, prices, and the positive constant a?

---

[16]More generally, the Lagrangian multiplier is often referred to as a *shadow value* that reflects the marginal rate of change in the objective function as the constraint is relaxed (see the Calculus Appendix at the end of the book).

Answer

Use Equations 3.29 and 3.30 to determine her budget shares. The share of her budget that Julia spends on pizza is her expenditure on pizza, $p_1 q_1$, divided by her budget, Y, or $p_1 q_1 / Y$. By multiplying both sides of Equation 3.29, $q_1 = aY/p_1$, by p_1, we find that $p_1 q_1 / Y = a$. Thus, a is both her budget share of pizza and the exponent on the units of pizza in her utility function. Similarly, from Equation 3.30, we find that her budget share of burritos is $p_2 q_2 / Y = 1 - a$.

Comment: The Cobb-Douglas functional form was derived to have this property. If an individual has a Cobb-Douglas utility function, we can estimate a and hence the utility function solely from information about the individual's budget shares. Indeed, that is how we obtained our estimate of Jackie's Cobb-Douglas utility function for recorded tracks and live music.

APPLICATION

Utility Maximization for Recorded Tracks and Live Music

We return to our typical consumer, Jackie, who has an estimated Cobb-Douglas utility function of $U = q_1^{0.4} q_2^{0.6}$ for music tracks, q_1, and live music, q_2. The average price of a track from iTunes, Amazon, Rhapsody, and other vendors was about $p_1 = £0.5$ in 2008, and we arbitrarily set the price of live music, p_2, at £1 per unit (so the units do not correspond to a concert or visit to a club). Jackie's budget constraint for purchasing these entertainment goods is

$$p_1 q_1 + p_2 q_2 = 0.5 q_1 + q_2 = 30 = Y,$$

given that Jackie, like the average 14-to-24-year-old British consumer, spends £30 on music per quarter.

Using Equations 3.29 and 3.30 from Solved Problem 3.6, we can solve for Jackie's optimal numbers of tracks and units of live music:

$$q_1 = 0.4 \frac{Y}{p_1} = 0.4 \times \frac{30}{0.5} = 24,$$

$$q_2 = 0.6 \frac{Y}{p_2} = 0.6 \times \frac{30}{1} = 18.$$

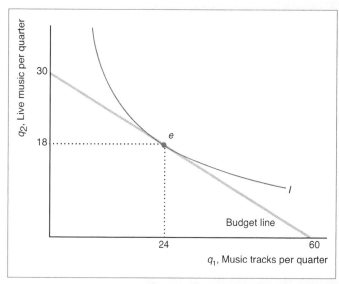

These quantities are the average quarterly purchases for a British youth in 2008. The figure shows that the optimal bundle is e where the indifference curve is tangent to the budget line.

We can use the result in Solved Problem 3.7 to confirm that the budget shares equal the exponents in Jackie's utility function. The share of Jackie's budget devoted to tracks is $p_1 q_1 / Y = (0.5 \times 24)/30 = 0.4$, which is the exponent on recorded tracks in her utility function. Similarly, the budget share she allocates to live music is $p_2 q_2 / Y = (1 \times 18)/30 = 0.6$, which is the live music exponent.

Minimizing Expenditure

Earlier, we showed how Lisa chooses quantities of goods so as to maximize her utility subject to a budget constraint. There is a related or *dual* constrained minimization problem in which Lisa wants to find that combination of goods that achieves a particular level of utility for the least expenditure.[17]

In Figure 3.8, we showed that, given the budget constraint that she faced, Lisa maximized her utility by picking a bundle of $q_1 = 30$ and $q_2 = 10$. She did that by choosing the highest indifference curve, I^2, that touched the budget constraint so that the indifference curve was tangent to the budget line.

Now, let's consider the alternative problem in which we ask how Lisa can make the lowest possible expenditure to maintain her utility at a particular level, $\bar{U}$, which corresponds to indifference curve I^2. Figure 3.11 shows three possible budget lines corresponding to budgets or expenditures of E_1, E_2, and E_3. The lowest of these budget lines with expenditure E_1 lies everywhere below I^2, so Lisa cannot achieve the level of utility on I^2 for such a small expenditure. Both the other budget lines cross I^2; however, the budget line with expenditure E_2 is the least expensive way for her to stay on I^2. The rule for minimizing expenditure while achieving a given level of utility is to choose the lowest expenditure such that the budget line touches—is tangent to—the relevant indifference curve.

The slope of all the expenditure or budget lines is $-p_2/p_1$ (see Equation 3.11), which depends only on the market prices and not on income or expenditure. Thus, the point of tangency in Figure 3.11 is the same as in Figure 3.8. Lisa purchases $q_1 = 30$ and $q_2 = 10$ because that is the bundle that minimizes her expenditure conditional on staying on I^2.

Thus, solving either of the two problems—maximizing utility subject to a budget constraint or minimizing the expenditure subject to maintaining a given level of utility—yields the same optimal values. It is sometimes more useful to use the expenditure-minimizing approach because expenditures are observable and utility levels are not.

Figure 3.11 Minimizing the Expenditure

The lowest expenditure that Lisa can make that will keep her on indifference curve I^2 is E_2. She buys 30 pizzas and 10 burritos.

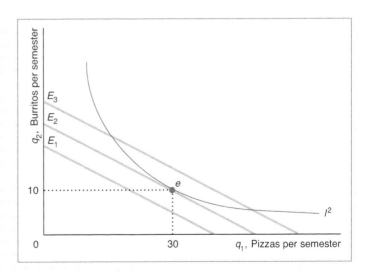

---

[17]For a formal calculus presentation, see "Duality" in **MyEconLab**'s textbook resources.

We can use calculus to solve the expenditure-minimizing problem. Lisa's objective is to minimize her expenditure, E, subject to the constraint that she hold her utility constant at $\bar{U} = U(q_1, q_2)$:

$$\min_{q_1, q_2} E = p_1 q_1 + p_2 q_2$$
$$\text{s.t. } \bar{U} = U(q_1, q_2). \quad (3.31)$$

The solution of this problem is an expression of the minimum expenditure as a function of the prices and the specified utility level:

$$E = E(p_1, p_2, \bar{U}). \quad (3.32)$$

We call this expression the **expenditure function**: the relationship showing the minimal expenditures necessary to achieve a specific utility level for a given set of prices.

SOLVED PROBLEM 3.8

Given that Julia has a Cobb-Douglas utility function $U = q_1^a q_2^{1-a}$, what is her expenditure function?

Answer

1. *Show Julia's Lagrangian function and derive her first-order conditions.* Julia's Lagrangian function is $\mathcal{L} = p_1 q_1 + p_2 q_2 + \lambda (\bar{U} - q_1^a q_2^{1-a})$. The first-order conditions for her to minimize her expenditure subject to remaining on a given indifference curve are obtained by differentiating the Lagrangian function with respect to q_1, q_2, and λ, and setting each derivative equal to zero:

$$\frac{\partial \mathcal{L}}{\partial q_1} = p_1 - \lambda a q_1^{a-1} q_2^{1-a} = p_1 - \lambda a \frac{U}{q_1} = 0, \quad (3.33)$$

$$\frac{\partial \mathcal{L}}{\partial q_2} = p_2 - \lambda (1-a) q_1^a q_2^{-a} = p_2 - \lambda (1-a) \frac{U}{q_2} = 0, \quad (3.34)$$

$$\frac{\partial \mathcal{L}}{\partial \lambda} = \bar{U} - q_1^a q_2^{1-a} = 0. \quad (3.35)$$

2. *Solve these three first-order equations for q_1 and q_2.* By equating the right-hand sides of the first two conditions, we obtain an equation that depends on q_1 and q_2, but not on λ:

$$p_1 q_1 / (aU) = p_2 q_2 / [(1-a)U], \text{ or}$$
$$(1-a) p_1 q_1 = a p_2 q_2. \quad (3.36)$$

This condition is the same as Equation 3.28, which we derived in Solved Problem 3.6 when we maximized Julia's utility subject to the budget constraint.

Rearranging Equation 3.36, we learn that $p_2 q_2 = p_1 q_1 (1-a)/a$. By substituting this expression into the expenditure definition, we find that

$$E = p_1 q_1 + p_2 q_2 = p_1 q_1 + p_1 q_1 (1-a)/a = p_1 q_1 / a.$$

Rearranging these terms, we find that

$$q_1 = a \frac{E}{p_1}. \quad (3.37)$$

Similarly, by rearranging Equation 3.36 to obtain $p_1 q_1 = p_2 q_2 a/(1-a)$, substituting that expression into the expenditure definition, and rearranging terms, we learn that

$$q_2 = (1-a)\frac{E}{p_2}. \qquad (3.38)$$

By substituting the expressions in Equations 3.37 and 3.38 into the indifference curve expression, Equation 3.35, we observe that

$$\overline{U} = q_1^a q_2^{1-a} = \left(a\frac{E}{p_1}\right)^a \left[(1-a)\frac{E}{p_2}\right]^{1-a} = E\left(\frac{a}{p}\right)^a \left(\frac{1-a}{p}\right)^{1-a}. \qquad (3.39)$$

Solving this expression for E, we can write the expenditure function as

$$E = \overline{U}\left(\frac{p_1}{a}\right)^a \left(\frac{p_2}{1-a}\right)^{1-a}. \qquad (3.40)$$

Equation 3.40 shows the minimum expenditure necessary to achieve utility level $\overline{U}$ given the prices p_1 and p_2. For example, if $a = 1 - a = 0.5$, then

$$E = \overline{U}(p_1/0.5)^{0.5}(p_2/0.5)^{0.5} = 2\overline{U}\sqrt{p_1 p_2}.$$

3.5 Behavioral Economics

So far, we have assumed that consumers are rational, maximizing individuals. A new field of study, **behavioral economics**, adds insights from psychology and empirical research on human cognition and emotional biases to the rational economic model to better predict economic decision making.[18] We discuss three applications of behavioral economics in this section: tests of transitivity, the endowment effect, and salience. Later in the book, we examine whether a consumer is influenced by the purchasing behavior of others (Chapter 11), whether individuals bid optimally in auctions (Chapter 13), why many people lack self-control (Chapter 17), and the psychology of decision making under uncertainty (Chapter 16).

Tests of Transitivity

In our presentation of the basic consumer choice model at the beginning of this chapter, we assumed that consumers make transitive choices. But do consumers actually make transitive choices?

A number of studies of both humans and animals show that preferences usually are transitive. Weinstein (1968) used an experiment to determine how frequently people give intransitive responses. None of the subjects knew the purpose of the experiment. They were given choices between ten goods, offered in pairs, in every possible combination. To ensure that the monetary value of the items would not affect people's calculations, they were told that all of the goods had a value of $3. Weinstein found that 93.5% of the responses of adults—people over 18 years old—were transitive. However, only 79.2% of children ages 9 through 12 gave transitive responses.

---

[18]The introductory chapter of Camerer et al. (2004) and DellaVigna (2009) are excellent surveys of the major papers in this field and heavily influenced the following discussion.

Psychologists have also tested for transitivity using preferences for colors, photos of faces, and so forth. Bradbury and Ross (1990) found that, given a choice of three colors, nearly half of 4- to 5-year-olds gave intransitive responses, compared to 15% of 11- to 13-year-olds, and 5% of adults. Bradbury and Ross showed that novelty (a preference for a new color) is responsible for most intransitive responses, and that this effect is especially strong in children.

Based on these results, one might conclude that it is appropriate to assume that adults exhibit transitivity for most economic decisions but that the theory should be modified when applied to children or when novel goods are introduced.

Economists normally argue that rational people should be allowed to make their own consumption choices so as to maximize their well-being. However, some people argue that children's lack of transitivity or rationality provides a justification for political and economic restrictions and protections placed on young people. For example, many governments effectively prevent youths from drinking.[19]

Endowment Effect

Experiments show that people have a tendency to stick with the bundle of goods that they currently possess. One important reason for this tendency is called the **endowment effect**, which occurs when people place a higher value on a good if they own it than they do if they are considering buying it.

We normally assume that an individual can buy or sell goods at the market price. Rather than rely on income to buy some mix of two goods, an individual who was *endowed* with several units of one good could sell some of them and use that money to buy units of another good.

We assume that a consumer's endowment does not affect the indifference map. In a classic buying and selling experiment, Kahneman et al. (1990) challenged this assumption. In an undergraduate law and economics class at Cornell University, 44 students were divided randomly into two groups. Members of one group were each given a coffee mug, which was available for sale at the student store for $6. Those students *endowed* with a mug were told that they could sell it and were asked the minimum price that they would accept for it. The subjects in the other group, who did not receive a mug, were asked how much they would pay to buy the mug. Given the standard assumptions of our model and that the subjects were chosen randomly, we would expect no difference between the selling and buying prices. However, the median selling price was $5.75 and the median buying price was $2.25, so sellers wanted more than twice what buyers would pay. This type of experiment has been repeated with many variations and typically an endowment effect is found.

However, some economists believe that this result has to do with how the experiment is designed. Plott and Zeiler (2005) argued that if you take adequate care to train the subjects in the procedures and make sure they understand them, the result didn't hold. List (2003) examined the actual behavior of sports memorabilia collectors and found that amateurs who do not trade frequently exhibited an endowment effect, unlike professionals and amateurs who traded a lot. Thus, experience may minimize or eliminate the endowment effect, and people who buy goods for resale may be less likely to become attached to these goods.

---

[19]U.S. federal law prevents drinking before the age of 21, but most other countries set the minimum drinking age between 16 and 18. It is 16 in Belgium, Denmark, and France; 18 in Australia, Sweden, and the United Kingdom; and 18 or 19 in Canada. A justification from limiting drinking is given by Carpenter and Dobkin (2009). They find that when U.S. youths start drinking alcohol legally at age 21, there is a 21% increase in the number of days on which they drink, which results in a 9% increase in their mortality rate.

Others accept the results and have considered how to modify the standard model to reflect the endowment effect (Knetsch, 1992). One implication of these experimental results is that people will only trade away from their endowments if prices change substantially. This resistance to trade could be captured by having a kink in the indifference curve at the endowment bundle. (We showed indifference curves with a kink at a 90° angle in panel b of Figure 3.5.) A kinked indifference curve could have an angle greater than 90° and be curved at points other than at the kink. If the indifference curve has a kink, the consumer does not shift to a new bundle in response to a small price change but does shift if the price change is large.

APPLICATION
How You Ask the Question Matters

The experimental design studies show that the behavior of consumers differs depending on how a choice is posed to them. One practical implication of this insight is that we can redesign programs to increase participation. Many workers are offered the choice of enrolling in their firm's voluntary tax-deferred retirement plan, called a 401(k) plan. The firm can pose the choice in two ways: It can automatically sign employees up for the program and let them opt out of the program, or it can tell them that they must sign up (opt in) to participate. These two approaches might seem identical, but the behaviors they lead to are not.

Madrian and Shea (2001, 2002) found that well over twice as many workers participate if they are automatically enrolled (but may opt out) than if they must opt in: 86% versus 37%. In short, inertia matters. As a consequence of this type of evidence, federal law was changed in 2006 and 2007 to make it easier for employers to enroll their employees in their 401(k) plans automatically. Labor Department officials estimate that retirement savings in 401(k) plans could increase by as much as $134 billion by 2034 as a consequence of these changes.

Salience

Except in the last two chapters of this book, we examine economic theories that are based on the assumption that decision makers are aware of all relevant information. In this chapter, we assume that consumers know their own income or endowment, the relevant prices, and their own tastes, and hence they make informed decisions.

Behavioral economists and psychologists have demonstrated that people are more likely to consider information if it is presented in a way that grabs their attention or if it takes relatively little thought or calculation to understand. Economists use the term *salience*, in the sense of *striking* or *obvious*, to describe this idea.

For example, *tax salience* is the awareness of a tax. If a store's posted price includes the sales tax, consumers observe a change in the price as the tax rises. On the other hand, if a store posts the pre-tax price and collects the tax at the cash register, consumers are less likely to be aware that the post-tax price increases when the tax rate increases.[20] Chetty et al. (2009) compare consumers' response to a rise in an ad valorem sales tax on beer (which is also called an *excise tax*) that is included in the posted price to an increase in a general ad valorem sales tax, which is collected at the cash register but not reflected in the posted price. An increase in either tax has the same effect on the final price, so an increase in either tax should have the same effect on purchases if consumers pay attention to both taxes.[21] However,

---

[20]See "Do Taxes Affect Click-versus-Brick Decisions?" in Supplemental Material to Chapter 3 in **MyEconLab**'s textbook resources.

[21]The final price consumers pay is $p^* = p(1 + \beta)(1 + \alpha)$, where p is the pretax price, α is the general sales tax, and β is the excise tax on beer.

a 10% increase in the posted price, which includes the excise tax, reduces beer consumption by 9%, whereas a 10% increase in the price due to a rise in the sales tax that is not posted reduces consumption by only 2%. Chetty et al. also conducted an experiment in which they posted tax-inclusive prices for 750 products in a grocery store and found that demand for these products fell by about 8% relative to control products in the store and comparable products at nearby stores.

One explanation for the lack of an effect of a tax on consumer behavior is consumer ignorance. For example, Furnham (2005) found that even by the age of 14 or 15, British youths do not fully understand the nature and purpose of taxes. Similarly, unless the tax-inclusive price is posted, many consumers ignore or forget about taxes.

An alternative explanation for ignoring taxes is **bounded rationality**: People have a limited capacity to anticipate, solve complex problems, or enumerate all options. To avoid having to perform hundreds of calculations when making purchasing decisions at a grocery store, many people chose not to calculate the tax-inclusive price. However, when post-tax price information is easily available to them, consumers make use of it. One way to modify the standard model is to assume that people incur a cost to making calculations—such as the time taken or the mental strain—and that deciding whether to incur this cost is part of their rational decision-making process.

People incur this calculation cost only if they think the gain from a better choice of goods exceeds the cost. More people pay attention to a tax when the tax rate is high or when their demand for the good is elastic (they are sensitive to price changes). Similarly, some people are more likely to pay attention to taxes when making large, one-time purchases—such as for a computer or car—rather than small, repeated purchases—such as for a bar of soap.

Tax salience has important implications for tax policy. In Chapter 2, we showed that the tax incidence on consumers is the same regardless of whether the tax is collected from consumers or sellers (where we implicitly assumed that everyone was aware of the tax). However, if consumers are inattentive to taxes, they're more likely to bear the tax burden if they're taxed. If a tax on consumers rises and consumers don't notice, their demand for the good is relatively inelastic, causing consumers to bear more of the tax incidence (see Equation 2.28). In contrast, if the tax is placed on sellers, and the sellers want to pass at least some of the tax on to consumers, they raise their prices, which consumers observe.

SUMMARY

Consumers maximize their utility (well-being) subject to constraints based on their incomes and the prices of goods.

1. **Preferences.** To predict consumers' responses to changes in these constraints, economists use a theory about individuals' preferences. One way of summarizing consumer preferences is with an indifference map. An indifference curve consists of all bundles of goods that give the consumer a particular level of utility. On the basis of observations of consumer behavior, economists assume that consumers' preferences have three properties: completeness, transitivity, and more-is-better. Given these three assumptions, indifference curves have the following properties:

   - Consumers get more pleasure from bundles on indifference curves the farther the curves are from the origin.
   - Indifference curves cannot cross.
   - There is an indifference curve through any given bundle.
   - Indifference curves cannot be thick.
   - Indifference curves slope downward.
   - Consumers are observed purchasing positive quantities of all relevant goods only where their indifference curves are convex to the origin.

   We also assume that consumers' preferences are continuous, and we use this assumption in our utility function analysis.

2. **Utility.** *Utility* is the set of numerical values that reflect the relative rankings of bundles of goods. Utility is an ordinal measure: By comparing the utility a consumer gets from each of two bundles, we know that the consumer prefers the bundle with the higher utility, but we can't tell by how much the consumer prefers that bundle. The utility function is unique only up to a positive monotonic transformation. The marginal utility from a good is the extra utility a person gets from consuming one more unit of it, holding the consumption of all other goods constant. The rate at which a consumer is willing to substitute one good for another, the marginal rate of substitution (*MRS*), depends on the relative amounts of marginal utility the consumer gets from each of the two goods.

3. **Budget Constraint.** The amount of goods consumers can buy at given prices is limited by their incomes. The greater their incomes and the lower the prices of goods, the better off consumers are. The rate at which they can exchange one good for another in the market, the marginal rate of transformation (*MRT*), depends on the relative prices of the two goods.

4. **Constrained Consumer Choice.** Each person picks an affordable bundle of goods to consume so as to maximize his or her pleasure. If an individual consumes both Good 1 and Good 2 (an interior solution), the individual's utility is maximized when the following four equivalent conditions hold:

   1. The consumer buys the bundle of goods that is on the highest obtainable indifference curve.
   2. The indifference curve between the two goods is tangent to the budget constraint.
   3. The consumer's marginal rate of substitution (the slope of the indifference curve) equals the marginal rate of transformation (the slope of the budget line).
   4. The last dollar spent on Good 1 gives the consumer as much extra utility as the last dollar spent on Good 2.

   However, consumers do not buy some of all possible goods (corner solutions). The last dollar spent on a good that is actually purchased gives a consumer more extra utility than would a dollar's worth of a good the consumer chose not to buy.

   We can use our model in which a consumer maximizes his or her utility subject to a budget constraint to predict the consumer's optimal choice of goods as a function of the consumer's income and market prices.

5. **Behavioral Economics.** Using insights from psychology and empirical research on human cognition and emotional biases, economists are starting to modify the rational economic model to better predict economic decision making. While adults tend to make transitive choices, children are less likely to do so, especially when novelty is involved. Consequently, some people would argue that ability of children to make economic choices should be limited. Consumers exhibit an endowment effect if they place a higher value on goods if they own them than they would if they were considering buying them. Such consumers are less sensitive to price changes and hence less likely to trade goods, as predicted by the standard consumer choice model. Many consumers fail to pay attention to sales taxes unless they are included in the product's final price, and thus ignore then when making purchasing decisions.

QUESTIONS

■ = exercise is available on **MyEconLab**; * = answer appears at the back of this book; V = video answer by James Dearden is available online.

1. Which of the following pairs of goods are complements (people like to consume them together), and which are substitutes (people are willing to trade off one good for the other)? Are the goods that are substitutes likely to be perfect substitutes for only some or all consumers?
    a. A popular novel and a gossip magazine
    b. A camera and film
    c. An economics textbook and a mathematics textbook
    d. A Panasonic DVD player and a JVC DVD player

2. Don is altruistic. Show the possible shape of his indifference curves between charitable contributions and all other goods.

*3. Arthur spends his income on bread and chocolate. He views chocolate as a good but is neutral about bread, in that he doesn't care if he consumes it or not. Draw his indifference map.

4. Miguel considers tickets to the Houston Grand Opera and to Houston Astros baseball games to be perfect substitutes. Show his preference map. What is his utility function?

*5. Sofia will consume hot dogs only with whipped cream. Show her preference map. What is her utility function?

6. Give as many reasons as you can why economists believe that indifference curves are convex.

7. Fiona requires a minimum level of consumption, a *threshold*, to derive additional utility: $U(X, Z)$ is 0 if $X + Z \leq 5$ and is $X + Z$ otherwise. Draw Fiona's

indifference curves. Which of our preference assumptions does this example violate?

*8. Gasoline was once less expensive in the United States than in Canada, but now gasoline costs less in Canada than in the United States due to a change in taxes. How will the gasoline-purchasing behavior of a Canadian who can easily buy gasoline in either country change? Answer using an indifference curve-budget line diagram.

*9. Governments frequently limit how much of a good a consumer can buy. During emergencies, governments may ration "essential" goods such as water, food, and gasoline rather than let their prices rise. Suppose that the government rations water, setting quotas on how much a consumer can purchase. If a consumer can afford to buy 12,000 gallons a month but the government restricts purchases to no more than 10,000 gallons a month, how do the consumer's budget line and opportunity set change?

10. What happens to a consumer's optimal choice of goods if all prices and the consumer's income double? (*Hint*: What happens to the intercepts of the budget constraint?)

11. Suppose that Boston consumers pay twice as much for avocados as they pay for tangerines, whereas San Diego consumers pay half as much for avocados as they pay for tangerines. Assuming that consumers maximize their utility, which city's consumers have a higher marginal rate of substitution of avocados for tangerines? Explain your answer.

12. Given Spenser's quasilinear indifference curves in Figure 3.9 and the same income and price of burritos, show that with a lower price of pizza—which leads to a flatter budget line—Spenser maximizes his utility by choosing an interior solution: a bundle with positive quantities of both goods.

13. Suppose that Solved Problem 3.4 were changed so that Nigel and Bob are buying a bundle of several cars and SUVs for their large families or businesses and have identical tastes, with the usual-shaped indifference curves. Use a figure to discuss how the different slopes of their budget lines affect the bundles of SUVs and cars that each chooses. Can you make any unambiguous statements about the quantity each can buy? Can you make an unambiguous statement if you know that Bob's budget line goes through Nigel's optimal bundle?

14. If a consumer has indifference curves that are convex to the origin but have a kink in them (similar to the perfect complements example, except the angle at the kink is greater than 90°), how can we determine the optimal bundle? Use a graph to illustrate your answer. Can we use all the conditions that we derived for determining an interior solution?

*15. What is the effect of a 50% income tax on Dale's budget line and opportunity set?

16. Goolsbee (2000) finds that people who live in high sales tax areas are much more likely than other consumers to purchase over the Internet, where they are generally exempt from the sales tax if the firm is located in another state. The National Governors Association (NGA) proposed a uniform tax of 5% on all Internet sales. Goolsbee estimates that the NGA's flat 5% tax would lower the number of online customers by 18% and total sales by 23%. Alternatively, if each state imposed its own taxes (which average 6.33%), the number of buyers would fall by 24% and spending by 30%. Use an indifference curve–budget line diagram to illustrate the reason for his results.

17. In 2006, Michigan passed legislation that provides greater incentives to drivers who buy ethanol by lowering the state tax on each gallon of ethanol-blended fuel to 12¢, down from the 19¢ per gallon tax on regular gas. Show the effects of such a subsidy on a consumer who is indifferent between using ethanol-blended fuel and regular gasoline and on another consumer who views the two types of gasoline as imperfect substitutes.

18. Some of the largest import tariffs, the tax on imported goods, are on shoes. Strangely, the higher the tariff, the cheaper the shoes. The highest U.S. tariff, 67%, is on a pair of $3 canvas sneakers, whereas the tariff on $12 sneakers is 37%, while $300 Italian leather imports have no tariff. (Adam Davidson, "U.S. Tariffs on Shoes Favor Well-Heeled Buyers," National Public Radio, June 12, 2007, www.npr.org/templates/story/story.php?storyId=10991519.) Laura buys either inexpensive, canvas sneakers ($3 before the tariff) or more expensive gym shoes ($12 before the tariff) for her many children. Use an indifference curve-budget line analysis to show how imposing the unequal tariffs affects the bundle of shoes she buys compared to what she would have bought in the absence of tariffs. Can you confidently predict whether she'll buy relatively more expensive gym shoes after the tariff? Why or why not?

19. Illustrate the logic of the endowment effect using a kinked indifference curve. Let the angle be greater than 90°. Suppose that the prices change, so the slope of the budget line through the endowment changes. Use the diagram to explain why an individual whose endowment point is at the kink will only trade from the endowment point if the price change is substantial.

PROBLEMS

20. Elise consumes cans of anchovies, A, and boxes of biscuits, B. Each of her indifference curves reflects strictly diminishing marginal rates of substitution. Where $A = 2$ and $B = 2$, her marginal rate of substitution between cans of anchovies and boxes of biscuits equals -1 ($= MU_A/MU_B$). Will she prefer a bundle with three cans of anchovies and a box of biscuits to a bundle with two of each? Why?

*21. Andy purchases only two goods, apples (a) and kumquats (k). He has an income of $40 and can buy apples at $2 per pound and kumquats at $4 per pound. His utility function is $U(a, k) = 3a + 5k$. What is his marginal utility for apples, and what is his marginal utility for kumquats? What bundle of apples and kumquats should he purchase to maximize his utility? Why?

*22. What is the marginal rate of substitution for a quasilinear utility function, $U(q_1, q_2) = u(q_1) + q_2$? Using this expression for the *MRS*, explain why the indifference curves must be parallel and have the same slope for a given q_1.

*23. David's utility function is $U = B + 2Z$. Describe the location of his optimal bundle (if possible) in terms of the relative prices of B and Z.

24. Mark consumes only cookies and books. At his current consumption bundle, his marginal utility from books is 10 and from cookies is 5. Each book costs $10, and each cookie costs $2. Is he maximizing his utility? Explain. If he is not, how can he increase his utility while keeping his total expenditure constant?

*25. Nadia likes spare ribs, R, and fried chicken, C. Her utility function is

$$U = 10R^2C.$$

Her weekly income is $90, which she spends on only ribs and chicken.

a. If she pays $10 for a slab of ribs and $5 for a chicken, what is her optimal consumption bundle? Show her budget line, indifference curve, and optimal bundle, e_1, in a diagram.

b. Suppose the price of chicken doubles to $10. How does her optimal consumption of chicken and ribs change? Show her new budget line and optimal bundle, e_2, in your diagram.

26. Steve's utility function is $U = BC$, where B = veggie burgers per week and C = packs of cigarettes per week. Here, $MU_B = C$ and $MU_C = B$. What is his marginal rate of substitution if veggie burgers are on the vertical axis and cigarettes are on the horizontal axis? Steve's income is $120, the price of a veggie burger is $2, and that of a pack of cigarettes is $1. How many burgers and how many packs of cigarettes does Steve consume to maximize his utility? When a new tax raises the price of a burger to $3, what is his new optimal bundle? Illustrate your answers in a graph.

27. Linda loves buying shoes and going out to dance. Her utility function for pairs of shoes, S, and the number of times she goes dancing per month, T, is $U(S, T) = 2ST$. What is her marginal utility from shoes, and what is her marginal utility from dancing? It costs Linda $50 to buy a new pair of shoes or to spend an evening out dancing. Assume that she has $500 to spend on clothing and dancing.

a. What is the equation for Linda's budget line? Draw it (with T on the vertical axis), and label the slope and intercepts.

b. What is her marginal rate of substitution? Explain.

c. Solve mathematically for her optimal bundle. Show in a diagram how to determine this bundle using indifference curves and a budget line.

28. Diogo has a utility function, $U(q_1, q_2) = q_1^{0.75} q_2^{0.25}$, where q_1 is pizza and q_2 is burritos. If the price of burritos, p_2, is $2, the price of pizzas, p_1, is $1, and Y is $100, what is Diogo's optimal bundle?

29. Vasco's utility function is $U = q_1 q_2^2$. The price of pizza, q_1, is $p_1 = 5, the price of burritos, q_2, is $p_2 = 10, and his income is $Y = 150. What is his optimal consumption bundle? Show it in a graph.

30. If José Maria's utility function is $U(q_1, q_2) = q_1 + Aq_1^a q_2^b + q_2$, what is his marginal utility from q_2? What is his marginal rate of substitution between these two goods?

31. Ann's utility function is $U = q_1 q_2/(q_1 + q_2)$. Solve for her optimal values of q_1 and q_2 as a function of p_1, p_2, and Y.

*32. Suppose we calculate the *MRS* at a particular bundle for a consumer whose utility function is $U(q_1, q_2)$. If we use a positive monotonic transformation, F, to obtain a new utility function, $V(q_1, q_2) = F(U(q_1, q_2))$, then this new utility function contains the same information about the consumer's rankings of bundles. Prove that the *MRS* is the same as with the original utility function.

33. The application "Indifference Curves Between Food and Clothing" postulates that there are minimum levels of food and clothing necessary to support life. Suppose that the amount of food one has is F, the minimum level to sustain life is $\underline{F}$, the amount of clothing one has is C, and the minimum necessary is $\underline{C}$. We can then modify the Cobb-Douglas utility

function to reflect these minimum levels: $U(C, F) = (C - \underline{C})^a(F - \underline{F})^{1-\alpha}$, where $C \geq \underline{C}$ and $F \geq \underline{F}$. Using the approach similar to that in Solved Problem 3.6, derive the optimal amounts of food and clothing as a function of prices and a person's income. To do so, introduce the idea of *extra income*, Y^*, which is the income remaining after paying for the minimum levels of food and clothing: $Y^* = Y - p_C\underline{C} - p_F\underline{F}$. Show that the demand for clothing is $C = \underline{C} + aI^*/p_C$ and that the demand for food is $F = \underline{F} + (1 - a)I^*/p_F$. Derive formulas for the share of income devoted to each good.

34. Use the substitution approach rather than the Lagrangian method in Solved Problem 3.6 to obtain expressions for the optimal levels of q_1 and q_2 given a Cobb-Douglas utility function. (*Hint:* It may help to take logarithms of both sides of the utility expression before you differentiate.)

35. We argued earlier that if all prices and income doubled, we would not expect an individual's choice of an optimal bundle to change. We say that a function $f(X, Y)$ is homogeneous of degree γ if, when we multiply each argument by a constant α, we have $f(\alpha X, \alpha Y) = \alpha^\gamma f(X, Y)$. Thus, if a function is homogeneous of degree zero, $f(\alpha X, \alpha Y) = \alpha^0 f(X, Y) = f(X, Y)$, because $\alpha^0 = 1$. Show that optimality conditions we derived based on the Cobb-Douglas utility function in Solved Problem 3.6 are homogeneous of degree zero. Explain why that result is consistent with our intuition about what happens if we double all prices and income.

36. In 2005, Americans bought 9.1 million home radios for $202 million and 3.8 million home-theater-in-a-box units for $730 million (*TWICE*, March 27, 2006, www.twice.com/article/CA6319031.html). Suppose that the average consumer has a Cobb-Douglas utility function and buys only these two goods. Given the results in Solved Problem 3.7, estimate a plausible Cobb-Douglas utility function such that the consumer would allocate income in the proportions actually observed.

*37. The constant elasticity of substitution (CES) utility function is $U(q_1, q_2) = (q_1^\rho + q_2^\rho)^{1/\rho}$, where ρ is a positive constant. Show that there is a positive monotonic transformation such that there is an equivalent utility function (one with the same preference ordering) $U(q_1, q_2) = q_1^\rho + q_2^\rho$.

*38. What is the *MRS* for the CES utility function $U(q_1, q_2) = q_1^\rho + q_2^\rho$?

39. For the CES utility function $U(q_1, q_2) = q_1^\rho + q_2^\rho$, derive the expressions for the optimal levels of q_1 and q_2.

40. Jen's utility for chocolate, q_1, and coffee, q_2, is $U = q_1^{0.5} + q_2^{0.5}$. Derive Jen's expenditure function. Does more money make Jen better off, and does less money reduce her well-being? V

41. Jim spends most of his time in Jazzman's, a coffee shop on the south side of Bethlehem, Pennsylvania. Jim has $12 a week to spend on coffee and muffins. Jazzman's sells muffins for $2 each and coffee for $1.20 per cup. Jim consumes q_c cups of coffee per week and q_m muffins per week. His utility function for coffee and muffins is $U(q_c, q_m) = q_c^{0.5} + q_m^{0.5}$.

   a. Draw Jim's budget line.

   b. Use the Lagrange technique to find Jim's optimal bundle.

   c. Now Jazzman's has introduced a frequent-buyer card: For every five cups of coffee purchased at the regular price of $1.20 per cup, Jim receives a free sixth cup. Draw Jim's new budget line. Is Jim's new budget line actually composed of more than one straight line?

   d. With the frequent-buyer card, does Jim consume more coffee? V

4 Demand

I have enough money to last me the rest of my life, unless I buy something. —Jackie Mason

Alexx's employer wants to transfer him from the firm's Miami office to its Paris office. Although Alexx likes the idea of living in Paris, he's concerned about the high cost of living there. The firm offers to pay him enough in euros so he can buy the same combination of goods in Paris that he currently buys in the United States. Does this higher income fully compensate or more-than-fully compensate Alexx for the higher Parisian prices? Could the firm induce him to move at a lower cost?

How much can Apple profitably raise its price for the iPhone above its cost of producing the phone? If the government cuts the income tax rate, will tax revenues rise or fall? If the government substantially increases the tax on gasoline, how much of a subsidy would the government have to give poor people who buy gasoline to keep them as well off as they were before the tax? The answers to these questions and to many, if not most, important economic questions turn critically on how consumers' demands respond to changes in prices or in their incomes.

In Chapter 3, we introduced consumer theory, which explains how consumers make choices when faced with constraints. We begin this chapter by using consumer theory to determine the shape of a demand curve for a good by varying the good's price, holding other prices and income constant. Firms use information about the shape of demand curves when setting prices. Governments also use this information to predict the impact of policies such as taxes and price controls.

We then apply consumer theory to show how an increase in people's incomes causes a demand curve to shift. Firms use information about the relationship between income and demand to predict which less-developed countries will substantially increase their demand for the firms' products when incomes rise.

Next, we discover that an increase in the price of a good has two effects on demand. First, consumers buy less of the now relatively more expensive good even if they are compensated with cash for the price increase. Second, holding consumers' incomes constant, an increase in price forces them to buy less of at least some goods.

We use the analysis of these two demand effects of a price increase to show why the government's measure of inflation, the Consumer Price Index (CPI), overestimates the amount of inflation. If you signed a long-term lease for an apartment in which your rent payments increase over time in proportion to the change in the CPI, you lose and your landlord gains from the bias.

Finally, having determined that we can infer how a consumer will behave based on the person's preferences, we use a *revealed preference* approach to show the opposite: that we can infer what a consumer's preferences are if we know the consumer's behavior. Using revealed preference, we can demonstrate that consumers substitute away from a good when its price rises.

In this chapter, we examine five main topics	1. **Deriving Demand Curves.** We use consumer theory to derive demand curves, showing how a change in a product's price causes a movement along its demand curve. 2. **Effects of an Increase in Income.** We use consumer theory to determine how an increase in consumers' incomes results in their buying more of some or all goods. 3. **Effects of a Price Increase.** A change in price has two effects on demand, one relating to a change in relative prices and the other concerning a change in consumers' opportunities. 4. **Cost-of-Living Adjustment.** Using the analysis of the two effects of price changes, we show that the CPI overestimates the rate of inflation. 5. **Revealed Preference.** Observing a consumer's choice at various prices allows us to infer what the consumer's preferences are and show that the consumer substitutes away from a good when its price increases.

4.1 Deriving Demand Curves

An increase in the price of a good—holding people's tastes, their incomes, and the prices of other goods constant—causes a *movement along the demand curve* for the good (Chapter 2). We use consumer theory to show how a consumer's choice changes as the price changes, thereby tracing out the demand curve.

System of Demand Equations

In Chapter 3, we used calculus to maximize the utility of a consumer subject to a budget constraint. In doing so, we solved for the optimal quantities of sets of goods that the consumer chooses as functions of prices and the consumer's income. That is, we solved for the consumer's system of demand functions for the goods. For example, Lisa chooses between pizzas, q_1, and burritos, q_2, so her demand functions are of the form

$$q_1 = Z(p_1, p_2, Y),$$
$$q_2 = B(p_1, p_2, Y),$$

where p_1 is the price of pizza, p_2 is the price of burritos, and Y is her income.

As we showed in Chapter 3, we can determine how the quantities an individual demands vary with prices and income if we know an individual's utility function. We illustrate this approach with four examples where a consumer chooses between two goods.

Constant Elasticity of Substitution. Usually, each of the two demand curves depends on both goods' prices and the consumer's income. We provided an example with this property in Solved Problem 3.5, where Michael has a constant elasticity of substitution (CES) utility function,

$$U(q_1, q_2) = \left(q_1^\rho + q_2^\rho\right)^{\frac{1}{\rho}}, \ 0 \neq \rho \leq 1.$$

He maximizes his utility subject to his budget constraint $Y = p_1 q_1 + p_2 q_2$ to obtain the system of demand functions, Equations 3.18 and 3.19:

$$q_1 = \frac{Y p_1^{z-1}}{p_1^z + p_2^z},$$

$$q_2 = \frac{Y p_2^{z-1}}{p_1^z + p_2^z},$$

where $z = \rho/[\rho - 1]$. Thus, each of Michael's demand functions depends on the prices of both the goods and his income.

Cobb-Douglas. In contrast, the demand functions corresponding to a Cobb-Douglas utility function, $U(q_1, q_2) = q_1^a q_2^{1-a}$, depend on the consumer's income and each good's *own price*, but not on the price of the other good. In Solved Problem 3.6, we showed that the Cobb-Douglas demand functions are Equations 3.29 and 3.30:

$$q_1 = a \frac{Y}{p_1},$$

$$q_2 = (1-a) \frac{Y}{p_2}.$$

Panel a of Figure 4.1 shows the demand curve for q_1, which we plot by holding Y fixed and varying p_1.

Figure 4.1 Cobb-Douglas and Perfect Substitute Demand Curves

(a) The Cobb-Douglas demand curve for $q_1 = aY/p_1$ is a smooth curve that approaches the horizontal, q_1-axis as p_1 becomes small. (b) Mahdu demands no cans of Coca-Cola when the price of Coke, p_1, is greater than the price of Pepsi, p_2. When the two prices are equal, he wants a total number of cans equal to $Y/p_1 = Y/p_2$, but he is indifferent as to how many are Coke and how many are Pepsi. If $p_1 < p_2$, he only buys Coke, and his demand curve is $q_1 = Y/p_1$.

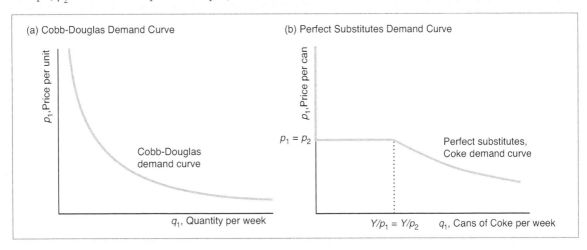

Perfect Substitutes. The demand curves depend on the consumer's income and the prices of both goods if the goods are perfect substitutes. Because Mahdu views Coca-Colas, q_1, and Pepsi Cola, q_2, as perfect substitutes, his utility function is $U(q_1, q_2) = q_1 + q_2$. The price of a 12-ounce can of Coke is p_1, while the price of a 12-ounce can of Pepsi is p_2. As Solved Problem 3.4 showed, a consumer is indifferent as to which good to buy if the goods' prices are the same, but the consumer buys the less expensive good if the prices differ. If $p_1 < p_2$, and his income is Y, then Mahdu buys as much of q_1 as he can afford: $q_1 = Y/p_1$. If $p_1 > p_2$, then his demand is $q_1 = 0$. Finally, if $p_1 = p_2$, he is indifferent between buying any quantity of q_1 between 0 and Y/p_1. If he buys $q_1 < Y/p_2$, he buys enough of q_2 so that $q_1 + q_2 = Y/p_1 = Y/p_2$. Panel b of Figure 4.1 shows his demand curve for q_1 for a given p_2 and Y.

Quasilinear. If Jim has a quasilinear utility function, Equation 3.9, $U(q_1, q_2) = u(q_1) + q_2$, then both his demand curves depend on both prices, but only one demand curve depends on income. We can rewrite his budget constraint, $Y = p_1 q_1 + p_2 q_2$, as $q_2 = Y/p_2 - (p_1/p_2)q_1$. If we substitute this expression into his utility function, the utility function becomes $u(q_1) + Y/p_2 - (p_1/p_2)q_1$. He now faces an unconstrained maximization problem, where he chooses only q_1:

$$\max_{q_1} u(q_1) + \frac{Y}{p_2} - \frac{p_1}{p_2}q_1.$$

We assume that he chooses to consume both goods (an interior solution, Chapter 3). His first-order condition is

$$\frac{du(q_1)}{dq_1} - \frac{p_1}{p_2} = 0.$$

This condition states that, at the optimum, Jim's marginal utility of the first good, $du(q_1)/dq_1$, equals the price ratio p_1/p_2. The first-order condition determines the consumer's demand curve and shows that we can write the demand function as $q_1(p_1/p_2)$ because the quantity of q_1 demanded depends on the relative prices of the two goods but not on his income. Consequently, the income elasticity of demand for the first good is zero. For example, if $p_2 = 1$, $u(q_1) + q_2 = 100q_1 - \frac{1}{2}(q_1)^2 + q_2$, and $q_1 \leq 100$, then the first-order condition is $100 - q_1 - p_1 = 0$, so the demand function for the first good is linear: $q_1 = 100 - p_1$.

We can derive the consumer's demand function for the second good using the budget constraint: $q_2 = Y/p_2 - (p_1/p_2)q_1(p_1/p_2)$. This demand function depends on both prices and income. Because the quantity of q_1 does not change as the consumer's income rises, the consumer spends any additional income on q_2.[1]

Graphical Interpretation

We can derive the demand curves using a graphical approach. If we increase the price of a product while holding other prices, the consumer's tastes, and income constant, we cause the consumer's budget constraint to rotate, prompting the consumer to choose a new optimal bundle. This change in the quantity demanded is the information we need to draw the demand curve.

---

[1] The statement that the q_1 demand function does not depend on income is true only if Jim buys both q_1 and q_2 (an interior solution). If Jim were at a corner solution in which he bought no q_2, then, from the budget constraint, his demand function for the first good would be $q_1 = Y/p_1$.

Figure 4.2 Deriving Mimi's Demand Curve

If the price of beer falls, holding the price of wine, the budget, and tastes constant, the typical American consumer, Mimi, buys more beer, according to our estimates. (a) At the actual budget line, L^1, where the price of beer is $12 per unit and the price of wine is $35 per unit, the average consumer's indifference curve I^1 is tangent at Bundle e_1, 26.7 gallons of beer per year and 2.8 gallons of wine per year. If the price of beer falls to $6 per unit, the new budget constraint is L^2, and the average consumer buys 44.5 gallons of beer per year and 4.3 gallons of wine per year. (b) By varying the price of beer, we trace out Mimi's demand curve for beer. The beer price-quantity combinations E_1, E_2, and E_3 on the demand curve for beer in panel b correspond to optimal bundles e_1, e_2, and e_3 in panel a.

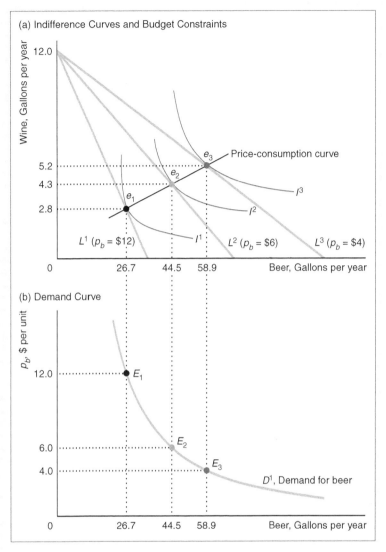

We start by estimating a utility function between wine and beer, using data for U.S. consumers.[2] Panel a of Figure 4.2 shows three of the corresponding estimated indifference curves for the average U.S. consumer, whom we call Mimi.[3] These indifference curves are convex to the origin because Mimi views beer and wine as imperfect substitutes (Chapter 3).

---

[2] I estimated the utility function that underlies Figure 4.2 using an almost ideal demand system, which is a more flexible, functional form than the Cobb-Douglas, and which includes the Cobb-Douglas as a special case.

[3] My mother, Mimi, wanted the most degenerate character in the book named after her. I hope that you do not consume as much beer or wine as the typical American in this example. ("One reason I don't drink is that I want to know when I am having a good time." Nancy, Lady Astor.)

The vertical axis in panel a measures the number of gallons of wine Mimi consumes each year, and the horizontal axis measures the number of gallons of beer she drinks per year. Mimi spends $Y = \$419$ per year on beer and wine. The price of beer, p_b, is \$12 per unit, and the price of wine, p_w, is \$35 per unit.[4] The slope of her budget line, L^1, is $-p_b/p_w = -12/35 \approx -\frac{1}{3}$. At those prices, Mimi consumes Bundle e_1, 26.7 gallons of beer per year and 2.8 gallons of wine per year, a combination that is determined by the tangency of indifference curve I^1 and budget line L^1.[5]

If the price of beer is cut in half to \$6 per unit while the price of wine and her budget remain constant, Mimi's budget line rotates outward to L^2. If she were to spend all her money on wine, she could buy the same 12 ($\approx 419/35$) gallons of wine per year as before, so the intercept on the vertical axis of L^2 is the same as for L^1. However, if she were to spend all her money on beer, she could buy twice as much as before (70 instead of 35 gallons of beer), so L^2 hits the horizontal axis twice as far from the origin as L^1. As a result, L^2 has a flatter slope than L^1, about $-\frac{1}{6}$ ($\approx -6/35$).

Because beer is now relatively less expensive, Mimi drinks relatively more beer. She chooses Bundle e_2, 44.5 gallons of beer per year and 4.3 gallons of wine per year, where her indifference curve I^2 is tangent to L^2. If the price of beer falls to \$4 per unit, Mimi consumes Bundle e_3, 58.9 gallons of beer per year and 5.2 gallons of wine per year. The lower the price of beer, the happier Mimi is because she can consume more on the same budget: She is on a higher indifference curve (or perhaps just higher).

Panel a also shows the *price-consumption curve*, which is the line through the optimal bundles, such as e_1, e_2, and e_3, that Mimi would consume at each price of beer, when the price of wine and Mimi's budget are held constant. Because the price-consumption curve is upward sloping, we know that Mimi's consumption of both beer and wine increases as the price of beer falls.

We can use the same information in the price-consumption curve to draw Mimi's demand curve, D^1, for beer in panel b. Corresponding to each possible price of beer on the vertical axis of panel b, we record on the horizontal axis the quantity of beer demanded by Mimi from the price-consumption curve.

Points E_1, E_2, and E_3 on the demand curve in panel b correspond to Bundles e_1, e_2, and e_3 on the price-consumption curve in panel a. Both e_1 and E_1 show that when the price of beer is \$12, Mimi demands 26.7 gallons of beer per year. When the price falls to \$6 per unit, Mimi increases her consumption to 44.5 gallons of beer, point E_2. The demand curve for beer is downward sloping, as predicted by the Law of Demand.

We can use the relationship between the points in panels a and b to show that Mimi's utility is lower at point E_1 on D^1 than at point E_2. Point E_1 corresponds to Bundle e_1 on indifference curve I^1, whereas E_2 corresponds to Bundle e_2 on indifference curve I^2, which is farther from the origin than I^1, so Mimi's utility is higher at E_2 than at E_1. Mimi is better off at E_2 than at E_1 because the price of beer is lower at E_2, so she can buy more goods with the same budget.

---

[4] To ensure that the prices are whole numbers, we state the prices with respect to an unusual unit of measure (not gallons).

[5] These figures are the U.S. average annual per capita consumption of wine and beer. These numbers are surprisingly high given that they reflect an average of teetotalers and (apparently very heavy) drinkers. According to the World Health Organization statistics for 2008, consumption of liters of pure alcohol per capita by people 15 years and older was 8.6 in the United States compared to 0.2 in Algeria, 4.6 in Mexico, 5.5 in Norway, 7.0 in Iceland, 7.8 in Canada, 8.0 in Italy, 9.0 in Australia, 9.7 in New Zealand, 9.7 in the Netherlands, 10.8 in Switzerland, 11.4 in France, 11.5 in Portugal, 11.8 in the United Kingdom, 12.0 in Germany, 13.0 in the Czech Republic, 13.7 in Ireland, and 15.6 in Luxembourg.

APPLICATION

Calling It Quits on Smoking

I phoned my dad to tell him I had stopped smoking. He called me a quitter.
—Steven Pearl

Tobacco use, one of the biggest public health threats the world has ever faced, killed 100 million people in the twentieth century. Today, tobacco kills 5.4 million people a year, and half of all users. Of the more than one billion smokers in the world, more than 80% live in low- and middle-income countries.

One way to get people to quit smoking is to raise the relative price of tobacco to that of other goods (thereby changing the slope of the budget constraints that individuals face). In poorer countries, smokers are giving up cigarettes to buy cell phones. As cell phones have recently become affordable in many poorer countries, the price ratio of cell phones to tobacco has fallen substantially. To pay for mobile phones, consumers reduce their expenditures on other goods including tobacco (see Question 2 at the end of the chapter).

According to Labonne and Chase (2008), in 2003 before cell phones were common, 42% of households in the Philippine villages they studied used tobacco, and 2% of total village income was spent on tobacco in 2003. After mobile phone ownership quadrupled from 2003 to 2006, mobile phone ownership led to a drop in tobacco consumption by a fifth for the entire population and by a third in households in which at least one member had smoked.

In developed countries, cigarette taxes are often used to increase the price of cigarettes relative to other goods. Lower-income and younger populations are more likely than others to quit smoking if the price rises. Colman and Remler (2008) estimated that price elasticities of demand for cigarettes among low-, middle-, and high-income groups, are -0.37, -0.35, and -0.20, respectively. Several economic studies estimate that the price elasticity of demand is between -0.3 and -0.6 for the U.S. population and between -0.6 and -0.7 for children. When the after-tax price of cigarettes in Canada increased 158% from 1979 to 1991 (after adjusting for inflation), teenage smoking dropped by 61%, and overall smoking fell by 38%.

But what happens to those who continue to smoke heavily? To pay for their now more expensive habit, they have to reduce their expenditures on other goods, such as housing and food. Busch et al. (2004) found that a 10% increase in the price of cigarettes causes poor smoking families to cut back on cigarettes by 9%, alcohol and transportation by 11%, food by 17%, and health care by 12%. Poor smoking families allocate 36% of their expenditures to housing compared to 40% for nonsmokers. Thus, to continue to smoke, these people cut back on many basic goods.

4.2 Effects of an Increase in Income

It is better to be nouveau riche than never to have been riche at all.

An increase in an individual's income, holding tastes and prices constant, causes a *shift of the demand curve*. An increase in income causes a parallel shift of the budget constraint away from the origin, prompting a consumer to choose a new optimal bundle with more of some or all of the goods.

How Income Changes Shift Demand Curves

We illustrate the relationship between the quantity demanded and income by examining how Mimi's behavior changes when her income rises while the prices of beer and wine remain constant. Figure 4.3 shows three ways of looking at the relation-

Figure 4.3 Effect of a Budget Increase

As the annual budget for wine and beer, Y, increases from $419 to $628 and then to $837, holding prices constant, the typical consumer buys more of both products, as the upward slope of the income-consumption curve illustrates (a). That the typical consumer buys more beer as income increases is shown by the outward shift of the demand curve for beer (b) and the upward slope of the Engel curve for beer (c).

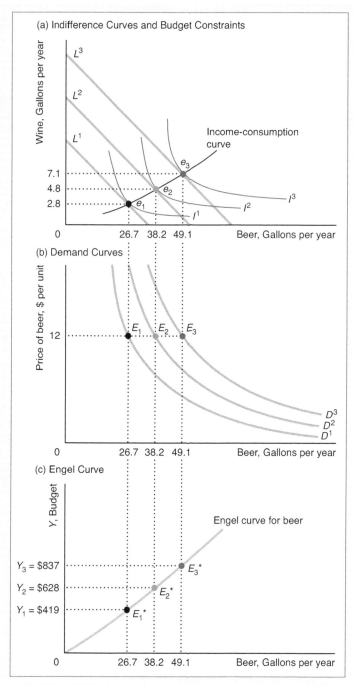

ship between income and the quantity demanded. All three diagrams have the same horizontal axis: the quantity of beer consumed per year. In the consumer theory diagram, panel a, the vertical axis is the quantity of wine consumed per year. In the demand curve diagram, panel b, the vertical axis is the price of beer per unit. Finally, in panel c, which directly shows the relationship between income and the quantity of beer demanded, the vertical axis is Mimi's budget, Y.

A rise in Mimi's income causes a parallel shift out of the budget constraint in panel a, which increases Mimi's opportunity set. Her budget constraint L^1 at her original income, $Y = \$419$, is tangent to her indifference curve I^1 at e_1.

As before, Mimi's demand curve for beer is D^1 in panel b. Point E_1 on D^1, which corresponds to point e_1 in panel a, shows how much beer, 26.7 gallons per year, Mimi consumes when the price of beer is \$12 per unit and the price of wine is \$35 per unit.

Now suppose that Mimi's beer and wine budget, Y, increases by roughly 50% to \$628 per year. Her new budget line, L^2 in panel a, is farther from the origin but parallel to her original budget constraint, L^1, because the prices of beer and wine are unchanged. Given this larger budget, Mimi chooses Bundle e_2. The increase in her income causes her demand curve to shift to D^2 in panel b. Holding Y at \$628, we can derive D^2 by varying the price of beer in the same way that we derived D^1 in Figure 4.2. When the price of beer is \$12 per unit, she buys 38.2 gallons of beer per year, E_2 on D^2. Similarly, if Mimi's income increases to \$837 per year, her demand curve shifts to D^3.

The *income-consumption curve* through Bundles e_1, e_2, and e_3 in panel a shows how Mimi's consumption of beer and wine increases as her income rises.[6] As Mimi's income goes up, her consumption of both wine and beer increases.

We can show the relationship between the quantity demanded and income directly rather than by shifting demand curves to illustrate the effect. In panel c, we plot an **Engel curve**, which shows the relationship between the quantity demanded of a single good and income, holding prices constant. Income is on the vertical axis, and the quantity of beer demanded is on the horizontal axis. On Mimi's Engel curve for beer, points E_1^*, E_2^*, and E_3^* correspond to points E_1, E_2, and E_3 in panel b and to e_1, e_2, and e_3 in panel a.

SOLVED PROBLEM 4.1	Mahdu views Coke and Pepsi as perfect substitutes: He is indifferent as to which one he drinks. The price of a 12-ounce can of Coke, p_1, is less than the price of a 12-ounce can of Pepsi, p_2. What does Mahdu's Engel curve for Coke look like? How much does his weekly cola budget have to rise for Mahdu to buy one more can of Coke per week?

Answer

1. *Use indifference curves to derive Mahdu's optimal choice.* Because Mahdu views the two brands as perfect substitutes, his indifference curves, such as I and I^* in panel a of the graph, are straight lines with a slope of -1 (see Chapter 3). When his income is Y, his budget line hits the Pepsi axis at Y/p_2 and his Coke axis at Y/p_1. Mahdu maximizes his utility by consuming Y/p_1 cans of the less expensive Coke and no Pepsi (corner solution). As his income rises, say, to Y^*, his budget line shifts outward and is parallel to the original line, with the same slope of $-p_1/p_2$. Thus, at each income level, his budget lines are flatter than his indifference curves, so his equilibria lie along the Coke axis.

2. *Use the first figure to derive his Engel curve.* Because his entire budget, Y, goes to buying Coke, Mahdu buys $q_1 = Y/p_1$ cans of Coke. This expression, which

---

[6]*Jargon alert*: Some economists refer to the income-consumption curve as the *income-expansion path*.

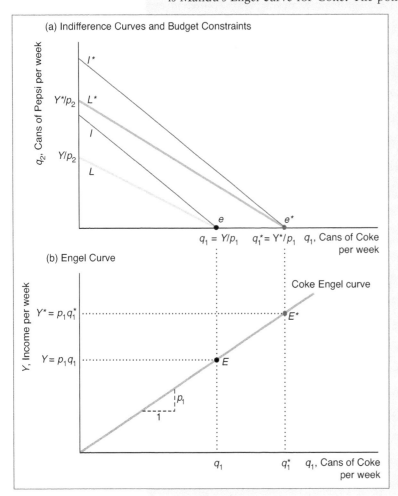

shows the relationship between his income and the quantity of Coke he buys, is Mahdu's Engel curve for Coke. The points E and E^* on the Engel curve in panel b correspond to e and e^* in panel a. We can rewrite this expression for his Engel curve as $Y = p_1 q_1$. Panel b shows that the Engle curve is a straight line. As q_1 increases by one can (the "run"), Y increases by p_1 (the "rise"), so the slope of this Engel curve is p_1 (= rise/run = $p_1/1$). Because his entire cola budget goes to buy Coke, his income needs to rise by only p_1 for him to buy one more can of Coke per week.

Consumer Theory and Income Elasticities

Income elasticities tell us how much the quantity demanded of a product changes as income increases. We can use income elasticities to summarize the shape of the Engel curve or the shape of the income-consumption curve. Such knowledge is useful. For example, firms use income elasticities to predict the impact that a change in the income tax will have on the demand for their goods.

Income Elasticity. The *income elasticity of demand* (or *income elasticity*) is the percentage change in the quantity demanded of a product in response to a given percentage change in income, Y (Chapter 2):

$$\xi = \frac{\text{percentage change in quantity demanded}}{\text{percentage change in income}} = \frac{\Delta Q/Q}{\Delta Y/Y} = \frac{\partial Q}{\partial Y} \frac{Y}{Q},$$

where ξ is the Greek letter xi.

Mimi's income elasticity of beer, ξ_b, is 0.88 and that of wine, ξ_w, is 1.38 (based on our estimates for the average American consumer). When her income goes up by 1%, she consumes 0.88% more beer and 1.38% more wine. Similarly, as her income falls by 1%, she reduces her consumption of beer by 0.88% and wine by 1.38%. Contrary to frequent (and unsubstantiated) claims in the media, average Americans do not drink more as their incomes fall during a recession—they drink less.

Some goods have negative income elasticities: $\xi < 0$. A good is called an **inferior good** if less of it is demanded as income rises. No value judgment is intended by the use of the term *inferior*. An inferior good need not be defective or of low quality. Some of the better-known examples of inferior goods are starchy foods such as potatoes and cassava, which very poor people typically eat in large quantities because they cannot afford meats or other foods. Some economists—apparently seriously—claim that human meat is an inferior good: Only when the price of other foods is very high and people are starving will they turn to cannibalism. Bezmen and Depken (2006) estimate that pirated goods are inferior: A 1% increase in per-capita income leads to a 0.25% reduction in piracy.

A good is called a **normal good** if more of it is demanded as income rises. Thus, a good is a normal good if its income elasticity is greater than or equal to zero: $\xi \geq 0$. Most goods, including beer and wine, have positive income elasticities and thus are called normal goods.

If the quantity demanded of a normal good rises more than in proportion to a person's income, $\xi > 1$, we say it is a *luxury good*. On the other hand, if the quantity demanded rises less than or in proportion to the person's income ($0 \leq \xi \leq 1$), we say it is a *necessity*. Because Mimi's income elasticities are 0.88 for beer but 1.38 for wine, Mimi views beer as a necessity and wine as a luxury according to our terminology.

A good that is inferior for some people may be superior for others. One strange example concerns treating children as a consumption good. Even though people can't buy children in a market, people can decide how many children to have. Willis (1973) estimated the income elasticity for the number of children in a family. He found that children are an inferior good, $\xi = -0.18$, if the wife has relatively little education and the family has an average income: These families have fewer children as their income increases. In contrast, children are a normal good, $\xi = 0.044$, in families in which the wife is relatively well educated. However, for both types of families, the income elasticities are close to zero, so the number of children demanded by either family is not very sensitive to income.

Income-Consumption Curves and Income Elasticities. The shape of the income-consumption curve for two goods tells us the sign of their income elasticities: whether the income elasticities for those goods are positive or negative. To illustrate the relationship between the slope of the income-consumption curve and the sign of income elasticities, we examine Peter's choices of food and housing. Peter purchases Bundle e in Figure 4.4 when his budget constraint is L^1. When his income increases so that his budget constraint is L^2, he selects a bundle on L^2. Which bundle he buys depends on his tastes—his indifference curves.

The horizontal and vertical dotted lines through e divide the new budget line, L^2, into three sections. The section where the new optimal bundle is located determines Peter's income elasticities of food and clothing.

Suppose that Peter's indifference curve is tangent to L^2 at a point in the upper-left section of L^2 (to the left of the vertical dotted line that goes through e) such as a. If Peter's income-consumption curve is ICC^1, which goes from e through a, he buys more housing and less food as his income rises, so housing is a normal good for Peter and food is an inferior good. (Although we draw these possible ICC curves as straight lines for simplicity, they could be curves.)

Figure 4.4 Income-Consumption Curves and Income Elasticities

At the initial income, the budget constraint is L^1 and the optimal bundle is e. After income rises, the new constraint is L^2. With an upward-sloping income-consumption curve such as ICC^2, both goods are normal. With an income-consumption curve such as ICC^1, which goes through the upper-left section of L^2 (to the left of the vertical dotted line through e), housing is normal and food is inferior. With an income-consumption curve such as ICC^3, which cuts L^2 in the lower-right section (below the horizontal dotted line through e), food is normal and housing is inferior.

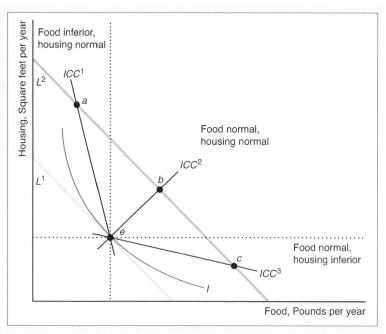

If instead the new optimal bundle is located in the middle section of L^2 (above the horizontal dotted line and to the right of the vertical dotted line), such as at b, his income-consumption curve ICC^2 through e and b is upward sloping. He buys more of both goods as his income rises, so both food and housing are normal goods.

Finally, suppose that his new optimal bundle is in the bottom-right segment of L^2 (below the horizontal dotted line). If his new optimal bundle is c, his income-consumption curve ICC^3 slopes downward from e through c. As his income rises, Peter consumes more food and less housing, so food is a normal good and housing is an inferior good.

Some Goods Must Be Normal. It is impossible for all goods to be inferior, as Figure 4.4 illustrates. At his original income, Peter faces budget constraint L^1 and buys the combination of food and housing e. When his income goes up, his budget constraint shifts outward to L^2. Depending on his tastes (the shape of his indifference curves), he may buy more housing and less food, such as Bundle a; more of both, such as b; or more food and less housing, such as c. Therefore, either both goods are normal or one good is normal and the other is inferior.

If both goods were inferior, Peter would buy less of both goods as his income rises—which makes no sense. Were he to buy less of both, he would be buying a bundle that lies inside his original budget constraint, L^1. Even at his original, relatively low income, he could have purchased that bundle but chose not to, buying e instead.[7]

A good may be normal at some income levels and inferior at others. When Gail was poor and her income increased slightly, she ate meat more frequently, and her

---

[7]Even if an individual does not buy more of the usual goods and services, that person may put the extra money into savings. We can use the consumer theory model to treat savings as a good if we allow for multiple periods. Empirical studies find that savings is a normal good.

meat of choice was hamburger. Thus, when her income was low, hamburger was a normal good. As her income increased further, however, she switched from hamburger to steak. Thus, at higher incomes, Gail views hamburger as an inferior good.

We show Gail's choice between hamburger (horizontal axis) and all other goods (vertical axis) in panel a of Figure 4.5. As Gail's income increases, her budget line shifts outward, from L^1 to L^2, and she buys more hamburger: Bundle e_2 lies to the right of e_1. As her income increases further, shifting her budget line outward to L^3, Gail reduces her consumption of hamburger: Bundle e_3 lies to the left of e_2.

Gail's Engel curve for hamburger in panel b captures the same relationship. At low incomes, her Engel curve is upward sloping, indicating that she buys more hamburger as her income rises. At higher incomes, her Engel curve is backward bending.

As their incomes rise, many consumers switch between lower-quality (hamburger) and higher-quality (steak) versions of the same good. This switching behavior explains the pattern of income elasticities across different qualities of cars. For example, the income elasticity of demand for a Jetta is 2.1, for an Accord is 2.2, for a BMW 700 Series is 4.4, and for a Jaguar X-Type is 4.5 (Bordley and McDonald, 1993).

Figure 4.5 A Good That Is Both Inferior and Normal

When she was poor and her income increased, Gail bought more hamburger. However, when she became wealthier and her income rose, she bought less hamburger and more steak. (a) The forward slope of the income-consumption curve from e_1 to e_2 and the backward bend from e_2 to e_3 show this pattern. (b) The forward slope of the Engel curve at low incomes, E_1 to E_2, and the backward bend at higher incomes, E_2 to E_3, also show this pattern.

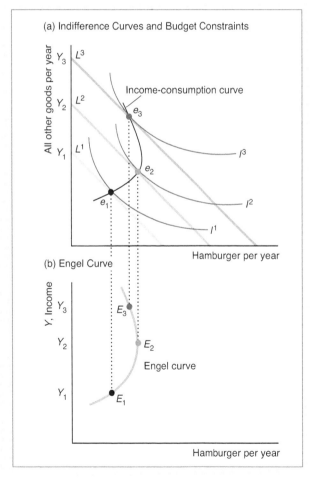

Weighted Income Elasticities. We just argued using graphical and verbal reasoning that a consumer cannot view all goods as inferior. We can derive a stronger result: The weighted sum of a consumer's income elasticities equals one. Firms and governments use this result to make predictions about income effects.

We start with the consumer's budget constraint where there are n goods consumed, p_i is the price, and q_i is the quantity for Good i:

$$p_1 q_1 + p_2 q_2 + \cdots + p_n q_n = Y.$$

By differentiating this equation with respect to income, we obtain

$$p_1 \frac{dq_1}{dY} + p_2 \frac{dq_2}{dY} + \cdots + p_n \frac{dq_n}{dY} = 1.$$

Multiplying and dividing each term by $q_i Y$, we can rewrite this equation as

$$\frac{p_1 q_1}{Y} \frac{dq_1}{dY} \frac{Y}{q_1} + \frac{p_2 q_2}{Y} \frac{dq_2}{dY} \frac{Y}{q_2} + \cdots + \frac{p_n q_n}{Y} \frac{dq_n}{dY} \frac{Y}{q_n} = 1.$$

If we define the budget share of Good i as $\theta_i = p_i q_i / Y$ and note that the income elasticities are $\xi_i = (dq_i/dY)(Y/q_i)$, we can rewrite this expression to show that the weighted sum of the income elasticities equals one:

$$\theta_1 \xi_1 + \theta_2 \xi_2 + \cdots + \theta_n \xi_n = 1. \tag{4.1}$$

We can use this formula to make predictions about income elasticities. If we know the budget share of a good and a little bit about the income elasticities of some goods, we can calculate bounds on other, unknown income elasticities. Being able to obtain bounds on income elasticities is very useful to governments and firms. For example, over the last couple of decades, many Western manufacturing firms, learning that Chinese incomes were rising rapidly, have tried to estimate the income elasticities for their products among Chinese consumers to decide whether to enter the Chinese market.

SOLVED PROBLEM 4.2

A firm is considering building a plant in a developing country to sell manufactured goods in that country. The firm expects incomes to start rising soon and wants to know the income elasticity for goods other than food. The firm knows that the budget share spent on food is θ and that food is a necessity (its income elasticity, ξ_f, is between 0 and 1). The firm wants to know "How large could the income elasticity of all other goods, ξ_o, be? How small could it be?" What were the bounds on ξ_o for Chinese urban consumers whose θ was 60% in 1983? What are the bounds today when θ is 37%?[8]

Answer

1. *Write Equation 4.1 in terms of ξ_f, ξ_o, and θ, and then use algebra to rewrite this expression with the income elasticity of other goods on the left-hand side.* By substituting ξ_f, ξ_o, and θ into Equation 4.1, we find that

$$\theta \xi_f + (1 - \theta) \xi_o = 1.$$

We can rewrite this expression with the income elasticity of other goods—the number we want to estimate—on the left-hand side:

$$\xi_o = \frac{1 - \theta \xi_f}{1 - \theta}. \tag{4.2}$$

---

[8]State Statistical Bureau, *Statistical Yearbook of China*, State Statistical Bureau Publishing House, Beijing, China, various years.

2. *Use Equation 4.2 and the bounds on ξ_f to derive bounds on ξ_o.* Because $\xi_o = (1 - \theta\xi_f)/(1 - \theta)$, ξ_o is smaller the larger is ξ_f. Given that food is a necessity, the largest ξ_o can be is $1/(1 - \theta)$, where $\xi_f = 0$. The smallest it can be is $\xi_o = 1$, which occurs if $\xi_f = 1$. [*Note*: If ξ_f equals one, $\xi_o = (1 - \theta)/(1 - \theta) = 1$ regardless of food's budget share, θ.]

3. *Substitute for the two Chinese values of ω to determine the upper bounds.* The upper bound for ξ_o was $1/(1 - \theta) = 1/0.4 = 2.5$ in 1983 and $1/0.63 \approx 1.59$ now.

Comment: The upper bound on the income elasticity of non-food goods in the United States is lower than in China because the share of consumption of food in the United States is smaller. The U.S. share of expenditures on food was 22% for welfare recipients and 14% for others in 2001–2002 (Paszkiewicz, 2005). Thus, the upper bound on ξ_o was about 1.28 for welfare recipients and 1.16 for others. From Equation 4.2, $\xi_o = (1 - \theta\xi_f)/(1 - \theta) \approx 1.16 - 0.16\xi_f$ for non-welfare recipients. Most estimates of the U.S. ξ_f range between 0.4 and 0.9, so ξ_o must range from about 1.02 to 1.10 for this group.

4.3 Effects of a Price Increase

Holding tastes, other prices, and income constant, an increase in a price of a good has two effects on an individual's demand. One is the **substitution effect**: the change in the quantity of a good that a consumer demands when the good's price rises, holding other prices and the consumer's utility constant. If the consumer's utility is held constant as the price of the good increases, the consumer *substitutes* other goods that are now relatively cheaper for this now more expensive good.

The other effect is the **income effect**: the change in the quantity of a good a consumer demands because of a change in income, holding prices constant. An increase in price reduces a consumer's buying power, effectively reducing the consumer's *income* or opportunity set and causing the consumer to buy less of at least some goods. A doubling of the price of all the goods the consumer buys is equivalent to a drop in the consumer's income to half its original level. Even a rise in the price of only one good reduces a consumer's ability to buy the same amount of all goods previously purchased. For example, when the price of food increases in a poor country in which half or more of the population's income is spent on food, the effective purchasing power of the population falls substantially.

When the price of a product rises, the total change in the quantity purchased is the sum of the substitution effect and the income effect. When economists estimate the effect of a product's price change on the quantity an individual demands, they decompose the combined effect into the two separate components. By doing so, they gain extra information that they can use to answer questions about whether inflation measures are accurate, whether an increase in tax rates will raise tax revenue, and what the effects are of government policies that compensate some consumers. For example, President Jimmy Carter, when advocating a tax on gasoline, and President Bill Clinton, when calling for an energy tax, proposed providing an income compensation for poor consumers to offset the harms of the tax. We can use our knowledge of the substitution and income effects from energy price changes to evaluate the effect of these policies.

Income and Substitution Effects with a Normal Good

To illustrate the substitution and income effects, we return to Jackie's choice between music tracks and live music based on our estimate of the average person's Cobb-Douglas utility function (see the application "*MRS Between Recorded Tracks and Live Music*" in Chapter 3). The price of a unit of live music is $p_2 = £1$, and the price of downloading a music track is $p_1 = £0.5$. Now, suppose that the price of music tracks rises to £1, causing Jackie's budget constraint to rotate inward from L^1 to L^2 in Figure 4.6. The new budget constraint, L^2, is twice as steep ($-p_1/p_2 = -1/1 = -1$) as L^1 ($-0.5/1 = -0.5$).

Because of the price increase, Jackie's opportunity set is smaller, so she must choose between fewer bundles of music tracks and live music than she could at the lower price. The area between the two budget constraints reflects the decrease in her opportunity set owing to the increase in the price of music tracks.

In Chapter 3, we determined that Jackie's demand functions for music tracks (songs), q_1, and live music, q_2, were

$$q_1 = 0.4 \frac{Y}{p_1}, \qquad (4.3)$$

$$q_2 = 0.6 \frac{Y}{p_2}. \qquad (4.4)$$

At the original price of tracks and with an entertainment budget of £30 per quarter, Jackie chooses Bundle e_1, $q_1 = 0.4 \times 30/0.5 = 24$ tracks and $q_2 = 0.6 \times 30/1 = 18$ units of live music per quarter, where her indifference curve I^1 is tangent to her budget constraint L^1. When the price of tracks rises, Jackie's new optimal bundle is e_2 (where she buys $q_1 = 0.4 \times 30/1 = 12$ tracks), which occurs where her indifference curve I^2 is tangent to L^2.

Figure 4.6 Substitution and Income Effects with Normal Goods

An increase in the price of music tracks from £0.5 to £1 causes Jackie's budget line to rotate from L^1 to L^2. The imaginary budget line L^* has the same slope as L^2 and is tangent to indifference curve I^1. The shift of the optimal bundle from e_1 to e_2 is the *total effect* of the price change. The total effect can be decomposed into the *substitution effect*—the movement from e_1 to e^*—and the *income effect*—the movement from e^* to e_2.

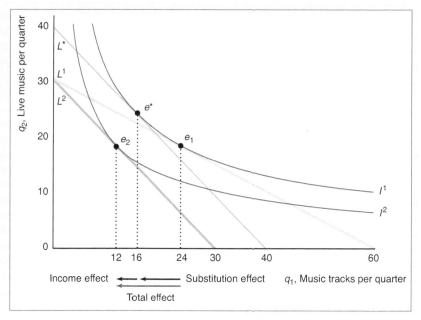

The movement from e_1 to e_2 is the total change in her consumption owing to the rise in the price of music tracks. In particular, the *total effect* on Jackie's consumption of tracks from the rise in their price is that she now buys 12 (= 24 − 12) fewer tracks per quarter. In the figure, the red arrow pointing to the left labeled "Total effect" shows this decrease. We can break the total effect into a substitution effect and an income effect.

As the price increases, Jackie's opportunity set shrinks even though her income is unchanged. If, as a thought experiment, we compensate her for this loss by giving her extra income, we can determine her substitution effect. The substitution effect is the change in the quantity demanded from a *compensated change in the price* of music tracks, which occurs when we increase Jackie's income by enough to offset the rise in price so that her utility stays constant. To determine the substitution effect, we draw an imaginary budget constraint, L^*, that is parallel to L^2 and tangent to Jackie's original indifference curve, I^1. This imaginary budget constraint, L^*, has the same slope, −1, as L^2 because both curves are based on the new, higher price of tracks. For L^* to be tangent to I^1, we need to increase Jackie's budget from £30 to £40 to offset the harm from the higher price of music tracks. If Jackie's budget constraint were L^*, she would choose Bundle e^*, where she buys $q_1 = 0.4 \times 40/1 = 16$ tracks.

Thus, if the price of tracks rises relative to that of live music and we hold Jackie's utility constant by raising her income, Jackie's optimal bundle shifts from e_1 to e^*, which is the substitution effect. She buys 8 (= 24 − 16) fewer tracks per quarter, as the arrow pointing to the left labeled "Substitution effect" shows.

Jackie also faces an income effect because the increase in the price of tracks shrinks Jackie's opportunity set, so that Jackie must buy a bundle on a lower indifference curve. As a thought experiment, we can ask how much we would have to lower her income while holding prices constant for her to choose a bundle on this new, lower indifference curve. The *income effect* is the change in the quantity of a good a consumer demands because of a change in income, holding prices constant. The parallel shift of the budget constraint from L^* to L^2 captures this effective decrease in income. The movement from e^* to e_2 is the income effect, as the arrow pointing to the left labeled "Income effect" shows. As her budget decreases from £40 to £30, Jackie consumes 4 (= 16 − 12) fewer tracks per quarter.

The *total effect* from the price change is the *sum of the substitution and income effects*, as the arrows show. Jackie's total effect (in tracks per quarter) from a rise in the price of tracks is

$$\text{total effect} = \text{substitution effect} + \text{income effect}$$
$$-12 \quad = \quad -8 \quad + \quad (-4).$$

Because indifference curves are convex to the origin, *the substitution effect is unambiguous*: Less of a good is consumed when its price rises. A consumer always substitutes a less-expensive good for a more expensive one, if we hold the consumer's utility constant. The substitution effect causes a *movement along an indifference curve*.

The income effect causes a shift to another indifference curve due to a change in the consumer's opportunity set. The direction of the income effect depends on the income elasticity. Because a music track is a normal good for Jackie, her income effect is negative. Thus, both Jackie's substitution effect and her income effect move in the same direction, so the total effect of the price rise must be negative.

Income and Substitution Effects with an Inferior Good

If a good is inferior, the income effect and the substitution effect move in opposite directions. For most inferior goods, the income effect is smaller than the substitution effect. As a result, the total effect moves in the same direction as the substitution effect, but the total effect is smaller. However, the income effect can more than offset the substitution effect for a *Giffen good*. A good is called a **Giffen good** if a decrease in its price causes the quantity demanded to fall.[9]

If music tracks are a Giffen good for Steven, a price decrease for tracks saves him money that he uses to see more live music. Indeed, he decides to increase his spending on live music even further by reducing his purchase of the tracks. Thus, the demand curve for a Giffen good has an *upward* slope. (In Question 4 at the end of the chapter, you are asked to draw an example in which you show that the Giffen good effect results from an income effect that more than offsets the substitution effect.)

However, the Law of Demand (Chapter 2) says that demand curves slope downward: Quantity demanded falls as the price rises. You're no doubt wondering how I'm going to worm my way out of this apparent contradiction. I have two explanations. The first is that I claimed that the Law of Demand is an empirical regularity, not a theoretical necessity. Although it's theoretically possible for a demand curve to slope upward, other than rice consumption in Hunan China (Jensen and Miller, 2008), economists have found few, if any, real-world examples of Giffen goods.[10] My second explanation is that the Law of Demand must hold theoretically for compensated demand curves, which we examine next.

Compensated Demand Curve

So far, the demand curves that we have derived graphically and mathematically allow a consumer's utility to vary as the price of the good increases. For example, a consumer's utility falls if the price of one of the goods rises. Consequently, the consumer's demand curve reflects both the substitution and income effects as the price of the product changes.

As panel a of Figure 4.2 illustrates, Mimi chooses a bundle on a lower indifference curve as the price of beer rises, so her utility level falls. Along her demand curve for beer, we hold other prices, income, and her tastes constant, while allowing her utility to vary. We can observe this type of demand curve by seeing how the purchases of a product change as its price increases. It is called *the* demand curve, the Marshallian demand curve (after Alfred Marshall, who popularized this approach), or the *uncompensated demand curve*. (Unless otherwise noted, when we talk about a demand curve, we mean the uncompensated demand curve.)

Alternatively, we could derive a *compensated demand curve*, which shows how the quantity demanded changes as the price rises, holding utility constant, so that the change in the quantity demanded reflects only the pure substitution effect from a price change. It is called the compensated demand curve because we would have to compensate an individual—give the individual extra income—as the price rises so as to hold the individual's utility constant. The compensated demand curve is also called the Hicksian demand curve, after John Hicks, who introduced the idea.

The compensated demand function for the first good is

$$q_1 = H(p_1, p_2, \overline{U}), \tag{4.5}$$

---

[9]Robert Giffen, a nineteenth-century British economist, argued that poor people in Ireland increased their consumption of potatoes when the price rose because of a potato blight. However, more recent studies of the Irish potato famine dispute this observation.

[10]However, Battalio, Kagel, and Kogut (1991) showed in an experiment that quinine water is a Giffen good for lab rats.

where we hold utility constant at $\bar{U}$. We cannot observe the compensated demand curve directly because we do not observe utility levels. Because the compensated demand curve reflects only substitution effects, the Law of Demand must hold: A price increase causes the compensated demand for a good to fall.

In Figure 4.7, we derive Jackie's compensated demand function, H, evaluated at her initial indifference curve, I, where her utility is $\bar{U}$. In 2008, the price of music tracks was $p_1 = £0.5$ and the price per unit of live music was $p_2 = £1$. At those prices, Jackie's budget line, L, has a slope of $-p_1/p_2 = -0.5/1 = -\tfrac{1}{2}$ and is tangent to I at e_2 in panel a. At this optimal bundle, she buys 24 tracks. The corresponding point E_2 on her compensated demand curve in panel b shows that she buys 24 tracks when they cost £0.5 each.

Figure 4.7 Deriving Jackie's Compensated Demand Curve

Initially, Jackie's optimal bundle is determined by the tangency of budget line L and indifference curve I in panel a. If we vary the price of music tracks but change her budget so that the new line (segments) are tangent to the same indifference curve, we can determine how the quantity that she demands varies with price, holding her utility constant. Hence, the corresponding quantities in panel b on her compensated demand curve reflect the pure substitution effect of a price change.

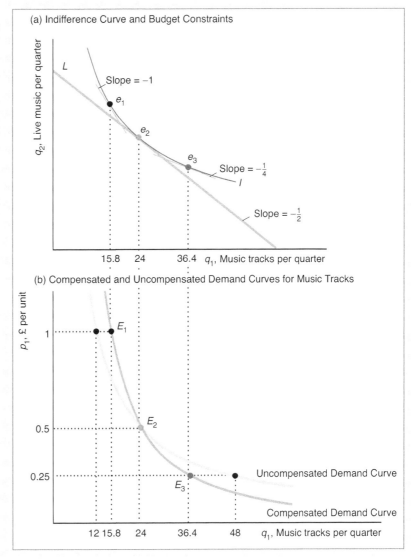

The two thin blue line segments in panel a show portions of other budget lines where we change p_1 and adjust Jackie's income to keep her on indifference curve I. At the budget line segment in the upper left, the price of tracks is £1, so Jackie's budget line's slope is -1. Her budget is increased enough that her new budget line is tangent to the original indifference curve, I, at e_1. This optimal bundle corresponds to E_1 on her compensated demand curve in panel b. Similarly, when p_1 is £0.25, we decrease her budget so that this budget line is tangent to her original indifference curve at e_3, which corresponds to E_3 on her compensated demand curve.

Panel b also shows Jackie's uncompensated demand curve: Equation 4.3, $q_1 = 0.4Y/p_1$. Her compensated and uncompensated demand curves *must* cross at the original price, $p_1 = £0.5$, where the original budget line, L, is tangent to I along which utility is $\bar{U}$. At that price, and only at that price, both demand curves are derived using the same budget line. The compensated demand curve is steeper than the uncompensated curve around this common point. The reason is that the compensated demand curve reflects only the substitution effect, unlike the uncompensated demand curve, along which the income effect reinforces the substitution effect (because a music track is a normal good for Jackie).

One way to derive the compensated demand curve is to use the expenditure function, Equation 3.32,

$$E = E(p_1, p_2, \bar{U}),$$

where E is the smallest expenditure that allows the consumer to achieve utility level $\bar{U}$, given market prices. If we differentiate the expenditure function with respect to the price of the first good, we obtain the compensated demand function for that good:[11]

$$\frac{\partial E}{\partial p_1} = H(p_1, p_2, \bar{U}) = q_1. \tag{4.6}$$

One informal explanation for Equation 4.6 is that if p_1 increases by \$1 on each of the q_1 units that the consumer buys, then the minimum amount the consumer must spend to keep his or her utility constant must increase by $\$q_1$. This expression can also be interpreted as the pure substitution effect on the quantity demanded because we are holding the consumer's utility constant as we change the price.

Slutsky Equation

We have shown graphically that the total effect from a price change can be decomposed into a substitution effect and an income effect. That same relationship can be derived mathematically. We can use this relationship in a variety of ways. For example, we can apply it to determine how likely a good is to be a Giffen good based on whether the consumer spends a relatively large or small share of the budget on this

---

[11]This result is called Shephard's lemma. As we showed in Solved Problem 3.8, we can use Lagrange's method to derive the expenditure function, where we want to minimize $E = p_1 q_1 + p_2 q_2$ subject to $\bar{U} = U(q_1, q_2)$. The Lagrangian equation is

$$\lambda = p_1 q_1 + p_2 q_2 + l[\bar{U} - U(q_1, q_2)].$$

According to the envelope theorem (see the Calculus Appendix), at the optimum,

$$\frac{\partial E}{\partial p_1} = \frac{\partial \mathcal{L}}{\partial p_1} = q_1,$$

which is Equation 4.6. It shows that the derivative of the expenditure function with respect to p_1 is q_1, the quantity that the consumer demands.

SOLVED PROBLEM 4.3

A consumer has a Cobb-Douglas utility function $U = q_1^a q_1^{1-a}$. Derive the compensated demand function for good q_1. Given that $a = 0.4$ in Jackie's utility function, what is her compensated demand function for music tracks, q_1?

Answer

1. *Write the formula for the expenditure function for this Cobb-Douglas utility function.* We derived this expenditure function in Solved Problem 3.8:

$$E = \overline{U}\left(\frac{p_1}{a}\right)^a \left(\frac{p_2}{1-a}\right)^{1-a}. \tag{4.7}$$

2. *Differentiate the expenditure function in Equation 4.7 with respect to p_1 to obtain the compensated demand function for q_1, making use of Equation 4.6.* The compensated demand function is

$$q_1 = \frac{E}{p_1} = \overline{U}\left(\frac{a}{1-a}\frac{p_2}{p_1}\right)^{1-a}. \tag{4.8}$$

3. *Substitute Jackie's value of a in Equation 4.7 to obtain her expenditure function, and in Equation 4.8 to obtain her compensated demand function for tracks.* Given that her $a = 0.4$, Jackie's expenditure function is

$$E = \overline{U}\left(\frac{p_1}{0.4}\right)^{0.4}\left(\frac{p_2}{0.6}\right)^{0.6} \approx 1.96\overline{U}p_1^{0.4}p_2^{0.6}, \tag{4.9}$$

and her compensated demand function for tracks is

$$q_1 = \overline{U}\left(\frac{0.4}{0.6}\frac{p_2}{p_1}\right)^{0.6} \approx 0.784\overline{U}\left(\frac{p_2}{p_1}\right)^{0.6}. \tag{4.10}$$

Comment: We showed above that when Jackie's quarterly budget is $Y = £30$ and she faces prices of $p_1 = £0.5$ and $p_2 = £1$, she chooses $q_1 = 24$ and $q_2 = 18$. The corresponding indifference curve is $\overline{U} = 24^{0.4}18^{0.6} \approx 20.2$. Thus, at the initial prices, her compensated demand for tracks, Equation 4.10, is $q_1 \approx 0.784 \times 20.2(1/0.5)^{0.6} \approx 24$, which is reassuring because the compensated and uncompensated demand curves must cross at the initial prices.

---

good. We can also use the relationship to determine the effect of government policies that compensate some consumers.

The usual price elasticity of demand, ε, captures the total effect of a price change—that is, the change along an uncompensated demand curve. We can break this price elasticity of demand into two terms involving elasticities that capture the substitution and income effects. We measure the substitution effect using the pure *substitution elasticity of demand*, ε^*, which is the percentage that the quantity demanded falls for a given percentage increase in price if we compensate the consumer to keep the consumer's utility constant. That is, ε^* is the elasticity of the compensated demand curve. The income effect is the income elasticity, ξ, times the share of the budget spent on that good, θ. This relationship among the price elasticity of demand, ε, the substitution elasticity of demand, ε^*, and the income elasticity of demand, ξ, is the *Slutsky equation* (named after its discoverer, the Russian economist Eugene Slutsky):[12]

$$\text{total effect} = \text{substitution effect} + \text{income effect}$$
$$\varepsilon = \varepsilon^* + (-\theta\xi). \qquad (4.11)$$

If a consumer spends little on a good, a change in its price does not affect the person's total budget significantly. For example, if the price of garlic triples, your purchasing power will hardly be affected (unless perhaps you are a vampire slayer). Thus, the total effect, ε, for garlic hardly differs from the substitution effect, ε^*, because the price change has little effect on the consumer's income.

In Mimi's original optimal bundle, e_1 in Figure 4.2, where the price of beer was $12 and Mimi bought 26.7 gallons of beer per year, Mimi spent about three-quarters of her $419 beverage budget on beer: $\theta = 0.76 = (12 \times 26.7)/419$. Her income elasticity is $\xi = 0.88$, her price elasticity is $\varepsilon = -0.76$, and her substitution price elasticity is $\varepsilon^* = -0.09$. Thus, Mimi's Slutsky equation is

$$\varepsilon = \varepsilon^* - \theta\xi$$
$$-0.76 \approx -0.09 - 0.76 \times 0.88.$$

Because beer is a normal good for Mimi, the income effect reinforces the substitution effect. Indeed, the size of the total change, $\varepsilon = -0.76$, is due more to the income effect, $-\theta\xi = -0.67$, than to the substitution effect, $\varepsilon^* = -0.09$. If the price of beer rises by 1% but Mimi is given just enough extra income so that her utility remains constant, Mimi would reduce her consumption of beer by less than a tenth of a percent (substitution effect). Without compensation, Mimi reduces her consumption of beer by about three-quarters of a percent (total effect).

Similarly, in Jackie's original optimum, e_1 in Figure 4.6, the price of a track was £0.5, and Jackie bought 24 tracks per year. She spent $\theta = 0.4$ share of her budget on tracks (see Solved Problem 3.7). Her uncompensated demand function, Equation 4.3, is $q_1 = 0.4Y/p_1$, so her price elasticity of demand is $\varepsilon = -1$, and her income elasticity is $\xi = 1$.[13] Her compensated demand function, Equation 4.10, is $q_1 = 0.784\overline{U}(p_2/p_1)^{0.6} = 0.784\overline{U}p_2^{0.6}p_1^{-0.6}$. Because it is a constant elasticity demand

---

[12]When we derived the compensated demand function, H, we noted that it equals the uncompensated demand function, D, at the initial optimum where utility is $\overline{U}$.

$$q_1 = H(p_1, p_2, \overline{U}) = D(p_1, p_2, Y) = D(p_1, p_2, E(p_1, p_2, \overline{U})),$$

and Y equals the minimum expenditure needed to achieve that level of utility, as given by the expenditure function. If we differentiate with respect to p_1, we find that

$$\frac{\partial H}{\partial p_1} = \frac{\partial D}{\partial p_1} + \frac{\partial D}{\partial E}\frac{\partial E}{\partial p_1} = \frac{\partial D}{\partial p_1} + \frac{\partial D}{\partial E}q_1,$$

where we know that $\partial E/\partial p_1 = q_1$ from Equation 4.6. Rearranging terms and multiplying all terms by p_1/q_1, and the last term by Y/Y, we obtain

$$\frac{\partial D}{\partial p_1}\frac{p_1}{q_1} = \frac{\partial H}{\partial p_1}\frac{p_1}{q_1} - q_1\frac{\partial D}{\partial E}\frac{p_1}{q_1}\frac{E}{E}.$$

This last expression is the Slustky Equation 4.11, where $\varepsilon = (\partial D/\partial p_1)(p_1/q_1)$, $\varepsilon^* = (\partial H/\partial p_1)(p_1/q_1)$, $\theta = p_1q_1/E$, and $\xi = (\partial D/\partial E)(p_1/E)$.

[13]We can equivalently write the demand curve as $\ln q_1 = \ln(0.4) + \ln Y - \ln p_1$, which is a constant-elasticity demand curve. We can find the price elasticity using the method in Solved Problem 2.2. Similarly, differentiating with respect to Y, we find that $(dq_1/dY)/q_1 = 1/Y$. Rearranging terms, we learn that $\xi = (dq_1/dY)(Y/q_1) = 1$.

function where the exponent on p_1 is –0.6, we know that $\varepsilon^* = -0.6$. Thus, her Slutsky equation is

$$\begin{array}{rcccc}\varepsilon & = & \varepsilon^* & - & \theta\xi \\ -1 & = & -0.6 & - & 0.4 \times 1.\end{array}$$

For a Giffen good to have an upward-sloping demand curve, ε must be positive. The substitution elasticity, ε^*, is always negative: Consumers buy less of a good when its price increases, holding utility constant. Thus, for a good to be a Giffen good and have an upward-sloping demand curve, the income effect, $-\theta\xi$, must be positive and large relative to the substitution effect. The income effect is more likely to be a large positive number if the good is very inferior (that is, ξ is a large negative number, which is not common) and the budget share, θ, is large (closer to one than to zero). One reason we don't see upward-sloping demand curves is that the goods on which consumers spend a large share of their budget, such as housing, are usually normal goods rather than inferior goods.

SOLVED PROBLEM 4.4

Next to its plant, a manufacturer of dinner plates has an outlet store that sells plates of both first quality (perfect plates) and second quality (plates with slight blemishes). The outlet store sells a relatively large share of second-quality plates (or seconds). At its regular stores elsewhere, the firm sells many more first-quality plates than second-quality plates. Why? (Assume that consumers' tastes with respect to plates are the same everywhere and that there is a cost, s, of shipping each plate from the factory to the firm's other stores.)

Answer

1. *Determine how the relative prices of plates differ between the two types of stores.* The slope of the budget line that consumers face at the factory outlet store is $-p_1/p_2$, where p_1 is the price of first-quality plates, and p_2 is the price of seconds. It costs the same, s, to ship a first-quality plate as a second because they weigh the same and have to be handled in the same way. At all retail stores, the firm adds the cost of shipping to the price it charges at its factory outlet store, so the price of a first-quality plate is $p_1 + s$ and the price of a second is $p_2 + s$. As a result, the slope of the budget line that consumers face at the retail stores is $-(p_1 + s)/(p_2 + s)$. The seconds are relatively less expensive at the factory outlet than they are at the other stores. For example, if $p_1 = \$2$, $p_2 = \$1$, and $s = \$1$ per plate, the slope of the budget line is -2 at the outlet store and $-3/2$ elsewhere. Thus, a first-quality plate costs twice as much as a second at the outlet store but only 1.5 times as much elsewhere.

2. *Use the relative price difference to explain why relatively more seconds are bought at the factory outlet.* Holding a consumer's income and tastes fixed, if the price of seconds rises relative to that of firsts (as we go from the factory outlet to the other retail shops), most consumers will buy relatively more firsts. The substitution effect is unambiguous: Were they compensated so that their utilities were held constant, consumers would unambiguously substitute firsts for seconds. It is possible that the income effect could go in the other direction (if plates are an inferior good); however, as most consumers spend relatively little of their total budgets on plates, the income effect is presumably small relative to the substitution effect. Thus, we expect relatively fewer seconds to be bought at the retail stores than at the factory outlet.

APPLICATION

Shipping the Good Stuff Away

According to the economic theory discussed in Solved Problem 4.4, we expect that the relatively larger the share is of higher-quality goods shipped, the greater the per-unit shipping fee will be. Is this theory true, and is the effect large? To answer these questions, Hummels and Skiba (2004) examined shipments between 6,000 country pairs for more than 5,000 goods. They found that doubling per-unit shipping costs results in a 70% to 143% increase in the average price of a good (excluding the cost of shipping) as a larger share of top-quality products is shipped.

The greater the distance between the trading countries, the higher was the cost of shipping. Hummels and Skiba speculate that the relatively high quality of Japanese goods is due to that country's relatively great distance from major importers.

4.4 Cost-of-Living Adjustment

In spite of the cost of living, it's still popular. —Kathleen Norris

By knowing both the substitution and income effects, we can answer questions that we could not answer if we knew only the total effect of a price change. One particularly important use of consumer theory is to analyze how accurately the government measures inflation.

Many long-term contracts and government programs include *cost-of-living adjustments* (*COLAs*), which raise prices or incomes in proportion to an index of inflation. Not only business contracts, but also rental contracts, alimony payments, salaries, pensions, and Social Security payments, are frequently adjusted in this manner over time. We will use consumer theory to show that the cost-of-living measure that governments commonly use overestimates how the true cost of living changes over time. Because of this overestimation, you overpay your landlord if the rent on your apartment rises with this measure.

Inflation Indexes

The prices of most goods rise over time. We call the increase in the overall price level *inflation*.

The actual price of a good is called the *nominal price*. The price adjusted for inflation is the *real price*. Because the overall level of prices rises over time, nominal prices usually increase more rapidly than real prices. For example, the nominal price of a McDonald's hamburger rose from 15¢ in 1955 to 89¢ in early 2010, a six-fold increase. However, the real price of the burger fell because the prices of other goods rose more rapidly than that of the burger.

How do we adjust for inflation to calculate the real price? Governments measure the cost of a standard bundle of goods, or market basket, to compare prices over time. This measure is called the Consumer Price Index (CPI). Each month, the government reports how much it costs to buy the bundle of goods that an average consumer purchased in a *base* year (with the base year changing every few years).

By comparing the cost of buying this bundle over time, we can determine how much the overall price level has increased. In the United States, the CPI was 26.8 in

1955 and 216.7 in January 2010.[14] The cost of buying the bundle of goods increased 809% ($\approx$ 216.7/26.8) from 1955 to 2010.

We can use the CPI to calculate the real price of a McDonald's hamburger over time. In terms of 2010 dollars, the real price of the hamburger in 1955 was

$$\frac{\text{CPI for 2010}}{\text{CPI for 1955}} \times \text{price of a burger} = \frac{216.7}{26.8} \times 15¢ = \$1.21.$$

If you could have purchased the hamburger in 1955 with 2010 dollars—which are worth less than 1955 dollars—the hamburger would have cost $1.21. The real price in 2010 dollars (and the nominal price) of the hamburger in 2010 was only 89¢. Thus, the real price fell by about 26%. If we compared the real prices in both years using 1955 dollars, we would reach the same conclusion that the real price of hamburgers fell by about 26%.

The government collects data on the quantities and prices of 364 individual goods and services, such as housing, dental services, watch and jewelry repairs, college tuition fees, taxi fares, women's hairpieces and wigs, hearing aids, slipcovers and decorative pillows, bananas, pork sausage, and funeral expenses. These prices rise at different rates. If the government merely reported all these price increases separately, most of us would find this information overwhelming. It is much more convenient to use a single summary statistic, the CPI, which tells us how prices rose *on average*.

We can use an example with only two goods, clothing and food, to show how the CPI is calculated. In the first year, consumers buy C_1 units of clothing and F_1 units of food at prices p_C^1 and p_F^1. We use this bundle of goods, C_1 and F_1, as our base bundle for comparison. In the second year, consumers buy C_2 and F_2 units at prices p_C^2 and p_F^2.

The government knows from its survey of prices each year that the price of clothing in the second year is p_C^2/p_C^1 times as large as the price the previous year. Similarly, the price of food is p_F^2/p_F^1 times as large as the price the previous year. For example, if the price of clothing were $1 in the first year and $2 in the second year, the price of clothing in the second year would be $\frac{2}{1} = 2$ times, or 100%, larger than in the first year.

One way we can average the price increases of each good is to weight them equally. But do we really want to do that? Do we want to give as much weight to the price increase for skateboards as to the price increase for automobiles? An alternative approach is to assign a larger weight to the price change of goods with relatively large budget shares. In constructing its averages, the CPI weights using budget shares.[15]

The CPI for the first year is the amount of income it took to buy the market basket that was actually purchased that year:

$$Y_1 = p_C^1 C_1 + p_F^1 F_1. \tag{4.12}$$

The cost of buying the first year's bundle in the second year is

$$Y_2 = p_C^2 C_1 + p_F^2 F_1. \tag{4.13}$$

---

[14]The number 216.7 is not an actual dollar amount. Rather, it is the actual dollar cost of buying the bundle divided by a constant. That constant was chosen so that the average expenditure in the period 1982–1984 was 100.

[15]This discussion of the CPI is simplified in a number of ways. Sophisticated adjustments are made to the CPI that are ignored here, including repeated updating of the base year (chaining). See Pollak (1989) and Diewert and Nakamura (1993).

That is, in the second year, we use the prices for the second year but the quantities from the first year.

To calculate the rate of inflation, we determine how much more income it took to buy the first year's bundle in the second year, which is the ratio of Equation 4.13 to Equation 4.12:

$$\frac{Y_2}{Y_1} = \frac{p_C^2 C_1 + p_F^2 F_1}{p_C^1 C_1 + p_F^1 F_1}.$$

For example, from January 2009 to January 2010, the U.S. CPI rose by $1.027 \approx Y_2/Y_1$ from $Y_1 = 211.1$ to $Y_2 = 216.7$. Thus, it cost on average 2.7% more in early 2010 than in early 2009 to buy the same bundle of goods.

The ratio Y_2/Y_1 reflects how much prices rise on average. By multiplying and dividing the first term in the numerator by p_C^1 and multiplying and dividing the second term by p_F^1, we find that this index is equivalent to

$$\frac{Y_2}{Y_1} = \frac{\left(\frac{p_C^2}{p_C^1}\right) p_C^1 C_1 + \left(\frac{p_F^2}{p_F^1}\right) p_F^1 F_1}{Y_1} = \left(\frac{p_C^2}{p_C^1}\right)\theta_C + \left(\frac{p_F^2}{p_F^1}\right)\theta_F,$$

where $\theta_C = p_C^1 C_1/Y_1$ and $\theta_F = p_F^1 F_1/Y_1$ are the budget shares of clothing and food in the first, or base, year. The CPI is a *weighted average* of the price increase for each good, p_C^2/p_C^1 and p_F^2/p_F^1, where the weights are each good's budget share in the base year, θ_C and θ_F.

Effects of Inflation Adjustments

A CPI adjustment of prices in a long-term contract overcompensates for inflation. We use an example involving an employment contract to illustrate the difference between using the CPI to adjust a long-term contract and using a true cost-of-living adjustment, which holds utility constant.

CPI Adjustment. Klaas signed a long-term contract when he was hired. According to the COLA clause in his contract, his employer increases his salary each year by the same percentage that the CPI increases. If the CPI this year is 5% higher than last year, Klaas's salary rises automatically by 5%.

Klaas spends all his money on clothing and food. His budget constraint in the first year is $Y_1 = p_C^1 C + p_F^1 F$, which we rewrite as

$$C = \frac{Y_1}{p_C^1} - \frac{p_F^1}{p_C^1} F.$$

The intercept of the budget constraint, L^1, on the vertical (clothing) axis in Figure 4.8 is Y_1/p_C^1, and the slope of the constraint is $-p_F^1/p_C^1$. The tangency of his indifference curve I^1 and the budget constraint L^1 determine his optimal consumption bundle in the first year, e_1, where he purchases C_1 and F_1.

In the second year, his salary rises with the CPI to Y_2, so his budget constraint in that year, L^2, is

$$C = \frac{Y_2}{p_C^2} - \frac{p_F^2}{p_C^2} F.$$

The new constraint, L^2, has a flatter slope, $-p_F^2/p_C^2$ than L^1 because the price of clothing rose more than the price of food. The new constraint goes through the orig-

Figure 4.8 CPI Adjustment

In the first year, when Klaas has an income of Y_1, his optimal bundle is e_1, where indifference curve I^1 is tangent to his budget constraint, L^1. In the second year, the price of clothing rises more than the price of food. Because his salary increases in proportion to the CPI, his second-year budget constraint, L^2, goes through e_1, so he can buy the same bundle as in the first year. His new optimal bundle, however, is e_2, where I^2 is tangent to L^2. The CPI adjustment overcompensates Klaas for the increase in prices: He is better off in the second year because his utility is greater on I^2 than on I^1. With a smaller true cost-of-living adjustment, Klaas's budget constraint, L^*, is tangent to I^1 at e^*.

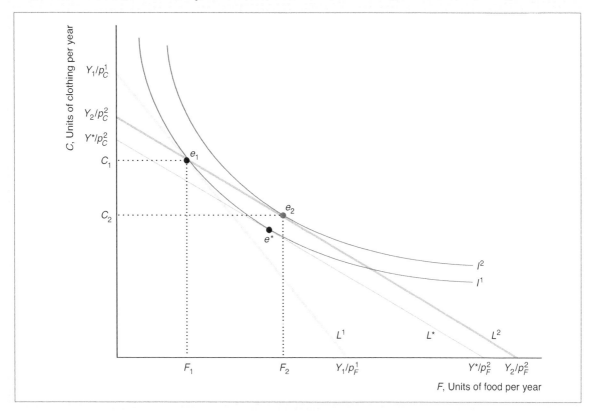

inal optimal bundle, e_1, because by increasing his salary according to the CPI, the firm ensures that Klaas can buy the same bundle of goods in the second year that he bought in the first year.

He *can* buy the same bundle, but *does* he? The answer is no. His optimal bundle in the second year is e_2, where indifference curve I^2 is tangent to his new budget constraint, L^2. The movement from e_1 to e_2 is the *total effect* from the changes in the real prices of clothing and food. *This adjustment to his income does not keep him on his original indifference curve, I^1.*

Indeed, Klaas is better off in the second year than in the first. The CPI adjustment *overcompensates* him for the change in inflation in the sense that his utility increases.

Klaas is better off because the prices of clothing and food did not increase by the same amount. Suppose that the price of clothing and food had both increased by *exactly* the same amount. After a CPI adjustment, Klaas's budget constraint in the second year, L^2, would be exactly the same as in the first year, L^1, so he would choose exactly the same bundle, e_1, in the second year as he chose in the first year.

Because the price of food rose by less than the price of clothing, L^2 is not the same as L^1. Food became cheaper relative to clothing. So by consuming more food and less clothing, Klaas has a higher utility in the second year.

Had clothing become relatively less expensive, Klaas would have raised his utility in the second year by consuming relatively more clothing. Thus, it doesn't matter which good becomes relatively less expensive over time for Klaas to benefit from the CPI compensation; it's necessary only for one of the goods to become a relative bargain.

True Cost-of-Living Adjustment. We now know that a CPI adjustment overcompensates for inflation. What we want is a *true cost-of-living index*: an inflation index that holds utility constant over time.

How big an increase in Klaas' salary would leave him exactly as well off in the second year as he was in the first? We can answer this question by applying the same technique we used to identify the substitution and income effects. Suppose that his utility function is $U = 20\sqrt{CF}$, where C is his units of clothing and F is his units of food. We draw an imaginary budget line, L^* in Figure 4.8, that is tangent to I^1 so that Klaas's utility remains constant but has the same slope as L^2. The income, Y^*, corresponding to that imaginary budget constraint is the amount that leaves Klaas' utility constant. Had Klaas received Y^* instead of Y_2 in the second year, he would have chosen Bundle e^* instead of e_2. Because e^* is on the same indifference curve, I^1, as e_1, Klaas' utility would be the same in both years.

The numerical example in Table 4.1 illustrates how the CPI overcompensates Klaas. Suppose that p_C^1 is \$1, p_C^2 is \$2, p_F^1 is \$4, and p_F^2 is \$5. In the first year, Klaas spends his income, $Y_1 = \$400$, on $C_1 = 200$ units of clothing and $F_1 = 50$ units of food, and he has a utility of 2,000, which is the level of utility on I^1. If his income did not increase in the second year, he would substitute toward the relatively inexpensive food, cutting his consumption of clothing in half but reducing his consumption of food by only a fifth. His utility would fall to 1,265.

If his second-year income increases in proportion to the CPI, he can buy the same bundle, e_1, in the second year as in the first. His second-year income is $Y_2 = \$650$ ($= p_C^2 C_1 + p_F^2 F_1 = \$2 \times 200 + \$5 \times 50$). However, instead of buying the same bundle, he can substitute toward the relatively inexpensive food, buying less clothing than in the first year. This bundle is depicted by e_2. His utility then rises from 2,000 to approximately 2,055 (the level of utility on I^2). Clearly, Klaas is better off if his income increases to Y_2. In other words, the CPI adjustment overcompensates him.

How much would his income have to rise to leave him *only* as well off as he was in the first year? If his second-year income is $Y^* \approx \$632.50$, by substituting toward food and the Bundle e^*, he can achieve the same level of utility, 2,000, as in the first year.

Table 4.1 Cost-of-Living Adjustments

	p_C	p_F	Income, Y	Clothing	Food	Utility, U
First year	\$1	\$4	\$400	200	50	2,000
Second year	\$2	\$5				
No adjustment			\$400	100	40	1,265
CPI adjustment			\$650	162.5	65	2,055
True COLA			\$632.50	158.1	63.2	2,000

We can use the income that just compensates Klaas for the price changes, Y^*, to construct a true cost-of-living index. In our numerical example, the true cost-of-living index rose 58.1% [≈ (632.50 − 400)/400], while the CPI rose 62.5% [= (650 − 400)/400].

SOLVED PROBLEM 4.5

Alexx doesn't care about where he lives, but he does care about what he eats. Alexx spends all his money on restaurant meals at either American or French restaurants. His firm offers to transfer him from its Miami office to its Paris office, where he will face different prices. The firm will pay him a salary in euros such that he can buy the same bundle of goods in Paris that he is currently buying in Miami. Will Alexx benefit by moving to Paris?

Answer

1. *Show Alexx's optimum bundle in the United States.* Alexx's optimal bundle, a, in the United States is determined by the tangency of his indifference curve I^1 and his American budget constraint L^A in the graph.

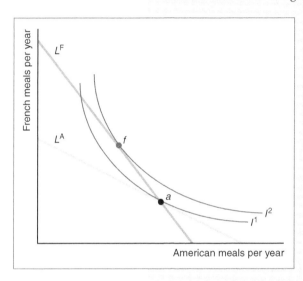

2. *Discuss what happens if prices are higher in France but the relative prices between American and French meals are the same.* If the prices of both French and American meals are x times higher in France than in the United States, the relative costs of French and American meals are the same. If the firm raises Alexx's income x times, his budget line does not change. Thus, if relative prices are the same in Miami and Paris, his budget line and optimal bundle are unchanged, so his level of utility is unchanged.

3. *Show the new optimum if relative prices in France differ from those in the United States.* Alexx's firm adjusts his income so that he can buy the same bundle, a, as he bought in the United States, so his new budget line in France, L^F, must go through a. Suppose that French meals are relatively less expensive than American meals in Paris. If Alexx spends all his money on French meals, he can buy more in Paris than he could in the United States, and if he spends all his money on American meals, he can buy fewer in Paris than he could in the United States. As a result, the L^F line hits the vertical axis at a higher point than the L^A line and cuts the L^A line at Bundle a. Alexx's new optimal bundle, f, is determined by the tangency of I^2 and L^F. Thus, if relative prices are different in Paris and Miami, Alexx is better off with the transfer. He was on I^1 and is now on I^2. Alexx could buy his original bundle, a, but chooses to substitute toward French meals, which are relatively inexpensive in France, thereby raising his utility.[16]

Comment: The overadjustment here is analogous to the upward bias in the CPI's COLA.

---

[16] A similar issue arises in making cross-country comparisons of income or wealth. See "Wealth of Developing Countries" in the Supplemental Material to Chapter 4 in **MyEconLab**'s textbook resources.

APPLICATION

Paying Workers to Relocate

International firms are increasingly relocating employees throughout their home countries and internationally. For example, KPMG, an international accounting and consulting firm, had about 2,500 of its 120,000 global employees on foreign assignment in 2008, but plans to increase that number to 5,000 by 2010. Its goal is to have 25% to 30% of its professional staff gain international experience at some point.

As you might expect, workers are not always enthusiastic about being relocated. In a 2008 survey by Runzheimer International, 79% of relocation managers responded that they experienced resistance from employees who were asked to relocate to high-cost locations. A survey of some of their employees found that 81% objected to moving because of their fear that their standard of living would fall.

One possible approach to convince employees to relocate is for the firm to assess the goods and services consumed by employees in the original home office location and then pay those employees enough to allow them to consume essentially the same items in their new locations. According to a survey by Organization Resource Counselors, Inc., 79% of international firms reported that they provided their workers with enough income abroad to maintain their home lifestyle.

Size of the CPI Substitution Bias. We have just demonstrated that the CPI has an *upward bias* in the sense that an individual's utility rises if we increase the person's income by the same percentage by which the CPI rises. If we make the CPI adjustment, we are implicitly assuming—incorrectly—that consumers do not substitute toward relatively inexpensive goods when prices change, but keep buying the same bundle of goods over time. We call this overcompensation a *substitution bias*.[17]

The CPI calculates the increase in prices as Y_2/Y_1. We can rewrite this expression as

$$\frac{Y_2}{Y_1} = \frac{Y^*}{Y_1} \frac{Y_2}{Y^*}.$$

The first term to the right of the equal sign, Y^*/Y_1, is the increase in the true cost of living. The second term, Y_2/Y^*, reflects the substitution bias in the CPI. It is greater than one because $Y_2 > Y^*$. In the example in Table 4.1, $Y_2/Y^* = 650/632.50 \approx 1.028$, so the CPI overestimates the increase in the cost of living by about 2.8%.

There is no substitution bias if all prices increase at the same rate so that relative prices remain constant. The faster some prices rise relative to others, the more pronounced the upward bias caused by the substitution that occurs toward less expensive goods.

---

[17]The CPI has other biases as well. For example, Bils (2009) argues that CPI measures for consumer durables largely capture shifts to newer product models that display higher prices, rather than a price increase for a given set of goods. He estimates that as much as two-thirds of the price increase for new models is due to quality growth. Consequently, the CPI inflation for durables may have been overstated by almost two percentage points per year.

APPLICATION

Fixing the CPI Substitution Bias

Several studies estimate that, due to the substitution bias, the CPI inflation rate is about half a percentage point too high per year. What can be done to correct this bias? One approach is to estimate utility functions for individuals and use those data to calculate a true cost-of-living index. However, given the wide variety of tastes across individuals, as well as various technical estimation problems, this approach is not practical.

A second method is to use a *Paasche* index, which weights prices using the current quantities of goods purchased. In contrast, the CPI (which is also called a *Laspeyres* index) uses quantities from the earlier, base period. A Paasche index is likely to overstate the degree of substitution and thus to understate the change in the cost-of-living index. Hence, replacing the traditional Laspeyres index with the Paasche would merely replace an overestimate with an underestimate of the rate of inflation.

A third, compromise approach is to take an average of the Laspeyres and Paasche indexes because the true cost-of-living index lies between these two biased indexes. The most widely touted average is the *Fisher* index, which is the geometric mean of the Laspeyres and Paasche indexes (the square root of their product). If we use the Fisher index, we are implicitly assuming that there is a unitary elasticity of substitution among goods so that the share of consumer expenditures on each item remains constant as relative prices change (in contrast to the Laspeyres approach, where we assume that the quantities remain fixed).

Not everyone agrees that averaging the Laspeyres and Paasche indexes would be an improvement. For example, if people do not substitute, the CPI (Laspeyres) index is correct and the Fisher index, based on the geometric average, underestimates the rate of inflation.

Nonetheless, in recent years, the Bureau of Labor Statistics (BLS), which calculates the CPI, has made several adjustments to its CPI methodology, including using averaging. Starting in 1999, the BLS replaced the Laspeyres index with a Fisher approach to calculate almost all of its 200 basic indexes (such as "ice cream and related products") within the CPI. It still uses the Laspeyres approach for a few of the categories in which it does not expect much substitution, such as utilities (electricity, gas, cable television, and telephones), medical care, and housing, and it uses the Laspeyres method to combine the basic indexes to obtain the final CPI.

Now, the BLS updates the CPI weights (the market basket shares of consumption) every two years instead of only every decade or so, as the Bureau had done before 2002. More frequent updating reduces the substitution bias in a Laspeyres index because market basket shares are frozen for a shorter period of time. According to the BLS, had it used updated weights between 1989 and 1997, the CPI would have increased by only 31.9% rather than the reported 33.9%. Thus, the BLS predicts that this change will reduce the rate of increase in the CPI by approximately 0.2 percentage points per year.

Overestimating the rate of inflation has important implications for U.S. society because Social Security, various retirement plans, welfare, and many other programs include CPI-based cost-of-living adjustments. According to one estimate, the bias in the CPI alone makes it the fourth-largest "federal program" after Social Security, health care, and defense. For example, the U.S. Postal Service (USPS) has a CPI-based COLA in its union contracts. In 2009, a typical employee earned about $53,000 a year. Consequently, the estimated substitution bias of half a percent a year cost the USPS nearly $265 per employee, or about $202 million, because the USPS had about 764,000 employees at the time.

4.5 Revealed Preference

We have seen that we can predict a consumer's purchasing behavior if we know that person's preferences. We can also do the opposite: We can infer a consumer's preferences from observing the consumer's buying behavior. If we observe a consumer's choice at many different prices and income levels, we can derive the consumer's indifference curves using the *theory of revealed preference* (Samuelson, 1947). We can also use this theory to demonstrate the substitution effect. Economists can use this approach to estimate demand curves merely by observing the choices consumers make over time.

Recovering Preferences

The basic assumption of the theory of revealed preference is that a consumer chooses bundles to maximize utility subject to a budget constraint: The consumer chooses the best bundle that the consumer can afford. We also assume that the consumer's indifference curve is convex to the origin so that the consumer picks a unique bundle on any budget constraint.

If such a consumer chooses a more expensive bundle of goods, a, over a less expensive bundle, b, then we say that the consumer *prefers* Bundle a to b. In panel a of Figure 4.9, when Linda's budget constraint is L^1, she chooses Bundle a, showing that she prefers a to b, which costs less than a because it lies strictly within her opportunity set.

Figure 4.9 Revealed Preference

(a) Linda chooses Bundle a on budget constraint L^1, so she prefers it to b, which costs less. On L^2, she chooses b, so she prefers it to c, which costs less. Thus, due to transitivity, Linda prefers a to c or any other of the *worse bundles*. She prefers the bundles in the shaded area above and to the right of a according to the more-is-better property. (b) With more budget lines and choices, we learn more about the *better bundles*. Linda's indifference curve through a must lie in the white area between the worse and better bundles.

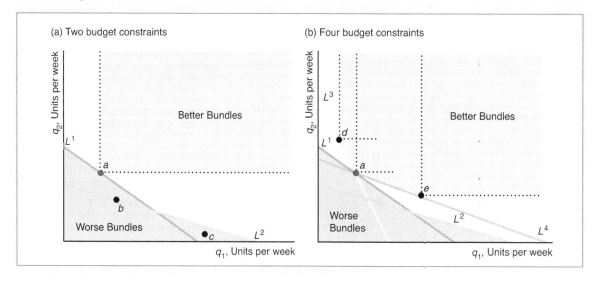

If the consumer prefers Bundle a to b and Bundle b to c, then the consumer must prefer Bundle a to c because the consumer's preferences are transitive. In panel a, Linda chooses Bundle a over b when the budget line is L^1, and she picks Bundle b over c when the constraint is L^2; so, by transitivity, Linda prefers a to c. We say that Bundle a is *revealed to be preferred* to Bundle c if Linda chooses a over c directly, or if we learn indirectly that Linda prefers a to b and b to c. We know that Linda prefers a to any other bundle in the shaded area, labeled "Worse Bundles," by a sequence of direct or indirect comparisons. Due to the more-is-better property (Chapter 3), Linda prefers bundles in the area above and to the right of a. Thus, the indifference curve through a must lie within the white area between the worse and better bundles.

If we learn that Linda chooses d when faced with budget line L^3 and e given line L^4 as panel b shows, we can expand her *better bundle* area. We know that her indifference curve through a must lie in the white area between the better and worse bundle areas. Thus, if we observe a large number of choices, we can determine the shape of her indifference curves, which summarizes her preferences.

Substitution Effect

One of the clearest and most important results from consumer theory is that the substitution effect is negative: The Law of Demand holds for compensated demand curves. This result stems from utility maximization, given that indifference curves are convex to the origin. The theory of revealed preference provides an alternative justification without appealing to unobservable indifference curves or utility functions.

Suppose that Steven is indifferent between Bundle a, which consists of M_a music tracks and C_a candy bars, and Bundle b, with M_b tracks and C_b candy bars. That is, the bundles are on the same indifference curve.

The price of candy bars, C, remains fixed at p_C, but the price of songs changes. We observe that when the price for M is p_M^a, Steven chooses Bundle a—that is, a is revealed to be preferred to b. Similarly, when the price is p_M^b, he chooses b over a.

Because Steven is indifferent between the two bundles, the cost of the chosen bundle must be less than or equal to that of the other bundle. Thus, if he chooses a when the price is p_M^a, then $p_M^a M_a + p_C C_a \leq p_M^a M_b + P_C C_b$, or

$$p_M^a(M_a - M_b) + p_C(C_a - C_b) \leq 0. \tag{4.14}$$

And, if he chooses b when the price is p_M^b, then $p_M^b M_b + p_C C_b \leq p_M^b M_a + P_C C_a$, or

$$p_M^b(M_b - M_a) + p_C(C_b - C_a) \leq 0. \tag{4.15}$$

Adding Equations 4.14 and 4.15 together, we learn that

$$(p_M^a - p_M^b)(M_a - M_b) \leq 0. \tag{4.16}$$

Equation 4.16 shows that the product of the difference in prices times the difference in quantities of music purchased is nonpositive. That result can be true only if the price and the quantity move in opposite directions: When the price rises, the quantity falls. Thus, we were able to derive the substitution effect result without using utility functions or making any assumption about the curvature of indifference curves.

SUMMARY

1. **Deriving Demand Curves.** We can derive an individual demand curve using the information about the consumer's tastes, which are summarized in an indifference or preference map. Varying the price of one good, holding other prices and income constant, we find how the quantity demanded of a good varies with its price, which is the information we need to draw the demand curve. Consumers' tastes, which are captured by the indifference curves, determine the shape of the demand curve.

2. **Effects of an Increase in Income.** A consumer's demand curve shifts as the consumer's income rises. By varying income while holding prices constant, we determine how quantity demanded shifts with income, which is the information we need to show how the consumer's demand curve shifts. An Engel curve summarizes the relationship between income and quantity demanded, holding prices constant.

3. **Effects of a Price Increase.** An increase in the price of a good causes both a substitution effect and an income effect. The substitution effect is the amount by which a consumer's demand for a good changes as a result of a price increase when we compensate the consumer for the price increase by raising the individual's income by just enough that the consumer's utility does not change. The direction of the substitution effect is unambiguous: A compensated rise in a good's price always causes consumers to buy less of the good. The increase in price rise reduces the consumer's opportunity set because the consumer can now buy less than before with the same income. As a consequence, the consumer buys a new bundle on a lower indifference curve. We determine how much we would have to lower the consumer's income, holding prices constant, so that the consumer would choose a bundle on this new lower indifference curve. The income effect is the change in the quantity demanded due to such an income adjustment. The income effect can be positive or negative. If a good is normal (income elasticity is positive), the income effect is negative.

4. **Cost-of-Living Adjustment.** The government's major index of inflation, the Consumer Price Index (CPI), overestimates inflation by ignoring the substitution effect.

5. **Revealed Preference.** If we observe a consumer's choice at various prices and income levels, we can infer the consumer's preferences: the shape of the consumer's indifference curves. We can also use the theory of revealed preference to show that a consumer substitutes away from a good as its price rises.

QUESTIONS

■ = exercise is available on **MyEconLab**; * = answer appears at the back of this book; **V** = video answer by James Dearden is available online.

1. Manufactured diamonds have become as big and virtually indistinguishable from the best natural diamonds (Dan Mitchell, "Fake Gems, Genuine Appeal," *New York Times*, June 21, 2008). Suppose consumers change from believing that manufactured diamonds, q_1, were imperfect substitutes for natural diamonds, q_2, to perfect substitutes, so that their utility function becomes $U(q_1, q_2) = q_1 + q_2$. What effect will that have on the demand for manufactured diamonds? Derive the new demand curve for manufactured diamonds and draw it.

2. Draw a figure to illustrate the application "Calling It Quits on Smoking." That is, show why as the price of cell phones drops, less tobacco is consumed. (*Hint*: Draw a figure like panel a of Figure 4.2 with cell phones on the horizontal axis and tobacco on the vertical axis. However, unlike in Figure 4.2, the price-consumption curve should slow downward.)

3. Have your folks given you cash or promised to leave you money after they're gone? If so, your parents may think of such gifts as a good. They must decide whether to spend their money on fun, food, drink, cars, or on transfers to you. Hmmm. Altonji and Villanueva (2007) estimate that, for every extra dollar of expected lifetime resources, parents give their adult offspring between 2¢ and 3¢ in bequests and about 3¢ in transfers. Those gifts are about one-fifth of what they give their children under 18 and spend on college. Illustrate how an increase in your parents' income affects their allocations between bequests to you and all other goods ("fun") in two related graphs, where you show an income-consumption curve in one and an Engel curve for bequests in the other.

4. Under what conditions does the income effect reinforce the substitution effect? Under what conditions does it have an offsetting effect? If the income effect more than offsets the substitution effect for a good, what do we call that good? Illustrate that the income effect can more than offset the substitution effect in a figure.

5. Michelle spends all her money on food and clothing. When the price of clothing decreases, she buys more clothing.
   a. Does the substitution effect cause her to buy more or less clothing? Explain. (If the direction of the effect is ambiguous, say so.)
   b. Does the income effect cause her to buy more or less clothing? Explain. (If the direction of the effect is ambiguous, say so.)

*6. Don spends his money on food and on operas. Food is an inferior good for Don. Does he view an opera performance as an inferior or a normal good? Why? In a diagram, show a possible income-consumption curve for Don.

*7. Alix consumes only coffee and coffee cake and consumes them only together (they are perfect complements). If we calculate a CPI using only these two goods, by how much will this CPI differ from the true cost-of-living index?

8. Are relatively more high-quality navel oranges sold in California or in New York? Why?

*9. Draw a figure to illustrate the verbal answer given in Solved Problem 4.4. Use math and a figure to show how applying an ad valorem tax rather than a specific tax changes the analysis (if it does).

10. During his first year at school, Ximing buys eight new college textbooks at a cost of $50 each. Used books cost $30 each. When the bookstore announces a 20% price increase in new texts and a 10% increase in used texts for the next year, Ximing's father offers him $80 extra. Is Ximing better off, the same, or worse off after the price change? Why?

11. Jean views coffee and cream as perfect complements. In the first year, Jean picks an optimal bundle of coffee and cream, e_1. In the second year, inflation occurs, the prices of coffee and cream change by different amounts, and Jean receives a cost-of-living adjustment (COLA) based on the consumer price index (CPI) for these two goods. After the price changes and she receives the COLA, her new optimal bundle is e_2. Show the two equilibria in a figure. Is she better off, worse off, or equally well off at e_2 compared to e_1? Explain why.

12. Ann's only income is her annual college scholarship, which she spends exclusively on gallons of ice cream and books. Last year, when ice cream cost $10 and used books cost $20, Ann spent her $250 scholarship on 5 gallons of ice cream and 10 books. This year, the price of ice cream rose to $15 and the price of books increased to $25. So that Ann can afford the same bundle of ice cream and books that she bought last year, her college raised her scholarship to $325. Ann has the usual-shaped indifference curves. Will Ann change the amount of ice cream and books that she buys this year? If so, explain how and why. Will Ann be better off, as well off, or worse off this year than last year? Why?

13. The *Economist* magazine publishes the Big Mac Index, which is an index based on the price of a Big Mac hamburger at McDonald's in various countries over time. Under what circumstances would people find this index to be as useful as or more useful than the consumer price index in measuring how their true cost of living changes over time?

14. Illustrate that the Paasche cost-of-living index (see the application "Fixing the CPI Substitution Bias") underestimates the rate of inflation when compared to the true cost-of-living index.

15. In Spenser's state, a sales tax of 10% is applied to clothing but not to food. Using indifference curves, show the effect of the tax on Spenser's choice between food and clothing.

16. Minnesota customers of Earthlink, Inc., a high-speed Internet service provider, get broadband access from a cable modem and pay no tax. In contrast, Earthlink customers who use telephone digital subscriber lines pay $3.10 a month in state and local taxes and other surcharges (Matt Richtel, "Cable or Phone? Difference Can Be Taxing," *New York Times,* April 5, 2004, C1, C6). Suppose that, were it not for the tax, Earthlink would set its prices for the two services so that Sven would be indifferent between using cable or phone service. Describe his indifference curves. Given the tax, Earthlink raises its price for the phone service but not its cable service. Use a figure to show how Sven chooses between the two services.

17. Ralph usually buys one pizza and two colas from the local pizzeria. The pizzeria announces a special: All pizzas after the first one are half price. Show the original and the new budget constraints. What can you say about the bundle Ralph will choose when faced with the new constraint?

18. The local swimming pool charges nonmembers $10 per visit. If you join the pool, you can swim for $5 per visit, but you have to pay an annual fee of F. Use an indifference curve diagram to find the value of F such that you are indifferent between joining and not joining. Suppose that the pool charged you exactly F. Would you go to the pool more or fewer times than if you did not join? For simplicity, assume that the price of all other goods is $1.

19. In Solved Problem 4.5, suppose that French meals are relatively more expensive than American meals in Paris, so the L^F budget line cuts the L^A budget line from below rather than from above as in the solved problem's figure. Show that the conclusion that Alexx is better off after his move still holds. Explain the logic behind the following statement: "The analysis holds as long as the relative prices differ in the two cities. Whether both prices, one price, or neither price in Paris is higher than in Miami is irrelevant to the analysis."

20. Pat eats eggs and toast for breakfast and insists on having three pieces of toast for every two eggs he eats. Derive his utility function. If the price of eggs increases but we compensate Pat to make him just as "happy" as he was before the price change, what happens to his consumption of eggs? Draw a graph and explain your diagram. Does the change in his consumption reflect a substitution or an income effect?

PROBLEMS

21. How would your answer to Question 1 about the demand curve for manufactured diamonds change if consumers have diminishing marginal utility of diamonds (of either type), so that the new utility function is $U = \ln(q_1 + q_2)$?

22. Because people dislike commuting to work, homes closer to employment centers tend to be more expensive. The price of a home in a given employment center is $60 per day. The daily rental price for housing drops by $2.50 per mile for each mile farther from the employment center. The price of gasoline per mile of the commute is p_g (which is less than $2.50). Thus, the net cost of traveling an extra mile to work is $p_g - 2.5$. Lan chooses the distance she lives from the job center, D (where D is at most 50 miles), and all other goods, A. The price of A is $1 per unit. Lan's utility function is $U = (50 - D)^{0.5} A^{0.5}$, and her income is Y, which for technical reasons is between $60 and $110.

    a. Is D an economic bad (the opposite of a good)? To answer this question, find $\partial U/\partial D$.
    b. Draw Lan's budget constraint.
    c. Use the Lagrange method to derive Lan's demands for A and D.
    d. Show that, as the price of gasoline increases, Lan chooses to live closer to the employment center. That is, show that $\partial D^*/\partial p_G < 0$.
    e. Show that, as Lan's income increases, she chooses to live closer to the employment center. Reportedly, increases in gasoline prices hit the poor especially hard because they live father from their jobs, consume more gasoline in commuting, and spend a greater fraction of their income on gasoline (Ball, "For Many Low-Income Workers, High Gasoline Prices Take a Toll," *Wall Street Journal*, July 12, 2004, A1). Demonstrate that as Lan's income decreases, she spends more per day on gasoline. That is, show that $\partial D^*/\partial Y < 0$. V

23. Research by economists Cutler, Glaeser, and Shapiro (2003) on Americans' increasing obesity points to improved technology in the preparation of tasty and more caloric foods as a possible explanation of weight gain. Before World War II, people rarely prepared french fries at home because of the significant amount of peeling, cutting, and cooking required. Today, french fries are prepared in factories using low-cost labor, shipped frozen, and then simply reheated in homes. Paul consumes two goods: potatoes and leisure, N. The number of potatoes Paul consumes does not vary, but their tastiness, T, does. For each extra unit of tastiness, he must spend p_t hours in the kitchen. Thus, Paul's time constraint is $N + p_t T = 24$. Paul's utility function is $U = TN^{0.5}$.

    a. What is Paul's marginal rate of substitution, MU_T/MU_N?
    b. What is the marginal rate of transformation, p_T/p_N?
    c. What is Paul's optimal choice (T^*, N^*)?
    d. With a decrease in the price of taste (the ability to produce a given level of tastiness faster), does Paul consume more taste (and hence gain weight) or spend more of his time in leisure? Does a decrease in the price of taste contribute to weight gain? V

24. According to the U.S. Consumer Expenditure Survey for 2008, Americans with incomes below $20,000 spend about 39% of their income on housing. What are the limits on their income elasticities of housing if all other goods are collectively normal? Given that they spend about 0.2% on books and other reading material, what are the limits on their income elasticities for reading matter if all other goods are collectively normal?

*25. In 2005, a typical U.S. owner of a home theater (a television and a DVD player) bought 12 music CDs (q_1) per year and 6 Top-20 movie DVDs (q_2) per year. The average price of a CD was about $p_1 = \$15$, the average price of a DVD was roughly $p_2 = \$20$, and the typical consumer spent $300 on these entertainment goods.[18] We'll call this typical consumer Barbara. We estimate her Cobb-Douglas utility function as $U = q_1^{0.6} q_2^{0.4}$. Redraw Figure 4.2 using

---

[18]We estimated the Cobb-Douglas utility function using budget share information and obtained prices and quantities from www.leesmovieinfo.net/Video-Sales.php, www.usatoday.com/life/music/news/2005-12-28-music-sales_x.htm, quickfacts.census.gov/qfd/states/00000.html, www.nytimes.com/ 2004/12/27/business/media/27music.html ?ex= 1261803600&en=49d1239df6399ffe&ei=5090&partner=rssuserland, bigpicture.typepad.com/comments/2004/12/ music_industry_.html, and www .ce.org/Press/CEA_Pubs/834.asp.

Barbara's utility function. Explain the shape of the price-consumption curve.

26. Derive the income elasticity of demand for individuals with (a) Cobb-Douglas, (b) perfect substitutes, and (c) perfect complements utility functions.

*27. Guerdon always puts half a sliced banana, q_1, on his bowl of cereal, q_2—the two goods are perfect complements. What is his utility function? Derive his demand curve for bananas graphically and mathematically.

28. Derive and plot Olivia's demand curve for pie if she eats pie only à la mode and does not eat either pie or ice cream alone (she views pie and ice cream as perfect complements). How much does her weekly budget have to rise for her to buy one more piece of pie per week?

*29. Given Barbara's estimated Cobb-Douglas utility function from Problem 23, $U = q_1^{0.6} q_2^{0.4}$, for CDs, q_1, and DVDs, q_2, derive her Engel curve for movie DVDs. Illustrate in a figure.

30. Ryan has a constant elasticity of substitution (CES) utility function $U = q_1^\rho + q_2^\rho$. Derive his Engel curve.

31. Derive Ryan's demand curve for q_1, given his CES utility function $U = q_1^\rho + q_2^\rho$.

*32. Philip's quasilinear utility function is $U = \sqrt{q_1} + q_2$. Derive his demand curves assuming that he consumes some of both goods and that $p_2 = 1$. Discuss how the demand curves depend on his income. (*Hint*: The quantity demanded cannot be completely independent of his income: You cannot buy goods if you have no income.) Discuss the substitution, income, and total effect on the demand for q_1 if its price, p_1, increases.

33. David consumes two things: gasoline (G) and bread (B). David's utility function is $U(G, B) = 10G^{0.25} B^{0.75}$.

  a. Use the Lagrange technique to solve for David's optimal choices of gasoline and bread as a function of the price of gasoline, p_G, the price of bread, p_B, and his income, Y.

  b. With recent increases in the price of gasoline, does David reduce his consumption of gasoline?

  c. For David, how does $\partial G/\partial p_G$ depend on his income? That is, how does David's change in gasoline consumption due to an increase in the price of gasoline depend on his income level? To answer these questions, find the cross-partial derivative, $\partial^2 G/(\partial p_G \partial Y)$. V

5 Consumer Welfare and Policy Analysis

The welfare of the people is the ultimate law. —Cicero

The U.S. government and many other governments around the world provide child care subsidies to poor parents so that they can work and better provide for themselves and their children. But does a price subsidy of this kind offer the most benefit to families? Or would a comparable amount of unrestricted cash or direct provision of child care services benefit poor families more?

To answer these types of questions, we will first use consumer theory to develop various measures of consumer welfare. We will then examine how several types of government policies affect consumer well-being. Finally, we will use consumer theory to study individuals' labor supply and analyze the impact of income taxes.

In this chapter, we examine five main topics

1. **Consumer Welfare.** The degree to which a consumer is helped or harmed by a change in the equilibrium price can be measured by using information from a consumer's demand curve or utility function.

2. **Expenditure Function and Consumer Welfare.** We can use the expenditure function to calculate how much more money we would have to give a consumer to offset the harm from a price increase.

3. **Market Consumer Surplus.** The market consumer surplus—the sum of the welfare effect across all consumers—can be measured using the market demand curve.

4. **Effects of Government Policies on Consumer Welfare.** We use our consumer welfare measures to determine the degree to which consumers are helped or harmed by quotas, food stamps, and child care subsidies.

5. **Deriving Labor Supply Curves.** We derive a worker's labor supply curve using the individual's demand curve for leisure. We use the labor supply curve to determine how a reduction in the income tax rate affects consumer welfare, the supply of labor, and tax revenues.

5.1 Consumer Welfare

Economists and policymakers want to know how much consumers are helped or harmed by shocks that affect the equilibrium price and quantity of goods and services. Prices change when new inventions reduce costs or when a government imposes a tax or subsidy. Quantities change when a government sets a quota. To determine how these changes affect consumers, we need a measure of consumers' welfare.

If we knew a consumer's utility function, we could directly answer the question of how government actions, natural disasters, and other events affect consumers' welfare. If the price of beef increases, the budget line of someone who eats beef rotates inward, so the consumer is on a lower indifference curve at the new equilibrium. If we knew the levels of utility associated with the original indifference curve and the new indifference curve, we could measure the impact of the tax in terms of the change in the consumer's utility level.

However, this approach is not practical for a couple of reasons. First, we rarely know individuals' utility functions. Second, even if we had utility measures for various consumers, we would have no obvious way to compare the measures. One person might say that he gets 1,000 utils (units of utility) from the same bundle that another consumer says gives her 872 utils of pleasure. The first person is not necessarily happier—he may just be using a different scale.

As a result, *we measure consumer welfare in terms of dollars.* Instead of asking the question "How many utils would you lose if your daily commute increased by 15 minutes?" we could ask, "How much would you pay to avoid having your daily commute grow a quarter of an hour longer?" or "How much would it cost you in forgone earnings if your daily commute were 15 minutes longer?" It is more practical to compare dollars rather than utils across people.

Consumer welfare from a good is the benefit a consumer gets from consuming that good in excess of its cost. How much pleasure do you get from a good above and beyond its price? If you buy a good for exactly what it's worth to you, you are indifferent between making that transaction and not making it. Frequently, however, you buy things that are worth more to you than what they cost. Imagine that you've played tennis in the hot sun and are very thirsty. You can buy a soft drink from a vending machine for 75¢, but you'd be willing to pay much more because you are so thirsty. As a result, you're much better off making this purchase than not.

In this section, we first examine *consumer surplus*, which is the most widely used measure of consumer welfare. Consumer surplus is relatively easy to calculate using the uncompensated demand function and is a good, but not exact, measure of the true value of a consumer's welfare. We then discuss approaches that provide exact values using compensated demand functions and examine how close consumer surplus comes to the exact values.

Willingness to Pay

If we can measure how much more you'd be willing to pay than you actually paid for a product, we'd know how much you gained from the transaction. Luckily for us, the demand curve contains the information we need to make this measurement. For convenience in most of the following discussion, we use the equivalent *inverse demand function*, which rearranges the demand function, $Q = D(p)$, so as to express a product's price as a function of the quantity of it demanded, $p = p(Q)$. For example, if the demand function is $Q = a - bp$, then the inverse demand function is $p = a/b - Q/b$.

To develop a welfare measure based on the inverse demand curve, we need to know what information is contained in an inverse demand curve. The inverse demand curve reflects a consumer's *marginal willingness to pay*: the maximum amount a consumer will spend for an extra unit. The consumer's marginal willingness to pay for a product is the *marginal value* the consumer places buying one more unit.

David's inverse demand curve for magazines per week in panel a of Figure 5.1 indicates his marginal willingness to pay for various numbers of magazines. If David has no magazines and is considering buying one, he places a value of $5 on that first magazine. As a result, if the price of a magazine is $5, David buys one magazine,

Figure 5.1 Consumer Surplus

(a) David's inverse demand curve for magazines has a step-like shape. When the price is $3, he buys three magazines, point c. David's marginal value for the first magazine is $5, areas $CS_1 + E_1$, and his expenditure is $3, area E_1, so his consumer surplus is $CS_1 = \$2$. His consumer surplus is $1 for the second magazine, area CS_2, and is $0 for the third (he is indifferent between buying and not buying it). Thus, his total consumer surplus is the blue shaded area $CS_1 + CS_2 + CS_3 = \$3$, and his total expenditure is the tan shaded area $E_1 + E_2 + E_3 = \$9$. (b) Steven's willingness to pay for trading cards is the height of his smooth inverse demand curve. At price p_1, Steven's expenditure is $E (= p_1 q_1)$, his consumer surplus is CS, and the total value he places on consuming q_1 trading cards per year is $CS + E$.

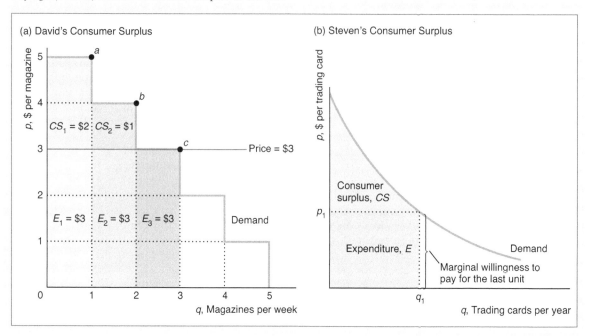

which corresponds to point *a* on the inverse demand curve. His marginal willingness to buy a second magazine is $4, so if the price falls to $4, he buys two magazines, *b*. His marginal willingness to buy three magazines is $3, so if the price of magazines is $3, he buys three magazines, *c*.

Consumer Surplus. The monetary difference between the maximum amount that a consumer is willing to pay for the quantity of the good purchased and what the good actually costs is called **consumer surplus** (*CS*). Consumer surplus is a dollar-value measure of the extra pleasure the consumer receives from the transaction beyond its price.

Measuring Consumer Surplus. David's consumer surplus from each additional magazine is his marginal willingness to pay minus what he pays to obtain the magazine. His marginal willingness to pay for the first magazine, $5, is area $CS_1 + E_1$. If the price is $3, his expenditure to obtain the magazine is area $E_1 = \$3$. Thus, his consumer surplus on the first magazine is area $CS_1 = (CS_1 + E_1) - E_1 = \$5 - \$3 = \$2$. Because his marginal willingness to pay for the second magazine is $4, his consumer surplus for the second magazine is the smaller area, $CS_2 = \$1$. His marginal willingness to pay for the third magazine is $3, which equals what he must pay to obtain it, so his consumer surplus is zero, $CS_3 = \$0$. He is indifferent between buying and not buying the third magazine.

At a price of \$3, David buys three magazines. His total consumer surplus from the three magazines he buys is the sum of the consumer surplus he gets from each of these magazines: $CS_1 + CS_2 + CS_3 = \$2 + \$1 + \$0 = \$3$. This total consumer surplus of \$3 is the extra amount that David is willing to spend for the right to buy three magazines at \$3 each. David is unwilling to buy a fourth magazine unless the price drops to \$2 or less. If David's mother gives him a fourth magazine as a gift, the marginal value that David puts on that fourth magazine, \$2, is less than what it cost his mother, \$3.

Thus, an individual's consumer surplus is

- the extra value that a consumer gets from buying the desired number of units of a good in excess of the amount paid,
- the amount that a consumer would be willing to pay for the right to buy as many units as desired at the specified price, and
- the area under the consumer's inverse demand curve and above the market price up to the quantity of the product the consumer buys.

We can determine the consumer surplus associated with smooth inverse demand curves in the same way as we did with David's unusual stair-like inverse demand curve. Steven has a smooth inverse demand curve for baseball trading cards, panel b of Figure 5.1. The height of this inverse demand curve measures his willingness to pay for one more card. This willingness varies with the number of cards he buys in a year. The total value he places on obtaining q_1 cards per year is the area under the inverse demand curve up to q_1, the areas CS and E. Area E is his actual expenditure on q_1 cards. Because the price is p_1, his expenditure is p_1q_1. Steven's consumer surplus from consuming q_1 trading cards is the value of consuming those cards, areas CS and E, minus his actual expenditures E to obtain them, or CS. Thus, his consumer surplus, CS, is the area under the inverse demand curve and above the horizontal line at the price p_1 up to the quantity he buys, q_1.

Just as we measure the consumer surplus for an individual by using that individual's inverse demand curve, we measure the consumer surplus of all consumers in a market by using the market inverse demand curve. *Market consumer surplus is the area under the market inverse demand curve above the market price up to the quantity consumers buy.*

To summarize, individual and market consumer surplus are practical and convenient measures of consumer welfare. There are two advantages to using consumer surplus rather than utility to discuss the welfare of consumers. First, the dollar-denominated consumer surplus of several individuals can be easily compared or combined, whereas the utility of various individuals cannot be easily compared or combined. Second, it is relatively easy to measure consumer surplus, whereas it is difficult to get a meaningful measure of utility directly. To calculate consumer surplus, all we have to do is measure the area under an inverse demand curve.

APPLICATION

Willingness to Pay and Consumer Surplus on eBay

People differ in their willingness to pay for a given item. We can determine willingness to pay of individuals for a 238 AD Roman coin—a sesterce (originally equivalent in value to four asses) of the image of Emperor Balbinus—by how much they bid in an eBay auction that ended September 6, 2009. On its Web site, eBay correctly argues (as we show in Chapter 13) that an individual's best strategy is to bid his or her *willingness to pay*: the maximum value that the bidder places on the item. From what eBay reports, we know the maximum bid of each person except the winner: eBay uses a *second-price auction*, where the winner pays the second-highest amount bid plus an increment. (The increment depends on the size of the bid. It is $1 for the bids between $25 and $100 and $25 for bids between $1,000 and $2,499.99.)

In the figure, the bids for the coin are arranged from highest to lowest. Because each bar on the graph indicates the bid for one coin, the figure shows how many units could have been sold to this group of bidders at various prices. That is, it is the market inverse demand curve.

Bapna et al. (2008) set up a Web site, www.Cniper.com (no longer active), that automatically bid on eBay at the last moment (a process called sniping). To use the site, an individual had to specify a maximum willingness to pay, so that the authors knew the top bidder's willingness to pay. Bapna et al. found that the median consumer surplus was $4 on goods that cost $14 on average. They estimated the CS and the expenditures, E, for all eBay buyers and calculated that $CS/E = 30\%$. That is, bidders' consumer surplus gain is 30% of their expenditures.

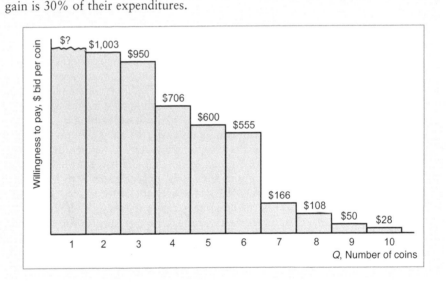

Effect of a Price Change on Consumer Surplus. If the price of a good rises, purchasers of that good lose consumer surplus. To illustrate this loss, we return to Jackie's estimated Cobb-Douglas utility, $U = q_1^{0.4} q_2^{0.6}$, between music tracks, q_1, and live music, q_2 (Chapters 3 and 4). In Chapter 3, we showed that her uncompensated demand curve for tracks is $q_1 = 0.4Y/p_1 = 12/p_1$ given that her music budget per quarter is $Y = £30$. At the initial price of tracks $p_1 = £0.5$, she bought $q_1 = 12/0.5 = 24$ song tracks.

Suppose that a government tax or an iTunes price increase causes the price of tracks to double to £1. Jackie now buys $q_1 = 12/1 = 12$ tracks. As Figure 5.2 illustrates, she loses the amount of consumer surplus (ΔCS) equal to area $A + B$: the area between £0.5 and £1 on the price axis to the left of her uncompensated demand curve. Due to the price rise, she now buys 12 tracks for which she pays £0.5 (= £1 − £0.5) more than originally, so area $A = £6 = £0.5 \times 12$. In addition, she loses surplus from no longer consuming 12 (= 24 − 12) of the original 24 tracks, area B.[1]

---

[1] If we replace the curved demand curve with a straight line, we slightly overestimate area B as the area of a triangle: $\frac{1}{2} \times £0.5 \times 12 = £3$. We calculate the exact amount in Solved Problem 5.1.

Figure 5.2 A Change in Consumer Surplus

As the price increases from £0.5 to £1, Jackie loses consumer surplus equal to areas $A + B$.

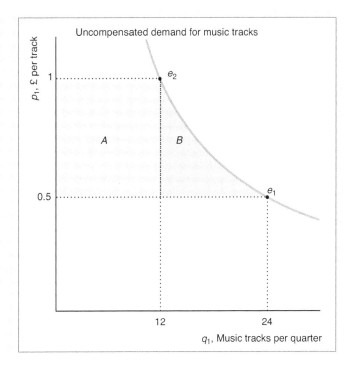

SOLVED PROBLEM 5.1

What is the exact change in Jackie's consumer surplus, $A + B$, in Figure 5.2? How large is area B?

Answer

1. *State Jackie's uncompensated demand function of music tracks given her initial budget.* From Chapters 3 and 4, we know that her demand function for tracks is $q_1 = 12/p_1$.

2. *Integrate between £0.5 and £1 to the left of Jackie's uncompensated demand curve for tracks.* Her lost consumer surplus is

$$\Delta CS = -\int_{0.5}^{1} \frac{12}{p_1} dp_1 = -12 \ln p_1 \Big|_{0.5}^{1}$$
$$= -12(\ln 1 - \ln 0.5) \approx -12 \times 0.69 \approx -8.28,$$

where we put a minus sign in front of the integrated area because the price increased, causing a loss of consumer surplus.

3. *Determine the size of area B residually.* Because $-\Delta CS =$ area $A + B$ and area $A = £6$ ($= [£1 - £0.5] \times 12$), area B is £2.28 ($= £8.28 - £6$).

Comment: A 100% increase in price causes Jackie's consumer surplus to fall by £8.28, which is 69% of the £12 she spends on tracks.

5.2 Expenditure Function and Consumer Welfare

Our desired consumer surplus measure is the income that we would need to give a consumer to offset the harm of an increase in price. That is, it is the extra income we would have to provide so that the consumer's utility would not change. Equivalently, this measure is the dollar value of the change in utility in the absence of compensation.

So far in this chapter, we have measured the effect of a price increase by a change in consumer surplus using an uncompensated demand curve, which provides an inexact measure of consumer welfare. An uncompensated demand curve does not hold a consumer's utility constant as the price changes. Along an uncompensated demand curve, as the price rises, the change in the quantity that the consumer buys reflects both a substitution and an income effect (Chapter 4). Economists frequently use the uncompensated demand curve to calculate consumer surplus because they usually have estimates of only the uncompensated demand curve.

However, if economists have an estimated compensated demand curve, they can calculate the pure income effect measure. Indeed, a compensated demand curve is constructed to answer the question of how much less of a product a consumer would purchase in response to a price increase if the consumer is given extra income to offset the price increase so as to hold the consumer's utility constant. That is, along a compensated demand curve, as the price rises, the change in the quantity demanded by the consumer reflects a pure substitution effect. The corresponding amount of income compensation is the measure we seek.

Luckily, we already have a means to calculate the relevant income compensation: the expenditure function, Equation 3.32, which is the minimal expenditure necessary to achieve a specific utility level, $\bar{U}$, for a given set of prices,

$$E = E(p_1, p_2, \bar{U}) \tag{5.1}$$

The expenditure function contains the same information as the compensated demand curve.

In Chapter 4, we showed that the compensated demand function for q_1 is the partial derivative of the expenditure function with respect to p_1: The compensated demand function is $\partial E(p_1, p_2, \bar{U})\partial p_1$. Thus, if we integrate with respect to price to the left of the compensated demand function, we get the expenditure function.*

We can calculate the consumer welfare loss of a price increase from p_1 to p_1^* as the difference between the expenditures at these two prices:

$$\text{welfare change} = E(p_1, p_2, \bar{U}) - E(p_1^*, p_2, \bar{U}). \tag{5.2}$$

In Equation 5.2, an increase in the price causes a drop in welfare.

However, to use this approach, we have to decide which level of utility, $\bar{U}$, to use. We could use the level of utility corresponding to the original indifference curve or the level on the indifference curve of the optimal bundle after the price change. We call the first of these measures the *compensating variation* and the second one the *equivalent variation*.

The **compensating variation** (*CV*) is the amount of money one would have to give a consumer to offset completely the harm from a price increase—to keep the consumer on the original indifference curve. This measure of the welfare harm of a price increase is called the compensating variation because we give money to the consumer; that is, we compensate the consumer.

The **equivalent variation** (*EV*) is the amount of money one would have to take from a consumer to harm the consumer by as much as the price increase. This measure is the same, or equivalent, harm as that due to the price increase: It moves the consumer to the new, lower indifference curve.

Indifference Curve Analysis

We can use indifference curves to determine CV and EV effects of an increase in price. Again, we use the example based on Jackie's estimated utility function, in which she chooses between music tracks and live music. Initially, Jackie pays $p_1 = £0.5$ for each music track and $p_2 = £1$ for each unit of live music. In Figure 5.3, her original budget constraint is L^a and has a slope of $-p_1/p_2 = -p_1 = -0.5$. The budget constraint is tangent to indifference curve I at her optimal bundle, a, where she buys 24 tracks.

Now, the price of tracks doubles to $p_1^* = £1$, so that Jackie's budget line rotates to L^b and has a slope of -1. The new budget line is tangent to indifference curve I^* at her new optimal bundle, b, where she buys 12 tracks. Jackie is harmed by the price increase: She is on a lower indifference curve I^* (utility level $\overline{U}^*$) instead of on I (utility level $\overline{U}$).

Figure 5.3 Compensating Variation and Equivalent Variation

At the initial price, Jackie's budget constraint, L^a, is tangent to her initial indifference curve I at a, where she buys 24 tracks. After the price of tracks doubles, her new budget constraint, L^b, is tangent to her indifference curve I^* at b, where she buys 12 tracks. Because the price of a unit of live music is £1, L^b hits the vertical axis at Y. If Jackie were given CV extra income to offset the price increase, her budget line would be L^{CV} (which is parallel to L^b), and she would be tangent to her original indifference curve, I, at point c. The budget line L^{CV} hits the vertical axis at $Y + CV$, so the difference between where this budget line and the L^b line strike the vertical axis equals CV. Similarly, at the original price, if we removed income equal to EV, her budget line would shift down to L^{EV}, and Jackie would choose bundle d on I^*. Thus, taking EV away harms her as much as the price increase. The gap between where L^b and L^{EV} touch the vertical axis equals EV.

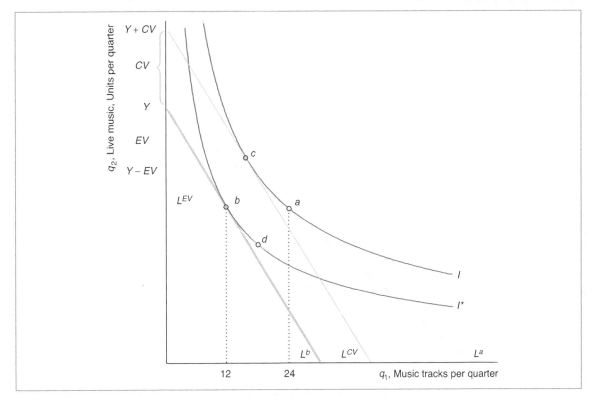

Compensating Variation. The amount of money that would fully compensate Jackie for a price increase is the compensating variation, CV. Suppose that after the price of tracks increases to £1, Jackie is given enough extra income, CV, so that her utility remains at $\bar{U}$. At this new income, $Y + CV$, Jackie's budget line is L^{CV}, which has the same slope, -1, as L^b. After the price changes and she receives this income compensation, she buys Bundle c.

How large is CV? Because the price of a unit of live music is £1 per unit, the before-compensation budget line, L^b, hits the live music axis at $Y = £30$, and the after-compensation budget line, L^{CV}, hits at $Y + CV$. Thus, the gap between the two intercepts is CV.

This analysis is the same one we engaged in to determine the substitution and income effects of a price change in Chapter 4. The compensating variation measure is the income (CV) involved in the income effect (the movement from b to c).

Equivalent Variation. The amount of income that, if taken from Jackie, would lower her utility by the same amount as the price increase for tracks from £0.5 to £1 is the equivalent variation, EV. The increase in price harms Jackie by as much as a loss of income equal to EV would if the price remained at £0.5. That is, Jackie's income would have to fall by enough to shift the original budget constraint, L^a, down to L^{EV}, where it is tangent to I^* at Bundle d. Because the price of a unit of live music is £1, EV is the distance between the intercept of L^a and that of L^{EV} on the live music axis. The key distinction between these two measures is that the equivalent variation is calculated by using the new, lower utility level, whereas the compensating variation is based on the original utility level.

APPLICATION

Compensating Variation for Television

How much do you value watching television? Fewer than one in four Americans (23%) say that they would be willing to "give up watching absolutely all types of television" for the rest of their lives in exchange for $25,000. Almost half (46%) say they would refuse to give up TV for anything under $1 million. One in four Americans wouldn't give it up for $1 million. Indeed, one-quarter of those who earn under $20,000 a year wouldn't give up TV for $1 million—more than they will earn in 50 years.

Thus, if you ask how much consumer surplus people receive from television, you will get many implausibly high answers. For this reason, economists typically calculate consumer surplus by using estimated inverse demand curves, which are based on actual observed behavior, or by conducting surveys that ask consumers to choose between relatively similar bundles of goods. A more focused survey of families in Great Britain and Northern Ireland in 2000 found that families were willing to pay £10.40 ($15.60) per month to keep their current, limited television service (BBC1, BB2, ITV, Channel 4, and Channel 5) and that they received £2 ($3) per month of consumer surplus (the cost of the service was £2 less than they were willing to pay).

Comparing the Three Welfare Measures

Economists usually think of the change in consumer surplus as an approximation of the compensating variation and equivalent variation measures. Which consumer welfare measure is larger depends on the income elasticity of the product. If the good is a normal good (as a music track is for Jackie), $|CV| > |\Delta CS| > |EV|$. If the good is an inferior good, $|CV| < |\Delta CS| < |EV|$.

5.2 Expenditure Function and Consumer Welfare

An Example. We illustrate the relative size of the three measures based on our earlier example using Jackie's estimated Cobb-Douglas utility, in which a government tax causes the price of music tracks, p_1, to double from £0.5 to £1, so that she now buys 12 rather than 24 tracks per quarter.

In Figure 5.4, her lost consumer surplus, ΔCS, is areas $A + B$: the area between £0.5 and £1 on the price axis to the left of her uncompensated demand curve. Her compensating variation is $A + B + C$, which is the area between £0.5 and £1 to the left of the compensated demand curve corresponding to the original utility level, H^{CV}. This amount of money is just large enough to offset the harm of the higher price, so that Jackie will remain on her initial indifference curve. Finally, her equivalent variation is A, which is the area between £0.5 and £1 to the left of the compensated demand curve, corresponding to the new, lower utility level, H^{EV}. Losing this amount of money would harm Jackie as much as would the price increase. We can calculate CV and EV as the change in Jackie's expenditure function as the price rises, holding the price of a unit of live music constant at $p_2 = £1$.[2] Substituting this price into Equation 4.9, we know that Jackie's expenditure function is

$$E = \bar{U}\left(\frac{p_1}{0.4}\right)^{0.4}\left(\frac{p_2}{0.6}\right)^{0.6} \approx 1.96\bar{U}p_1^{0.4}p_2^{0.6} = 1.96\bar{U}p_1^{0.4}. \quad (5.3)$$

Figure 5.4 Comparing CV, EV, and ΔCS

When the price rises from $15 to $20, Jackie loses consumer surplus, ΔCS, equal to $A + B$. Using her compensated demand curve at her initial utility level, H^{CV}, an increase of income or compensating variation, CV, equal to area $A + B + C$ would offset the harm from the price increase. Based on her compensated demand curve at the new utility level, H^{EV}, Jackie's loss from the price increase is equal to a loss of income of EV = area A.

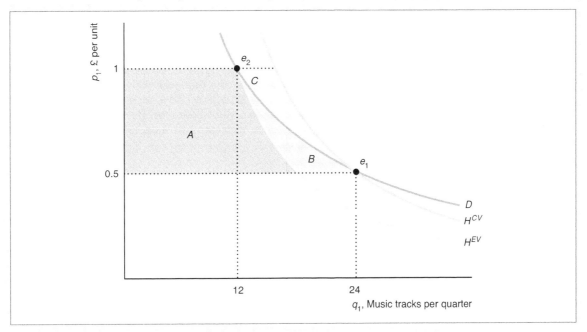

---

[2]We would get the same answer if we integrate to the left of the relevant compensated demand curve, as we did with the uncompensated demand curve to get our consumer surplus measure.

At Jackie's initial optimum, where $q_1 = 24$ and $q_2 = 18$, her utility is $\bar{U} = 24^{0.4}18^{0.6} \approx 20.20$. Thus, the expenditure function at the original equilibrium is $E \approx 39.59 p_1^{0.4}$. At her new optimum after the price change, where $q_1 = 12$ and $q_2 = 18$, the utility level $\bar{U}^* = 12^{0.4}18^{0.6} \approx 15.31$, so the new expenditure function is $E^* \approx 30.01 p_1^{0.4}$. Thus,

$$CV = E(0.5) - E(1) = 39.59(0.5^{0.4} - 1^{0.4}) \approx 39.59 \times (-0.24) \approx -8.63, \quad (5.4)$$

$$EV = E^*(0.5) - E^*(1) = 30.01(0.5^{0.4} - 1^{0.4}) \approx 30.01 \times (-0.24) \approx -7.20. \quad (5.5)$$

As Figure 5.4 shows, Jackie's equivalent variation, $EV = A + B + C = -£7.20$, is a smaller loss (in absolute value) than her consumer surplus loss, $\Delta CS = A + B = -£8.28$, which is a smaller loss than her compensating variation, $CV = C = -£8.63$.

Differences Between the Three Measures. Although the three measures of welfare could in principle differ substantially, for many goods they do not differ much for small changes in price. According to the Slutsky equation (Equation 4.11),

$$\varepsilon = \varepsilon^* - \theta \xi,$$

the uncompensated elasticity of demand, ε, equals the compensated elasticity of demand (pure substitution elasticity), ε^*, minus the budget share of the good, θ, times the income elasticity, ξ. The smaller the income elasticity or the smaller the budget share, the closer the substitution elasticity is to the total elasticity, and the closer the compensated and uncompensated demand curves are. Thus, the smaller the income elasticity or budget share, the closer the three welfare measures are to each other.

Because the budget shares of most goods are small, the three measures are often very close. Even for an aggregate good on which consumers spend a relatively large share of their budget, these differences may be small. Table 5.1 gives estimates of these three measures for various aggregate goods based on an estimated system of U.S. demand curves for a typical consumer. For each good, the table shows the income elasticity, the budget share, the ratio of compensating variation to the change in consumer surplus, $CV/\Delta CS$, and the ratio of the equivalent variation to the change in consumer surplus, $EV/\Delta CS$, for a 50% increase in price.

The three welfare measures are virtually identical for the alcohol and tobacco category, which has the smallest income elasticity and budget share of any of the goods.

Table 5.1 Welfare Measures

	Income Elasticity, ξ	Budget Share (%)	$\dfrac{EV}{\Delta CS}$	$\dfrac{CV}{\Delta CS}$
Alcohol & tobacco	0.39	4	99%	100.4%
Food	0.46	17	97	103
Clothing	0.88	8	97	102
Utilities	1.00	4	98	101
Transportation	1.04	8	97	103
Medical	1.37	9	95	104
Housing	1.38	15	93	107

Source: Calculations based on Blanciforti (1982).

Because housing has the largest income elasticity and budget share, it has a relatively large gap between the measures. However, even for housing, the difference between the change in uncompensated consumer surplus and either of the compensating consumer surplus measures is only 7%.

Willig (1976) showed theoretically that the three measures vary little for small price changes regardless of the size of the income effect. Indeed, for the seven goods in the table, if the price change were only 10%—instead of the 50% in the table—the differences between CV or EV and ΔCS are a small fraction of a percentage point for all goods except housing, where the difference is only about 1%.

Thus, the three measures of the welfare effect of a small price change give very similar answers even for aggregate goods. As a result, economists frequently use the change in consumer surplus, which is relatively easy to calculate because it is based on the uncompensated demand curve.

SOLVED PROBLEM 5.2

Lucy has a quasilinear utility function, Equation 3.9, $U(q_1, q_2) = u(q_1) + q_2$. When she maximizes her utility subject to her budget constraint, she chooses to consume both goods (an interior solution). The price of the second good, p_2, equals one. The price of q_1 increases from $\underline{p}_1$ to $\bar{p}_1$. Show that her compensating variation, CV, equals her equivalent variation, EV, and equals the change in her consumer surplus, ΔCS.

Answer

1. *Discuss Lucy's demand function for q_1 and write her utility function in terms of her expenditures.* From Chapter 4, we know that Lucy's demand for q_1 is a function of its price, $q_1(p_1)$. We can rewrite Lucy's expenditure function, $E = p_1 q_1 + q_2$, as $q_2 = E - p_1 q_1$. Substituting this expression into her utility function, we can write her utility as $u(q_1) + E - p_1 q_1$.

2. *Calculate the compensating variation at the two prices.* At $\underline{p}_1$, Lucy demands $\underline{q}_1 = q_1(\underline{p}_1)$ and her utility is $u(\underline{q}_1) + E - \underline{p}_1 \underline{q}_1$. At $\bar{p}_1$, $\bar{q}_1 = q_1(\bar{p}_1)$ and $u(\bar{q}_1) + E - \bar{p}_1 \bar{q}_1$. The compensating variation, CV, is the amount of extra money that she needs to receive if her utility is to remain constant despite the increase in price: $u(\underline{q}_1) + E - \underline{p}_1 \underline{q}_1 = u(\bar{q}_1) + E + CV - \bar{p}_1 \bar{q}_1$. Solving the equation for CV, we find that
$$CV = u(\underline{q}_1) - u(\bar{q}_1) + \bar{p}_1 \bar{q}_1 - \underline{p}_1 \underline{q}_1.$$

3. *Calculate the equivalent variation at the two prices and compare it to the compensating variation.* By similar reasoning, her equivalent variation, EV, is the amount that would have to be taken from her at the original price to lower her utility to that at the higher price. It is determined by $u(\underline{q}_1) + E - EV - \underline{p}_1 \underline{q}_1 = u(\bar{q}_1) + E - \bar{p}_1 \bar{q}_1$. Solving for EV, we learn that
$$EV = u(\underline{q}_1) - u(\bar{q}_1) + \bar{p}_1 \bar{q}_1 - \underline{p}_1 \underline{q}_1.$$
Thus, for a quasilinear utility function, $CV = EV$.

4. *Show that her consumer surplus equals the other two measures.* Because ΔCS lies between EV and CV, if $EV = CV$, then $EV = CV = \Delta CS$.

Comment: We noted earlier that $|CV| > |\Delta CS| > |EV|$ for a normal good (positive income effect) and that $|CV| < |\Delta CS| < |EV|$ for an inferior good (negative income effect). With a quasilinear utility function, there is no income effect for the first good, so $|CV| = |\Delta CS| = |EV|$.

5.3 Market Consumer Surplus

A change in total consumer surplus captures the effects of a shock on all consumers in a market. Because the market demand curve is the (horizontal) sum of the individual demand curves, the market consumer surplus is the sum of each individual's consumer surplus.

We first measure the effect of a price increase on the market consumer surplus using an estimated market demand curve for sweetheart and hybrid tea roses sold in the United States.[3] We then discuss in which markets consumers are likely to suffer the greatest loss of consumer surplus due to a price increase.

Loss of Market Consumer Surplus from a Higher Price

Suppose that a new tax causes the (wholesale) price of roses to rise from the original equilibrium price of 30¢ to 32¢ per rose stem, which reflects a movement along the market inverse demand curve in Figure 5.5. The consumer surplus is area $A + B + C = \$173.74$ million per year at a price of 30¢, but it is only area $A = \$149.64$ million at a price of 32¢.[4] Thus, the loss in consumer surplus from the increase in the price is $B + C = \$24.1$ million per year.

Markets in Which Consumer Surplus Losses Are Large

In general, as the price of a good increases, consumer surplus falls more (1) the greater the initial revenue spent on the good and (2) the less elastic the demand curve at the equilibrium.[5] More is spent on a good when its demand curve is farther to the right, so that areas like A, B, and C in Figure 5.5 are larger. The larger $B + C$ is, the greater the drop in consumer surplus from a given percentage increase in price. Similarly, the less elastic a demand curve is (the closer it is to vertical), the less willing consumers are to give up the good, so consumers do not cut their consumption much as the price increases, and hence suffer a greater consumer surplus loss.

Higher prices cause a greater loss of consumer surplus in some markets than in others. Consumers would benefit if policymakers, before imposing a tax, considered in which market the tax would be likely to harm consumers the most.

---

[3]This model was estimated using data from the *Statistical Abstract of the United States, Floriculture Crops, Floriculture and Environmental Horticulture Products*, and **usda.mannlib.cornell.edu**. The prices are in real 1991 dollars.

[4]The height of triangle A is 25.8¢ = 57.8¢ − 32¢ per stem, and the base is 1.16 billion stems per year, so its area is $\frac{1}{2} \times \$0.258 \times 1.16$ billion = \$149.64 million per year. The area of rectangle B is \$0.02 × 1.16 billion = \$23.2 million. The area of triangle C is $\frac{1}{2} \times \$0.02 \times 0.09$ billion = \$0.9 million.

[5]If the demand curve is linear, as in Figure 5.5, the lost consumer surplus is area $B + C$. If Q is the initial quantity, 1.25, then the new quantity is $Q + \Delta Q$, 1.16 (where $\Delta Q = -0.09$), so area B is a rectangle, of $(Q + \Delta Q)\Delta p$, with length $Q + \Delta Q$ and height Δp. Similarly, area C is a triangle, $-\frac{1}{2}\Delta Q \Delta p$, of length $-\Delta Q$ and height Δp. For small changes in price, we can approximate any demand curve with a straight line, so $\Delta CS = (Q + \Delta Q)\Delta p - \frac{1}{2}\Delta Q \Delta p = (Q + \frac{1}{2}\Delta Q)\Delta p$ is a reasonable approximation of the true change in consumer surplus (a rectangle plus a triangle). We can rewrite this expression for ΔCS as

$$\Delta p \left(Q + \frac{1}{2}\Delta Q\right) = Q\Delta p \left[1 + \frac{1}{2}\left(\frac{\Delta Q}{Q} \frac{p}{\Delta p}\right)\frac{\Delta p}{p}\right] = (pQ)\frac{\Delta p}{p}\left(1 + \frac{1}{2}\varepsilon\frac{\Delta p}{p}\right) = Rx\left(1 + \frac{1}{2}\varepsilon x\right),$$

where $x = \Delta p/p$ is the percentage increase in the price, $R\ (= pQ)$ is the initial revenue from the sale of good Q, and ε is the elasticity of demand. This equation is used to calculate the last column in Table 5.2.

Figure 5.5 A Fall in Market Consumer Surplus as the Price of Roses Rises

As the price of roses rises 2¢ per stem from 30¢ per stem, the quantity demanded decreases from 1.25 to 1.16 billion stems per year. The loss in market consumer surplus from the higher price, areas B and C, is $24.1 million per year.

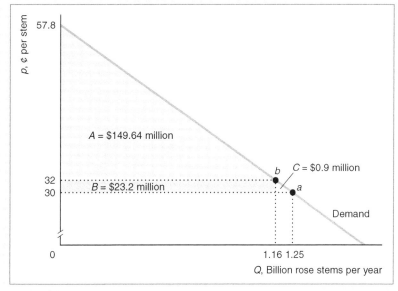

We can use estimates of demand curves to predict for which good a price increase causes the greatest loss of consumer surplus. Table 5.2 shows the consumer surplus loss in billions of 2008 dollars from a 10% increase in the price of various goods. The table shows that the loss in consumer surplus is larger, the larger the initial revenue (price times quantity) that is spent on a good. A 10% increase in price causes a $149 billion loss of consumer surplus if the increase is imposed on medical services where annual revenue is $1,554 billion, but only a $19 loss of consumer surplus if the increase is imposed on alcohol and tobacco where annual revenue is $192 billion.

At first glance, the relationship between elasticities of demand and the loss in consumer surplus in Table 5.2 looks backward: A given percent change in prices has a larger effect on consumer surplus for the relatively elastic demand curves. However, this relationship is coincidental: The large-revenue goods happen to have

Table 5.2 The Effect of a 10% Price Increase on Consumer Surplus
(Revenue and Consumer Surplus in Billions of 2008 Dollars)

	Revenue	Elasticity of Demand, ε	Change in Consumer Surplus, ΔCS
Medical	1,554	−0.604	−151
Housing	1,543	−0.633	−149
Food	669	−0.245	−66
Clothing	338	−0.405	−33
Transportation	301	−0.461	−29
Utilities	308	−0.448	−30
Alcohol & tobacco	192	−0.162	−19

Sources: Revenues are from National Income and Product Accounts (NIPA), www.bea.gov; elasticities are based on Blanciforti (1982).

148 Chapter 5 *Consumer Welfare and Policy Analysis*

relatively elastic demand curves. The effect of a price change depends on both revenue and the demand elasticity. In this table, the relative size of the revenues is more important than the relative elasticities.

However, if we could hold the revenue constant and vary the elasticity, we would find that the consumer surplus lost from a price increase is larger as the demand curve becomes less elastic. If the demand curve for alcohol and tobacco were 10 times more elastic, −1.62, while the revenue stayed the same (so that the demand curve were flatter at the initial price and quantity), the consumer surplus loss would be nearly $1.2 billion less.

SOLVED PROBLEM 5.3

Suppose that two linear demand curves go through the initial equilibrium, e_1. One demand curve is less elastic than the other at e_1. For which demand curve will a price increase cause the larger consumer surplus loss?

Answer

1. *Draw the two demand curves, and indicate which one is less elastic at the initial equilibrium.* Two demand curves cross at e_1 in the diagram. The steeper demand curve is less elastic at e_1.[6]

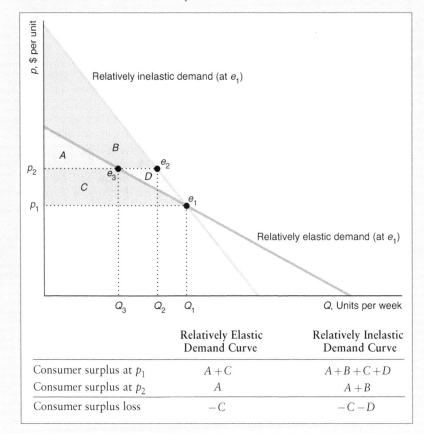

	Relatively Elastic Demand Curve	Relatively Inelastic Demand Curve
Consumer surplus at p_1	$A+C$	$A+B+C+D$
Consumer surplus at p_2	A	$A+B$
Consumer surplus loss	$-C$	$-C-D$

---

[6]The price elasticity of demand, $\varepsilon = (dQ/dp)(p/Q)$, equals 1 over the slope of the demand curve, dp/dQ, times the ratio of the price to the quantity (Chapter 2). Thus, at the point of intersection where both demand curves have the same price, p_1, and the same quantity, Q_1, the steeper the demand curve, the lower the elasticity of demand.

2. *Illustrate that a price increase causes a larger consumer surplus loss with the less elastic demand curve.* If the price rises from p_1 to p_2, the consumer surplus falls by only $-C$ with the relatively elastic demand curve and by $-C - D$ with the relatively inelastic demand curve.

5.4 Effects of Government Policies on Consumer Welfare

The various consumer welfare measures are used to answer questions about the effect on consumers of government programs and other events that shift consumers' budget constraints. If the government imposes a quota, which reduces the number of units that a consumer buys, or provides a consumer with a certain amount of a good (such as food), the government creates a kink in the consumer's budget constraint. In contrast, if the government subsidizes the price of a good (such as a child care subsidy) or provides cash to the consumer, it causes a rotation or a parallel shift of the budget line.

Quotas

Consumers' welfare is reduced if they cannot buy as many units of a good as they want. As a promotion, firms often sell a good at an unusually low price but limit the number of units that one can purchase. Governments, too, frequently limit how much of a good one can buy by setting a quota.

During emergencies, for example, governments sometimes ration "essential" goods such as water, food, energy, and flu vaccines rather than let these goods' prices rise. In the last couple of years, water quotas were imposed in areas of the United Kingdom, Fiji, China, Cyprus, Australia, and the United States (California, Georgia, North Carolina, Massachusetts, Oklahoma, and Texas). In recent years, legislation was proposed in the United States, Britain, and other countries to limit energy use. Under the Domestic Tradable Quotas proposed by the United Kingdom, individuals would be issued a "carbon card" from which points would be deducted every time the cardholder purchased fossil fuel—for example, when filling up a gas tank or taking a flight. Also, in recent years, many nations have rationed bird, swine, and other flu vaccines.

To illustrate the effect of a quota, we return to Jackie's choice between music tracks and live music. As Figure 5.6 shows, before the quota is imposed, Jackie's downward-sloping budget constraint consists of two line segments, L^1 and L^2. Her optimal bundle e_1, where she purchases 24 tracks and 18 units of live music per quarter, occurs where L^2 is tangent to I^1.

Now suppose that a government (or her mother) limits Jackie's purchases to no more than 12 tracks per quarter. Her new budget constraint is the same as the original for fewer than 12 tracks, L^1, and is vertical at 12 tracks. She loses part of the original opportunity set: the shaded triangle, area A, determined by the vertical line at 12 tracks, L^2, and the horizontal axis. Now, her best option is to purchase Bundle e_2— 12 tracks and 24 units of live music—which is the point where the highest indifference curve, I^2, touches the new constraint. However, I^2 is not tangent to the budget constraint. Thus with a quota, a consumer could have an interior solution in which she buys some of all the goods, but the tangency condition does not hold because the limit causes a kink in the budget constraint (as in the corner solution in Chapter 3).

Figure 5.6 The Equivalent Variation of a Quota

Originally, Jackie faces a budget constraint consisting of the line segments L^1 and L^2 and buys 24 song tracks and 18 units of live music at e_1 on indifference curve I^1. When a quota limits purchases of tracks to 12 per quarter (vertical line at 12), the L^2 segment is no longer available and the shaded triangle, A, is lost from the opportunity set. The best that Jackie can do now is to purchase e_2 on indifference curve I^2. Suppose that Jackie did not face a quota but lost an amount of income equal to EV that caused her budget constraint to shift down to L^3, which is tangent to indifference curve I^2 at e_3. Thus, the effect on her utility of losing EV amount of income—shifting her from I^1 to I^2—is equivalent to the effect of the quota.

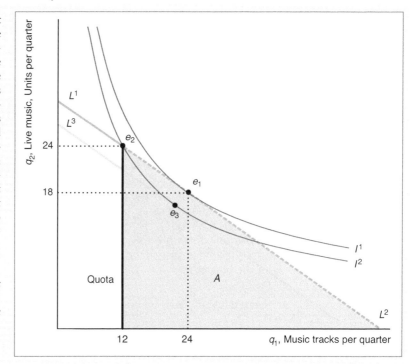

The quota harms Jackie because she is now on indifference curve I^2, which is below her original indifference curve, I^1. To determine by how much she is harmed, we can calculate the equivalent variation: the amount of money we would have to take from Jackie to harm her as much as the quota does. We draw a budget line, L^3, that is parallel to L^2 but that just barely touches I^2. The difference between the expenditure on the original budget line and the new expenditure is Jackie's equivalent variation.

As we know, Jackie's original expenditure is £30. We can use her expenditure function, Equation 5.3, $E \approx 1.96\bar{U}p_1^{0.4}$, to determine the expenditure on L^3. Substituting $p_1 = £0.5$ and her utility on I^2 at e_2, $\bar{U} = 12^{0.4}24^{0.6} \approx 18.19$, into her expenditure function, we find that her expenditure on L^3 is about £27. Thus, Jackie's equivalent variation is £3 (= £30 − £27).

APPLICATION
Water Quota

Since 2001, a major drought, the "Big Dry," has reduced the amount of water in storage throughout much of South-East Australia. Australian state governments and water utilities imposed quotas to reduce the amount of water demanded by banning various outdoor water uses. At least 75% of Australians faced mandatory water restrictions in 2008, and restrictions continued into 2010.

Grafton and Ward (2008) compared the consumer surplus loss from restricting water use rather than allowing the price to rise so as to clear the market. To achieve the same reduction in the water demanded on the original demand curve, the price would have had to rise substantially from $1.01 to $2.35 per kiloliter. (Of course, raising price instead of imposing a quota would have created a hardship for poor people unless they received compensating financial help.) They estimated that the loss in consumer surplus from using mandatory water restrictions rather than price adjustments was $235 million—about $150 per household, which was a little less than half the average Sydney household's annual water bill. This loss occurs because consumers who were willing to pay more to use water outdoors were prevented from doing so.

Food Stamps

I've known what it is to be hungry, but I always went right to a restaurant.
—Ring Lardner

We can use the theory of consumer choice to analyze whether poor people are better off receiving food or a comparable amount of cash. Federal, state, and local governments work together to provide food subsidies for poor Americans. According to a 2008 U.S. Department of Agriculture report, 11.1% of U.S. households worry about having enough money to buy food, and 4.1% report that they suffer from inadequate food at some point during the year. Households that meet income, asset, and employment eligibility requirements receive coupons—food stamps—that they can use to purchase food from retail stores.

The U.S. Food Stamp Plan started in 1939. The modern version, the Food Stamp Program, was permanently funded starting in 1964. In 2008, it was renamed the Supplemental Nutrition Assistance Program (SNAP). SNAP is one of the nation's largest social welfare programs, with expenditures of $34.6 billion for 28.4 million people in 2008, and 32.6 million in 2009. Of recipient households, 83% have a child or an elderly or disabled person, and these households receive 88% of all benefits. During the 2009 recession, food stamps fed one in eight Americans and one in four children. Americans receiving food stamps included 28% of blacks, 15% of Latinos, and 8% of whites. According to Professor Mark Rank, by the time they reach 20 years of age, half of all Americans and 90% of black children have received food stamps at least briefly.[7]

Since the food stamp programs started, economists, nutritionists, and policymakers have debated "cashing out" food stamps by providing checks or cash instead of coupons that can be spent only on food. Legally, food stamps may not be sold, though a black market for them exists. Because of technological advances in electronic fund transfers, switching from food stamps to a cash program would lower administrative costs and reduce losses due to fraud and theft.

Would a switch to a comparable cash subsidy increase the well-being of food stamp recipients? Would the recipients spend less on food and more on other goods?

Why Cash Is Preferred to Food Stamps. Poor people who receive cash have more choices than those who receive a comparable amount of food stamps. Only food can be obtained with food stamps. With cash, either food or other goods can be purchased. As a result, a cash grant increases a recipient's opportunity set by more than do food stamps of the same value.

In Figure 5.7, we made both the price of a unit of food and the price of all other goods $1 by choosing the units for each such that $1 buys one unit of each. Felicity has a monthly income of Y, so her budget line hits both axes at Y. Her opportunity set is area A.

If Felicity receives a subsidy of $100 in cash per month, her new monthly income is $Y + \$100$. Her new budget constraint with cash hits both axes at $Y + 100$ and is

---

[7]DeParle, Jason, and Gebeloff, Robert, "The Safety Net: Food Stamp Use Soars, and Stigma Fades," *New York Times*, November 29, 2009.

Figure 5.7 Food Stamps Versus Cash

The lighter line shows the original budget line of an individual with Y income per month. The heavier line shows the budget constraint with $100 worth of food stamps. The budget constraint with a grant of $100 in cash is a line between Y + 100 on both axes. The opportunity set increases by area B with food stamps but by B + C with cash. An individual with these indifference curves consumes Bundle d (with less than 100 units of food) with no subsidy, e (Y units of all other goods and 100 units of food) with food stamps, and f (more than Y units of all other goods and less than 100 units of food) with a cash subsidy. This individual's utility is greater with a cash subsidy than with food stamps.

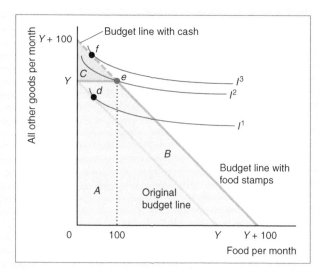

parallel to the original budget constraint. Her opportunity set increases by $B + C$ to $A + B + C$.

If instead Felicity receives $100 worth of food stamps, her food stamp budget constraint has a kink. Because the food stamps can be spent only on food, the budget constraint shifts 100 units to the right for any quantity of other goods up to Y units. For example, if Felicity buys only food, now $Y + 100$ units of food can be purchased. If she buys only other goods with the original Y income, she can get Y units of other goods plus 100 units of food. Because the food stamps cannot be turned into other goods, Felicity can't buy $Y + 100$ units of other goods, as she could under a cash transfer program. The food stamps opportunity set is area $A + B$, which is larger than the pre-subsidy opportunity set by B. The opportunity set with food stamps is smaller than with the cash transfer program by C.

Felicity benefits as much from cash or an equivalent amount of food stamps if she would have spent at least $100 on food if given cash. In other words, she is indifferent between cash and food stamps if her indifference curve is tangent to the downward-sloping section of the food stamp budget constraint. Here, the equivalent variation is $100.

Conversely, if she would not spend at least $100 on food if given cash, she prefers receiving cash to food stamps. If she has the indifference curves shown in Figure 5.7, she prefers cash to food stamps. She chooses Bundle e (Y units of all other goods and 100 units of food) if she receives food stamps, but Bundle f (more than Y units of all other goods and less than 100 units of food) if she is given cash. She is on a higher indifference curve, I^2 rather than I^1, if given cash rather than food stamps. If we draw a budget line with the same slope as the original one (−1) that is tangent to I^2, we can calculate the equivalent variation as the difference between the expenditure on that budget line and the original one. The equivalent variation is less than $100.

APPLICATION

Benefiting from Food Stamps

If recipients of food stamps received cash instead of the stamps, their utility would remain the same or rise, some recipients would consume less food and more of other goods, potential recipients would be more likely to participate, and the administrative costs of these welfare programs would fall.

Whitmore (2002) finds that a sizable minority of food stamp recipients would be better off if they were given cash instead of an equivalent value in food stamps. She estimates that between 20% and 30% of food stamp recipients would spend less on food than their food stamp benefit amount if they received cash instead of stamps, and therefore would be better off with cash. Of those who would trade their food stamps for cash, the average food stamp recipient values the stamps at 80% of their face value (although the average price on the underground market is only 65%). Thus, across all such recipients, $500 million is wasted by giving food stamps rather than cash.

As the theory suggests, Hoynes and Schanzenbach (2009) find that food stamps result in a decrease in out-of-pocket expenditures on food and an increase in overall food expenditures. For those households that would prefer cash to food stamps—those that spend relatively little of their income on food—food stamps cause them to increase their food consumption by about 22%, compared to 15% for other recipients, and 18% overall. Based on her statistical study of the types of food that recipients consume, Whitmore (2002) concludes that giving cash would not lower their nutrition and might reduce their odds of obesity.

It is also possible that the stigma of using food stamps discourages some people from participating in food stamp programs. Only about two-thirds (67.3%) of eligible people participated in the Food Stamps Program in 2006. To make participating easier and to reduce the stigma associated with presenting food stamps at a grocery store, the federal government required that all states replace paper food stamps with ATM-like cards. After June 2009, food stamp coupons were no longer in use. Using these cards instead of stamps reduced administrative costs by half in some states.

Why We Give Food Stamps. Two groups in particular object to giving cash instead of food stamps: some policymakers, because they fear that cash might be spent on booze or drugs, and some nutritionists, who worry that poor people will spend the money on housing or other goods and get too little nutrition. In response, many economists argue that poor people are the best judges of how to spend their scarce resources. The question of whether it is desirable to let poor people choose what to consume is normative (a question of values), and economic theory cannot answer it. How poor people will change their behavior, however, is a positive (scientific) question, one that we *can* analyze. Experiments to date find that cash recipients consume slightly lower levels of food but receive at least adequate levels of nutrients and that they prefer receiving cash.

Given that recipients are as well off or better off receiving cash as they are receiving food stamps, why do we have programs that provide food stamps instead of programs that provide cash? The introduction to a report by the U.S. Department of Agriculture's Food and Nutrition Service, which administers the food stamp program (Fasciano et al., 1993, p. 6), offers this explanation:

> From the perspective of recipient households, cash is more efficient than coupons in that it permits each household to allocate its resources as it sees fit.... But in a more general sense, recipients' welfare clearly depends on public support for the program. And what evidence we have suggests that taxpayers are more comfortable providing in-kind, rather than cash, benefits and may consequently be more generous in their support of a coupon-based program. Thus, the question of which benefit form best promotes the welfare of financially needy households is more complex than it might appear.

Child Care. The high cost of child care prevents some poor mothers from working.[8] Consequently, countries around the world provide child care subsidies to poor parents. Instead of subsidizing the price of child care, governments could provide unrestricted lump-sum payments for poor parents to spend on day care or on all other goods, such as food and housing. (A third alternative is to provide parents with vouchers for child care services. We would analyze such a program as we did food stamps.)

Would a price subsidy or a lump-sum subsidy provide greater benefit to recipients for a given government expenditure? Which program increases the demand for day care services by more? Which approach benefits poor families most?

To answer these questions, we use an indifference curve–budget line analysis in which a poor family chooses between hours of day care per day, Q, and all other goods per day (with a price of $1 per unit). Given that its initial budget constraint is L^o, a poor family chooses Bundle e_1 on indifference curve I^1. The family consumes Q_1 hours of day care services in Figure 5.8.

Figure 5.8 Child Care Subsidies

Given the initial budget constraint L^o, the family obtains Q_1 hours of day care per day. If the government subsidizes the price of day care, the budget line rotates out to L^{PS} and the family consumes Q_2 hours of day care. Conditional on obtaining Q_2 hours of day care, the family could have spent Y_o on other goods originally, but it can now buy Y_2 amount. If the government gives the family $Y_2 - Y_o$ instead of the price subsidy, the family's budget constraint is L^{LS}, and it buys only Q_3 hours of day care. The family is better off with the lump sum than with the price subsidy because it is on indifference curve I^3 rather than I^2.

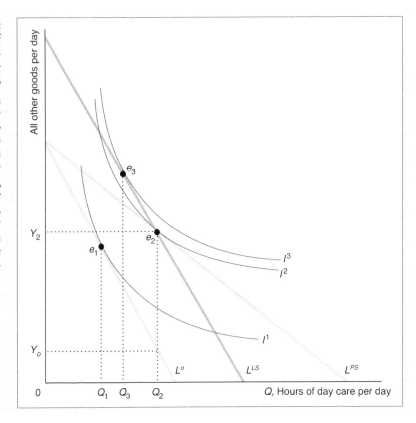

---

[8]The increased employment of mothers outside the home has led to a steep rise in the use of child care over the past several decades. In the United States, 6 out of 10 mothers work today—twice the rate in 1970. 6 out of 10 children under the age of 6 are in child care, as are 45% of children under age 1. 8 of 10 employed mothers with children under age 6 are likely to have some form of nonparental child care arrangement. In the United States, child care expenses for children under the age of 5 absorb 25% of the earnings for families with annual incomes under $14,400 but only 6% for families with incomes of $54,000 or more.

If the government gives the family a day care price subsidy, which lowers the daily price of day care, the new budget line L^{PS} rotates out along the day care axis. Now, the family consumes Bundle e_2 on the higher indifference curve I^2. The family consumes more hours of day care, Q_2, because day care is now less expensive and is a normal good.

One way to measure the value of the subsidy that the family receives is to calculate the equivalent variation. Given that the family consumes Q_2 hours of day care, the family could have consumed Y_o other goods with the original budget constraint and Y_2 with the price-subsidy budget constraint. Given that Y_2 is the family's remaining income after paying for child care, the family buys Y_2 units of all other goods. That is, $Y_2 - Y_o$ is the extra amount of money that the family spends on other goods.

If, instead of receiving a day-care price subsidy, the family were to receive a lump-sum payment of $Y_2 - Y_o$, taxpayers' costs for the two programs would be the same. The family's budget constraint after receiving a lump-sum payment, L^{LS}, has the same slope as the original budget constraint, L^o, given that the relative prices of day care and all other goods have not changed. This budget constraint must go through e_2 because the family has just enough money to buy that bundle. However, the family will be better off if it buys Bundle e_3 on indifference curve I^3 (the reasoning is the same as in Solved Problem 4.5 and the Consumer Price Index analysis in Figure 4.8). The family consumes less day care with the lump-sum subsidy: Q_3 rather than Q_2.

Thus, the lump-sum payment of $Y_2 - Y_o$ is slightly more than the equivalent variation of the price subsidy. (If we draw a budget line that is parallel to L^o but tangent to I^2, then the equivalent variation is the difference between the intersection of that budget line with the vertical axis and the intersection of L^o with the vertical axis.)

Poor families prefer the lump-sum payment to the price subsidy because the indifference curve I^3 is above I^2. Taxpayers should be indifferent between the two programs because they both cost the same. The day care industry prefers the price subsidy because the demand curve for its service is farther to the right: At any given price, more child care is demanded by poor families who receive a price subsidy rather than a lump-sum subsidy.

Given that most of the directly affected groups should prefer lump-sum payments to price subsidies, why are price subsidies so heavily used? One possible explanation is that the day care industry has very effectively lobbied for price supports, but there is little evidence that such lobbying occurred. Second, politicians might believe that poor families will not make intelligent choices about day care, so the politicians might see price subsidies as a way of inducing these families to consume relatively more (or better-quality) day care than they would choose if they were given lump-sum payments they could spend on any goods. Third, politicians may prefer that poor people consume more day care so that poor people can work more hours, thereby increasing society's wealth. Fourth, politicians may not understand this analysis.

APPLICATION
Child Care Subsidies

Child care or day care subsidies are common throughout the world. The United States and the United Kingdom spend 0.6% of GDP on child care, compared to 0.2% in Canada and Ireland, 0.3% in Japan, 0.4% in Australia and New Zealand, 1% in Norway, 1.2% in France and Sweden, and 1.6% in Denmark (Currie and Gahvari, 2008).

A 1996 U.S. welfare law, the Personal Responsibility and Work Opportunity Reconciliation Act (PRWORA), sought to help people transition from welfare to work and to keep low-income parents employed. It aimed to double the number of children from poor families receiving federal child care assistance between 1997 and 2003. Since then, Congress has reauthorized the program twice. The

amount spent on the child care program rose from $10.4 billion in 2001 to $12.3 billion in 2003, but fell to $11.9 billion in 2004 and to $11.7 billion in 2005, while the average number of children served remained essentially constant over this period, resulting in less assistance per child.

Child care programs vary substantially across states in their generosity and in the form of the subsidy. Some states provide an ad valorem subsidy, while others use a specific subsidy (Chapter 2) to lower the hourly rate that a poor family pays for day care. We can use Figure 5.8 to analyze either a specific subsidy or an ad valorem subsidy if the families are free to choose the total number of hours of child care because the figure is based on the after-subsidy price of child care for the last hour of care. However, states generally limit the amount of the subsidy. In 2009, a family's maximum child care subsidy was 85% of the cost of care in Nevada and 70% in Louisiana, $72.50 per week in Alabama, 10% of gross income in Maine, and $153 per month plus $5 per month for each extra child in Mississippi. A binding limit on the subsidy creates a kink in the budget constraint. (Question 17 asks you to show how a limit changes the analysis.)

5.5 Deriving Labor Supply Curves

Throughout Chapters 3, 4, and 5, we've used consumer theory to examine consumers' demand behavior. Perhaps surprisingly, we can also apply the consumer theory model to derive a person's supply curve of labor. We do so by using consumer theory to obtain the person's demand curve for leisure time and then using that demand curve to derive the supply curve, which shows the hours the individual wants to work as a function of the wage. We then use our labor supply model to analyze how a change in the income tax rate affects the supply of labor and the revenue that the government collects.

Labor-Leisure Choice

The human race is faced with a cruel choice: work or daytime television.

People choose between working to earn money to buy goods and services and consuming *leisure*: all their time spent not working for pay. In addition to sleeping, eating, and playing, leisure—or more accurately nonwork, N—includes time spent cooking meals and fixing things around the house.

Hugo spends his total income, Y, on various goods. For simplicity, we assume that the price of these goods is $1 per unit, so he buys Y goods. His utility, U, depends on how many goods, Y, and how much leisure, N, he consumes:

$$U = U(Y, N). \tag{5.6}$$

He faces an hours-worked constraint and an income constraint. The number of hours he works per day, H, equals 24 minus the hours he spends on leisure:

$$H = 24 - N. \tag{5.7}$$

The total income, Y, that Hugo has to spend on goods equals his earned income—his wage times the number of hours he works, wH—and his unearned income, Y^*, such as income from an inheritance or a gift from his parents:

$$Y = wH + Y^*. \tag{5.8}$$

Using consumer theory, we can determine Hugo's demand curve for leisure once we know the price of leisure. What does it cost you to watch TV or go to school or do anything other than work for an hour? It costs you the wage, w, you could have earned from an hour's work: The price of leisure is forgone earnings. The higher your wage, the more an hour of leisure costs you. For this reason, taking an afternoon off costs a lawyer who earns $250 an hour much more than it costs a fast food server who earns the minimum wage.

Panel a of Figure 5.9 shows Hugo's choice between leisure and goods. The vertical axis shows how many goods, Y, Hugo buys. The horizontal axis shows both

Figure 5.9 The Demand Curve for Leisure

(a) Hugo chooses between leisure, N, and other goods, Y, subject to a time constraint (the vertical line at 24 hours) and a budget constraint, L^1, which is $Y = w_1 H = w_1 \times (24 - N)$, and has a slope of $-w_1$. The tangency of his indifference curve I^1 with his budget constraint L^1 determines his optimal bundle, e_1, where he has $N_1 = 16$ hours of leisure and works $H_1 = 24 - N_1 = 8$ hours. If his wage rises from w_1 to w_2, Hugo shifts from optimal bundle e_1 to e_2. (b) Bundles e_1 and e_2 correspond to E_1 and E_2 on his leisure demand curve.

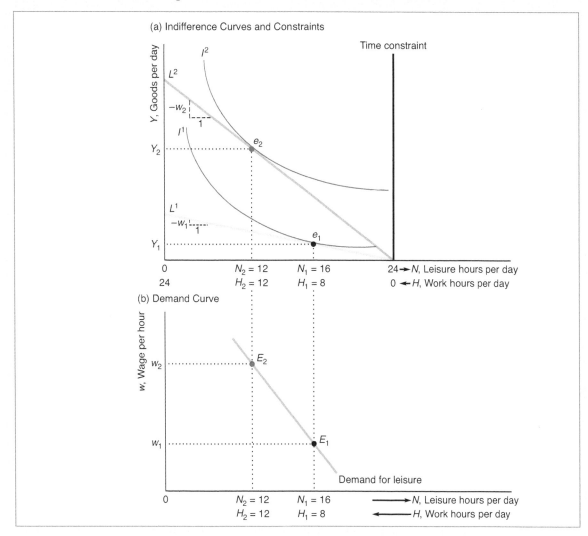

hours of leisure, N, which are measured from left to right, and hours of work, H, which are measured from right to left. Hugo maximizes his utility given the *two* constraints he faces. First, he faces a time constraint, which is a vertical line at 24 hours of leisure. There are only 24 hours in a day; all the money in the world won't buy him more hours in a day. Second, Hugo faces a budget constraint. Because Hugo has no unearned income, his initial budget constraint, L^1, is $Y = w_1 H = w_1(24 - N)$. The slope of his budget constraint is $-w_1$, because each extra hour of leisure he consumes costs him w_1 goods.

Hugo picks his optimal hours of leisure, $N_1 = 16$, so he is on the highest indifference curve, I^1, that touches his budget constraint. He works $H_1 = 24 - N_1 = 8$ hours per day and earns an income of $Y_1 = w_1 H_1 = 8w_1$.

We derive Hugo's demand curve for leisure using the same method by which we derived Mimi's demand curve for beer in Chapter 4. We raise the price of leisure—the wage—in panel a of Figure 5.9 to trace out Hugo's demand curve for leisure in panel b. As the wage increases from w_1 to w_2, leisure becomes more expensive, and Hugo demands less of it.

We can also solve this problem using calculus. Hugo maximizes his utility, Equation 5.6, subject to the time constraint, Equation 5.7, and the income constraint, Equation 5.8. Although we can analyze this problem using Lagrangian techniques, it is easier to do so by substitution. By substituting Equations 5.7 and 5.8 into 5.6, we can convert this constrained problem into an unconstrained maximization problem, where Hugo maximizes his utility through his choice of how many hours to work per day:

$$\max_H U = U(Y, N) = U(wH, 24 - H). \tag{5.9}$$

By using the chain rule of differentiation, we find that the first-order condition for an interior maximum to the problem in Equation 5.9 is

$$\frac{\partial U}{\partial Y}\frac{dY}{dH} + \frac{\partial U}{\partial N}\frac{dN}{dH} = U_Y w - U_N = 0, \tag{5.10}$$

where $U_Y = \partial U/\partial Y$ is the marginal utility of goods or income and $U_N = \partial U/\partial N$ is the marginal utility of leisure.[9] That is, Hugo sets his marginal rate of substitution of income for leisure, $MRS = -U_N/U_Y$, equal to his marginal rate of transformation of income for leisure, $MRT = -w$, in the market:

$$MRS = -\frac{U_N}{U_Y} = -w = MRT. \tag{5.11}$$

Equivalently, the last dollar's worth of leisure, U_N/w, equals the marginal utility from the last dollar's worth of goods, U_Y.

By subtracting Hugo's demand for leisure at each wage—his demand curve for leisure in panel a of Figure 5.10—from 24, we construct his labor supply curve—the hours he is willing to work as a function of the wage, $H(w)$—in panel b. His supply curve for hours worked is the mirror image of the demand curve for leisure: For every extra hour of leisure that Hugo consumes, he works one hour less.

---

[9]The second-order condition for an interior maximum is
$$\frac{\partial^2 U}{\partial Y^2}w^2 - 2\frac{\partial^2 U}{\partial Y \partial N}w + \frac{\partial^2 U}{\partial N^2} < 0.$$

Figure 5.10 The Labor Supply Curve

(a) Hugo's demand for leisure is downward sloping. (b) At any given wage, the number of hours that Hugo works, h, and the number of hours of leisure, n, that he consumes add to 24. Thus, his supply curve for hours worked, which equals 24 hours minus the number of hours of leisure he demands, is upward sloping.

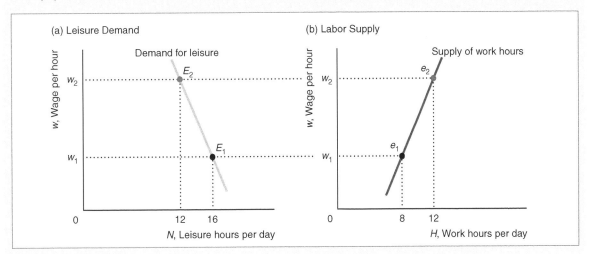

SOLVED PROBLEM 5.4

If Sofia has a Cobb-Douglas utility function, $U = (wH)^a(24 - H)^{1-a}$, what is her labor supply function? What is her supply function if $a = \frac{1}{3}$?

Answer

1. *To find the values that maximize her utility, set the derivative of Sofia's utility function with respect to H equal to zero.* This first-order condition is $aw(wH)^{a-1}(24 - H)^{1-a} - (1 - a)(wH)^a(24 - H)^{-a} = 0$. Simplifying, we find that $H = 24a$. Thus, Sofia works a fixed number of hours regardless of the wage.

2. *Substitute in the value $a = \frac{1}{3}$ to obtain the specific hours-worked function.* Given that $a = \frac{1}{3}$, she works $H = 8$ hours a day whether the wage is 50¢ or $50 per hour.

Income and Substitution Effects

An increase in the wage causes both income and substitution effects, which alter an individual's demand for leisure and supply of hours worked. The *total effect* of an increase in Hugo's wage from w_1 to w_2 is the movement from e_1 to e_2 in Figure 5.11. Hugo works $H_2 - H_1$ fewer hours and consumes $N_2 - N_1$ more hours of leisure.

By drawing an imaginary budget constraint, L^*, that is tangent to Hugo's original indifference curve and has the slope of the new wage, we can divide the total effect into substitution and income effects. The *substitution effect*, the movement from e_1 to e^*, must be negative: A compensating wage increase causes Hugo to consume fewer hours of leisure, N^*, and to work more hours, H^*. As his wage rises, if Hugo works the same number of hours as before, he has a higher income. The *income effect* is the movement from e^* to e_2. The figure shows that his income effect

Figure 5.11 The Income and Substitution Effects of a Wage Change

A wage change causes both a substitution and an income effect. As the wage rises, Hugo's optimal bundle changes from e_1 to e_2. The movement from e_1 to e^* is the substitution effect, the movement from e^* to e_2 is the income effect, and the movement from e_1 to e_2 is the total effect. The compensating variation is $Y^* - Y_2$.

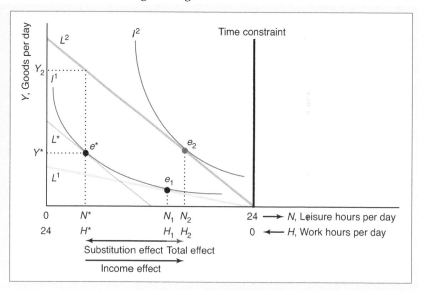

is positive—he consumes more leisure as his income rises—because he views leisure as a normal good.

When leisure is a normal good, the substitution and income effects work in opposite directions. Which effect dominates depends on the relative size of the two effects. In Figure 5.11, Hugo's income effect dominates the substitution effect, so the total effect for leisure is positive: $N_2 > N_1$. Given that the total number of hours in a day is fixed, if Hugo consumes more leisure when his wage rises, then he must work fewer hours. That is, he is in a backward-bending section of his supply curve (his supply curve has the opposite slope of the one in panel b of Figure 5.10). If, alternatively, Hugo viewed leisure as an inferior good, both his substitution effect and income effect would work in the same direction, so that an increase in the wage would cause his hours of leisure to fall and his work hours to rise (as in Figure 5.10).

In Figure 5.11, by removing $Y^* - Y_2$ income from Hugo, we could offset the benefit of the wage increase by keeping him on indifference curve I^1. Thus, $Y^* - Y_2$ is the compensating variation.[10]

SOLVED PROBLEM 5.5

Enrico receives a no-strings-attached scholarship that pays him an extra Y^* per day. How does this scholarship affect the number of hours he wants to work? Does his utility increase?

Answer

1. *Show his consumer equilibrium without unearned income.* When Enrico had no unearned income, his budget constraint, L^1 in the graphs, hit the hours-leisure axis at 0 hours and had a slope of $-w$.

2. *Show how the unearned income affects his budget constraint.* The extra income causes a parallel upward shift of Y^*. His new budget constraint, L^2,

---

[10]See "Leisure-Income Choices of Textile Workers" in the supplemental material to Chapter 5 in **MyEconLab**'s textbook resources for an example of substitution and income effects based on estimated utility functions of workers.

has the same slope as before because his wage does not change. The extra income cannot buy Enrico more time, of course, so L^2 cannot extend to the right of the time constraint. As a result, L^2 is vertical at 0 hours up to Y^*: His income is Y^* if he works no hours. Above Y^*, L^2 slants toward the goods axis with a slope of $-w$.

3. *Show that the relative position of the new to the original equilibrium depends on his tastes.* The change in the number of hours he works depends on Enrico's tastes. Panels a and b show two possible sets of indifference curves. In both diagrams, when facing budget constraint L^1, Enrico chooses to work H_1 hours. In panel a, leisure is a normal good, so as his income rises, Enrico consumes more leisure: He moves from Bundle e_1 to Bundle e_2. In panel b, he views leisure as an inferior good and consumes fewer hours of leisure than at first: He moves from e_1 to e_3. (Another possibility is that the number of hours he works is unaffected by the extra unearned income.)

4. *Discuss how his utility changes.* Regardless of his tastes, Enrico has more income in the new equilibrium and is on a higher indifference curve after receiving the scholarship. In short, he believes that more money is better than less.

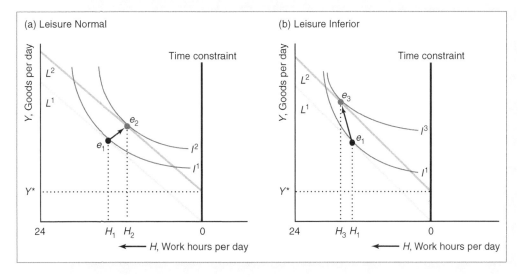

Shape of the Labor Supply Curve

Whether the labor supply curve slopes upward, bends backward, or has sections with both properties depends on the income elasticity of leisure. Suppose that a worker views leisure as an inferior good at low wages and a normal good at high wages. As the wage increases, the worker's demand for leisure first falls and then rises, and the hours supplied to the market first rise and then fall. (Alternatively, the labor supply curve may slope upward and then backward even if leisure is normal at all wages: At low wages, the substitution effect—working more hours—dominates the income effect—working fewer hours—while the opposite occurs at higher wages.)

The budget line rotates upward from L^1 to L^2 as the wage rises in panel a of Figure 5.12. Because leisure is an inferior good at low incomes, in the new optimal

Figure 5.12 A Labor Supply Curve That Slopes Upward and Then Bends Backward

At low incomes, an increase in the wage causes the worker to work more hours: the movement from e_1 to e_2 in panel a or from E_1 to E_2 in panel b. At higher incomes, an increase in the wage causes the worker to work fewer hours: the movement from e_2 to e_3 or from E_2 to E_3.

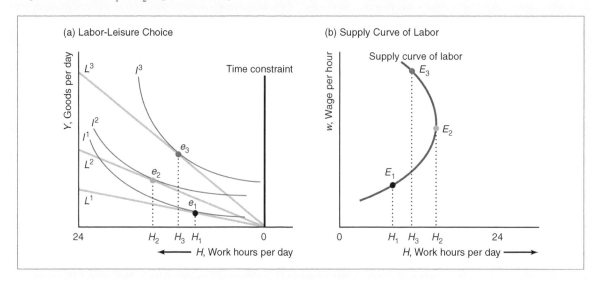

bundle, e_2, this worker consumes less leisure and buys more goods than at the original bundle, e_1.

At higher incomes, however, leisure is a normal good. At an even higher wage, the new equilibrium is e_3 on budget line L^3, where the quantity of leisure demanded is higher and the number of hours worked is lower. Thus, the corresponding supply curve for labor slopes upward at low wages and bends backward at higher wages in panel b.

Do labor supply curves slope upward or backward? Economic theory alone cannot answer this question, as both forward-sloping and backward-bending supply curves are *theoretically* possible. Empirical research is necessary to resolve this question.

Most studies (Killingsworth, 1983; MaCurdy et al., 1990; Saez et al., 2009) find that the labor supply curves for British and American men are virtually vertical because both the income and the substitution effects are offsetting or both small. Similar results are found in other countries such as Japan (Kuroda and Yamamoto, 2008) and the Netherlands (Evers et al., 2008). Studies find that wives' labor supply curves are also nearly vertical: slightly backward bending in Canada and the United States and slightly forward sloping in the United Kingdom and Germany. In contrast, some studies of the labor supply of single women find relatively large positive supply elasticities of 4.0 and even higher. Thus, only single women tend to work substantially more hours when their wages rise.

APPLICATION
Working After Winning the Lottery

Would you stop working if you won a lottery jackpot or inherited a large sum? Economists want to know how unearned income affects the amount of labor people are willing to supply because this question plays a crucial role in many government debates on taxes and welfare. For example, some legislators oppose negative income tax and welfare programs because they claim that giving money to poor people will stop them from working. Is that assertion true?

We could clearly answer this question if we could observe the behavior of a large group of people, only some of whom were randomly selected to receive varying but large amounts of unearned income each year for decades. Luckily for us, governments conduct such experiments by running lotteries.

Imbens et al. (2001) compared the winners of major prizes to others who played the Massachusetts Megabucks lottery. Major prizes ranged from $22,000 to $9.7 million, with an average of $1.1 million, and were paid in yearly installments over two decades.

A typical player in this lottery earned $16,100. The average winner received $55,200 in prize money per year and chose to work slightly fewer hours so that his or her labor earnings fell by $1,877 per year. That is, winners increased their consumption and savings but did not substantially decrease how much they worked.

For every dollar of unearned income, winners reduced their work effort and hence their labor earnings by 11¢ on average. Men and women, big and very big prize winners, and people of all education levels behaved the same way. However, the behavior of winners differed by age and by income groups. People ages 55 to 65 reduced their labor efforts by about a third more than younger people did, presumably because they decided to retire early. Most striking, people with no earnings in the year before winning the lottery tended to increase their labor earnings after winning.

Kuhn et al. (2008) examined the Dutch Postcode Lottery in which prizes are awarded weekly to lottery participants living in randomly selected postal codes. On average, the prizes are equal to about eight months of income. Household heads who received prizes did not change how many hours they worked.

Income Tax Rates and the Labor Supply Curve

The wages of sin are death, but by the time taxes are taken out, it's just sort of a tired feeling. —Paula Poundstone

Why do we care about the shape of labor supply curves? One reason is that we can tell from the shape of the labor supply curve whether an increase in the income tax rate—a percent of earnings—will cause a substantial reduction in the hours of work.[11] An increase in the income tax rate lowers workers' after-tax wages. If workers' supply curves are backward bending, a small increase in the tax rate increases hours worked (reducing leisure hours), boosts production, and increases the tax revenue collected. On the other hand, if people's supply curves are upward sloping, a small increase in the wage tax rate reduces hours worked, decreases production, and may lower the tax revenue collected.

Although they have been unwilling to emulate Lady Godiva's tax-fighting technique—allegedly, her husband, Leofric, the Earl of Mercia, agreed to her request to eliminate taxes if she rode naked through the Coventry marketplace—various U.S. presidents have advocated tax cuts. Presidents John Kennedy, Ronald Reagan, and George W. Bush argued that cutting the *marginal tax rate*—the percentage of the last dollar earned that the government takes in taxes—would induce people to work

---

[11]Although taxes are ancient, the modern income tax was introduced in 1798 by William Pitt the Younger: The British assessed 10% on annual incomes above £60 to finance the war with Napoleon. The U.S. Congress followed suit in 1861, collecting 3% on annual incomes over $800 to pay for the Civil War.

longer and produce more, both desirable effects. President Reagan predicted that the government's tax receipts would increase due to the additional work.

Because tax rates have changed substantially over time, we have a natural experiment to test this hypothesis. The Kennedy tax cuts lowered the top federal personal marginal tax rate from 91% to 70%. Due to the Reagan tax cuts, the maximum rate fell to 50% in 1982–1986, 38.5% in 1987, and 28% in 1988–1990. The rate rose to 31% in 1991–1992 and to 39.6% in 1993–2000. The Bush tax cuts reduced this rate to 38.6% for 2001–2003, 37.6% for 2004–2005, and 35% since 2006. (President Obama expanded two tax cuts for the working poor, but proposed raising the top rate to 39.6%.)

Many other countries' central governments have also lowered their top marginal tax rates in recent years. The top U.K. rate fell sharply during the Thatcher administration from 83% to 60% in 1979 and to 40% in 1988 (although it is scheduled to rise to 50% in April 2010). Japan's top rate fell from 75% in 1983 to 60% in 1987, 50% in 1988, and to 37% in 1999 (but it rose to 40% in 2007). In 1988, Canada raised the marginal tax rates for the two lowest income groups and lowered them for those falling into the top nine brackets.

Of more concern to individuals than the federal marginal tax rate is the tax rate that includes taxes collected by all levels of government. According to the Organization for Economic Cooperation and Development (OECD), the top all-inclusive marginal tax rate in 2008 was 22.5% in the Slovak Republic, 29.6% in Mexico, 39.0% in New Zealand, 41.0% in the United Kingdom, 43.2% in the United States (on average across the states), 46.4% in Canada, 46.5% in Australia, 47.8 in Japan, 59.4% in Belgium, and 63% in Denmark.

If the tax does not affect the pretax wage, the effect of imposing a tax rate of $\tau = 25\% = 0.25$ is to reduce the effective wage from w to $(1 - \tau)w = 0.75w$.[12] The tax reduces the after-tax wage by 25%, so a worker's budget constraint rotates downward, similar to rotating the budget constraint downward from L^2 to L^1, in Figure 5.12.

As we discussed, if the budget constraint rotates downward, the hours of work may increase or decrease, depending on whether a person considers leisure to be a normal or an inferior good. The worker in panel b of Figure 5.12 has a labor supply curve that at first slopes upward and then bends backward. If the worker's wage is very high, the worker is in the backward-bending section of the labor supply curve.

If so, the relationship between the marginal tax rate, τ, and tax revenue, $\tau w H$, is bell-shaped, as in Figure 5.13. This figure is the estimated U.S. tax revenue curve (Trabandt and Uhlig, 2009). At the marginal rate for the typical person, $\tau = 28\%$, the government collects 100% of the amount of tax revenue it's currently collecting. At a zero tax rate, a small increase in the tax rate *must* increase the tax revenue because no revenue was collected when the tax rate was zero. However, if the tax rate rises a little more, the tax revenue collected must rise even higher, for two rea-

---

[12]Under a progressive income tax system, the marginal tax rate increases with income. The average tax rate differs from the marginal tax rate. Suppose that the marginal tax rate is 20% on the first $10,000 earned and 30% on the second $10,000. Someone who earned $20,000 would pay $2,000 (=0.2 × $10,000) on the first $10,000 of earnings and $3,000 on the next $10,000. That taxpayer's average tax rate is 25% (=[$2,000 + $3,000]/$20,000). For simplicity, in the following analysis, we assume that the marginal tax rate is a constant, τ, so the average tax rate is also τ. In 2009, if you were a single person with a taxable income of $500,000, your marginal rate was 35%, but your average rate was 23.54%. (To see your marginal and average tax rates, use the calculator at www.smartmoney.com/tax/filing/index.cfm?story=taxbracket.)

Figure 5.13 The Relationship of U.S. Tax Revenue to the Marginal Tax Rate

This curve shows how U.S. income tax revenue varies with the marginal income tax rate, τ, according to Trabandt and Uhlig (2009). The typical person pays τ = 28%, which corresponds to 100% of the current tax revenue that the government collects. The tax revenue would be maximized at 130% of its current level if the marginal rate were set at τ* = 63%. For rates below τ*, an increase in the marginal rate raises larger tax revenue. However at rates above τ*, an increase in the marginal rate decreases tax revenue.

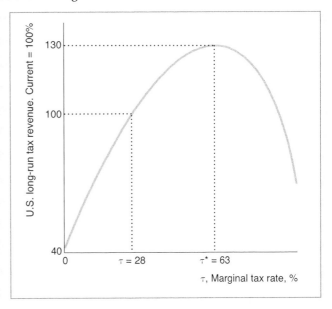

sons: First, the government collects a larger percentage of every dollar earned because the tax rate is higher. Second, employees work more hours as the tax rate rises because workers are in the backward-bending sections of their labor supply curves.

As the marginal rate increases, tax revenue rises until the marginal rate reaches τ* = 63%, where the U.S. tax revenue would be 130% of its current level. If the marginal tax rate increases more, workers are in the upward-sloping sections of their labor supply curves, so an increase in the tax rate reduces the number of hours worked. When the tax rate rises high enough, the reduction in hours worked more than offsets the gain from the higher rate, so the tax revenue falls.

It makes little sense for a government to operate at very high marginal tax rates in the downward-sloping portion of this bell-shaped curve. The government could get more output *and* more tax revenue by cutting the marginal tax rate.

What is the effect on the tax revenue collected when the income tax rate increases? To answer this question, we let τ be the constant marginal income tax rate and w be the worker's wage, so that for every w a worker is paid, the government receives τw. (We ignore unearned income and the possibility that the tax rate varies with income.)

Suppose the government collects τ share of the wage. If w is the worker's wage, then the government takes τw, and the worker's after-tax wage is $\omega = (1 - \tau)w$. The government's tax revenue, T, is

$$T = \tau w H\left[(1-\tau)w\right] = \tau w H(\omega), \tag{5.12}$$

where $H(\omega)$ is the hours of labor that a worker supplies given the after-tax wage ω.

By differentiating Equation 5.12 with respect to τ, we can show how revenue changes as the tax rate increases:

$$\frac{dT}{d\tau} = wH(\omega) - \tau w^2 \frac{dH}{d\omega}. \tag{5.13}$$

Thus, a change in the tax rate has two effects. First, the government collects more revenue because of the higher tax rate: A one-unit increase in τ causes the tax revenue to increase by $wH(\omega)$, the amount that the worker earns. Second, the change in the tax alters the hours worked. As the rate goes up, before-tax labor earnings, $wH(\omega)$, decrease if the labor supply is upward sloping, $dH/d\omega > 0$, which reduces the tax revenue by $\tau w^2 dH/d\omega$.

The government can raise the amount of tax revenue collected by lowering the tax rate if the economy is on the downward sloping part of the tax-revenue curve to the right of τ^* in Figure 5.13. In Equation 5.13, for the tax revenue to decrease when the tax rate increases (or to rise when the tax rate decreases), we need $dT/d\tau = wH - \tau w^2 dH/d\omega < 0$. Using algebra, we can rewrite this condition as

$$\frac{1}{\tau} < \frac{dH}{d\omega} \frac{w}{H(\omega)}.$$

If we multiply both sides of this expression by $(1 - \tau)$, we obtain the condition that

$$\frac{1-\tau}{\tau} < \frac{dH}{d\omega} \frac{\omega}{H(\omega)} = \eta, \tag{5.14}$$

where $\eta = [dH/d\omega][\omega/H(\omega)]$ is the elasticity of supply of work hours with respect to after-tax wages, ω.

Thus, for the tax revenue the government collects to fall from a small increase in the tax rate, the elasticity of supply of labor must be greater than $(1 - \tau)/\tau$. In the United States in 2009, a single person earning between \$33,950 and \$82,250 had a marginal tax rate of $\tau = 25\%$. For a small increase in this rate to lower the tax revenue collected, such a person's η had to be greater than 3 (= 0.75/0.25), which was not likely. In the past, some countries had very high tax rates where this condition could be hold. For example, if $\tau = 90\%$, the condition is met if the elasticity of supply is greater than 1/9.

APPLICATION

Maximizing Income Tax Revenue

If a country's marginal income tax rate is initially on the upward sloping section to the left of the peak of the bell-shaped tax revenue curve below τ^*, then raising τ increases tax revenue, but causes people to work fewer hours. If the initial rate is on the "wrong side" of the revenue curve to the right of τ^*, then reducing τ will raise tax revenues and hours worked.

Trabandt and Uhlig (2009) calculated the potential revenue gains from adjusting the tax rate to τ^*. The following table summarizes their results for the United States and 14 EU countries, where EU-14 is the average for the 14 EU countries and all numbers are percentages. The first column is the typical marginal tax-rate percentage, τ; the second column shows the rate that maximizes tax collections, τ^*; and the final column is the maximum possible percentage increase in tax revenue that can be obtained in the long run, by raising or lowering τ to equal τ^*. Denmark is (slightly) on the wrong side of the curve. If Denmark were to lower its marginal tax rate by 2 percentage points, it would increase the number of hours its citizens worked and raise the nation's tax revenue by 1%. All the other countries can increase their tax revenues by raising their marginal income tax rates. The United States and Ireland could gain the most additional revenue, 30%, by more than doubling their current tax rates.

	τ	τ*	Maximum Additional Tax Revenue
United States	28	63	30
EU-14	41	62	8
Ireland	27	68	30
United Kingdom	28	59	17
Portugal	31	59	14
Spain	36	62	13
Germany	41	64	10
Netherlands	44	67	9
Greece	41	60	7
France	46	63	5
Italy	47	62	4
Belgium	49	61	3
Finland	49	62	3
Austria	50	61	2
Sweden	56	63	1
Denmark	57	55	1

SUMMARY

1. **Consumer Welfare.** The pleasure a consumer receives from a good in excess of its cost is called *consumer surplus*. Consumer surplus is the extra value that a consumer gets from a transaction over and above the amount paid, the amount that a consumer would be willing to pay for the right to buy as many units as desired at the specified price, and the area under the consumer's inverse demand curve and above the market price up to the quantity the consumer buys. The degree to which consumers are harmed by an increase in a product's price is measured by the reduction in consumer surplus.

2. **Expenditure Function and Consumer Welfare.** If we measure the harm to a consumer from a price increase using consumer surplus, we are not holding a consumer's utility constant. We can use the expenditure function to obtain two other measures that hold utility constant. The expenditure function enables us to determine how much a consumer's income (expenditure) would have to change to offset a change in price so as to hold the consumer's utility constant. The *compensating variation* is the amount of money one would have to give a consumer to offset completely the harm from a price increase—to keep the consumer on the original indifference curve. The *equivalent variation* is the amount of money one would have to take from a consumer to harm the consumer by as much as the price increase would. For small price changes, the three measures of the effect of a price increase on a consumer's well-being—the change in consumer surplus, the compensating variation, and the equivalent variation—are typically close. The smaller the income elasticity or the smaller the budget share of the good, the smaller the differences between these three measures.

3. **Market Consumer Surplus.** The market consumer surplus—the sum of the welfare effect across all consumers—is the area under the market inverse demand curve above the market price. The more revenue that is spent on the good and the less elastic the demand curve is, the larger the market consumer surplus.

4. **Effects of Government Policies on Consumer Welfare.** A government quota on the consumption of a good, food stamps, or a child care price subsidy creates a kink in a consumer's budget constraint, which affects how much consumers purchase and their well-being. Many, but not all, consumers would be better

off if the government gave them an amount of money equal to the value of the food stamps or the child care subsidy instead of these subsidies.

5. **Deriving Labor Supply Curves.** Using consumer theory, we can derive a person's daily demand curve for leisure (time spent on activities other than work), which shows how hours of leisure vary with the wage rate, which is the price of leisure. The number of hours that a person works equals 24 minus that person's leisure hours, so we can determine a person's daily labor supply curve from that person's demand curve for leisure. The labor supply curve is upward sloping if leisure is an inferior good and backward bending if it is a normal good. Whether a cut in the income tax rate will cause government tax revenue to rise or fall depends on the shape of the labor supply curve.

QUESTIONS

■ = exercise is available on **MyEconLab**; * = answer appears at the back of this book; V = video answer by James Dearden is available online.

1. According to Hong and Wolak (2008), a 5% postal price increase, such as the one in 2006, reduces postal revenue by $215 million and lowers consumer surplus loss by $333 million. Illustrate these results in a figure similar to that of Figure 5.2, and indicate the dollar amounts of areas A and B in the figure.

2. Hong and Wolak (2008) find that recent postal price increases and the wider use of personal computers and phones by U.S. households led to similar reductions on postal expenditure. Using the information in the previous question, illustrate how the greater use of computers and phones affects the demand curve for postal services. Assuming that the price of postal services remains constant, show how consumer surplus from postal services changes.

3. In the "Compensating Variation for Television" application, people are asked how much they would be willing to pay to watch television or how much they'd have to be paid never to watch again. Graph what is being measured. What alternative question could have been asked that would have provided more details on the value consumers place on watching an extra hour of television?

4. What happens to the budget line if the government applies a specific tax of $1 per gallon on gasoline but does not tax other goods? What happens to the budget line if the tax applies only to purchases of gasoline in excess of 10 gallons per week?

5. Max chooses between water and all other goods. If he spends all his money on water, he can buy 12,000 gallons per week. At current prices, his optimal bundle is e_1. Show in a diagram. During a drought, the government limits the number of gallons per week that he may purchase to 10,000. Using diagrams, discuss under which conditions his new optimal bundle, e_2, will be the same as e_1. If the two bundles differ, can you state where e_2 must be located?

6. Since 1979, low-income recipients have been given food stamps without charge. However before 1979, people bought food stamps at a subsidized rate. For example, to get $1 worth of food stamps, a household paid about 15¢ (the exact amount varied by household characteristics and other factors). Show the budget constraint facing an individual if that individual is allowed to buy up to $100 per month in food stamps at 15¢ per each $1 coupon.

7. Is a poor person more likely to benefit from $100 a month worth of food stamps (that can be used only to buy food) or $100 a month worth of clothing stamps (that can be used only to buy clothing)? Why?

8. If a relatively wealthy person spends more on food than a poor person before receiving food stamps, is the wealthy person less likely than the poor person to have a tangency at a point such as f in Figure 5.7?

9. Is a wealthy person more likely than a poor person to prefer to receive a government payment of $100 in cash to $100 worth of food stamps? Why or why not?

10. Federal housing assistance programs provide allowances that can be spent only on housing. Several empirical studies find that recipients increase their non-housing expenditures by 10% to 20% (Harkness and Newman, 2003). Show that recipients might—but do not necessarily—increase their spending on non-housing, depending on their tastes.

11. Federal housing and food stamp subsidy programs are two of the largest in-kind transfer programs for the poor. In President George W. Bush's proposed 2006 budget, the Food Stamp Program (FSP) provided approximately $33.1 billion in benefits and the housing program added another $38.4 billion. Many poor people are eligible for both programs: 30% of housing assistance recipients also used food stamps, and 38% of FSP participants also received housing assistance (Harkness and Newman, 2003). Suppose Jill's income is $500 a month, which she spends on food and housing. The prices of food and housing are each $1 per unit. Draw her budget line. If she receives $100 in food stamps and $200 in a housing subsidy (which she can spend only on housing), how do her budget line and opportunity set change?

12. In 2002, the Supreme Court ruled that school voucher programs do not violate the Establishment Clause of the First Amendment, provided that parents, not the state, direct to which schools the money goes. Educational vouchers are increasingly used in various parts of the United States. Suppose that the government offers poor people $5,000 education vouchers that can be used only to pay for education. Doreen would be better off with $5,000 in cash than with the educational voucher. In a graph, determine the cash value, V, Doreen places on the education voucher (that is, the amount of cash that would leave her as well off as with the voucher). Show how much education and "all other goods" she would consume with the educational voucher versus the cash payment of V.

13. A poor person who has an income of $1,000 receives $100 worth of food stamps. Draw the budget constraint if the food stamp recipient can sell these coupons on the black market for less than their face value.

14. Show how much an individual's opportunity set increases if the government gives people food stamps rather than sells them at subsidized rates.

*15. How do parents who do not receive subsidies feel about the two child care programs analyzed in Figure 5.8? (*Hint*: Use a supply-and-demand analysis from Chapter 2.)

*16. How could the government set a smaller lump-sum subsidy that would make poor parents as well off as with the hourly child care subsidy yet cost the government less? Given the tastes shown in Figure 5.8, what would be the effect on the number of hours of child care service that these parents buy? Are you calculating a compensating variation or an equivalent variation (given that the original family is initially at e_1 in the figure)?

17. The "Child Care Subsidies" application notes that many states limit the amount of a subsidy that a family may receive. How does that limit affect the analysis in Figure 5.8?

18. Under a welfare plan, poor people are given a lump-sum payment of L. If they accept this welfare payment, they must pay a high tax, $\tau = \frac{1}{2}$, on anything they earn. If they do not accept the welfare payment, they do not have to pay a tax on their earnings. Show that whether an individual accepts welfare depends on the individual's tastes.

19. If an individual's labor supply curve slopes forward at low wages and bends backward at high wages, is leisure a Giffen good? If so, is leisure a Giffen good at high or low wage rates?

20. Bessie, who can currently work as many hours as she wants at a wage of w, chooses to work 10 hours a day. Her boss decides to limit the number of hours that she can work to 8 hours per day. Show how her budget constraint and choice of hours change. Is she unambiguously worse off as a result of this change? Why or why not?

21. Suppose that Roy could choose how many hours to work at a wage of w and chose to work seven hours a day. The employer now offers him time-and-a-half wages ($1.5w$) for every hour he works beyond a minimum of eight hours per day. Show how his budget constraint changes. Will he choose to work more than seven hours a day?

22. Jerome moonlights: He holds down two jobs. The higher-paying job pays w, but he can work at most eight hours. The other job pays w^*, but he can work as many hours as he wants. Show how Jerome determines how many total hours to work.

23. Suppose that the job in the previous question with no restriction on hours was the higher-paying job. How do Jerome's budget constraint and behavior change?

24. Taxes during the fourteenth century were very progressive. The 1377 poll tax on the Duke of Lancaster was 520 times the tax on a peasant. A poll tax is a lump-sum (fixed amount) tax per person, which is independent of the hours a person works or earns. Use a graph to show the effect of a poll tax on the labor-leisure decision. Does knowing that the tax was progressive tell us whether a nobleman or a peasant—assuming they have identical tastes—worked more hours?

25. Today, most developed countries have progressive income taxes. Under such a taxation program, is the marginal tax higher than, equal to, or lower than the average tax?

*26. Several political leaders, including some recent candidates for the presidency, have proposed a flat income tax, where the marginal tax rate is constant. As of January 1, 2009, 24 countries—including 20 formerly centrally planned economies of Central and Eastern Europe and Eurasia—switched to a flat personal income tax rate (Duncan and Peter, 2009). Show that if each person is allowed a "personal deduction" where the first $10,000 earned by the person is untaxed, the flat tax can be a *progressive* tax in which rich people pay a higher average tax rate than poor people.

27. Inheritance taxes are older than income taxes. Caesar Augustus instituted a 5% tax on all inheritances (except gifts to children and spouses) to provide retirement funds for the military. During the last

couple of decades, congressional Republicans and Democrats have vociferously debated the wisdom of cutting income taxes and inheritance taxes (which the Republicans call the death tax) to stimulate the economy by inducing people to work harder. Presumably, the government cares about a tax's effect on work effort and tax revenues.

a. Suppose George views leisure as a normal good. He works at a job that pays w an hour. Use a labor-leisure analysis to compare the effects on the hours he works from a marginal tax rate on his wage, τ, or a lump-sum tax (a tax collected regardless of the number of hours he works), T. If the per-hour tax is used, he works 10 hours and earns $10w(1 - \tau)$. The government sets $T = 10w\tau$, so that it collects the same amount of money from either tax.

b. Now suppose that the government wants to raise a given amount of revenue through taxation by imposing either an inheritance tax or an income (wage) tax. Which is likely to reduce George's hours of work more, and why?

*28. Prescott (2004) argued that U.S. employees work 50% more than do German, French, and Italian employees because European employees face lower marginal tax rates. Assuming that workers in all four countries have the same tastes toward leisure and goods, must it necessarily be true that U.S. employees work longer hours? Use graphs to illustrate your answer, and explain why it is true or is not true. Does Prescott's evidence indicate anything about the relative sizes of the substitution and income effects? Why or why not?

*29. Originally, Julia could work as many hours as she wanted at a wage of w. She chose to work 12 hours per day. Then, her employer told her that, in the future, she may work as many hours as she wants up to a maximum of 8 hours (and she can find no additional part-time job). How does her optimal choice between leisure and goods change? Does this change hurt her?

PROBLEMS

*30. According to Hong and Wolak (2008), a 5% postal price increase, such as the one in 2006, reduces the revenue earned by the U.S. Postal Services by $215 million and lowers consumer surplus by $333 million.

a. Hong and Wolak estimate that the elasticity of demand for postal services is –1.6. Assume that there is a constant elasticity of demand function, $Q = Xp^{-1.6}$, where X is a constant. In 2006, the price of a first-class stamp went from 37¢ to 39¢. Given the information in the problem about the effect of the price increase on revenue, calculate X.

b. Calculate the size of the triangle corresponding to the lost consumer surplus (area B in Question 1). *Note*: You will get a slightly larger total surplus loss than the amount estimated by Hong and Wolak because they estimated a slightly different demand function.

31. Using calculus, show the effect of a change in the wage on the amount of leisure that an individual wants to consume.

32. Cynthia buys gasoline and other goods. The government considers imposing a lump-sum tax, L dollars per person, or a tax on gasoline of τ dollars per gallon. If L and τ are such that either tax will raise the same amount of tax revenue from Cynthia, which tax does she prefer and why? Show your answer using a graph or calculus.

33. Suppose that Joe's wage varies with the hours he works: $w(H) = \alpha H$, $\alpha > 0$. Use both a graph and calculus to show how the number of hours he chooses to work depends on his tastes.

34. Jim's utility function is $U(q_1, q_2) = \min(q_1, q_2)$. The price of each good is $1, and his monthly income is $2,000. His firm wants him to relocate to another city where the price of q_2 is $2, but the price of q_1 and his income remain constant. Obviously, Jim would be worse off due to the move. What would be his equivalent variation or compensating variation?

35. Jane's utility function is $U(q_1, q_2) = q_1 + q_2$. The price of each good is $1, and her monthly income is $2,000. Her firm wants her to relocate to another city where the price of q_2 is $2, but the price of q_1 and her income remain constant. What would be her equivalent variation or compensating variation?

36. Compare the welfare effects on a consumer between a lump-sum tax and an equal ad valorem (percentage) tax on all goods that raise the same amount of tax revenue.

37. Use the numbers for the alcohol and tobacco category from Table 5.2 to draw a figure that illustrates the roles that the revenue and the elasticity of demand play in determining the loss of consumer surplus due to an increase in price. Indicate how the various areas of your figure correspond to the equation derived in footnote 7.

38. Suppose that the inverse market demand for an upcoming Bruce Springsteen concert at Philadelphia's 20,000-seat Wachovia Center is $p = 1,000 - 0.04\, Q$.

Mr. Springsteen and his promoters consider whether to auction the tickets to the concert. The auction works as follows: An auctioneer orders the bids from highest to lowest, and the price of each ticket equals the 20,000th highest bid. The tickets go to the highest bidders. In the auction, assume that each person bids his or her willingness to pay.

a. What is the price of the tickets? What is the market consumer surplus?

b. Instead, suppose that Mr. Springsteen, for the benefit of his fans, decides to sell each ticket for $100. Based on the demand function, there are 22,500 people who are willing to pay $100 or more. So, not everyone who wants to see the concert at the $100 price can purchase a ticket. Of these 22,500 people, suppose that each of the 20,000 people who actually acquires a ticket has a lower willingness to pay than each of the 2,500 people who does not. What is the consumer surplus?

c. Suppose Bruce Springsteen's objective in choosing whether to auction the tickets or to set a price of $100 is to maximize the market consumer surplus. Which does he choose: an auction or a $100 ticket price? V

39. Joe won $365,000 a year for life in the state lottery. Use a labor-leisure choice analysis to answer the following questions:

a. Show how Joe's lottery winnings affect the position of his budget line.

b. Joe's utility function for goods per day (Y) and hours of leisure per day (N) is $U = Y + 240N^{0.50}$. After winning the lottery, does Joe continue to work the same number of hours each day? What is the income effect of Joe's lottery gains on the amount of goods he buys per day? V

6 Firms and Production

Hard work never killed anybody, but why take a chance?
—Charlie McCarthy

The Ghirardelli Chocolate Company converts chocolate and other inputs into an output of 144,000 wrapped chocolate bars and 340,000 wrapped chocolate squares each day. The material inputs include chocolate, other food products, and various paper goods for wrapping and boxing the candy. The labor inputs include chefs, assembly-line workers, and various mechanics and technicians. The capital inputs are the manufacturing plant, the land on which the plant is located, conveyor belts, molds, wrapping machines, and various other types of equipment.

Over time, Ghirardelli has changed how it produces its finished product, increasing the ratio of machines to workers. Several years ago, to minimize employees' risk of repetitive motion injuries, the company spent $300,000 on robots, which pack the wrapped chocolate and place it on pallets. The use of robotic arms resulted in greatly reduced downtime, increased production, and improved working conditions.

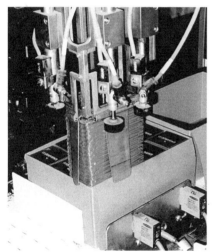

By using robotic equipment to pack finished, wrapped chocolate, the Ghirardelli Chocolate Company benefits from reduced downtime and increased production.

In this chapter, we look at the types of decisions that the owners of firms have to make. First, a decision must be made as to how a firm is owned and managed. Ghirardelli, for example, is a corporation—it is not owned by an individual or partners—and is run by professional managers. Second, the firm must decide how to produce. Ghirardelli now uses relatively more machines and robots and fewer workers than in the past. Third, if a firm wants to expand output, it must decide how to do so in the short run *and* the long run. In the short run, Ghirardelli can expand output by extending the workweek to six or seven days and by using extra materials. To expand output further, Ghirardelli would have to install more equipment (such as extra robotic arms), hire more workers, and eventually build a new plant, all of which take time. Fourth, given its ability to change its output level, a firm must decide how large to grow. Ghirardelli determines its current investments based on its beliefs about future demand and costs.

This chapter examines the nature of firms and how they choose their inputs so as to produce efficiently. Chapter 7 considers how firms choose the least costly among all possible efficient production processes. Then, Chapter 8 combines this information about costs with information about revenues to determine how firms select the output level that maximizes profit.

The main lesson of this chapter and the next is that firms are not black boxes that mysteriously transform inputs (such as labor, capital, and material) into outputs.

Economic theory explains how firms make decisions about production processes, types of inputs to use, and the volume of output to produce.

In this chapter, we examine six main topics

1. **The Ownership and Management of Firms.** Decisions must be made about how a firm is owned and managed.
2. **Production.** A firm converts inputs into outputs using one of possibly many available technologies.
3. **Short-Run Production: One Variable and One Fixed Input.** In the short run, only some inputs can be varied, so the firm changes its output by adjusting its variable inputs.
4. **Long-Run Production: Two Variable Inputs.** The firm has more flexibility in how it produces and how it changes its output level in the long run, when all factors can be varied.
5. **Returns to Scale.** How the ratio of output to input varies with the size of the firm is an important factor in determining a firm's size.
6. **Productivity and Technical Change.** The amount of output that can be produced with a given quantity of inputs varies across firms and over time.

6.1 The Ownership and Management of Firms

A **firm** is an organization that converts *inputs* such as labor, materials, and capital into *outputs*, the goods and services that it sells. U.S. Steel combines iron ore, machinery, and labor to create steel. A local restaurant buys raw food, cooks it, and serves it. A landscape designer hires gardeners, rents machines, buys trees and shrubs, transports them to a customer's home, and supervises the project.

Private, Public, and Nonprofit Firms

Organizations that pursue economic activity fit into three broad categories: the private sector, the public sector, and the nonprofit sector. The *private sector*, sometimes referred to as the *for-profit private sector*, consists of firms owned by individuals or other non-governmental entities and whose owners try to earn a profit. Throughout this book, we concentrate on these firms. In almost every country, this sector contributes the most to the gross domestic product (a measure of a country's total output).

The *public sector* consists of firms and organizations that are owned by governments or government agencies. For example, the National Railroad Passenger Corporation (Amtrak) is owned primarily by the U.S. government. The armed forces and the court system are also part of the public sector, as are most schools, colleges, and universities. The government produces less than one-fifth of the total GDP in most developed countries, including Switzerland (9%), the United States (11%), Ireland (12%), Canada (13%), Australia (16%), and the United Kingdom (17%).[1] The government's share is higher in some developed countries that provide

---

[1]The data in this paragraph are from Heston, Alan, Robert Summers, and Bettina Aten, Penn World Table Version 6.2, Center for International Comparisons of Production, Income and Prices at the University of Pennsylvania, September 2006: **pwt.econ.upenn.edu/php_site/pwt62/pwt62_form.php**. Western governments' shares increased markedly (but presumably temporarily) during the major 2008 to 2010 recession, when they bought part or all of a number of private firms to keep them from going bankrupt.

many government services or maintain a relatively large army including Iceland (20%), the Netherlands (21%), Sweden (22%), and Israel (24%). The government's share varies substantially in less-developed countries, ranging from very low levels in Nigeria (4%) to very high levels in Eritrea (94%). Strikingly, a number of former communist countries such as Albania (20%) and China (28%) now have public sectors of comparable relative size to developed countries and hence must rely primarily on the private sector for economic activity.

The *not-for-profit sector* consists of organizations that are neither government-owned nor intended to earn a profit. Organizations in this sector typically pursue social or public interest objectives. Well-known examples include Greenpeace, Alcoholics Anonymous, and the Salvation Army, along with many other charitable, educational, health, and religious organizations. According to the U.S. Census Bureau's 2009 *U.S. Statistical Abstract*, the private sector created 77% of the U.S. gross domestic product, the government sector was responsible for 11%, and nonprofits and households produced the remaining 12%.

The Ownership of For-Profit Firms

The legal structure of a firm determines who is liable for its debts. Within the private sector, there are three primary legal forms of organization: a sole proprietorship, a general partnership, or a corporation.

Sole proprietorships are firms owned by a single individual who is personally liable for the firm's debts.

General partnerships (often called *partnerships*) are businesses jointly owned and controlled by two or more people who are personally liable for the firm's debts. The owners operate under a partnership agreement. In most legal jurisdictions, if any partner leaves, the partnership agreement ends and a new partnership agreement is created if the firm is to continue operations.

Corporations are owned by *shareholders* in proportion to the number of shares or amount of stock they hold. The shareholders elect a board of directors to represent them. In turn, the board of directors usually hires managers to oversee the firm's operations. Some corporations are very small and have a single shareholder; others are very large and have thousands of shareholders. A fundamental characteristic of corporations is that the owners are not personally liable for the firm's debts; they have **limited liability**: The personal assets of corporate owners cannot be taken to pay a corporation's debts even if it goes into bankruptcy. Because corporations have limited liability, the most that shareholders can lose is the amount they paid for their stock, which typically becomes worthless if the corporation declares bankruptcy.[2]

The purpose of limiting liability was to allow firms to raise funds and grow beyond what was possible when owners risked personal assets on any firm in which they invested. According to the 2009 *U.S. Statistical Abstract*, U.S. corporations are responsible for 83% of business receipts and 70% of net business income, although they comprise only 19% of all nonfarm firms. Nonfarm sole proprietorships are 72% of all firms but receive only 4% of sales and earn 10% of net income. Partnerships comprise 9% of firms, account for 13% of receipts, and earn 20% of net income. These statistics show that larger firms tend to be corporations, whereas smaller firms are often sole proprietorships.

---

[2]Recently, the United States (1996), the United Kingdom (2000), and other countries have allowed any sole proprietorship, partnership, or corporation to register as a *limited liability company* (LLC). Thus, all firms—not just corporations—can now obtain limited liability.

The Management of Firms

In a small firm, the owner usually manages the firm's operations. In larger firms, typically corporations and larger partnerships, a manager or a management team usually runs the company. In such firms, owners, managers, and lower-level supervisors are all decision makers.

As revelations about Enron and WorldCom illustrate, various decision makers may have conflicting objectives. What is in the best interest of the owners may not be in the best interest of managers or other employees. For example, a manager may want a fancy office, a company car, a corporate jet, and other perks, but an owner would likely oppose those drains on profit.

The owner replaces the manager if the manager pursues personal objectives rather than the firm's objectives. In a corporation, the board of directors is responsible for ensuring that the manager stays on track. If the manager and the board of directors are ineffective, the shareholders can fire both or change certain policies through votes at the corporation's annual shareholders' meeting. Until Chapter 19, we'll ignore the potential conflict between managers and owners and assume that the owner *is* the manager of the firm and makes all the decisions.

What Owners Want

Economists usually assume that a firm's owners try to maximize profit. Presumably, most people invest in a firm to make money—lots of money, they hope. They want the firm to earn a positive profit rather than suffer a loss (a negative profit). A firm's **profit**, π, is the difference between its revenue, R, which is what it earns from selling a good, and its cost, C, which is what it pays for labor, materials, and other inputs:

$$\pi = R - C. \tag{6.1}$$

Typically, revenue is p, the price, times q, the firm's quantity: $R = pq$. (For simplicity, we will assume that the firm produces only one product.)

In reality, some owners have other objectives, such as running as large a firm as possible, owing a fancy building, or keeping risks low. However, Chapter 8 shows that a firm in a highly competitive market is likely to be driven out of business if it doesn't maximize its profit.

To maximize its profit, a firm must produce as efficiently as possible. A firm engages in **efficient production** (achieves **technological efficiency**) if it cannot produce its current level of output with fewer inputs, given its existing knowledge about technology and how to organize production. Equivalently, a firm produces efficiently if, given the quantity of inputs used, no more output can be produced using existing knowledge.

If a firm does not produce efficiently, it cannot maximize its profit—so efficient production is a *necessary condition* for maximizing profit. Even if a firm efficiently produces a given level of output, it will not maximize its profit if that output level is too high or too low or if it uses an excessively expensive production process. Thus, efficient production alone is not a *sufficient condition* to ensure that a firm's profit is maximized.

A firm may use engineers and other experts to determine the most efficient ways to produce using a known method or technology. However, this knowledge does not indicate which of the many technologies, each of which uses different combinations of inputs, allows for production at the lowest cost or with the highest possible profit. How to produce at the lowest cost is an economic decision typically made by the firm's manager (see Chapter 7).

6.2 Production

A firm uses a *technology* or *production process* to transform *inputs* or *factors of production* into *outputs*. Firms use many types of inputs, most of which fall into three broad categories:

1. **Capital services** (K): Use of long-lived inputs such as land, buildings (such as factories and stores), and equipment (such as machines and trucks)
2. **Labor services** (L): Hours of work provided by managers, skilled workers (such as architects, economists, engineers, and plumbers), and less-skilled workers (such as custodians, construction laborers, and assembly-line workers)
3. **Materials** (M): Natural resources and raw goods (such as oil, water, and wheat) and processed products (such as aluminum, plastic, paper, and steel) that are typically consumed in producing, or incorporated in making, the final product

We typically refer to *capital services* as *capital* and *labor services* as *labor* for brevity. The output can be a *service* such as an automobile tune-up by a mechanic, or a *physical product* such as a computer chip or a potato chip.

Production Functions

Firms can transform inputs into outputs in many different ways. Candy manufacturing companies differ in the skills of their workforce and the amount of equipment they use. While all employ a chef, a manager, and relatively unskilled workers, some candy firms also use skilled technicians and modern equipment. In small candy companies, the relatively unskilled workers shape the candy, decorate it, package it, and box it by hand. In slightly larger firms, these same-level workers use conveyor belts and other industrial equipment. In modern large-scale plants, the relatively unskilled laborers work with robots and other state-of-the-art machines that are maintained by skilled technicians. Before deciding which production process to use, a firm must consider its options.

The various ways that a firm can transform inputs into output are summarized in the **production function**: the relationship between the quantities of inputs used and the *maximum* quantity of output that can be produced, given current knowledge about technology and organization. The production function for a firm that uses labor and capital only is

$$q = f(L, K), \tag{6.2}$$

where q units of output (wrapped candy bars) are produced using L units of labor services (days of work by relatively unskilled assembly-line workers) and K units of capital (the number of conveyor belts).

The production function shows only the *maximum* amount of output that can be produced from given levels of labor and capital, because the production function includes efficient production processes only. A profit-maximizing firm is not interested in production processes that are inefficient and wasteful: Why would the firm want to use two workers to do a job that one worker can perform as efficiently?

Time and the Variability of Inputs

A firm can more easily adjust its inputs in the long run than in the short run. Typically, a firm can vary the amount of materials and relatively unskilled labor it uses comparatively quickly. However, it needs more time to find and hire skilled workers, order new equipment, or build a new manufacturing plant.

The more time a firm has to adjust its inputs, the more factors of production it can alter. The **short run** is a period of time so brief that at least one factor of production cannot be varied practically. A factor that a firm cannot vary practically in the short run is called a **fixed input**. In contrast, a **variable input** is a factor of production whose quantity the firm can change readily during the relevant time period. The **long run** is a long enough period of time that all inputs can be varied. There are no fixed inputs in the long run—all factors of production are variable inputs.

Suppose that one day a painting company has more work than its crew can handle. Even if it wanted to, the firm does not have time to buy or rent an extra truck and buy another compressor to run a power sprayer; these inputs are fixed in the short run. To complete the day's work, the firm uses its only truck to drop off a temporary worker, equipped with only a brush and a can of paint, at the last job. However in the long run, the firm can adjust all its inputs. If the firm wants to paint more houses every day, it can hire more full-time workers, purchase a second truck, get another compressor to run a power sprayer, and buy a computer to track its projects.

The time it takes for all inputs to be variable depends on the factors a firm uses. For a janitorial service whose only major input is workers, the long run is a brief period of time. In contrast, an automobile manufacturer may need many years to build a new manufacturing plant or design and construct a new type of machine. A pistachio farmer needs about a decade before newly planted trees yield a substantial crop of nuts.

For many firms over a short period, say a month, materials and often labor are variable inputs. However, labor is not always a variable input. Finding additional highly skilled workers may take substantial time. Similarly, capital may be a variable or a fixed input. A firm can rent small capital assets (trucks and personal computers) quickly, but it may take years to obtain larger capital assets (buildings and large specialized pieces of equipment).

To illustrate the greater flexibility a firm has in the long run than in the short run, we examine the production function in Equation 6.2, in which output is a function of only labor and capital. We first look at the short-run and then at the long-run production process.

6.3 Short-Run Production: One Variable and One Fixed Input

In the short run, we assume that capital is a fixed input and that labor is a variable input, so the firm can increase output only by increasing the amount of labor it uses. In the short run, the firm's production function is

$$q = f(L, \bar{K}), \tag{6.3}$$

where q is output, L is workers, and $\bar{K}$ is the fixed number of units of capital. The short-run production function is also referred to as the **total product of labor**—the amount of output (or *total product*) that a given amount of labor can produce holding the quantity of other inputs fixed.

Chapter 6 Firms and Production

The exact relationship between *output* or *total product* and *labor* is given in Equation 6.3. The **marginal product of labor** (MP_L) is the change in total output resulting from using an extra unit of labor, holding other factors (capital) constant. The marginal product of labor is the partial derivative of the production function with respect to labor,

$$MP_L = \frac{\partial q}{\partial L} = \frac{\partial f(L, K)}{\partial L}.$$

The **average product of labor** (AP_L) is the ratio of output to the number of workers used to produce that output,[3]

$$AP_L = \frac{q}{L}.$$

SOLVED PROBLEM 6.1

A computer assembly firm's production function is $q = 0.1LK + 3L^2K - 0.1L^3K$. What is its short-run production function if capital is fixed at $\bar{K} = 10$? Give the formulas for its marginal product of labor and its average product of labor. Draw two figures, one above the other. In the top figure, show the relationship between output (total product) and labor. In the bottom figure, show the MP_L and AP_L curves. Is this production function valid for all values of labor?

Answer

1. *Write the formula for the short-run production function by replacing K in the production function with its fixed short-run value.* To obtain a production function in the form of Equation 6.3, set capital in the production function equal to 10:

$$q = 0.1L(10) + 3L^2(10) - 0.1L^3(10) = L + 30L^2 - L^3.$$

2. *Determine the MP_L by differentiating the short-run production function with respect to labor.* The marginal product of labor is[4]

$$MP_L = \frac{dq}{dL} = \frac{d(L + 30L^2 - L^3)}{dL} = 1 + 60L - 3L^2.$$

3. *Determine the AP_L by dividing the short-run production function by labor.* The average product of labor is

$$AP_L = \frac{q}{L} = \frac{L + 30L^2 - L^3}{L} = 1 + 30L - L^2.$$

4. *Draw the requested figures by plotting the short-run production function, MP_L, and AP_L equations.* Figure 6.1 shows how the total product of labor, marginal product of labor, and average product of labor vary with the number of workers.

5. *Show that the production function equation does not hold for all values of labor by noting that, beyond a certain level, extra workers lower output.* In the figure, the total product curve to the right of $L = 20$ is a dashed line,

---

[3] *Jargon alert*: Some economists call the MP_L the marginal physical product of labor and the AP_L the average physical product of labor.

[4] Because the short-run production function is solely a function of labor, $MP_L = dq/dL$. An alternative way to derive the MP_L is to differentiate the production function with respect to labor and then set capital equal to 10: $MP_L = \partial q/\partial L = \partial(0.1LK + 3L^2K - 0.1L^3K)/\partial L = 0.1K + 6LK - 0.3L^2K$. Evaluating at $\bar{K} = 10$, we obtain $MP_L = 1 + 60L - 30L^2$.

indicating that this section is not part of the true production function. Because output falls—the curve decreases—as the firm uses more than 20 workers, a rational firm would never use more than 20 workers. From the definition of a production function, we want the maximum quantity of output that can be produced from the given inputs, so if the firm had more than 20 workers, it could increase its output by sending the extra employees home. (The portions of the MP_L and AP_L curves beyond 20 workers also appear as dashed lines because they correspond to irrelevant sections of the short-run production function equation.)

Figure 6.1 Production Relationships with Variable Labor

(a) The short-run total product of labor curve, $q = L + 30L^2 - L^3$, shows how much output, q, can be assembled with 10 units of capital, which is fixed in the short run. Where extra workers reduce the amount of output produced, the total product of labor curve is a dashed line, which indicates that such production is inefficient production and not part of the production function. The slope of the line from the origin to point B is the average product of labor for 15 workers. (b) The marginal product of labor, MP_L, equals the average product of labor, AP_L, at the peak of the average product curve where the firm employs 15 workers.

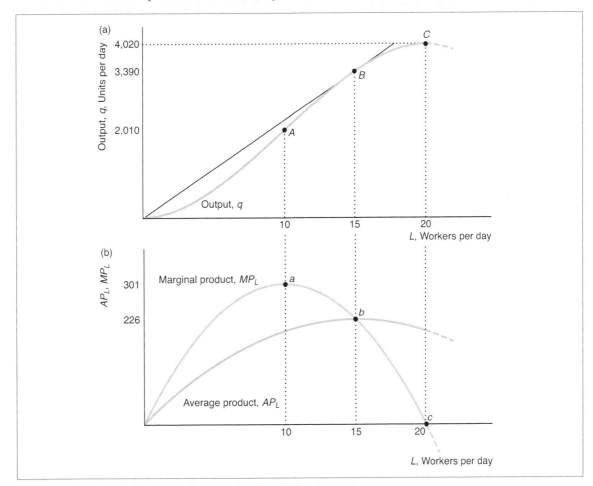

Interpretation of Graphs

Figure 6.1 shows how the total product of labor (computers assembled), the average product of labor, and the marginal product of labor vary with the number of workers. The figures are smooth curves because the firm can hire a "fraction of a worker" by employing a worker for a fraction of a day. The total product of labor curve in panel a shows that output rises with labor until the firm employs 20 workers.

Panel b illustrates how the average product of labor and the marginal product of labor vary with the number of workers. By lining up the two panels vertically, we can show the relationships between the total product of labor, marginal product of labor, and average product of labor curves.

In most production processes—and as Figure 6.1 shows—the average product of labor first rises and then falls as labor increases. For example, the AP_L curve may initially rise because it helps to have more than two hands when assembling a computer. One worker holds a part in place while another worker bolts it down. As a result, output increases more than in proportion to labor, so the average product of labor rises. Similarly, output may initially rise more than in proportion to labor because of greater specialization of activities. With greater specialization, workers are assigned to tasks at which they are particularly adept, and time is saved by not having workers move from one task to another.

However, as the number of workers rises further, output may not increase by as much per worker because workers have to wait to use a particular piece of equipment or because they get in each other's way. In Figure 6.1, as the number of workers exceeds 15, total output increases less than in proportion to labor, so the average product falls.

The three curves are geometrically related. First, we use panel b to illustrate the relationship between the average and marginal product of labor curves. Then, we use panels a and b to show the relationship between the total product of labor curve and the other two curves.

The average product of labor curve slopes upward where the marginal product of labor curve is above it and slopes downward where the marginal product curve is below it. If an extra worker adds more output—that worker's marginal product—than the average product of the initial workers, the extra worker raises the average product. As panel b shows, when there are fewer than 15 workers, the marginal product curve is above the average product curve, so the average product curve is upward sloping.

Similarly, if the marginal product of labor for a new worker is less than the former average product of labor, then the average product of labor falls. In the figure, the average product of labor falls beyond 15 workers. Because the average product of labor curve rises when the marginal product of labor curve is above it, and the average product of labor falls when the marginal product of labor is below it, the average product of labor curve reaches a peak, point *b* in panel b, where the marginal product of labor curve crosses it.[5]

---

[5]We can use calculus to prove that the MP_L curve intersects the AP_L at its peak. Because capital is fixed, we can write the production function solely in terms of labor: $q = f(L)$. In the figure, $MP_L = dq/dL = df/dL > 0$ and $d^2f/dL^2 < 0$. A necessary condition to identify the amount of labor where the average product of labor curve, $AP_L = q/L = f(L)/L$, reaches a maximum is that the derivative of AP_L with respect to L equals zero:

$$\frac{dAP_L}{dL} = \left(\frac{dq}{dL} - \frac{q}{L}\right)\frac{1}{L} = 0.$$

(At the L determined by this first-order condition, AP_L is maximized if the second-order condition is negative: $d^2AP_L/dL^2 = d^2f/dL^2 < 0$.) From the necessary condition, $MP_L = dq/dL = q/L = AP_L$, at the peak of the AP_L curve.

We can determine the average product of labor curve, shown in panel b of Figure 6.1, using the total product of labor curve, shown in panel a. The AP_L for L workers equals the slope of a straight line from the origin to a point on the total product of labor curve for L workers in panel a. The slope ("rise over run") of this line equals output ("rise") divided by the number of workers ("run"), which is the definition of the average product of labor. For example, the slope of the straight line drawn from the origin to point B ($L = 15$, $q = 3{,}390$) is 226, which is the height of the AP_L curve in panel b when $L = 15$.

The marginal product of labor also has a geometric interpretation in terms of the total product of labor curve. The slope of the total product of labor curve at a given point, dq/dL, equals the MP_L. That is, the MP_L equals the slope of a straight line that is tangent to the total output curve for a given number of workers. For example, at point C in panel a where there are 20 workers, the line tangent to the total product curve is flat, so the MP_L is zero: A little extra labor has no effect on output. The total product curve is upward sloping when there are fewer than 20 workers, so the MP_L is positive. If the firm is foolish enough to hire more than 20 workers, the total product curve slopes downward (dashed line), so the MP_L would be negative: Extra workers lower output. Again, this portion of the MP_L curve is not part of the production function.

When there are 15 workers, the average product of labor equals the marginal product of labor. The reason is that the line from the origin to point B in panel a is tangent to the total product curve, so the slope of that line, 226, is the marginal product of labor and the average product of labor at point b in panel b.

SOLVED PROBLEM 6.2

Tian and Wan (2000) estimated the production function for rice in China as a function of labor, fertilizer, and other inputs such as seed, draft animals, and equipment. Holding the other inputs besides labor fixed, the total product of labor is $\ln q = 4.63 + 1.29 \ln L - 0.2 (\ln L)^2$. What is the marginal product of labor? What is the relationship of the marginal product of labor to the average product of labor? What is the elasticity of output with respect to labor?

Answer

1. *Totally differentiate the short-run production function to obtain the marginal product of labor.* Differentiating $\ln q = 4.63 + 1.29 \ln L - 0.2(\ln L)^2$ with respect to q and L, we obtain

$$\frac{dq/dL}{q} = \frac{1.29 - 0.4 \ln L}{L}.$$

By rearranging terms, we find that the $MP_L = dq/dL = (q/L)(1.29 - 0.4 \ln L)$.

2. *Determine the relationship between MP_L and AP_L using the expression for MP_L.* Using the definition for $AP_L = q/L$, we can rewrite the expression we derived for the marginal product of labor as $MP_L = AP_L(1.29 - 0.4 \ln L)$, so the MP_L is $(1.29 - 0.4 \ln L)$ times as large as is the AP_L. Equivalently, $MP_L/AP_L = 1.29 - 0.4 \ln L$.

3. *Show that the elasticity of output with respect to labor is the ratio of the marginal product of labor to the average product of labor and make use of the equation relating the MP_L to the AP_L.* Given the general definition of an elasticity, the elasticity of output produced with respect to labor is $(dq/dL)(L/q)$. By substituting into this expression the definitions of $MP_L = dq/dL$ and $AP_L = q/L$, we find that the elasticity of output with respect to labor is $(dq/dL)(L/q) = MP_L/AP_L = 1.29 - 0.4 \ln L$.

Law of Diminishing Marginal Returns

Next to *supply equals demand*, probably the most commonly used phrase of economic jargon is the *law of diminishing marginal returns*. This "law" determines the shapes of the total product and marginal product of labor curves as a firm uses more and more labor. As with the "law" of supply and demand, this "law" is not theoretically necessary, but it is an empirical regularity.

The *law of diminishing marginal returns* (or *diminishing marginal product*) holds that *if a firm keeps increasing an input, holding all other inputs and technology constant, the corresponding increases in output will eventually become smaller*. That is, if only one input is increased, *the marginal product of that input will eventually diminish*. The marginal product of labor diminishes if $\partial MP_L/\partial L = \partial(\partial q/\partial L)/\partial L = \partial^2 q/\partial L^2 = \partial^2 f(L, K)/\partial L^2 < 0$. That is, the marginal product falls with increased labor if the second partial derivative of the production function with respect to labor is negative.

Panel b of Figure 6.1 illustrates diminishing marginal product of labor. At low levels of labor, the marginal product of labor rises with the number of workers. However, when the number of workers exceeds 10, each additional worker reduces the marginal product of labor.

Unfortunately, when attempting to cite this empirical regularity, many people overstate it. Instead of talking about "diminishing *marginal* returns," they talk about "diminishing returns." These phrases have different meanings. Where there are "diminishing marginal returns," the MP_L curve is falling—beyond 10 workers in panel b of Figure 6.1—but it may be positive, as the solid MP_L curve between 10 and 20 workers shows. With "diminishing returns," extra labor causes *output* to fall. There are diminishing total returns for more than 20 workers, and consequently the MP_L is negative, as the dashed MP_L line in panel b shows.

Thus, saying that there are diminishing returns is much stronger than saying that there are diminishing marginal returns. We often observe successful firms producing with diminishing marginal returns to labor, but we never see a well-run firm operating with diminishing total returns. Such a firm could produce more output by using fewer inputs.

A second common misinterpretation of this law is the claim that marginal products must fall as we increase an input without requiring that technology and other inputs remain constant. If we increase labor while simultaneously increasing other factors or adopting superior technologies, the marginal product of labor may rise indefinitely. Thomas Malthus provided the most famous example of this fallacy (as well as the reason economics is referred to as the "dismal science").

APPLICATION

Malthus and the Green Revolution

In 1798, Thomas Malthus—a clergyman and professor of modern history and political economy—predicted that population (if unchecked) would grow more rapidly than food production because the quantity of land was fixed. The problem, he believed, was that the fixed amount of land would lead to diminishing marginal product of labor, so output would rise less than in proportion to the increase in farm workers. Malthus grimly concluded that mass starvation would result. Brander and Taylor (1998) argue that such a disaster may have occurred on Easter Island around 500 years ago.

Today, the earth supports a population almost seven times as great as it was when Malthus made his predictions. Why haven't most of us starved to death? The simple explanation is that fewer workers using less land can produce much more food today than was possible when Malthus was alive. Two hundred years

ago, most of the population had to work in agriculture to prevent starvation. As of 2009, only 1% of the U.S. population works in agriculture (2% live on farms), and the share of land devoted to farming has fallen constantly over many decades. Since World War II, the U.S. population has doubled but U.S. food production has tripled.

Two key factors (in addition to birth control) are responsible for the rapid increase in food production per capita in most countries. First, agricultural technology—such as disease-resistant seeds and better land management practices—has improved substantially, so more output can be produced with the same inputs. Second, although the amounts of land and labor used have remained constant or fallen in most countries in recent years, the use of other inputs such as fertilizer and tractors has increased significantly, so output per acre of land has risen.

In 1850, it took more than 80 hours of labor to produce 100 bushels of corn. Introducing mechanical power cut the required labor in half. Labor hours were again cut in half by the introduction of hybrid seed and chemical fertilizers, and then in half again by the advent of herbicides and pesticides. Biotechnology, with the 1996 introduction of herbicide-tolerant and insect-resistant crops, has reduced the labor required to produce 100 bushels of corn to about two hours. Today, the output of a U.S. farm worker is 215% of that of a worker just 50 years ago.

Of course, the risk of starvation is more severe in developing countries. Luckily, one man decided to defeat the threat of Malthusian disaster personally. Do you know anyone who saved a life? A hundred lives? Do you know the name of the man who probably saved the most lives in history? According to some estimates, during the second half of the twentieth century, Norman Borlaug and his fellow scientists prevented a *billion deaths* with their *green revolution*, which used modified seeds, tractors, irrigation, soil treatments, fertilizer, and various other ideas to increase production. Thanks to these innovations, wheat, rice, and corn production increased significantly in many low-income countries. In the late 1960s, Dr. Borlaug and his colleagues brought the techniques they developed in Mexico to India and Pakistan because of the risk of mass starvation there. The results were stunning. In 1968, Pakistan's wheat crop soared to 146% of the 1965 pre-green revolution crop. By 1970, it was 183% of the 1965 crop. (Hear Dr. Borlaug's story in his own words: **webcast.berkeley.edu/event_details.php?webcastid=9955**).

However, as Dr. Borlaug noted in his 1970 Nobel Prize speech, superior science is not the complete answer to preventing starvation. A sound economic system is needed as well. It is the lack of a sound economic system that has doomed many Africans. Per capita food production has fallen in sub-Saharan Africa over the past two decades and widespread starvation has plagued some African countries in recent years. The United Nations reports that 140 million people are substantially underweight, including nearly 50% of all children under five in Southern Asia (India, Pakistan, Bangladesh and nearby countries) and 28% in sub-Saharan Africa. Unfortunately, 15 million children die of hunger each year.

Although droughts have contributed, these tragedies are primarily due to political problems such as wars and the breakdown of economic production and distribution systems. Further, "neo-Malthusians" point to other areas of concern, emphasizing the role of global climate change in disrupting food production, and claiming that current methods of food production are not sustainable in view of environmental damage and continuing rapid population growth in many parts of the world.[6] If these economic and political problems cannot be solved, Malthus may prove to be right for the wrong reason.

6.4 Long-Run Production: Two Variable Inputs

Eternity is a terrible thought. I mean, where's it going to end? —Tom Stoppard

We started our analysis of production functions by looking at a short-run production function in which one input, capital, is fixed, and the other, labor, is variable. In the long run, however, both of these inputs are variable. With both factors variable, a firm can produce a given level of output by using a great deal of labor and very little capital, a great deal of capital and very little labor, or moderate amounts of each. That is, the firm can substitute one input for another while continuing to produce the same level of output, in much the same way that a consumer can maintain a given level of utility by substituting one good for another.

Typically, a firm can produce in various ways, some of which require more labor than others. For example, a lumberyard can produce 200 planks an hour with 10 workers using hand saws, or 4 workers using handheld power saws, or 2 workers using bench power saws.

We can illustrate the basic idea using a Cobb-Douglas production function,

$$q = AL^a K^b, \tag{6.4}$$

where A, a, and b are constants.[7] If we redefine a unit of output as $1/A$, we can write the production function as $q = L^a K^b$, which is the form we generally use. Hsieh (1995) estimated that using a Cobb-Douglas production function for a U.S. firm producing electronics and other electrical equipment,

$$q = L^{0.5} K^{0.5}, \tag{6.5}$$

where L is labor (workers) per day and K is capital services per day. From inspection, there are many combinations of labor and capital that will produce the same level of output.

Isoquants

We can summarize the possible combinations of inputs that will produce a given level of output using an **isoquant**, which is a curve that shows the efficient combinations of labor and capital that can produce a single (*iso*) level of output (*quant*ity).

---

[6]There is some hope for another set of dramatic improvements in agricultural productivity—based largely on genetic engineering (Andrew Pollack, "Monsanto Seeks Big Increase in Crop Yields," *New York Times*, June 5, 2008: www.nytimes.com/2008/06/05/business/worldbusiness/05crop.html).

[7]The Cobb-Douglas production function (named after its inventors, Charles W. Cobb, a mathematician, and Paul H. Douglas, an economist and U.S. senator) is the most commonly used production function. The Cobb-Douglas production function has the same functional form as the Cobb-Douglas utility function, which we studied in Chapters 3 through 5. Unlike in those chapters, we do not require that $b = 1 - a$ in this chapter.

If the production function is $q = f(L, K)$, then the equation for an isoquant where output is held constant at $\bar{q}$ is

$$\bar{q} = f(L, K). \tag{6.6}$$

For our particular production function, Equation 6.5, the isoquant is $\bar{q} = L^{0.5}K^{0.5}$.

Figure 6.2 shows an isoquant for $q = 6$, $q = 9$, and $q = 12$, which are three of the many possible isoquants. The isoquants show a firm's flexibility in producing a given level of output. These isoquants are smooth curves because the firm can use fractional units of each input.

There are many combinations of labor and capital, (L, K), that will produce 6 units of output, including (1, 36), (2, 18), (3, 12), (4, 9), (6, 6), (9, 4), (12, 3), (18, 2), and (36, 1). Figure 6.2 shows some of these combinations as points *a* through *f* on the $q = 6$ isoquant.

Properties of Isoquants. Isoquants have most of the same properties as indifference curves. The main difference is that an isoquant holds quantity constant, whereas an indifference curve holds utility constant. The quantities associated with isoquants have cardinal properties (for example, an output of 12 is twice as much as an output of 6), while the utilities associated with indifference curves have only ordinal properties (for example, 12 utils are associated with more pleasure than 6, but not necessarily twice as much pleasure).

We now consider four major properties of isoquants. Most of these properties result from efficient production by firms.

First, *the farther an isoquant is from the origin, the greater the level of output.* That is, the more inputs a firm uses, the more output it gets if it produces efficiently. At point *e* in Figure 6.2, the electronics firm is producing 6 units of output with 12

Figure 6.2 Family of Isoquants for a U.S. Electronics Manufacturing Firm

These isoquants for a U.S. firm producing electronics and other electrical equipment (Hsieh, 1995) show the combinations of labor and capital that produce various levels of output. Isoquants farther from the origin correspond to higher levels of output. Points *a*, *b*, *c*, *d*, *e*, and *f* are various combinations of labor and capital that the firm can use to produce $q = 6$ units of output. If the firm holds capital constant at 12 and increases labor from 3 (point *b*) to 12 (point *g*), the firm shifts from operating on the $q = 6$ isoquant to producing on the $q = 12$ isoquant.

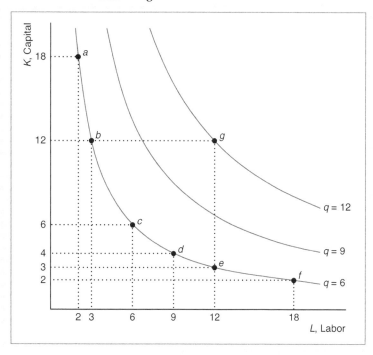

workers and 3 units of capital. If the firm holds the number of workers constant and adds 9 more units of capital, it produces at point g. Point g must be on an isoquant with a higher level of output—here, 12 units—if the firm is producing efficiently and not wasting the extra labor.

Second, *isoquants do not cross*. Such intersections are inconsistent with the requirement that the firm always produces efficiently. For example, if the $q = 15$ and $q = 20$ isoquants crossed, the firm could produce at either output level with the same combination of labor and capital. The firm must be producing inefficiently if it produces $q = 15$ when it could produce $q = 20$. Thus, that labor-capital combination should not lie on the $q = 15$ isoquant, which should include only efficient combinations of inputs. So, efficiency requires that isoquants do not cross.

Third, *isoquants slope downward*. If an isoquant sloped upward, the firm could produce the same level of output with relatively few inputs or relatively many inputs. Producing with relatively many inputs would be inefficient. Consequently, because isoquants show only efficient production, an upward-sloping isoquant is impossible.

Fourth, *isoquants must be thin*. This result follows from virtually the same argument we just used to show that isoquants slope downward.

Shape of Isoquants. The curvature of an isoquant shows how readily a firm can substitute one input for another. The two extreme cases are production processes in which inputs are perfect substitutes and those in which inputs cannot be substituted for each other.

If the inputs are perfect substitutes, each isoquant is a straight line. Suppose either potatoes from Maine, x, or potatoes from Idaho, y, both of which are measured in pounds per day, can be used to produce potato salad, q, measured in pounds. This technology has a *linear production function,*

$$q = x + y.$$

A pound of potato salad can be produced by using one pound of Idaho potatoes and no Maine potatoes, one pound of Maine potatoes and no Idaho potatoes, or a half pound of each. The isoquant for $q =$ one pound of potato salad is $1 = x + y$, or $y = 1 - x$. The slope of this straight-line isoquant is -1. Panel a of Figure 6.3 shows the $q = 1, 2,$ and 3 isoquants.

Sometimes it is impossible to substitute one input for the other: Inputs must be used in fixed proportions. Such a technology is called a *fixed-proportions production function*. For example, the inputs needed to produce a 12-ounce box of cereal, q, are cereal (12-ounce units per day), g, and cardboard boxes (boxes per day), b. This fixed-proportions production function is

$$q = \min(g, b),$$

where the min function means "the minimum number of g or b." For example, if the firm has $g = 4$ units of cereal and $b = 3$ boxes, it can produce only $q = 3$ boxes of cereal. Thus, in panel b of Figure 6.3, the only efficient points of production are the large dots along the 45° line, where the firm uses equal quantities of both inputs. Dashed lines show that the isoquants would be right angles if isoquants could include inefficient production processes.

Other production processes allow imperfect substitution between inputs. These isoquants are convex (so the middle of the isoquant is closer to the origin than it would be if the isoquant were a straight line). They do not have the same slope at every point, unlike the straight-line isoquants. Most isoquants are smooth, slope downward, curve away from the origin, and lie between the extreme cases of straight lines (perfect substitutes) and right angles (nonsubstitutes), as panel c of Figure 6.3 illustrates.

Figure 6.3 Substitutability of Inputs

(a) If the inputs are perfect substitutes, each isoquant is a straight line. (b) If the inputs cannot be substituted at all, the isoquants are right angles (the dashed lines show that the isoquants would be right angles if we included ineffi- cient production). (c) Typical isoquants lie between the extreme cases of straight lines and right angles. Along a curved isoquant, the ability to substitute one input for another varies.

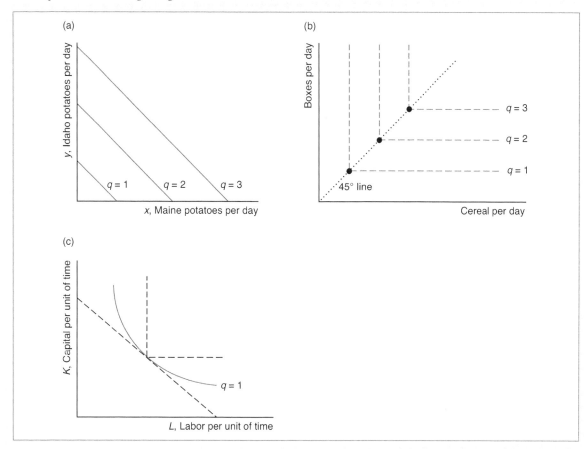

APPLICATION

A Semiconductor Integrated Circuit Isoquant

We can show why isoquants curve away from the origin by deriving an isoquant for semiconductor integrated circuits (ICs, or "chips"). ICs—the "brains" of computers and other electronic devices—are made by building up layers of conductive and insulating materials on silicon wafers. Each wafer contains many ICs, which are subsequently cut into individual chips, called *dice*.

Semiconductor manufacturers ("fabs") buy the silicon wafers and then use labor and capital to produce the chips. A semiconductor IC's several layers of conductive and insulating materials are arranged in patterns that define the function of the chip.

During the manufacture of ICs, a track moves a wafer into a machine, where the wafer is spun and a light-sensitive liquid called photoresist is applied to its whole surface. Next, the photoresist is hardened. Then, the wafer advances along the track to a point where photolithography is used to define patterns in the photoresist. In photolithography, light transfers a pattern from a template, called a photomask, to the photoresist, which is then "developed" like film, creating a pattern by removing the resist from certain areas. A subsequent process can then add to or etch away those areas not protected by the resist.

In a repetition of this entire procedure, additional layers are created on the wafer. Because the conducting and insulating patterns in each layer interact with those in the previous layers, the patterns must line up correctly.

To align layers properly, firms use combinations of labor and equipment. In the least capital-intensive technology, employees use machines called *aligners*. Operators look through microscopes and line up the layers by hand, and then expose the entire surface. An operator running an aligner can produce 250 layers, or 25 ten-layer chips per day.

A second, more capital-intensive technology uses machines called *steppers*. The stepper picks a spot on the wafer, automatically aligns the layers, and then exposes that area to light. Then the machine moves—*steps* to other sections—lining up and exposing each area in turn until the entire surface has been aligned and exposed. This technology requires less labor: A single worker can run two steppers and produce 500 layers, or 50 ten-layer chips per day.

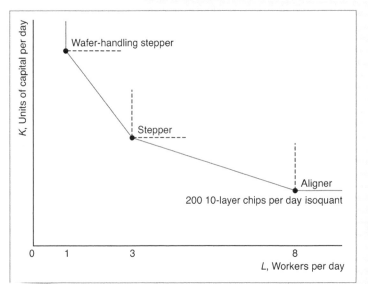

A third, even more capital-intensive technology uses a stepper with wafer-handling equipment, which reduces the amount of labor even more. By linking the tracks directly to a stepper and automating the chip transfer process, human handling can be greatly reduced. A single worker can run four steppers with wafer-handling equipment and produce 1,000 layers, or 100 ten-layer chips per day.

Only steppers can be used if the chip requires line widths of one micrometer or less. We show an isoquant for producing 200 ten-layer chips with lines that are more than one micrometer wide, for which any of the three technologies can be used.

All these technologies use labor and capital in fixed proportions. Producing 200 chips takes 8 workers and 8 aligners, 3 workers and 6 steppers, or 1 worker and 4 steppers with wafer-handling capabilities. The accompanying graph shows the three right-angle isoquants corresponding to each of these technologies.

Some fabs, however, employ a combination of these technologies; some workers use one type of machine while others use different types. A fab that implements this process can produce using intermediate combinations of labor and capital, as the solid-line, kinked isoquant illustrates. A fab would *not* use a combination of the aligner and the wafer-handling stepper technologies because those combinations are less efficient than using the plain stepper (the line connecting the aligner and wafer-handling stepper technologies is farther from the origin than the lines between those technologies and the plain stepper technology).

New processes are constantly being invented. As they are introduced, the isoquant will have more and more kinks (one for each new process) and will begin to resemble the usual smooth-shaped isoquants.

Substituting Inputs

The slope of an isoquant shows the ability of a firm to replace one input with another while holding output constant. The slope of an isoquant is called the *marginal rate of technical substitution*:

$$MRTS = \frac{\text{change in capital}}{\text{change in labor}} = \frac{\Delta K}{\Delta L} = \frac{dK}{dL}.$$

The **marginal rate of technical substitution** (*MRTS*) tells us how many units of capital the firm can replace with an extra unit of labor while holding output constant. Because isoquants slope downward, the *MRTS* is negative.

To determine the slope at a point on an isoquant, we totally differentiate the isoquant, $\bar{q} = f(L, K)$, with respect to L and K. Along the isoquant, we can write capital as an implicit function of labor: $K(L)$. That is, for a given quantity of labor, there is a level of capital such that $\bar{q}$ units are produced. Differentiating with respect to labor (and realizing that output does not change along the isoquant as we change labor), we have

$$\frac{d\bar{q}}{dL} = 0 = \frac{\partial f}{\partial L} + \frac{\partial f}{\partial K}\frac{dK}{dL} = MP_L + MP_K\frac{dK}{dL}, \quad (6.7)$$

where $MP_K = \partial f/\partial K$ is the marginal product of capital.

There is an appealing intuition behind Equation 6.7. As we move down and to the right along an isoquant (such as the ones in Figure 6.2), we increase the amount of labor slightly, so we must decrease the amount of capital to stay on the same isoquant. A little extra labor produces MP_L amount of extra output, the marginal product of labor. For example, if the MP_L is two and the firm hires one extra worker, its output rises by two units. Similarly, a little extra capital increases output by MP_K, so the change in output due to the drop in capital in response to the increase in labor is $MP_K \times dK/dL$. If we are to stay on the same isoquant—that is, hold output constant—these two effects must offset each other: $MP_L = -MP_K \times dK/dL$.

By rearranging Equation 6.7, we find that the marginal rate of technical substitution, which is the change in capital relative to the change in labor, equals the negative of the ratio of the marginal products:

$$MRTS = \frac{dK}{dL} = -\frac{MP_L}{MP_K}. \quad (6.8)$$

SOLVED PROBLEM 6.3

What is the marginal rate of technical substitution for a general Cobb-Douglas production function, Equation 6.4, $q = AL^aK^b$?

Answer

1. *Calculate the marginal products of labor and capital by differentiating the Cobb-Douglas production function first with respect to labor and then with respect to capital.* The marginal product of labor is $MP_L = \partial q/\partial L = aAL^{a-1}K^b = aq/L$, and the marginal product of capital is $MP_K = \partial q/\partial K = bAL^aK^{b-1} = bq/K$.

2. *Substitute the expression for MP_L and MP_K into Equation 6.8 to determine the MRTS.* Making the indicated substitutions,

$$MRTS = -\frac{MP_L}{MP_K} = -\frac{a\dfrac{q}{L}}{b\dfrac{q}{K}} = -\frac{a}{b}\frac{K}{L}. \quad (6.9)$$

Thus, the MRTS for a Cobb-Douglas production function is a constant, $-a/b$, times the capital-labor ratio, K/L.

Diminishing Marginal Rates of Technical Substitution

We can illustrate how the MRTS changes along an isoquant using the estimated $q = 6 = L^{0.5}K^{0.5}$ isoquant for an electronics firm from Figure 6.2, which is reproduced in Figure 6.4. Setting $a = b = 0.5$ in Equation 6.9, we find that the slope along this isoquant is $MRTS = -K/L$.

At point c in Figure 6.4, where $K = 12$ and $L = 3$, the $MRTS = -4$. The dashed line that is tangent to the isoquant at that point has the same slope. In contrast, the $MRTS = -1$ at d ($K = 6$, $L = 6$), and the $MRTS = -0.25$ at e ($K = 3$, $L = 12$). Thus, as we move down and to the right along this curved isoquant, the slope becomes flatter—the slope gets closer to zero—because the ratio K/L grows closer to zero.

The curvature of the isoquant away from the origin reflects *diminishing marginal rates of technical substitution*. The more labor the firm has, the harder it is to replace the remaining capital with labor, so the MRTS falls as the isoquant becomes flatter.

In the special case in which isoquants are straight lines, isoquants do not exhibit diminishing marginal rates of technical substitution because neither input becomes more valuable in the production process: The inputs remain perfect substitutes. In our earlier example of producing potato salad, the MRTS is -1 at every point along the isoquant: one pound of Idaho potatoes always can be replaced by one pound of

Figure 6.4 How the Marginal Rate of Technical Substitution Varies Along an Isoquant

Moving from point c to d, a U.S. electronics firm (Hsieh, 1995) can produce the same amount of output, $q = 6$, using six fewer units of capital, $\Delta K = -6$, if it uses three more workers. The slope of the isoquant, the MRTS, at a point is the same as the slope of the dashed tangent line. The MRTS goes from -4 at point c to -1 at d to -0.25 at e. Thus, as we move down and to the right, the isoquant becomes flatter: The slope gets closer to zero. Because it curves away from the origin, this isoquant exhibits a diminishing marginal rate of technical substitution: With each extra worker, the firm reduces capital by a smaller amount as the ratio of capital to labor falls.

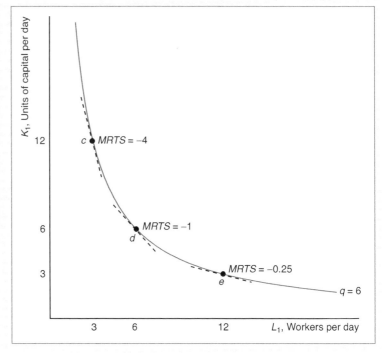

Maine potatoes. In the other special case of fixed proportions, where isoquants are right angles (or, perhaps more accurately, single points), no substitution is possible.

The Elasticity of Substitution

We've just seen that the marginal rate of technical substitution, the slope of the isoquant at a single point, varies as we move along a curved isoquant. It is useful to have a measure of this curvature, which reflects the ease with which a firm can substitute capital for labor. The best-known measure of the ease of substitution is the **elasticity of substitution**, σ (the Greek letter sigma), which is the percentage change in the capital-labor ratio divided by the percentage change in the MRTS:

$$\sigma = \frac{\frac{d(K/L)}{K/L}}{\frac{dMRTS}{MRTS}} = \frac{d(K/L)}{dMRTS}\frac{MRTS}{K/L}. \tag{6.10}$$

This measure tells us how the input factor ratio changes as the slope of the isoquant changes. If the elasticity is large—a small change in the slope results in a big increase in the factor ratio—the isoquant is relatively flat. As the elasticity falls, the isoquant becomes more curved. As we move along the isoquant, both K/L and the absolute value of the MRTS change in the same direction (see Figure 6.4), so the elasticity is positive.

Both the factor ratio, K/L, and the absolute value of the MRTS, $|MRTS|$, are positive numbers, so the logarithm of each is meaningful. It is often helpful to write the elasticity of substitution as a logarithmic derivative:[8]

$$\sigma = \frac{d\ln(K/L)}{d\ln|MRTS|}. \tag{6.11}$$

Constant Elasticity of Substitution Production Function. In general, the elasticity of substitution varies along an isoquant. An exception is the *constant elasticity of substitution* (CES) production function,

$$q = \left(aL^\rho + bK^\rho\right)^{\frac{d}{\rho}}, \tag{6.12}$$

where ρ is a positive constant. For simplicity, we assume that $a = b = d = 1$, so

$$q = \left(L^\rho + K^\rho\right)^{\frac{1}{\rho}}. \tag{6.13}$$

The marginal rate of technical substitution for a CES isoquant is[9]

$$MRTS = -\left(\frac{L}{K}\right)^{\rho-1}. \tag{6.14}$$

---

[8] By totally differentiating, we find that $d\ln(K/L) = d(K/L)/(K/L)$ and $d\ln|MRTS| = dMRTS/MRTS$, so $[d\ln(K/L)]/[d\ln|MRTS|] = [d(K/L)/dMRTS][MRTS/(K/L)] = \sigma$.

[9] Using the chain rule, we know that the $MP_L = (1/\rho)(L^\rho + K^\rho)^{1/\rho - 1}\rho L^{\rho - 1} = (L^\rho + K^\rho)^{1/\rho - 1}L^{\rho - 1}$. Similarly, the $MP_K = (L^\rho + K^\rho)^{1/\rho - 1}K^{\rho - 1}$. Thus, the $MRTS = -MP_L/MP_K = -(L/K)^{\rho - 1}$.

That is, the *MRTS* varies with the labor-capital ratio. At every point on a CES isoquant, the constant elasticity of substitutions is[10]

$$\sigma = \frac{1}{1-\rho}. \quad (6.15)$$

The linear, fixed-proportion, and Cobb-Douglas production functions are special cases of the constant elasticity production function.

Linear Production Function. Setting $\rho = 1$ in Equation 6.13, we get the linear production function $q = L + K$. At every point along a linear isoquant, the elasticity of substitution, $\sigma = 1/(1 - \rho) = 1/0$, is infinite: The two inputs are perfect substitutes for each other.

Cobb-Douglas Production Function. As ρ approaches zero, the CES isoquants approach the Cobb-Douglas isoquants, and hence the CES production function approaches the Cobb-Douglas production function. According to Equation 6.14 for the CES production function, $MRTS = -(K/L)^{\rho-1}$. In the limit as ρ approaches zero, $MRTS = -K/L$. Similarly, setting $a = b$ in Equation 6.9, we find that the Cobb-Douglas *MRTS* is the same. The elasticity of substitution is $\sigma = 1/(1 - \rho) = 1/1 = 1$ at every point along a Cobb-Douglas isoquant.[11]

Fixed-Proportion Production Function. As ρ approaches negative infinity, this production function approaches the fixed-proportion production function, which has right-angle isoquants (or, more accurately, single-point isoquants).[12] The elasticity of substitution is $\sigma = 1/(-\infty)$, which approaches zero: Substitution between the inputs is impossible.

SOLVED PROBLEM 6.4

What is the elasticity of substitution for the general Cobb-Douglas production function, Equation 6.4, $q = AL^aK^b$? (*Comment:* We just showed that the elasticity of substitution is one for a Cobb-Douglas production function where $a = b$. We want to know if that result holds for the more general Cobb-Douglas production function.)

Answer

1. *Using the formula for the marginal rate of technical substitution, determine* d(K/L)/dMRTS *and* MRTS/(K/L), *which are needed for the elasticity of substitution formula*. The marginal rate of technical substitution of a general Cobb-Douglas production function, Equation 6.9, is $MRTS = -(a/b)(K/L)$. Rearranging these terms:

$$\frac{K}{L} = -\frac{b}{a}MRTS. \quad (6.16)$$

---

[10]From the *MRTS* Equation 6.14, we know that $K/L = |MRTS|^{1/(1-\rho)}$. Taking logarithms of both sides of this expression, we find that $\ln(K/L) = [1/(1-\rho)]\ln|MRTS|$. We use the logarithmic derivative of the elasticity of substitution, Equation 6.11, to show that $\sigma = (d \ln K/L)/(d \ln |MRTS|) = 1/(1-\rho)$.

[11]Balistreri et al. (2003) used a CES production function to estimate substitution elasticities for 28 industries that cover the entire U.S. economy and found that the estimated CES substitution elasticity did not differ significantly from the Cobb–Douglas elasticity in 20 of the 28 industries.

[12]As ρ approaches $-\infty$, the CES isoquant approaches the right-angle, fixed-proportions isoquant. According to Equation 6.15, the $MRTS = -(L/K)^{-\infty}$. Thus, the *MRTS* is zero if $L > K$, and the *MRTS* goes to infinity if $K > L$.

Differentiating Equation 6.16, we find that $d(K/L)/dMRTS = -b/a$. By rearranging the terms in Equation 6.16, we also know that $MRTS/(K/L) = -a/b$.

2. *Substitute the two expressions from Step 1 into the elasticity of substitution formula and simplify.* The elasticity of substitution for a Cobb-Douglas production function is

$$\sigma = \frac{d(K/L)}{dMRTS}\frac{MRTS}{K/L} = \left(-\frac{b}{a}\right)\left(-\frac{a}{b}\right) = 1. \qquad (6.17)$$

6.5 Returns to Scale

So far, we have examined the effects of increasing one input while holding the other input constant (the shift from one isoquant to another), or decreasing the other input by an offsetting amount (the movement along an isoquant). We now turn to the question of *how much output changes if a firm increases all its inputs proportionately.* The answer to this question helps a firm determine its *scale* or size in the long run.

In the long run, a firm can increase its output by building a second plant and staffing it with the same number of workers as in the first plant. The firm's decision about whether to build a second plant partly depends on whether its output increases less than in proportion, in proportion, or more than in proportion to its inputs.

Constant, Increasing, and Decreasing Returns to Scale

If, when all inputs are increased by a certain percentage, output increases by that same percentage, the production function is said to exhibit **constant returns to scale** (*CRS*). A firm's production process has constant returns to scale if, when the firm doubles its inputs—for example, builds an identical second plant and uses the same amount of labor and equipment as in the first plant—it doubles its output: $f(2L, 2K) = 2f(L, K)$. [More generally, a production function is homogeneous of degree γ if $f(xL, xK) = x^{\gamma}f(L, K)$, where x is a positive constant. Thus, constant returns to scale is homogeneity of degree one.]

We can check whether the linear potato salad production function has constant returns to scale. If a firm uses x_1 pounds of Idaho potatoes and y_1 pounds of Maine potatoes, it produces $q_1 = x_1 + y_1$ pounds of potato salad. If it doubles both inputs, using $x_2 = 2x_1$ Idaho potatoes and $y_2 = 2y_1$ Maine potatoes, it doubles its output:

$$q_2 = x_2 + y_2 = 2x_1 + 2y_1 = 2q_1.$$

Thus, the potato salad production function exhibits constant returns to scale.

If output rises more than in proportion to an equal percentage increase in all inputs, the production function is said to exhibit **increasing returns to scale** (*IRS*). A technology exhibits increasing returns to scale if doubling inputs more than doubles the output: $f(2L, 2K) > 2f(L, K)$.

Why might a production function have increasing returns to scale? One reason is that although a firm could duplicate its small factory and double its output, it might be able to more than double its output by building a single large plant, which may allow for greater specialization of labor or capital. In the two smaller plants, workers must perform many unrelated tasks such as operating, maintaining, and fixing machines. In the single large plant, some workers may specialize in maintaining and fixing machines, thereby increasing efficiency. Similarly, a firm may use specialized equipment in a large plant but not in a small one.

If output rises less than in proportion to an equal percentage increase in all inputs, the production function exhibits **decreasing returns to scale** (*DRS*). A technology exhibits decreasing returns to scale if doubling inputs causes output to rise less than in proportion: $f(2L, 2K) < 2f(L, K)$.

One reason for decreasing returns to scale is that the difficulty of organizing, coordinating, and integrating activities increases with firm size. An owner may be able to manage one plant well but may have trouble running two plants. In some sense, the owner's difficulties in running a larger firm may reflect our failure to consider some factor such as management in our production function. When the firm increases the various inputs, it does not increase the management input in proportion. Therefore, the "decreasing returns to scale" is really due to a fixed input. Another reason is that large teams of workers may not function as well as small teams in which each individual has greater personal responsibility.

SOLVED PROBLEM 6.5

Under what conditions does a general Cobb-Douglas production function, $q = AL^aK^b$, exhibit decreasing, constant, or increasing returns to scale?

Answer

1. *Show how output changes if both inputs are doubled.* If the firm initially uses L and K amounts of inputs, it produces $q_1 = AL^aK^b$. After the firm doubles the amount of both labor and capital, it produces

$$q_2 = A(2L)^a (2K)^b = 2^{a+b} AL^aK^b. \qquad (6.18)$$

That is, q_2 is 2^{a+b} times q_1. If we define $\gamma = a + b$, then Equation 6.18 tells us that

$$q_2 = 2^\gamma q_1. \qquad (6.19)$$

Thus, if the inputs double, output increases by 2^γ.

2. *Give a rule for determining the returns to scale.* If we set $\gamma = 1$ in Equation 6.19, we find that $q_2 = 2^1 q_1 = 2q_1$. That is, output doubles when the inputs double, so the Cobb-Douglas production function has constant returns to scale. If $\gamma < 1$, then $q_2 = 2^\gamma q_1 < 2q_1$ because $2^\gamma < 2$ if $\gamma < 1$. That is, when input doubles, output increases less than in proportion, so this Cobb-Douglas production function exhibits decreasing returns to scale. Finally, the Cobb-Douglas production function has increasing returns to scale hold if $\gamma > 1$ so that $q_2 > 2q_1$. Thus, the rule for determining returns to scale for a Cobb-Douglas production function is that the returns to scale are decreasing if $\gamma < 1$, constant if $\gamma = 1$, and increasing if $\gamma > 1$.

Comment: Thus, γ is a measure of the returns to scale. It is a *scale elasticity*: If all inputs increase by 1%, output increases by γ%.

APPLICATION

Returns to Scale in U.S. Manufacturing

Increasing, constant, and decreasing returns to scale are commonly observed. The table shows estimates of Cobb-Douglas production functions and rates of returns in various U.S. manufacturing industries (based on Hsieh, 1995).

The table shows that the estimated returns to scale measure for a tobacco firm is $\gamma = 0.51$: A 1% increase in the inputs causes output to rise by 0.51%. Because

	Labor, a	Capital, b	Scale, $\gamma = a + b$
Decreasing Returns to Scale			
Tobacco products	0.18	0.33	0.51
Food and kindred products	0.43	0.48	0.91
Transportation equipment	0.44	0.48	0.92
Constant Returns to Scale			
Apparel and other textile products	0.70	0.31	1.01
Furniture and fixtures	0.62	0.40	1.02
Electronic and other electric equipment	0.49	0.53	1.02
Increasing Returns to Scale			
Paper and allied products	0.44	0.65	1.09
Petroleum and coal products	0.30	0.88	1.18
Primary metal	0.51	0.73	1.24

output rises less than in proportion to the inputs, the tobacco production function exhibits decreasing returns to scale. In contrast, firms that manufacture primary metals have increasing returns to scale production functions, in which a 1% increase in all inputs causes output to rise by 1.24%.

The accompanying graphs use isoquants to illustrate the returns to scale for the electronics, tobacco, and primary metal firms. We measure the units of labor, capital, and output so that, for all three firms, 100 units of labor and 100 units of capital produce 100 units of output on the $q = 100$ isoquant in the three panels. For the constant returns to scale electronics firm, panel a, if both labor and capital are doubled from 100 to 200 units, output doubles to 200 ($= 100 \times 2^1$, multiplying the original output by the rate of increase using Equation 6.19).

That same doubling of inputs causes output to rise to only 142 ($\approx 100 \times 2^{0.51}$) for the tobacco firm, panel b. Because output rises less than in proportion to inputs, the production function exhibits decreasing returns to scale. If the

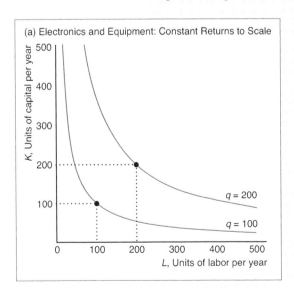

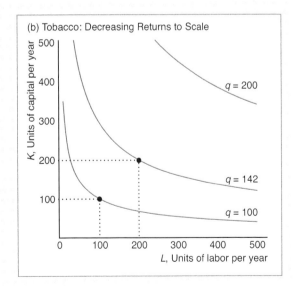

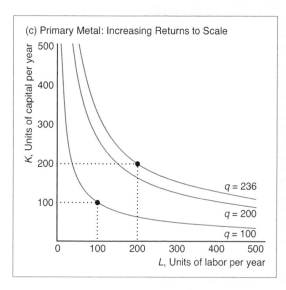

primary metal firm doubles its inputs, panel c, its output more than doubles, to 236 ($\approx 100 \times 2^{1.24}$), so the production function has increasing returns to scale.

These graphs illustrate that the spacing of the isoquant determines the returns to scale. The closer the $q = 100$ and $q = 200$ isoquants, the greater the returns to scale.

The returns to scale in these industries are estimated to be the same at all levels of output. A production function's returns to scale may vary, however, as the scale of the firm changes.

Varying Returns to Scale

Many production functions have increasing returns to scale for small amounts of output, constant returns for moderate amounts of output, and decreasing returns for large amounts of output. When a firm is small, increasing labor and capital may produce gains from cooperation between workers and greater specialization of workers and equipment—*returns to specialization*—so there are increasing returns to scale. As the firm grows, returns to scale are eventually exhausted. There are no more returns to specialization, so the production process has constant returns to scale. If the firm continues to grow, managing the staff becomes more difficult, so the firm suffers from decreasing returns to scale.

Figure 6.5 shows such a pattern. Again, the spacing of the isoquants reflects the returns to scale. Initially, the firm has one worker and one piece of equipment, point a, and produces one unit of output on the $q = 1$ isoquant. If the firm doubles its inputs, it produces at b, where $L = 2$ and $K = 2$, which lies on the dashed line through the origin and point a. Output more than doubles to $q = 3$, so the production function exhibits increasing returns to scale in this range. Another doubling of inputs to c causes output to double to $q = 6$, so the production function has constant returns to scale in this range. Another doubling of inputs to d causes output to increase by only one-third, to $q = 8$, so the production function has decreasing returns to scale in this range.

6.6 Productivity and Technical Change

Because firms may use different technologies and different methods of organizing production, the amount of output that one firm produces from a given amount of inputs may differ from that produced by another. Moreover, after a technical or managerial innovation, a firm can produce more today from a given amount of inputs than it could in the past.

Figure 6.5 Varying Scale Economies

This production function exhibits varying returns to scale. Initially, the firm uses one worker and one unit of capital, point a. It repeatedly doubles these inputs to points b, c, and d, which lie along the dashed line. The first time the inputs are doubled, a to b, output more than doubles from $q = 1$ to $q = 3$, so the production function has increasing returns to scale. The next doubling, b to c, causes a proportionate increase in output, constant returns to scale. At the last doubling, from c to d, the production function exhibits decreasing returns to scale.

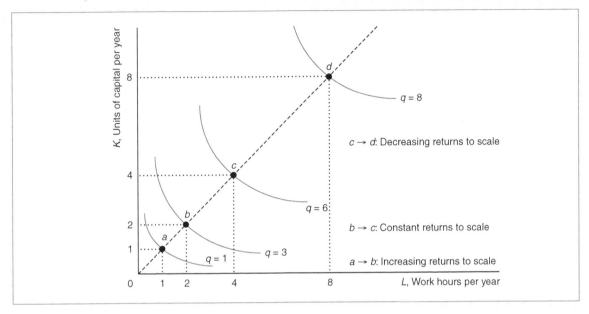

Relative Productivity

This chapter has assumed that firms produce efficiently. A firm must produce efficiently to maximize its profit. However, even if each firm in a market produces as efficiently as possible, firms may not be equally *productive*—one firm may be able to produce more than another from a given amount of inputs.

A firm may be more productive than another if its management knows a better way to organize production or if it has access to a new invention. Union-mandated work rules, racial or gender discrimination, government regulations, or other institutional restrictions that affect only certain firms may lower the relative productivity of those firms.

We can measure the *relative productivity* of a firm by expressing the firm's actual output, q, as a percentage of the output that the most productive firm in the industry could have produced, q^*, from the same amount of inputs: $100q/q^*$. The most productive firm in an industry has a relative productivity measure of 100% (= $100q^*/q^*$ percent). Caves and Barton (1990) reported that the average productivity of firms across U.S. manufacturing industries ranged from 63% to 99%.

Differences in productivity across markets may be due to differences in the degree of competition. In competitive markets, where many firms can enter and exit easily, less productive firms lose money and are driven out of business, so the firms that actually continue to produce are equally productive (see Chapter 8). In a less competitive market with few firms and no possibility of entry by new ones, a less productive firm may be able to survive, so firms with varying levels of productivity are observed.

APPLICATION

U.S. Electric Generation Efficiency

Prior to the mid-1990s, more than 90% of the electricity was produced and sold to consumers by investor-owned utility monopolies that were subject to government regulation of the prices they charged. Beginning in the mid-1990s, some states mandated that electric production be *restructured*. In those states, the utility monopoly was forced to sell its electric generation plants to several other firms. These new firms sold the electricity they generated to the utility monopoly, which delivered the electricity to final consumers. Because they expected these new electric generator firms to compete with each other, state legislators hoped that this increased competition would result in greater production efficiency.

Fabrizio, Rose, and Wolfram (2007) found that, in anticipation of greater competition, the generation plant operators in states that restructured reduced their labor and non-fuel expenses by 3% to 5% (holding output constant) relative to investor-owned utility monopoly plants in states that did not restructure. When compared to plants run by government- and cooperatively owned utility monopolies that were not exposed to restructuring incentives, these gains were even greater: 6% in labor and 13% in non-fuel expenses. Thus, restructuring, which led to greater competition, resulted in increased productivity.

Innovations

Maximum number of miles that Ford's most fuel-efficient 2003 car could drive on a gallon of gas: 36. Maximum number its 1912 Model T could: 35.
—Harper's Index 2003

In its production process, a firm tries to use the best available technological and managerial knowledge. An advance in knowledge that allows more output to be produced with the same level of inputs is called **technical progress**. The invention of new products is a form of technical innovation. The use of robotic arms increases the number of automobiles produced with a given amount of labor and raw materials. Better *management or organization of the production process* similarly allows the firm to produce more output from given levels of inputs.

Technical Progress. A technological innovation changes the production process. Last year, a firm produced

$$q_1 = f(L, K)$$

units of output using L units of labor services and K units of capital service. Due to a new invention employed by the firm, this year's production function differs from last year's, so the firm produces 10% more output with the same inputs:

$$q_2 = 1.1 f(L, K).$$

This firm has experienced *neutral technical change*, in which it can produce more output using the same ratio of inputs. For example, a technical innovation in the form of a new printing press allows more output to be produced using the same ratio of inputs as before: one worker to one printing press.

Many empirical studies find that systematic neutral technical progress occurs over time. In these studies, the production function is

$$q = A(t)f(L, K), \tag{6.20}$$

where $A(t)$ is a function of time, t, that shows how much output grows over time for any given mix of inputs. Table 6.1 shows estimates of the annual rate at which computer and related goods output grew for given levels of inputs in several countries. According to this estimate, the U.S. computer production function, Equation 6.20, is $q = e^{0.017t}f(L, K)$, so that output grows at a 1.7% rate per year.

Non-neutral technical changes are innovations that alter the proportion in which inputs are used. If a printing press that requires two people to operate is replaced by a press that can be run by one worker, the technical change is *labor saving*. The ratio of labor to the other inputs used to produce a given level of output falls after the innovation.[13] Similarly, the ratio of output to labor, the average product of labor, rises.

Organizational Change. Organizational change may also alter the production function and increase the amount of output produced by a given amount of inputs. In 1904, King C. Gillette used automated production techniques to produce a new type of razor blade that could be sold for 5¢—a fraction of the price charged by rivals—allowing working men to shave daily.

In the early 1900s, Henry Ford revolutionized mass production through two organizational innovations. First, he introduced interchangeable parts, which cut the time required to install parts because workers no longer had to file or machine individually made parts to get them to fit. Second, Ford introduced a conveyor belt and an assembly line to his production process. Before Ford, workers walked around the car, and each worker performed many assembly activities. In Ford's plant, each worker specialized in a single activity such as attaching the right rear fender to the chassis. A conveyor belt moved the car at a constant speed from worker to worker along the assembly line. Because his workers gained proficiency from specializing in only a few activities, and because the conveyor belts reduced the number of movements workers had to make, Ford could produce more automobiles with the same number of workers. In 1908, the Ford Model T sold for $850, when rival vehicles sold for $2,000. By the early 1920s, Ford had increased production from fewer than a thousand cars per year to 2 million cars per year.

Table 6.1 Annual Percentage Rates of Neutral Productivity Growth for Computer and Related Capital Goods

	1990–1995	1995–2002
Australia	1.4	1.5
Canada	0.4	1.0
France	0.8	1.4
Japan	0.8	0.6
United Kingdom	1.2	0.9*
United States	0.8	1.3

*United Kingdom rate is for 1995–2001.
Source: OECD Productivity Database, December 17, 2004.

---

[13]See "More Productive Death" and "Rolls Royce" in the Supplemental Material to Chapter 8 in **MyEconLab**'s textbook resources.

APPLICATION

Tata Nano's Technical and Organizational Innovations

In 2009, the automotive world was stunned when India's new Tata Motors introduced the Nano, its tiny, fuel-efficient four-passenger car. With a base price of less than $2,500, it is by far the world's least expensive car. The next cheapest car in India, the Maruti 800, sells for about $4,800.

The Nano's dramatically lower price is not the result of amazing new inventions. Although Tata Motors filed for 34 patents related to the design of the Nano (compared to the roughly 280 patents awarded to General Motors annually), most of these patents are for mundane items such as the two-cylinder engine's balance shaft and the configuration of the transmission gears. Instead of relying on innovations, Tata reduced manufacturing costs at every stage of the process with a no-frills design, decreased vehicle weight, and major production improvements.

The Nano has a single windshield wiper, one side view mirror, no power steering, a simplified door opening lever, three nuts on the wheels instead of the customary four, and a trunk that does not open from the outside—it is accessed by folding down the rear seats. The Nano has smaller overall dimensions than the Maruti, but about 20% more seating capacity because of design decisions, such as putting the wheels at the extreme edges of the car. The Nano is much lighter than comparable models due to the reduced amount of steel, the use of lightweight steel, and the use of aluminum in the engine. The ribbed roof structure is not only a style element but also a strength structure, which is necessary because the design uses thin-gauge sheet metal. Because the engine is in the rear, the driveshaft doesn't need complex joints as in a front-engine car with front-wheel drive. To cut costs further, the company reduced the number of tools needed to make the components and thereby increased the life of the dies used by three times the norm. In consultation with their suppliers, Tata's engineers determined how many useful parts the design required, which helped them determine that some functions could be integrated in parts.

Tata's major innovation was its open distribution. The Nano's modular design enables an experienced mechanic to assemble the car in a workshop. Therefore, Tata Motors can distribute a complete knock-down (CKD) kit to be assembled and serviced by local assembly hubs and entrepreneurs closer to consumers. The cost of transporting these kits, produced at a central manufacturing plant, is charged directly to the customer. This approach is expected to speed up the distribution process, even to the more remote locations of India.

SUMMARY

1. **The Ownership and Management of Firms.** Firms can be sole proprietorships, partnerships, or corporations. In small firms (particularly sole proprietorships and partnerships), the owners usually run the company. In large firms (such as most corporations), the owners hire managers to run the firms. Owners want to maximize profits. If managers have different objectives than owners, owners must keep a close watch to ensure that profits are maximized.

2. **Production.** Inputs, or factors of production—labor, capital, and materials—are combined to produce output using the current state of knowledge about technology and management. To maximize profits, a firm must produce as efficiently as possible: It must get the maximum amount of output from the inputs it uses, given existing knowledge. A firm may have access to many efficient production processes that use different combinations of inputs to produce a given level of output. New technologies or new forms of organization can increase the amount of output that can be produced from a given combination of inputs. A production function shows how much output can be produced efficiently from various levels of inputs.

A firm can vary all its inputs in the long run but only some of its inputs in the short run.

3. **Short-Run Production: One Variable and One Fixed Input.** In the short run, a firm cannot adjust the quantity of some inputs, such as capital. The firm varies its output by adjusting its variable inputs, such as labor. If all factors are fixed except labor, and a firm that was using very little labor increases its labor, its output may rise more than in proportion to the increase in labor because of greater specialization of workers. Eventually, however, as more workers are hired, the workers get in each other's way or wait to share equipment, so output increases by smaller and smaller amounts. This phenomenon is described by the law of diminishing marginal returns: The marginal product of an input—the extra output from the last unit of input—eventually decreases as more of that input is used, holding other inputs fixed.

4. **Long-Run Production: Two Variable Inputs.** In the long run, when all inputs are variable, firms can substitute between inputs. An isoquant shows the combinations of inputs that can produce a given level of output. The marginal rate of technical substitution is the slope of the isoquant. Usually, the more of one input the firm uses, the more difficult it is to substitute that input for another input. That is, there are diminishing marginal rates of technical substitution as the firm uses more of one input. The elasticity of substitution reflects the ease of replacing one input with another in the production process, or, equivalently, the curvature of an isoquant.

5. **Returns to Scale.** If, when a firm increases all inputs in proportion, its output increases by the same proportion, the production process exhibits constant returns to scale. If output increases less than in proportion to inputs, the production process has decreasing returns to scale; if it increases more than in proportion, it has increasing returns to scale. All these types of returns to scale are commonly observed in various industries. Many production processes first exhibit increasing, then constant, and finally decreasing returns to scale as the size of the firm increases.

6. **Productivity and Technical Change.** Although all firms in an industry produce efficiently, given what they know and what institutional and other constraints they face, some firms may be more productive than others: They can produce more output from a given bundle of inputs. Due to innovations such as technical progress and new methods of organizing production, firms can produce more today than they could in the past from the same bundle of inputs. Such innovations change the production function.

QUESTIONS

■ = exercise is available on **MyEconLab**; * = answer appears at the back of this book; V = video answer by James Dearden is available online.

*1. If each extra worker produces an extra unit of output, how do the total product of labor, the average product of labor, and the marginal product of labor vary with the number of workers?

2. Each extra worker produces an extra unit of output, up to six workers. After six, no additional output is produced. Draw the total product of labor, average product of labor, and marginal product of labor curves.

3. What are the differences between an isoquant and an indifference curve?

4. Why must isoquants be thin?

5. Suppose that a firm has a fixed-proportions production function in which one unit of output is produced using one worker and two units of capital. If the firm has an extra worker and no more capital, it still can produce only one unit of output. Similarly, one more unit of capital produces no extra output.
   a. Draw the isoquants for this production function.
   b. Draw the total product of labor, average product of labor, and marginal product of labor curves (you will probably want to use two diagrams) for this production function.

*6. To produce a recorded CD, $q = 1$, a firm uses one blank disc, $D = 1$, and the services of a recording machine, $M = 1$, for one hour. Draw an isoquant for this production process. Explain the reason for its shape.

7. Michelle's business produces ceramic cups using labor, clay, and a kiln. She can manufacture 25 cups a day with one worker and 35 cups with two workers. Does her production process illustrate *diminishing returns to scale* or *diminishing marginal returns to scale*? Give a plausible explanation for why output does not increase proportionately with the number of workers.

8. The production function at Ginko's Copy Shop is $q = 1{,}000 \times \min(L, 3K)$, where q is the number of copies per hour, L is the number of workers, and K is the number of copy machines. As an example, if $L = 4$ and $K = 1$, then $\min(L, 3K) = 3$, and $q = 3{,}000$.
   a. Draw the isoquants for this production function.
   b. Draw the total product of labor, average product of labor, and marginal product of labor curves for this production function for some fixed level of capital.

9. Why might we expect the law of diminishing marginal product to hold?

*10. Mark launders his white clothes using the production function $q = B + 2G$, where B is the number of cups of Clorox bleach and G is the number of cups of generic bleach that is half as potent. Draw an isoquant. What is the marginal product of B? What is the marginal rate of technical substitution at each point on an isoquant?

11. To speed relief to isolated South Asian communities that were devastated by the December 2004 tsunami, the U.S. Navy doubled the number of helicopters from 45 to 90 soon after the first ship arrived. Navy Admiral Thomas Fargo, head of the U.S. Pacific Command, was asked if doubling the number of helicopters would "produce twice as much [relief]." He replied, "Maybe pretty close to twice as much." (Vicky O'Hara, *All Things Considered,* National Public Radio, January 4, 2005, www.npr.org/dmg/dmg.php?prgCode=ATC&showDate=04-Jan-2005&segNum=10&NPRMediaPref=WM&getAd=1).
Identify the inputs and outputs and describe the production process. Is the admiral discussing a production process with nearly constant returns to scale, or is he referring to another property of the production process?

12. Alfred's Print Shop can use any one of three fixed-proportion technologies. Each involves one printer and one worker. Describe the possible shapes of the firm's isoquant. (*Hint*: Review the discussion in the application "A Semiconductor Integrated Circuit Isoquant.")

13. From the ninth century BC until the proliferation of gunpowder in the fifteenth century AD, the ultimate weapon of mass destruction was the catapult (John N. Wilford, "How Catapults Married Science, Politics and War," *New York Times,* February 24, 2004, D3). As early as the fourth century BC, rulers set up research and development laboratories to support military technology. Research on improving the catapult was by trial and error until about 200 BC, when the engineer Philo of Byzantium reported that, using mathematics, it was determined that each part of the catapult was proportional to the size of the object it was designed to propel. For example, the weight and length of the projectile was proportional to the size of the torsion springs (bundles of sinews or ropes that were tightly twisted to store enormous power). Mathematicians devised precise reference tables of specifications for builders and soldiers on the firing line. The Romans had catapults capable of delivering 60-pound boulders at least 500 feet. (Legend has it that Archimedes' catapults used stones that were three times heavier than those boulders.) If the output of the production process is measured as the weight of a delivered projectile, how does the amount of capital needed vary with output? If the amount of labor to operate the catapult did not vary substantially with the projectile's size, what can you say about the marginal productivity of capital and scale economies?

14. Until the mid-eighteenth century, when spinning became mechanized, cotton was an expensive and relatively unimportant textile (Virginia Postrel, "What Separates Rich Nations from Poor Nations?" *New York Times,* January 1, 2004). Where it used to take an Indian hand-spinner 50,000 hours to hand-spin 100 pounds of cotton, an operator of a 1760s-era hand-operated cotton mule spinning machine could produce 100 pounds of stronger thread in 300 hours. After 1825, when the self-acting mule spinner automated the process, the time dropped to 135 hours, and cotton became an inexpensive, common cloth. Was this technological progress neutral? In a figure, show how these technological changes affected isoquants.

15. Draw a circle in a diagram with labor services on one axis and capital services on the other. This circle represents all the combinations of labor and capital that produce 100 units of output. Now, draw the isoquant for 100 units of output. (*Hint*: Remember that the isoquant includes only the efficient combinations of labor and capital.)

16. In a manufacturing plant, workers use a specialized machine to produce belts. A new labor-saving machine is invented. With the new machine, the firm can use fewer workers and still produce the same number of belts as it did using the old machine. In the long run, both labor and capital (the machine) are variable. From what you know, what is the effect of this invention on the AP_L, MP_L, and returns to scale? If you require more information to answer this question, specify what else you need to know.

17. Show in a diagram that a production function can have diminishing marginal returns to a factor and constant returns to scale.

18. If a firm lays off workers during a recession, how will the firm's marginal product of labor change?

*19. During recessions, American firms lay off a larger proportion of their workers than Japanese firms do. (It has been claimed that Japanese firms continue to produce at high levels and store the output or sell it at relatively low prices during recessions.) Assuming that the production function remains unchanged over a period that is long enough to include many recessions and expansions, would you expect the average product of labor to be higher in Japan or in the United States? Why?

20. Does it follow that, because we observe that the average product of labor is higher for Firm 1 than for Firm 2, Firm 1 is more productive in the sense that it can produce more output from a given amount of inputs? Why or why not?

PROBLEMS

21. By studying, Will can produce a higher grade, G_W, on an upcoming economics exam. His production function depends on the number of hours he studies marginal analysis problems, A, and the number of hours he studies supply and demand problems, R. Specifically, $G_W = 2.5A^{0.36}R^{0.64}$. His roommate David's grade production function is $G_D = 2.5A^{0.25}R^{0.75}$.
    a. What is Will's marginal productivity from studying supply and demand problems? What is David's?
    b. What is Will's marginal rate of technical substitution between studying the two types of problems? What is David's?
    c. Is it possible that Will and David have different marginal productivity functions but the same marginal rate of technical substitution functions? Explain. V

*22. Suppose that the production function is $q = L^{0.75}K^{0.25}$.
    a. What is the average product of labor, holding capital fixed at K?
    b. What is the marginal product of labor?
    c. Does this production function have increasing, constant, or decreasing returns to scale?

23. What is the production function if L and K are perfect substitutes and each unit of q requires one unit of L or one unit of K (or a combination of these inputs that equals one)?

*24. At $L = 4$ and $K = 4$, the marginal product of labor is 2 and the marginal product of capital is 3. What is the marginal rate of technical substitution?

25. In the short run, a firm cannot vary its capital, $K = 2$, but it can vary its labor, L. It produces output q. Explain why the firm will or will not experience diminishing marginal returns to labor in the short run if its production function is:
    a. $q = 10L + K$
    b. $q = L^{0.5}K^{0.5}$

26. Under what conditions do the following production functions exhibit decreasing, constant, or increasing returns to scale?
    a. $q = L + K$, a linear production function
    b. $q = AL^a K^b$, a general Cobb-Douglas production function
    c. $q = L + L^a K^b + K$
    d. $q = (aL^\rho + bK^\rho)^{d/\rho}$, a general CES production function

*27. Firm 1 and Firm 2 use the same type of production function, but Firm 1 is only 90% as productive as Firm 2. That is, the production function of Firm 2 is $q_2 = f(L, K)$, and the production function of Firm 1 is $q_1 = 0.9f(L, K)$. At a particular level of inputs, how does the marginal product of labor differ between the firms?

28. Is it possible that a firm's production function exhibits increasing returns to scale while exhibiting diminishing marginal productivity of each of its inputs? To answer this question, calculate the marginal productivities of capital and labor for the production of electronics and equipment, tobacco, and primary metal using the information listed in the "Returns to Scale in U.S. Manufacturing" application. V

*29. The production function for the automotive and parts industry is $q = L^{0.27}K^{0.16}M^{0.61}$, where M is energy and materials (based loosely on Klein, 2003). What kind of returns to scale does this production function exhibit? What is the marginal product of energy and materials?

30. A production function is said to be homogeneous of degree γ if $f(xL, xK) = x^\gamma f(L, K)$, where x is a positive constant. That is, the production function has the same returns to scale for every combination of inputs. For such a production function, show that the marginal product of labor and marginal product of capital functions are homogeneous of degree $\gamma - 1$.

31. Show that with a constant returns to scale production function, the $MRTS$ between labor and capital depends only on the K/L ratio and not on the scale of production. (*Hint*: Use your result from Problem 30.)

32. Prove Euler's theorem that, if $f(L, K)$ is homogeneous of degree γ (see Problem 30), then $L(\partial f/\partial L) + K(\partial f/\partial K) = \gamma f(L, K)$. Given this result, what can you conclude if a production function has constant returns to scale? Express your results in terms of the marginal products of labor and capital.

33. Show that $f(L, K) = (aL^\rho + bK^\rho)^{1/\rho}$, a CES production function, can be written as
$$f(L, K) = B(\rho)[cL^\rho + (1 - c) \times K^\rho]^{1/\rho}.$$

34. Ben's swim coach estimates that his time, t, in the 100-yard butterfly at a big upcoming meet, as a function of the number of yards he swims per week, y, is $t = 47 + 7e^{-0.00005y}$. Based on this production function, his coach determines that if Ben swims 20,000 yards per week, his time will be 49.57 seconds, and he will finish in tenth place. If he swims 40,000 yards per week, his time will be 47.94 seconds, and he will come in third. If he swims 60,000 yards per week, his time will be 47.34 seconds, and he will win the race.

   a. Use calculus to determine Ben's marginal productivity of time given the number of yards he practices. Is there diminishing marginal productivity of practice yards?

   b. In terms of Ben's place in the big meet, what is his marginal productivity of the number of yards he practices? Is there diminishing marginal productivity of practice yards? V

*35. In recent years, professional sports teams have used sabermetrics (the application of statistics to measuring player productivity) to study the productivity of professional baseball players. Sabermetrics is now being used to study the contributions of individual players to the productivity of their teams. (See Allen St. John, "An NBA MBA," *Wall Street Journal,* Nov. 3, 2006, p. W5.)

   a. In the CES basketball production function, $q = (a_1 L_1^\rho + \cdots + a_n L_n^\rho)^{d/\rho}$, q is the number of points per game that a team scores, and L_i is the number of minutes in a game that player i is on the court. According to sabermetric analyses, a player's productivity depends on how the player and the other four on the court interact. What is the plausible range of values of the ρ parameter? V

   b. In the CES baseball production function, $q = (a_1 L_1^\rho + \cdots + a_n L_n^\rho)^{d/\rho}$, q is the number of team hits per game, and L_i is the number of times that player i bats in a game. The statisticians who study player contributions contend that in baseball, a player's batting contribution is independent of his teammates' productivity. What is the value of the ρ parameter given this statistical evidence? Now, suppose that q represents the number of team *runs* per game in the CES production function. What is the range of values of the ρ parameter?

7

Costs

An economist is a person who, when invited to give a talk at a banquet, tells the audience there's no such thing as a free lunch.

A semiconductor manufacturer can produce a chip by using many pieces of equipment and relatively few workers' labor or by using many workers and relatively few machines. How does the firm make its choice?

The firm uses a two-step procedure to determine how to produce a certain amount of output efficiently. It first determines which production processes are *technologically efficient* so that it can produce the desired level of output with the least amount of inputs. As we saw in Chapter 6, the firm uses engineering and other information to determine its production function, which summarizes the many technologically efficient production processes available.

The firm's second step is to select the technologically efficient production process that is also **economically efficient**, minimizing the cost of producing a specified amount of output. To determine which process minimizes its cost of production, the firm uses information about the production function and the cost of inputs.

By reducing its cost of producing a given level of output, a firm can increase its profit. Any profit-maximizing competitive, monopolistic, or oligopolistic firm minimizes its cost of production.

In this chapter, we examine five main topics

1. **Measuring Costs.** Economists count both explicit costs and implicit (opportunity) costs.

2. **Short-Run Costs.** To minimize its costs in the short run, a firm can adjust its variable factors (such as labor), but it cannot adjust its fixed factors (such as capital).

3. **Long-Run Costs.** To minimize its costs in the long run, a firm can adjust all its inputs because all inputs are variable.

4. **Lower Costs in the Long Run.** Long-run cost is as low or lower than short-run cost because the firm has more flexibility in the long run, technological progress occurs, and workers and managers learn from experience.

5. **Cost of Producing Multiple Goods.** If a firm produces several goods simultaneously, the cost of each may depend on the quantity of all the goods it produces.

Business people and economists need to understand the relationship between the costs of inputs and production to determine the most cost-efficient way to produce. Economists have an additional reason for wanting to understand costs. As we'll see in later chapters, the relationship between output and costs plays an important role in determining the nature of a market—how many firms are in the market and how high price is relative to cost.

7.1 Measuring Costs

How much would it cost you to stand at the wrong end of a shooting gallery?
—S. J. Perelman

To show how a firm's cost varies with its output, we first have to measure costs. Businesspeople and economists often measure costs differently. Economists include all relevant costs. To run a firm profitably, a manager must think like an economist and consider all relevant costs. However, this same manager may direct the firm's accountant or bookkeeper to measure costs in ways that are more consistent with tax laws and other laws so as to make the firm's financial statements look good to stockholders or to minimize the firm's taxes.[1]

To produce a particular amount of output, a firm incurs costs for the required inputs such as labor, capital, energy, and materials. A firm's manager (or accountant) determines the cost of labor, energy, and materials by multiplying the price of the factor by the number of units used. If workers earn $20 per hour and work 100 hours per day, then the firm's cost of labor is $20 × 100 = $2,000 per day. The manager can easily calculate these *explicit costs*, which are its direct, out-of-pocket payments for inputs to its production process within a given time period. While calculating explicit costs is straight forward, some costs are *implicit* in that they reflect only a forgone opportunity rather than an explicit, current expenditure. Properly taking account of forgone opportunities requires particularly careful attention when dealing with durable capital goods as past expenditures for an input may be irrelevant to current cost calculations if that input has no current, alternative use.

Opportunity Costs

The **economic cost** or **opportunity cost** of a resource is the value of the best alternative use of that resource. Explicit costs are opportunity costs. If a firm purchases an input in a market and uses that input immediately, the input's opportunity cost is the amount the firm pays for it, the market price. After all, if the firm does not use the input in its production process, its best alternative would be to sell it to someone else at the market price. The concept of an opportunity cost becomes particularly useful when the firm uses an input that is not available for purchase in a market or that was purchased in a market in the past.

A key example of such an opportunity cost is the value of a manager's time. For example, Maoyong owns and manages a firm. He pays himself only a small monthly salary of $1,000 because he also receives the firm's profit. However, Maoyong could work for another firm and earn $11,000 a month. Thus, the opportunity cost of his time is $11,000—from his best alternative use of his time—not the $1,000 he actually pays himself.

The classic example of an implicit opportunity cost is captured in the phrase "There's no such thing as a free lunch." Suppose that your parents offer to take you

---
[1] See "Tax Rules" in **MyEconLab**'s textbook resources for Chapter 7.

to lunch tomorrow. You know that they'll pay for the meal, but you also know that this lunch will not truly be free. Your opportunity cost for the lunch is the best alternative use of your time. Presumably, the best alternative use of your time is studying this textbook, but other possible alternatives include working at a job or watching TV. Often, such an opportunity cost is substantial. (What are you giving up to study opportunity costs?)

APPLICATION

The Opportunity Cost of an MBA

During the sharp economic downturn in 2008, did applications to MBA programs fall, hold steady, or take off as tech stocks did during the first Internet bubble? Knowledge of opportunity costs helps us answer this question.

For many potential students, the biggest cost of attending an MBA program is the opportunity cost of giving up a well-paying job. Someone who leaves a job that pays $5,000 per month to attend an MBA program is, in effect, incurring a $5,000-per-month opportunity cost, in addition to the tuition and cost of textbooks (although this one is well worth the money).

Thus, it is not surprising that MBA applications rise in bad economic times when outside opportunities decline. People thinking of going back to school face a reduced opportunity cost of entering an MBA program if they think they may be laid off or might not be promoted during an economic downturn. As Stacey Kole, deputy dean for the MBA program at the University of Chicago Graduate School of Business observed in 2008, "When there's a go-go economy, fewer people decide to go back to school. When things go south the opportunity cost of leaving work is lower."

In 2008, when U.S. unemployment rose sharply and the economy was in poor shape, the number of people seeking admission to MBA programs rose sharply. The number of applicants to MBA programs in 2008 increased from 2007 by 79% in the U.S., 77% in the U.K., and 69% in other European programs.

SOLVED PROBLEM 7.1

Meredith's firm sends her to a conference for managers and has paid her registration fee. Included in the registration fee is free admission to a class on how to price derivative securities such as options. She is considering attending, but her most attractive alternative opportunity is to attend a talk by Warren Buffett about his investment strategies, which is scheduled at the same time. Although she would be willing to pay $100 to hear his talk, the cost of a ticket is only $40. Given that there are no other costs involved in attending either event, what is Meredith's opportunity cost of attending the derivatives talk?

Answer

To calculate her opportunity cost, determine the benefit that Meredith would forgo by attending the derivatives class. Because she incurs no additional fee to attend the derivatives talk, Meredith's opportunity cost is the forgone benefit of hearing the Buffett speech. Because she values hearing the Buffett speech at $100, but only has to pay $40, her net benefit from hearing that talk is $60 (= $100 − $40). Thus, her opportunity cost of attending the derivatives talk is $60.

Capital Costs

Determining the opportunity cost of capital, such as land or equipment, requires special considerations. Capital is a **durable good**: a product that is usable for a long period, typically for many years. Two problems may arise in measuring the cost of capital. The first is how to allocate the initial purchase cost over time. The second is what to do if the value of the capital changes over time.

We can avoid these two measurement problems if capital is rented instead of purchased. For example, suppose a firm can rent a small pick-up truck for $400 a month or buy it outright for $20,000. If the firm rents the truck, the rental payment is the relevant opportunity cost per month. The truck is rented month-to-month, so the firm does not have to worry about how to allocate the purchase cost of a truck over time. Moreover, the rental rate will adjust if the cost of trucks changes over time. Thus, if the firm can rent capital for short periods of time, it calculates the cost of this capital in the same way that it calculates the cost of nondurable inputs such as labor services or materials.

The firm faces a more complex problem in determining the opportunity cost of the truck if it purchases the truck. The firm's accountant may *expense* the truck's purchase price by treating the full $20,000 as a cost at the time that the truck is purchased, or the accountant may *amortize* the cost by spreading the $20,000 over the life of the truck, following rules set by an accounting organization or by a relevant government authority such as the Internal Revenue Service (IRS).

A manager who wants to make sound decisions does not expense or amortize the truck using such rules. The true opportunity cost of using a truck that the firm owns is the amount that the firm could earn if it rented the truck to others. That is, regardless of whether the firm rents or buys the truck, the manager views the opportunity cost of this capital good as the rental rate for a given period of time. If the value of an older truck is less than that of a newer one, the rental rate for the truck falls over time.

But what if there is no rental market for trucks available to the firm? It is still important to determine an appropriate opportunity cost. Suppose that the firm has two choices: It can choose not to buy the truck and keep the truck's purchase price of $20,000, or it can use the truck for a year and sell it for $17,000 at the end of the year. If the firm does not purchase the truck, it will deposit the $20,000 in a bank account that pays 5% per year, so the firm will have $21,000 at the end of the year. Thus, the opportunity cost of capital of using the truck for a year is $21,000 − $17,000 = $4,000.[2] This $4,000 opportunity cost equals the $3,000 depreciation of the truck (= $20,000 − $17,000) plus the $1,000 in forgone interest that the firm could have earned over the year if the firm had invested the $20,000.

Because the values of trucks, machines, and other equipment decline over time, their rental rates fall, so the firm's opportunity costs decline. In contrast, the value of some land, buildings, and other forms of capital may rise over time. To maximize profit, a firm must properly measure the opportunity cost of a piece of capital even if its value rises over time. If a beauty parlor buys a building when similar buildings in the area rent for $1,000 per month, the opportunity cost of using the building is $1,000 a month. If land values increase so that rents in the area rise to $2,000 per month, the beauty parlor's opportunity cost of its building rises to $2,000 per month.

APPLICATION

Swarthmore College's Cost of Capital

Many nonprofit institutions, such as universities and governmental agencies, are notorious for ignoring the implicit cost of their capital. When setting tuition rates and making other plans, Swarthmore College in Pennsylvania estimates its annual cost at $90,000 per student, based on the cost of salaries, academic and general institutional support, maintenance and additions to the physical plant,

---

[2]The firm would also pay for gasoline, insurance, licensing fees, and other operating costs, but these items would all be expensed as operating costs and would not appear in the firm's accounts as capital costs.

dining services, and other annual expenses such as student aid. This cost calculation is a gross underestimate, however, because it ignores the opportunity cost of the campus real estate—the amount the college could earn by renting out its land and buildings. Including the opportunity cost of its land and buildings raises the college's true annual economic cost per student to about $115,000 in 2009.

Sunk Costs

An opportunity cost is not always easy to observe but should always be taken into account when deciding how much to produce. In contrast, a **sunk cost**—a past expenditure that cannot be recovered—though easily observed, is not relevant to a manager when deciding how much to produce now. If an expenditure is sunk, it is not an opportunity cost.[3]

If a firm buys a forklift for $25,000 and can resell it for the same price, it is not a sunk expenditure, and the opportunity cost of the forklift is $25,000. If instead the firm buys a specialized piece of equipment for $25,000 and cannot resell it, then the original expenditure is a sunk cost. Because this equipment has no alternative use and cannot be resold, its opportunity cost is zero, and it should not be included in the firm's current cost calculations. If the specialized equipment that originally cost $25,000 can be resold for $10,000, then only $15,000 of the original expenditure is a sunk cost, and the opportunity cost is $10,000.

To illustrate why a sunk cost should not influence a manager's current decisions, consider a firm that paid $300,000 for a piece of land for which the market value has fallen to $200,000. Now, the land's true opportunity cost is $200,000. The $100,000 difference between the $300,000 purchase price and the current market value of $200,000 is a sunk cost that has already been incurred and cannot be recovered. The land is worth $240,000 to the firm if it builds a plant on this parcel. Is it worth carrying out production on this land or should the land be sold for its market value of $200,000? If the firm uses the original purchase price in its decision-making process, the firm will falsely conclude that using the land for production will result in a $60,000 loss: the $240,000 value of using the land minus the purchase price of $300,000. Instead, the firm should use the land because it is worth $40,000 more as a production facility than if the firm sells the land for $200,000, its next best alternative. Thus, the firm should use the land's opportunity cost to make its decisions and ignore the land's sunk cost. In short, "There's no use crying over spilt milk."

7.2 Short-Run Costs

To make profit-maximizing decisions, a firm needs to know how its cost varies with output. A firm's cost rises as it increases its output. The short run is the period over which some inputs, such as labor, can be varied, while other inputs, such as capital, are fixed (Chapter 6). In contrast, the firm can vary all its inputs in the long run. For simplicity in our graphs, we concentrate on firms that use only two inputs: labor and capital. We focus on the case in which labor is the only variable input in the

---

[3]Nonetheless, a sunk cost paid for a specialized input should still be deducted from income before paying taxes even if that cost is sunk, and must therefore appear in financial accounts.

short run, and both labor and capital are variable in the long run. However, we can generalize our analysis to examine a firm that uses any number of inputs.

We start by examining various measures of cost, which we use to show the distinction between short-run and long-run costs. Then we show how the shapes of the short-run cost curves are related to the firm's production function.

Short-Run Cost Measures

We start by using a numerical example to illustrate the basic cost concepts. We then examine the graphic relationship between these concepts.

Fixed Cost, Variable Cost, and Total Cost. To produce a given level of output in the short run, a firm incurs costs for both its fixed and variable inputs. A **fixed cost** (*F*) is a cost that does not vary with the level of output. Fixed costs, which include expenditures on land, office space, production facilities, and other *overhead* expenses, cannot be avoided by reducing output and must be incurred as long as the firm stays in business.

Fixed costs are often sunk costs, but not always. For example, a restaurant rents space for $2,000 per month on a month-to-month lease. This rent does not vary with the number of meals served (its output level), so it is a fixed cost. Because the restaurant has already paid this month's rent, this fixed cost is also a sunk cost: The restaurant cannot recover the $2,000 even if it goes out of business. Next month, if the restaurant stays open, it will have to pay the $2,000 rent. If the lease is a month-to-month rental agreement, this fixed cost of $2,000 is an *avoidable cost*, not a sunk cost. The restaurant can shut down, cancel its rental agreement, and avoid paying this fixed cost. Therefore, in planning for next month, the restaurant should treat the $2,000 rent as a fixed cost but not as a sunk cost. Thus, the fixed cost of $2,000 per month is a fixed cost in both the short run (this month) and the long run, but it is a sunk cost only in the short run.

A firm's **variable cost** (*VC*) is the production expense that changes with the quantity of output produced. The variable cost is the cost of the variable inputs—the inputs the firm can adjust to alter its output level, such as labor and materials.

A firm's **cost** (or **total cost,** *C*) is the sum of a firm's variable cost and fixed cost:

$$C = VC + F.$$

Because variable cost changes with the level of output, total cost also varies with the level of output.

To decide how much to produce, a firm uses measures of marginal and average costs. We derive four such measures using the fixed cost, the variable cost, and the total cost.

Marginal Cost. A firm's **marginal cost** (*MC*) is the amount by which a firm's cost changes if it produces one more unit of output. The marginal cost is

$$MC = \frac{dC(q)}{dq}. \tag{7.1}$$

Because only variable cost changes with output, we can also define marginal cost as the change in variable cost from a small increase in output,

$$MC = \frac{dVC(q)}{dq},$$

where $VC(q)$ is the firm's variable cost function. Chapter 8 will show that a firm uses its marginal cost to decide whether changing its output level pays off.

Average Cost. Firms use three average cost measures. The **average fixed cost** (AFC) is the fixed cost divided by the units of output produced: $AFC = F/q$. The average fixed cost falls as output rises because the fixed cost is spread over more units: $dAFC/dq = -F/q^2 < 0$. It approaches zero as the output level grows very large.

The **average variable cost** (AVC) is the variable cost divided by the units of output produced: $AVC = VC/q$. Because the variable cost increases with output, the average variable cost may either increase or decrease as output rises. As Chapter 8 shows, a firm uses the average variable cost to determine whether to shut down operations when demand is low.

The **average cost** (AC)—or average total cost—is the total cost divided by the units of output produced: $AC = C/q$. Because total cost equals variable cost plus fixed cost, $C = VC + F$, when we divide both sides of the equation by q, we learn that

$$AC = \frac{C}{q} = \frac{VC}{q} + \frac{F}{q} = AVC + AFC. \tag{7.2}$$

That is, the average cost is the sum of the average variable cost and the average fixed cost. A firm uses its average cost to determine if it is making a profit.

SOLVED PROBLEM 7.2

A manufacturing plant has a short-run cost function of $C(q) = 100q - 4q^2 + 0.2q^3 + 450$. What is the firm's short-run fixed cost and variable cost function? Derive the formulas for its marginal cost, average fixed cost, average variable cost, and average cost. Draw two figures, one above the other. In the top figure, show the fixed cost, variable cost, and total cost curves. In the bottom figure, show the corresponding marginal cost curve and three average cost curves.

Answer

1. *Identify the fixed cost as the part of the short-run cost function that does not vary with output, q, and the remaining part of the cost function as the variable cost function.* The fixed cost is $F = 450$, the only part that does not vary with q. The variable cost function, $VC(q) = 100q - 4q^2 + 0.2q^3$, is the part of the cost function that varies with q.

2. *Determine the marginal cost by differentiating the short-run cost function (or variable cost function) with respect to output.* Differentiating, we find that

$$MC = \frac{dC(q)}{dq} = \frac{d(100q - 4q^2 + 0.2q^3 + 450)}{dq} = 100 - 8q + 0.6q^2.$$

3. *Calculate the three average cost functions using the definitions.* By definition,

$$AFC = \frac{F}{q} = \frac{450}{q},$$

$$AVC = \frac{V(q)}{q} = \frac{100q - 4q^2 + 0.2q^3}{q} = 100 - 4q + 0.2q^2,$$

$$AC = \frac{C(q)}{q} = \frac{100q - 4q^2 + 0.2q^3 + 450}{q}$$
$$= 100 - 4q + 0.2q^2 + \frac{450}{q} = AVC + AFC.$$

4. *Use these cost, marginal cost, and average cost functions to plot the specified figures.* Figure 7.1 shows these plots.

Figure 7.1 Short-Run Cost Curves

(a) Because the total cost differs from the variable cost by the fixed cost, $F = \$450$, the cost curve, C, is parallel to the variable cost curve, VC. (b) The marginal cost curve, MC, cuts the average variable cost, AVC, and average cost, AC, curves at their minimums. The height of the AC curve at point a equals the slope of the line from the origin to the cost curve at A. The height of the AVC at b equals the slope of the line from the origin to the variable cost curve at B. The height of the marginal cost is the slope of either the C or VC curve at that quantity.

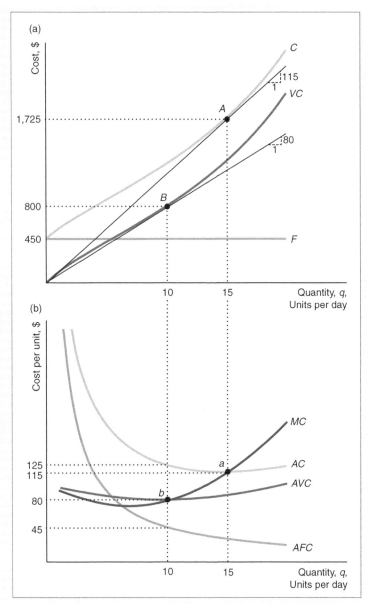

Short-Run Cost Curves

We illustrate the relationship between output and the various cost measures using the example in Solved Problem 7.2. Panel a of Figure 7.1 shows the variable cost, fixed cost, and total cost curves. The fixed cost, which does not vary with output, is a horizontal line at $450. The variable cost curve is zero when output is zero and rises as output increases. The total cost curve, which is the vertical sum of the variable cost curve and the fixed cost line, is $450 higher than the variable cost curve at every output level, so the variable cost and total cost curves are parallel.

Panel b shows the average fixed cost, average variable cost, average cost, and marginal cost curves. The average fixed cost curve falls as output increases. It approaches zero as output gets larger because the fixed cost is spread over many units of output. The average cost curve is the vertical sum of the average fixed cost and average variable cost curves. For example, at 10 units of output, the average variable cost is $80 and the average fixed cost is $45, so the average cost is $125.

The marginal cost curve cuts the U-shaped average cost and the average variable cost curves at their minimums.[4] The average cost (or average variable cost) curve rises where it lies below the marginal cost curve and falls where it lies above the marginal cost curve, so the marginal cost curve must cut the average cost curve at its minimum (by similar reasoning to that used in Chapter 6, where we discussed average and marginal products).

Production Functions and the Shape of Cost Curves

The production function determines the shape of a firm's cost curves. It shows the amount of inputs needed to produce a given level of output. The firm calculates its cost by multiplying the quantity of each input by its price and then summing.

If a firm produces output using capital and labor and its capital is fixed in the short run, the firm's variable cost is its cost of labor. Its labor cost is the wage per hour, w, times the number of hours of labor, L: $VC = wL$.

If input prices are constant, the production function determines the shape of the variable cost curve. We can write the short-run production function as $q = f(L, \bar{K}) = g(L)$ because capital does not vary. By inverting, we know that the amount of labor we need to produce any given amount of output is $L = g^{-1}(q)$. If the wage of labor is w, the variable cost function is $V(q) = wL = wg^{-1}(q)$. Similarly, the cost function is $C(q) = V(q) + F = wg^{-1}(q) + F$.

In the short run, when the firm's capital is fixed, the only way the firm can increase its output is to use more labor. If the firm increases its labor enough, it reaches the point of *diminishing marginal returns to labor*, where each extra worker increases output by a smaller amount. Because the variable cost function is the inverse of the short-run production function, its properties are determined by the short-run production function. If the production function exhibits diminishing marginal returns, then the variable cost rises more than in proportion as output increases.

Because the production function determines the shape of the variable cost curve, it also determines the shape of the marginal, average variable, and average cost curves. We now examine the shape of each of these cost curves in detail, because firms rely more on these per-unit cost measures than on total variable cost to make decisions about labor and capital.

---

[4]To determine the output level q where the average cost curve, $AC(q)$, reaches its minimum, we set the derivative of average cost with respect to q equal to zero:

$$\frac{dAC(q)}{dq} = \frac{d[C(q)/q]}{dq} = \left[\frac{dC(q)}{dq} - \frac{C(q)}{q}\right]\frac{1}{q} = 0.$$

This condition holds at the output q where $dC(q)/dq = C(q)/q$, or $MC = AC$. If the second-order condition holds at the same level for q, the average cost curve reaches its minimum at that quantity. The second-order condition requires that the average cost curve be falling to the left of this quantity and rising to the right. Similarly, $dAVC/dq = d[VC(q)/q]/dq = [dVC/dq - VC(q)/q](1/q) = 0$, so $MC = AVC$ at the minimum of the average variable cost curve.

Shape of the Marginal Cost Curve. The marginal cost is the change in variable cost as output increases by one unit: $MC = dVC/dq$. In the short run, capital is fixed, so the only way a firm can produce more output is to use extra labor. The extra labor required to produce one more unit of output is $dL/dq = 1/MP_L$. The extra labor costs the firm w per unit, so the firm's cost rises by $w(dL/dq)$. As a result, the firm's marginal cost is

$$MC = \frac{dV(q)}{dq} = w\frac{dL}{dq}.$$

The marginal cost equals the wage times the extra labor necessary to produce one more unit of output.

How do we know how much extra labor is needed to produce one more unit of output? This information comes from the production function. The marginal product of labor—the amount of extra output produced by another unit of labor, holding other inputs fixed—is $MP_L = dq/dL$. Thus, the extra labor needed to produce one more unit of output, dL/dq, is $1/MP_L$, so the firm's marginal cost is

$$MC = \frac{w}{MP_L}. \tag{7.3}$$

According to Equation 7.3, the marginal cost equals the wage divided by the marginal product of labor. If it takes four extra hours of labor services to produce one more unit of output, the marginal product of an hour of labor is $\frac{1}{4}$. Given a wage of $5 an hour, the marginal cost of one more unit of output is $5 divided by $\frac{1}{4}$ or $20.

Equation 7.3 shows that the marginal cost moves in the opposite direction to that of the marginal product of labor. At low levels of labor, the marginal product of labor commonly rises with additional workers who may help the original workers to collectively make better use of the firm's equipment (Chapter 6). As the marginal product of labor rises, the marginal cost falls.

Eventually, however, as the number of workers increases, workers must share the fixed amount of equipment and may get in each other's way Consequently, the marginal cost curve slopes upward due to diminishing marginal returns to labor. As a result, the marginal cost first falls and then rises, as panel b of Figure 7.1 illustrates.

Shape of the Average Cost Curve. Because diminishing marginal returns to labor affect the shape of the variable cost curve, they also determine the shape of the average variable cost curve. The average variable cost is the variable cost divided by output: $AVC = VC/q$. For a firm that has labor as its only variable input, variable cost is wL, so average variable cost is

$$AVC = \frac{VC}{q} = \frac{wL}{q}.$$

Because the average product of labor is q/L, average variable cost is the wage divided by the average product of labor:

$$AVC = \frac{w}{AP_L}. \tag{7.4}$$

With a constant wage, the average variable cost moves in the opposite direction to that of the average product of labor in Equation 7.4. As we saw in Chapter 6, the average product of labor tends to rise and then fall, so the average cost tends to fall and then rise, as in panel b of Figure 7.1.

The average cost curve is the vertical sum of the average variable cost curve and the average fixed cost curve, as in panel b. If the average variable cost curve is U-shaped, adding the strictly falling average fixed cost makes the average cost fall more steeply than the average variable cost curve at low output levels. At high output levels, the average cost and average variable cost curves differ by ever smaller amounts, as the average fixed cost, F/q, approaches zero. Thus, the average cost curve is also U-shaped.

APPLICATION

Short-Run Cost Curves for a Furniture Manufacturer

We can derive the various short-run cost curves for a typical furniture firm using its Cobb-Douglas production function (as estimated by Hsieh, 1995) and the prices of the inputs, which we assume are $w = \$24$ and $r = \$8$. The figure shows that the short-run average cost curve for this firm is U-shaped, even though its average variable cost is strictly upward sloping. The graph shows the firm's various short-run cost curves where the firm's capital is fixed at $\bar{K} = 100$.

Given that the rental rate of a unit of capital is \$8, the fixed cost, F, is $800(= \$8 \times \bar{K})$. The figure shows that the average fixed cost, $AFC = F/q = 800/q$, falls as output, q, increases.

We can use the production function to derive the variable cost. The estimated production function is

$$q = 1.52\, L^{0.6} K^{0.4}, \qquad (7.5)$$

where labor, L, is measured in hours and K is the number of units of capital. We start by determining how output and labor are related. Setting capital, $K = \bar{K} = 100$ units in the production function, we find that the output produced in the short run is solely a function of labor:

$$q = 1.52 L^{0.6} 100^{0.4} \approx 9.59 L^{0.6}.$$

Rearranging this expression, we can write the number of workers per year, L, needed to produce q units of output, as a function solely of output:

$$L(q) = \left(\frac{q}{1.52 \times 100^{0.40}}\right)^{1.67} \approx 0.023 q^{1.67}.$$

Now that we know how labor and output are related, we can calculate variable cost directly. The only variable input is labor, so if the wage is $w = \$24$, the firm's variable cost is $VC(q) = wL(q) = 24L(q)$. Substituting for $L(q)$, we see how variable cost varies with output:

$$V(q) = 24L(q) = 24\left(\frac{q}{1.52 \times 100^{0.40}}\right)^{1.67} \approx 0.55 q^{1.67}.$$

Using this expression for variable cost, we can construct the other cost measures.

We obtain the average variable cost as a function of output, $AVC(q)$, by dividing both sides of this last equation by q:

$$AVC(q) = \frac{V(q)}{q} = \frac{24L(q)}{q} \approx 24\left(\frac{0.023 q^{1.67}}{q}\right) = 0.55 q^{0.67}.$$

As the figure shows, the average variable cost is strictly increasing.

To obtain the equation for marginal cost as a function of output, we differentiate the variable cost, $V(q)$, with respect to output:

$$MC(q) = \frac{dV(q)}{dq} \approx \frac{d(0.55 q^{1.67})}{dq} = 1.67 \times 0.55 q^{0.67} \approx 0.92 q^{0.67}.$$

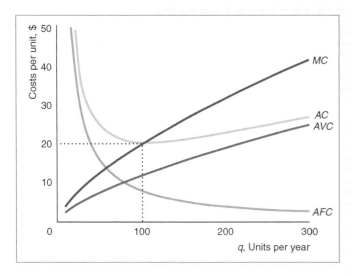

The firm's average fixed cost (AFC) curve falls as output increases. The firm's average variable cost (AVC) curve is strictly increasing. The average cost (AC) curve is the vertical sum of the average variable cost and average fixed cost curves. Because the average fixed cost curve falls with output and the average variable cost curve rises with output, the average cost curve is U-shaped. The firm's marginal cost curve lies above the rising average variable cost curve for all positive quantities of output and cuts the average cost curve at its minimum at $q = 100$.

Effects of Taxes on Costs

Taxes applied to a firm shift some or all of the marginal and average cost curves. For example, suppose that the government collects a specific tax of $10 per unit of output. This specific tax, which varies with output, affects the firm's variable cost but not its fixed cost. As a result, it affects the firm's average cost, average variable cost, and marginal cost curves but not its average fixed cost curve.

At every quantity, the average variable cost and the average cost rise by the full amount of the tax. Thus, the firm's after-tax average variable cost, AVC^a, is its average variable cost of production—the before-tax average variable cost, AVC^b—plus the tax per unit, $10: AVC^a = AVC^b + \$10$.

The average cost equals the average variable cost plus the average fixed cost. For example, in the last application, the furniture firm's before-tax average cost is $AC^b = AVC + AFC = 0.55q^{0.67} + 800/q$. Because the tax increases average variable cost by $10 and does not affect the average fixed cost, average cost increases by $10: $AC^a = AC^b + 10 = 0.55q^{0.67} + 800/q + 10$. The tax also increases the firm's marginal cost by $10 per unit. The furniture firm's pre-tax marginal cost is $MC^b = 0.92q^{0.67}$, so its after-tax marginal cost is $MC^a = 0.92q^{0.67} + 10$.

Figure 7.2 shows these shifts in the marginal and average cost curves. The new marginal cost curve and average cost curve are parallel to the old ones: $10 higher at each quantity. At first, it may not look like the shift of the average cost curve is parallel, but you can convince yourself that it is a parallel shift by using a ruler.

Similarly, we can analyze the effect of a franchise tax on costs. A franchise tax—also called a business license fee—is a lump sum that a firm pays for the right to operate a business. For example, a tax of $800 per year is levied "for the privilege of doing business in California." A three-year license to sell hot dogs in front of New York City's Metropolitan Museum of Art costs $900,600. These taxes do not vary with output, so they affect firms' fixed costs only—not their variable costs (see Questions 10 and 11 at the end of the chapter).

Figure 7.2 Effect of a Specific Tax on a Furniture Firm's Cost Curves

A specific tax of $10 per unit shifts both the marginal cost and average cost curves upward by $10. Because of the parallel upward shift of the average cost curve, the minimum of both the before-tax average cost curve, AC^b, and the after-tax average cost curve, AC^a, occurs at the same output, 100 units.

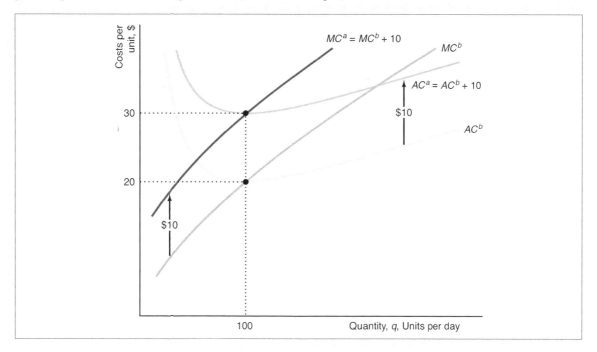

Short-Run Cost Summary

We have examined three cost-level curves—total cost, fixed cost, and variable cost—and four cost-per-unit curves—average cost, average fixed cost, average variable cost, and marginal cost. Understanding the shapes of these curves and the relationships among them is crucial to understanding the analysis of a firm's behavior in the rest of this book. The following four basic concepts capture most of what you need to know about the relationships among the curves and their shapes:

1. In the short run, the cost associated with inputs that cannot be adjusted is fixed, while the cost from inputs that can be adjusted is variable.
2. Given constant input prices, the shapes of the cost, variable cost, marginal cost, and average cost curves are determined by the production function.
3. Where a variable input has diminishing marginal returns, the variable cost and cost curves become relatively steep as output increases, so the average cost, average variable cost, and marginal cost curves rise with output.
4. Both the average cost curve and the average variable cost curve fall at quantities where the marginal cost curve is below them and rise where the marginal cost is above them, so the marginal cost curve cuts both of these average cost curves at their minimum points.

7.3 Long-Run Costs

In the long run, a firm adjusts all its inputs to keep its cost of production as low as possible. The firm can change its plant size, design and build new equipment, and otherwise adjust inputs that were fixed in the short run.

Although firms may incur fixed costs in the long run, these fixed costs are *avoidable* rather than *sunk* costs, as in the short run. The rent of F per month paid by a restaurant is a fixed cost because it does not vary with the number of meals (output) served. In the short run, this fixed cost is also a sunk cost: The firm must pay F even if the restaurant does not operate. In the long run, this fixed cost is avoidable: The firm does not have to pay the rent if it shuts down. The long run is determined by the length of the rental contract, during which time the firm is obligated to pay rent.

The examples throughout this chapter assume that all inputs can be varied in the long run, so there are no long-run fixed costs ($F = 0$). As a result, the long-run total cost equals the long-run variable cost: $C = VC$. Thus, our firm concentrates on only three cost concepts in the long run—total cost, average cost, and marginal cost—rather than the seven cost concepts that it uses in the short run.

To produce a given quantity of output at minimum cost, our firm uses information about the production function and the price of labor and capital. In the long run, the firm chooses how much labor and capital to use, whereas in the short run, when capital is fixed, it chooses only how much labor to use. As a consequence, the firm's long-run cost is lower than its short-run cost of production if it has to use the "wrong" level of capital in the short run. This section shows how a firm determines which combinations of inputs are cost-minimizing in the long run.

Input Choice

A firm can produce a given level of output using many different *technologically efficient* combinations of inputs, as summarized by an isoquant (Chapter 6). From among the technologically efficient combinations of inputs, a firm wants to choose the particular bundle with the lowest cost of production, which is the *economically efficient* combination of inputs. To do so, the firm combines information about technology from the isoquant with information about the cost of labor and capital.

We now show how information about cost can be summarized in an *isocost line*. Then we show how a firm can combine the information in isoquant and isocost lines to determine the economically efficient combination of inputs.

Isocost Line. The cost of producing a given level of output depends on the price of labor and capital. The firm hires L hours of labor services at a wage of w per hour, so its labor cost is wL. The firm rents K hours of machine services at a rental rate of r per hour, so its capital cost is rK. (If the firm owns the capital, r is the implicit rental rate.) The firm's total cost is the sum of its labor and capital costs:

$$C = wL + rK. \tag{7.6}$$

The firm can hire as much labor and capital as it wants at these constant input prices.

The firm can use many combinations of labor and capital that cost the same amount. These combinations of labor and capital are plotted on an **isocost line**, which indicates all the combinations of inputs that require the same (*iso*) total expenditure (*cost*). Along an isocost line, cost is fixed at a particular level, $\bar{C}$, so by setting cost at $\bar{C}$ in Equation 7.6, we can write the equation for the $\bar{C}$ isocost line as

$$\bar{C} = wL + rK. \tag{7.7}$$

Figure 7.3 shows three isocost lines for the furniture manufacturer where the fixed cost is $\bar{C} = \$1{,}000$, $\$2{,}000$, or $\$3{,}000$; $w = \$24$ per hour; and $r = \$8$ per hour.

Using algebra, we can rewrite Equation 7.7 to show how much capital the firm can buy if it spends a total of $\bar{C}$ and purchases L units of labor:

$$K = \frac{\bar{C}}{r} - \frac{w}{r}L. \tag{7.8}$$

The equation for the isocost lines in the figure is $K = \bar{C}/8 - (24/8)L = \bar{C}/8 - 3L$. We can use Equation 7.8 to derive three properties of isocost lines.

First, the point where the isocost lines hit the capital and labor axes depends on the firm's cost, $\bar{C}$, and the input prices. The $\bar{C}$ isocost line intersects the capital axis

Figure 7.3 Cost Minimization

The furniture manufacturer minimizes its cost of producing 100 units of output by producing at x ($L = 50$ and $K = 100$). This cost-minimizing combination of inputs is determined by the tangency between the $q = 100$ isoquant and the lowest isocost line, $\$2{,}000$, that touches that isoquant. At x, the isocost is tangent to the isoquant, so the slope of the isocost, $-w/r = -3$, equals the slope of the isoquant, which is the negative of the marginal rate of technical substitution. That is, the rate at which the firm can trade capital for labor in the input markets equals the rate at which it can substitute capital for labor in the production process.

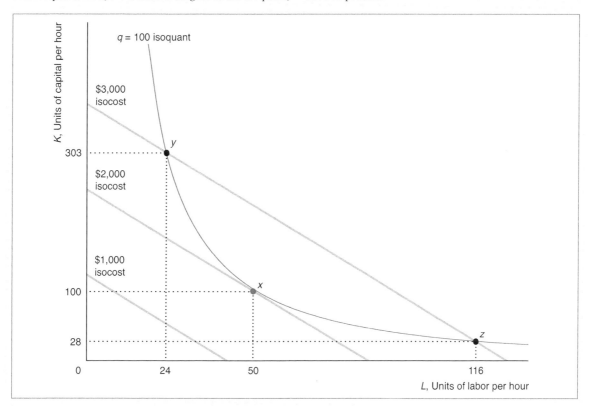

where the firm uses only capital. Setting $L = 0$ in Equation 7.8, we find that the firm buys $K = \bar{C}/r$ units of capital. Similarly, the intersection of the isocost line with the labor axis is at $\bar{C}/w$, which is the amount of labor the firm hires if it uses only labor.

Second, isocosts that are farther from the origin have higher costs than those closer to the origin. Because the isocost lines intersect the capital axis at $\bar{C}/r$ and the labor axis at $\bar{C}/w$, an increase in the cost shifts these intersections with the axes proportionately outward.

Third, the slope of each isocost line is the same. By differentiating Equation 7.8, we find that the slope of any isocost line is

$$\frac{dK}{dL} = -\frac{w}{r}.$$

Thus, the slope of the isocost line depends on the relative prices of the inputs. Because all isocost lines are based on the same relative prices, they all have the same slope, so they are parallel.

The role of the isocost line in the firm's decision making is similar to the role of the budget line in a consumer's decision making. Both an isocost line and a budget line are straight lines with slopes that depend on relative prices. There is an important difference between them, however. The consumer has a single budget line determined by the consumer's income. The firm faces many isocost lines, each of which corresponds to a different level of expenditures the firm might make. A firm may incur a relatively low cost by producing relatively little output with few inputs, or it may incur a relatively high cost by producing a relatively large quantity.

Minimizing Cost. By combining the information about costs contained in the isocost lines with information about efficient production that is summarized by an isoquant, a firm determines how to produce a given level of output at the lowest cost. We examine how our furniture manufacturer picks the combination of labor and capital that minimizes its cost of producing 100 units of output. Figure 7.3 shows the isoquant for 100 units of output and the isocost lines where the rental rate of a unit of capital is $8 per hour and the wage rate is $24 per hour.

The firm can choose any of three equivalent approaches to minimize its cost:

1. **Lowest-isocost rule.** Pick the bundle of inputs where the lowest isocost line touches the isoquant.
2. **Tangency rule.** Pick the bundle of inputs where the isoquant is tangent to the isocost line.
3. **Last-dollar rule.** Pick the bundle of inputs where the last dollar spent on one input gives as much extra output as the last dollar spent on any other input.

Using the *lowest-isocost rule,* the firm minimizes its cost by using the combination of inputs on the isoquant that lies on the lowest isocost line to touch the isoquant. The lowest possible isoquant that will allow the furniture manufacturer to produce 100 units of output is tangent to the $2,000 isocost line. This isocost line touches the isoquant at the bundle of inputs x, where the firm uses $L = 50$ workers and $K = 100$ units of capital.

How do we know that x is the least costly way to produce 100 units of output? We need to demonstrate that other practical combinations of inputs produce fewer than 100 units or produce 100 units at greater cost.

If the firm spent less than $2,000, it could not produce 100 units of output. Each combination of inputs on the $1,000 isocost line lies below the isoquant, so the firm cannot produce 100 units of output for $1,000.

The firm can produce 100 units of output using other combinations of inputs besides x, but using these other bundles of inputs is more expensive. For example, the firm can produce 100 units of output using the combinations y ($L = 24$, $K = 303$) or z ($L = 116$, $K = 28$). Both these combinations, however, cost the firm $3,000.

If an isocost line crosses the isoquant twice, as the $3,000 isocost line does, there must be another lower isocost line that also touches the isoquant. The lowest possible isocost line to touch the isoquant, the $2,000 isocost line, is tangent to the isoquant at a single bundle, x. Thus, the firm may use the *tangency rule*: The firm chooses the input bundle where the relevant isoquant is tangent to an isocost line to produce a given level of output at the lowest cost.

We can interpret this tangency or cost minimization condition in two ways. At the point of tangency, the slope of the isoquant equals the slope of the isocost. As we saw in Chapter 6, the slope of the isoquant is the marginal rate of technical substitution (*MRTS*). The slope of the isocost is the negative of the ratio of the wage to the cost of capital, $-w/r$. Thus, to minimize its cost of producing a given level of output, a firm chooses its inputs so that the marginal rate of technical substitution equals the negative of the relative input prices:

$$MRTS = -\frac{w}{r}. \qquad (7.9)$$

The firm chooses inputs so that the rate at which it can substitute capital for labor in the production process, the *MRTS*, exactly equals the rate at which it can trade capital for labor in input markets, $-w/r$.

Equation 6.8 shows that, for a Cobb-Douglas production function, $MRTS = -(a/b)(K/L)$. Thus, the furniture manufacturer's marginal rate of technical substitution is $-1.5K/L$, because $a = 0.6$ and $b = 0.4$. At $K = 100$ and $L = 50$, its *MRTS* is -3, which equals the negative of the ratio of its input prices, $-w/r = -24/8 = -3$. In contrast, at y the isocost cuts the isoquant so that the slopes are not equal. At y, the *MRTS* is -18.9375, which is greater than the ratio of the input price, 3. Because the slopes are not equal at y, the firm can produce the same output at lower cost. As the figure shows, the cost of producing at y is $3,000, whereas the cost of producing at x is only $2,000.

We can interpret the condition in Equation 7.9 in another way. The marginal rate of technical substitution equals the negative of the ratio of the marginal product of labor to that of capital: $MRTS = -MP_L/MP_K$ (Chapter 6). Thus, the cost-minimizing condition in Equation 7.9 is (taking the absolute value of both sides)

$$\frac{MP_L}{MP_K} = \frac{w}{r}. \qquad (7.10)$$

This expression may be rewritten as

$$\frac{MP_L}{w} = \frac{MP_K}{r}. \qquad (7.11)$$

Equation 7.11 states the *last-dollar rule*: Cost is minimized if inputs are chosen so that the last dollar spent on labor adds as much extra output as the last dollar spent on capital.

Because the furniture manufacturer's production function is $q = 1.52L^{0.6}K^{0.4}$, Equation 7.5, its marginal product of labor is $MP_L = 0.6 \times 1.52L^{0.6-1}K^{0.4} = 0.6q/L$, and its marginal product of capital is $MP_K = 0.4q/K$. At Bundle x, the furniture firm's marginal product of labor is 1.2 ($= 0.6 \times 100/50$) and its marginal product of capital is 0.4. The last dollar spent on labor gets the firm

$$\frac{MP_L}{w} = \frac{1.2}{24} = 0.05$$

more output. Spending its last dollar on capital, the firm produces

$$\frac{MP_K}{r} = \frac{0.4}{8} = 0.05$$

extra output. Therefore, spending one more dollar on labor at x gets the firm as much extra output as spending the same amount on capital. Equation 7.11 holds, so the firm is minimizing its cost of producing 100 units of output.

If instead the firm produced at y, where it uses more capital and less labor, its MP_L is 2.5 (= 0.6 × 100/24) and its MP_K is approximately 0.13 (≈ 0.4 × 100/303). As a result, the last dollar spent on labor gets $MP_L/w \approx 0.1$ more unit of output, whereas the last dollar spent on capital gets only one-fourth as much extra output, $MP_K/r \approx 0.017$. At y, if the firm shifts \$1 from capital to labor, output falls by 0.017 because there is less capital and increases by 0.1 because there is more labor, for a net gain of 0.083 more output at the same cost. The firm should shift even more resources from capital to labor—thereby increasing the marginal product of capital and decreasing the marginal product of labor—until Equation 7.10 holds with equality at x.

To summarize, there are three equivalent rules that the firm can use to determine the lowest-cost combination of inputs that will produce a given level of output when isoquants are smooth: the lowest-isocost rule; the tangency rule, Equations 7.9 and 7.10; and the last-dollar rule, Equation 7.11. If the isoquant is not smooth, the lowest-cost method of production cannot be determined by using the tangency rule or the last-dollar rule. The lowest-isocost rule always works—even when isoquants are not smooth—as "Rice Milling on Java" in **MyEconLab**'s textbook resources for Chapter 7 illustrates.

Using Calculus to Minimize Cost. Formally, the firm minimizes its cost, Equation 7.6, subject to the information about the production function that is contained in the isoquant expression: $\bar{q} = F(L, K)$. The corresponding Lagrangian problem is

$$\min_{L,K,\lambda} \mathcal{L} \approx wL + rK + \lambda[\bar{q} - f(L, K)]. \tag{7.12}$$

Assuming that we have an interior solution where both L and K are positive, the first-order conditions are

$$\frac{\partial \mathcal{L}}{\partial L} = w - \lambda \frac{\partial f}{\partial L} = 0, \tag{7.13}$$

$$\frac{\partial \mathcal{L}}{\partial K} = r - \lambda \frac{\partial f}{\partial K} = 0, \tag{7.14}$$

$$\frac{\partial \mathcal{L}}{\partial \lambda} = \bar{q} - f(L, K) = 0. \tag{7.15}$$

Dividing Equation 7.13 by Equation 7.14 and rearranging terms, we obtain the same expression as in Equation 7.10:

$$\frac{w}{r} = \frac{\frac{\partial f}{\partial L}}{\frac{\partial f}{\partial K}} = \frac{MP_L}{MP_K}. \tag{7.16}$$

That is, we find that cost is minimized where the factor-price ratio equals the ratio of the marginal products.[5]

Maximizing Output An equivalent or "dual" problem to minimizing the cost of producing a given quantity of output is maximizing output for a given level of cost. (In a similar pair of problems in Chapter 3, we examined how firms maximize utility for a given budget constraint and minimize expenditure for a given level of utility.) Here, the Lagrangian problem is

$$\max_{L, K, \lambda} \mathcal{L} = f(L, K) + \lambda(\bar{C} - wL - rK). \tag{7.17}$$

Assuming that we have an interior solution where both L and K are positive, the first-order conditions are

$$\frac{\partial \mathcal{L}}{\partial L} = \frac{\partial f}{\partial L} - \lambda w = 0, \tag{7.18}$$

$$\frac{\partial \mathcal{L}}{\partial K} = \frac{\partial f}{\partial K} - \lambda r = 0, \tag{7.19}$$

$$\frac{\partial \mathcal{L}}{\partial \lambda} = \bar{C} - wL - rK = 0. \tag{7.20}$$

By examining the ratio of the first two conditions, Equations 7.18 and 7.19, we obtain the same condition as when we minimized cost by holding output constant: $MP_L/MP_K = (\partial f/\partial L)/(\partial f/\partial K) = w/r$. That is, at the maximum, the slope of the isoquant equals the slope of the isocost line. Figure 7.4 shows that the firm maximizes

Figure 7.4 Output Maximization

The furniture manufacturer maximizes its production at a cost of $2,000 by producing 100 units of output at x using $L = 50$ and $K = 100$. The $q = 100$ isoquant is the highest one that touches the $2,000 isocost line. The firm operates where the $q = 100$ isoquant is tangent to the $2,000 isocost line.

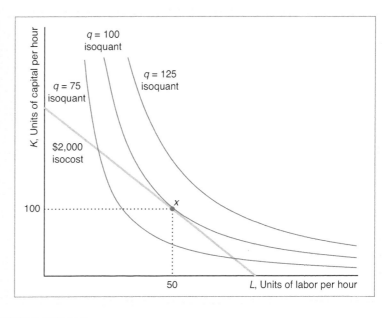

---

[5]Using Equations 7.13, 7.14, and 7.16, we find that $\lambda = w/MP_L = r/MP_K$. That is, the Lagrangian multiplier, λ, equals the ratio of the input price to the marginal product for each factor. As we already know, the input price divided by the factor's marginal product equals the marginal cost. Thus, the Lagrangian multiplier equals the marginal cost of production: It measures how much the cost increases if we produce one more unit of output.

its output for a given level of cost by operating where the highest feasible isoquant, $q = 100$, is tangent to the $2,000 isocost line.

Factor Price Changes Once the furniture manufacturer determines the lowest-cost combination of inputs to produce a given level of output, it uses that method as long as the input prices remain constant. How should the firm change its behavior if the cost of one of the factors changes?

Suppose that the wage falls from $24 to $8 but the rental rate of capital stays constant at $8. Because of the wage decrease, the new isocost line in Figure 7.5 has a flatter slope, $-w/r = -8/8 = -1$, than the original isocost line, $-w/r = -24/8 = -3$. The change in the wage does not affect technological efficiency, so it does not affect the isoquant. The relatively steep original isocost line is tangent to the 100-unit isoquant at Bundle x ($L = 50$, $K = 100$), while the new, flatter isocost line is tangent to the isoquant at Bundle v ($L = 77$, $K = 52$). Because labor is now relatively less expensive, the firm uses more labor and less capital as labor becomes relatively less expensive. Moreover, the firm's cost of producing 100 units falls from $2,000 to $1,032 as a result of the decrease in the wage. This example illustrates that a change in the relative prices of inputs affects the combination of inputs that a firm selects and its cost of production.

Formally, we know from Equation 7.10 that the ratio of the factor prices equals the ratio of the marginal products: $w/r = MP_L/MP_K$. As we've already determined, this expression is $w/r = 1.5K/L$ for the furniture firm. Holding r fixed for a small

Figure 7.5 Change in Factor Price

Originally the wage was $24 and the rental rate of capital was $8, so the lowest isocost line ($2,000) was tangent to the $q = 100$ isoquant at x ($L = 50$, $K = 100$). When the wage fell to $8, the isocost lines became flatter: Labor became relatively less expensive than capital. The slope of the isocost lines falls from $-w/r = -24/8 = -3$ to $-8/8 = -1$. The new lowest isocost line ($1,032) is tangent at v ($L = 77$, $K = 52$). Thus, when the wage falls, the firm uses more labor and less capital to produce a given level of output, and the cost of production falls from $2,000 to $1,032.

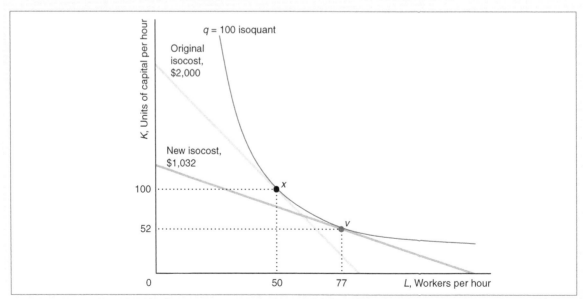

change in w, the change in the factor ratio is $d(K/L)/dw = 1/(1.5r)$. For the furniture manufacturer, where $r = 8$, $d(K/L)/dw = 1/12 \approx 0.083$. Because this derivative is positive, a small change in the wage leads to a higher capital-labor ratio because the firm substitutes some relatively less expensive capital for labor.

APPLICATION
Semiconductor Outsourcing

U.S. semiconductor manufacturing firms have moved much of their production abroad since 1961, when Fairchild Semiconductor built a plant in Hong Kong. According to the Semiconductor Industry Association (www.sia-online.org), worldwide semiconductor September billings from the Americas dropped from 66% in 1976 to 34% in 1998, and to 17% in early 2010. Firms move their production abroad to benefit from lower taxes, lower labor costs, and capital grants provided by foreign governments to induce firms to move production to their countries. Such grants can reduce the cost of owning and operating an overseas semiconductor fabrication facility by as much as 25% compared with the costs of a U.S.-based plant.

A manager of a semiconductor manufacturing firm, who can choose from many different production technologies, must determine whether the firm should use the same technology in a foreign plant that it uses in its domestic plant. If relative factor prices (and hence slopes of isocost lines) are different abroad than at home, a firm with smooth isoquants uses a different factor combination when producing abroad, as Figure 7.5 illustrates. However, if isoquants are not smooth curves, the firm does not necessarily use a different factor mix. The following solved problem shows that small differences in factor prices may not induce the firm to change technologies or factor mixes if isoquants have kinks.[6]

SOLVED PROBLEM 7.3

A U.S. semiconductor manufacturing company plans to move its production abroad. Its technologies are described in the application "A Semiconductor Integrated Circuit Isoquant" (Chapter 6). The firm currently produces using a wafer-handling stepper. The cost of equipment is the same everywhere; however, the wage is lower abroad. Will the firm necessarily use a different technology when it produces abroad? Why might it use a different technology?

Answer

1. *Show the isoquant and the relevant domestic isoquant.* The figure shows the same isoquant as in Chapter 6. We are told there that the firm produces at home using the wafer-handling stepper technology, so its initial C^1 isocost line must hit the isoquant at that technology. Note that the isoquant is kinked at the wafer-handling stepper technology.

2. *State what happens to the slope of the isocost line if the firm produces abroad.* The firm's new isocost line will be flatter than the C^1 isocost line. The slope of the isocost is $-w/r$, where w is the wage and r is the rental cost of the machine. Thus, the smaller w is, the less steeply sloped the isocost curve.

3. *Show that a flatter isocost might but does not necessarily hit the isoquant at a different technology.* Because the isoquant has kinks, a small change in the relative input prices does not necessarily induce a change in technique. The C^2

---

[6]In Problem 33 at the end of the chapter, you are asked to show that, if all foreign factor prices are proportionally lower than domestic prices, the firm will use the same technology as at home. Problems 34–36 ask you to show what happens in a typical case with smooth isoquants.

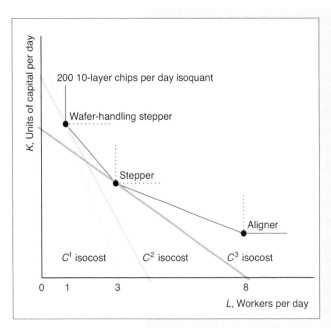

and C^3 isocost lines are both flatter than the C^1 isocost line. If the wage drops a small amount, so that the C^2 isocost is only slightly flatter, the firm still uses the capital-intensive wafer-handling stepper technology. However, with a larger drop in the wage, the much flatter C^3 isocost line hits the isoquant at the stepper technology (if it were even flatter, it could hit at the aligner technology).

Comment: The firm's cost drops due to the lower wage even if it uses the same technology: $C^2 < C^1$. However, if the wage is low enough that it can shift to a more labor-intensive technology, its costs will be even lower: $C^3 < C^2$. If the isoquant were smooth (without kinks), any change in relative factor costs would induce the firm to change the technology (labor-capital ratio) that it uses.

How Long-Run Cost Varies with Output

We now know how a firm determines the cost-minimizing combination of inputs for any given level of output. By repeating this analysis for different output levels, the firm determines how its cost varies with output.

Expansion Path. Panel a of Figure 7.6 shows the relationship between the lowest-cost factor combinations and various levels of output for the furniture manufacturer when input prices are held constant at $w = \$24$ and $r = \$8$. The curve through the tangency points is the long-run **expansion path**: the cost-minimizing combination of labor and capital for each output level. The lowest-cost method of producing 100 units of output is to use the labor and capital combination x ($L = 50$ and $K = 100$), which lies on the \$2,000 isocost line. Similarly, the lowest-cost way to produce 200 units is to use z, which lies on the \$4,000 isocost line. The expansion path for the furniture manufacturer is a straight line through the origin and x, y, and z, which has a slope of 2: At any given output level, the firm uses twice as much capital as labor. (In general, the expansion path need not be a straight line but can curve up or down as input use increases.)

SOLVED PROBLEM 7.4

What is the expansion path function for a constant-returns-to-scale Cobb-Douglas production function $q = AL^a K^{1-a}$? What is the path for the estimated furniture firm production function: $q = 1.52 L^{0.6} K^{0.4}$?

Answer

Use the tangency condition between the isocost and the isoquant that determines the cost-mimizing factor ratio to derive the expansion path. Because the marginal product of labor is $MP_L = aq/L$ and the marginal product of capital is $MP_K = (1 - a)q/K$, the tangency condition is

$$\frac{w}{r} = \frac{aq/L}{(1-a)q/K} = \frac{a}{1-a}\frac{K}{L}.$$

Using algebra to rearrange this expression, we obtain the expansion path formula:

$$K = \frac{(1-a)}{a}\frac{w}{r}L. \tag{7.21}$$

For the furniture firm in panel a of Figure 7.6, the expansion path, Equation 7.21, is $K = (0.4/0.6)(24/8)L = 2L$.

Long-Run Cost Function. The furniture manufacturer's expansion path contains the same information as its long-run cost function, $C(q)$, which shows the relationship between the cost of production and output. As the expansion path plot in Figure 7.6 shows, to produce q units of output requires $K = q$ units of capital and $L = q/2$ units of labor. Thus, the long-run cost of producing q units of output is

$$C(q) = wL + rK = wq/2 + rq = (w/2 + r)q = (24/2 + 8)q = 20q.$$

Figure 7.6 Expansion Path and Long-Run Cost Curve

(a) The curve through the tangency points between isocost lines and isoquants, such as x, y, and z, is called the expansion path. The points on the expansion path are the cost-minimizing combinations of labor and capital for each output level. (b) The furniture manufacturer's expansion path shows the same relationship between long-run cost and output as the long-run cost curve.

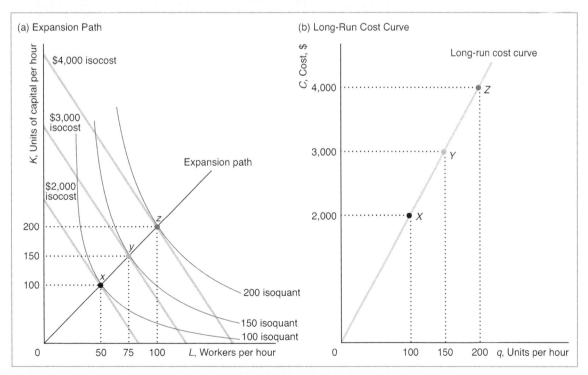

That is, the long-run cost function corresponding to this expansion path is $C(q) = 20q$. This cost function is consistent with the expansion path in panel a: $C(100) = \$2,000$ at x on the expansion path, $C(150) = \$3,000$ at y, and $C(200) = \$4,000$ at z.

Panel b of Figure 7.6 plots this long-run cost curve. Points X, Y, and Z on the cost curve correspond to points x, y, and z on the expansion path. For example, the $\$2,000$ isocost line hits the $q = 100$ isoquant at x, which is the lowest-cost combination of labor and capital that can produce 100 units of output. Similarly, X on the long-run cost curve is at $\$2,000$ and 100 units of output. Consistent with the expansion path, the cost curve shows that as output doubles, cost doubles.

Solving for the cost function from the production function is not always easy. However, a cost function is relatively simple to derive from the production function if the production function is homogeneous of degree γ so that $q = f(xL^*, xK^*) = x^\gamma f(L^*, K^*)$, where x is a positive constant and L^* and K^* are particular values of labor and capital. That is, the production function has the same returns to scale for any given combination of inputs. Important examples of such production functions include the Cobb-Douglas ($q = AL^aK^b$, $\gamma = a + b$), constant elasticity of substitution (CES), linear, and fixed-proportions production functions (see Chapter 6).

We know that a firm's cost identity is $C = wL + rK$ (Equation 7.6). Were we to double the inputs, we would double the cost. More generally, if we multiplied each output by x, the new cost would be $C = (wL^* + rK^*)x = \theta x$, where $\theta = wL^* + rK^*$. Solving the production function for x, we know that $x = q^{1/\gamma}$. Substituting that expression in the cost identity, we find that the cost function for any homogeneous production function of degree γ is $C = \theta q^{1/\gamma}$. The constant in this cost function depends on factor prices and two constants, L^* and K^*. We would prefer to express the constant in terms of only the factor prices and parameters. We can do so by noting that the firm chooses the cost-minimizing combination of labor and capital, as summarized in the expansion path equation, as we illustrate in the following solved problem.

SOLVED PROBLEM 7.5

A firm has a Cobb-Douglas production function that is homogeneous of degree one: $q = AL^aK^{1-a}$. Derive the firm's long-run cost function as a function of only output and factor prices. What is the cost function that corresponds to the estimated furniture firm production function $q = 1.52L^{0.6}K^{0.4}$?

Answer

1. *Combine the cost identity, Equation 7.6, with the expansion path, Equation 7.21, which shows how the cost-minimizing factor ratio varies with factor prices, to derive expressions for the inputs as a function of cost and factor prices.* From the expansion path, we know that $rK = wL(1 - a)/a$. Substituting for rK in the cost identity gives $C = wL + wL(1 - a)/a$. Simplifying shows that $L = aC/w$. Repeating this process to solve for K, we find that $K = (1 - a)C/r$.

2. *To derive the cost function, substitute these expressions of labor and capital into the production function.* By combining this information with the production function, we can obtain a relationship between cost and output. By substituting, we find that

$$q = A\left(\frac{aC}{w}\right)^a \left[\frac{(1-a)C}{r}\right]^{1-a}. \tag{7.22}$$

We can rewrite Equation 7.22 as $C = q\theta$, where $\theta = w^a r^{1-a}/[Aa^a(1-a)^{1-a}]$.

3. *To derive the long-run cost function for the furniture firm, substitute the parameter values into $C = q\theta$.* For the furniture firm,

$$C = q 24^{0.6} 8^{0.4}/(1.52 \times 0.6^{0.6} 0.4^{0.4}) \approx 20q.$$

The Shape of Long-Run Cost Curves

The shapes of the average cost and marginal cost curves depend on the shape of the long-run cost curve. The relationships among total, marginal, and average costs are the same for both the long-run and short-run cost functions. For example, if the long-run average cost curve is U-shaped, the long-run marginal cost curve cuts it at its minimum.

The long-run average cost curve may be U-shaped, but the reason for this shape differs from those given for the short-run average cost curve. A key explanation for why the short-run average cost initially slopes downward is that the average fixed cost curve is downward sloping: Spreading the fixed cost over more units of output lowers the average fixed cost per unit. Because there are no fixed costs in the long run, fixed costs cannot explain the initial downward slope of the long-run average cost curve.

A major reason why the short-run average cost curve slopes upward at higher levels of output is diminishing marginal returns. In the long run, however, all factors can be varied, so diminishing marginal returns do not explain the upward slope of a long-run average cost curve.

As with the short-run curves, the shape of the long-run curves is determined by the production function relationship between output and inputs. In the long run, returns to scale play a major role in determining the shape of the average cost curve and the other cost curves. As we discussed in Chapter 6, increasing all inputs in proportion may cause output to increase more than in proportion (increasing returns to scale) at low levels of output, in proportion (constant returns to scale) at intermediate levels of output, and less than in proportion (decreasing returns to scale) at high levels of output. If a production function has this returns-to-scale pattern and the prices of inputs are constant, the long-run average cost curve must be U-shaped.

A cost function is said to exhibit **economies of scale** if the average cost of production falls as output expands. We would expect economies of scale in the range where the production function has increasing returns to scale: Doubling inputs more than doubles output, so average cost falls with higher output.

With constant returns to scale, doubling the inputs causes output to double as well, so the average cost remains constant. If an increase in output has no effect on average cost—the average cost curve is flat—there are *no economies of scale*. In the range where the production function has constant returns to scale, the average cost remains constant, so the cost function has *no economies of scale*. Finally, in the range where the production function has decreasing returns to scale, average cost increases. A firm suffers from **diseconomies of scale** if average cost rises when output increases.

Average cost curves can have many different shapes. Perfectly competitive firms typically show U-shaped average cost curves. Average cost curves in noncompetitive markets may be U-shaped, L-shaped (average cost at first falls rapidly and then levels off as output increases), everywhere downward sloping, everywhere upward sloping, or take other shapes altogether. The shape of the average cost curve indicates whether the production process results in economies or diseconomies of scale.

Table 7.1 summarizes the shapes of average cost curves of firms in various Canadian manufacturing industries (as estimated by Robidoux and Lester, 1992). The table shows that U-shaped average cost curves are the exception rather than the rule in Canadian manufacturing and that nearly one-third of these average cost curves are L-shaped. Cement firms provide an example of such a cost curve.

Some of the L-shaped average cost curves may be part of a U-shaped curve with long, flat bottoms, where we don't observe any firm producing enough to exhibit diseconomies of scale.

Table 7.1 Shape of Average Cost Curves in Canadian Manufacturing

Scale Economies	Share of Manufacturing Industries, %	
Economies of scale: Initially downward-sloping AC	57	
Everywhere downward-sloping AC		18
L-shaped AC (downward sloping, then flat)		31
U-shaped AC		8
No economies of scale: Flat AC	23	
Diseconomies of scale: Upward-sloping AC	14	

Source: Robidoux and Lester (1992).

APPLICATION

Innovations and Economies of Scale

Before the introduction of robotic assembly lines in the tire industry, firms had to produce large runs of identical products to take advantage of economies of scale and thereby keep their per-unit costs low. A traditional plant might be half a mile in length and be designed to produce popular models in batches of a thousand or more. To change to a different model, workers in traditional plants labored for eight hours or more to switch molds and set up the machinery.

In contrast, in its modern plant in Rome, Georgia, Pirelli Tire uses a modular integrated robotized system (MIRS) to produce small batches of a large number of products without driving up the cost per tire. A MIRS production unit has a dozen robots that feed a group of rubber-extruding and ply-laying machines. Tires are fabricated around metal drums gripped by powerful robotic arms. The robots pass materials into the machinery at various angles, where strips of rubber and reinforcements are built up to form the tire's structure. One MIRS system can simultaneously build 12 different tire models. At the end of the process, robots load the unfinished tires into molds that emboss the tread pattern and sidewall lettering. By producing only as needed, Pirelli avoids the inventory cost of storing large quantities of expensive raw materials and finished tires.

Because Pirelli can practically produce as few as four tires at a time, it can build some wild variations. "We make tires for ultra-big bling-bling wheels in small numbers, but they are quite profitable," brags Gaetano Mannino, the president of Pirelli Tire North America. Thus, with this new equipment, Pirelli can manufacture specialized tires at relatively low costs without the need for large-scale production.

Estimating Cost Curves Versus Introspection

Economists use statistical methods to estimate a cost function. However, we can sometimes infer the shape through casual observation and deductive reasoning.

For example, in the good old days, the Good Humor Company sent out herds of ice cream trucks to purvey its products. It seems likely that the company's production process had fixed proportions and constant returns to scale: If it wanted to sell more, Good Humor dispatched one more truck and one more driver. Drivers and trucks are almost certainly nonsubstitutable inputs (the isoquants are right angles). If the cost of a driver is w per day, the rental cost is r per day, and q is the quantity of ice cream sold in a day, then the cost function is $C = (w + r)q$.

Such deductive reasoning can lead one astray, as I once discovered. A water heater manufacturing firm provided me with many years of data on the inputs it used and the amount of output it produced. I also talked to the company's engineers about the production process and toured the plant (which resembled a scene from Dante's *Inferno,* with deafening noise levels and flames everywhere).

A water heater consists of an outside cylinder of metal, a liner, an electronic control unit, hundreds of tiny parts, and a couple of rods that slow corrosion. Workers cut out the metal for the cylinder, weld it together, and add the other parts. "OK," I said to myself, "this production process must be one of fixed proportions because the firm needs one of each input to produce a water heater. How could you substitute a cylinder for an electronic control unit? Or substitute labor for metal?"

I then used statistical techniques to estimate the production and cost functions. Following the usual procedure, I did not assume that I knew the exact form of the functions. Rather, I allowed the data to "tell" me the type of production and cost functions. To my surprise, the estimates indicated that the production process was not one of fixed proportions. Rather, the firm could readily substitute between labor and capital.

"Surely I've made a mistake," I said to the plant manager after describing these results.

"No," he said, "that's correct. There's a great deal of substitutability between labor and metal."

"How can they be substitutes?"

"Easy," he said. "We can use a lot of labor and waste very little metal by cutting out exactly what we want and being very careful. Or we can use relatively little labor, cut quickly, and waste more metal. When the cost of labor is relatively high, we waste more metal. When the cost of metal is relatively high, we cut more carefully." This practice, as the manager explained, minimizes the firm's cost.

7.4 Lower Costs in the Long Run

In its long-term planning, a firm selects a plant size and makes other investments to minimize its long-run cost on the basis of how many units it produces. Once it chooses its plant size and equipment, these inputs are fixed in the short run. Thus, the firm's long-run decisions determine its short-run cost. Because the firm cannot vary its capital in the short run but can in the long run, its short-run cost is at least as high as long-run cost and is higher if the "wrong" level of capital is used in the short run.

Long-Run Average Cost as the Envelope of Short-Run Average Cost Curves

As a result, the long-run average cost is always equal to or less than the short-run average cost. Panel a of Figure 7.7 shows a firm with a U-shaped long-run average cost curve. Suppose initially that the firm has only three possible plant sizes. The firm's short-run average cost curve is $SRAC^1$ for the smallest possible plant. The average cost of producing q_1 units of output using this plant, point *a* on $SRAC^1$, is $10. If instead the firm used the next larger plant size, its cost of producing q_1 units of output, point *b* on $SRAC^2$, would be $12. Thus, if the firm knows that it will produce only q_1 units of output, it minimizes its average cost by using the smaller plant. Its average cost of producing q_2 is lower on the $SRAC^2$ curve, point *e*, than on the $SRAC^1$ curve, point *d*.

Figure 7.7 Long-Run Average Cost as the Envelope of Short-Run Average Cost Curves

(a) If there are only three possible plant sizes, with short-run average costs $SRAC^1$, $SRAC^2$, and $SRAC^3$, the long-run average cost curve is the solid, scalloped portion of the three short-run curves. $LRAC$ is a smooth, U-shaped long-run average cost curve if there are many possible short-run average cost curves. (b) Because the furniture firm's production function has constant returns to scale, its long-run average cost and marginal cost curves are horizontal.

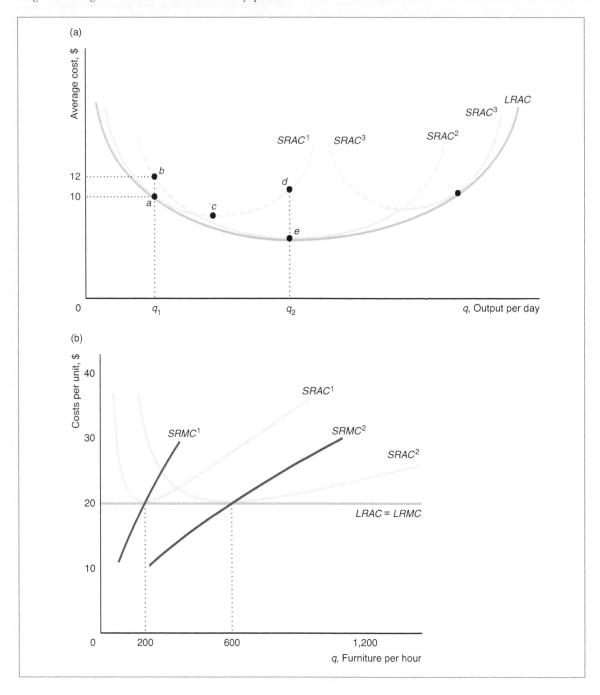

In the long run, the firm chooses the plant size that minimizes its cost of production, so it selects the plant size with the lowest average cost for each possible output level. At q_1, it opts for the small plant, whereas at q_2, it uses the medium plant. Therefore, the long-run average cost curve is the solid, scalloped section of the three short-run cost curves.

But if there are many possible plant sizes, the long-run average curve, $LRAC$, is smooth and U-shaped. The $LRAC$ includes one point from each possible short-run average cost curve. This point, however, is not necessarily the minimum point from a short-run curve. For example, the $LRAC$ includes point a on $SRAC^1$ and not the curve's minimum point, c. A small plant operating at minimum average cost cannot produce at as low an average cost as a slightly larger plant that takes advantage of economies of scale.

Panel b of Figure 7.7 shows the relationship between short-run and long-run average cost curves for the furniture manufacturer. Because this production function has constant returns to scale, doubling both inputs doubles output, so the long-run average cost, $LRAC$, is constant at $20, as we saw earlier. If capital is fixed at 200 units, the firm's short-run average cost curve is $SRAC^1$. If the firm produces 200 units of output, its short-run and long-run average costs are equal. At any other output, its short-run cost is higher than its long-run cost.

The short-run marginal cost curves, $SRMC^1$ and $SRMC^2$, are upward sloping and equal the corresponding U-shaped short-run average cost curves, $SRAC^1$ and $SRAC^2$, only at their minimum points of $20. In contrast, because the long-run average cost is horizontal at $20, the long-run marginal cost curve, $LRMC$, is horizontal at $20. Thus, the long-run marginal cost curve is not the envelope of the short-run marginal cost curves.

APPLICATION

Choosing an Inkjet or Laser Printer

In 2010, you can buy a personal laser printer for $100 or an inkjet printer for $30 that prints 16 pages a minute at 1,200 dots per inch. If you buy the inkjet, you save $69 right off the bat. The laser printer costs less per page to operate, however. The cost of ink and paper is about 4¢ per page for a laser compared to about 7¢ per page for an inkjet. The average cost per page of operating a laser is $100/q + 0.04$, where q is the number of pages, while the average cost for an inkjet is $30/q + 0.07$. Thus, the average cost per page is lower with the inkjet until q reaches 2,300 pages, and thereafter the laser is less expensive per page.

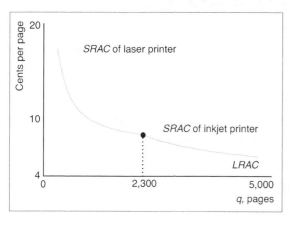

The graph shows the short-run average cost curves for the laser printer and the inkjet printer. The inkjet printer is the lower-cost choice if you're printing fewer than 2,300 pages, and the laser printer if you're printing more.

So, should you buy the laser printer? If you print more than 2,300 pages over its lifetime, the laser is less expensive to operate than the inkjet. If the printers last two years and you print 23 or more pages per week, then the laser printer is cost effective.

Short-Run and Long-Run Expansion Paths

Long-run cost is lower than short-run cost because a firm has more flexibility in the long run. To show the advantage of flexibility, we can compare the short-run and long-run expansion paths, which correspond to the short-run and long-run cost curves.

The furniture manufacturer has greater flexibility in the long run. The tangency of the firm's isoquants and isocost lines determines the long-run expansion path in Figure 7.8. The firm expands output by increasing both its labor and capital, so its long-run expansion path is upward sloping. To increase its output from 100 to 200 units (that is, move from x to z), the firm doubles its capital from 100 to 200 units and its labor from 50 to 100 workers. As a result, its cost increases from $2,000 to $4,000.

In the short run, the firm cannot increase its capital, which is fixed at 100 units. The firm can increase its output only by using more labor, so its short-run expansion path is horizontal at $K = 100$. To expand its output from 100 to 200 units (move from x to y), the firm must increase its labor from 50 to 159 workers, and its cost rises from $2,000 to $4,616. Doubling output increases long-run cost by a factor of 2 and short-run cost by approximately 2.3.

How Learning by Doing Lowers Costs

Long-run cost is lower than short-run cost for three reasons. First, firms have more flexibility in the long run. Second, technological progress (Chapter 6) may lower cost over time. Third, the firm may benefit **learning by doing:** the productive skills

Figure 7.8 Long-Run and Short-Run Expansion Paths

In the long run, the furniture manufacturer increases its output by using more of both inputs, so its long-run expansion path is upward sloping. In the short run, the firm cannot vary its capital, so its short-run expansion path is horizontal at the fixed level of output. That is, it increases its output by increasing the amount of labor it uses. Expanding output from 100 to 200 raises the furniture firm's long-run cost from $2,000 to $4,000 but raises its short-run cost from $2,000 to $4,616.

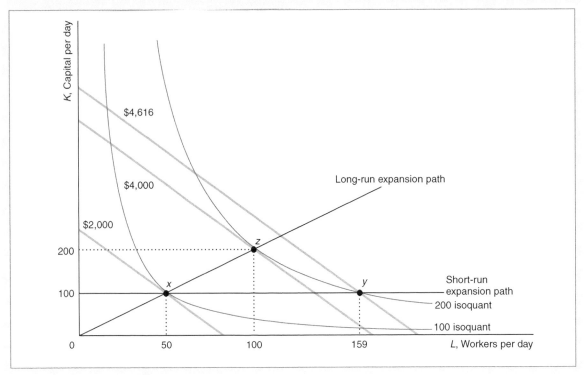

and knowledge of better ways to produce that workers and managers gain from experience. Workers who are given a new task may perform it slowly the first few times they try, but their speed increases with practice. Over time, managers may learn how to organize production more efficiently, determine which workers to assign to which tasks, and discover where inventories need to be increased and where they can be reduced. Engineers may optimize product designs by experimenting with various production methods. For these and other reasons, the average cost of production tends to fall over time, and the effect is particularly strong with new products.

Learning by doing might be a function of the time elapsed since a particular product or production process is introduced. More commonly, learning is a function of *cumulative output*: workers become increasingly adept the more often they perform a task. We summarize the relationship between average costs and cumulative output by a **learning curve**. The learning curve for Intel central processing units (CPUs) in panel a of Figure 7.9 shows that Intel's average cost fell very rapidly with the first

Figure 7.9 Learning by Doing

(a) As Intel produces more cumulative central processing units (CPUs), the average cost of production per unit falls (Salgado, 2008). The horizontal axis measures the cumulative production. (b) In the short run, extra production reduces a firm's average cost owing to economies of scale: Because $q_1 < q_2 < q_3$, A is higher than B, which is higher than C. In the long run, extra production reduces average cost as a result of learning by doing. To produce q_2 this period costs B on AC^1, but to produce that same output in the next period would cost only b on AC^2. If the firm produces q_3 instead of q_2 in this period, its average cost in the next period is AC^3 instead of AC^2 due to additional learning by doing. Thus, extra output in this period lowers the firm's cost in two ways: It lowers average cost in this period due to economies of scale and lowers average cost for any given output level in the next period due to learning by doing.

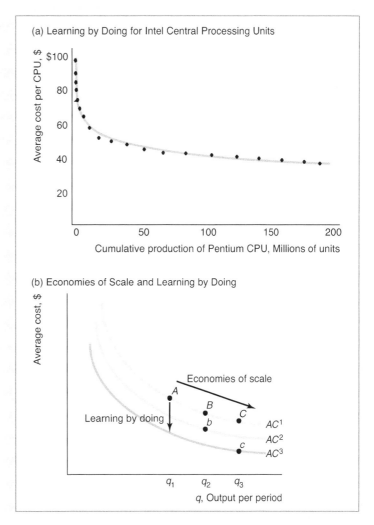

few million units of cumulative output, but then dropped relatively slowly with additional units (Salgado, 2008).

If a firm operates in the economies-of-scale section of its average cost curve, expanding output lowers its cost for two reasons: Its average cost falls today due to economies of scale, and for any given level of output, its average cost will be lower in the next period as a result of learning by doing.

In panel b of Figure 7.9, the firm currently produces q_1 units of output at point A on average cost curve AC^1. If it expands its output to q_2, its average cost falls in this period to point B due to economies of scale. Learning by doing in this period results in a lower average cost, AC^2, in the next period. If the firm continues to produce q_2 units of output in the next period, its average cost will fall to point b on AC^2.

If instead of expanding output to q_2 in Period 1, the firm expands to q_3, its average cost is even lower in Period 1 (C on AC^1) due to even greater economies of scale. Moreover, its average cost curve, AC^3, in Period 2 is even lower due to the extra experience gained from producing more output in Period 1. If the firm continues to produce q_3 in Period 2, its average cost is c on AC^3. Thus, all else being the same, if learning by doing depends on cumulative output, firms have an incentive to produce more in the short run than they otherwise would to lower their costs in the future.

APPLICATION

Learning by Drilling

Learning by doing can substantially reduce the cost of drilling oil wells. Two types of firms work together to drill oil wells: oil production companies and oil drilling companies. Oil production companies, such as ExxonMobil and Chevron, design and plan wells to be drilled. The actual drilling is performed by companies that own and staff drilling rigs. The time it takes to drill a well varies across fields, which vary in terms of the types of rock covering the oil and the depth of the oil.

Kellogg (2009) found that the more experience a firm has—the cumulative number of wells drilled by the oil production firm in the field over the past two years—the less time it takes the firm to drill another well. His estimated learning curve shows that drilling time decreases rapidly at first, falling by about 15% after the first 25 wells are drilled, but does not fall much more with additional experience.

This decrease in drilling time is the sum of the benefits from two types of experience. The time it takes to drill a well falls as the production company (1) drills more wells in the field, and (2) drills more wells in that field with a particular drilling company. The second effect occurs because the two firms learn to work better together in a particular field. Because neither firm can apply its learning with a particular partner to its work with another partner, production companies prefer to continue to work with same drilling rig firms over time.

The reduction in drilling time from a production firm's average stand-alone experience over the past two years is 6.4% or 1.5 fewer days to drill a well. This time savings reduces the cost of drilling a well by about $16,300. The relationship-specific learning from experience due to working with a drilling company for the average duration over two years reduces drilling time per well by 3.8%, or about $9,700 per well. On average, the reduction in drilling time from working with one rig crew regularly is twice as much as from working with rigs that frequently switch from one production firm to another.

7.5 Cost of Producing Multiple Goods

If a firm produces two or more goods, the cost of one good may depend on the output level of the other. Outputs are linked if a single input is used to produce both of them. For example, mutton and wool come from sheep, cattle provide beef and hides, and oil supplies heating fuel and gasoline. It is less expensive to produce beef and hides together than separately. If the goods are produced together, a single steer yields one unit of beef and one hide. If beef and hides are produced separately (throwing away the unused good), the same amount of output requires two steers and more labor.

We say that there are **economies of scope** if it is less expensive to produce goods jointly than separately (Panzar and Willig, 1977, 1981). A measure of the degree to which there are economies of *scope* (*SC*) is

$$SC = \frac{C(q_1, 0) + C(0, q_2) - C(q_1, q_2)}{C(q_1, q_2)},$$

where $C(q_1, 0)$ is the cost of producing q_1 units of the first good by itself, $C(0, q_2)$ is the cost of producing q_2 units of the second good, and $C(q_1, q_2)$ is the cost of producing both goods together. If the cost of producing the two goods separately, $C(q_1, 0) + C(0, q_2)$, is the same as the cost of producing them together, $C(q_1, q_2)$, then SC is zero. If it is cheaper to produce the goods jointly, SC is positive. If SC is negative, there are *diseconomies* of scope, and the two goods should be produced separately.

To illustrate this idea, suppose that Laura spends one day collecting mushrooms and wild strawberries in the woods. Her **production possibility frontier**—the maximum amount of outputs (mushrooms and strawberries) that can be produced from a fixed amount of input (Laura's effort during one day)—is PPF^1 in Figure 7.10. The production possibility frontier summarizes the trade-off Laura faces: She picks fewer mushrooms if she collects more strawberries in a day.

Figure 7.10 Joint Production

If there are economies of scope, the production possibility frontier bows away from the origin, PPF^1. If instead the production possibility frontier is a straight line, PPF^2, the cost of producing both goods does not fall if they are produced together.

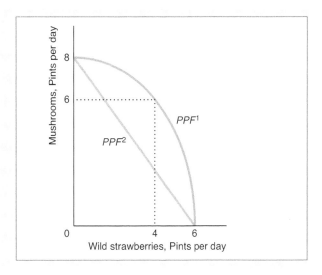

If Laura spends all day collecting only mushrooms, she picks eight pints; if she spends all day picking strawberries, she collects six pints. If she picks some of each, however, she can harvest more total pints: six pints of mushrooms and four pints of strawberries. The product possibility frontier is concave (the middle of the curve is farther from the origin than it would be if it were a straight line) because of the diminishing marginal returns to collecting only one of the two goods. If she collects only mushrooms, she must walk past wild strawberries without picking them. As a result, she has to walk farther if she collects only mushrooms than if she picks both. Thus, there are economies of scope in jointly collecting mushrooms and strawberries.

If instead the production possibility frontier were a straight line, the cost of producing the two goods jointly would not be lower. Suppose, for example, that mushrooms grow in one section of the woods and strawberries in another section. In that case, Laura can collect only mushrooms without passing any strawberries. That production possibility frontier is a straight line, PPF^2 in Figure 7.10. By allocating her time between the two sections of the woods, Laura can collect any combination of mushrooms and strawberries by spending part of her day in one section of the woods and part in the other.

APPLICATION
Economies of Scope

Empirical studies show that some processes have economies of scope, others have none, and some have diseconomies of scope. In Japan, there are substantial economies of scope in producing and transmitting electricity, $SC = 0.2$ (Ida and Kuwahara, 2004), and broadcasting television and radio, $SC = 0.12$ (Asai 2006).

In Switzerland, some utility firms provide gas, electric, and water, while others provide only one or two of these utilities. Farsi et al. (2008) estimates that most firms have scope economies. The SC ranges between 0.04 and 0.15 for median-sized firms, but scope economies can reach 20% to 30% of total costs for small firms, which may help explain why only some firms provide multiple utilities.

Friedlaender, Winston, and Wang (1983) found that for American automobile manufacturers, it is 25% less expensive ($SC = 0.25$) to produce large cars together with small cars and trucks than to produce large cars separately and small cars and trucks together. However, there are no economies of scope from producing trucks together with small and large cars. Producing trucks separately from cars is efficient.

Kim (1987) found substantial diseconomies of scope in using railroads to transport freight and passengers together. It is 41% less expensive ($SC = -0.41$) to transport passengers and freight separately than together. In the early 1970s, passenger service in the United States was transferred from the private railroad companies to Amtrak, and the services are now separate. Kim's estimates suggest that this separation is cost-effective.

SUMMARY

From all available technologically efficient production processes, a firm chooses the one that is economically efficient. The economically efficient production process is the technologically efficient process for which the cost of producing a given quantity of output is lowest, or the one that produces the most output for a given cost.

1. **Measuring Costs.** The economic or opportunity cost of a good is the value of its next best alternative use. Economic cost includes both explicit and implicit costs.

2. **Short-Run Costs.** In the short run, a firm can vary the costs of the factors that are adjustable, but the costs of other factors are fixed. The firm's average fixed cost falls as its output rises. If a firm has a short-run average cost curve that is U-shaped, its marginal cost curve lies below the average cost curve when average

cost is falling and above the average cost curve when it is rising, so the marginal cost curve cuts the average cost curve at its minimum.

3. **Long-Run Costs.** In the long run, all factors can be varied, so all costs are variable. As a result, average cost and average variable cost are identical. A firm chooses the best combination of inputs to minimize its cost. To produce a given output level, it chooses the lowest isocost line to touch the relevant isoquant, which is tangent to the isoquant. Equivalently, to minimize cost, the firm adjusts inputs until the last dollar spent on any input increases output by as much as the last dollar spent on any other input. If the firm calculates the cost of producing every possible output level given current input prices, it knows its cost function: Cost is a function of the input prices and the output level. If the firm's average cost falls as output expands, its cost function exhibits economies of scale. If the firm's average cost rises as output expands, it exhibits diseconomies of scale.

4. **Lower Costs in the Long Run.** The firm can always do in the long run what it does in the short run, so its long-run cost can never be greater than its short-run cost. Because some factors are fixed in the short run, the firm, to expand output, must greatly increase its use of other factors, a relatively costly choice. In the long run, the firm can adjust all factors, a process that keeps its cost down. Long-run cost may also be lower than short-run cost if technological progress or learning by doing occurs.

5. **Cost of Producing Multiple Goods.** If it is less expensive for a firm to produce two goods jointly rather than separately, there are economies of scope. With diseconomies of scope, it is less expensive to produce the goods separately.

QUESTIONS

■ = exercise is available on **MyEconLab**; * = answer appears at the back of this book; V = video answer by James Dearden is available online.

*1. "There are certain fixed costs when you own a plane," [Andre] Agassi explained during a break in the action at the Volvo/San Francisco tennis tournament, "so the more you fly it, the more economic sense it makes. . . . The first flight after I bought it, I took some friends to Palm Springs for lunch." (Ostler, Scott, "Andre Even Flies like a Champ," *San Francisco Chronicle*, February 8, 1993, C1.) Discuss whether Agassi's analysis is reasonable.

2. The only variable input a janitorial service firm uses to clean offices is workers who are paid a wage, w, of $8 an hour. Each worker can clean four offices in an hour. Use math to determine the variable cost, the average variable cost, and the marginal cost of cleaning one more office. Draw a diagram similar to Figure 7.1 to show the variable cost, average variable cost, and marginal cost curves.

*3. A firm builds shipping crates out of wood. How does the cost of producing a 1-cubic-foot crate (each side is 1 foot square) compare to the cost of building an 8-cubic-foot crate if wood costs $1 per square foot and the firm has no labor or other costs? More generally, how does cost vary with volume?

*4. You have 60 minutes to complete an exam with two questions. You want to maximize your score. Toward the end of the exam, the more time you spend on either question, the fewer extra points per minute you get for that question. How should you allocate your time between the two questions? (*Hint*: Think about producing an output of a score on the exam using inputs of time spent on each of the problems. Then use an equation similar to Equation 7.11.)

5. Boxes of cereal are produced using a fixed-proportion production function: One box and one unit (8 ounces) of cereal produce one box of cereal. What is the expansion path?

6. Suppose that your firm's production function has constant returns to scale. What is the long-run expansion path?

7. The production process of the firm you manage uses labor and capital services. How does the long-run expansion path change when the wage increases while the rental rate of capital stays constant?

8. A U-shaped long-run average cost curve is the envelope of U-shaped short-run average cost curves. On what part of the curve (downward sloping, flat, or upward sloping) does a short-run curve touch the long-run curve? (*Hint*: Your answer should depend on where the two curves touch on the long-run curve.)

9. Suppose that the government subsidizes the cost of workers by paying for 25% of the wage (the rate offered by the U.S. government in the late 1970s under the New Jobs Tax Credit program). What effect does this subsidy have on the firm's choice of labor and capital to produce a given level of output?

*10. What is the effect of a lump-sum franchise tax $\mathcal{L}$ on the quantity at which a firm's after-tax average cost curve reaches its minimum, given that the firm's before-tax average cost curve is U-shaped?

11. Suppose in the previous problem that the government charges the firm a franchise tax each year instead of only once. Describe the effect of this tax on the

marginal cost, average variable cost, short-run average cost, and long-run average cost curves.

12. Over the last century, department stores and supermarkets have largely replaced smaller specialty stores, as consumers have found it more efficient to go to one rather than to many stores. Consumers incur a transaction cost (or search cost) to shop, primarily the opportunity cost of their time. This transaction cost includes a fixed cost of traveling to and from the store and a variable cost that rises with the number of different types of items the consumer looks for on the shelves. By going to a supermarket that carries meat, fruit, vegetables, and other items, consumers can avoid some of the fixed transaction costs of traveling to a separate butcher shop, produce mart, and so forth. Use math or figures to explain why a shopper's average costs are lower when buying at a single supermarket than when buying from many stores. (*Hint*: Define the goods as the items that are purchased and brought home.)

*13. The all-American baseball is made using cork from Portugal, rubber from Malaysia, yarn from Australia, and leather from France, and it is stitched (108 stitches exactly) by workers in Costa Rica. To assemble a baseball takes one unit of each of these inputs. Ultimately, the finished product must be shipped to its final destination—say, Cooperstown, New York. The materials used cost the same in any location. Labor costs are lower in Costa Rica than in a possible alternative manufacturing site in Georgia, but shipping costs from Costa Rica are higher. Would you expect the production function to exhibit decreasing, increasing, or constant returns to scale? What is the cost function? What can you conclude about shipping costs if it is less expensive to produce baseballs in Costa Rica than in Georgia?

14. The Bouncing Ball Ping Pong Company sells table tennis sets, which include two paddles and one net. What is the firm's long-run expansion path if it incurs no costs other than what it pays for paddles and nets, which it buys at market prices? How does its expansion path depend on the relative prices of paddles and nets?

*15. A bottling company uses two inputs to produce bottles of the soft drink Sludge: bottling machines, K, and workers, L. The isoquants have the usual smooth shape. The machine costs $1,000 per day to run, and the workers earn $200 per day. At the current level of production, the marginal product of the machine is an additional 200 bottles per day, and the marginal product of labor is 50 more bottles per day. Is this firm producing at minimum cost? If it is minimizing cost, explain why. If it is not minimizing cost, explain how the firm should change the ratio of inputs it uses to lower its cost. (*Hint*: Examine the conditions for minimizing cost: Equations 7.10 and 7.11.)

16. Rosenberg (2004) reports the invention of a new machine that serves as a mobile station for receiving and accumulating packed flats of strawberries close to where they are picked, reducing workers' time and the burden of carrying full flats of strawberries. A machine-assisted crew of 15 pickers produces as much output, q^*, as that of an unaided crew of 25 workers. In a 6-day, 50-hour workweek, the machine replaces 500 worker hours. At an hourly wage cost of $10, a machine saves $5,000 per week in labor costs, or $130,000 over a 26-week harvesting season. The cost of machine operation and maintenance expressed as a daily rental is $200, or $1,200 for a six-day week. Thus, the net savings equal $3,800 per week, or $98,800 for 26 weeks.

  a. Draw the q^* isoquant assuming that only two technologies are available (pure labor and labor-machine). Label the isoquant and axes as thoroughly as possible.

  b. Add an isocost line to show which technology the firm chooses. (Be sure to measure wage and rental costs on a comparable time basis.)

  c. Draw the corresponding cost curves (with and without the machine), assuming constant returns to scale, and label the curves and the axes as thoroughly as possible.

17. In February 2003, Circuit City Stores, Inc., replaced skilled sales representatives who earn up to $54,000 per year with relatively unskilled workers who earned $14 to $18 per hour (Carlos Tejada and Gary McWilliams, "New Recipe for Cost Savings: Replace Highly Paid Workers," *Wall Street Journal*, June 11, 2003). Suppose that sales representatives sold one specific Sony high-definition TV model. Let q represent the number of TVs sold per hour, s the number of skilled sales representatives per hour, and u the number of unskilled representatives per hour. Working eight hours per day, each skilled worker sold six TVs per day, and each unskilled worker sold four. The wage rate of the skilled workers was $w_s = $26 per hour, and the wage rate of the unskilled workers was $w_u = $16 per hour.

  a. Show the isoquant for $q = 4$ with both skilled and unskilled sales representatives. Are they substitutes?

  b. Draw the isocost line for $C = $104 per hour.

  c. Using an isocost-isoquant diagram, identify the cost-minimizing number of skilled and unskilled reps to sell $q = 4$ TVs per hour. V

18. Many corporations allow CEOs to use their firm's corporate jet for personal travel. The Internal Revenue Service (IRS) requires that the firm report personal use of its corporate jet as taxable executive income, and the Securities and Exchange Commission (SEC) requires that publicly traded corporations report the value of this benefit to shareholders. An important issue is the determination of the value of this benefit. *The Wall Street Journal* (Mark Maremont, "Amid Crackdown, the Jet Perk Suddenly Looks a Lot Pricier," May 25, 2005, A1) reports three valuation techniques. The IRS values a CEO's personal flight at or below the price of a first-class ticket. The SEC values the flight at the "incremental" cost of the flight: the additional costs to the corporation of the flight. The third alternative is the market value of chartering an aircraft. Of the three methods, the first-class ticket is least expensive and the chartered flight is most expensive.

   a. What factors (such as fuel) determine the marginal explicit cost to a corporation of an executive's personal flight? Does any one of the three valuation methods correctly determine the marginal explicit cost?

   b. What is the marginal opportunity cost to the corporation of an executive's personal flight? V

19. In 1796, Gottfried Christoph Härtel, a German music publisher, calculated the cost of printing music using an engraved plate technology and used these estimated cost functions to make production decisions. Härtel figured that the fixed cost of printing a musical page—the cost of engraving the plates—was 900 pfennigs. The marginal cost of each additional copy of the page was 5 pfennigs (Scherer, 2001).

   a. Graph the total cost, average total cost, average variable cost, and marginal cost functions.

   b. Is there a cost advantage to having only one music publisher print a given composition? Why?

   c. Härtel used his data to do the following type of analysis: Suppose he expected to sell exactly 300 copies of a composition at 15 pfennigs per page. What is the highest price the publisher would be willing to pay the composer per page of the composition? V

*20. In Solved Problem 7.3, show that for some wage and rental cost of capital the firm is indifferent between using the wafer-handling stepper technology and the stepper technology. How does this wage/cost-of-capital ratio compare to those in the C^2 and C^3 isocosts?

21. What can you say about Laura's economies of scope if her time is valued at $5 an hour and her production possibility frontier is PPF^1 in Figure 7.10?

PROBLEMS

22. Give the formulas for and plot *AFC*, *MC*, *AVC*, and *AC* if the cost function is

    a. $C = 10 + 10q$
    b. $C = 10 + q^2$
    c. $C = 10 + 10q - 4q^2 + q^3$

23. The short-run cost function of a U.S. furniture manufacturer (the Application "Short-Run Cost Curves for a Furniture Manufacturer") is approximately $C(q) = 0.55q^{1.67} + 800/q$. At what positive quantity does the average cost function reach its minimum? If a $400 lump-sum tax is applied to the firm, at what positive quantity is the after-tax average cost minimized? (*Hint*: See Solved Problem 7.2.)

*24. What is the long-run cost function if the production function is $q = L + K$?

25. Gail works in a flower shop, where she produces 10 floral arrangements per hour. She is paid $10 an hour for the first eight hours she works and $15 an hour for each additional hour. What is the firm's cost function? What are its *AC*, *AVC*, and *MC* functions? Draw the *AC*, *AVC*, and *MC* curves.

26. A firm's cost curve is $C = F + 10q - bq^2 + q^3$, where $b > 0$.

    a. For what values of b are cost, average cost, and average variable cost positive? (From now on, assume that all these measures of cost are positive at every output level.)

    b. What is the shape of the *AC* curve? At what output level is the *AC* minimized?

    c. At what output levels does the *MC* curve cross the *AC* and the *AVC* curves?

    d. Use calculus to show that the *MC* curve must cross the *AVC* at its minimum point.

27. A firm has two plants that produce identical output. The cost functions are $C_1 = 10q - 4q^2 + q^3$ and $C_2 = 10q - 2q^2 + q^3$.

    a. At what output level does the average cost curve of each plant reach its minimum?

    b. If the firm wants to produce four units of output, how much should it produce in each plant?

28. For a Cobb-Douglas production function, how does the expansion path change if the wage increases while the rental rate of capital stays the same?

29. A firm has a Cobb-Douglas production function, $Q = AL^aK^b$, where $a + b < 1$. On the basis of this information, what properties does its cost function have?

*30. A firm's average cost is $AC = \alpha q^\beta$, where $\alpha > 0$. How can you interpret α? (*Hint:* Suppose that $q = 1$.) What sign must β have if learning by doing takes place? What happens to average cost as q increases? Draw the average cost curve as a function of output for particular values of α and β.

31. A U.S. chemical firm has a production function of $q = 10L^{0.32}K^{0.56}$ (Hsieh, 1995). It faces factor prices of $w = 10$ and $r = 20$. What are its short-run marginal and average variable cost curves?

32. A glass manufacturer's production function is $q = 10L^{0.5}K^{0.5}$ (Hsieh, 1995). Suppose that its wage, w, is $1 per hour and the rental cost of capital, r, is $4.

   a. Draw an accurate figure showing how the glass firm minimizes its cost of production.

   b. What is the equation of the (long-run) expansion path for a glass firm? Illustrate in a graph.

   c. Derive the long-run total cost curve equation as a function of q.

33. If it manufactures at home, a firm faces input prices for labor and capital of $\hat{w}$ and $\hat{r}$ and produces $\hat{q}$ units of output using $\hat{L}$ units of labor and $\hat{K}$ units of capital. Abroad, the wage and cost of capital are half as much as at home. If the firm manufactures abroad, will it change the amount of labor and capital it uses to produce $\hat{q}$? What happens to its cost of producing $\hat{q}$?

34. A U.S. electronics firm is considering moving its production to a plant in Mexico. Its estimated production function is $q = L^{0.5}K^{0.5}$ (based on Hsieh, 1995). The U.S. factor prices are $w = r = 10$. In Mexico, the wage is half that in the United States, but the firm faces the same cost of capital: $w^* = 5$ and $r^* = r = 10$. What are L and K, and what is the cost of producing $q = 100$ units in both countries?

*35. A U.S. electronics firm is considering moving its production to a plant in Asia. Its estimated production function is $q = L^{0.5}K^{0.5}$ (based on Hsieh, 1995). In the United States, $w = 10 = r$. At its Asian plant, the firm will pay a 10% lower wage and a 10% higher cost of capital: $w^* = 10/1.1$ and $r^* = 1.1 \times 10 = 11$. What are L and K, and what is the cost of producing $q = 100$ units in both countries? What would the cost of production be in Asia if the firm had to use the same factor quantities as in the United States?

36. A U.S. apparel manufacturer is considering moving its production abroad. Its production function is $q = L^{0.7}K^{0.3}$ (based on Hsieh, 1995). In the United States, $w = 7$ and $r = 3$. At its Asian plant, the firm will pay a 50% lower wage and a 50% higher cost of capital: $w = 7/1.5$ and $r = 3 \times 1.5$. What are L and K, and what is the cost of producing $q = 100$ units in both countries? What would the cost of production be in Asia if the firm had to use the same factor quantities as in the United States?

37. A production function is homogeneous of degree γ and involves three inputs, L, K, and M (materials). The corresponding factor prices are w, r, and e. Derive the long-run cost curve.

38. Equation 7.22 gives the long-run cost function of a firm with a constant-returns-to-scale Cobb-Douglas production function. Show how, for a given output level, cost changes as the wage, w, increases. Explain why.

39. Derive the long-run cost function for the constant elasticity of substitution production function, Equation 6.12, $q = (L^\rho + K^\rho)^{1/\rho}$.

40. Consider a water heater manufacturing company. The number of water heaters manufactured per day, q, is a function of the number of workers per day, L, and the number of square feet of sheet metal per day, S. Specifically, its (general) CES production function is $q = (L^{-2} + S^{-2}/40)^{-0.5}$. The hourly wage rate is $20, and the price per square foot of sheet metal is 50¢.

   a. What is the marginal productivity of labor? What is the marginal productivity of capital?

   b. What is the formula needed to draw the expansion path? Draw the expansion path.

   c. Derive the long-run cost function.

   d. Suppose the price of sheet metal decreases to 25¢. Draw the new expansion path. With this 50% decrease in the price (50¢ to 25¢), discuss the magnitude of the shift in the expansion path. V

41. Swim coach Rob teaches athletes how to swim freestyle while keeping their hips raised. Let q represent the number of swimmers that learn the technique, and let h represent the number of hours of individual training Rob provides in which the swimmers focus on their hips. The team's production function is $q = h^{0.5}$. Rob is paid $150 per hour of practice.

   a. What is the cost function $C(q)$? What is the marginal cost function $m(q)$?

   b. Now suppose that Rob has learned a new method to teach swimmers how to swim with their hips raised. His new team production function is $q = h^{0.75}$. What is the cost function? What is the marginal cost function?

   c. Compare the marginal cost functions of parts a and b. V

Competitive Firms and Markets

8

The love of money is the root of all virtue. —George Bernard Shaw

One of the major questions that a firm faces is how much should it produce? To pick a level of output that maximizes profit, a firm must consider its cost function and how much it can sell at a given price. The amount the firm thinks it can sell depends in turn on the market demand of consumers and the firm's beliefs about how other firms in the market will behave. The behavior of firms depends on the **market structure**: the number of firms in the market, the ease with which firms can enter and leave the market, and the ability of firms to differentiate their products from those of their rivals.

In this chapter, we look at **perfect competition**: a market structure in which buyers and sellers are price takers. That is, neither firms nor consumers can sell or buy except at the market price. If a firm were to try to charge more than the market price, it would be unable to sell any of its output because consumers would buy the good at a lower price from other firms in the market. The market price summarizes everything that a firm needs to know about the demand of consumers *and* the behavior of its rivals. Thus, a competitive firm can ignore the specific behavior of individual rivals when deciding how much to produce.[1]

> **In this chapter, we examine four main topics**
>
> 1. **Perfect Competition.** A perfectly competitive firm is a price taker, and as such, it faces a horizontal demand curve.
> 2. **Profit Maximization.** To maximize profit, any firm must make two decisions: what output level maximizes its profit (or minimizes its loss) and whether to produce at all.
> 3. **Competition in the Short Run.** In the short run, variable costs determine a profit-maximizing, competitive firm's supply curve, the market supply curve, and, with the market demand curve, the competitive equilibrium.
> 4. **Competition in the Long Run.** Firm supply, market supply, and competitive equilibrium are different in the long run than in the short run because firms can vary inputs that were fixed in the short run and new firms can enter the market.

---

[1] In contrast, in a market with a small number of firms, each firm must consider the behavior of each of its rivals, as we discuss in Chapter 14.

8.1 Perfect Competition

Competition is a common market structure with very desirable properties, so it is useful to compare other market structures to competition. In this section, we examine the properties of competitive firms and markets.

Price Taking

When most people talk about "competitive firms," they mean firms that are rivals for the same customers. By this interpretation, any market with more than one firm is competitive. However, to an economist, only some of these multifirm markets are competitive.

Economists say that a market is perfectly competitive if each firm in the market is a price taker that cannot significantly affect the market price for its output or the prices at which it buys inputs. Why would a competitive firm be a price taker? It has no choice. The firm *has* to be a price taker if it faces a demand curve that is horizontal at the market price. If the demand curve is horizontal at the market price, the firm can sell as much as it wants at that price, so it has no incentive to lower its price. Similarly, the firm cannot increase the price at which it sells by restricting its output because it faces an infinitely elastic demand (see Chapter 2): A small increase in price results in its demand falling to zero.

Why a Firm's Demand Curve Is Horizontal

Firms are likely to be price takers in markets that have some or all of the following properties:

- The market contains a large number of firms.
- Firms sell *identical products*.
- Buyers and sellers have full information about the prices charged by all firms.
- Transaction costs—the expenses of finding a trading partner and completing the trade beyond the price paid for the good or service—are low.
- Firms can freely enter and exit the market.

Large Number of Buyers and Sellers. If there are enough sellers in a market, no one firm can raise or lower the market price. The more firms in a market, the less any one firm's output affects the market output and hence the market price.

For example, the 107,000 U.S. soybean farmers are price takers. If a typical grower drops out of the market, market supply falls by only $1/107{,}000 = 0.00093\%$, so the market price would not be noticeably affected. A soybean farm can sell any feasible output it produces at the prevailing market equilibrium price. In other words, *the firm's demand curve is a horizontal line at the market price.*

Similarly, perfect competition requires that buyers be price takers as well. For example, if firms have to sell to a single buyer—for example, producers of advanced weapons are allowed to sell only to their government—then the buyer sets the price.

Identical Products. Firms in a perfectly competitive market sell *identical* or *homogeneous* products. Consumers do not ask which farm grew a Granny Smith apple because they view all Granny Smith apples as essentially identical. If the products of all firms are identical, it is difficult for a single firm to raise its price above the going price charged by other firms.

In contrast, in the automobile market—which is not perfectly competitive—the characteristics of a BMW and a Honda Civic differ substantially. These products are *differentiated* or *heterogeneous*. Competition from Civics would not in itself be a very strong force preventing BMW from raising its price.

Full Information. Because buyers know that different firms produce identical products and know the prices charged by all firms, it is very difficult for any one firm to unilaterally raise its price above the market equilibrium price. If it did, consumers would simply switch to a different firm.

Negligible Transaction Costs. Perfectly competitive markets have very low transaction costs. Buyers and sellers do not have to spend much time and money finding each other or hiring lawyers to write contracts to execute a trade.[2] If transaction costs are low, it is easy for a customer to buy from a rival firm if the customer's usual supplier raises its price.

In contrast, if transaction costs are high, customers might absorb a price increase from a traditional supplier. For example, because some consumers prefer to buy milk at a local convenience store rather than travel several miles to a supermarket, the convenience store can charge slightly more than the supermarket without losing all its customers.

In some perfectly competitive markets, many buyers and sellers are brought together in a single room, so transaction costs are virtually zero. For example, transaction costs are very low at FloraHolland's daily flower auctions in the Netherlands, which attract 7,000 suppliers and 4,500 buyers from around the world. There are 125,000 auction transactions every day, with 12 billion cut flowers and 1.3 billion plants trading in a year.

Free Entry and Exit. The ability of firms to enter and exit a market freely leads to a large number of firms in a market and promotes price taking. Suppose a firm can raise its price and increase its profit. If other firms are not able to enter the market, the firm will not be a price taker. However, if other firms can quickly and easily enter the market, the higher profit will encourage entry until the price is driven back to the original level. Free exit is also important: If firms can freely enter a market but cannot exit easily if prices decline, they might be reluctant to enter the market in response to a short-run profit opportunity in the first place.[3]

Deviations from Perfect Competition

A good example of perfect competition is the wheat market, which has many *price-taking* buyers and sellers. Many thousands of farmers produce virtually *identical products*. Wheat is sold in formal exchanges or markets such as the Chicago Commodity Exchange, where buyers and sellers have *full information* about products and prices. Market participants can easily place, buy, or sell orders in person, by phone, or electronically, so *transaction costs are negligible*. No time is wasted finding someone who wants to trade, and transactions are virtually instantaneous without much paperwork. Moreover, *buyers and sellers can easily enter this market*.

However, there are many markets that do not exhibit all the characteristics of perfect competition but are still highly competitive, in which buyers and sellers are,

---

[2]Average number of hours per week that an American and a Chinese person, respectively, spend shopping: 4, 10.—*Harper's Index*, 2008.

[3]For example, some governments require that firms give workers six months warning before they exit a market.

for all practical purposes, still price takers. For example, a government may limit entry into a market, but if there are still many buyers and sellers, they may still be price takers. Similarly, even if only some customers have full information about prices, that may be sufficient to prevent firms from deviating significantly from price taking.

Economists often use the terms *competition* and *competitive* when describing these markets where firms are, for all practical purposes, price takers even though the market does not fully possess all the characteristics of perfect competition. A firm in such a market might have a slight but insignificant ability to raise prices without losing its customer base. From now on, we will not distinguish between markets that are perfectly competitive and those that are highly competitive. We will use the terms *competition* and *competitive* to refer to all markets in which no buyer or seller can significantly affect the market price.

Derivation of a Competitive Firm's Demand Curve

Are the demand curves faced by individual competitive firms actually flat? To answer this question, we use a modified supply-and-demand diagram to derive the demand curve for an individual firm.

An individual firm faces a **residual demand curve**: the market demand that is not met by other sellers at any given price. The firm's residual demand function, $D^r(p)$, shows the quantity demanded from the firm at price p. A firm sells only to people who have not already purchased the good from another seller. We can determine how much demand is left for a particular firm at each possible price using the market demand curve and the supply curve for all *other* firms in the market. The quantity the market demands is a function of the price: $Q = D(p)$. The supply curve of the other firms is $S^o(p)$. The residual demand function equals the market demand function, $D(p)$, minus the supply function of all other firms:

$$D^r(p) = D(p) - S^o(p). \tag{8.1}$$

At prices so high that the amount supplied by other firms, $S^o(p)$, is greater than the quantity demanded by the market, $D(p)$, the residual quantity demanded, $D^r(p)$, is zero.

In Figure 8.1, we derive the residual demand for a Canadian manufacturing firm that produces metal chairs. Panel b shows the market demand curve, D, and the supply of all but one manufacturing firm, S^o.[4] At $p = \$66$ per chair, the supply of other firms, 500 units (where a unit is 1,000 metal chairs) per year, equals the market demand (panel b), so the residual quantity demanded of the remaining firm (panel a) is zero.

At prices below \$66, the other chair firms are not willing to supply as much as the market demands. At $p = \$63$, for example, the market demand is 527 units, but other firms want to supply only 434 units. As a result, the residual quantity demanded from the individual firm at $p = \$63$ is 93 ($= 527 - 434$) units. Thus, the residual demand curve at any given price is the horizontal difference between the market demand curve and the supply curve of the other firms.

The residual demand curve that the firm faces in panel a is much flatter than the market demand curve in panel b. As a result, the elasticity of the residual demand curve is much higher than the market elasticity.

---

[4]The figure uses constant elasticity demand and supply curves (Chapter 2). The elasticity of supply is based on the estimated cost function from Robidoux and Lester (1988) for Canadian office furniture manufacturers. I estimate that the market elasticity of demand is $\varepsilon = -1.1$, using data from *Statistics Canada, Office Furniture Manufacturers*.

Figure 8.1 Residual Demand Curve

The residual demand curve, $D^r(p)$, faced by a single office furniture manufacturing firm is the market demand, $D(p)$, minus the supply of the other firms in the market, $S^o(p)$. The residual demand curve is much flatter than the market demand curve.

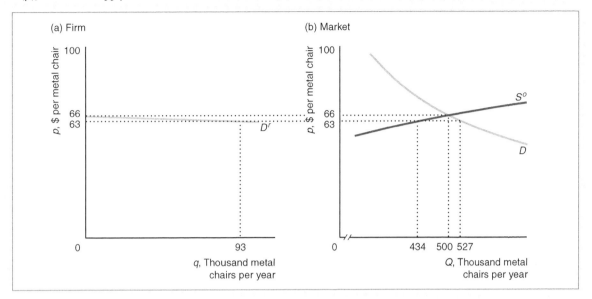

If there are n identical firms in the market, the elasticity of demand, ε_i, facing Firm i is

$$\varepsilon_i = n\varepsilon - (n-1)\eta_o, \tag{8.2}$$

where ε is the market elasticity of demand (a negative number), η_o is the elasticity of supply of each of the other firms (typically a positive number), and $n - 1$ is the number of other firms.[5]

There are $n = 78$ firms manufacturing metal chairs in Canada. If they are identical, the elasticity of demand facing a single firm is

$$\varepsilon_i = n\varepsilon - (n-1)\eta_o = [78 \times (-1.1)] - (77 \times 3.1) = -85.8 - 238.7 = -324.5.$$

---

[5]To derive Equation 8.2, we start by differentiating the residual demand function, Equation 8.1, with respect to p:

$$\frac{dD^r}{dp} = \frac{dD}{dp} - \frac{dS^o}{dp}.$$

Because the n firms in the market are identical, each firm produces $q = Q/n$, where Q is total output. The output produced by the other firms is $Q_o = (n-1)q$. Multiplying both sides of the previous expression by p/q and multiplying and dividing the first term on the right-hand side by Q/Q and the second term by Q_o/Q_o, this expression may be rewritten as

$$\frac{dD^r}{dp}\frac{p}{q} = \frac{dD}{dp}\frac{p}{Q}\frac{Q}{q} - \frac{dS^o}{dp}\frac{p}{Q_o}\frac{Q_o}{q},$$

where $q = D^r(p)$, $Q = D(p)$, and $Q_o = S^o(p)$. This expression can be rewritten as Equation 8.2 by noting that $Q/q = n$, $Q_o/q = (n-1)$, $(dD^r/dp)(p/q) = \varepsilon_i$, $(dD/dp)(p/Q) = \varepsilon$, and $(dS^o/dp)(p/Q_o) = \eta_o$.

That is, a typical firm faces a residual demand elasticity, $\varepsilon_i = -324.5$, that's nearly 300 times the market elasticity, -1.1. If a firm raises its price by one-tenth of a percent, the quantity it can sell falls by nearly one-third. Therefore, the competitive model assumption that this firm faces a horizontal demand curve with an infinite price elasticity is not much of an exaggeration.

As Equation 8.2 shows, a firm's residual demand curve is more elastic the more firms, n, are in the market, the more elastic the market demand, ε, and the larger the elasticity of supply of the other firms, η_o. If the supply curve slopes upward, the residual demand elasticity, ε_i, must be at least as elastic as $n\varepsilon$ (because the second term makes the estimate only more elastic), so using $n\varepsilon$ as an approximation is conservative. For example, even though the market elasticity of demand for soybeans is very inelastic at about -0.2, because there are roughly 107,000 soybean farms, so the residual demand facing a single farm must be at least $n\varepsilon = 107{,}000 \times (-0.2) = -21{,}400$, which is extremely elastic.

Why Perfect Competition Is Important

Perfectly competitive markets are important for two reasons. First, many markets can be reasonably described as competitive. Many agricultural and other commodity markets, stock exchanges, retail and wholesale, building construction, and other types of markets have many or all of the properties of a perfectly competitive market. The competitive supply-and-demand model works well enough in these markets that it accurately predicts the effects of changes in taxes, costs, incomes, and other factors on market equilibrium.

Second, a perfectly competitive market has many desirable properties. Economists use this model as the ideal against which real-world markets are compared. Throughout the rest of this book, we consider that society as a whole is worse off if the properties of the perfectly competitive market fail to hold. From this point on, for brevity, we use the phrase *competitive market* to mean a *perfectly competitive market* unless we explicitly note an imperfection.

8.2 Profit Maximization

"Too caustic?" To hell with the cost. If it's a good picture, we'll make it.
—Samuel Goldwyn

Economists usually assume that *all* firms—not just competitive firms—want to maximize their profits. One reason is that many businesspeople say that their objective is to maximize profits. A second reason is that a firm—especially a competitive firm—that does not maximize profit is likely to lose money and be driven out of business. In this section, we examine how any type of firm—not just a competitive firm—maximizes its profit.

Profit

A firm's *profit*, π, is the difference between its revenues, R, and its cost, C:

$$\pi = R - C.$$

If profit is negative, $\pi < 0$, the firm makes a *loss*.

Measuring a firm's revenue sales is straightforward: revenue is price times quantity. Measuring cost is more challenging. From the economic point of view, the correct measure of cost is the *opportunity cost* or *economic cost*: the value of the best alternative use of any input the firm employs. As discussed in Chapter 7, the full opportunity cost of inputs used might exceed the explicit or out-of-pocket costs recorded in financial accounting statements. This distinction is important because a firm may make a serious mistake if it incorrectly measures profit by ignoring some relevant opportunity costs.

We always refer to *profit* or **economic profit** as revenue minus opportunity (economic) cost. For tax or other reasons, *business profit* may differ. For example, if a firm uses only explicit cost, then its reported profit may be larger than its economic profit.

A couple of examples illustrate the difference between the two profit measures and the importance of this distinction. Suppose you start your own firm.[6] You have to pay explicit costs such as workers' wages and the price of materials. Like many owners, you do not pay yourself a salary. Instead, you take home a business profit based on explicit costs only of $20,000 per year.

Economists (well-known spoilsports) argue that your profit is less than $20,000. Economic profit equals your business profit minus any additional opportunity cost. Suppose that instead of running your own business, you could have earned $25,000 a year working for someone else. The opportunity cost of your time working for your business is $25,000—your forgone salary. So even though your firm made a business profit of $20,000, your economic loss (negative economic profit) is $5,000. Put another way, the price of being your own boss is $5,000.

By looking at only the explicit cost and ignoring opportunity cost, you conclude that running your business is profitable. However, if you consider economic profit, you realize that working for others maximizes your income.

Similarly, when a firm decides whether to invest in a new venture, it must consider the next best alternative use of its funds. A firm considering setting up a new branch in Tucson must evaluate all the alternatives: placing the branch in Santa Fe, depositing the money it would otherwise spend on the new branch in the bank where it earns interest, and so on. If the best alternative use of the money is to put it in the bank and earn $10,000 per year in interest, the firm should build the new branch in Tucson only if it expects to make $10,000 or more per year in business profit. That is, the firm should create a Tucson branch only if its economic profit from the new branch is zero or greater. If its economic profit is zero, then it is earning the same return on its investment as it would from putting the money into its next best alternative, the bank.

APPLICATION

Breaking Even on Christmas Trees

On the day after Thanksgiving each year, Tom Ruffino begins selling Christmas trees in Lake Grove, New York. The table is an accounting statement of his seasonal explicit costs.

Mr. Ruffino sells trees for 29 days at the market price of $25 each. To break even, he has to sell an average of 45 trees per day, so his average cost is $25. If he can sell an average of 52 trees per day (1,508 trees total), he makes an accounting profit of $5,090 for the season.

To calculate his economic profit, he must subtract his forgone earnings at another job and the interest he would have earned on the money he paid at the beginning of the month (on his fixed costs and the price of the trees, $27,110) if

---

[6]Michael Dell started a mail-order computer company while he was in college. Today, his company is the world's largest personal computer company. In 2010, *Forbes* estimated Mr. Dell's wealth at $13.5 billion.

he had invested that money elsewhere, such as a bank, for a month. Although the forgone interest is small, his alternative earnings could be a large proportion of his business profit.

Fixed Costs	
Permit	$300
Security (guard patrol to prevent theft when the lot is closed)	360
Insurance	700
Electricity	1,000
Lot rental (undeveloped land across from a major shopping mall)	2,500
Miscellaneous (fences, lot cleanup, snow removal)	2,000
Total fixed costs:	$6,860
Variable Costs	
Labor (two full-time employees at $12 an hour for 50 hours a week, plus some part-time workers)	$5,500
Trees (1,500 trees bought from a Canadian tree farm at $11.50 each)	17,250
Shipping (1,500 trees at $2 each)	3,000
Total variable costs:	$25,750
Total Accounting Costs	$32,610

Two Steps to Maximizing Profit

Any firm (not just a competitive firm) uses a two-step process to maximize profit. Because both revenue and cost vary with output, a firm's profit varies with its output level. Its profit function is

$$\pi(q) = R(q) - C(q), \tag{8.3}$$

where $R(q)$ is its revenue function and $C(q)$ is its cost function. To maximize its profit, a firm must answer two questions:

1. **Output decision:** If the firm produces, what output level, q^*, maximizes its profit or minimizes its loss?
2. **Shutdown decision:** Is it more profitable to produce q^* or to shut down and produce no output?

We use the profit curve in Figure 8.2 to illustrate these two basic decisions. This firm makes losses at very low and very high output levels and makes positive profits at moderate output levels. The profit curve first rises and then falls, reaching a maximum profit of π^* when its output is q^*. Because the firm makes a positive profit at that output, it chooses to produce q^* units of output.

Output Rules. A firm can use one of three equivalent rules to choose how much output to produce. All types of firms maximize profit using the same rules.

The most straightforward rule is:

Output Rule 1: *The firm sets its output where its profit is maximized.*
The profit curve in Figure 8.2 is maximized at π^* when output is q^*. If the firm knows its entire profit curve, it can immediately set its output to maximize its profit.

Figure 8.2 Maximizing Profit

By setting its output at q^*, the firm maximizes its profit at π^*, where $d\pi/dq = 0$.

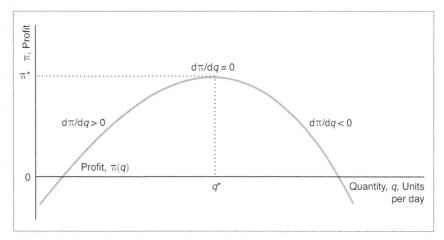

Even if the firm does not know the exact shape of its profit curve, it may be able to find the maximum by experimenting: The firm slightly increases its output. If profit increases, the firm increases the output more. The firm keeps increasing output until its profit does not change. At that output, the firm is at the peak of the profit curve. If profit falls when the firm first increases its output, the firm tries decreasing its output. It keeps decreasing its output until it reaches the peak of the profit curve.

What the firm is doing is experimentally determining the slope of the profit curve. The slope of the profit curve is the firm's **marginal profit**: the change in the profit the firm gets from selling one more unit of output, $d\pi/dq$. In the figure, the marginal profit or slope is positive when output is less than q^*, zero when output is q^*, and negative when output is greater than q^*.

Thus,

Output Rule 2: *A firm sets its output where its marginal profit is zero.*

We obtain this result formally using the first-order condition for a profit maximum. We set the derivative of the profit function, Equation 8.3, with respect to quantity equal to zero:

$$\frac{d\pi(q^*)}{dq} = 0. \tag{8.4}$$

Equation 8.4 states that a necessary condition for profit to be maximized is that the quantity be set at q^* where the firm's marginal profit with respect to quantity equals zero.

Equation 8.4 is a necessary condition for profit to be maximized. Sufficiency requires, in addition, that the second-order condition hold:

$$\frac{d^2\pi(q^*)}{dq^2} < 0. \tag{8.5}$$

That is, for profit to be maximized at q^*, when we increase the output beyond q^*, the marginal profit must decline.

Because profit is a function of revenue and cost, we can state this last condition in one additional way. We can obtain another necessary condition for profit maximization by setting the derivative of $\pi(q) = R(q) - C(q)$ with respect to output equal to zero:

$$\frac{d\pi(q^*)}{dq} = \frac{dR(q^*)}{dq} - \frac{dC(q^*)}{dq} = MR(q^*) - MC(q^*) = 0. \quad (8.6)$$

The derivative of cost with respect to output, $dC(q)/dq = MC(q)$, is its marginal cost (Chapter 7). The firm's **marginal revenue**, MR, is the change in revenue it gains from selling one more unit of output: dR/dq. Equation 8.6 shows that a necessary condition for profit to be maximized is that the firm set its quantity at q^* where the difference between the firm's marginal revenue and marginal cost is zero. Thus, a third, equivalent rule is:

Output Rule 3: *A firm sets its output where its marginal revenue equals its marginal cost,*

$$MR(q^*) = MC(q^*). \quad (8.7)$$

For profit to be maximized at q^*, the second-order condition must hold:

$$\frac{d^2\pi(q^*)}{dq^2} = \frac{d^2R(q^*)}{dq^2} - \frac{d^2C(q^*)}{dq^2} = \frac{dMR(q^*)}{dq} - \frac{dMC(q^*)}{dq} < 0. \quad (8.8)$$

That is, for profit to be maximized at q^*, the slope of the marginal revenue curve, dMR/dq, must be less than the slope of the marginal cost curve, dMC/dq.

Shutdown Rule. The firm chooses to produce q^* if it can make a profit. But even if the firm maximizes its profit at q^*, it does not necessarily follow that the firm is making a positive profit. If the firm makes a loss, does it shut down? Surprisingly, the answer is "It depends." The general rule, which holds for all types of firms in both the short and long run, is:

Shutdown Rule 1: *The firm shuts down only if it can reduce its loss by doing so.*
In the short run, the firm has variable costs, such as from labor and materials, and fixed plant and equipment costs (Chapter 7). If the fixed cost is a *sunk* cost, this expense cannot be avoided by stopping operations—the firm pays this cost whether it shuts down or not. Thus, the sunk fixed cost is irrelevant to the shutdown decision. By shutting down, the firm stops receiving revenue and stops paying avoidable costs, but it is still stuck with its fixed cost. Thus, it pays for the firm to shut down only if its revenue is less than its avoidable cost.

Suppose that the firm's revenue is $R = \$2,000$, its variable cost is $VC = \$1,000$, and its fixed cost is $F = \$3,000$, which is the price it paid for a machine that it cannot resell or use for any other purpose. This firm is making a short-run loss:

$$\pi = R - VC - F = \$2,000 - \$1,000 - \$3,000 = -\$2,000.$$

If the firm shuts down, it still has to pay its fixed cost of $3,000, and hence it loses $2,000. Because its fixed cost is sunk, the firm should ignore it when making its shutdown decision. Ignoring the fixed cost, the firm sees that its $2,000 revenue exceeds its $1,000 avoidable, variable cost by $1,000, so it does not shut down. The extra $1,000 can be used to offset some of the fixed cost.

However, if its revenue is only $500, it cannot cover the $1,000 avoidable, variable cost, and loses $500. Adding this $500 loss to the $3,000 it must pay in fixed cost, the firm's total loss is $3,500. Because the firm can reduce its loss from $3,500 to $3,000 by ceasing operations, it shuts down. (Remember the shutdown rule: The firm shuts down only if it can reduce its loss by doing so.)

In conclusion, the firm compares its revenue to its variable cost only when deciding whether to stop operating. Because the fixed cost is *sunk*—the expense cannot be avoided by stopping operations (Chapter 7)—the firm pays this cost whether it shuts down or not. Thus, the sunk fixed cost is irrelevant to the shutdown decision.

We usually assume that fixed cost is *sunk* (Chapter 7). However, if a firm can sell its capital for as much as it paid, its fixed cost is *avoidable* and should be taken into account when the firm is considering whether to shut down. A firm with a fully avoidable fixed cost always shuts down if it makes a short-run loss. If a firm buys a specialized piece of machinery for $1,000 that can be used only for its business but can be sold for scrap metal for $100, then $100 of the fixed cost is avoidable and $900 is sunk. Only the avoidable portion of a fixed cost is relevant for the shutdown decision.

In the long run, all costs are avoidable because the firm can eliminate them all by shutting down. Thus, in the long run, where the firm can avoid all losses by not operating, it pays to shut down if the firm faces any loss at all. As a result, we can restate the shutdown rule, which holds for all types of firms in both the short run and the long run, as:

Shutdown Rule 2: *The firm shuts down only if its revenue is less than its avoidable cost.*

8.3 Competition in the Short Run

Having considered how firms maximize profit in general, we now examine the profit-maximizing behavior of competitive firms, paying careful attention to firms' shutdown decisions. In this section, we focus on the short run.

Short-Run Competitive Profit Maximization

A competitive firm, like other firms, first determines the output at which it maximizes its profit (or minimizes its loss). Second, it decides whether to produce or to shut down.

Short-Run Output Decision. We've already seen that *any* firm maximizes its profit at the output where its marginal profit is zero or, equivalently, where its marginal cost equals its marginal revenue. *Because it faces a horizontal demand curve, a competitive firm can sell as many units of output as it wants at the market price, p.* Thus, a competitive firm's revenue, $R(q) = pq$, increases by p if it sells one more unit of output, so its marginal revenue equals the market price: $MR = d(pq)/dq = p$. A competitive firm maximizes its profit by choosing its output such that

$$\frac{d\pi(q^*)}{dq} = \frac{dpq^*}{dq} - \frac{dC(q^*)}{dq} = p - MC(q^*) = 0. \tag{8.9}$$

That is, because a competitive firm's marginal revenue equals the market price, a profit-maximizing competitive firm produces the amount of output q^* at which its *marginal cost equals the market price*: $MC(q^*) = p$.

For the quantity determined by Equation 8.9 to maximize profit, the second-order condition must hold: $d^2\pi(q^*)/dq^2 = dp/dq - dMC(q^*)/dq < 0$. Because the firm's marginal revenue, p, does not vary with q, $dp/dq = 0$. Thus, the second-order condition requires that the second derivative of the cost function (the first derivative of the marginal cost function) with respect to quantity evaluated at the profit-maximizing quantity is positive:

$$\frac{dMC(q^*)}{dq} > 0. \tag{8.10}$$

Equation 8.10 requires that the marginal cost curve be upward sloping at q^*.

To illustrate how a competitive firm maximizes its profit, we examine a typical Canadian lime manufacturing firm (based on the estimates of the variable cost function by Robidoux and Lester, 1988). Lime is a nonmetallic mineral used in mortars, plasters, cements, bleaching powders, steel, paper, glass, and other products. The lime plant's estimated cost curve, C, in panel a of Figure 8.3 rises less rapidly with output at low quantities than at higher quantities.[7] If the market price of lime is $p = 8$, the competitive firm faces a horizontal demand curve at 8 (in panel b), so the revenue curve, $R = pq = 8q$, in panel a is an upward-sloping straight line with a slope of 8.

By producing 284 units (where a unit is 1,000 metric tons), the firm maximizes its profit at $\pi^* = \$426,000$, which is the height of the profit curve and the difference between the revenue and cost curves at that quantity in panel a. At the competitive firm's profit-maximizing output, determined by Equation 8.9, its marginal cost equals the market price of \$8 at point e in panel b.

Point e is the competitive firm's equilibrium. Were the firm to produce less than the equilibrium quantity, 284 units, the market price would be above its marginal cost. As a result, the firm could increase its profit by expanding output because it earns more on the next ton, $p = 8$, than it costs to produce it, $MC < 8$. If the firm were to produce more than 284 units, so that market price was below its marginal cost, $MC > 8$, the firm could increase its profit by reducing its output. Thus, the firm does not want to change the quantity that it sells only if it is producing where its marginal cost equals the market price.

The firm's maximum profit, $\pi^* = \$426,000$, is the shaded rectangle in panel b. The length of the rectangle is the number of units sold, $q = 284$ units. The height of the rectangle is the firm's average profit, which is the difference between the market price, or average revenue, and its average cost:

$$\frac{\pi}{q} = \frac{R}{q} - \frac{C}{q} = \frac{pq}{q} - \frac{C}{q} = p - AC. \tag{8.11}$$

Here, the average profit per unit is $p - AC(284) = \$8 - \$6.50 = \$1.50$.

As panel b illustrates, the firm chooses its output level to maximize its total profit rather than its profit per ton. By producing 140 units, where its average cost is minimized at \$6, the firm could maximize its average profit at \$2. Although the firm gives up 50¢ in profit per ton when it produces 284 units instead of 140 units, it more than compensates for that by selling an extra 144 units. The firm's profit is \$146,000 higher at 284 units than at 140 units.

Using the $MC = p$ rule, a firm can decide how much to alter its output in response to a change in its cost due to a new tax. For example, only one of the many lime plants in Canada is in the province of Manitoba. If that province taxes that lime firm, the Manitoba firm is the only one in the lime market affected by the tax, so the tax will not affect market price. Solved Problem 8.1 shows how a profit-maximizing competitive firm would react to a tax that affected it alone.

---

[7]In the figure, we assume that the minimum of the average variable cost curve is \$5 at 50,000 metric tons of output. Based on information from *Statistics Canada*, we set the fixed cost so that the average cost is \$6 at 140,000 tons.

Figure 8.3 How a Competitive Firm Maximizes Profit

(a) A competitive lime manufacturing firm produces 284 units of lime so as to maximize its profit at $\pi^* =$ $426,000 (Robidoux and Lester, 1988). (b) The firm's profit is maximized where its marginal revenue, MR, which is the market price $p = \$8$, equals its marginal cost, MC.

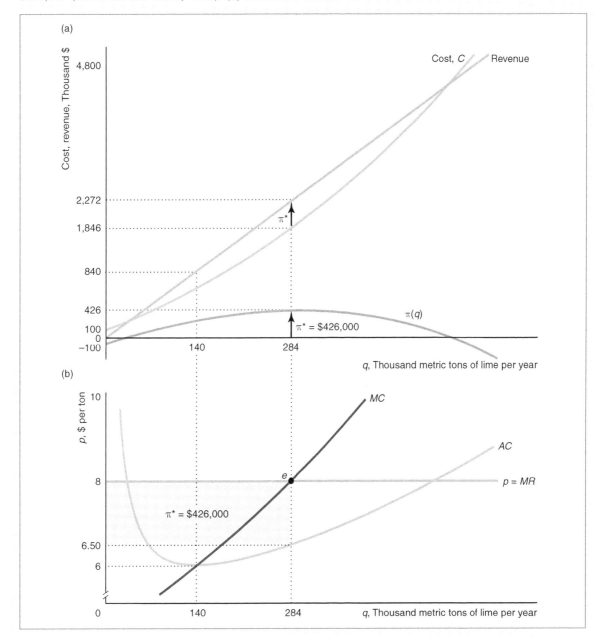

SOLVED PROBLEM 8.1

A specific tax of τ is collected from only one competitive firm. What is the firm's before-tax, profit-maximizing output level? What is its profit-maximizing output after the tax is imposed? How does its output change due to the tax? How does its profit change due to the tax? Answer using both calculus and a graph.

Answer

1. *Use calculus to find the firm's profit-maximizing output before the tax is imposed.* The firm's before-tax profit function is $\pi = pq - C(q)$. According to its first-order condition for a profit maximum, it sets its output at q_1 where $d\pi(q_1)/dq = p - dC(q_1)/dq = 0$, or $p = MC(q_1)$. As the figure shows, the firm maximizes its profit at e_1, where its MC^1 marginal cost curve crosses the market price line.

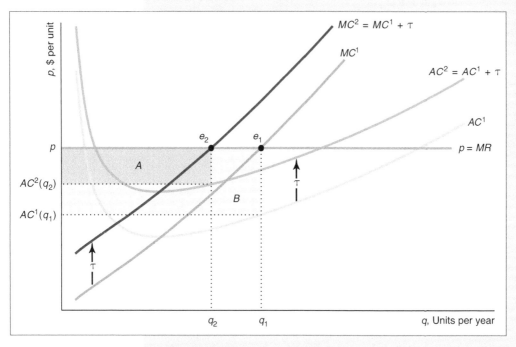

2. *Use calculus to find the firm's profit-maximizing output after the tax is imposed.* The after-tax profit is $\bar{\pi} = pq - C(q) - \tau q$. The firm maximizes its profit at q_2 where

$$\frac{d\bar{\pi}(q_2)}{dq} = p - \frac{dC(q_2)}{dq} - \tau = 0, \qquad (8.12)$$

or $p = MC(q_2) + \tau$. (If $\tau = 0$, we obtain the same result as in our before-tax analysis.) The figure shows that the firm's after-tax marginal cost curve shifts from MC^1 to $MC^2 = MC^1 + \tau$. Because the firm is a price taker and the tax is applied to only this one firm, its marginal revenue before and after the tax is the market price, p. In the figure, the firm's new maximum is at e_2.

3. *Use comparative statics to determine how a change in the tax rate affects output.* Given the first-order condition, Equation 8.12, we can write the optimal quantity as a function of the tax rate: $q(\tau)$. Differentiating the first-order condition with respect to τ, we obtain

$$-\frac{d^2C}{dq^2}\frac{dq}{d\tau} - 1 = -\frac{dMC}{dq}\frac{dq}{d\tau} - 1 = 0.$$

The second-order condition for a profit maximum, Equation 8.10, requires that dMC/dq be negative, so

$$\frac{dq}{d\tau} = -\frac{1}{dMC/dq} < 0. \tag{8.13}$$

At $\tau = 0$, the firm chooses q_1. As τ increases, the firm reduces its output as Equation 8.13 shows. The figure shows that the tax shifts the firm's after-tax marginal cost curve up by τ, so it produces less, reducing its output from q_1 to q_2. (*Note*: The figure shows a relatively large change in tax, whereas the calculus analysis examines a marginal change.)

4. *Show that the profit must fall using the definition of a maximum or by showing that profit falls at every output.* Because the firm's before-tax profit is maximized at q_1, when the firm reduces its output in response to the tax, its before-tax profit falls: $\pi(q_2) < \pi(q_1)$. Because its after-tax profit is lower than its before-tax profit at *any given output level*, $\underline{p}(q_2) = \pi(q_2) - \tau q_2 < \pi(q_2)$, its profit must fall after the tax: $\bar{\pi}(q_2) < \pi(q_1)$.

We can also show this result by noting that the firm's average cost curve shifts up by τ from AC^1 to $AC^2 = AC^1 + \tau$ in the figure, so the firm's profit at every output level falls because the market price remains constant. The firm sells fewer units (because of the increase in marginal cost) and makes less profit per unit (because of the increase in average cost). The after-tax profit is area $A = \bar{\pi}(q_2) = [p - AC(q_2) - \tau]q_2$, and the before-tax profit is area $A + B = \pi(q_1) = [p - AC(q_1)]q_1$, so profit falls by area B due to the tax.

Short-Run Shutdown Decision. Does the competitive lime firm operate or shut down? At the market price of $8 in Figure 8.3, the lime firm makes an economic profit, so it chooses to operate.

If the market price falls below $6, which is the minimum of the average cost curve, the price does not cover average cost, so average profit, Equation 8.11, is negative, and the firm suffers a loss. (A firm cannot "lose a little on every sale but make it up on volume.") The firm shuts down only if doing so reduces or eliminates its loss. This shutdown may be temporary: When the market price rises, the firm resumes producing.

The firm can gain by shutting down only if its revenue is less than its short-run variable cost:

$$pq < VC(q). \tag{8.14}$$

By dividing both sides of Equation 8.14 by output, we can write this condition as

$$p < \frac{VC(q)}{q} = AVC. \tag{8.15}$$

A competitive firm shuts down if the market price is less than the minimum of its short-run average variable cost curve.

We illustrate this rule in Figure 8.4 using the Canadian lime firm's cost curves. The minimum of the average variable cost, point *a*, is $5 at 50 units (one unit again

Figure 8.4 The Short-Run Shutdown Decision

The competitive lime manufacturing plant operates if price is above the minimum of the average variable cost curve, point a, at $5. With a market price of $5.50, the firm produces 100 units because that price is above AVC(100) = $5.14, so the firm more than covers its out-of-pocket, variable costs. At that price, the firm suffers a loss of area A = $62,000 because the price is less than the average cost of $6.12. If it shuts down, its loss is its fixed cost, area A + B = $98,000. Therefore, the firm does not shut down.

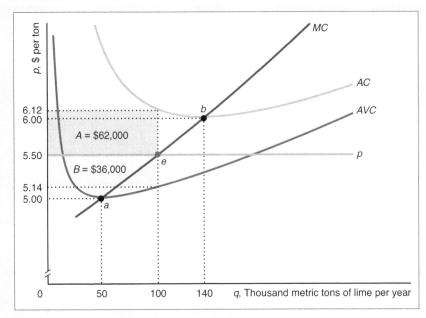

being 1,000 metric tons). If the market price is less than $5 per ton, the firm shuts down. The firm stops hiring labor, buying materials, and paying for energy, thereby avoiding these variable costs. If the market price rises above $5, the firm starts operating again.

In this figure, the market price is $5.50 per ton. Because the minimum of the firm's average cost, $6 (point b), is more than $5.50, the firm loses money if it produces.

If the firm produces, it sells 100 units at e, where its marginal cost curve intersects its demand curve, which is horizontal at $5.50. By operating, the firm loses area A, or $62,000. The length of A is 100 units, and the height is the average loss per ton, or 62¢, which equals the price of $5.50 minus the average cost at 100 units of $6.12.

The firm is better off producing than shutting down. If the firm shuts down, it has no revenue or variable cost, so its loss is the fixed cost, $98,000, which equals area A + B. The length of this box is 100 units, and its height is the lost average fixed cost of 98¢, which is the difference between the average variable cost and the average cost at 100 units.

The firm saves area B = $36,000 by producing rather than shutting down. This amount is the money left over from the revenue after paying for the variable cost, which helps cover part of the fixed cost. Thus, even if $p < AC$ so that the firm makes a loss, the firm continues to operate if $p > AVC$ because it more than covers its variable costs.

In summary, a competitive firm uses a two-step decision-making process to maximize its profit. First, the competitive firm determines the output that maximizes its profit or minimizes its loss when its marginal cost equals the market price (which is its marginal revenue): $MC = p$. Second, the firm chooses to produce that quantity unless it would lose more by operating than by shutting down. The firm shuts down only if the market price is less than the minimum of its average variable cost, $p < AVC$.

APPLICATION

Oil, Oil Sands, and Oil Shale Shutdowns

Oil production starts and stops as prices fluctuate. In 1998–1999, 74,000 of the 136,000 oil wells in the United States were temporarily shut down or permanently abandoned. At the time, Terry Smith, the general manager of Tidelands Oil Production Company, who had shut down 327 of his company's 834 wells, said that he would operate these wells again when the price rose above $10 a barrel—his minimum average variable cost. Getting oil from oil wells is relatively easy. It is harder and more costly to obtain oil from other sources, so firms that use those alternative sources have higher shutdown points.

Canada has enormous quantities of one such alternate source. As a consequence, it has the second-largest known oil reserves in the world, 180 billion barrels, trailing only Saudi Arabia's 259 billion barrels, and far exceeding third-place Iraq's 113 billion and the Arctic National Wildlife Refuge's estimated 10 billion. You rarely see discussions of Canada's vast oil reserves in newspapers because 97% of those reserves are oil sands, which cover an area the size of Florida.

Oil sands are a mixture of heavy petroleum (bitumen), water, and sandstone. Producing oil from oil sands is extremely expensive and polluting. To liberate four barrels of crude from the sands, a processor must burn the equivalent of a fifth barrel. With the technology available in 2006, two tons of sand yielded a single barrel (42 gallons) of oil and produced more greenhouse gas emissions than do four cars operating for a day. Today's limited production draws from the one-fifth of the oil sands deposits that lie close enough to the surface to allow strip mining. Going after deeper deposits will be even more expensive. The Alberta government estimates that 173 billion barrels of oil are economically recoverable today but that more than 300 billion barrels may one day be produced from the oil sands.

The first large oil sands mining began in the 1960s, but as oil prices were often less than the $25-per-barrel average variable cost of recovering crude from the sand, production was frequently halted. From mid 2009 through the first quarter of 2010, a barrel of oil sold for between $60 and $80 a barrel and technological improvements had lowered the average variable cost to $18 a barrel, so firms produced oil from oil sands. Because they expect oil prices to remain adequately high, virtually every large U.S. oil firm and one Chinese firm have Canadian oil sands projects, and their planned investments over the next decade exceed $25 billion.

Even these gigantic oil sands deposits may be exceeded by oil shale. According to some current estimates, oil shale deposits in Colorado and neighboring areas of Utah and Wyoming contain 800 billion recoverable barrels, the equivalent of 40 years of U.S. oil consumption. The United States has between 1 and 2 trillion recoverable barrels from oil shale, which is at least four times Saudi Arabia's proven reserves. A 2007 federal task force report concluded that the United States will be able to produce 3 million barrels of oil a day from oil shale and sands by 2035. Oil shale is much more difficult to extract and to transform into crude oil than are oil sands. Shell Oil now believes that it will be profitable to extract oil from shale at $30 a barrel. As soon as that occurs, if current oil prices stay as high as they currently are, oil shale production facilities will start operating, joining oil wells and oil sand producers.

Short-Run Firm Supply Curve

We just analyzed how a competitive firm chooses its output for a given market price to maximize its profit. By repeating this analysis at different possible market prices, we can derive the firm's short-run supply curve, which shows how the quantity supplied by the competitive firm varies with the market price.

Tracing Out the Short-Run Supply Curve. As the market price increases from $p_1 = \$5$ to $p_2 = \$6$ to $p_3 = \$7$ to $p_4 = \$8$, the lime firm increases its output from 50 to 140 to 215 to 285 units per year, as Figure 8.5 shows. The equilibrium at each market price, e_1 through e_4, is determined by the intersection of the relevant demand curve—market price line—and the firm's marginal cost curve. That is, as the market price increases, the equilibria trace out the marginal cost curve.

If the price falls below the firm's minimum average variable cost of \$5, the firm shuts down. Thus, the competitive firm's short-run supply curve is its marginal cost curve above its minimum average variable cost.

The firm's short-run supply curve, S, is a thick line in the figure. At prices above \$5, the short-run supply curve is the same as the marginal cost curve. The supply is zero when price is less than the minimum of the AVC curve of \$5. (From now on, for simplicity, the graphs will not show the supply curve at prices below the minimum AVC.)

Figure 8.5 How the Profit-Maximizing Quantity Varies with Price

As the market price increases, the lime manufacturing firm produces more output. The change in the price traces out the marginal cost curve of the firm.

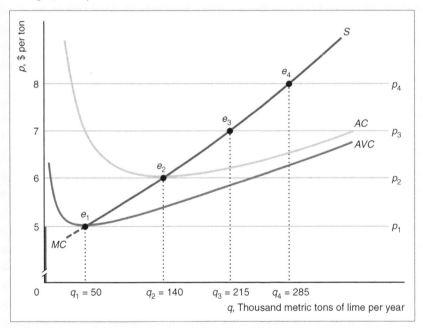

SOLVED PROBLEM 8.2

Given that a competitive firm's short-run cost function is $C(q) = 100q - 4q^2 + 0.2q^3 + 450$, what is the firm's short-run supply curve? If the price is $p = 115$, how much output does the firm supply?

Answer

1. *Determine the firm's supply curve by calculating for which output levels the firm's marginal cost is greater than its minimum average variable cost.* The firm's supply curve is its marginal cost above its minimum average variable cost. From Solved Problem 7.2, we know that $MC(q) = dC(q)/dq 100 - 8q + 0.6q^2$ and $AVC(q) = VC(q)/q = 100 - 4q + 0.2q^2$. We also know that the marginal cost cuts the average variable cost at its minimum (Chapter 7), so we can determine the $\underline{q}$ where the AVC reaches its minimum by equating the AVC and MC functions: $AVC = 100 - 4\underline{q} + 0.2\underline{q}^2 = 100 - 8\underline{q} + 0.6\underline{q}^2 = MC$. Solving, the minimum is $\underline{q} = 10$, as Figure 7.1 illustrates. Thus, the supply curve is the MC curve for output greater than or equal to 10.

2. *Determine the quantity where $p = MC = 115$.* The firm operates where price equals marginal cost. At $p = 115$, the firm produces the quantity q such that $115 = MC = 100 - 8q + 0.6q^2$, or $q = 15$ (see Figure 7.1).

Factor Prices and the Short-Run Firm Supply Curve. An increase in factor prices causes the production costs of a firm to rise, shifting the firm's supply curve to the left. If all factor prices double, it costs the firm twice as much as before to produce a given level of output. If only one factor price rises, costs rise less than in proportion.

To illustrate the effect of an increase in a single factor price on supply, we examine a typical Canadian vegetable oil mill (based on the estimates of the variable cost function for vegetable oil mills by Robidoux and Lester, 1988). This firm uses vegetable oil seed to produce canola and soybean oils, which customers use in commercial baking and soap making as lubricants, and for other purposes. At the initial factor prices, the oil mill's average variable cost curve, AVC^1, reaches its minimum of $7 at 100 units of vegetable oil (where one unit is 100 metric tons), in Figure 8.6. As a result, the firm's initial short-run supply curve, S^1, is the initial marginal cost curve, MC^1, above $7.

Figure 8.6 Effect of an Increase in the Cost of Materials on the Vegetable Oil Supply Curve

Materials are 95% of variable costs, so when the price of materials rises by 25%, variable costs rise by 23.75% (95% of 25%). As a result, the supply curve of a vegetable oil mill shifts upward from S^1 to S^2. If the market price is $12, the quantity supplied falls from 178 to 145 units.

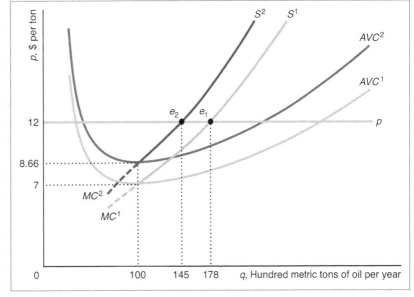

If the wage, the price of energy, or the price of oil seeds increases, the oil mill's cost of production rises. The mill cannot substitute between oil seeds and other factors of production. The cost of oil seeds is 95% of the variable cost. Thus, if the price of raw materials increases by 25%, variable cost rises by 95% × 25%, or 23.75%. This increase in the price of oil seeds causes the marginal cost curve to shift from MC^1 to MC^2 and the average variable cost curve to shift from AVC^1 to AVC^2 in the figure. As a result, the mill's short-run supply curve shifts upward from S^1 to S^2. The price increase causes the shutdown price to rise from $7 per unit to $8.66. At a market price of $12 per unit, at the original factor prices, the mill produces 178 units. After the increase in the price of vegetable oil seeds, the mill produces only 145 units if the market price remains constant.

Short-Run Market Supply Curve

The market supply curve is the horizontal sum of the supply curves of all the individual firms in the market (see Chapter 2). In the short run, the maximum number of firms in a market, n, is fixed because new firms need time to enter the market. If all the firms in a competitive market are identical, each firm's supply curve is identical, so the market supply at any price is n times the supply of an individual firm. Where firms have different shutdown prices, the market supply reflects a different number of firms at various prices even in the short run. We examine competitive markets first with firms that have identical costs and then with firms that have different costs.

Short-Run Market Supply with Identical Firms. To illustrate how to construct a short-run market supply curve, we suppose that the lime manufacturing market has $n = 5$ competitive firms with identical cost curves. Panel a of Figure 8.7 plots the short-run supply curve, S^1, of a typical firm—the MC curve above the minimum AVC—where the horizontal axis shows the firm's output, q, per year. Panel b illus-

Figure 8.7 Short-Run Market Supply with Five Identical Lime Firms

(a) The short-run supply curve, S^1, for a typical lime manufacturing firm is its MC above the minimum of its AVC. (b) The market supply curve, S^5, is the horizontal sum of the supply curves of each of the five identical firms. The curve S^4 shows what the market supply curve would be if there were only four firms in the market.

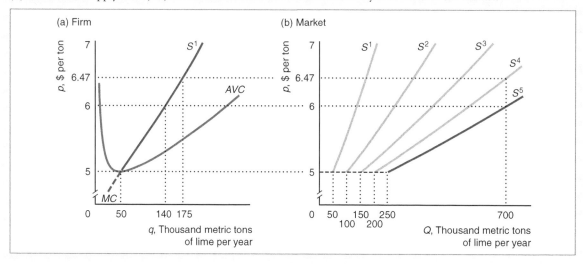

trates the competitive market supply curve, the dark line S^5, where the horizontal axis is market output, Q, per year. The price axis is the same in the two panels.

If the market price is less than $5 per ton, no firm supplies any output, so the market supply is zero. At $5, each firm is willing to supply $q = 50$ units, as in panel a. Consequently, the market supply is $Q = 5q = 250$ units in panel b. At $6 per ton, each firm supplies 140 units, so the market supply is 700 (= 5 × 140) units.

Suppose, however, that there were fewer than five firms in the short run. The light-colored lines in panel b show the market supply curves for various other numbers of firms. The market supply curve is S^1 if there is one price-taking firm, S^2 with two firms, S^3 with three firms, and S^4 with four firms. The market supply curve flattens as the number of firms in the market increases because the market supply curve is the horizontal sum of more and more upward-sloping firm supply curves. As the number of firms grows very large, the market supply curve approaches a horizontal line at $5. Thus, *the more identical firms producing at a given price, the flatter (more elastic) the short-run market supply curve at that price.* As a result, the more firms in the market, the less the price has to increase for the short-run market supply to increase substantially. Consumers pay $6 per ton to obtain 700 units of lime if there are five firms but must pay $6.47 per ton to obtain that amount with only four firms.

Short-Run Market Supply with Firms That Differ. If the firms in a competitive market have different minimum average variable costs, not all firms produce at every price, a situation that affects the shape of the short-run market supply curve. Suppose that the only two firms in the lime market are our typical lime firm with a supply curve of S^1 and another firm with a higher marginal and minimum average cost with the supply curve of S^2 in Figure 8.8. The first firm produces if the market price is at least $5, whereas the second firm does not produce unless the price is $6 or more. At $5, the first firm produces 50 units, so the quantity on the market

Figure 8.8 Short-Run Market Supply with Two Different Lime Firms

The supply curve S^1 is the same as for the typical lime firm in Figure 8.7. A second firm has an MC that lies to the left of the original firm's cost curve and a higher minimum AVC. Thus, its supply curve, S^2, lies above and to the left of the original firm's supply curve, S^1. The market supply curve, S, is the horizontal sum of the two supply curves. When prices are high enough for both firms to produce, at $6 and above, the market supply curve is flatter than the supply curve of either individual firm.

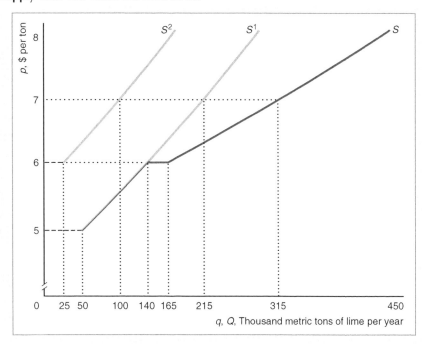

supply curve, S, is 50 units. Between $5 and $6, only the first firm produces, so the market supply, S, is the same as the first firm's supply, S^1. If the price is $6 or more, both firms produce, so the market supply curve is the horizontal summation of their two individual supply curves. For example, at $7, the first firm produces 215 units, and the second firm supplies 100 units, so the market supply is 315 units.

As with the identical firms, where both firms produce, the market supply curve is flatter than that of either firm. Because the second firm does not produce at as low a price as the first firm, the short-run market supply curve has a steeper slope (less elastic supply) at relatively low prices than it would if the firms were identical.

Where firms differ, only the low-cost firm supplies goods at relatively low prices. As the price rises, the other, higher-cost firm starts supplying, creating a stair-like market supply curve. The more suppliers there are with differing costs, the more steps there are in the market supply curve. As price rises and more firms supply goods, the market supply curve flattens, so it takes a smaller increase in price to increase supply by a given amount. Stated another way, the more firms differ in costs, the steeper the market supply curve at low prices. Differences in costs are one explanation for why some market supply curves are upward sloping.

Short-Run Competitive Equilibrium

By combining the short-run market supply curve and the market demand curve, we can determine the short-run competitive equilibrium. We examine first how to determine the equilibrium in the lime market and then how the equilibrium changes when firms are taxed.

Suppose that there were five identical firms in the short-run equilibrium for the lime manufacturing industry. Panel a of Figure 8.9 shows the short-run cost curves

Figure 8.9 Short-Run Competitive Equilibrium in the Lime Market

(a) The short-run supply curve is the marginal cost above the minimum average variable cost of $5. At a price of $5, each firm makes a short-run loss of $(p - AC)q = ($5 - $6.97) \times 50,000 = -$98,500$, area $A + C$. At a price of $7, the short-run profit of a typical lime firm is $(p - AC)q = ($7 - $6.20) \times 215,000 = $172,000$, area $A +$ B. (b) If there are five firms in the lime market in the short run so that the market supply is S, and the market demand curve is D^1, then the short-run equilibrium is E_1, the market price is $7, and market output is $Q_1 = 1,075$ units. If the demand curve shifts to D^2, the market equilibrium is $p = 5 and $Q_2 = 250$ units.

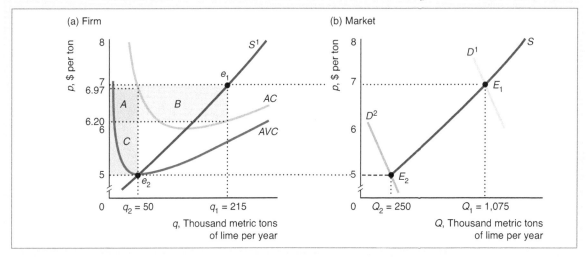

and the supply curve, S^1, for a typical firm, and panel b shows the corresponding short-run competitive market supply curve, S.

In panel b, the initial demand curve D^1 intersects the market supply curve at E_1, the market equilibrium. The equilibrium quantity is $Q_1 = 1{,}075$ units of lime per year, and the equilibrium market price is $7.

In panel a, each competitive firm faces a horizontal demand curve at the equilibrium price of $7. Each price-taking firm chooses its output where its marginal cost curve intersects the horizontal demand curve at e_1. Because each firm maximizes its profit at e_1, no firm wants to change its behavior, so e_1 is each firm's equilibrium. In panel a, each firm makes a short-run profit of area $A + B = \$172{,}000$, which is the average profit per ton, $p - AC = \$7 - \$6.20 = 80¢$, times the firm's output, $q_1 = 215$ units. The equilibrium market output, Q_1, is the number of firms, n, times the equilibrium output of each firm: $Q_1 = nq_1 = 5 \times 215$ units $= 1{,}075$ units (panel b).

Now suppose that the demand curve shifts to D^2. The new market equilibrium is E_2, where the price is only $5. At that price, each firm produces $q = 50$ units, and market output is $Q = 250$ units. In panel a, each firm loses $98{,}500$, area $A + C$, because it makes an average per ton of $(p - AC) = (\$5 - \$6.97) = -\$1.97$ and it sells $q_2 = 50$ units. However, such a firm does not shut down because the price equals the firm's average variable cost, so the firm is able to cover its out-of-pocket expenses.

SOLVED PROBLEM 8.3

What is the effect on the short-run equilibrium of a specific tax of τ per unit that is collected from all n identical firms in a market? Does the consumer bear the full incidence of the tax (the share of the tax that falls on consumers)?

Answer

1. *Show how the tax shifts a typical firm's marginal cost and average cost curves and hence its supply curve.* In Solved Problem 8.1, we showed that such a tax causes the marginal cost curve, the average cost curve, and (hence) the minimum average cost of the firm to shift up by τ, as illustrated in panel a of the figure. As a result, the short-run supply curve of the firm, labeled $S^1 + \tau$, shifts up by τ from the pretax supply curve, S^1.

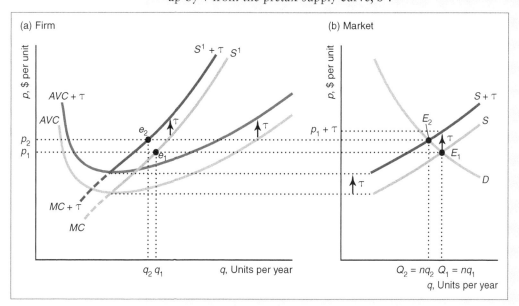

2. *Show how the market supply curve shifts.* The market supply curve is the sum of all the individual firm's supply curves, so it also shifts up by τ, from S to $S + \tau$ in panel b of the figure.

3. *Determine how the short-run market equilibrium changes.* The pre-tax short-run market equilibrium is E_1, where the downward-sloping market demand curve D intersects S in panel b. In that equilibrium, price is p_1 and quantity is Q_1, which equals n (the number of firms) times the quantity q_1 that a typical firm produces at p_1. The after-tax short-run market equilibrium, E_2, determined by the intersection of D and the after-tax supply curve, $S + \tau$, occurs at p_2 and Q_2. Because the after-tax price p_2 is above the after-tax minimum average variable cost, all the firms continue to produce, but they produce less than before: $q_2 < q_1$. Consequently, the equilibrium quantity falls from $Q_1 = nq_1$ to $Q_2 = nq_2$.

4. **Discuss the incidence of the tax.** The equilibrium price increases, but by less than the full amount of the tax: $p_2 < p_1 + \tau$. The incidence of the tax is shared between consumers and producers because both the supply and the demand curves are sloped (Chapter 2).[8]

8.4 Competition in the Long Run

I think there is a world market for about five computers.
—Thomas J. Watson, IBM chairman, 1943

In the long run, competitive firms can vary inputs that were fixed in the short run, so the long-run firm and market supply curves differ from the short-run curves. After briefly looking at how a firm determines its long-run supply curve that maximizes its profit, we examine the relationship between short-run and long-run market supply curves and competitive equilibria.

Long-Run Competitive Profit Maximization

A firm's two profit-maximizing decisions—how much to produce and whether to produce at all—are simpler in the long run than in the short run. In the long run, typically all costs are variable, so the firm does not have to consider whether fixed costs are sunk or avoidable costs.

Long-Run Output Decision. The firm chooses the quantity that maximizes its profit using the same rules as in the short run. The company will pick the quantity that maximizes long-run profit, which is the difference between revenue and long-run cost. Equivalently, it operates where long-run marginal profit is zero and where marginal revenue equals long-run marginal cost.

Long-Run Shutdown Decision. After determining the output level, q^*, that maximizes its profit or minimizes its loss, the firm decides whether to produce or shut down. The firm shuts down if its revenue is less than its avoidable or variable cost. In the long run, however, all costs are variable. As a result, in the long run, the firm shuts down if it would suffer an economic loss by continuing to operate.

---

[8] See Chapter 2 for the calculus analysis of the incidence of a specific tax in a competitive market.

Long-Run Firm Supply Curve

A firm's long-run supply curve is its long-run marginal cost curve above the minimum of its long-run average cost curve (because all costs are variable in the long run). The firm is free to choose its capital in the long run, so the firm's long-run supply curve may differ substantially from its short-run supply curve.

The firm chooses a plant size to maximize its long-run economic profit in light of its beliefs about the future. If its forecast is wrong, it may be stuck with a plant that is too small or too large for its chosen level of production in the short run. The firm corrects this mistake in plant size in the long run.

The firm in Figure 8.10 has different short- and long-run cost curves. In the short run, the firm uses a plant that is smaller than the optimal long-run size if the price is $35. The firm produces 50 units of output per year in the short run, where its short-run marginal cost, $SRMC$, equals the price, and makes a short-run profit equal to area A. The firm's short-run supply curve, S^{SR}, is its short-run marginal cost above the minimum, $20, of its short-run average variable cost, $SRAVC$.

If the firm expects the price to remain at $35, it builds a larger plant in the long run. Using the larger plant, the firm produces 110 units per year, where its long-run marginal cost, $LRMC$, equals the market price. It expects to make a long-run profit, area $A + B$, which is greater than its short-run profit by area B because it sells 60 more units, and its equilibrium long-run average cost, $LRAC = \$25$, is lower than its short-run average cost in equilibrium, $28.

The firm does not operate at a loss in the long run when all inputs are variable. It shuts down if the market price falls below the firm's minimum long-run average cost of $24. Thus, the competitive firm's long-run supply curve is its long-run marginal cost curve above $24.

Figure 8.10 The Short-Run and Long-Run Supply Curves

The firm's long-run supply curve, S^{LR}, is zero below its minimum average cost of $24 and equals the long-run marginal cost, $LRMC$, at higher prices. The firm produces more in the long run than in the short run, 110 units instead of 50 units, and earns a higher profit, area $A + B$, instead of just area A.

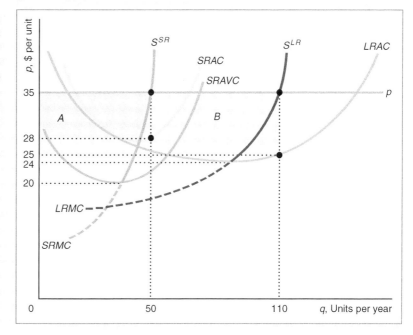

Long-Run Market Supply Curve

The competitive market supply curve is the horizontal sum of the supply curves of the individual firms in both the short run and the long run. Because the maximum number of firms in the market is fixed in the short run, we add the supply curves of a known number of firms to obtain the short-run market supply curve. The only way for the market to supply more output in the short run is for existing firms to produce more.

In the long run, firms can enter or leave the market. Thus, before we can add all the relevant firm supply curves to obtain the long-run market supply curve, we need to determine how many firms are in the market at each possible market price.

To construct the long-run market supply curve properly, we also have to determine how input prices vary with output. As the market expands or contracts substantially, changes in factor prices may shift firms' cost and supply curves. If so, we need to determine how such shifts in factor prices affect firm supply curves so that we can properly construct the market supply curve. The effect of changes in input prices is greater in the long run than in the short run because market output can change more dramatically in the long run.

We now look in detail at how entry and changing factor prices affect long-run market supply. We first derive the long-run market supply curve, assuming that the price of inputs remains constant as market output increases, so as to isolate the role of entry. We then examine how the market supply curve is affected if the price of inputs changes as market output rises.

Entry and Exit. The number of firms in a market in the long run is determined by the *entry* and *exit* of firms. In the long run, each firm decides whether to enter or exit, depending on whether it can make a long-run profit.

In many markets, firms face barriers to entry or must incur significant costs to enter. For example, many city governments limit the number of cab drivers, creating an insurmountable barrier that prevents additional firms from entering. In some markets, a new firm considering entry must hire consultants to determine the profit opportunities, pay lawyers to write contracts, and incur other expenses. Typically, such costs of entry (or exit) are fixed costs.

Even if existing firms are making positive profits, no entry occurs in the short run if entering firms need time to find a location, build a new plant, and hire workers. In the long run, firms enter the market if they can make profits by so doing. The costs of entry are often lower, and hence the profits from entering are higher, if a firm takes its time to enter. As a result, firms may enter markets long after profit opportunities first appear. For example, Starbucks announced that it planned to enter the Puerto Rican market in 2002 but that it would take up to two years to reach 16 stores from its initial 11. Starbucks had 22 stores in Puerto Rico by 2007 and 28 by the beginning of 2009.

In contrast, firms usually react faster to losses than to potential profits. We expect firms to shut down or exit the market quickly in the short run when price is below average variable cost.

In markets without barriers or fixed costs to entry, firms can freely enter and exit. For example, many construction firms, which have no capital and provide only labor services, engage in *hit-and-run* entry and exit: They enter the market whenever they can make a profit and exit whenever they can't. These firms may enter and exit markets several times a year.

In such markets, a shift of the market demand curve to the right entices firms to enter. For example, home builders often enter and exit the market repeatedly during a year. If the housing demand curve shifts to the right, the market price rises, and existing firms make unusually high profits in the short run. Seeing these profits, other builders enter the market, causing the market supply curve to shift to the right and the market price to fall. Entry occurs until the last firm to enter—the *marginal firm*—makes zero long-run profit.

Similarly, if the demand curve shifts to the left so that the market price drops, firms suffer losses. Firms with minimum average costs above the new, lower market price exit the market. Firms continue to leave the market until the next firm considering leaving, the marginal firm, again earns a zero long-run profit.

Thus, in a market with free entry and exit:

- A firm enters the market if it can make a long-run profit, $\pi > 0$.
- A firm exits the market to avoid a long-run loss, $\pi < 0$.

If firms in a market are making zero long-run profit, they are indifferent between staying in the market and exiting. We presume that if they are already in the market, they stay in the market when they are making zero long-run profit.

Most transportation markets are thought to have free entry and exit unless governments regulate them. Relatively few airline, trucking, or shipping firms may serve a particular route, but they face extensive potential entry. Other firms can and will quickly enter and serve a route if a profit opportunity appears. Entrants shift their highly mobile equipment from less profitable routes to more profitable ones. See "Threat of Entry in Shipping" in **MyEconLab**'s textbook resources for Chapter 8.

Entry and exit are relatively difficult in many manufacturing and mining industries as well as in government-regulated industries such as public utilities and insurance. In contrast, firms can enter and exit easily in many agriculture, construction, wholesale and retail trade, and service industries.

In the United States, an estimated 627,200 new firms that employ worker began operations and 595,600 firms exited in 2008.[9] The annual rates of entry and exit of firms employing workers are both about 10% per year. The corresponding rates for firms that do not employ workers are three times as high.

Long-Run Market Supply with Identical Firms and Free Entry. The *long-run market supply curve is flat* at the minimum long-run average cost *if firms can freely enter and exit* the market, an unlimited number of *firms have identical costs,* and *input prices are constant*. This result follows from our reasoning about the short-run supply curve, in which we showed that the more firms there are in the market, the flatter the market supply curve. With many firms in the market in the long run, the market supply curve is effectively flat. ("Many" is 10 firms in the vegetable oil market.)

The long-run supply curve of a typical vegetable oil mill, S^1 in panel a of Figure 8.11, is the long-run marginal cost curve above a minimum long-run average cost of $10. Because each firm shuts down if the market price is below $10, the long-run market supply curve is zero at a price below $10. If the price rises above $10, firms make positive profits, so new firms enter, expanding market output until profits are driven to zero, where price is again $10. The long-run market supply curve in panel b is a horizontal line at the minimum long-run average cost of the typical firm, $10. At a price of $10, each firm produces $q = 150$ units (where one unit equals 100 metric tons). Thus, the total output produced by n firms in the market is $Q = nq = n \times 150$ units. Extra market output is obtained by new firms entering the market.

In summary, the long-run market supply curve is horizontal if the market has free entry and exit, an unlimited number of firms have identical costs, and input prices are constant. When these strong assumptions do not hold, the long-run market supply curve has a slope, as we now show.

---

[9]www.sba.gov/advo/stats/sbfaq.pdf, September 2009.

Figure 8.11 Long-Run Firm and Market Supply with Identical Vegetable Oil Firms

(a) The long-run supply curve of a typical vegetable oil mill, S^1, is the long-run marginal cost curve above the minimum average cost of $10. (b) The long-run market supply curve is horizontal at the minimum of the long-run minimum average cost of a typical firm. Each firm produces 150 units, so market output is $150n$, where n is the number of firms.

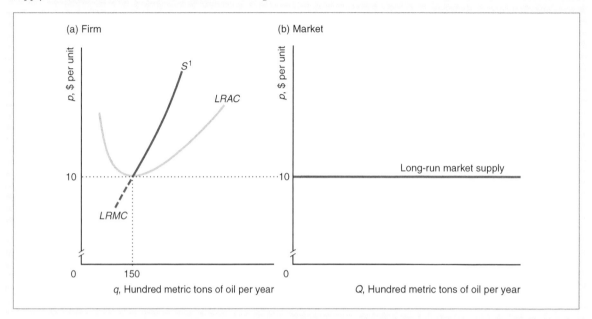

Long-Run Market Supply When Entry Is Limited. If the number of firms in a market is limited in the long run, the market supply curve slopes upward. The number of firms is limited if the government restricts that number, if firms need a scarce resource, or if entry is costly. An example of a scarce resource is the limited number of lots on which a luxury beachfront hotel can be built in Miami. High entry costs restrict the number of firms in a market because firms enter only if the long-run economic profit is greater than the cost of entering.

The only way to increase output if the number of firms is limited is for existing firms to produce more. Because individual firms' supply curves slope upward, the long-run market supply curve is also upward sloping. The reasoning is the same as in the short run, as panel b of Figure 8.7 illustrates, given that no more than five firms can enter. The market supply curve is the upward-sloping S^5 curve, which is the horizontal sum of the five firms' upward-sloping marginal cost curves above minimum average cost.

Long-Run Market Supply When Firms Differ. A second reason why some long-run market supply curves slope upward is that firms differ. Because firms with relatively low minimum long-run average costs are willing to enter the market at lower prices than others, an upward-sloping long-run market supply curve results. The long-run supply curve is upward sloping due to differences in costs across firms *only* if the amount that lower-cost firms can produce is limited. If there were an unlimited number of the lowest-cost firms, we would never observe any higher-cost firms produce. Effectively, then, the only firms producing in the market would have the same low costs of production.

APPLICATION

Upward-Sloping Long-Run Supply Curve for Cotton

Many countries produce cotton. Production costs differ among countries because of differences in the quality of land, rainfall, the costs of irrigation and labor, and other factors.

The length of each step-like segment of the long-run supply curve of cotton in the graph is the quantity produced by the named country. The amount that the low-cost countries can produce must be limited, or we would not observe production by the higher-cost countries.

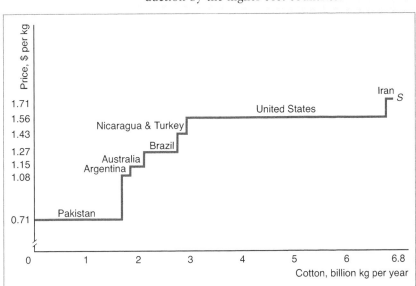

The height of each segment of the supply curve is the typical minimum average cost of production in that country. The average cost of production in Pakistan is less than half that in Iran. The supply curve has a step-like appearance because we are using an average of the estimated average cost in each country, which is a single number. If we knew the individual firms' supply curves in each of these countries, the market supply curve would have a smoother shape.

As the market price rises, the number of countries producing rises. At market prices below $1.08 per kilogram, only Pakistan produces. If the market price is below $1.50, the United States and Iran do not produce. If the price increases to $1.56, the United States supplies a large amount of cotton. In this range of the supply curve, supply is very elastic. For Iran to produce, the price has to rise to $1.71. Price increases in that range result in only a relatively small increase in supply. Thus, the supply curve is relatively inelastic at prices above $1.56.

Long-Run Market Supply When Input Prices Vary with Output. A third reason why market supply curves may slope is non-constant input prices. In markets where factor prices rise or fall when output increases, the long-run supply curve slopes even if firms have identical costs and can freely enter and exit.

If a relatively small share of the total quantity of a factor of production is used in a specific market, as that market's output expands, the price of the factor is unlikely to be affected. For example, dentists do not hire enough receptionists to affect the market wage for receptionists.

In contrast, if a very large share of a factor is used in one market, the price of that input is more likely to vary with that market's output. As jet plane manufacturers expand and buy more jet engines, the price of these engines rises because the jet plane manufacturers are the sole purchasers of these engines.

To produce more goods, firms must use more inputs. If the prices of some or all inputs rise when more inputs are purchased, the cost of producing the final good also rises. We call a market in which input prices rise with output an *increasing-cost market*. Few steelworkers have no fear of heights and are willing to construct tall buildings, so their supply curve is steeply upward sloping. As more skyscrapers are built at one time, the demand curve for these workers shifts to the right, driving up their wage.

We assume that all firms in a market have the same cost curves and that input prices rise as market output expands. We use the cost curves of a representative firm in panel a of Figure 8.12 to derive the upward-sloping market supply curve in panel b.

When input prices are relatively low, each identical firm has the same long-run marginal cost curve, MC^1, and average cost curve, AC^1, in panel a. A typical firm produces at minimum average cost, e_1, and sells q_1 units of output. The market supply is Q_1 in panel b when the market price is p_1. The n_1 firms collectively sell $Q_1 = n_1 q_1$ units of output, which is point E_1 on the market supply curve in panel b.

If the market demand curve shifts outward, the market price rises to p_2, new firms enter, and market output rises to Q_2, causing input prices to rise. As a result, the marginal cost curve shifts from MC^1 to MC^2, and the average cost curve rises from AC^1 to AC^2. The typical firm produces at a higher minimum average cost, e_2. At this higher price, there are n_2 firms in the market, so market output is $Q_2 = n_2 q_2$ at point E_2 on the market supply curve.

Thus, in both an increasing-cost market and a *constant-cost market*—where input prices remain constant as output increases—firms produce at minimum average cost in the long run. The difference is that the minimum average cost rises as market output increases in an increasing-cost market, whereas minimum average cost remains constant in a constant-cost market. In conclusion, *the long-run supply curve is upward sloping in an increasing-cost market and flat in a constant-cost market*.

Figure 8.12 Long-Run Market Supply in an Increasing-Cost Market

At a relatively low market output, Q_1 in panel b, the firm's long-run marginal and average cost curves are MC^1 and AC^1 in panel a. At the higher market quantity Q_2, the cost curves shift upward to MC^2 and AC^2 as a result of the higher input prices. Given identical firms, each firm produces at minimum average cost, such as points e_1 and e_2. Long-run market supply, S, is upward sloping.

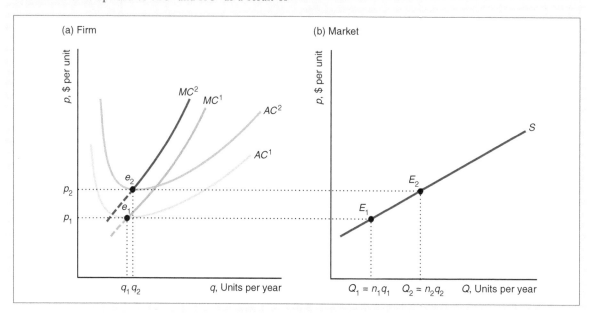

In a decreasing-cost market, as market output rises, at least some factor prices fall. As a result, in a decreasing-cost market, the long-run market supply curve is downward sloping.

Increasing returns to scale may cause factor prices to fall. For example, when DVD drives were first introduced, relatively few were manufactured, and their cost of manufacturing was relatively high. Both due to the high price of DVD drives and the lack of DVDs, there was much less demand for DVD drives than there is today. As demand for DVD drives increased, it became practical to automate more of the production process so that drives could be produced at a lower average cost. The resulting decrease in the price of these drives lowered the cost of personal computers.

To summarize, theory tells us that competitive long-run market supply curves may be flat, upward sloping, or downward sloping. If all firms are identical in a market in which firms can freely enter and input prices are constant, the long-run market supply curve is flat. If entry is limited, firms differ in costs, or input prices rise with output, the long-run supply curve is upward sloping. Finally, if input prices fall with market output, the long-run supply curve may be downward sloping. (See "Slope of Long-Run Market Supply Curves" in **MyEconLab**'s textbook resources for Chapter 8.)

Long-Run Market Supply Curve with Trade. Cotton, oil, and many other goods are traded on world markets. The world equilibrium price and quantity for a good are determined by the intersection of the world supply curve—the horizontal sum of the supply curves of each producing country—and the world demand curve—the horizontal sum of the demand curves of each consuming country.

A country that imports a good has a supply curve that is the horizontal sum of its domestic industry's supply curve and the import supply curve. The domestic supply curve is the competitive long-run supply curve that we have just derived. However, we need to determine the import supply curve.

A country's import supply curve is the world's **residual supply curve**: the quantity that the market supplies that is not consumed by other demanders at any given price.[10] Because the country buys only that part of the world supply, $S(p)$, that is not consumed by any *other* demander elsewhere in the world, $D^o(p)$, its residual supply function, $S^r(p)$, is

$$S^r(p) = S(p) - D^o(p). \tag{8.16}$$

At prices so low that $D^o(p)$ is greater than $S(p)$, the residual supply, $S^r(p)$, is zero.

In Figure 8.13, we derive Japan's residual supply curve for cotton in panel a using the world supply curve, S, and the demand curve of the rest of the world, D^o, in panel b. The scales differ for the quantity axes in the two panels. At a price of \$850 per metric ton, the demand in other countries exhausts world supply (D^o intersects S at 32 million metric tons per year), so there is no residual supply for Japan. At a much higher price, \$935, Japan's excess supply, 4 million metric tons, is the difference between the world supply, 30 million tons, and the quantity demanded elsewhere, 34 million tons. As the figure illustrates, the residual supply curve facing Japan is much closer to horizontal than the world supply curve.

The elasticity of residual supply, η_r, facing a given country is[11]

$$\eta_r = \frac{\eta}{\theta} - \frac{1-\theta}{\theta}\varepsilon_o, \tag{8.17}$$

---

[10]*Jargon alert*: It is traditional to use the expression *excess supply* when discussing international trade and *residual supply* otherwise, though the terms are equivalent.

[11]The derivation of this equation is similar to that of Equation 8.2. See Problem 36.

Figure 8.13 Excess or Residual Supply Curve

Japan's excess supply curve, S^r, for cotton is the horizontal difference between the world's supply curve, S, and the demand curve of the other countries in the world, D^o.

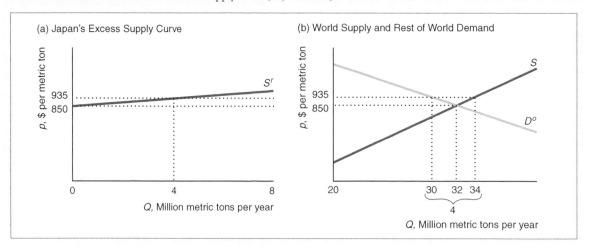

where η is the market supply elasticity, ε_o is the demand elasticity of the other countries, and $\theta = Q_r/Q$ is the importing country's share of the world's output.

If a country imports a small fraction of the world's supply, we expect it to face an almost perfectly elastic, horizontal residual supply curve. On the other hand, a relatively large consumer of the good might face an upward-sloping residual supply curve.

We can illustrate this difference for cotton, where $\eta = 0.5$ and $\varepsilon = -0.7$ (Green et al., 2005). The United States imports only $\theta = 0.1\%$ of the world's cotton, so its residual supply elasticity is

$$\eta_r = \frac{\eta}{0.001} - \frac{0.999}{0.001}\varepsilon_o$$
$$= 1{,}000\eta - 999\varepsilon_o$$
$$= (1{,}000 \times 0.5) - [999 \times (-0.)7] = 1{,}199.3,$$

which is 2,398.6 times more elastic than the world's supply elasticity. Canada's import share is 10 times larger, $\theta = 1\%$, so its residual supply elasticity is "only" 119.3. Nonetheless, its residual supply curve is nearly horizontal: A 1% increase in the price would induce imports to more than double, rising by 119.3%. Even Japan's $\theta = 2.5\%$ leads to a relatively elastic $\eta_r = 46.4$. In contrast, China imports 18.5% of the world's cotton, so its residual supply elasticity is 5.8. Even though its residual supply elasticity is more than 11 times larger than the world's elasticity, it is still small enough for its excess supply curve to be upward sloping.

Thus, if a country is "small"—it imports a small share of the world's output—then it faces a horizontal import supply curve at the world equilibrium price. If its domestic supply curve lies stirictly above the world price, then the country only imports and faces a horizontal supply curve. If some portion of its upward-sloping domestic supply curve lies below the world price, then its total supply curve is the same as the upward-sloping domestic supply curve up to the world price and is horizontal at the world price (Chapter 9 shows this type of supply curve for oil).

APPLICATION

Reformulated Gasoline Supply Curves

This analysis of trade applies to trade within a country too. The following application shows that it can be used to look at trade across geographic areas or jurisdictions such as states.

You can't buy the gasoline sold in Milwaukee in other parts of Wisconsin. Houston gas isn't the same as western Texas gas. California, Minnesota, and Nevada and most of America's biggest cities use one or more of at least 46 specialized blends (sometimes referred to as *boutique fuels*), while the rest of the country uses regular gas. Because special blends are often designed to cut air pollution, they are more likely to be required by the U.S. Clean Air Act Amendments, state laws, or local ordinances in areas with serious pollution problems. For example, the objective of the federal Reformulated Fuels Program (RFG) is to reduce ground-level ozone-forming pollutants. It specifies both content criteria (such as benzene content limits) and emissions-based performance standards for refiners.

The number of working U.S. refineries has dropped from 324 in 1981 to 141 in 2009. Many of these remaining refiners produce regular gasoline, which is sold throughout most of the country. Wholesalers are willing to ship regular gas across state lines in response to slightly higher prices in neighboring states. If the price rises slightly in New Hampshire, firms will quickly send gasoline from Vermont or Maine to New Hampshire. As a consequence, the residual supply curve for regular gasoline for a given state is close to horizontal.

In contrast, gasoline is usually not imported into jurisdictions that require special blends. Few refiners produce any given special blend. Only 13 California refineries can produce California's special low-polluting blend of gasoline, California Reformulated Gasoline (CaRFG). Because refineries require expensive upgrades to produce a new kind of gas, they generally do not switch from producing one type to another type of gas. Thus, even if the price of gasoline rises in California, wholesalers in other states do not send gasoline to California, because they cannot legally sell regular gasoline in California and it would cost too much to start producing CaRFG.

Consequently, unlike the nearly horizontal residual supply curve for regular gasoline, the reformulated gasoline residual supply curve is eventually upward sloping. At relatively small quantities, refineries can produce more gasoline without incurring higher costs, so the supply curve in this region is relatively flat. However, to produce much larger quantities of gasoline, refiners have to run their plants around the clock and convert a larger fraction of each gallon of oil into gasoline, incurring higher costs of production. As a result of this higher cost, they are willing to sell larger quantities in this range only at a higher price, so the supply curve slopes upward. When the refineries reach capacity, no matter how high the price gets, firms cannot produce more gasoline (at least until new refineries go online), so the supply curve becomes vertical. California normally operates in the steeply upward-sloping section of its supply curve. At the end of the summer of 2009, when gas prices fell in the rest of the nation, California's gas price jumped an extra 30¢ per gallon relative to the average national price due to a series of production problems at its refineries.

Brown et al. (2008) found that when the RFG was first imposed, prices in regulated metropolitan areas increased by an average of 3¢ per gallon relative to unregulated areas—and the jump was over 7¢ in some cities such as Chicago—as the demand curve went from intersecting the supply curve in the flat section to intersecting it in the upward sloping section.

SOLVED PROBLEM 8.4

In the short run, what happens to the competitive market price of gasoline if the demand curve in a state shifts to the right as more people move to the state or start driving gas-hogging SUVs? In your answer, distinguish between areas in which regular gasoline is sold and jurisdictions that require special blends.

Answer

1. *Show the effect of a shift of the demand curve in areas that use regular gasoline.* In an area using regular gasoline, the supply curve is horizontal, as panel a of the figure shows. Thus, as the demand curve shifts to the right from D^1 to D^2, the equilibrium shifts along the supply curve from e_1 to e_2, and the price remains at p_1.

2. *Show the effects of both a small and large shift of the demand curve in a jurisdiction that uses a special blend.* The supply curve in panel b is drawn as described in the previous application. If the demand curve shifts slightly to the

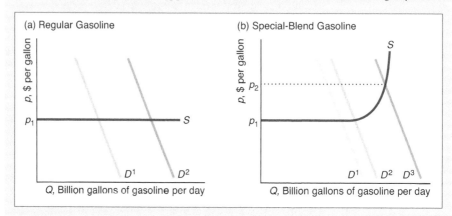

right from D^1 to D^2, the price remains unchanged at p_1 because the demand curve continues to intersect the supply curve in the flat region. However, if the demand curve shifts farther to the right to D^3, then the new intersection is in the upward-sloping section of the supply curve and the price increases to p_2. Consequently, unforeseen "jumps" in demand are more likely to cause a *price spike*—a large increase in price—in jurisdictions that use special blends.[12]

Long-Run Competitive Equilibrium

The intersection of the long-run market supply and demand curves determines the long-run competitive equilibrium. With identical firms, constant input prices, and free entry and exit, the long-run competitive market supply is horizontal at minimum long-run average cost, so the equilibrium price equals long-run average cost. A shift in the demand curve affects only the equilibrium quantity and not the equilibrium price, which remains constant at the minimum long-run average cost.

The market supply curve is different in the short run than in the long run, so the long-run competitive equilibrium differs from the short-run equilibrium. The relationship between the short- and long-run equilibria depends on where the market

---

[12] The gasoline wholesale market may not be completely competitive, especially in areas where special blends are used. Moreover, gas can be stored. Hence price differences across jurisdictions may be due to other factors as well. See Borenstein et al. (2004.)

demand curve crosses the short- and long-run market supply curves. Figure 8.14 illustrates this point using the short- and long-run supply curves for the vegetable oil mill market.

The short-run supply curve for a typical firm in panel a is the marginal cost curve above the minimum of the average variable cost, $7. At a price of $7, each firm produces 100 units, so the 20 firms in the market in the short run collectively supply 2,000 (= 20 × 100) units of oil in panel b. At higher prices, the short-run market supply curve slopes upward because it is the horizontal summation of the firm's upward-sloping marginal cost curves.

We assume that the firms use the same size plant in the short run and the long run so that the minimum average cost is $10 in both the short run and the long run. Because all firms have the same costs and can enter freely, the long-run market supply curve is flat at the minimum average cost, $10, in panel b. At prices between $7 and $10, firms supply goods at a loss in the short run but not in the long run.

If the market demand curve is D^1, the short-run market equilibrium, F_1, lies below and to the right of the long-run market equilibrium, E_1. This relationship is reversed if the market demand curve is D^2.[13]

In the short run, if the demand is as low as D^1, the market price in the short-run equilibrium, F_1, is $7. At that price, each of the 20 firms produces 100 units, at f_1 in panel a. The firms lose money because the price of $7 is below average cost at 100 units. These losses drive some of the firms out of the market in the long run, so market output falls and the market price rises. In the long-run equilibrium, E_1, price

Figure 8.14 The Short-Run and Long-Run Equilibria for Vegetable Oil

(a) A typical vegetable oil mill is willing to produce 100 units of oil at a price of $7, 150 units at $10, or 165 units at $11. (b) The short-run market supply curve, S^{SR}, is the horizontal sum of 20 individual firms' short-run marginal cost curves above minimum average variable cost, $7. The long-run market supply curve, S^{LR}, is horizontal at the minimum average cost, $10. If the demand curve is D^1 in the short-run equilibrium, F_1, 20 firms sell 2,000 units of oil at $7. In the long-run equilibrium, E_1, 10 firms sell 1,500 units at $10. If demand is D^2, the short-run equilibrium is F_2 ($11; 3,300 units; 20 firms) and the long-run equilibrium is E_2 ($10; 3,600 units; 24 firms).

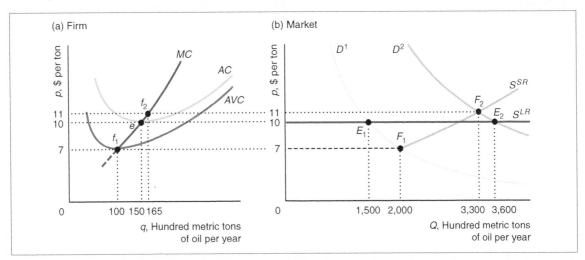

---

[13]Using data from *Statistics Canada*, I estimated that the elasticity of demand for vegetable oil is −0.8. Both D^1 and D^2 are constant −0.8 elasticity demand curves, but the demand at any price on D^2 is 2.4 times that on D^1.

is $10, and each firm produces 150 units, e, and breaks even. As the market demands only 1,500 units, only 10 (= 1,500/150) firms produce, so half the firms that produced in the short run exit the market.[14] Thus, with the D^1 demand curve, price rises and output falls in the long run.

If demand expands to D^2 in the short run, each of the 20 firms expands its output to 165 units, f_2, and the price rises to $11, where the firms make profits: The price of $11 is above the average cost at 165 units. These profits attract entry in the long run, and the price falls. In the long-run equilibrium, each firm produces 150 units, e, and 3,600 units are sold by the market, E_2, by 24 (= 3,600/150) firms. Thus, with the D^2 demand curve, price falls and output rises in the long run.

Because firms may enter and exit in the long run, taxes can have a counterintuitive effect on the competitive equilibrium. For example, as the following solved problem shows, a lump-sum franchise tax causes the competitive equilibrium output of a firm to increase even though market output falls.

SOLVED PROBLEM 8.5

If the government starts collecting a lump-sum franchise tax of $\mathscr{L}$ each year from each identical firm in a competitive market with free entry and exit and an unlimited number of potential firms, how do the long-run market and firm equilibria change? Answer using a graph. (In Problem 38, you are asked for a calculus solution.)

Answer

1. *Show that the franchise tax causes the minimum long-run average cost to rise.* Panel a shows a typical firm's cost curves, while panel b shows the market equilibrium. In panel a, a lump-sum franchise tax shifts the typical firm's average cost curve upward from AC^1 to $AC^2 = AC^1 + \mathscr{L}/q$ but does not affect the marginal cost (see Solved Problem 7.2). As a result, the minimum average cost rises from e_1 to e_2.

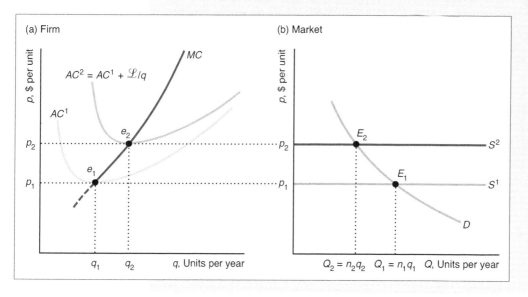

---

[14]How do we know which firms leave? If the firms are identical, the theory says nothing about which ones leave and which ones stay. The firms that leave make zero economic profit, and those that stay make zero economic profit, so firms are indifferent as to whether to stay or exit.

2. *Show that the shift in the minimum average cost causes the market supply curve to shift upward, equilibrium quantity to fall, and equilibrium price to rise.* The long-run market supply is horizontal at minimum average cost. Thus, the market supply curve shifts upward by the same amount that the minimum average cost increases in panel b. With a downward-sloping market demand curve, the new equilibrium, E_2, has a lower quantity, $Q_2 < Q_1$, and higher price, $p_2 > p_1$, than the original equilibrium, E_1.

3. *Show that the increase in the equilibrium price causes the output of an individual firm to rise.* Because the market price rises, the quantity that a firm produces rises from q_1 to q_2. Thus, if the firm remains in the market, it will produce more.

4. *Use the market quantity and individual firm quantity to determine how the number of firms changes.* At the initial equilibrium, the number of firms was $n_1 = Q_1/q_1$. The new equilibrium number of firms, $n_2 = Q_2/q_2$, must be smaller than n_1 because $Q_2 < Q_1$ and $q_2 > q_1$. Thus, there are fewer firms but each remaining firm produces more output at the new equilibrium.

SUMMARY

1. **Perfect Competition.** Competitive firms are price takers that cannot influence market price. Markets are likely to be competitive if a large number of buyers and sellers transact in a market, all firms produce identical products, all market participants have full information about price and product characteristics, transaction costs are negligible, and firms can easily enter and exit the market. A competitive firm faces a horizontal demand curve at the market price.

2. **Profit Maximization.** Most firms maximize economic profit, which is revenue minus economic cost (explicit and implicit costs). Because business profit, which is revenue minus explicit cost, does not include implicit cost, economic profit, which includes implicit cost, tends to be less than business profit. A firm earning zero economic profit is making as much as it could if its resources were devoted to their best alternative uses. To maximize profit, all firms (not just competitive firms) must make two decisions. First, the firm must determine the quantity of output at which its profit is highest. Profit is maximized when marginal profit is zero or, equivalently, when marginal revenue equals marginal cost. Second, the firm must decide whether to produce at all.

3. **Competition in the Short Run.** Because a competitive firm is a price taker, its marginal revenue equals the market price. As a result, a competitive firm maximizes its profit by setting its output so that its short-run marginal cost equals the market price. The firm shuts down if the market price is less than its minimum average variable cost. Thus, a profit-maximizing competitive firm's short-run supply curve is its marginal cost curve above its minimum average variable cost. The short-run market supply curve, which is the sum of the supply curves of the fixed number of firms producing in the short run, is flat at low output levels and upward sloping at larger levels. The short-run competitive equilibrium is determined by the intersection of the market demand curve and the short-run market supply curve. The effect of an increase in demand depends on whether demand intersects the market supply in the flat or upward-sloping section.

4. **Competition in the Long Run.** In the long run, a competitive firm sets its output where the market price equals its long-run marginal cost. It shuts down if the market price is less than the minimum of its long-run average cost because all costs are variable in the long run. Consequently, the competitive firm's supply curve is its long-run marginal cost above its minimum long-run average cost. The long-run supply curve of a firm may have a different slope than the short-run curve because the firm can vary its fixed factors in the long run. The long-run market supply curve is the horizontal sum of the supply curves of all the firms in the market. If all firms are identical, entry and exit are easy, and input prices are constant, the long-run market supply curve is flat at minimum average cost. If firms differ, entry is difficult or costly, or input prices vary with output, the long-run market supply curve has an upward slope. The long-run market

supply curve slopes upward if input prices increase with output and slopes downward if input prices decrease with output. The long-run market equilibrium price and quantity are different from the short-run price and quantity.

QUESTIONS

■ = exercise is available on **MyEconLab**; * = answer appears at the back of this book; V = video answer by James Dearden is available online.

1. Should a competitive firm ever produce when it is losing money? Why or why not?

*2. A competitive firm's bookkeeper, upon reviewing the firm's books, finds that the company spent twice as much on its plant, a fixed cost, as the firm's manager had previously thought. Should the manager change the output level as a result of this new information? How does this new information affect profit?

*3. Many marginal cost curves are U-shaped. As a result, it is possible that the marginal cost curve hits the demand or price line at two output levels. Which is the profit-maximizing output? Why?

4. In 2003 and 2004, virtually every U.S. food company seemed to "Atkinize," introducing low-carbohydrate foods by removing sugar and starch. In 1999, few food or beverage products were marketed as "no-carb" or "low-carb." In 2003, some 500 products carried such labels, and by 2004, more than 3,000 products made such a claim (Melanie Warner, "Is the Low-Carb Boom Over?" *New York Times*, December 5, 2004, 3.1 and 3.9). But low-carb product sales rose only 6% in the 13 weeks ending September 24, 2004, compared to double-digit gains in the corresponding period in 2003 and triple-digit gains in the beginning of 2004. By 2005, low-carb products were disappearing rapidly. Assume that food firms can be properly viewed as being competitive. Use side-by-side firm and market diagrams to show why firms quickly entered and then quickly exited the low-carb market. Did the firms go wrong by introducing so many low-carb products? (Answer in terms of fixed costs and expectations about demand.)

5. The war in Iraq has caused Defense Department purchases from contractors to soar (Todd Wallack, "Business Booms for Bay Area Contractors: $5.5 Billion Flowed from the Defense Dept. to Local Firms Last Year," *San Francisco Chronicle*, March 18, 2004, A1, A15), including firms as diverse as ice-cream vendors and armored vehicle manufacturers. Use side-by-side firm-market diagrams to show the effects (number of firms, price, output, profits) of such a shift in demand in one such industry in both the short run and the long run. Explain how your answer depends on whether the shift in demand is expected to be temporary or permanent.

6. The Internet is affecting holiday shipping. In years past, the busiest shipping period was Thanksgiving week. Now, as people have become comfortable with e-commerce, they postpone purchases to the last minute and are more likely to have their purchases shipped (rather than purchasing locally). FedEx, along with Amazon.com and other e-commerce firms, have to hire extra workers during the holiday period, and many regular workers log substantial overtime hours (up to 60 a week).

   a. Are a firm's marginal and average costs likely to rise or fall with this extra business? (Discuss economies of scale and the slopes of marginal and average cost curves.)

   b. Use side-by-side firm-market diagrams to show the effects on the number of firms, equilibrium price and output, and profits of such a seasonal shift in demand for e-retailers in both the short run and the long run. Explain your reasoning.

7. Carol Skonberg, a housewife and part-time piano teacher, thought she was filling a crying need with her wineglass jewelry (Eve Tahmincioglu, "Even the Best Ideas Don't Sell Themselves," *New York Times*, October 9, 2003, C9). Her Wine Jewels are sterling silver charms of elephants, palm trees, and other subjects that hook onto wineglass stems so that people don't misplace their drinks at parties. In 2000, her first year, she signed with 90 stores in Texas to carry her charms. Then, almost overnight, orders disappeared as rival companies—with names such as Wine Charms, Stemmies, and That Wine Is Mine—offered similar products at lower prices. Ellen Petti started That Wine Is Mine in 1999. She set up a national network of sales representatives and got the product in national catalogs. Her company's sales surged from $250,000 the first year to $6 million in 2001, before falling to $4.5 million in 2002, when she sold the company. Tina Matte's firm started selling Stemmies in late 2000, earning $90,000 in its first year, before sales fell to $75,000 the following year. Assume that this market is competitive and use side-by-side firm and market diagrams to show what happened to prices, quantities, number of firms, and profit as this market evolved over a couple of years. (*Hint*: Consider the possibility that firms' cost functions differ.)

8. Dairy farms can produce Grade A milk, which meets the highest sanitation standards designed for the fluid

market, or Grade B milk, which meets the lower sanitation standards designed for the cheese, butter, and nonfluid markets (Caputo and Paris, 2005). Substantial additional physical and human capital is necessary to produce Grade A rather than Grade B milk. From 1949 to 1999, the share of Grade A milk produced in the United States rose from 57% to 97%, as most dairy farms adopted the necessary technology. Use graphs to explain why Caputo and Paris conclude that "the rising relative price of Grade A milk gave dairy farmers the incentive to adopt the technology for Grade A milk production since such adoption resulted in higher future expected profits than did Grade B milk production."

*9. For Red Delicious apple farmers in Washington, 2001 was a terrible year (Linda Ashton, "Bumper Crop a Bummer for Struggling Apple Farmers," *San Francisco Chronicle*, January 9, 2001, C7). The average price for Red Delicious apples was $10.61 per box, well below the shutdown level of $13.23. Many farmers did not pick the apples from their trees. Other farmers bulldozed their trees, getting out of the Red Delicious business for good, removing 25,000 acres from production. Why did some farmers choose not to pick apples, and others to bulldoze their trees? (*Hint*: Consider the average variable cost and expectations about future prices.)

10. According to the Application "Oil, Oil Sands, and Oil Shale Shutdowns," due to technological advances, the minimum average variable cost of processing oil sands dropped from $25 a barrel in the 1960s to $18 today. In a figure, show how this change affects the supply curve of a typical competitive firm and the supply curve of all the firms producing oil from oil sands.

11. The African country Lesotho gains most of its export earnings—90% in 2004—from its garment and textile factories. The T-shirts you purchased in Wal-Mart and the fleece sweats you bought in JCPenney probably were made in Lesotho. In 2005, the demand curve for Lesotho products shifted downward precipitously due to increased Chinese supply with the end of textile quotas on China and the resulting increase in Chinese exports and the plunge of the U.S. dollar exchange rate against China's currency. Lesotho's garment factories had to sell roughly $55 worth of clothing in the United States to cover a factory worker's monthly wage in 2002, but in 2005, they had to sell an average of $109 to $115, in part due to changes in the exchange rate between U.S. and Lesotho's currencies. Consequently, in the first quarter of 2005, 6 of Lesotho's 50 clothes factories shut down, as the world price plummeted below their minimum average variable cost. These shutdowns eliminated 5,800 of the 50,000 garment jobs. Layoffs at other factories eliminated another 6,000. Since 2002, Lesotho has lost an estimated 30,000 textile jobs.

   a. What is the shape of the demand curve facing Lesotho textile factories, and why? (*Hint*: They are price takers in the world market.)
   b. Use figures to show how the increase in Chinese exports affected the demand curve the Lesotho factories face.
   c. Discuss how the change in the exchange rate affected their demand curve, and explain why.
   d. Use figures to explain why the factories have temporarily or permanently shut down. How does a factory decide whether to shut down temporarily or permanently?

12. Chinese art factories are flooding the world's generic art market (Keith Bradsher, "Own Original Chinese Copies of Real Western Art!" *New York Times*, July 15, 2005). The value of bulk shipments of Chinese paintings to the United States nearly tripled from slightly over $10 million in 1996 to $30.5 million in 2004 (and early 2005 sales were up 50% from the corresponding period in 2004). A typical artist earns less than $200 a month, plus modest room and board, or $360 a month without food and housing. Using a step-like supply function (similar to the one in the "Upward-Sloping Long-Run Supply Curve for Cotton" application), show how the entry of the Chinese affects the world supply curve and how this change affects the equilibrium (including who produces art). Explain.

13. Cheap handheld video cameras have revolutionized the hard-core pornography market. Previously, making movies required expensive equipment and some technical expertise. Today, anyone with a couple thousand dollars and a moderately steady hand can buy and use a video camera to make a movie. Consequently, many new firms have entered the market, and the supply curve of porn movies has slithered substantially to the right. Whereas only 1,000 to 2,000 video porn titles were released annually in the United States from 1986 to 1991, that number grew to 10,300 in 1999 and to 13,588 by 2005.[15] Use a side-by-side diagram to illustrate how this technological innovation affected the long-run supply curve and the equilibrium in this market.

14. In June 2005, Eastman Kodak announced that it would no longer produce black-and-white photographic paper—the type used to develop photographs by a traditional darkroom process. Kodak based its

decision on the substitution of digital photography for traditional photography. In making its exit decision, did Kodak compare the price of its paper and average variable cost (at its optimal output)? Alternatively, did Kodak compare the price of its paper and average total cost (again, at its optimal output)? V

15. During the winter of 2004–2005, wholesale gasoline prices rose rapidly. Although retail gasoline prices increased, retailers' profit per gallon fell. The difference between price and average variable cost for self-service regular gasoline averaged 7.7¢ a gallon in the first quarter of 2005 compared with 9.1¢ for all of 2004. Further, many gasoline retailers exited the market (Thaddeus Herrick, "Pumping Profits from Gas Sales Is Tough to Do," *Wall Street Journal*, May 25, 2005, B1).

   a. Show how an increase in wholesale gasoline prices affects the individual retailer's marginal cost and supply curves.
   b. Show how shifts in the individual retailer's supply curves affect the market supply curve.
   c. Show and explain why an $x per gallon increase in wholesale gasoline prices results in a retail market price increase that is less than $x.
   d. Identify the effect of wholesale gasoline price increases on the profit margins of an individual gasoline retailer.
   e. Why has the increase in wholesale gasoline prices prompted many gasoline retailers to exit the market? V

16. When natural gas prices rose in the first half of 2004, producers considered using natural gas fields that once had been passed over because of the high costs of extracting the gas (Russell Gold, "Natural Gas Is Likely to Stay Pricey," *Wall Street Journal*, June 14, 2004, A2).

   a. In a figure, show what this statement implies about the shape of the natural gas extraction cost function.
   b. Use the cost function you drew in part a to show how an increase in the market price of natural gas affects the amount of gas that a competitive firm extracts. Show the change in the firm's equilibrium profit. V

17. In late 2004 and early 2005, the price of raw coffee beans jumped as much as 50% from the previous year. In response, the price of roasted coffee rose about 14%. Why would firms increase the price less than in proportion to the rise in the cost of raw beans?

18. Fierce storms in October 2004 caused TomatoFest Organic Heirlooms Farm to end its tomato harvest two weeks early. According to Gary Ibsen, a partner in this small business (Carlyn Said, "Tomatoes in Trouble," *San Francisco Chronicle,* October 29, 2004, C1, C2), TomatoFest lost about 20,000 pounds of tomatoes that would have sold for about $38,000; however, because he did not have to hire pickers and rent trucks during these two weeks, his net loss was about $20,000. In calculating the revenue lost, he used the post-storm price, which was double the pre-storm price. Assume that TomatoFest's experience was typical of that of many small tomato farms.

    a. Draw a diagram for a typical farm next to one for the market to show what happened as a result of the storm.
    b. Did TomatoFest suffer an economic loss? What extra information (if any) do you need to answer this question? How do you define "economic loss" in this situation?

19. If we plot a firm's profit against the number of vacation days taken by its owner, Julia, we find that profit first rises with vacation days (a few days of vacation improve Julia's effectiveness as a manager the rest of the year) but eventually falls as she takes more vacation days. Use a diagram to determine whether Julia takes the number of vacation days that maximizes profit given that she has usual-shaped indifference curves between profit and vacation days. Explain.

20. The "Upward-Sloping Long-Run Supply Curve for Cotton" application shows a supply curve for cotton. Discuss the equilibrium if the world demand curve crosses this supply curve in either (a) a flat section labeled "Brazil" or (b) the vertical section to its right. What do farms in the United States do?

21. Mercedes-Benz of San Francisco advertises on the radio that it has been owned and operated by the same family in the same location for 48 years (as of 2010). It then makes two claims: first, that because it has owned this land for 48 years, it has lower overhead than other nearby auto dealers, and second, because of its lower overhead, it charges a lower price for its cars. Discuss the logic of these claims.

22. In Solved Problem 8.5, would it make a difference to the analysis whether the franchise tax was collected annually or only once when the firm starts operation? How would each of these franchise taxes affect the firm's long-run supply curve? Explain.

23. Answer Solved Problem 8.5 for the short run rather than for the long run. (*Hint*: The answer depends on

where the demand curve intersects the original short-run supply curve.)

24. A San Francisco supervisor called for a tax on plastic grocery store bags collected from the stores (Suzanne Herel, "Grocery Store Bag Fee Lacks Public Support; Supervisors Ponder Lower Charge, Other Ways to Reduce Use," *San Francisco Chronicle*, May 13, 2005, B1, B4). He said that he had never intended that this surcharge be passed on to consumers. Does such a tax affect marginal cost? By how much? How much of the tax would a store likely pass on to consumers? In 2007, San Francisco's Board of Supervisors instead banned plastic bags. Compare the grocery store equilibrium with a tax and a ban.

25. *What is the effect on firm and market equilibrium of the U.S. law requiring a firm to give its workers six months' notice before it can shut down its plant?

26. Redraw Figure 8.10 to show the situation where the short-run plant size is too large, relative to the optimal long-run plant size.

27. Is it true that the long-run supply curve for a good is horizontal only if the long-run supply curves of all factors are horizontal? Explain.

28. Navel oranges are grown in California and Arizona. If Arizona starts collecting a specific tax per orange from its firms, what happens to the long-run market supply curve? (*Hint*: You may assume that all firms initially have the same costs. Your answer may depend on whether unlimited entry occurs.)

29. In 1994, Americans bought 33 million real Christmas trees and 40 million artificial trees. (By 2008, 28.2 million real trees were sold compared to 11.7 million artificial trees.) The number of tree producers had fallen by about one-third over the previous 10 years, to about 2,000 in 1994, due to artificial tree sales. That year, trees sold for an average of $26.50, about 50¢ more than the previous year. Retailers' average cost was $20. In 1998, 33 million trees sold for an average of $29.25. Use graphs to illustrate this information.

30. Bribes paid by Swiss companies to foreign officials, which had been tax deductible since 1946, are no longer deductible as of 1999. Use economic models from this chapter and Chapter 7 to show the likely effects of this ban on the bribing behavior of Swiss firms.

31. To reduce pollution, the California Air Resources Board in 1996 required the reformulation of gasoline sold in California. In 1999, a series of disasters at California refineries substantially cut the supply of gasoline and contributed to large price increases. Environmentalists and California refiners (who had sunk large investments to produce the reformulated gasoline) opposed imports from other states, which would have kept prices down. To minimize fluctuations in prices in California, Severin Borenstein and Steven Stoft suggest setting a 15¢ surcharge on sellers of standard gasoline. In normal times, none of this gasoline would be sold, because it costs only 8¢ to 12¢ more to produce the California version. However, when disasters trigger a large shift in the supply curve of gasoline, firms could profitably import standard gasoline and keep the price in California from rising more than about 15¢ above prices in the rest of the United States. Use figures to evaluate Borenstein and Stoft's proposal.

PROBLEMS

32. If the cost function for John's Shoe Repair is $C(q) = 100 + 10q - q^2 + \frac{1}{3}q^3$, what is the firm's marginal cost function? What is its profit-maximizing condition if the market price is p? What is its supply curve?

*33. If a competitive firm's cost function is $C(q) = a + bq + cq^2 + dq^3$, where a, b, c, and d are constants, what is the firm's marginal cost function? What is the firm's profit-maximizing condition?

34. Each firm in a competitive market has a cost function of $C = 16 + q^2$. The market demand function is $Q = 24 - p$. Determine the long-run equilibrium price, quantity per firm, market quantity, and number of firms.

*35. The finding that the average real price of abortions has remained relatively constant over the last 25 years suggests that the supply curve is horizontal. Medoff (1997) estimated that the price elasticity of demand for abortions ranges from -0.70 to -0.99. By how much would the market price of abortions and the number of abortions change if a lump-sum tax is assessed on abortion clinics raises their minimum average cost by 10%? Use a figure to illustrate your answer.

*36. Derive the residual supply elasticity in Equation 8.17 using the definition of the residual demand function in Equation 8.16. What is the formula if there are n identical countries?

*37. As of 2005, the federal specific tax on gasoline is 18.4¢ per gallon, and the average state specific tax is 20.2¢, ranging from 7.5¢ in Georgia to 25¢ in Connecticut (down from 38¢ in 1996). A statistical study (Chouinard and Perloff, 2004) finds that the incidence (Chapter 2) of the federal specific tax on consumers is substantially lower than that from state specific taxes. When the federal specific tax increases by 1¢, the retail price rises by about $\frac{1}{2}$¢: Retail consumers bear half the tax incidence. In contrast, when a state that uses regular gasoline increases its specific tax by 1¢, the incidence of the tax falls almost entirely on consumers: The retail price rises by nearly 1¢.

a. What are the incidences of the federal and state specific gasoline taxes on firms?

b. Explain why the incidence on consumers differs between a federal and a state specific gasoline tax, assuming that the market is competitive. (*Hint*: Consider the residual supply curve facing a state compared to the supply curve facing the nation.)

c. Using the residual supply elasticity in Equation 8.17, estimate how much more elastic is the residual supply elasticity to one state than is the national supply elasticity. (For simplicity, assume that all 50 states are identical.)

*38. Answer Solved Problem 8.5 using calculus. (*Note*: This comparative statics problem is difficult because you will need to solve two or three equations simultaneously, and hence you probably will need to use matrix techniques.)

39. What is the effect of an ad valorem tax of α (the share of the price that goes to the government) on a competitive firm's profit-maximizing output?

40. Consider the Christmas tree seller in the application "Breaking Even on Christmas Trees." Suppose that the seller's cost function is

$C = 6{,}860 + (p_T + t + 7/12)q + 37/27{,}000{,}000 q^3$,

where p_T is the wholesale price of each tree and t is the shipping price per tree. Suppose $p_T = \$11.50$ and $t = \$2.00$.

a. What is the seller's marginal cost function?

b. What is the shutdown price?

c. What is the seller's short-run supply function?

d. If the seller's supply curve is $S(q, t)$, what is $\partial(q, t)/\partial t$? Evaluate it at $p_T = \$11.50$ and $t = \$2.00$. V

41. Joey operates a lemonade stand. His cost of the lemons, sugar, and water per 8 oz. glass is 15¢. Joey's fixed cost is $180. Joey sells five glasses of lemonade per hour.

a. When he was eight years old, Joey had a near zero opportunity cost of time. What was Joey's total cost function? What was his marginal cost function? What was his shutdown price?

b. Joey is now 17. If he were not selling lemonade, he would be working six hours a day at $6 per hour and he would be spending the remainder of the day with his friends. Joey's total value of the time he spends with his friends, t, is $6t + t^2$. What is Joey's total cost function? What is his marginal cost function, $MC(q)$? What is his shutdown price?

c. Compare the shutdown prices of 8-year-old and 17-year-old Joey. V

Applications of the Competitive Model

9

No more good must be attempted than the public can bear.
—Thomas Jefferson

In 2009, China threatened to impose tariffs on U.S. exports of automotive products and chicken meat in retaliation for President Obama's decision to levy tariffs on Chinese tires. How do such trade conflicts and government actions affect consumers and producers? This chapter shows how the competitive model can answer this type of question. One of the major strengths of the competitive market model is that it can predict how trade wars, changes in government policies, global warming, and major cost-saving discoveries affect consumers and producers.

We start by examining the properties of a competitive market and then consider how government actions and other shocks affect the market and its properties. We concentrate on two main properties of such a market. First, firms in a competitive equilibrium generally make zero (economic) profit. Second, competition maximizes a measure of societal welfare. To many people, the term *welfare* refers to the government's payments to the poor. However, no such meaning is implied when economists employ the term. Economists use *welfare* to refer to the well-being of various groups such as consumers and producers. They call an analysis of the impact of a change on various groups' well-being a study of *welfare economics*. This chapter introduces a measure, *producer surplus*, that is closely related to profit and frequently employed by economists to determine whether firms gain or lose when the equilibrium of a competitive market changes. The sum of producer surplus and *consumer surplus* (Chapter 5) equals the measure of welfare that we use in this chapter. By predicting the effects of a proposed policy on consumer surplus, producer surplus, and welfare, economists can advise policymakers as to who will benefit, who will lose, and what the net effect of this policy will likely be. To decide whether to adopt a particular policy, policymakers may combine these predictions with their normative views (values), such as whether they are more interested in helping the group that gains or the group that loses.

In this chapter, we examine six main topics

1. **Zero Profit for Competitive Firms in the Long Run.** In the long-run competitive market equilibrium, profit-maximizing firms break even, so firms that do not try to maximize profits lose money and leave the market.

2. **Producer Welfare.** How much producers gain or lose from a change in the equilibrium price can be measured by using information from the marginal cost curve or by measuring the change in profits.

3. **How Competition Maximizes Welfare.** Competition maximizes a measure of social welfare based on consumer and producer welfare.
4. **Policies That Shift Supply Curves.** Government policies that limit the number of firms in competitive markets harm consumers and lower welfare.
5. **Policies That Create a Wedge Between Supply and Demand Curves.** Government policies such as taxes, price ceilings, price floors, and tariffs that create a wedge between the supply and demand curves reduce the equilibrium quantity, raise the equilibrium price to consumers, and therefore lower welfare.
6. **Comparing Both Types of Policies: Trade.** Policies that limit supply (such as quotas or bans on imports) or create a wedge between supply and demand (such as tariffs, which are taxes on imports) have different welfare effects when both policies reduce imports by equal amounts.

9.1 Zero Profit for Competitive Firms in the Long Run

Competitive firms earn zero profit in the long run whether or not entry is completely free. As a consequence, competitive firms must maximize profit.

Zero Long-Run Profit with Free Entry

The long-run supply curve is horizontal if firms are free to enter the market, firms have identical cost, and input prices are constant. All firms in the market operate at minimum long-run average cost. That is, they are indifferent about whether or not to shut down because they are earning zero profit.

One implication of the shutdown rule is that firms are willing to operate in the long run even if they are making zero profit. This conclusion may seem strange unless you remember that we are talking about *economic profit*, which is revenue minus opportunity cost. Because opportunity cost includes the value of the next best investment, at a zero long-run economic profit, firms earn the normal business profit that they could gain by investing elsewhere in the economy.

For example, if a firm's owner had not built the plant the firm uses to produce, the owner could have spent that money on another business or put the money in a bank. The opportunity cost of the current plant, then, is the forgone profit from what the owner could have earned by investing the money elsewhere.

The five-year after-tax accounting return on capital across all firms is 10.5%, indicating that the typical firm earned a business profit of 10.5¢ for every dollar it invested in capital (*Forbes*). These firms were earning roughly zero economic profit but positive business profit.

Because business cost does not include all opportunity costs, business profit is larger than economic profit. Thus, a profit-maximizing firm may stay in business if it earns zero long-run economic profit but it shuts down if it earns zero long-run business profit.

Zero Long-Run Profit When Entry Is Limited

In some markets, firms cannot enter in response to long-run profit opportunities. The number of firms in these markets may be limited because the supply of an input is limited. For example, only so much land is suitable for mining uranium.

One might think that firms could make positive long-run economic profits in such markets; however, that's not true. The reason firms earn zero economic profits is that firms bidding for the scarce input drive up its price until their profits are zero.

Suppose that the number of acres suitable for growing tomatoes is limited. Figure 9.1 shows a typical farm's average cost curve if the rental cost of land is zero (the average cost curve includes only the farm's costs of labor, capital, materials, and energy—not land). At the market price p^*, the firm produces q^* bushels of tomatoes and makes a profit of π^*, the shaded rectangle in the figure.

Thus, if the owner of the land does not charge rent, the farmer makes a profit. Unfortunately for the farmer, the landowner rents the land for π^*, so the farmer actually earns zero profit. Why does the landowner charge that much? The reason is that π^* is the opportunity cost of the land: The land is worth π^* to other potential farmers. These farmers will bid against each other to rent this land until the rent is driven up to π^*.

This rent is a fixed cost to the farmer because it does not vary with the amount of output. Thus, the rent affects the farm's average cost curve but not its marginal cost curve.

As a result, if the farm produces at all, it produces q^* where its marginal cost equals the market price, no matter what rent is charged. The higher average cost curve in the figure includes a rent equal to π^*. The minimum point of this average cost curve is p^* at q^* bushels of tomatoes, so the farmer earns zero economic profit.

If the demand curve shifts to the left so that the market price falls, the farmer suffers short-run losses. In the long run, the rental price of the land will fall enough that once again each farm earns zero economic profit.

Does it make a difference whether farmers own or rent the land? Not really. The opportunity cost to a farmer who owns superior land is the amount for which that land could be rented in a competitive land market. Thus, the economic profit of both owned and rented land is zero at the long-run equilibrium.

Good-quality land is not the only scarce resource. The price of any fixed factor will be bid up in a similar fashion until economic profit for the firm is zero in the

Figure 9.1 Rent

If farmers did not have to pay rent for their farms, a farmer with relatively high-quality land would earn a positive long-run profit of π^*. Due to competitive bidding for this land, however, the rent equals π^*, so the landlord reaps all the benefits of the superior land, and the farmer earns a zero long-run economic profit.

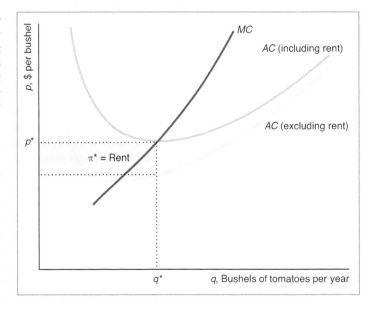

long run. Similarly, the government may require that a firm have a license to operate and then limit the number of licenses available. The price of the license gets bid up by potential entrants, driving profit to zero. For example, the license fee is $326,000 a year for a hot dog stand on the north side of the steps of the Metropolitan Museum of Art in New York City.

A scarce input—whether its fixed factor is a person with high ability or land—earns an extra opportunity value. This extra opportunity value is called a **rent**: a payment to the owner of an input beyond the minimum necessary for the factor to be supplied.

Bonnie manages a store for the salary of $40,000, the amount paid to a typical manager. Because she's a superior manager, however, the firm earns an economic profit of $50,000 a year. Other firms, seeing what a good job Bonnie is doing, offer her a higher salary. The bidding for her services drives her salary up to $90,000: her $40,000 base salary plus the $50,000 rent. After paying this rent to Bonnie, the store makes zero economic profit.

In short, if some firms in a market make short-run economic profits due to a scarce input, the other firms in the market bid for that input. This bidding drives up the price of the factor until all firms earn zero long-run profits. In such a market, the supply curve is flat because all firms have the same minimum long-run average cost.

People with unusual abilities can earn staggering rents. For example, by the time Cher ended her four-year "Never Can Say Goodbye" tour at the Hollywood Bowl on April 30, 2005, she had sold nearly $200 million worth of tickets. Though no law stops anyone from trying to become a professional entertainer, most of us do not have enough talent and charisma to entice millions to pay to watch us perform.[1]

APPLICATION
Tiger Woods' Rents

Tiger Woods was leading a charmed life as the world's great golfer and an advertising star—earning $100 million a year in endorsements—when he and much of his endorsement career came to a crashing halt as he smashed his car in front of his home at about 2:30 AM on November 27, 2009. A series of revelations about his personal life that followed over the next few days further damaged his pristine public reputation, and several endorsers either suspended using him in their advertisements or dropped him altogether.

Knittel and Stango (2010) assessed the financial damage to these firms' shareholders using an *event study* approach in which they compared the stock prices of firms using Mr. Woods in their promotions relative to the stock market prices as a whole and those of close competitor firms. They examine the period between the crash and when Mr. Woods announced on December 11 that he was taking an "indefinite" leave from golf. Their results tell us about the rents that he was receiving.

They estimated that shareholders of companies endorsed by Mr. Woods lost $5 to $12 billion in wealth, which reflects stock investors' estimates of the

---

[1] Major celebrities (or their estates) continue to collect rents even after they die. In 2009, Michael Jackson earned $90 million, Elvis Presley $55 million, writer J.R.R. Tolkien $50 million, and Peanuts cartoonist Charles Schulz $33 million. Even Albert Einstein raked in $10 million from use of his image for products such as in Disney's Baby Einstein learning tools and a McDonald's happy meal promotion. (Miller, Matthew, "Dead Celebs," *Forbes*, October 27, 2009.)

damage from the end of effective endorsements over future years. Mr. Woods' five major sponsors—Accenture, Electronic Arts, Gatorade (PepsiCo), Gillette, and Nike—collectively lost 2% to 3% of their aggregate market value after the accident. However, most of the loss was suffered by his main sports-related sponsors Electronic Arts, Gatorade, and Nike, which saw their market value plunge over 4%.

Mr. Woods' sports-related sponsors suffered more than his other sponsors. As Knittel and Stango point out, sponsorship from firms that are not sports-related, such as Accenture ("a global management consulting, technology services, and outsourcing company"), probably does not increase the overall value of the "Tiger" brand. Presumably, when Mr. Woods negotiated his original deal with Accenture, he captured all the excess profit generated for Accenture as a rent of about $20 million a year. Consequently, we would not expect Accenture to lose much from the end of their relationship with Mr. Woods, as Knittel and Stango's estimates show.

In contrast, partnering with sports-related firms such as Nike presumably increased the value of both the Nike and Tiger brands and created other financial opportunities for Mr. Woods. If so, Nike would likely have captured some of the profit generated by partnering with Tiger Woods above and beyond the $20 to $30 million Nike paid him annually. Consequently, the sports-related firms' shareholders suffered a sizable loss from Mr. Woods' fall from grace.

The Need to Maximize Profit

The worst crime against working people is a company which fails to operate at a profit. —Samuel Gompers, first president of the American Federation of Labor

In a competitive market with identical firms and free entry, if most firms are profit-maximizing, profits are driven to zero at the long-run equilibrium. Any firm that does not maximize profit—that is, any firm that sets its output so that its marginal cost exceeds the market price or that fails to use the most cost-efficient methods of production—will lose money. Thus *to survive in a competitive market, a firm must maximize its profit.*

9.2 Producer Welfare

Economists often use a measure that is closely related to profit when evaluating the effects of policies on firms' welfare. We developed a measure of consumer welfare—consumer surplus—in Chapter 5. A firm's gain from participating in the market is measured by its **producer surplus** (*PS*), which is the difference between the amount for which a good sells and the minimum amount necessary for the seller to be willing to produce the good. The minimum amount that a seller must receive to be willing to produce is the firm's avoidable production cost (the shutdown rule discussed in Chapter 8).

Measuring Producer Surplus Using a Supply Curve

To determine a competitive firm's producer surplus, we use its supply curve: its marginal cost curve above its minimum average variable cost (Chapter 8). The firm's

Figure 9.2 Producer Surplus

(a) The firm's producer surplus, $6, is the area below the market price, $4, and above the marginal cost (supply curve) up to the quantity sold, 4. The area under the marginal cost curve up to the number of units actually produced is the variable cost of production. (b) The market producer surplus is the area above the supply curve and below the line at the market price, p^*, up to the quantity produced, Q^*. The area below the supply curve and to the left of the quantity produced by the market, Q^*, is the variable cost of producing that level of output.

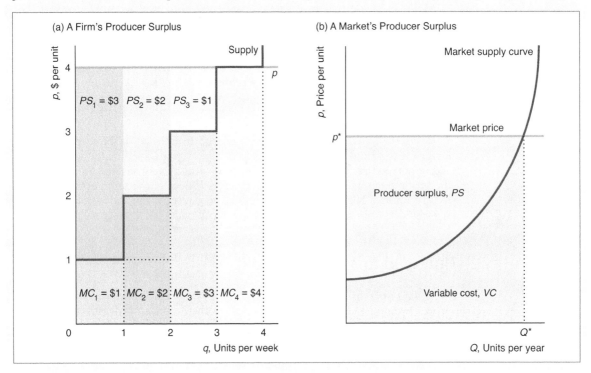

supply curve in panel a of Figure 9.2 looks like a staircase. The marginal cost of producing the first unit is $MC_1 = \$1$, which is the area below the marginal cost curve between 0 and 1. The marginal cost of producing the second unit is $MC_2 = \$2$, and so on. The variable cost, VC, of producing 4 units is the sum of the marginal costs for the first 4 units: $VC = MC_1 + MC_2 + MC_3 + MC_4 = \$1 + \$2 + \$3 + \$4 = \$10$.

If the market price, p, is $4, the firm's revenue from the sale of the first unit exceeds its cost by $PS_1 = p - MC_1 = \$4 - \$1 = \$3$, which is its producer surplus on the first unit. The firm's producer surplus is $2 on the second unit and $1 on the third unit. On the fourth unit, the price equals marginal cost, so the firm just breaks even. As a result, the firm's total producer surplus, PS, from selling 4 units at $4 each is the sum of its producer surplus on these 4 units: $PS = PS_1 + PS_2 + PS_3 + PS_4 = \$3 + \$2 + \$1 + \$0 = \$6$.[2]

Graphically, the total producer surplus is the area above the supply curve and below the market price up to the quantity actually produced. This same reasoning holds when the firm's supply curve is smooth, as in panel b.

---

[2] The firm is indifferent between producing the fourth unit or not. Its producer surplus would be the same if it produced only three units, because its marginal producer surplus from the fourth unit is zero.

The producer surplus is found by integrating the difference between the firm's demand function—the straight line at p—and its marginal cost function, $MC(q)$, up to the quantity produced, q^* (here $q^* = 4$ units):[3]

$$PS = \int_0^{q^*} [p - MC(q)]dq = pq^* - VC(q^*) = R(q^*) - VC(q^*), \tag{9.1}$$

where $R = pq^*$ is revenue. In panel a of Figure 9.2, revenue is $R = \$4 \times 4 = \$16$ and variable cost is $VC = \$10$, so producer surplus is $PS = \$6$.

Producer surplus is closely related to profit. Profit is revenue minus total cost, C, which equals variable cost plus fixed cost, F:

$$\pi = R - C = R - (VC + F). \tag{9.2}$$

Thus, the difference between producer surplus, Equation 9.1, and profit, Equation 9.2, is fixed cost, $PS - \pi = F$. If the fixed cost is zero (as often occurs in the long run), producer surplus equals profit.[4]

Another interpretation of producer surplus is as a gain to trade. In the short run, if the firm produces and sells a good—that is, if the firm trades—it earns a profit of $\pi = R - VC - F$. If the firm shuts down—does not trade—it loses its fixed cost of $-F$. Thus, producer surplus equals the profit from trading minus the loss (fixed costs) it incurs from not trading:

$$PS = (R - VC - F) - (-F) = R - VC.$$

Using Producer Surplus

Even in the short run, we can use producer surplus to study the effects of any shock that does not affect the fixed cost of firms, such as a change in the price of a substitute or an input. Such shocks change profit by exactly the same amount as they change producer surplus because fixed costs do not change.

A major advantage of producer surplus is that we can use it to measure the effect of a shock on *all* the firms in a market without having to measure the profit of each firm separately. We can calculate market producer surplus using the market supply curve in the same way that we calculate a firm's producer surplus using its supply curve. The market producer surplus in panel b of Figure 9.2 is the area above the supply curve and below the market price line at p^* up to the quantity sold, Q^*. The market supply curve is the horizontal sum of the marginal cost curves of each of the firms (Chapter 8).

SOLVED PROBLEM 9.1

Green et al. (2005) estimate the inverse supply curve for California processed tomatoes as $p = 0.693Q^{1.82}$, where Q is the quantity of processing tomatoes in millions of tons per year and p is the price in dollars per ton. If the price falls from \$60 (where the quantity supplied is about 11.6) to \$50 (where the quantity supplied is approximately 10.5), how does producer surplus change? Illustrate in a figure. Show that you can obtain a good approximation using rectangles and triangles. (Round results to the nearest tenth.)

---

[3] As we noted in Chapter 7, the marginal cost can be obtained by differentiating with respect to output either the variable cost function, $VC(q)$, or the total cost function, $C(q) = VC(q) + F$, because F is a constant. When we integrate under the marginal cost function, we obtain the variable cost function (that is, we cannot recover the constant fixed cost).

[4] Even though each competitive firm makes zero profit in the long run, owners of scarce resources used in that market may earn rents, as we discussed in Section 9.1. Thus, owners of scarce resources may receive positive producer surplus in the long run.

Answer

1. *Calculate the producer surplus at each price (or corresponding quantity) and take the difference to determine how producer surplus changes.* When price is $60, the producer surplus is

$$PS_1 = \int_0^{11.6} (60 - 0.693Q^{1.82})dQ = 60Q - \frac{0.693}{2.82}Q^{2.82}\Big|_0^{11.6} \approx 449.3.$$

The producer surplus at the new price is

$$PS_2 = \int_0^{10.5} (50 - 0.693Q^{1.82})dQ \approx 338.7.$$

Thus, the change in producer surplus is $\Delta PS = PS_2 - PS_1 \approx -110.6$.

2. *At each price, the producer surplus is the area above the supply curve below the price up to the quantity sold.* In the figure, area A corresponds to PS_2 because it is the area above the supply curve, below the price of $50, up to the quantity 10.5. Similarly, PS_1 is the sum of areas A and B, so the loss in producer surplus, ΔPS, is area B.

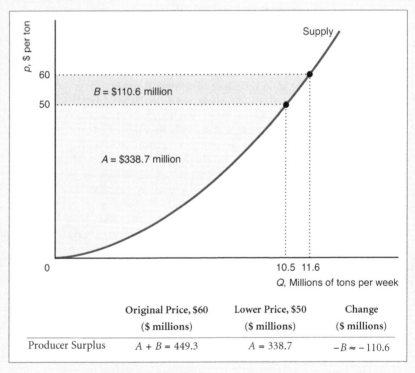

	Original Price, $60 ($ millions)	Lower Price, $50 ($ millions)	Change ($ millions)
Producer Surplus	A + B = 449.3	A = 338.7	−B ≈ −110.6

3. *Approximate area B as the sum of a rectangle and a triangle.* Area B consists of a rectangle with a height of 10 (= 60 − 50) and a length of 10.5 and a shape that's nearly a triangle with a height of 10 and a base of 1.1 (= 11.6 − 10.5). The sum of the areas of the rectangle and the triangle is $(10 \times 10.5) + (\frac{1}{2} \times 10 \times 1.1) = 110.5$, which is close to the value, 110.6, that we obtained by integrating.

9.3 How Competition Maximizes Welfare

How should we measure society's welfare? There are many reasonable answers to this question. One commonly used measure of the welfare of society, W, is the sum of consumer surplus (Chapter 5) plus producer surplus:

$$W = CS + PS.$$

This measure implicitly weights the well-being of consumers and producers equally. By using this measure, we are making a value judgment that the well-being of consumers and that of producers are equally important.

Not everyone agrees that society should try to maximize this measure of welfare. Groups of producers argue for legislation that benefits them even if it hurts consumers by more than the producers gain—as though only producer surplus matters. Similarly, some consumer advocates argue that we should care only about consumers, so social welfare should include only consumer surplus.

In this chapter, we use the consumer surplus plus producer surplus to measure welfare (and postpone a further discussion of other welfare concepts until Chapter 10). One of the most striking results in economics is that competitive markets maximize this measure of welfare. If either less or more output than the competitive level is produced, welfare falls.

Why Producing Less Than the Competitive Output Lowers Welfare

Producing less than the competitive output lowers welfare. At the competitive equilibrium in Figure 9.3, e_1, where output is Q_1 and price is p_1, consumer surplus equals area $CS_1 = A + B + C$, producer surplus is $PS_1 = D + E$, and total welfare is $W_1 = A + B + C + D + E$. If output is reduced to Q_2 so that price rises to p_2 at e_2, consumer surplus is $CS_2 = A$, producer surplus is $PS_2 = B + D$, and welfare is $W_2 = A + B + D$.

The change in consumer surplus is

$$\Delta CS = CS_2 - CS_1 = A - (A + B + C) = -B - C.$$

Consumers lose B because they have to pay $p_2 - p_1$ more than they would at the competitive price for the Q_2 units they buy. Consumers lose C because they buy only Q_2 rather than Q_1 at the higher price.

The change in producer surplus is

$$\Delta PS = PS_2 - PS_1 = (B + D) - (D + E) = B - E.$$

Producers gain B because they now sell Q_2 units at p_2 rather than at p_1. They lose E because they sell $Q_2 - Q_1$ fewer units.

The change in welfare is

$$\begin{aligned}
\Delta W &= W_2 - W_1 \\
&= (CS_2 + PS_2) - (CS_2 + PS_2) \\
&= (CS_2 - CS_1) + (PS_2 - PS_1) \\
&= \Delta CS + \Delta PS \\
&= (-B - C) + (B - E) \\
&= -C - E.
\end{aligned}$$

The area B is a transfer from consumers to producers—the extra amount consumers pay for the Q_2 units goes to the sellers—so it does not affect welfare. Welfare drops

Figure 9.3 Why Reducing Output from the Competitive Level Lowers Welfare

Reducing output from the competitive level Q_1 to Q_2 causes price to increase from p_1 to p_2. Consumers suffer: Consumer surplus is now A, a fall of $\Delta CS = -B - C$. Producers may gain or lose: Producer surplus is now $B + D$, a change of $\Delta PS = B - E$. Overall, welfare falls by $\Delta W = -C - E$, which is a deadweight loss (DWL) to society.

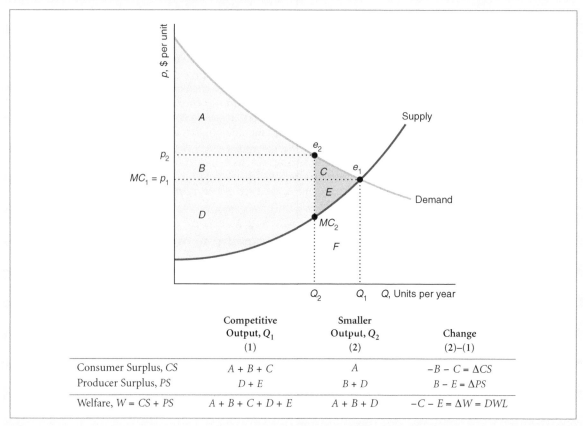

	Competitive Output, Q_1 (1)	Smaller Output, Q_2 (2)	Change (2)–(1)
Consumer Surplus, CS	$A + B + C$	A	$-B - C = \Delta CS$
Producer Surplus, PS	$D + E$	$B + D$	$B - E = \Delta PS$
Welfare, $W = CS + PS$	$A + B + C + D + E$	$A + B + D$	$-C - E = \Delta W = DWL$

because the consumer loss of C and the producer loss of E benefit no one. This drop in welfare, $\Delta W = -C - E$, is a **deadweight loss** (DWL): the net reduction in welfare from a loss of surplus by one group that is not offset by a gain to another group.

The deadweight loss results because consumers value extra output by more than the marginal cost of producing it. At each output between Q_2 and Q_1, consumers' marginal willingness to pay for another unit—the height of the demand curve—is greater than the marginal cost of producing the next unit—the height of the supply curve. For example, at e_2, consumers value the next unit of output at p_2, which is much greater than the marginal cost, MC_2, of producing it. Increasing output from Q_2 to Q_1 raises firms' variable cost by area F, the area under the marginal cost (supply) curve between Q_2 and Q_1. Consumers value this extra output by the area under the demand curve between Q_2 and Q_1, area $C + E + F$. Thus, consumers value the extra output by $C + E$ more than it costs to produce it.

Society would be better off producing and consuming extra units of this good than spending the deadweight loss, $C + E$, on other goods. In short, *the deadweight loss is the opportunity cost of giving up some of this good to buy more of another good.*

Why Producing More Than the Competitive Output Lowers Welfare

Increasing output beyond the competitive level also decreases welfare because the cost of producing this extra output exceeds the value consumers place on it. Figure 9.4 shows the effect of increasing output from the competitive level Q_1 to Q_2 and letting the price fall to p_2, point e_2 on the demand curve, so that consumers buy the extra output.

Because price falls from p_1 to p_2, consumer surplus rises by

$$\Delta CS = C + D + E,$$

which is the area between p_2 and p_1 to the left of the demand curve. At the original price, p_1, producer surplus was $C + F$. The cost of producing the larger output is the area under the supply curve up to Q_2, $B + D + E + G + H$. The firms sell this quantity for only $p_2 Q_2$, area $F + G + H$. Thus, the new producer surplus is $F - B - D - E$. As a result, the increase in output causes producer surplus to fall by

$$\Delta PS = -B - C - D - E.$$

Because producers lose more than consumers gain, the deadweight loss is

$$\Delta W = \Delta CS + \Delta PS = (C + D + E) + (-B - C - D - E) = -B.$$

Figure 9.4 Why Increasing Output from the Competitive Level Lowers Welfare

Increasing output from the competitive level Q_1, to Q_2 lowers the price from p_1 to p_2. Consumer surplus rises by $C + D + E$, producer surplus falls by $B + C + D + E$, and welfare falls by B, which is a deadweight loss to society.

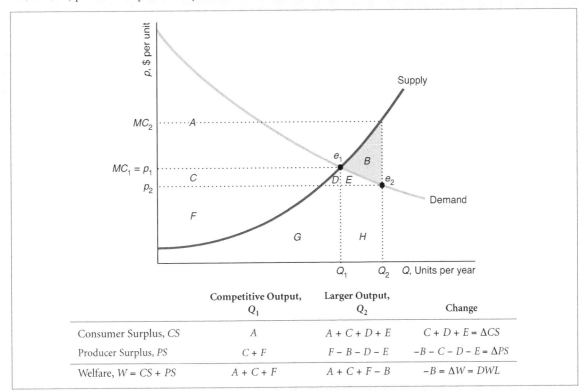

	Competitive Output, Q_1	Larger Output, Q_2	Change
Consumer Surplus, CS	A	$A + C + D + E$	$C + D + E = \Delta CS$
Producer Surplus, PS	$C + F$	$F - B - D - E$	$-B - C - D - E = \Delta PS$
Welfare, $W = CS + PS$	$A + C + F$	$A + C + F - B$	$-B = \Delta W = DWL$

A net loss occurs because consumers value the $Q_2 - Q_1$ extra output by only $E + H$, which is less than the extra cost, $B + E + H$, of producing it. The new price, p_2, is less than the marginal cost, MC_2, of producing Q_2. Too much output is being produced.

The reason that competition maximizes welfare is that price equals marginal cost at the competitive equilibrium. At the competitive equilibrium, demand equals supply, which ensures that price equals marginal cost. When price equals marginal cost, consumers value the last unit of output by exactly the amount that it costs to produce it. If consumers value the last unit by more than the marginal cost of production, welfare rises if more is produced. Similarly, if consumers value the last unit by less than its marginal cost, welfare is higher at a lower level of production.

A **market failure** is inefficient production or consumption, often because a price exceeds marginal cost. In the next application, we show that the surplus for the recipient of a gift is often less than the giver's cost, and hence gift giving is inefficient.

APPLICATION

Deadweight Loss of Christmas Presents

Just how much did you enjoy the expensive woolen socks with the dancing purple teddy bears that your Aunt Fern gave you last Christmas? Often the cost of a gift exceeds the value that the recipient places on it.

Only 10% to 15% of holiday gifts are monetary. A gift of cash typically gives at least as much pleasure to the recipient as a gift that costs the same but can't be exchanged for cash. (So what if giving cash is tacky?) Of course, it's possible that a gift can give more pleasure to the recipient than it cost the giver—but how often does that happen to you?

An *efficient gift* is one that the recipient values as much as the gift costs the giver, or more. The difference between the price of the gift and its value to the recipient is a deadweight loss to society. Joel Waldfogel (1993, 2009) asked Yale undergraduates just how large this deadweight loss is. He estimated that the deadweight loss is between 10% and 33% of the value of gifts. Waldfogel (2005) finds that consumers value their own purchases at 10% to 18% more, per dollar spent, than items received as gifts. He found that gifts from friends and "significant others" are most efficient, while noncash gifts from members of the extended family are least efficient (one-third of the value is lost). Luckily, grandparents, aunts, and uncles are most likely to give cash.

Given holiday expenditures of about $66 billion per year in 2007 in the United States, he concluded that a conservative estimate of the deadweight loss of Christmas, Hanukkah, and other holidays with gift-giving rituals is about $12 billion. (And that's not counting about 2.8 billion hours spent shopping.)

Gift recipients may exhibit an endowment effect (Chapter 3) in which their willingness to pay (WTP) for the gift is less than what they would have to be offered to give up the gift, their willingness to accept (WTA). Bauer and Schmidt (2008) asked students at the Ruhr University in Germany their WTP and WTA for three recently received Christmas gifts. On average over all students and gifts, the average WTP was 11% percent below the market price and the WTA was 18% above the market price.

The question remains why people don't give cash instead of presents.[5] If the reason is that they get pleasure from picking the "perfect" gift, the deadweight loss that adjusts for the pleasure of the giver is lower than these calculations suggest. (Bah, humbug!)

---

[5]People sometimes deal with a disappointing present by "regifting" it. Some families have been passing the same fruitcake among family members for decades. According to a survey just before Christmas in 2004, 33% of women and 19% of men admitted that they pass on an unwanted gift (and 28% of respondents said that they would not admit it if asked whether they had done so).

9.4 Policies That Shift Supply Curves

I don't make jokes. I just watch the government and report the facts. —Will Rogers

One of the main reasons that economists developed welfare tools was to predict the impact of government programs that alter a competitive equilibrium. Virtually all government actions affect a competitive equilibrium in one of two ways. Some government policies, such as limits on the number of firms in a market, shift the supply or demand curve. Others, such as sales taxes, create a wedge or gap between price and marginal cost so that they are not equal, even though they were in the original competitive equilibrium.

These government interventions move us from an unconstrained competitive equilibrium to a new, constrained competitive equilibrium. Because welfare was maximized at the initial competitive equilibrium, the examples of government-induced changes that we consider here lower welfare. In later chapters, we examine markets in which government intervention may raise welfare because welfare was not maximized initially.

Although government policies may cause either the supply curve or the demand curve to shift, we concentrate on policies that limit supply because they are used frequently and have clear-cut effects. The two most common types of government policies that shift the supply curve are limits on the number of firms in a market and quotas or other limits on the amount of output that firms may produce. We study restrictions on entry and exit of firms in this section and examine quotas later in the chapter.

Government policies that cause a decrease in supply at each possible price (that is, shift the supply curve to the left) lead to fewer purchases by consumers at higher prices, an outcome that lowers consumer surplus and welfare. Welfare falls when governments restrict the consumption of competitive products that we all agree are *goods*, such as food and medical services. In contrast, if most of society wants to discourage the use of certain products, such as hallucinogenic drugs and poisons, policies that restrict consumption may increase some measures of society's welfare.

Governments, other organizations, and social pressures limit the number of firms in at least three ways. The number of firms is restricted explicitly in some markets such as taxi service. In other markets, some members of society are barred from owning firms or performing certain jobs or services. In yet other markets, the number of firms is controlled indirectly by raising the cost of entry.

Restricting the Number of Firms

A limit on the number of firms causes the supply curve to shift to the left. As a result, the equilibrium price rises and the equilibrium quantity falls. Consumers are harmed: They do not buy as much as they would at lower prices. Firms that are in the market when the limits are first imposed benefit from higher profits.

To illustrate these results, we examine the regulation of taxicabs. Countries throughout the world regulate taxicabs. Many American cities limit the number of taxicabs. To operate a cab in these cities legally, you must possess a city-issued permit.

Two explanations are given for such regulation. First, using permits to limit the number of cabs raises the earnings of permit owners—usually taxi fleet owners—who lobby city officials for such restrictions. Second, some city officials contend that limiting cabs allows for better regulation of cabbies' behavior and protection of consumers. (However, it would seem possible that cities could directly regulate behavior and not restrict the number of cabs.)

298 Chapter 9 Applications of the Competitive Model

Whatever the justification for such regulation, the limit on the number of cabs raises the market prices. If the city does not limit entry, a virtually unlimited number of potential taxi drivers with identical costs can enter freely.

Panel a of Figure 9.5 shows a typical taxi owner's marginal cost curve, MC, and average cost curve, AC^1. The MC curve slopes upward because a typical cabbie's opportunity cost of working more hours increases as the cabbie works longer hours (drives more customers). An outward shift of the demand curve is met by new firms entering, so the long-run supply curve of taxi rides, S^1 in panel b, is horizontal at the minimum of AC^1 (Chapter 8). For the market demand curve in the figure, the equilibrium is E_1 where the equilibrium price, p_1, equals the minimum of AC^1 of a typical cab. The total number of rides is $Q_1 = n_1 q_1$, where n_1 is the equilibrium number of cabs and q_1 is the number of rides per month provided by a typical cab.

Consumer surplus, $A + B + C$, is the area under the market demand curve above p_1 up to Q_1. There is no producer surplus because the supply curve is horizontal at the market price, which equals marginal and average cost. Thus, welfare is the same as consumer surplus.

Figure 9.5 Effect of a Restriction on the Number of Cabs

A restriction on the number of cabs causes the supply curve to shift from S^1 to S^2 in the short run and the equilibrium to change from E_1 to E_2. The resulting lost surplus, C, is a deadweight loss to society. In the long run, the unusual profit, π, created by the restriction becomes a rent to the owner of the license. As the license owner increases the charge for using the license, the average cost curve rises to AC^2, so the cab driver earns a zero long-run profit. That is, the producer surplus goes to the permit holder, not to the cab driver.

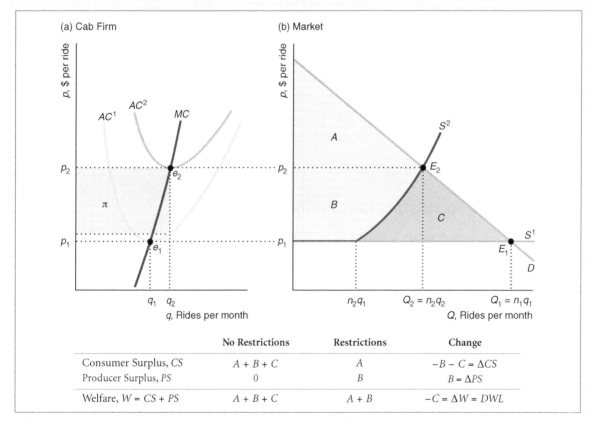

	No Restrictions	Restrictions	Change
Consumer Surplus, CS	$A + B + C$	A	$-B - C = \Delta CS$
Producer Surplus, PS	0	B	$B = \Delta PS$
Welfare, $W = CS + PS$	$A + B + C$	$A + B$	$-C = \Delta W = DWL$

Legislation limits the number of permits to operate cabs to $n_2 < n_1$. The market supply curve, S^2, is the horizontal sum of the marginal cost curves above the corresponding minimum average cost curves of the n_2 firms in the market. For the market to produce more than $n_2 q_1$ rides, the price must rise to induce the n_2 firms to supply more.

With the same demand curve as before, the equilibrium market price rises to p_2. At this higher price, each licensed cab firm produces more than before by operating longer hours, $q_2 > q_1$, but the total number of rides, $Q_2 = n_2 q_2$, falls because there are fewer cabs, n_2. Consumer surplus is A, producer surplus is B, and welfare is $A + B$.

Thus, because of the higher fares (prices) under a permit system, consumer surplus falls by

$$\Delta CS = -B - C.$$

The producer surplus of the lucky permit owners rises by

$$\Delta PS = B.$$

As a result, total welfare falls,

$$\Delta W = \Delta CS + \Delta PS = (-B - C) + B = -C,$$

which is a deadweight loss.

By preventing other potential cab firms from entering the market, limiting cab permits creates economic profit, the area labeled π in panel a, for permit owners. In many cities, these permits can be sold or rented, so the owner of the scarce resource, the permit, can capture this unusual profit, or rent. The rent for the permit or the implicit rent paid by the owner of a permit causes the cab driver's average cost to rise to AC^2. Because the rent allows the use of the cab for a certain period of time, it is a fixed cost that is unrelated to output. As a result, it does not affect the marginal cost.

Cab drivers earn zero economic profits because the market price, p_2, equals their average cost, the minimum of AC^2. The producer surplus, B, created by the limits on entry goes to the original owners of the permits rather than to the current cab drivers. Thus, the permit owners are the *only* ones who benefit from the restrictions, and their gains are less than the losses to others. If the government collected the rents each year in the form of an annual license, then these rents could be distributed to all citizens instead of to just a few lucky permit owners.

In many cities, the rents and welfare effects that result from these laws are large. The size of the loss to consumers and the benefit to permit holders depend on how severely a city limits the number of cabs.

APPLICATION	
Licensing Cabs	*Too bad the only people who know how to run the country are busy driving cabs and cutting hair.* —George Burns

Limiting the number of cabs has large effects in cities around the world. Some cities regulate the number of cabs much more strictly than others. Tokyo has five times as many cabs as New York City. San Francisco, which limits cabs, has only a tenth as many cabs as Washington, D.C., which has fewer people but does not restrict the number of cabs. The number of residents per cab is 757 in Detroit, 748 in San Francisco, 538 in Dallas, 533 in Baltimore, 350 in Boston, 301 in New Orleans, and 203 in Honolulu.

In 1937, when New York City started regulating the number of cabs, all 11,787 cab owners could buy a permit, called a medallion, for $10. Because New

York City allows these medallions to be sold, medallion holders do not have to operate a cab to benefit from the restriction on the number of cabs. A holder can sell a medallion for an amount that captures the unusually high future profits from the limit on the number of cabs. The number of medallions has hardly increased, reaching only 12,779 in 2006 plus another 308 hybrid-electric or "green" taxicabs in 2007. Because the number of users of cabs has increased substantially, this limit has become more binding over time, so the price of a medallion has soared. In July 2009, the owner of a New York cab medallion sold it for $766,000. The value of all New York City taxi licenses is $9.7 billion (much greater than the $2.6 billion insured value of the World Trade Center).

Medallion systems in other cities have also generated large medallion values. Taxi licenses usually sell for £25,000 ($44,400) in the United Kingdom and for more than $100,000 in Rome as of 2005. After Ireland's High Court relaxed the severe limit on taxis, the number of cabs in Dublin more than tripled from 2,722 to 8,609 and the value of a taxi license fell from I£90,000 to the new amount charged by the city, I£5,000.

Cab drivers do not make unusual returns. New York City cab drivers who lease medallions earn as little as $50 to $115 a day. In Boston, cabbies average 72 hours a week driving someone else's taxi, to net maybe $550. Permit holders capture the extra producer surplus, which would be eliminated if there were free entry into the market.

A 1984 study for the U.S. Department of Transportation estimated consumers' annual extra cost from restrictions on the number of taxicabs throughout the United States at nearly $2.1 billion (in 2009 dollars). The total lost consumer surplus is even greater because this amount does not include lost waiting time and other inconveniences associated with having fewer taxis. Movements toward liberalizing entry into taxi markets started in the United States in the 1980s and in Sweden, Ireland, the Netherlands, and the United Kingdom in the 1990s, but tight regulation remains common throughout the world.

Raising Entry and Exit Costs

Instead of directly restricting the number of firms that may enter a market, governments and other organizations may raise the cost of entering, thereby indirectly restricting that number. Similarly, raising the cost of exiting a market discourages some firms from entering.

Entry Barriers. If its cost will be greater than that of firms already in the market, a potential firm might not enter a market even if existing firms are making a profit. Any cost that falls only on potential entrants and not on current firms discourages entry. A long-run **barrier to entry** is an explicit restriction or a cost that applies only to potential new firms—existing firms are not subject to the restriction or do not bear the cost.

At the time they entered, incumbent firms had to pay many of the costs of entering a market that new entrants incur, such as the fixed costs of building plants, buying equipment, and advertising a new product. For example, the fixed cost to McDonald's and other fast-food chains of opening a new fast-food restaurant is about $2 million. These fixed costs are *costs of entry* but are *not* barriers to entry because they apply equally to incumbents and entrants. Costs incurred by both incumbents and entrants do not discourage potential firms from entering a market if existing firms are making money. Potential entrants know that they will do as well as existing firms once they begin operations, so they are willing to enter as long as profit opportunities exist.

Large sunk costs can be barriers to entry under two conditions. First, if capital markets do not work efficiently so that new firms have difficulty raising money, new firms may be unable to enter profitable markets. Second, if a firm must incur a large *sunk* cost, which increases the loss if it exits, the firm may be reluctant to enter a market in which it is uncertain of success.

Exit Barriers. Some markets have barriers that make it difficult (though typically not impossible) for a firm to exit by going out of business. In the short run, exit barriers can keep the number of firms in a market relatively high. In the long run, exit barriers may limit the number of firms in a market.

Why do exit barriers limit the number of firms in a market? Suppose that you are considering starting a construction firm with no capital or other fixed factors. The firm's only input is labor. You know that there is relatively little demand for construction during business downturns and in the winter. To avoid paying workers when business is slack, you plan to shut down during those periods. If you can avoid losses by shutting down during low-demand periods, you enter this market if your expected economic profits during good periods are zero or positive.

A law that requires you to give your workers six months' warning before laying them off prevents you from shutting down quickly. You know that you'll regularly suffer losses during business downturns because you'll have to pay your workers for up to six months during periods when you have nothing for them to do. Knowing that you'll incur these regular losses, you are less inclined to enter the market. Unless the economic profits during good periods are much higher than zero—high enough to offset your losses—you will not choose to enter the market. (See "Job Termination Laws," in **MyEconLab**'s textbook resources for Chapter 9.)

If exit barriers limit the number of firms, the same analysis that we used to examine entry barriers applies. Thus, exit barriers may raise prices, lower consumer surplus, and reduce welfare.

9.5 Policies That Create a Wedge Between Supply and Demand Curves

The most common government policies that create a wedge between supply and demand curves are sales taxes (or subsidies) and price controls. Because these policies create a gap between marginal cost and price, either too little or too much is produced. For example, a tax causes price to exceed marginal cost—that is, consumers value the good more than it costs to produce it—with the result that consumer surplus, producer surplus, and welfare fall (although tax revenue rises).

Welfare Effects of a Sales Tax

A new sales tax causes the price that consumers pay to rise (Chapter 2), resulting in a loss of consumer surplus, $\Delta CS < 0$, and the price that firms receive to fall, resulting in a drop in producer surplus, $\Delta PS < 0$. However, this tax provides the government with new tax revenue, $\Delta T = T > 0$, if tax revenue was zero before the new tax.

Assuming that the government does something useful with the tax revenue, we should include tax revenue in our definition of welfare:

$$W = CS + PS + T.$$

As a result, the change in welfare is

$$\Delta W = \Delta CS + \Delta PS + \Delta T.$$

Even when we include tax revenue in our welfare measure, a specific tax must lower welfare in, for example, the competitive market for tea roses. We show the welfare loss from a specific tax of $\tau = 11¢$ per rose stem in Figure 9.6, which is based on estimated demand and supply curves.

Without the tax, the intersection of the demand curve, D, and the supply curve, S, determines the competitive equilibrium, e_1, at a price of 30¢ per stem and a quan-

Figure 9.6 Welfare Effects of a Specific Tax on Roses

The $\tau = 11¢$ specific tax on roses creates an 11¢ per stem wedge between the price customers pay, 32¢, and the price producers receive, 21¢. Tax revenue is $T = \tau Q =$ $127.6 million per year. The deadweight loss to society is $C + E = \$4.95$ million per year.

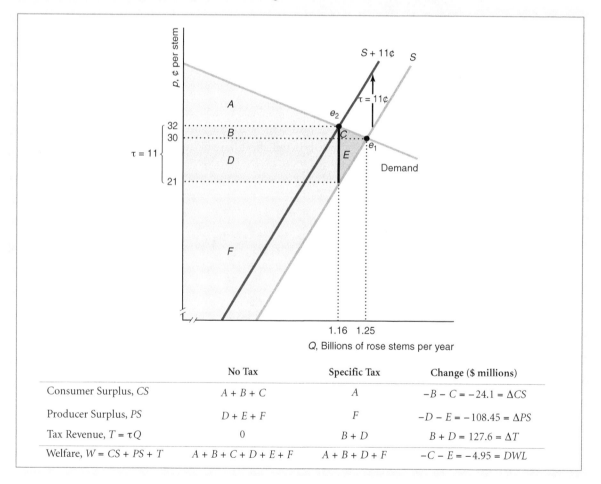

	No Tax	Specific Tax	Change ($ millions)
Consumer Surplus, CS	$A + B + C$	A	$-B - C = -24.1 = \Delta CS$
Producer Surplus, PS	$D + E + F$	F	$-D - E = -108.45 = \Delta PS$
Tax Revenue, $T = \tau Q$	0	$B + D$	$B + D = 127.6 = \Delta T$
Welfare, $W = CS + PS + T$	$A + B + C + D + E + F$	$A + B + D + F$	$-C - E = -4.95 = DWL$

tity of 1.25 billion rose stems per year. Consumer surplus is $A + B + C$, producer surplus is $D + E + F$, tax revenue is zero, and there is no deadweight loss.

The specific tax shifts the effective supply curve up by 11¢, creating an 11¢ wedge or differential between the price consumers pay, 32¢, and the price producers receive, $32¢ - \tau = 21¢$. Equilibrium output falls from 1.25 to 1.16 billion stems per year.

The extra 2¢ per stem that buyers pay causes consumer surplus to fall by $B + C$ = $24.1 million per year, as we showed in Figure 5.5. Due to the 9¢ drop in the price firms receive, they lose producer surplus of $D + E$ = $108.45 million per year (Solved Problem 9.1). The government gains tax revenue of $\tau Q = 11¢$ per stem × 1.16 billion stems per year = $127.6 million per year, area $B + D$.

The combined loss of consumer surplus and producer surplus is only partially offset by the government's gain in tax revenue, so welfare drops:

$$\Delta W = \Delta CS + \Delta PS + \Delta T = -\$24.1 - \$108.45 + \$127.6 = -\$4.95 \text{ million per year.}$$

This deadweight loss is area $C + E$.

Why does society suffer a deadweight loss? The reason is that the tax lowers output from the competitive level where welfare is maximized. An equivalent explanation for this inefficiency or loss to society is that the tax puts a wedge between price and marginal cost. At the new equilibrium, buyers are willing to pay $p = 32¢$ for one more rose stem, while the marginal cost to firms is only 21¢ ($= p - \tau$). Shouldn't more roses be produced and sold if consumers are willing to pay nearly a third more than the cost of producing it? That's what our welfare study indicates. See "Deadweight Loss from Wireless Taxes" in **MyEconLab**'s textbook resources for Chapter 9.

Welfare Effects of a Price Floor

In some markets, the government sets a *price floor*, or minimum price, which is the lowest price a consumer can legally pay for the good. For example, in most countries, the government sets price floors for at least some agricultural products, which guarantee producers that they will receive at least a price of $\underline{p}$ for their good. If the market price is above $\underline{p}$, the support program is irrelevant. If the market price is below $\underline{p}$, however, the government buys as much output as necessary to drive the price up to $\underline{p}$. Since 1929 (the start of the Great Depression), the U.S. government has used price floors or similar programs to keep the prices of many agricultural products above the price that competition would determine in unregulated markets.

My favorite program is the wool and mohair subsidy. The U.S. government instituted wool price supports after the Korean War to ensure "strategic supplies" for uniforms. Congress later added mohair subsidies, even though mohair has no military use. In some years, the mohair subsidy exceeded the amount consumers paid for mohair, and the subsidies on wool and mohair reached a fifth of a billion dollars over the first half-century of support. No doubt the Clinton-era end of these subsidies in 1995 endangered national security. Thanks to Senator Phil Gramm, a well-known fiscal conservative, and other patriots (primarily from Texas, where much mohair is produced), the subsidy was resurrected in 2000.[6] Representative Lamar Smith took vehement exception to people who questioned the need to subsidize mohair: "Mohair is popular! I have a mohair sweater! It's my favorite one!" The 2006 budget called for $11 million for wool and mohair with a loan rate of $4.20 per pound.

---

[6]As U.S. Representative Lynn Martin said, "No matter what your religion, you should try to become a government program, for then you will have everlasting life."

We now show the effect of a price support using estimated supply and demand curves for the soybean market (Holt, 1992). The intersection of the market demand curve and the market supply curve in Figure 9.7 determines the competitive equilibrium, e, in the absence of a price support program, where the equilibrium price is $p_1 = \$4.59$ per bushel and the equilibrium quantity is $Q_1 = 2.1$ billion bushels per year.

With a price support on soybeans of $\underline{p} = \$5.00$ per bushel and the government's pledge to buy as much output as farmers want to sell, quantity sold is $Q_s = 2.2$ billion bushels.[7] At $\underline{p}$, consumers buy less output, $Q_d = 1.9$ billion bushels, than the Q_1 they would have bought at the market-determined price p_1. As a result, con-

Figure 9.7 Effect of Price Supports in Soybeans

Without government price supports, the equilibrium is e, where $p_1 = \$4.59$ per bushel and $Q_1 = 2.1$ billion bushels of soybeans per year (based on estimates in Holt, 1992). With the price support at $\underline{p} = \$5.00$ per bushel, output sold increases to Q_s and consumer purchases fall to Q_d, so the government must buy $Q_g = Q_s - Q_d$ at a cost of $1.283 billion per year. The deadweight loss is $C + F + G = \$1.226$ billion per year, not counting storage and administrative costs.

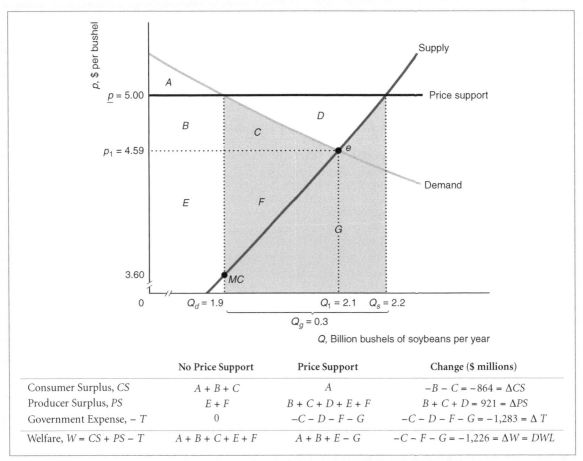

	No Price Support	Price Support	Change ($ millions)
Consumer Surplus, CS	A + B + C	A	−B − C = −864 = ΔCS
Producer Surplus, PS	E + F	B + C + D + E + F	B + C + D = 921 = ΔPS
Government Expense, − T	0	−C − D − F − G	−C − D − F − G = −1,283 = Δ T
Welfare, W = CS + PS − T	A + B + C + E + F	A + B + E − G	−C − F − G = −1,226 = ΔW = DWL

---

[7]In 1985, the price support was $5.02. The 2002 farm bill set the support at $5.80 from 2002 through 2007.

sumer surplus falls by $B + C = \$864$ million. The government buys $Q_g = Q_s - Q_d$ ≈ 0.3 billion bushels per year, which is the excess supply, at a cost of $T = \underline{p} \times Q_g$ $= C + D + F + G = \$1.283$ billion.

The government cannot resell the output domestically, because if it tried to do so, it would succeed only in driving down the price consumers pay. Instead, the government stores the output or sends it abroad.

Although farmers gain producer surplus of $B + C + D = \$921$ million, this program is an inefficient way to transfer money to them. Assuming that the government's purchases have no alternative use, the change in welfare is $\Delta W = \Delta CS + \Delta PS - T = -C - F - G = -\$1.226$ billion per year.[8] This deadweight loss reflects two distortions in this market:

1. **Excess production:** More output is produced than is consumed, so Q_g is stored, destroyed, or shipped abroad.
2. **Inefficiency in consumption:** At the quantity they actually buy, Q_d, consumers are willing to pay \$5 for the last bushel of soybeans, which is more than the marginal cost, $MC = \$3.60$, of producing that bushel.

Alternative Price Support. After price supports were first introduced, the U.S. government was buying and storing large quantities of grains and other foods, much of which was allowed to spoil. As a consequence, since 1938 the government has limited how much farmers can produce. Because there is uncertainty about how much farmers will produce, the government sets quotas, or limits, on the amount of land farmers can use, thereby restricting their output.[9] Today, the government uses an alternative subsidy program. The government sets a support price, $\underline{p}$. Farmers decide how much to grow, and they sell all of their produce to consumers at the price, p, that clears the market. The government then gives the farmers a *deficiency* payment equal to the difference between the support and actual prices, $\underline{p} - p$, for every unit sold so that farmers receive the support price on their entire crop.

SOLVED PROBLEM 9.2

What are the effects in the soybean market of a \$5-per-bushel deficiency-payment price support on the equilibrium price and quantity, consumer surplus, producer surplus, and deadweight loss?

Answer

1. *Describe how the program affects the equilibrium price and quantity.* Without a price support, the equilibrium is e_1 in the figure, where the price is $p_1 = \$4.59$ and the quantity is 2.1 billion bushels per year. With a support price of \$5 per bushel, the new equilibrium is e_2. Farmers produce at the quantity where the price support line hits their supply curve at 2.2 billion bushels. The equilibrium price is the height of the demand curve at 2.2 billion bushels, or approximately \$4.39 per bushel. Thus, the equilibrium price falls and the quantity increases.

---

[8] This measure of deadweight loss underestimates the true loss. The government also pays storage and administration costs. In 2005 the U.S. Department of Agriculture (USDA), which runs farm support programs, had 109,832 employees, or one worker for every eight farms that received assistance (although many of these employees had other job responsibilities). In 2009, the Secretary of Agriculture said that the USDA computer software was so out of date that he could not determine the number of employees.

[9] See Solved Problem 2 in **MyEconLab**'s textbook resources for Chapter 9.

2. *Show the welfare effects.* Because the price consumers pay drops from p_1 to p_2, consumer surplus rises by area $D + E$. Producers now receive $\underline{p}$ instead of p_1, so their producer surplus rises by $B + C$. Government payments are the difference between the support price, $\underline{p} = \$5$, and the price consumers pay, $p_2 = \$4.39$, times the number of units sold, 2.2 billion bushels per year, or the rectangle $B + C + D + E + F$. Because government expenditures exceed the gains to consumers and producers, welfare falls by the deadweight loss triangle F.[10]

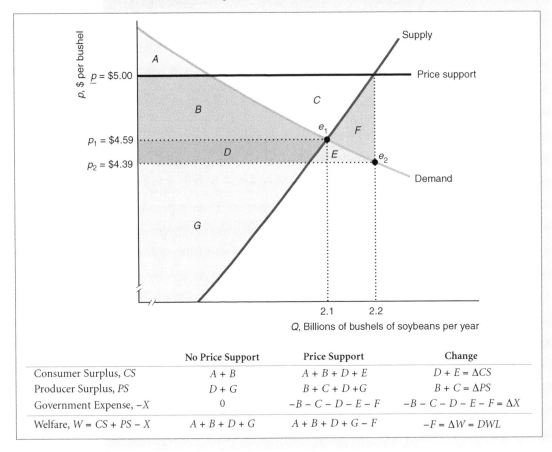

	No Price Support	Price Support	Change
Consumer Surplus, CS	$A + B$	$A + B + D + E$	$D + E = \Delta CS$
Producer Surplus, PS	$D + G$	$B + C + D + G$	$B + C = \Delta PS$
Government Expense, $-X$	0	$-B - C - D - E - F$	$-B - C - D - E - F = \Delta X$
Welfare, $W = CS + PS - X$	$A + B + D + G$	$A + B + D + G - F$	$-F = \Delta W = DWL$

Who Benefits? Presumably, the purpose of these programs is to help poor farmers, not to hurt consumers and taxpayers. However, the lion's share of American farm subsidies goes to large agricultural corporations, not to poor farmers. Three-quarters of U.S. farms have sales of less than $50,000 per year, yet these farms received only 16% of the total direct government payments for agriculture in 2003. In contrast, farms with over half a million dollars in annual sales are only 3.5% of all farms, yet they received 29% of all direct government payments. Farms with over a quarter of a million dollars in sales (the top 8% of all farms) received 50% of the payments.

---

[10]Compared to the soybean price support program in Figure 9.7, the deficiency payment approach results in a smaller deadweight loss (less than a tenth of the original one) and lower government expenditures (though the expenditures need not be smaller in general).

APPLICATION

Giving Money to Farmers

Virtually every country in the world showers its farmers with subsidies. For example, EU sugar producers received three times the world price of sugar in 2009.

Although government support to farmers has fallen in developed countries over the last decade, support remains high. Farmers in developed countries received $265 billion in direct agricultural producer support payments (subsidies) in 2008, including $150 billion in the European Union, $41 billion in Japan, $23 billion in the United States, and $18 billion in Korea. These payments are a large percentage of actual sales in many countries, averaging 21% in developed countries, and ranging from 62% in Norway, 58% in Switzerland, 48% in Japan, 25% in the European Union, 13% in Canada, 7% in the United States, 6% in Australia, to only 1% in New Zealand.

Total U.S. agricultural support payments were $96 billion, or about 0.67% of the U.S. gross domestic product. Each adult in the United States pays about $500 a year to support agriculture. Did you get full value for your money? (Cargill, Monsanto, and Archer Daniels Midland thank you.)

Welfare Effects of a Price Ceiling

In some markets, the government sets a *price ceiling*: the highest price that a firm can legally charge. If the government sets the ceiling below the unregulated competitive price, consumers demand more than the unregulated equilibrium quantity and firms supply less than that quantity (Chapter 2). Producer surplus must fall because firms receive a lower price and sell fewer units.

As a result of the price ceiling, consumers buy the good at a lower price but are limited in how much they can buy by sellers. Because less is sold than at the pre-control equilibrium, there is a deadweight loss: Consumers value the good more than the marginal cost of producing extra units.

This measure of the deadweight loss may *underestimate* the true loss for two reasons. First, because consumers want to buy more units than are sold, they may spend additional time searching for a store with units for sale. This (often unsuccessful) search activity is wasteful and thus an additional deadweight loss to society. Deacon and Sonstelie (1989) calculated that for every $1 consumers saved from lower prices due to U.S. gasoline price controls in 1973, they lost $1.16 in waiting time and other factors.[11]

Second, when a price ceiling creates excess demand, the customers who are lucky enough to buy the good may not be the consumers who value it most. In a market without a price ceiling, all consumers who value the good more than the market price buy it, and those who value it less do not, so that those consumers who value it most buy the good. In contrast with a price control where the good is sold on a first-come first-served basis, the consumers who reach the store first may not be the consumers with the highest willingness to pay. With a price control, if a lucky customer who buys a unit of the good has a willingness to pay of p_0, while someone who cannot buy it has a willingness to pay of $p_1 > p_0$, then the *allocative cost* to society of this unit being sold to the "wrong" consumer is $p_1 - p_0$.[12]

---

[11]Strangely, this type of wasteful search does not occur if the good is efficiently but inequitably distributed to people according to a discriminatory criteria such as race, gender, or attractiveness because people who are suffering discrimination know it is pointless to search.

[12]This allocative cost will be reduced or eliminated if there is a resale market where consumers who place a high value on the good can buy it from consumers who place a lower value on the good but were lucky enough to be able to buy it initially.

SOLVED PROBLEM 9.3

What is the effect on the equilibrium, consumer surplus, producer surplus, and welfare if the government sets a price ceiling, $\bar{p}$, below the unregulated competitive equilibrium price?

Answer

1. *Show the initial unregulated equilibrium.* The intersection of the demand curve and the supply curve determines the unregulated, competitive equilibrium e_1, where the equilibrium quantity is Q_1.

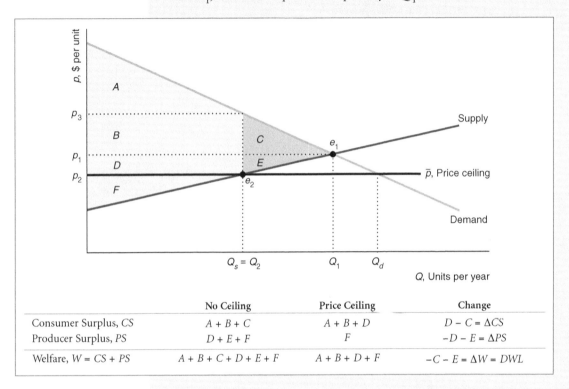

	No Ceiling	Price Ceiling	Change
Consumer Surplus, CS	A + B + C	A + B + D	D − C = ΔCS
Producer Surplus, PS	D + E + F	F	−D − E = ΔPS
Welfare, W = CS + PS	A + B + C + D + E + F	A + B + D + F	−C − E = ΔW = DWL

2. *Show how the equilibrium changes with the price ceiling.* Because the price ceiling, $\bar{p}$, is set below the equilibrium price of p_1, the ceiling binds. At this lower price, consumer demand increases to Q_d while the quantity that firms are willing to supply falls to Q_s, so only $Q_s = Q_2$ units are sold at the new equilibrium, e_2. Thus, the price control causes the equilibrium quantity and price to fall, but consumers have excess demand of $Q_d − Q_s$.

3. *Describe the welfare effects.* Because consumers are able to buy Q_s units at a lower price than before the controls, they gain area D. Consumers lose consumer surplus of C, however, because they can purchase only Q_s instead of Q_1 units of output. Thus, consumers gain net consumer surplus of $D − C$. Because they sell fewer units at a lower price, firms lose producer surplus $−D − E$. Part of this loss, D, is transferred to consumers in the form of lower prices, but the rest, E, is a loss to society. The deadweight loss to society—the change in welfare—is at least $\Delta W = \Delta CS + \Delta PS = -C - E$.

APPLICATION

The Social Cost of a Natural Gas Price Ceiling

From 1954 through 1989, U.S. federal law imposed a price ceiling on interstate sales of natural gas. The law did not apply to sales within the Southwest states that produced the gas—primarily Louisiana, Oklahoma, New Mexico, and Texas. Consequently, consumers in the Midwest and Northeast, where most of the gas was used, were less likely to be able to buy as much natural gas as they wanted, unlike consumers in the Southwest. Because they could not buy natural gas, some consumers who would have otherwise done so did not install natural gas heating. As heating systems last for years, even today, many homes use dirtier fuels such as heating oil due to this decades-old price control.

By comparing consumer behavior before and after the control period, Davis and Kilian (2008) estimated that demand for natural gas exceeded observed sales of natural gas by an average of 20.3% from 1950 through 2000. They calculated that the allocative cost averaged $4.6 billion annually during this half century. This additional loss is nearly half of the estimated annual deadweight loss from the price control of $10.5 billion (MacAvoy, 2000). The total loss is $15.1 (= $10.5 + $4.6) billion.[13]

9.6 Comparing Both Types of Policies: Trade

Traditionally, most of Australia's imports come from overseas.
—Keppel Enderbery, former Australian cabinet minister

We have examined examples of government policies that shift supply or demand curves and policies that create a wedge between supply and demand. Governments use both types of policies to control international trade.

Allowing imports of foreign goods benefits the importing country. If a government reduces imports of a good, the domestic price rises; the profits increase for domestic firms that produce the good but domestic consumers are hurt. Our analysis will show that the loss to consumers exceeds the gain to producers.

The government of the (potentially) importing country can use one of four trade (import) policies:

1. **Allow free trade**: Any firm can sell in the importing country without restrictions.
2. **Ban all imports**: The government sets a quota of zero on imports.
3. **Set a positive quota**: The government limits imports to $\bar{Q}$.
4. **Set a tariff**: The government imposes a tax called a **tariff** (or a *duty*) only on imported goods.

We compare welfare under free trade to welfare under bans and quotas, which change the supply curve, and to welfare under tariffs, which create a wedge between supply and demand.

To illustrate the differences in welfare under these various policies, we examine the U.S. market for crude oil. We also assume, for the sake of simplicity, that

---

[13]Consumers' share of the deadweight loss, area C in the figure in Solved Problem 9.3, is $9.3 billion annually; the sellers' share, area E, is $1.2 billion; so the entire deadweight loss is $10.5 billion. Consumers who are lucky enough to buy the gas gain area $D = $6.9 billion from paying a lower price, which represents a transfer from sellers. Thus, altogether consumers lose $7.0 (= $9.3 + $4.6 − $6.9) billion and firms lose $8.1 (= $1.2 + $6.9) billion.

transportation costs are zero and that the supply curve of the potentially imported good is horizontal at the world price p^*. Given these two assumptions, the importing country, the United States, can buy as much of this good as it wants at p^* per unit: It is a price taker in the world market because its demand is too small to influence the world price.

Free Trade Versus a Ban on Imports

No nation was ever ruined by trade. —Benjamin Franklin

Preventing imports raises the domestic market price. We now compare the equilibrium with and without free trade in the U.S. oil market.

The estimated U.S. daily demand function for oil is[14]

$$Q = D(p) = 35.4p^{-0.37}, \quad (9.3)$$

and the U.S. daily domestic supply function is

$$Q = S(p) = 3.35p^{0.33}. \quad (9.4)$$

Although the estimated U.S. domestic supply curve, S^a, in Figure 9.8 is upward sloping, the foreign supply curve is horizontal at the world price of \$14.70. The total U.S. supply curve, S^1, is the horizontal sum of the domestic supply curve and the foreign supply curve. Thus, S^1 is the same as the upward-sloping domestic supply curve for prices below \$14.70 and is horizontal at \$14.70. Under free trade, the United States imports crude oil if its domestic price in the absence of imports would exceed the world price, \$14.70 per barrel.

The free-trade equilibrium, e_1, is determined by the intersection of S^1 and the demand curve, where the U.S. price equals the world price, \$14.70. Substituting p = \$14.70 into demand function in Equation 9.3, we find that the equilibrium quantity is about $13.1 \approx 35.4(14.70)^{-0.37}$ million barrels per day. At the equilibrium price of \$14.70, domestic supply is about 8.2, so imports are 4.9 (= 13.1 − 8.2). U.S. consumer surplus is $A + B + C$, U.S. producer surplus is D, and U.S. welfare is $A + B + C + D$. Throughout our discussion of trade, we ignore welfare effects in other countries.

If imports are banned, the total U.S. supply curve, S^2, is the American domestic supply curve, S^a. The equilibrium is at e_2, where S^2 intersects the demand curve. The new equilibrium price is \$29.04, and the new equilibrium quantity, 10.2 million barrels per day, is produced domestically.[15] Consumer surplus is A, producer surplus is $B + D$, and welfare is $A + B + D$.

The ban helps producers but harms consumers. Because of the higher price, domestic firms gain producer surplus of $\Delta PS = B$. The change in consumer surplus is $\Delta CS = -B - C$. Does the ban help the United States? The change in total welfare, ΔW, is the difference between the gain to producers and the loss to consumers, $\Delta W = \Delta PS + \Delta CS = -C$, so the ban hurts society.

---

[14]These short-run, constant-elasticity supply and demand equations for crude oil in 1988 are based on the short-run supply and demand elasticities reported by Anderson and Metzger (1991).

[15]In equilibrium, the right-hand sides of Equations 9.3 and 9.4 are equal: $35.4p^{-0.37} = 3.35p^{0.33}$. By dividing both sides by $p^{-0.37}$ and 3.35, we find that $p^{0.7} \approx 10.57$. Raising both sides of this expression to the 1/0.7 = 1.43 power shows that the no-trade equilibrium price is about \$29.04. Substituting this price into Equation 9.3 or 9.4 gives us the equilibrium quantity, which is about 10.2.

9.6 Comparing Both Types of Policies: Trade 311

Figure 9.8 Loss from Eliminating Free Trade

Because the supply curve that foreigners face is horizontal at the world price of $14.70, the total U.S. supply curve of crude oil is S^1 when there is free trade. The free-trade equilibrium is e_1. With a ban on imports, the equilibrium e_2 occurs where the domestic supply curve, $S^a =$ S^2, intersects D. The ban increases producer surplus by B = $132.5 million per day and decreases consumer surplus by $B + C$ = $163.7 million per day, so the deadweight loss is C = $31.2 million per day or $11.4 billion per year.

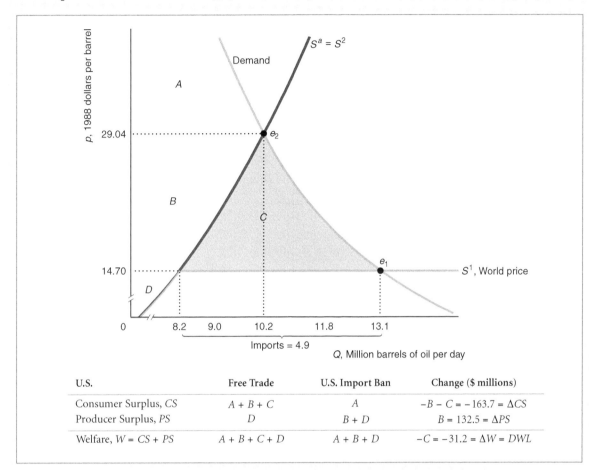

U.S.	Free Trade	U.S. Import Ban	Change ($ millions)
Consumer Surplus, CS	A + B + C	A	$-B - C = -163.7 = \Delta CS$
Producer Surplus, PS	D	B + D	$B = 132.5 = \Delta PS$
Welfare, W = CS + PS	A + B + C + D	A + B + D	$-C = -31.2 = \Delta W = DWL$

SOLVED PROBLEM 9.4

Based on the estimates of the U.S. daily oil demand function in Equation 9.3 and the supply function in 9.4, use calculus to determine the changes in producer surplus, consumer surplus, and welfare from eliminating free trade. (Round results to the nearest tenth.)

Answer

1. *Integrate with respect to price between the free-trade and no-trade prices to obtain the change in producer surplus.* If imports are banned, the gain in domestic producer surplus is the area to the left of the domestic supply curve

between the free-trade price, $14.70, and the price with the ban in effect, $29.04, which is area B in Figure 9.8.[16] Integrating, we find that

$$\Delta PS = \int_{14.70}^{29.04} S(p)\,dp = \int_{14.70}^{29.04} 3.35 p^{0.33}\,dp$$

$$= \frac{3.35}{1.33} p^{1.33} \Big|_{14.70}^{29.04} \approx 2.52(29.04^{1.33} - 14.70^{1.33}) \approx 132.5.$$

2. *Integrate with respect to price between the free-trade and no-trade prices to obtain the change in consumer surplus.* The lost consumer surplus is found by integrating to the left of the demand curve between the relevant prices:

$$\Delta CS = -\int_{14.70}^{29.04} D(p)\,dp = -\int_{14.70}^{29.04} 35.41 p^{-0.37}\,dp = -163.7.$$

3. *To determine the change in welfare, sum the changes in consumer surplus and producer surplus.* The change in welfare is $\Delta W = \Delta CS + \Delta PS = -163.7 + 132.5 = -\$31.2$ million per day or $-\$11.4$ billion per year. This deadweight loss is 24% of the gain to producers: Consumers lose $1.24 for every $1 that producers gain from a ban.

Free Trade Versus a Tariff

TARIFF, n. A scale of taxes on imports, designed to protect the domestic producer against the greed of his customers. —Ambrose Bierce

There are two common types of tariffs: *specific tariffs* (τ dollars per unit) and *ad valorem tariffs* (α percent of the sales price). In recent years, tariffs have been applied throughout the world, most commonly to agricultural products.[17] American policymakers have frequently debated the optimal tariff on crude oil as a way to raise revenue or to reduce "dependence" on foreign oil.

You may be asking yourself, "Why should we study tariffs if we've already looked at taxes? Isn't a tariff just another tax?" Good point! Tariffs are just taxes. If only imported goods were sold, the effect of a tariff in the importing country would be the same as for a sales tax. We study tariffs separately because a tariff is applied only to imported goods, so it affects domestic and foreign producers differently.

Because tariffs apply only to imported goods, all else the same, they do not raise as much tax revenue or affect equilibrium quantities as much as taxes applied to all goods in a market. De Melo and Tarr (1992) found that almost five times more tax revenue would be generated by a 15% additional ad valorem tax on petroleum products ($34.6 billion) than by a 25% additional import tariff on oil and gas ($7.3 billion).

---

[16]Earlier we noted that we can also calculate the producer surplus by integrating below the price, above the supply (or marginal cost) function, up to the relevant quantity.

[17]After World War II, most trading nations signed the General Agreement on Tariffs and Trade (GATT), which limited their ability to subsidize exports or limit imports using quotas and tariffs. The rules prohibited most export subsidies and import quotas, except when imports threatened "market disruption" (a term that unfortunately was not defined). The GATT also required that any new tariff be offset by a reduction in other tariffs to compensate the exporting country. Modifications of the GATT and agreements negotiated by its successor, the World Trade Organization, have reduced or eliminated many tariffs.

To illustrate the effect of a tariff, suppose that the government imposes a specific tariff of $\tau = \$5$ per barrel of crude oil. Given this tariff, firms will not import oil into the United States unless the U.S. price is at least \$5 above the world price, \$14.70. The tariff creates a wedge between the world price and the U.S. price. This tariff causes the total supply curve to shift from S^1 to S^3 in Figure 9.9. Given that

Figure 9.9 Effect of a Tariff (or Quota)

A tariff of $\tau = \$5$ per barrel of oil imported or a quota of $Q = 2.8$ drives the U.S. price of crude oil to \$19.70, which is \$5 more than the world price. Under the tariff, the equilibrium, e_3, is determined by the intersection of the S_3 total U.S. supply curve and the D demand curve. Under the quota, e_3 is determined by a quantity wedge of 2.8 million barrels per day between the quantity demanded, 9.0 million barrels per day, and the quantity supplied, 11.8 million barrels per day. Compared to free trade, producers gain $B = \$42.8$ million per day and consumers lose $B + C + D + E = \$61.9$ million per day from the tariff or quota. The deadweight loss under the quota is $C + D + E = \$19.1$ million per day. With a tariff, the government's tariff revenue increases by $D = \$14$ million a day, so the deadweight loss is only $C + E = \$5.1$ million per day.

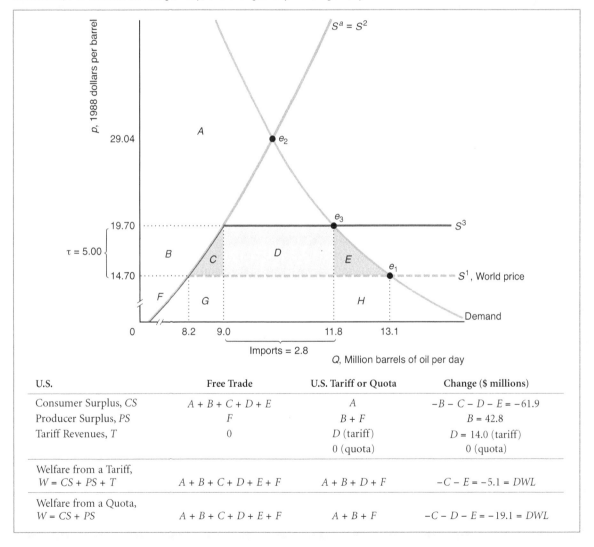

U.S.	Free Trade	U.S. Tariff or Quota	Change (\$ millions)
Consumer Surplus, CS	$A + B + C + D + E$	A	$-B - C - D - E = -61.9$
Producer Surplus, PS	F	$B + F$	$B = 42.8$
Tariff Revenues, T	0	D (tariff)	$D = 14.0$ (tariff)
		0 (quota)	0 (quota)
Welfare from a Tariff, $W = CS + PS + T$	$A + B + C + D + E + F$	$A + B + D + F$	$-C - E = -5.1 = DWL$
Welfare from a Quota, $W = CS + PS$	$A + B + C + D + E + F$	$A + B + F$	$-C - D - E = -19.1 = DWL$

the world's excess supply curve to the United States is horizontal at $14.70, a tariff shifts this supply curve upward so that it is horizontal at $19.70. As a result, the total U.S. supply curve with the tariff, S^3, equals the domestic supply curve for prices below $19.70 and is horizontal at $19.70.

The new equilibrium, e_3, occurs where S^3 intersects the demand curve. At this equilibrium, price is $19.70 and quantity is 11.8 million barrels of oil per day. At this higher price, domestic firms supply 9.0 million barrels, so imports are 2.8 (= 11.8 − 9.0).

The tariff *protects* American producers from foreign competition. The larger the tariff, the less oil is imported, and hence the higher the price that domestic firms can charge. (With a large enough tariff, nothing is imported, and the price rises to the no-trade level, $29.04.) With a tariff of $5, domestic firms' producer surplus increases by area $B = \$42.8$ million per day.

Because the price rises from $14.70 to $19.70, consumer surplus falls by $61.9 million per day. The government receives tariff revenues, T, equal to area $D = \$14$ million per day, which is $\tau = \$5$ times the quantity imported, 2.8.

The deadweight loss is $C + E = \$5.1$ million per day, or nearly $1.9 billion per year.[18] This deadweight loss equals almost 12% of the gain to producers. Consumers lose $1.45 for each $1 that domestic producers gain. Because the tariff does not completely eliminate imports, the welfare loss is smaller than it would be if all imports were banned.

We can interpret the two components of this deadweight loss. First, C is the loss from producing 9.0 million barrels per day instead of 8.2 million barrels per day. Domestic firms produce this extra output because the tariff drives up the price from $14.70 to $19.70. The cost of producing these extra 0.8 million barrels of oil per day domestically is $C + G$, the area under the domestic supply curve, S^a, between 8.2 and 9.0. Had Americans bought this oil at the world price, the cost would have been only $G = \$11.8$ million per day. Thus, C is the additional cost of producing the extra 0.8 million barrels of oil per day domestically instead of importing it.

Second, E is a *consumption distortion loss* from American consumers' buying too little oil, 11.8 instead of 13.1 million barrels, because the price rises from $14.70 to $19.70 owing to the tariff. American consumers value this extra output as $E + H$, the area under their demand curve between 11.8 and 13.1, whereas the value in international markets is only H, the area below the line at $14.70 between 11.8 and 13.1. Thus, E is the difference between the value at world prices and the value U.S. consumers place on this extra 1.3 million barrels per day.

SOLVED PROBLEM 9.5

Based on the estimates of the U.S. daily oil demand function in Equation 9.3 and supply function in 9.4 and the preceding discussion, use calculus to determine the change in equilibrium quantity, the amount supplied by domestic firms, and their producer surplus from a marginal increase in a tariff, evaluated where the tariff is initially zero.

Answer

1. *Discuss the effect of the tariff on the U.S. equilibrium quantity and on the domestic supply of oil at the free-trade equilibrium.* Without the tariff, the U.S. supply curve of oil is horizontal at a price of $14.70 ($S^1$ in Figure 9.9), and the equilibrium is determined by the intersection of this horizontal supply curve with the demand curve. With a new, small tariff of τ, the U.S. supply

---

[18]If the foreign supply is horizontal, welfare in the importing country must fall. However, if the foreign supply is upward sloping, welfare in the importing country may rise.

curve is horizontal at $\$14.70 + \tau$, and the new equilibrium quantity is determined by substituting $p = 14.70 + \tau$ into the demand function in Equation 9.3: $Q = 35.4(14.70 + \tau)^{-0.67}$. The domestic supply is determined by substituting $\$14.70 + \tau$ into the U.S. supply function in Equation 9.4: $Q = 3.35(\$14.70 + \tau)^{0.33}$. Evaluated at $\tau = 0$, the equilibrium quantity remains 13.1 and the domestic supply is still 8.2 million barrels of oil per day.

2. *Differentiate the expression for producer surplus with respect to τ and evaluate at $\tau = 0$.* The producer surplus is the area below $\$14.70$ and to the left of the supply curve (area $B + F$ in Figure 9.9):

$$PS = \int_0^{14.70+\tau} S(p)\,dp = \int_0^{14.70+\tau} 3.35 p^{0.33}\,dp.$$

To see how a change in τ affects producer surplus, we differentiate PS with respect to τ:[19]

$$\frac{dPS}{d\tau} = \frac{d}{d\tau}\int_0^{14.70+\tau} S(p)\,dp = S(14.70 + \tau)$$

$$= \frac{d}{d\tau}\int_0^{14.70+\tau} 3.35 p^{0.33}\,dp = 3.35(14.70 + \tau)^{0.33}.$$

If we evaluate this expression at $\tau = 0$, we find that $dPS/d\tau = S(14.70) = 3.35(14.70)^{0.33} \approx 8.2$ million. Equivalently, $dPS = S(14.70 + \tau)d\tau$. If $d\tau = 1¢$, then the change in producer surplus is about \$82,000. (Problem 37 asks about the effect of a change of τ on deadweight loss.)

Free Trade Versus a Quota

The effect of a positive quota is similar to that of a tariff. If the government limits imports to $\overline{Q} = 2.8$ million barrels per day, the quota is binding because 4.9 million barrels per day would be imported under free trade. Given this binding quota, at the equilibrium price, the quantity demanded minus the quantity supplied by domestic producers equals 2.8 million barrels per day. In Figure 9.9 where the price is \$19.70, the gap between the quantity demanded, 11.8 million barrels per day, and the quantity supplied, 9.0 million barrels per day, is 2.8 million barrels per day. Thus, a quota on imports of 2.8 million barrels leads to the same equilibrium, e_3, as a tariff of \$5.

The gain to domestic producers, B, and the loss to consumers, $C + E$, are the same as those with a tariff. However, unlike with a tariff, the government does not receive any revenue when it uses a quota (unless the government sells import licenses). Area D may go to foreign exporters. As a result, the deadweight loss from the quota, \$19.1 million per day, or \$7.0 billion per year, is greater than under the tariff. This deadweight loss is nearly half (45%) of the gains to producers.

---

[19]We are using Leibniz's rule for differentiating a definite integral. According to Leibniz's rule,

$$\frac{d}{d\tau}\int_{a(\tau)}^{b(\tau)} f(\tau, p)\,dp = \int_{a(\tau)}^{b(\tau)} \frac{\partial f(\tau, p)}{\partial \tau}\,dp + f[\tau, b(\tau)]\frac{db(\tau)}{d\tau} - f[\tau, a(\tau)]\frac{da(\tau)}{d(\tau)}.$$

In our problem, neither a nor f are functions of τ and $db(\tau)/d\tau = d(14.70 + \tau)d\tau = 1$.

Thus, the importing country fares better using a tariff than setting a quota that reduces imports by the same amount. Consumers and domestic firms do as well under the two policies, but the government gains tariff revenues, D, only when the tariff is used.

Rent Seeking

Given that tariffs and quotas hurt the importing country, why do the Japanese, U.S., and other governments impose tariffs, quotas, or other trade barriers? The reason is that domestic producers stand to make large gains from such government actions; hence it pays for them to organize and lobby the government to enact these trade policies. Although consumers as a whole suffer large losses, the loss to any one consumer is usually small. Moreover, consumers rarely organize to lobby the government about trade issues. Thus in most countries, producers are often able to convince (cajole, influence, or bribe) legislators or government officials to aid them, even though the loss to consumers exceeds the gain to domestic producers.

If domestic producers can talk the government into a tariff, quota, or other policy that reduces imports, they gain extra producer surplus (rents), such as area B in Figures 9.7 and 9.8. Economists call efforts and expenditures to gain a rent or a profit from government actions **rent seeking**. If producers or other interest groups bribe legislators to influence policy, the bribe is a transfer of income and hence does not increase deadweight loss (except to the degree that a harmful policy is chosen). However, if this rent-seeking behavior—such as hiring lobbyists and engaging in advertising to influence legislators—uses up resources, the deadweight loss from tariffs and quotas understates the true loss to society. The domestic producers may spend an amount up to the gain in producer surplus to influence the government.[20]

Indeed, some economists argue that the government revenues from tariffs are completely offset by administrative costs and rent-seeking behavior. If so (and if the tariffs and quotas do not affect world prices), the loss to society from tariffs and quotas equals the entire change in consumer surplus, such as area $B + C$ in Figure 9.8 and area $B + C + D + E$ in Figure 9.9.

Lopez and Pagoulatos (1994) estimated the deadweight loss and the additional losses due to rent-seeking activities in the United States in food and tobacco products. Table 9.1 summarizes their estimates for several industries in 2009 dollars. They estimated that the deadweight loss (in 2009 dollars) was $16.5 billion, which was 2.6% of the domestic consumption of these products. The largest deadweight losses were in milk products and sugar manufacturing, which primarily use import quotas to raise domestic prices. The gain in producer surplus is $59.6 billion, or 9.5% of domestic consumption. The government obtained $2.4 billion in tariff revenues, or 0.4% of consumption. If all of producer surplus and government revenues were expended in rent-seeking behavior and other wasteful activities, the total loss is $62.1 billion, or 12.5% of consumption, which is 4.75 times larger than the deadweight loss alone. In other words, the loss to society is somewhere between the deadweight loss of $16.5 billion and $78.6 billion.

---

[20]This argument was made in Tullock (1967) and Posner (1975). Fisher (1985) and Varian (1989) argued that the expenditure is typically less than the producer surplus.

Table 9.1 Welfare Cost of Trade Barriers (millions of 2009 dollars)

Industry	DWL	ΔPS	Government Revenues	ΔCS
Meat products	−34	2,867	83	−2,984
Dairy products[a]	−18,708	34,161	1,282	−50,151
Sugar confectionary[a]	−1,168	5,358	340	−6,866
Grain mill products	−12	1,394	12	−1,418
Fats and oils	−162	2,892	6	−3,060
Beverages	−11	1,337	179	−1,527
Tobacco	−250	4,668	116	−5,034
All food and tobacco	−16,483	59,637	2,419	−78,536

[a]Import quotas were the primary instrument of protection.
Note: As estimated, $\Delta CS = DWL - \Delta PS -$ government revenue. Dollar amounts were adjusted using the Consumer Price Index.
Source: Lopez and Pagoulatos (1994).

SUMMARY

1. **Zero Profit for Competitive Firms in the Long Run.** Although firms may make profits or losses in the short run, they earn zero economic profit in the long run. If necessary, the prices of scarce inputs adjust to ensure that competitive firms make zero long-run profit. Because profit-maximizing firms just break even in the long run, firms that do not try to maximize profits will lose money. Competitive firms must maximize profit to survive.

2. **Producer Welfare.** A firm's gain from trading is measured by its producer surplus. Producer surplus is the largest amount of money that could be taken from a firm's revenue and still leave the firm willing to produce. That is, the producer surplus is the amount that the firm is paid minus its variable cost of production, which is profit in the long run. It is the area below the price and above the supply curve up to the quantity that the firm sells. The effect of a change in price on a supplier is measured by the change in producer surplus.

3. **How Competition Maximizes Welfare.** A standard measure of welfare is the sum of consumer surplus and producer surplus. The more price is above marginal cost, the lower is this measure of welfare. In the competitive equilibrium, in which price equals marginal cost, welfare is maximized.

4. **Policies That Shift Supply Curves.** Governments frequently limit the number of firms in a market directly by licensing them, or indirectly by raising the costs of entry to new firms or by raising the cost of exiting. A reduction in the number of firms in a competitive market raises price, hurts consumers, helps producing firms, and lowers the standard measure of welfare. This reduction in welfare is a deadweight loss: The gain to producers is less than the loss to consumers.

5. **Policies That Create a Wedge Between Supply and Demand Curves.** Taxes, price ceilings, and price floors create a gap between the price consumers pay and the price firms receive. These policies force price above marginal cost, which raises the price to consumers and lowers the amount sold. The wedge between price and marginal cost results in a deadweight loss: The loss of consumer surplus and producer surplus is not offset by increased taxes or by benefits to other groups.

6. **Comparing Both Types of Policies: Trade.** A government may use either a quantity restriction such as a quota, which shifts the supply curve, or a tariff, which creates a wedge, to reduce imports or achieve other goals. These policies may have different welfare implications. A tariff that reduces imports by the

same amount as a quota has the same harms—a larger loss of consumer surplus than increased domestic producer surplus—but has a partially offsetting benefit—increased tariff revenues for the government. Rent-seeking activities are attempts by firms or individuals to influence a government to adopt a policy that favors them. By using up resources, rent seeking exacerbates the welfare loss beyond the deadweight loss caused by the policy itself. In a perfectly competitive market, government policies frequently lower welfare. As later chapters show, however, in markets that are not perfectly competitive, government policies may increase welfare.

QUESTIONS

■ = exercise is available on **MyEconLab**; * = answer appears at the back of this book; V = video answer by James Dearden is available online.

1. How would the quantitative effect of a specific tax on welfare change as demand becomes more elastic? As it becomes less elastic? (*Hint*: See Solved Problem 5.3.)

2. What were the welfare effects (who gained, who lost, what was the deadweight loss) of the gasoline price controls described in Chapter 2? Add the relevant areas to a drawing like Figure 2.14.

3. Use an indifference curve diagram (gift goods on one axis and all other goods on the other) to illustrate that one is better off receiving cash than a gift. (*Hint*: See the discussion of gifts in this chapter and the discussion of food stamps in Chapter 5.) Relate your analysis to the Application "Deadweight Loss of Christmas Presents."

*4. What is the long-run welfare effect of a profit tax (the government collects a specified percentage of a firm's profit) assessed on each competitive firm in a market?

5. What is the welfare effect of an ad valorem sales tax, α, assessed on each competitive firm in a market?

6. What are the welfare effects of a binding minimum wage? Use a graphical approach to show what happens if all workers are identical. Then describe in writing what is likely to happen to workers who differ by experience, education, age, gender, and race.

*7. What is the welfare effect of a lump-sum tax, $\mathcal{L}$, assessed on each competitive firm in a market? (*Hint*: See Chapter 8.)

8. In 2002, Los Angeles imposed a ban on new billboards. Owners of existing billboards did not oppose the ban. Why? What are the implications of the ban for producer surplus, consumer surplus, and welfare? Who are the producers and consumers in your analysis? How else does the ban affect welfare in Los Angeles?

9. The government wants to drive the price of soybeans above the equilibrium price, p_1, to p_2. It offers growers a payment of x to reduce their output from Q_1 (the equilibrium level) to Q_2, which is the quantity demanded by consumers at p_2. Show in a figure how large x must be for growers to reduce output to this level. What are the effects of this program on consumers, farmers, and total welfare? Compare this approach to (a) offering a price support of p_2, (b) offering a price support and a quota set at Q_1, and (c) offering a price support and a quota set at Q_2.

10. The park service wants to restrict the number of visitors to Yellowstone National Park to Q^*, which is fewer than the current volume. It considers two policies: (a) raising the price of admissions and (b) setting a quota. Compare the effects of these two policies on consumer surplus and welfare. Use a graph to show which policy is superior by your criterion.

11. By 1996, the world price for raw sugar, 11.75¢ per pound, was about half the domestic price, 22.5¢ per pound, due to quotas and tariffs on sugar imports. As a consequence, American-made corn sweetener, which costs 12¢ a pound to produce, could be sold profitably. Archer Daniels Midland made an estimated profit of $290 million in 1994 from selling corn sweetener. The U.S. Commerce Department says that quotas and price supports reduce American welfare by about $3 billion a year. If so, each dollar of Archer Daniels Midland's profit costs Americans about $10. Model the effects of a quota on sugar in both the sugar and corn sweetener markets.

12. A government is considering a quota and a tariff, both of which will reduce imports by the same amount. Why might the government prefer one of these policies to the other?

13. Given that the world supply curve is horizontal at the world price for a given good, can a subsidy on imports raise welfare in the importing country? Explain your answer.

14. Canada has 20% of the world's known freshwater resources, yet many Canadians believe that the country has little or none to spare. Over the years, U.S. and Canadian firms have struck deals to export bulk shipments of water to drought-afflicted U.S. cities and towns. Provincial leaders have blocked these deals in British Columbia and Ontario. Use graphs to show the likely outcome of such barriers to exports on the price and quantity of water used in Canada

and in the United States if markets for water are competitive. Show the effects on consumer and producer surplus in both countries.

15. A mayor wants to help renters in her city. She considers two policies that will benefit renters equally. One policy is a *rent control*, which places a price ceiling, p, on rents. The other is a government housing subsidy of s dollars per month that lowers the amount renters pay (to p). Who benefits and who loses from these policies? Compare the effects of the two policies on the quantity of housing consumed, consumer surplus, producer surplus, government expenditure, and deadweight loss. Does the comparison of deadweight loss depend on the elasticities of supply and demand? (*Hint*: Consider extreme cases.) If so, how?

16. The U.S. Supreme Court ruled in May 2005 that people can buy wine directly from out-of-state vineyards. In the 5–4 decision, the Court held that state laws requiring people to buy directly from wine retailers within the state violate the Constitution's commerce clause.

    a. Suppose the market for wine in New York is perfectly competitive both before and after the Supreme Court decision. Use the analysis of Section 9.6 to evaluate the effect of the Court's decision on the price of wine in New York.

    b. Evaluate the increase in New York consumer surplus.

    c. How does the increase in consumer surplus depend on the price elasticity of supply and demand? V

18. Ethanol, which is distilled from corn, is blended into gasoline (allegedly) to make the gasoline burn cleaner and to increase the supply of fuel. Given that ethanol is a close substitute for gasoline, its price in a competitive market would be closely tied to the price of gasoline. However, ethanol usually costs more to make than gasoline, so its usage depends on federal incentives and clean-air legislation mandates for oil companies to produce cleaner fuels.

    a. Suppose that without federal clean-air legislation mandates, ethanol and gasoline are perfect substitutes. Derive the wholesale-market demand function for ethanol. How does this market demand function depend on the price of gasoline?

    b. Suppose that federal clean-air legislation mandates that at least 5% of automobile fuel must contain ethanol. Derive the wholesale-market demand function for ethanol.

    c. Compare the wholesale-market demand functions of parts a and b.

    d. Suppose that for any refining plant output, q gallons per day, the marginal cost of ethanol refining, $MC_e(q)$, is greater than the marginal cost of gasoline refining, $MC_g(q)$. Compare the wholesale-market supply functions of ethanol and gasoline. Show that if the wholesale price of gasoline is sufficiently low, federal mandates are needed to ensure that ethanol is produced, but if the price of gasoline is sufficiently high, federal mandates are not necessary. V

18. Government policies affect who gets the scarce water in the western United States and how that water is used. In 2004, farmers in California's Central Valley paid as little as $10 per acre-foot, while in urban San Jose, a water agency shelled out $80 an acre-foot. Price differentials between agricultural and other uses can persist only if the groups cannot trade. Critics argue that eliminating the agricultural subsidy would encourage farmers to conserve water. The California Department of Water Resources estimates that doubling water prices would reduce agricultural water use by roughly 30% (Jim Carlton, "Is Water Too Cheap?" *Wall Street Journal*, March 17, 2004, B1). Further, farmers would use water more efficiently. [An alternative approach is to allow farmers to sell their (cheap) water in a competitive market—an approach some water agencies are using.]

    a. Based on the data in this description, what is the price elasticity of demand for water?

    b. What is the relationship between the price elasticity of demand for water and the effect of a price increase on water conservation? V

19. Google, Yahoo!, and other Internet search companies charge advertisers for each click on one of their ads (which sends the browser to the advertiser's Web site). Per-click advertising fees present an opportunity for "click fraud," an industry term describing someone (such as a rival firm or hacker) who clicks on a Web-search ad with ill intent. If the advertiser can demonstrate that a click was fraudulent, the search company does not bill for that click. A market for click-fraud detectives has developed to fight click fraud. The market demand for the detectives depends on the amount of fraud they can catch, which reduces the firm's advertising bill. Let p_C denote the per-click fee, n denote the number of clicks per month an advertiser generates, and X equal the fraction of clicks that are fraudulent. Let Z represent the fraction of fraudulent clicks that a detective can prove are fraudulent.

    a. Show how much money the advertiser can save by hiring a click-fraud detective in terms of p_C, n, X, and Z. What is the advertiser's willingness to pay for the detective services?

b. Suppose there are 500 advertisers with the following attributes: $p_C = \$5$, $n = 700$, $X = 0.2$, and $Z = 0.8$. There are 200 advertisers with the attributes $p_C = \$9$, $n = 600$, $X = 0.3$, and $Z = 0.8$. Finally, there are 300 advertisers with the attributes $p_C = \$12$, $n = 100$, $X = 0.1$, and $Z = 0.7$. Draw the inverse market demand curve for click-fraud detectives. [*Hint*: The demand curve is a "step" function (see panel a of Figure 9.2).]

c. Suppose the market supply curve for click-fraud detective services is perfectly price elastic with an intercept of $500 on the price axis. What is the consumer surplus to the advertisers? V

20. There are many possible ways to limit the number of cabs in a city. The most common method is an explicit quota using a fixed number of medallions that are good forever and can be resold. One alternative is to charge a high license fee each year, which would reduce supply by as much a medallion or license that lasts only a year. A third option is to charge a daily tax on taxicabs. Using figures, compare and contrast the equilibrium under each of these approaches. Discuss who wins and who loses from each plan, considering consumers, drivers, the city, and (if relevant) medallion owners.

21. Although 23 states barred the sale of self-service gasoline in 1968, most removed the bans by the mid-1970s. By 1992, self-service outlets sold nearly 80% of all U.S. gas, and only New Jersey and Oregon continued to ban self-service sales. Using predicted values for self-service sales for New Jersey and Oregon, Johnson and Romeo (2000) estimated that the ban in those two states raised the price of gasoline by approximately 3¢ to 5¢ per gallon. Why did the ban affect the price? Illustrate using a figure and explain. Show the welfare effects in your figure. Use a table to show who gains and who loses.

22. The U.S. Department of Agriculture's (USDA) minimum general recommendation is five servings of fruits and vegetables a day. Jetter et al. (2004) estimated that if consumers followed that guideline, the equilibrium price and quantity of most fruits and vegetables would increase substantially. For example, the price of salad would rise 7.2%, output would increase 3.5%, and growers' revenues would jump 7.3% (presumably, health benefits would occur as well). Use a diagram to illustrate as many of these effects as possible and to show how consumer surplus and producer surplus change. Discuss how to calculate the consumer surplus (given that the USDA's recommendation shifts consumers' tastes or behavior).

23. After Mexico signed the North American Free Trade Agreement (NAFTA) with the United States in 1994, corn imports from the United States doubled within a year, and today U.S. imports make up nearly one-third of the corn consumed in Mexico. According to Oxfam (2003), the price of Mexican corn has fallen more than 70% since NAFTA took effect. Part of the reason for this flow south of our border is that the U.S. government subsidizes corn production to the tune of $10 billion a year. According to Oxfam, the 2002 U.S. cost of production was $3.08 per bushel, but the export price was $2.69 per bushel, with the difference reflecting an export subsidy of 39¢ per bushel. The U.S. exported 5.3 metric tons. Use graphs to show the effect of such a subsidy on the welfare of various groups and on government expenditures in the United States and Mexico.

24. In 2004, the Bush administration made a preliminary ruling that China and Vietnam were dumping shrimp in the United States at below cost, and proposed duties as high as 112%. Suppose that China and Vietnam were subsidizing their shrimp fisheries. In a diagram, show who gains and who loses in the United States (compared to the equilibrium in which those nations do not subsidize their shrimp fisheries). Currently, the United States imposes a 10.17% antidumping duty (essentially a tariff) on shrimp from these and several other countries. Use your diagram to show how the large tariff would affect government revenues and the welfare of consumers and producers.

25. The United States not only subsidizes producers of cotton (in several ways, including a water subsidy and a price support) but also pays $1.7 billion to U.S. agribusiness and manufacturers to buy American cotton. It has paid $100 million each to Allenberg Cotton and Dunavant Enterprises and large amounts to more than 300 other firms (Elizabeth Becker, "U.S. Subsidizes Companies to Buy Subsidized Cotton," *New York Times*, November 4, 2003, C1, C2). Assume for simplicity that specific subsidies (dollars per unit) are used. Use a diagram to show how applying both subsidies changes the equilibrium from the no-subsidy case. Show who gains and who loses.

26. Using the information in "Deadweight Loss from Wireless Taxes" in **MyEconLab**'s textbook resources for Chapter 9, draw graphs to illustrate why the tax on landlines creates almost no deadweight loss whereas the tax on cell phones creates more substantial deadweight loss.

27. During the Napoleonic Wars, Britain blockaded North America, seizing U.S. vessels and cargo and impressing sailors. At President Thomas Jefferson's request, Congress imposed a nearly complete—perhaps 80%—embargo on international commerce from December 1807 to March 1809. Just before the embargo, exports were about 13% of the U.S. gross national product (GNP). Due to the embargo, U.S. consumers could not find acceptable substitutes for manufactured goods from Europe, and producers could not sell farm produce and other goods for as much as in Europe. According to Irwin (2005), the welfare cost of the embargo was at least 8% of the GNP in 1807. Use graphs to show the effects of the embargo on a market for an exported good and one for an imported good. Show the change in equilibria and the welfare effects on consumers and firms.

28. Show that if the importing country faces an upward-sloping foreign supply curve (excess supply curve), a tariff may raise welfare in the importing country.

*29. Suppose that the government gives rose producers a specific subsidy of $s = 11$¢ per stem. (Figure 9.6 shows the original demand and supply curves.) What is the effect of the subsidy on the equilibrium prices and quantity, consumer surplus, producer surplus, government expenditures, welfare, and deadweight loss? (*Hint*: A subsidy is a negative tax, so we can use the same approach of shifting a supply curve as we would use with a tax.)

PROBLEMS

*30. If the inverse demand function for toasters is $p = 60 - q$, what is the consumer surplus if the price is 30?

31. If the inverse demand function for radios is $p = a - bq$, what is the consumer surplus if the price is $a/2$?

32. If the supply function is $q = ap^\eta$, what is the producer surplus if price is p^*?

33. If the inverse demand function for books is $p = 60 - q$ and the supply function is $q = p$, what is the initial equilibrium? What is the welfare effect of a specific tax of $\tau = \$2$?

*34. Suppose that the demand curve for wheat is $q = 100 - 10p$ and the supply curve is $q = 10p$. The government imposes a price support at $p = 6$ using a deficiency payment program.

   a. What is the quantity supplied, the price that clears the market, and the deficiency payment?

   b. What effect does this program have on consumer surplus, producer surplus, welfare, and deadweight loss?

35. Suppose that the demand curve for wheat is $Q = 100 - 10p$ and that the supply curve is $Q = 10p$. The government imposes a specific tax of $\tau = 1$ per unit.

   a. How do the equilibrium price and quantity change?

   b. What effect does this tax have on consumer surplus, producer surplus, government revenue, welfare, and deadweight loss?

36. Suppose that the demand curve for wheat is $Q = 100 - 10p$ and the supply curve is $Q = 10p$. The government imposes a price ceiling of $p = 3$.

   a. Describe how the equilibrium changes.

   b. What effect does this ceiling have on consumer surplus, producer surplus, and deadweight loss?

*37. Based on the estimates of the U.S. daily oil demand function in Equation 9.3 and supply function in Equation 9.4, use calculus to determine the change in deadweight loss from a marginal increase in a tariff, evaluated where the tariff is initially zero. (*Hint*: You are being asked to determine how an area similar to that of $C + E$ in Figure 9.9 changes when a small tariff is initially applied.)

38. Suppose that the inverse market demand for silicone replacement tips for Sony EX71 earbud headphones is $p = p_N - 0.1Q$, where p is the price per pair of replacement tips, p_N is the price of a new pair of headphones, and Q is the number of tips per week. Suppose that the inverse supply function of the replacement tips is $p = 2 + 0.012 Q$.

   a. Find the effect of a change in the price of a new pair of headphones on the equilibrium price of replacement tips at the equilibrium, dp/dp_N.

   b. If $p_N = \$30$, what are the equilibrium p and Q? What is the consumer surplus? What is the producer surplus? V

39. Suppose that the market demand for 32-oz. wide mouth Nalgene bottles is $Q = 50,000p^{-1.076}$, where Q is the quantity of bottles per week and p is the price per bottle. The market supply is $Q = 0.01p^{7.208}$. What is the equilibrium price and quantity? What is the consumer surplus? What is the producer surplus? V

11 Monopoly

Monopoly: one parrot.

A **monopoly** is the only supplier of a good for which there is no close substitute. Monopolies have been common since ancient times. In the fifth century BC, the Greek philosopher Thales gained control of most of the olive presses during a year of exceptionally productive harvests. Similarly, the ancient Egyptian pharaohs controlled the sale of food. In England, until Parliament limited the practice in 1624, kings granted monopoly rights called royal charters or patents to court favorites. Today, virtually every country grants a *patent*—an exclusive right to sell that lasts for a limited time—to an inventor of a new product, process, substance, or design. Until 1999, the U.S. government gave one company, Network Solutions, the right to be the sole registrar of Internet domain names.

Consumers hate monopolies because monopolies charge high prices. A monopoly can *set* its price—it is not a price taker like a competitive firm is. A monopoly's output is the market output, and the demand curve a monopoly faces is the market demand curve. Because the market demand curve is downward sloping, the monopoly doesn't lose all its sales if it raises its price, unlike a competitive firm. As a consequence, the monopoly sets its price above marginal cost to maximize its profit. Consumers buy less at this high monopoly price than they would at the competitive price, which equals marginal cost.

In this chapter, we examine eight main topics

1. **Monopoly Profit Maximization.** Like all firms, a monopoly maximizes its profit by setting its price or output so that its marginal revenue equals its marginal cost.

2. **Market Power.** How much the monopoly's price is above its marginal cost depends on the shape of the demand curve that the monopoly faces.

3. **Welfare Effects of Monopoly.** By setting its price above marginal cost, a monopoly creates a deadweight loss.

4. **Taxes and Monopoly.** Specific and ad valorem taxes increase the deadweight loss due to monopoly, may have consumer incidences in excess of 100%, and affect welfare differently from each other.

5. **Cost Advantages That Create Monopolies.** A firm can use a cost advantage over other firms (due, say, to control of a key input or to economies of scale) to become a monopoly.

6. **Government Actions That Create Monopolies.** Governments create monopolies by establishing government monopoly firms, limiting entry of other firms to create a private monopoly, and issuing patents, which are temporary monopoly rights.

7. **Government Actions That Reduce Market Power.** The welfare loss of a monopoly can be reduced or eliminated if the government regulates the price the monopoly charges or allows other firms to enter the market.

8. **Monopoly Decisions over Time and Behavioral Economics.** If its current sales affect a monopoly's future demand curve, a monopoly that maximizes its long-run profit may choose not to maximize its short-run profit.

11.1 Monopoly Profit Maximization

Competitive firms and monopolies alike maximize their profits using a two-step procedure (Chapter 8). First, the firm determines the output at which it makes the highest possible profit. Second, the firm decides whether to produce at that output level or to shut down, using the rules described in Chapter 8.

For a competitive firm, we distinguished between a lowercase q, which represented a firm's output, and an uppercase Q, which reflected the market quantity. Because a monopoly sells the entire market quantity, we use Q to indicate both the monopoly's quantity and the market quantity.

The Necessary Condition for Profit Maximization

A monopoly's first step is to pick its optimal output level. A monopoly, like any firm (Chapter 8), maximizes its profit by operating where its marginal revenue equals its marginal cost, as we now show formally.

A monopoly's profit function is $\pi(Q) = R(Q) - C(Q)$, where $R(Q)$ is its revenue function and $C(Q)$ is its cost function. The necessary condition for the monopoly to maximize its profit is found by choosing that output Q^* such that the derivative of its profit function with respect to output equals zero:

$$\frac{d\pi(Q^*)}{dQ} = \frac{dR(Q^*)}{dQ} - \frac{dC(Q^*)}{dQ} = 0, \tag{11.1}$$

where $dR/dQ = MR$ is its marginal revenue function (Chapter 8) and $dC/dQ = MC$ is its marginal cost function (Chapter 7). Thus, Equation 11.1 requires the monopoly to choose that output level Q^* such that *its marginal revenue equals its marginal cost*: $MR(Q^*) = MC(Q^*)$.

The sufficient condition for a profit maximum requires that the second derivative of the profit function with respect to output be negative,

$$\frac{d^2\pi(Q^*)}{dQ^2} = \frac{d^2R(Q^*)}{dQ^2} - \frac{d^2C(Q^*)}{dQ^2} < 0, \tag{11.2}$$

where d^2R/dQ^2 is the second derivative of the revenue function with respect to Q and d^2C/dQ^2 is the second derivative of the cost function. By definition, $d^2R/dQ^2 = dMR/dQ$ is the slope of its marginal revenue curve. Similarly, $d^2C/dQ^2 = dMC/dQ$

is the slope of the marginal cost curve. Thus, Equation 11.2 requires that, at the critical point Q^*, the slope of the marginal revenue curve be less than that of the marginal cost curve: $d^2R(Q^*)/dQ^2 < d^2C(Q^*)/dQ^2$ or $dMR(Q^*)/dQ < dMC(Q^*)/dQ$. Typically, this condition is met because the marginal cost curve is constant or increasing with output ($dMC/dQ \geq 0$) and the monopoly's marginal revenue curve is downward sloping ($dMR/dQ < 0$), as we will now show.

Marginal Revenue and the Demand Curves

A firm's marginal revenue curve depends on its demand curve. We will demonstrate that a monopoly's marginal revenue curve is downward sloping and lies below its demand curve at any positive quantity because its demand curve is downward sloping. The following reasoning applies to any firm that faces a downward-sloping demand curve—not just to a monopoly.

The monopoly's inverse demand function shows the price it receives for selling a given quantity: $p(Q)$. That price, $p(Q)$, is the monopoly's *average revenue* for a given quantity, Q. Its revenue function is its average revenue or price times the number of units it sells: $R(Q) = p(Q)Q$.

Using the product rule of differentiation, we can write the monopoly's marginal revenue function as

$$MR(Q) = \frac{dR(Q)}{dQ} = \frac{dp(Q)Q}{dQ} = p(Q)\frac{dQ}{dQ} + \frac{dp(Q)}{dQ}Q = p(Q) + \frac{dp(Q)}{dQ}Q. \quad (11.3)$$

The first term on the right-hand side of Equation 11.3, $p(Q)$, is the price or average revenue. The second term is the slope of the demand curve, $dp(Q)/dQ$, times the number of units sold, Q. Because the monopoly's inverse demand curve slopes downward, $dp(Q)/dQ < 0$, this second term is negative. (In contrast, a competitive firm's inverse demand curve has a slope of zero because it is horizontal, so the second term is zero, and the competitive firm's marginal revenue equals the market price, as we saw in Chapter 8.) Thus, at a given positive quantity, a monopoly's marginal revenue is less than its price or average revenue by $[dp(Q)/dp]Q$. That is, *a monopoly's marginal revenue curve lies below its inverse demand curve at any positive quantity*.

Figure 11.1 illustrates the reason a monopoly's marginal revenue is less than its price. The monopoly, which is initially selling Q units at p_1, can increase the number of units it sells by one unit to $Q + 1$ by lowering its price to p_2.

The monopoly's initial revenue is $R_1 = p_1Q = A + C$. When it sells the extra unit, its revenue is $R_2 = p_2(Q + 1) = A + B$. Thus, its marginal revenue from selling one additional unit is

$$MR = R_2 - R_1 = (A + B) - (A + C) = B - C.$$

The monopoly sells the extra unit of output at the new price, p_2, so it gains extra revenue from that last unit of $B = p_2 \times 1 = p_2$, which corresponds to the $p(Q)$ term in Equation 11.3. Because it had to lower its price, the monopoly loses the difference between the new price and the original price, $\Delta p = (p_2 - p_1)$, on the Q units it originally sold, $C = \Delta pQ$, which corresponds to the $(dp/dQ)Q$ term in Equation 11.3. Thus, the monopoly's marginal revenue, $B - C = p_2 - C$, is less than the price it charges by an amount equal to area C.

In general, the relationship between the marginal revenue and demand curves depends on the shape of the demand curve. For all linear demand curves, the relationship between the marginal revenue and demand curve is the same.

Figure 11.1 Average and Marginal Revenue

The demand curve shows the average revenue or price per unit of output sold. The monopoly's marginal revenue is less than the price p_2 by area C (the revenue lost due to a lower price on the Q units originally sold). The monopoly's initial revenue is $R_1 = p_1 Q = A + C$. If it sells one more unit, its revenue is $R_2 = p_2(Q + 1) = A + B = A + p_2$. Thus, its marginal revenue (if one extra unit is a very small increase in its output) is $MR = R_2 - R_1 = B - C = p_2 - C$, which is less than p_2.

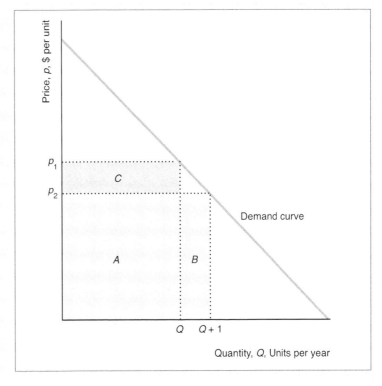

SOLVED PROBLEM 11.1

Show that if a monopoly's inverse demand curve is linear, its marginal revenue curve is also linear, has twice the slope of the inverse demand curve, intersects the vertical axis at the same point as the inverse demand curve, and intersects the horizontal axis at half the distance as does the inverse demand curve.

Answer

1. *Write a general formula for any downward-sloping linear inverse demand curve.* Any linear demand curve can be written as $p(Q) = a - bQ$, where a and b are positive constants.

2. *Derive the monopoly's revenue function and then derive its marginal revenue function by differentiating the revenue function with respect to its output.* The monopoly's revenue function is $R = p(Q)Q = aQ - bQ^2$. The marginal revenue function is the derivative of the revenue function with respect to quantity: $MR(Q) = dR/dQ = a - 2bQ$.

3. *Describe the properties of the marginal revenue function relative to those of the inverse demand function.* Both the marginal revenue function and the inverse demand functions are linear. Both hit the vertical (price) axis at a: $MR(0) = a - (2b \times 0) = a$ and $p(0) = a - (b \times 0) = a$. The slope of the marginal revenue curve, $dMR/dQ = -2b$, is twice the slope of the inverse demand curve $dp(Q)/dQ = -b$. Consequently, the MR curve hits the quantity axis at half the distance of the demand curve: $MR = 0 = a - 2bQ$, where $Q = a/(2b)$, and $p = 0 = a - bQ$, where $Q = a/b$.

Marginal Revenue Curve and the Price Elasticity of Demand

The marginal revenue at any given quantity depends on the inverse demand curve's height (the price) and the elasticity of demand. From Chapter 2, we know that the price elasticity of demand is $\varepsilon = (dQ/dp)/(p/Q) < 0$, which tells us the percentage by which quantity demanded falls as the price increases by 1%.

According to Equation 11.3, $MR = p + (dp/dQ)/Q$. By multiplying and dividing the second term by p, rearranging terms, and substituting using the definition of the elasticity of demand, we can write marginal revenue in terms of the elasticity of demand:

$$MR = p + \frac{dp}{dQ}Q = p + p\frac{dp}{dQ}\frac{Q}{p} = p\left[1 + \frac{1}{(dQ/dp)(p/Q)}\right] = p\left(1 + \frac{1}{\varepsilon}\right). \quad (11.4)$$

According to Equation 11.4, marginal revenue is closer to price as demand becomes more elastic. In the limit where $\varepsilon \to -\infty$, a monopoly faces a perfectly elastic demand curve (similar to that of a competitive firm), and its marginal revenue equals its price.

In Figure 11.2, we illustrate the relationship between the marginal revenue and the price elasticity of demand for a particular linear inverse demand function,

$$p(Q) = 24 - Q. \quad (11.5)$$

Figure 11.2 Elasticity of Demand and Total, Average, and Marginal Revenue

The demand curve (or the average revenue curve), $p = 24 - Q$, lies above the marginal revenue curve, $MR = 24 - 2Q$. Where the marginal revenue equals zero, $Q = 12$, and the elasticity of demand is $\varepsilon = -1$.

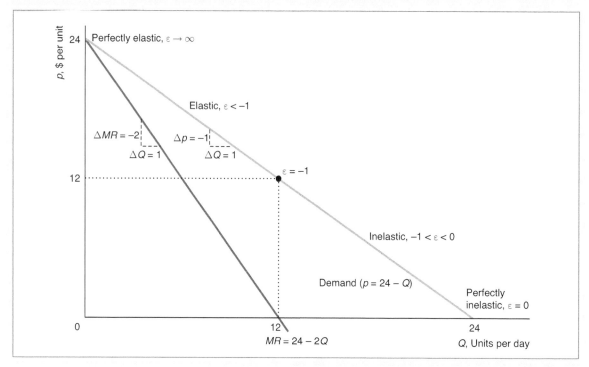

Its corresponding demand function is $Q(p) = 24 - p$. The slope of this demand function is $dQ/dp = -1$, so the elasticity of demand at a given output level is $\varepsilon = (dQ/dp)(p/Q) = -p/Q = -(24 - Q)/Q = 1 - 24/Q$.

From the results of Solved Problem 11.1, the monopoly's marginal revenue function is

$$MR(Q) = 24 - 2Q. \tag{11.6}$$

Where the demand curve hits the price axis ($Q = 0$), the demand curve is perfectly elastic, so the marginal revenue equals price: $MR = p$. At the midpoint of any linear demand curve, the demand elasticity is unitary (see Chapter 2), $\varepsilon = -1$, so, using Equation 11.4, we know that the marginal revenue is zero:

$$MR = p\,[1 + 1/\varepsilon] = p[1 + 1/(-1)] = 0.$$

In our example at the midpoint of the demand curve where $Q = 12$, the elasticity is $\varepsilon = 1 - 24/12 = -1$, and the marginal revenue is $MR = 24 - (2 \times 12) = 0$. To the right of the midpoint of the demand curve, the demand curve is inelastic, $-1 \le \varepsilon \le 0$, so the marginal revenue is negative.

An Example of Monopoly Profit Maximization

In Chapter 8, we found that any type of firm maximizes its profit by selling its output such that its marginal cost equals its marginal revenue. We now examine how a monopoly maximizes its profit using an example with the linear inverse demand function in Equation 11.5, $p(Q) = 24 - Q$, and a quadratic short-run cost function,

$$C(Q) = VC(Q) + F = Q^2 + 12, \tag{11.7}$$

where the monopoly's variable cost is $VC(Q) = Q^2$ and its fixed cost is $F = 12$ (see Chapter 7). The firm's marginal cost function is

$$MC(Q) = \frac{dC(Q)}{dQ} = 2Q. \tag{11.8}$$

The average variable cost is $AVC = Q^2/Q = Q$, so it is a straight line through the origin with a slope of 1. The average cost is $AC = C/Q = (Q^2 + 12)/Q = Q + 12/Q$, which is U-shaped. Panel a of Figure 11.3 shows the MC, AVC, and AC curves.

The Profit-Maximizing Output. The firm's highest possible profit is obtained by producing at the quantity Q^* where its marginal revenue equals its marginal cost function:

$$MR(Q^*) = 24 - 2Q^* = 2Q^* = MC(Q^*).$$

Solving this expression, we find that $Q^* = 6$. Panel a of Figure 11.3 shows that the monopoly's marginal revenue and marginal cost curves intersect at $Q^* = 6$.

Panel b shows the corresponding profit and revenue curves. The profit curve reaches its maximum at 6 units of output, where marginal profit—the slope of the profit curve—is zero. Because *marginal profit is marginal revenue minus marginal cost* (Chapter 8), marginal profit is zero where the marginal revenue curve intersects the marginal cost curve at 6 units in panel a. The height of the demand curve at the profit-maximizing quantity is $p = 18$. Thus, the monopoly maximizes its profit at point e, where it sells 6 units per day at a price of $18 per unit.

Why does the monopoly maximize its profit by producing 6 units where its marginal revenue equals its marginal cost? At smaller quantities, the monopoly's marginal revenue is greater than its marginal cost, so its marginal profit is positive. By increasing its output slightly, it raises its profit. Similarly, at quantities greater

Figure 11.3 Maximizing Profit

(a) At $Q = 6$, where marginal revenue, MR, equals marginal cost, MC, profit is maximized. The rectangle showing the maximum profit $60 is average profit per unit, $p - AC = \$18 - \$8 = \$10$, times six units. (b) Profit is maximized at a smaller quantity, $Q = 6$ (where marginal revenue equals marginal cost), than revenue is maximized, $Q = 12$ (where marginal revenue is zero).

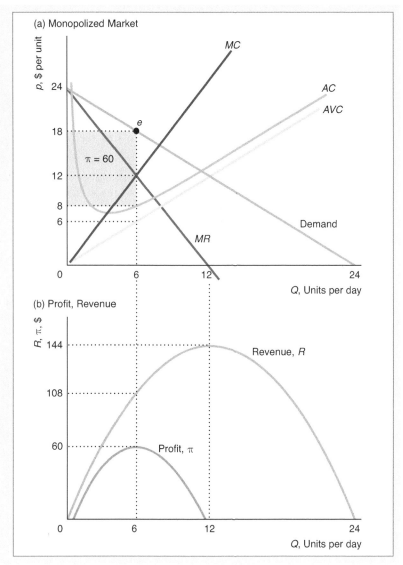

than 6 units, the monopoly's marginal cost is greater than its marginal revenue, so it can increase its profit by reducing its output slightly.

The profit-maximizing quantity is smaller than the revenue-maximizing quantity. The revenue curve reaches its maximum at $Q = 12$, where the slope of the revenue curve, the marginal revenue, is zero (panel a). In contrast, the profit curve reaches its maximum at $Q = 6$, where marginal revenue equals marginal cost. Because marginal cost is positive, marginal revenue must be positive when profit is maximized. Given that the marginal revenue curve has a negative slope, marginal revenue is positive at a smaller quantity than where it equals zero. Thus, the profit curve must reach a maximum at a smaller quantity, 6, than the revenue curve, 12.

As we already know, marginal revenue equals zero at the quantity where the demand curve has a unitary elasticity. Because a linear demand curve is more elastic at smaller quantities, *monopoly profit is maximized in the elastic portion of the demand curve.* (Here, profit is maximized at $Q = 6$ where the elasticity of demand is -3.) Equivalently, *a monopoly never operates in the inelastic portion of its demand curve.*

APPLICATION
Cable Cars and Profit Maximization

Since San Francisco's cable car system started operating in 1873, it has been one of the city's main tourist attractions. In mid-2005, the cash-strapped Municipal Railway raised the one-way fare by two-thirds from $3 to $5. Not surprisingly, the number of riders dropped substantially, and many residents called for a rate reduction.

The rate increase prompted many locals to switch to buses or other forms of transportation, but most tourists have a relatively inelastic demand curve for cable car rides. Frank Bernstein of Arizona, who visited San Francisco with his wife, two children, and mother-in-law, said that there was no way they would visit San Francisco without riding a cable car: "That's what you do when you're here." But the $50 cost for his family to ride a cable car from the Powell Street turnaround to Fisherman's Wharf and back "is a lot of money for our family. We'll do it once, but we won't do it again."

If the city ran the cable car system like a profit-maximizing monopoly, the decision to raise fares would be clearer. The 67% rate hike resulted in a 23% increase in revenue to $9,045,792 in the 2005–2006 fiscal year. For a reduction in rides (output) to raise revenue, the city must have been operating in the inelastic portion of its demand curve ($\varepsilon > -1$) where $MR = p(1 + 1/\varepsilon) < 0$ prior to the fare increase. With fewer riders, costs stay constant or fall (if the city chooses to run fewer than its traditional 40 cars). Thus, its profit must increase.

However, the city may not be interested in maximizing its profit on the cable cars. Mayor Gavin Newsom said that having fewer riders "was my biggest fear when we raised the fare. I think we're right at the cusp of losing visitors who come to San Francisco and want to enjoy a ride on a cable car." The mayor believes that enjoyable and inexpensive cable car rides attract tourists to the city, thereby benefiting many local businesses.[1] Newsom observed, "Cable cars are so fundamental to the lifeblood of the city, and they represent so much more than the revenue they bring in." The mayor decided to continue to run the cable cars at a price below the profit-maximizing level: The fare is still $5 in 2010.

The Shutdown Decision. Should a profit-maximizing monopoly produce at the output level determined by its first-order condition, Q^*, or shut down? In the short run, the monopoly shuts down if the monopoly-optimal price is less than its average variable cost. In our short-run example in Figure 11.3, at the profit-maximizing output, the average variable cost is $AVC(6) = 6$, which is less than the price, $p(6) = 18$, so the firm chooses to produce. Equivalently, the firm's revenue, $R(6) = p(6)6 = (24 - 6)6 = 108$, exceeds its variable (or avoidable) cost, $VC(6) = 6^2 = 36$, so the firm chooses to produce.

---

[1]That is, the mayor believes that cable cars provide a positive externality; see Chapter 16.

Indeed, the monopoly makes a positive profit. Because its profit is $\pi = p(Q)Q - C(Q)$, its average profit is $\pi/Q = p(Q) - C(Q)/Q = p(Q) - AC$. Thus, its average profit (and hence its profit) is positive only if price is above the average cost. At $Q^* = 6$, its average cost, $AC(6) = 8$, is above its price, $p(6) = 18$. Its profit is $\pi = 60$, which is the shaded rectangle with a height equal to the average profit per unit, $p(6) - AC(6) = 18 - 8 = 10$, and a width of 6 units.

Choosing Price or Quantity

Unlike a competitive firm, a monopoly can adjust its price, so it has the choice of setting its price *or* its quantity to maximize its profit. (A competitive firm must set its quantity to maximize profit because it cannot affect market price.)

The monopoly is constrained by the market demand curve. Because the demand curve slopes downward, the monopoly faces a trade-off between a higher price and a lower quantity or a lower price and a higher quantity. The monopoly chooses the point on the demand curve that maximizes its profit. Unfortunately for the monopoly, it cannot set both its quantity and its price and thereby pick a point that is above the demand curve. If it could, the monopoly would choose an extremely high price and an extremely high output level and would become exceedingly wealthy.

If the monopoly sets its price, the demand curve determines how much output it sells. If the monopoly picks an output level, the demand curve determines the price. Because the monopoly wants to operate at the price and output at which its profit is maximized, it chooses the same profit-maximizing solution whether it sets the price or the output. In this chapter, we assume that the monopoly sets the quantity.

Effects of a Shift of the Demand Curve

Shifts in the demand curve or marginal cost curve affect the monopoly optimum and can have a wider variety of effects in a monopolized market than in a competitive market. In a competitive market, the effect of a shift in demand on a competitive firm's output depends only on the marginal cost curve (Chapter 8). In contrast, the effect of a shift in demand on a monopoly's output depends on the marginal cost curve and the demand curve.

A competitive firm's marginal cost curve tells us everything we need to know about the amount that the firm will supply at any given market price. The competitive firm's supply curve is its upward-sloping marginal cost curve above its minimum average variable cost. A competitive firm's supply behavior does not depend on the shape of the market demand curve because the firm always faces a horizontal residual demand curve at the market price. Thus, if you know a competitive firm's marginal cost curve, you can predict how much the firm will produce at any given market price.

In contrast, a monopoly's output decision depends on its marginal cost curve and its demand curve. Unlike a competitive firm, *a monopoly does not have a supply curve*. Knowing the monopoly's marginal cost curve is not sufficient for us to predict how much a monopoly will sell at any given price.

Figure 11.4 illustrates that the relationship between price and quantity is unique in a competitive market but not in a monopoly market. If the market is competitive, the initial equilibrium is e_1 in panel a, where the original demand curve D^1 intersects the supply curve, MC, which is the sum of the marginal cost curves of a large number of competitive firms. When the demand curve shifts to D^2, the new competitive equilibrium, e_2, has a higher price and quantity. A shift of the demand curve maps

Figure 11.4 Effects of a Shift of the Demand Curve

(a) A shift of the demand curve from D^1 to D^2 causes the competitive equilibrium to move from e_1 to e_2 along the supply curve (the horizontal sum of the marginal cost curves of all the competitive firms). Because the competitive equilibrium lies on the supply curve, each quantity corresponds to only one possible equilibrium price. (b) With a monopoly, this same shift of demand causes the monopoly optimum to change from E_1 to E_2. The monopoly quantity stays the same, but the monopoly price rises. Thus, a shift in demand does not map out a unique relationship between price and quantity in a monopolized market: The same quantity, $Q_1 = Q_2$, is associated with two different prices, p_1 and p_2.

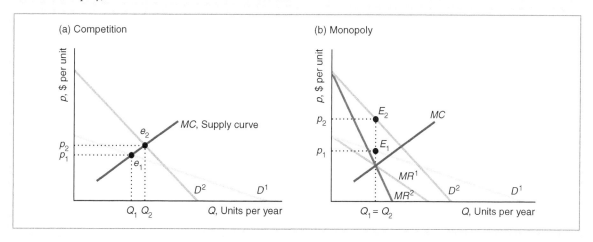

out competitive equilibria along the marginal cost curve, so for every equilibrium quantity, there is a single corresponding equilibrium price.

Panel b shows the corresponding situation with a monopoly. As demand shifts from D^1 to D^2, the monopoly optimum shifts from E_1 to E_2, so the price rises but the quantity stays constant, $Q_1 = Q_2$. Thus, *a given quantity can correspond to more than one monopoly-optimal price.* A shift in the demand curve may cause the monopoly-optimal price to stay constant and the quantity to change, or both price and quantity to change.

11.2 Market Power

What determines how high a price a monopoly can charge? A monopoly has **market power**: the ability of a firm to charge a price above marginal cost and earn a positive profit. In this section, we examine the factors that determine how much above its marginal cost a monopoly sets its price.

Market Power and the Shape of the Demand Curve

The degree to which the monopoly raises its price above its marginal cost depends on the shape of the demand curve at the profit-maximizing quantity. If the monopoly faces a highly elastic—nearly flat—demand curve at the profit-maximizing quantity, it would lose substantial sales if it raised its price by even a small amount. Conversely, if the demand curve is not very elastic (is relatively steep) at that quantity, the monopoly would lose fewer sales from raising its price by the same amount.

We can derive the relationship between market power and the elasticity of demand at the profit-maximizing quantity using the expression for marginal revenue in Equation 11.4 and the firm's profit-maximizing condition that marginal revenue equals marginal cost:

$$MR = p\left(1 + \frac{1}{\varepsilon}\right) = MC. \quad (11.9)$$

By rearranging terms, we can rewrite Equation 11.9 as

$$\frac{p}{MC} = \frac{1}{1 + (1/\varepsilon)}. \quad (11.10)$$

According to Equation 11.10, the ratio of the price to marginal cost depends *only* on the elasticity of demand at the profit-maximizing quantity.

In our linear demand example in panel a of Figure 11.3, the elasticity of demand is $\varepsilon = -3$ at the monopoly optimum where $Q^* = 6$. As a result, the ratio of price to marginal cost is $p/MC = 1/[1 + 1/(-3)] = 1.5$, or $p = 1.5MC$. The profit-maximizing price, $18, in panel a is 1.5 times the marginal cost of $12.

Table 11.1 illustrates how the ratio of price to marginal cost varies with the elasticity of demand. When the elasticity is -1.01, which is only slightly elastic, the monopoly's profit-maximizing price is 101 times larger than its marginal cost: $p/MC = 1/[1 + 1/(-1.01)] \approx 101$. As the elasticity of demand approaches negative infinity (becomes perfectly elastic), $1/\varepsilon$ approaches zero, so the ratio of price to marginal cost shrinks to $p/MC = 1$.

The table illustrates that not all monopolies can set high prices. A monopoly that faces a horizontal, perfectly elastic demand curve sets its price equal to its marginal cost—like a price-taking competitive firm does. If this monopoly were to raise its price, it would lose all its sales, so it maximizes its profit by setting its price equal to its marginal cost.

The more elastic the demand curve, the less a monopoly can raise its price without losing sales. All else the same, the more close substitutes for the monopoly's good there are, the more elastic the demand the monopoly faces. For example, Pearson has the monopoly right to produce and sell this textbook. However, many other publishers have the rights to produce and sell similar microeconomics textbooks (although you wouldn't like them as much). The demand Pearson faces is much more elastic than it would be if no substitutes were available. If you think this textbook is expensive, imagine the cost if no substitutes were published!

Table 11.1 Elasticity of Demand, Price, and Marginal Cost

Elasticity of Demand, ε	Price/Marginal Cost Ratio, $p/MC = 1/[1 + (1/\varepsilon)]$	Lerner Index, $(p - MC)/p = -1/\varepsilon$
-1.01	101	0.99
-1.1	11	0.91
-2	2	0.50
-3	1.5	0.33
-5	1.25	0.20
-10	1.11	0.10
-100	1.01	0.01
$-\infty$	1	0

↑ less elastic / ↓ more elastic

Lerner Index

Another way to show how the elasticity of demand affects a monopoly's price relative to its marginal cost is to look at the firm's **Lerner Index** (or *price markup*): the ratio of the difference between price and marginal cost to the price: $(p - MC)/p$.[2] This measure is zero for a competitive firm because a competitive firm cannot raise its price above its marginal cost. The greater the difference between price and marginal cost, the larger the Lerner Index and the greater the monopoly's ability to set price above marginal cost.

If the firm is maximizing its profit, we can express the Lerner Index in terms of the elasticity of demand by rearranging Equation 11.10:

$$\frac{p - MC}{p} = -\frac{1}{\varepsilon}. \tag{11.11}$$

Because $MC \geq 0$ and $p \geq MC$, $0 \leq p - MC \leq p$ and the Lerner Index ranges from 0 to 1 for a profit-maximizing firm.[3] Equation 11.11 confirms that a competitive firm has a Lerner Index of zero because its demand curve is perfectly elastic. As Table 11.1 illustrates, the Lerner Index for a monopoly increases as the demand becomes less elastic. If $\varepsilon = -5$, the monopoly's markup or Lerner Index is $\frac{1}{5} = 0.2$; if $\varepsilon = -2$, the markup is $\frac{1}{2} = 0.5$; and if $\varepsilon = -1.01$, the markup is 0.99. Monopolies that face demand curves that are only slightly elastic set prices that are multiples of their marginal cost and have Lerner Indexes close to 1.

APPLICATION
Apple's iPod

Apple introduced its iPod on October 23, 2001. Although the iPod was not the first hard-drive music player, it was the most elegant one at the time. Equipped with a tiny hard drive, it was about a quarter the size of its competitors, fit in one's pocket, and weighed only 6.5 ounces. Moreover, it was the only player to use a high-speed FireWire interface to transfer files, and it held a thousand songs. Perhaps most importantly, the iPod offered an intuitive interface, an attractive white case, and unusual ear buds.

People loved the iPod. Even at its extremely high price of $399, Apple enjoyed a virtual monopoly for five years. In 2004, the iPod had 95.6% of the hard-drive player market, and Apple reported that it still had more than 90% in 2005. In 2009, though, it claimed only 74%.

To keep ahead of potential competitors, Apple introduced subsequent generations of iPods in quick succession. Its proprietary iTunes media player software and its iTunes Music Store helped Apple maintain its stranglehold on the market.

SOLVED PROBLEM 11.2

When the iPod was introduced, Apple's constant marginal cost of producing its top-of-the-line iPod was $200, its fixed cost was $736 million, and its inverse demand function was $p = 600 - 25Q$, where Q is units measured in millions. What was Apple's average cost function? Assuming that Apple was maximizing short-run monopoly profit, what was its marginal revenue function? What were its profit-maximizing price and quantity, profit, and Lerner Index? What was the

---

[2]This index is named after its inventor, Abba Lerner.

[3]For the Lerner Index to be above 1, ε would have to be a negative fraction, indicating that the demand curve was inelastic at the monopoly optimum. However, a profit-maximizing monopoly never operates in the inelastic portion of its demand curve.

elasticity of demand at the profit-maximizing level? Show Apple's profit-maximizing solution in a figure.[4]

Answer

1. *Derive the average cost function using the information about Apple's marginal and fixed costs.* Given that Apple's marginal cost was constant, its average variable cost equaled its marginal cost, $200. Its average fixed cost was its fixed cost divided by the quantity produced, $736/Q$. Thus, its average cost was $AC = 200 + 736/Q$.

2. *Derive Apple's marginal revenue function using the information about its demand function.* Because the inverse demand function was $p = 600 - 25Q$, Apple's revenue function was $R = 600Q - 25Q^2$, so $MR = dR/dQ = 600 - 50Q$.

3. *Derive Apple's profit-maximizing price and quantity by equating the marginal revenue and marginal cost functions and solving.* Apple maximized its profit where

$$MR = 600 - 50Q = 200 = MC.$$

Solving this equation for the profit-maximizing output, we find that $Q = 8$ million units. By substituting this quantity into the inverse demand equation, we determine that the profit-maximizing price was $p = \$400$ per unit, as the figure shows.

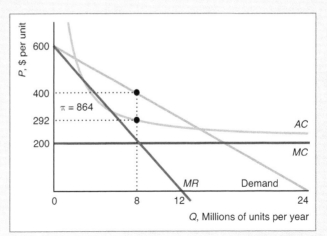

4. *Calculate Apple's profit using the profit-maximizing price and quantity and the average cost.* The firm's profit was $\pi = (p - AC)Q = [400 - (200 + 736/8)]8 = \$864$ million. The figure shows that the profit is a rectangle with a height of $(p - AC)$ and a length of Q.

---

[4]The marginal cost estimate came from www.eetimes.com. Although we assume that the marginal cost curve is constant, there is some evidence from Apple's other lines that it might be downward sloping. The quantity in 2004 is from In-Stat market research (reported in www.tomshardware.com). We assumed that the company's gross profit margin for 2004, www.apple.com/pr/library/2004/oct/13results.html, held for the iPod line and used that to calculate the fixed cost. We derived the linear demand curve by assuming Apple maximizes profit and using the information on price, marginal cost, and quantity. Assuming that Apple maximizes its short-run profit may not be completely realistic, as we discuss in the last section of this chapter.

5. *Determine the Lerner Index by substituting into the Lerner definition.* Apple's Lerner Index is

$$\frac{p - MC}{p} = \frac{400 - 200}{400} = \frac{1}{2}.$$

6. *Use Equation 11.11 to infer the elasticity.* According to that equation, a profit-maximizing monopoly operates where $(p - MC)/p = -1/\varepsilon$. Combining that equation with the Lerner Index from the previous step, we learn that $\frac{1}{2} = -1/\varepsilon$, or $\varepsilon = -2$.

Sources of Market Power

When will a monopoly face a relatively elastic demand curve and hence have little market power? Ultimately, the elasticity of demand of the market demand curve depends on consumers' tastes and options. The more consumers want a good—the more willing they are to pay "virtually anything" for it—the less elastic is the demand curve.

All else the same, the demand curve that a firm (not necessarily a monopoly) faces becomes more elastic as *better substitutes* for the firm's product are introduced, as *more firms* enter the market selling the same product, or as firms that provide the same service *locate closer* to the firm. The demand curves for Xerox, the U.S. Postal Service, and McDonald's have become more elastic in recent decades for these three reasons.

When Xerox started selling its plain-paper copier, no other firm sold a close substitute. Other companies' machines produced copies on special slick paper that yellowed quickly. As other firms developed plain-paper copiers, the Xerox's demand curve became more elastic.

The U.S. Postal Service (USPS) has a monopoly in first-class mail service. Today, phone calls, faxes, and e-mail are excellent substitutes for many types of first-class mail. The USPS had a monopoly in overnight-delivery services until 1979. Today, FedEx, United Parcel Service (UPS), and many other firms compete with the USPS to provide overnight deliveries. Because of this increased competition, the USPS's share of business and personal correspondence fell from 77% in 1988 to 59% in 1996, and its overnight-mail market fell to 4%.[5] Thus, over time the demand curves that the USPS has faced for first-class mail and overnight services have shifted downward and become more elastic.

As you drive down a highway, you may notice that McDonald's restaurants are spaced a fixed number of miles apart. The purpose of this spacing is to reduce the likelihood that two McDonald's outlets compete for the same customer. Although McDonald's can prevent its own restaurants from competing with each other, it cannot prevent Wendy's or Burger King from locating near its restaurants. As other fast-food restaurants open near a McDonald's, that restaurant faces a more elastic demand.

What happens as a profit-maximizing monopoly faces more elastic demand? It has to lower its price.[6]

---

[5]Passell, Peter, "Battered by Its Rivals," *New York Times*, May 15, 1997:C1. However, the USPS's share of air shipments rose to 38% by 2005 (**www.cygnusb2b.com**, January 13, 2007).

[6]See "Airport Monopolies" in the Supplemental Material to Chapter 11 in **MyEconLab**'s textbook resources for Chapter 11 for an illustration of how a monopoly adjusts its price as it changes its beliefs about the elasticity of demand that it faces.

11.3 Welfare Effects of Monopoly

Welfare, W, defined as the sum of consumer surplus, CS, and producer surplus, PS, is lower under monopoly than it is under competition. Chapter 9 showed that competition maximizes welfare because price equals marginal cost. Because a monopoly sets its price above its marginal cost, consumers buy less than the competitive level of the good, and society suffers from a deadweight loss.

We illustrate this loss using our linear example. If the monopoly were to act like a competitive market and operate where its inverse demand curve, Equation 11.5, intersects its marginal cost (supply) curve, Equation 11.8,

$$p = 24 - Q = 2Q = MC,$$

it would sell $Q_c = 8$ units of output at a price of $16, as Figure 11.5 shows. At this competitive price, consumer surplus is area $A + B + C$ and producer surplus is area $D + E$.

Figure 11.5 Deadweight Loss of Monopoly

A competitive market would produce $Q_c = 8$ at $p_c = 16, where the demand curve intersects the marginal cost (supply) curve. A monopoly produces only $Q_m = 6$ at $p_m = 18, where the marginal revenue curve intersects the marginal cost curve. Under monopoly, consumer surplus is A, producer surplus is $B + D$, and the lost welfare or deadweight loss of monopoly is $-C - E$.

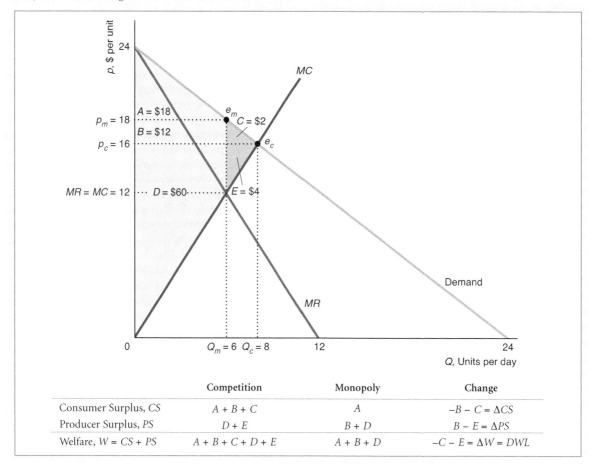

	Competition	Monopoly	Change
Consumer Surplus, CS	$A + B + C$	A	$-B - C = \Delta CS$
Producer Surplus, PS	$D + E$	$B + D$	$B - E = \Delta PS$
Welfare, $W = CS + PS$	$A + B + C + D + E$	$A + B + D$	$-C - E = \Delta W = DWL$

If the firm acts like a monopoly and operates where its marginal revenue equals its marginal cost, only 6 units are sold at the monopoly price of $18, and consumer surplus is only A. Part of the lost consumer surplus, B, goes to the monopoly; but the rest, C, is lost.

By charging the monopoly price of $18 instead of the competitive price of $16, the monopoly receives $2 more per unit and earns an extra profit of area $B = \$12$ on the $Q_m = 6$ units it sells. The monopoly loses area E, however, because it sells less than the competitive output. Consequently, the monopoly's producer surplus increases by $B - E$ over the competitive level. We know that its producer surplus increases, $B - E > 0$, because the monopoly had the option of producing at the competitive level and chose not to do so.

Social welfare with a monopoly is lower than with a competitive industry. The deadweight loss of monopoly is $-C - E$, which represents the consumer surplus and producer surplus lost because less than the competitive output is produced. As in the analysis of a tax in Chapter 9, the deadweight loss is due to the gap between price and marginal cost at the monopoly output. At $Q_m = 6$, the price, $18, is above the marginal cost, $12, so consumers are willing to pay more for the last unit of output than it costs to produce it.

11.4 Taxes and Monopoly

Monopolies may face specific taxes (the government charges τ dollars per unit) or ad valorem taxes (the government collects αp per unit of output, where α is the tax rate, a fraction, and p is the price it charges consumers). Both types of tax raise the price that consumers pay and lower welfare—the same effect as when a tax is applied to a competitive market (Chapter 2). However, taxes affect a monopoly differently than they affect a competitive industry in two ways. First, the tax incidence on consumers—the change in the consumers' price divided by the change in the tax—can exceed 100% in a monopoly market but not in a competitive market. Second, if tax rates α and τ are set so that the after-tax output is the same with either an ad valorem or a specific tax, the government raises the same amount of tax revenue from either tax in a competitive market (Chapter 2), but raises more by using an ad valorem tax than a specific tax in a market with a monopoly.

Effects of a Specific Tax

If the government imposes a specific tax of τ dollars per unit on a monopoly, the monopoly will reduce its output and raise its price. The incidence of the tax on consumers may exceed 100%.

Comparative Statics. The monopoly's before-tax cost function is $C(Q)$, so its after-tax cost function is $C(Q) + \tau Q$. The monopoly's after-tax profit is $R(Q) - C(Q) - \tau Q$. A necessary condition for the monopoly to maximize its after-tax profit is found by equating the derivative of its after-tax profit to zero:

$$\frac{dR(Q)}{dQ} - \frac{dC(Q)}{dQ} - \tau = 0, \qquad (11.12)$$

where dR/dQ is its marginal revenue and $dC/dQ + \tau$ is its after-tax marginal cost. That is, the monopoly equals its marginal revenue with its relevant (after-tax) marginal cost. At $\tau = 0$, this condition gives the before-tax necessary condition for profit maximization, Equation 11.1. The sufficient condition is the same as the before-tax Equation 11.2, $d^2R/dQ^2 - d^2C/dQ^2 < 0$, because $d\tau/dQ = 0$.

We can use comparative statics techniques to determine the effect of imposing a specific tax by asking how output changes as τ goes from zero to a small positive value. Based on the necessary condition, Equation 11.2, we can write the monopoly's optimal quantity as a function of the tax: $Q(\tau)$. Differentiating the necessary condition with respect to τ, we find that

$$\frac{d^2R}{dQ^2}\frac{dQ}{d\tau} - \frac{d^2C}{dQ^2}\frac{dQ}{d\tau} - 1 = 0,$$

or

$$\frac{dQ}{d\tau} = \frac{1}{\frac{d^2R}{dQ^2} - \frac{d^2C}{dQ^2}}. \quad (11.13)$$

The denominator of the right-hand-side of Equation 11.13 is negative by the sufficient condition, Equation 11.2, so $dQ/d\tau < 0$. That is, as the specific tax rises, the monopoly reduces its output. Because its demand curve is downward sloping, when the monopoly lowers its output, it raises its price by $dp(Q(\tau))/d\tau = (dp/dQ)(dQ/d\tau) > 0$.

Tax Incidence on Consumers. In a competitive market, the incidence of a specific or ad valorem tax on consumers is less than or equal to 100% of the tax, and the incidence on consumers plus the incidence on suppliers is 100% (Chapter 2). In contrast in a monopoly market, the incidence of a specific tax falling on consumers can exceed 100%: The price consumers pay may rise by an amount greater than the tax.

To demonstrate this possibility, we suppose that a monopoly's marginal cost is constant at m and that its demand curve has a constant elasticity of ε, so its inverse demand function is $p = Q^{1/\varepsilon}$. Consequently, the monopoly's revenue function is $R = pQ = Q^{1+1/\varepsilon}$. The monopoly's marginal revenue is $MR = dQ^{1+1/\varepsilon}/dQ = (1 + 1/\varepsilon)Q^{1/\varepsilon}$.

To maximize its profit, the monopoly equates its after-tax marginal cost, $m + \tau$, with its marginal revenue function:

$$m + \tau = \left(1 + \frac{1}{\varepsilon}\right)Q^{1/\varepsilon}.$$

Solving this equation for the profit-maximizing output, the monopoly produces $Q = [(m + \tau)/(1 + 1/\varepsilon)]^\varepsilon$. The monopoly substitutes that value of Q into its inverse demand function, $p = Q^{1/\varepsilon}$, to choose the price it sets:

$$p = \frac{m + \tau}{1 + 1/\varepsilon}. \quad (11.14)$$

To determine the effect of a change in the tax on the price that consumers pay, we differentiate Equation 11.14 with respect to the tax: $dp/d\tau = 1/(1 + 1/\varepsilon)$. We know that $dp/d\tau$ is greater than one because $\varepsilon < -1$ (a monopoly never operates in the inelastic portion of its demand curve). Thus, the incidence of the tax that falls on consumers exceeds 100%. However, for other types of demand curves, the tax incidence on consumers may be less than 100%, as the following solved problem shows.

SOLVED PROBLEM 11.3

If the government imposes a specific tax of $\tau = \$8$ per unit on the monopoly in the linear example in Figure 11.3, how does the monopoly change its profit-maximizing quantity and price? Use a figure to show how the tax affects tax revenue, consumer surplus, producer surplus, welfare, and deadweight loss. What is the incidence of the tax on consumers?

Answer

1. *Determine how imposing the tax affects the monopoly's optimum quantity by equating marginal revenue and after-tax marginal cost, and substitute the optimum quantity into the inverse demand function to find the profit-maximizing price.* The monopoly's marginal revenue, Equation 11.6, is $MR = 24 - 2Q$. Its before-tax marginal cost, Equation 11.8, is $2Q$, so its after-tax marginal cost is $MC = 2Q + 8$. The monopoly picks the output, Q^*, that equates its marginal revenue and its after-tax marginal cost: $24 - 2Q^* = 2Q^* + 8$. Solving, we find that $Q^* = 4$. Because the monopoly's inverse demand function, Equation 11.5, is $p = 24 - Q$, it charges $p^* = 24 - 4 = 20$.

The graph shows that the intersection of the marginal revenue curve, MR, and the before-tax marginal cost curve, MC^1, determines the before-tax monopoly's optimum quantity, $Q_1 = 6$. At the before-tax optimum, e_1, the price is $p_1 = \$18$. The specific tax causes the monopoly's before-tax marginal cost curve, $MC^1 = 2Q$, to shift upward by \$8 to $MC^2 = MC^1 + 8 = 2Q + 8$. After the tax is applied, the monopoly operates where $MR = 24 - 2Q = 2Q + 8 = MC^2$. In the after-tax monopoly optimum, e_2, the quantity is $Q_2 = 4$ and the price is $p_2 = \$20$. Thus, output falls by $\Delta Q = 2$ units and the price increases by $\Delta p = \$2$.

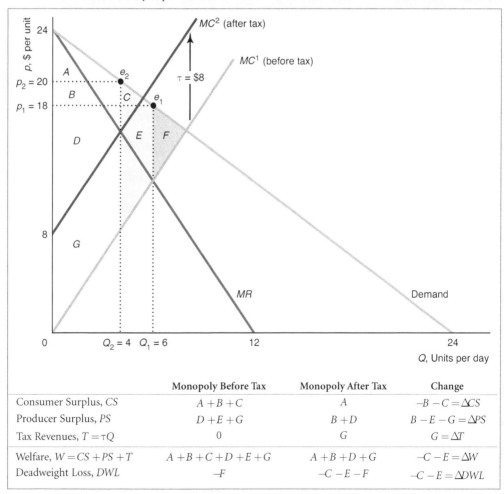

	Monopoly Before Tax	Monopoly After Tax	Change
Consumer Surplus, CS	$A + B + C$	A	$-B - C = \Delta CS$
Producer Surplus, PS	$D + E + G$	$B + D$	$B - E - G = \Delta PS$
Tax Revenues, $T = \tau Q$	0	G	$G = \Delta T$
Welfare, $W = CS + PS + T$	$A + B + C + D + E + G$	$A + B + D + G$	$-C - E = \Delta W$
Deadweight Loss, DWL	$-F$	$-C - E - F$	$-C - E = \Delta DWL$

2. *Show the change in tax revenue and the various welfare measures.* In the figure, area G is the tax revenue collected by the government, $32, because its height is the distance between the two marginal cost curves, $\tau = \$8$, and its length is the output the monopoly produces after the tax is imposed, $Q = 4$. The tax reduces consumer and producer surplus and increases the deadweight loss. Consumer surplus falls by area $B + C$ from $A + B + C$ to A. The monopoly's producer surplus drops from $D + E + G$ to $B + D$, so its net decrease is $B - E - G$. We know that producer surplus falls because (a) the monopoly could have produced this reduced output level in the absence of the tax but did not because it was not the profit-maximizing output, so its before-tax profit falls, and (b) the monopoly must now pay taxes. The before-tax deadweight loss due to monopoly pricing was $-F$. The after-tax deadweight loss is $-C - E - F$, so the increase in deadweight loss (or loss in welfare) due to the tax is $-C - E$.

3. *Calculate the incidence of the tax.* Because the tax goes from $0 to $8, the change in the tax is $\Delta \tau = \$8$. The incidence of the tax on consumers is $\Delta p / \Delta \tau = \$2/\$8 = \frac{1}{4}$. That is, the monopoly absorbs $6 of the tax and passes on only $2.

Welfare Effects of Ad Valorem Versus Specific Taxes

Governments typically use an ad valorem tax rather than a specific tax. Why do governments generally use ad valorem sales taxes? A government raises more tax revenue with an ad valorem tax α applied to a monopoly than with a specific tax τ when α and τ are set so that the after-tax output is the same with either tax, as we now show.[7]

In Figure 11.6, the before-tax market demand curve is D, and the corresponding marginal revenue is MR. The before-tax monopoly optimum is e_1. The MR curve intersects the MC curve at Q_1 units, which sell at a price of p_1.

If the government imposes a specific tax τ, the monopoly's after-tax demand curve is D^s, which is the market demand curve D shifted downward by τ dollars.[8] The corresponding marginal revenue curve, MR^s, intersects the marginal cost curve at Q_2. In this after-tax equilibrium, e_2, consumers pay p_2 and the monopoly receives $p_s = p_2 - \tau$ per unit. The government's revenue from the specific tax is area $A = \tau Q_2$.

If the government imposes an ad valorem tax α, the demand curve facing the monopoly is D^a. The gap between D^a and D, which is the tax per unit, αp, is greater at higher prices. By setting α appropriately, the corresponding marginal revenue curve, MR_a, intersects the marginal cost curve at Q_2, where consumers again pay p_2. Although the ad valorem tax reduces output by the same amount as the specific tax, the ad valorem tax raises more revenue, area $A + B = \alpha p_2 Q_2$.

Both sales taxes harm consumers by the same amount because they raise the price consumers pay from p_1 to p_2 and reduce the quantity purchased from Q_1 to Q_2. The ad valorem tax transfers more revenue from the monopoly to the government, so the government prefers the ad valorem tax and the monopoly prefers the specific tax. (Equivalently, if the government set τ and α so that they raised the same amount

---

[7] Chapter 2 shows that both taxes raise the same tax revenue in a competitive market. However, the taxes raise different amounts when applied to monopolies or other noncompetitive firms. See Delipalla and Keen (1992), Skeath and Trandel (1994), and Hamilton (1999).

[8] Instead, we could capture the effect of a specific tax by shifting the marginal cost curve upward by τ as in our answer to Solved Problem 11.3.

Figure 11.6 Ad Valorem Versus Specific Tax

A specific tax (τ) and an ad valorem tax (α) that reduce the monopoly output by the same amount (from Q_1 to Q_2) raise different amounts of tax revenues for the government. The tax revenue from the specific tax is area $A = \tau Q_2$. The tax revenue from the ad valorem tax is area $A + B = \alpha p_2 Q_2$.

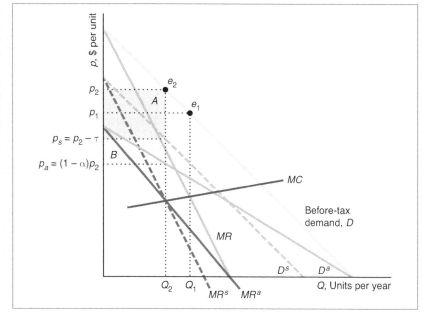

of tax revenue, the ad valorem tax would reduce output and consumer surplus less than the specific tax.) Amazingly, it makes sense for the government to employ an ad valorem tax, and most state and local governments use ad valorem taxes for most goods.[9]

11.5 Cost Advantages That Create Monopolies

Why are some markets monopolized? Two key reasons are that a firm has a cost advantage over other firms or a government created the monopoly.[10] If a low-cost firm profitably sells at a price so low that potential competitors with higher costs would incur losses, no other firm enters the market.

Sources of Cost Advantages

A firm can have a cost advantage over potential rivals for various reasons. One reason is that the firm controls an **essential facility**: a scarce resource that a rival needs

---

[9]However, as Professor Stearns and his students at the University of Maryland inform me, the federal government uses many specific taxes (on alcohol, tobacco products, gasoline and other fuels, international air travel, tires, vaccines, ship passengers, and ozone-depleting chemicals) as well as ad valorem taxes (on telephone service, transportation of property by air, sport fishing equipment, bow and arrow components, gas-guzzling autos, foreign insurance, and firearms).

[10]In later chapters, we discuss three other means by which monopolies are created. First, a merger into a single firm (Chapter 14) of all the firms in an industry creates a monopoly if new firms fail to enter the market. Second, firms may coordinate their activities and set their prices as a monopoly would (Chapter 14). Firms that act collectively in this way are called a *cartel*. Third, the first firm in a market may use strategies that discourage other firms from entering the market (Chapter 13).

to use to survive. For example, a firm that owns the only quarry in a region is the only firm that can profitably sell gravel to local construction firms.

A second important reason why a firm may have lower costs is that the firm uses a superior technology or has a better way of organizing production. Henry Ford's methods of organizing production using assembly lines and standardization allowed him to produce cars at lower cost than rival firms until they copied his organizational techniques.

When a firm develops a better production method that provides an advantage—possibly enough of an advantage for the firm to be a monopoly—the firm must either keep the information secret or obtain a patent, which provides government protection from imitation. According to a survey of 650 research and development managers of U.S. firms (Levin, Klevorick, Nelson, and Winter, 1987), secrecy is more commonly used than patents to prevent duplication of new or improved processes by rival firms but is less commonly used to protect new products.

APPLICATION

China's New Monopolies

China has replaced the United States as the world's major supplier of *rare earth elements* or *metals*: 17 elements from the periodic table, found in minerals—primarily in bastnäsite and laterite nickel ore—in the earth's crust. In 2009, China's mines supplied 93% of these elements, and more than 99% of two of these elements, dysprosium and terbium. Dysprosium—used in the manufacture of lasers, fuel injectors for diesel engines, and compact discs—sells for $110 a kilogram, or about $50 a pound. Terbium—used in solid-state devices, fuel cells that operate at high temperatures, sonar systems and sensors, and fluorescent lamps and color TV tubes—goes for $300 a kilogram, or nearly $150 a pound. Because these elements are crucial for a variety of green energy technologies and military applications, such as missiles, China has many potential buyers.

In the last five years, the United States stopped mining these elements (though some previous mined concentrates are still being processed). Moreover, Chinese firms have been trying to acquire a majority stakes in the few remaining mines in Africa, South America, and Australia. As China increases its stranglehold on these essential resources, it exercises its increased market power by reducing its exports of rare earths. Moreover, China is trying to force manufacturers that rely on these rare earths to build their factories in China.

Natural Monopoly

A market has a **natural monopoly** if one firm can produce the total output of the market at lower cost than several firms could. If the cost for any firm to produce q is $C(q)$, the condition for a natural monopoly is

$$C(Q) < C(q_1) + C(q_2) + \cdots + C(q_n), \qquad (11.15)$$

where $Q = q_1 + q_2 + \cdots + q_n$ is the sum of the output of any $n \geq 2$ firms and where the condition holds for all output levels that could be demanded by the market. With a natural monopoly, it is more efficient to have only one firm produce than to have more than one firm produce.[11] Believing that they are natural monopolies, gov-

---

[11]A natural monopoly is the most efficient market structure only in the sense that the single firm produces at lowest cost. However, society's welfare may be greater with more than one firm in the industry producing at higher cost, because competition drives down the price from the monopoly level. A solution that allows society to maximize welfare is for the government to allow only one firm to produce and where the government regulates that firm to force it to charge a price equal to marginal cost (as we discuss later in this chapter).

ernments frequently grant monopoly rights to *public utilities* to provide essential goods or services such as water, gas, electric power, and mail delivery.

Suppose that a public utility has economies of scale (Chapter 7) at all levels of output, so its average cost curve falls as output increases for any observed level of output. If all potential firms have the same strictly declining average cost curve, this market has a natural monopoly, as we now consider.[12]

A company that supplies water to homes incurs a high fixed cost, F, to build a plant and connect houses to the plant. The firm's marginal cost, m, of supplying water is constant, so its marginal cost curve is horizontal and its average cost, $AC = m + F/Q$, declines as output rises. (The iPod cost function in Solved Problem 11.2 has this functional form.)

Figure 11.7 shows such marginal and average cost curves where $m = \$10$ and $F = \$60$. If the market output is 12 units per day, one firm produces that output at an average cost of $15, or a total cost of $180 (= $15 × 12). If two firms each produce 6 units, the average cost is $20, and the cost of producing the market output is $240 (= $20 × 12), which is greater than the cost with a single firm.

If the two firms were to divide the total production in any other way, their costs of production would still exceed the cost of a single firm (as Solved Problem 11.4 asks you to prove).[13] The reason is that the marginal cost per unit is the same no matter how many firms produce, but each additional firm adds a fixed cost, which raises the cost of producing a given quantity. If only one firm provides water, the cost of building a second plant and a second set of pipes is avoided.

Figure 11.7 Natural Monopoly

This natural monopoly has a strictly declining average cost.

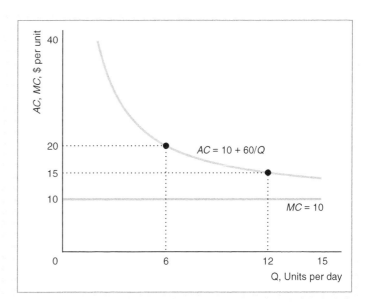

---

[12]A firm may be a natural monopoly even if its cost curve does not fall at all levels of output. If a U-shaped average cost curve reaches its minimum at 100 units of output, it may be less costly for only one firm to produce an output of 101 units even though its average cost curve is rising at that output. Thus, a cost function with economies of scale everywhere is a sufficient but not a necessary condition for a natural monopoly.

[13]See "Electric Power Utilities" in **MyEconLab**'s textbook resources for Chapter 11.

> **SOLVED PROBLEM 11.4**
>
> A firm that delivers Q units of water to households has a total cost of $C(Q) = mQ + F$. If any entrant would have the same cost, does this market have a natural monopoly?
>
> **Answer**
>
> *Determine whether costs rise if two firms produce a given quantity.* Let q_1 be the output of Firm 1 and q_2 be the output of Firm 2. The combined cost of these firms producing $Q = q_1 + q_2$ is
>
> $$C(q_1) + C(q_2) = (mq_1 + F) + (mq_2 + F) = m(q_1 + q_2) + 2F = mQ + 2F.$$
>
> If a single firm produces Q, its cost is $C(Q) = mQ + F$. Thus the cost of producing any given Q is greater with two firms than with one firm, so this market has a natural monopoly.

11.6 Government Actions That Create Monopolies

I think it's wrong that only one company makes the game Monopoly.
—Steven Wright

Governments create many monopolies. Sometimes governments own and manage monopolies. In the United States, as in most other countries, the postal service is a government monopoly. Indeed, the U.S. Constitution explicitly grants the government the right to establish a postal service. Many local governments own and operate public utility monopolies that provide garbage collection, electricity, water, gas, phone services, and other utilities.

Frequently, however, governments create monopolies by preventing competing firms from entering a market. For example, when a government grants a patent, it limits entry and allows the patent-holding firm to earn a monopoly profit from an invention—a reward for developing the new product.

Barriers to Entry

By preventing other firms from entering a market, governments create monopolies. Governments typically create monopolies in one of three ways: by making it difficult for new firms to obtain a license to operate, by granting a firm the rights to be a monopoly, or by auctioning the rights to be a monopoly.

Licenses to Operate. Frequently, firms need government licenses to operate. If a government makes it difficult for new firms to obtain licenses, the first firm to become licensed can maintain its monopoly. Until recently, many U.S. cities required new hospitals or other inpatient establishments to demonstrate the need for a new facility by securing a certificate of need, which allowed them to enter the market.

Grants of Monopoly Rights. Government grants of monopoly rights have been common for public utilities. Instead of running a public utility itself, a government gives a private company the monopoly rights to operate the utility. A government may capture some of the monopoly's profits by charging a high rent to the monopoly. Alternatively, government officials may capture the rents for monopoly rights through bribery.

Auctions of Monopoly Rights. Governments around the world have privatized many state-owned monopolies in the past several decades. By selling its monopolies to private firms, a government can capture the future value of monopoly earnings.[14]

Patents

If a firm cannot prevent imitation by keeping its discovery secret, it may obtain government protection to prevent other firms from duplicating its discovery and entering the market. Virtually all countries provide such protection through a **patent**: an exclusive right granted to the inventor to sell a new and useful product, process, substance, or design for a fixed time. A patent grants an inventor the right to be the monopoly provider of the good for a number of years. (Similarly, a copyright gives its owner the exclusive production, publication, or sales rights to artistic, dramatic, literary, or musical works.)

Patent Length. The length of a patent varies across countries. The U.S. Constitution explicitly gives the government the right to grant authors and inventors exclusive rights to their writings (copyrights) and to their discoveries (patents) for limited periods of time. Traditionally, U.S. patents lasted 17 years from the date they were *granted*, but in 1995, the United States agreed to change its patent law as part of an international agreement. Now, U.S. patents last for 20 years after the date the inventor *files* for patent protection. The length of protection is likely to be shorter under the new rules because frequently it takes more than three years after filing to obtain final approval of a patent.

Patents Stimulate Research. A firm with a patent monopoly sets a high price, which results in deadweight loss. Why, then, do governments grant patent monopolies? The main reason is that inventive activity would fall if there were no patent monopolies or other incentives to inventors. The costs of developing a new drug or new computer chip are often hundreds of millions or even billions of dollars. If anyone could copy a new drug or computer chip and compete with the inventor, few individuals or firms would undertake the costly research. Thus, the government is explicitly trading-off the long-run benefits of additional inventions against the shorter-term harms of monopoly pricing during the period of patent protection.[15]

APPLICATION

Botox Patent Monopoly

Ophthalmologist Dr. Alan Scott turned the deadly poison botulinum toxin into a miracle drug to treat two eye conditions: strabismus, a condition in which the eyes are not properly aligned, and blepharospasm, an uncontrollable closure of the eyes. Strabismus affects about 4% of children and blepharospasm left about 25,000 Americans functionally blind before Scott's discovery. His patented drug, Botox, is sold by Allergan, Inc.

---

[14]See "Government Sales of Monopolies" in **MyEconLab**'s textbook resources for Chapter 11. However, for political or other reasons, governments frequently sell at a lower price that does not capture all future profits. See "Iceland's Government Creates Genetic Monopoly" in **MyEconLab**'s textbook resources for Chapter 11.

[15]Although patents may increase innovation, abuses of patent law may inhibit innovation. For example, *patent trolls* obtain minor patents that they use in lawsuits to block other more serious inventors unless they are paid a *ransom*. In addition, the large number of patents and patent holders in many areas, such as information technology and biotechnology, impose large transaction costs on potential inventors. Thus, while a well-designed patent system provides strong incentives for innovation, a poorly designed system can be counter-productive.

Dr. Scott has been amused to see several of the unintended beneficiaries of his research at the annual Academy Awards. Even before it was explicitly approved for cosmetic use, many doctors were injecting Botox into the facial muscles of actors, models, and others to smooth out their wrinkles. (The drug paralyzes the muscles, so those injected with it also lose their ability to frown or smile—and, some would say, act.) The treatment is only temporary, lasting up to 120 days, so repeated injections are necessary. In 2002, Allergan had expected to sell $400 million worth of Botox. However, in April of that year, the Federal Food and Drug Administration approved the use of Botox for cosmetic purposes. The FDA ruling allows the company to advertise the drug widely.

Allergan sold $800 million worth of Botox in 2004 and $1.3 billion in 2008. Allergan has a near-monopoly in the treatment of wrinkles, although plastic surgery, as well as injections of collagen, Restylane, hyaluronic acid, and other fillers, provide limited competition. Between 2002 and 2004, the number of facelifts dropped 3% to about 114,000, according to the American Society of Plastic Surgeons, while the number of Botox injections skyrocketed 166%. Indeed, Botox injections rose 388% from 2000 to 2005.

Dr. Scott can produce a vial of Botox in his lab for about $25. Allergan sells the potion to doctors for about $400. Assuming that the firm is setting its price to maximize its short-run profit, we can rearrange Equation 11.9 to determine the elasticity of demand for Botox:

$$\varepsilon = -\frac{p}{p - MC} = -\frac{400}{400 - 25} \approx -1.067.$$

Thus, the demand that Allergan faces is only slightly elastic: A 1% increase in price causes quantity to fall by slightly more than 1%.

If we assume that the demand curve is linear and given that the elasticity of demand is -1.067 at the 2002 monopoly optimum, e_m (1 million vials sold at

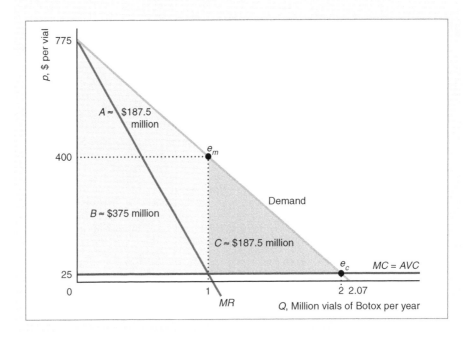

$400 each, producing revenue of $400 million), then Allergan's inverse demand function is[16]

$$p = 775 - 375Q.$$

This demand curve (see the graph) has a slope of -375 and hits the price axis at $775 and the quantity axis at about 2.07 million vials per year. The corresponding marginal revenue curve,

$$MR = 775 - 750Q,$$

strikes the price axis at $775 and has twice the slope, -750, of the demand curve.

The intersection of the marginal revenue and marginal cost curves,

$$MR = 775 - 750Q = 25 = MC,$$

determines the monopoly equilibrium at the profit-maximizing quantity of 1 million vials per year and at a price of $400 per vial.

Were the company to sell Botox at a price equal to its marginal cost of $25 (as a competitive industry would), consumer surplus would equal area $A + B + C$. The height of triangle $A + B + C$ is $750 = $775 - $25, and its length is 2 million vials, so its area is $750 ($= \frac{1}{2} \times 750 \times 2$) million. At the higher monopoly price of $400, the consumer surplus is $A = \$187.5$ million. Compared to the competitive solution, e_c, buyers lose consumer surplus of $B + C = \$562.5$ million per year. Part of this loss, $B = \$375$ million per year, is transferred from consumers to Allergan. The rest, $C = \$187.5$ million per year, is the deadweight loss from monopoly pricing. Allergan's profit is its producer surplus, B, minus its fixed costs.

Alternatives to Patents. A government that wanted to induce innovation could avoid the monopoly distortion and other patent-related problems by subsidizing research or offering prizes. The U.S. Congress allocated $2.4 billion to encourage development of plug-in vehicles and advanced batteries. In the last couple of years, governments, firms, and nonprofit organizations have offered prizes to spur research on lightweight batteries for military use (U.S. government), energy saving refrigerators (industry organization), rockets capable of moon exploration (Google), and meat substitutes (People for the Ethical Treatment of Animals).

APPLICATION

Property Rights and Piracy

Protecting owners of intellectual property, such as music and software, that is covered by copyrights or patents from unauthorized copying has proved increasingly difficult in recent years. Many users download music, movies, and books over the Internet without paying. Condemning these actions as piracy, music and software publishers have sued individuals and firms that facilitate copying and have instituted copy protection schemes. These attempts to prevent copying have had limited success.

In 2009, the Business Software Alliance (BSA) reported that computer software piracy rates in the previous year were 95% in Georgia; 92% in Armenia, Bangladesh, and Zimbabwe; 80% in China; 41% in France; 32% in Canada;

---

[16]The graph shows an inverse linear demand curve of the form $p = a - bQ$. Such a linear demand curve has an elasticity of $\varepsilon = -(1/b)(p/Q)$. Given that the elasticity of demand is $-400/375 = -(1/b)(400/1)$, where Q is measured in millions of vials, then $b = 375$. Solving $p = 400 = a - 375$, we find that $a = 775$.

27% in the United Kingdom; 26% in Australia; and 20% in the United States. The BSA estimated that the worldwide PC software piracy rate is 38% and that software companies suffered annual revenue losses of $53.0 billion.[17]

In the short run, artists and producers are harmed by piracy. If consumers benefit by purchasing music or software for less or stealing it, the overall short-run welfare effect of piracy is ambiguous. For example, in the extreme case where downloaders would not have bought the product, piracy raises welfare and harms no one.

Rob and Waldfogel (2006) surveyed college students at the University of Pennsylvania and elsewhere. They found that each album illegally downloaded reduces purchases by one-fifth album. Students reported downloading almost as many albums as they purchased and admitted that if downloading had not been possible, they would have purchased 26% of the albums they downloaded. Among Penn undergrads, downloading reduced their personal expenditures on hit albums from $126 to $100 but raised their per capita consumer surplus by $70. Thus, for this group, the increase in consumer surplus more than offset the loss in revenues.

Regardless of the short-run welfare effects, the more serious harm occurs in the long run. Reduced copyright and patent protection lowers the drive to create or to innovate, as artists and inventors do not capture the full social value of their work.

11.7 Government Actions That Reduce Market Power

Some governments act to reduce or eliminate monopolies' market power. Many governments directly regulate monopolies, especially those created by the government, such as public utilities. Most Western countries have designed laws to prevent a firm from driving other firms out of the market so as to monopolize it. A government may destroy a monopoly by breaking it up into smaller, independent firms (as the government did with Alcoa, the former aluminum monopoly).

Regulating Monopolies

Governments limit monopolies' market power in various ways. For example, most utilities are subject to direct regulation. Alternatively, governments may limit the harms of a monopoly by imposing a ceiling on the price it can charge.

Optimal Price Regulation. In some markets, the government can eliminate the deadweight loss of a monopoly by requiring that it charge no more than the competitive price. We use our earlier linear example to illustrate this type of regulation in Figure 11.8.

If the government doesn't regulate the profit-maximizing monopoly, the monopoly optimum is e_m, at which 6 units are sold at the monopoly price of $18. Suppose that the government sets a ceiling price of $16, the price at which the marginal cost curve intersects the market demand curve. Because the monopoly can-

---

[17]However, they calculate the loss as the retail price times the number of illegal copies, which creates an upward bias.

Figure 11.8 Optimal Price Regulation

If the government sets a price ceiling at $16, where the monopoly's marginal cost curve hits the demand curve, the new demand curve that the monopoly faces has a kink at 8 units, and the corresponding marginal revenue curve, MR_r, "jumps" at that quantity. The regulated monopoly sets its output where $MR_r = MC$, selling the same quantity, 8 units, at the same price, $16, as a competitive industry would. The regulation eliminates the monopoly deadweight loss, $C + E$. Consumer surplus, $A + B + C$, and producer surplus, $D + E$, are the same as under competition.

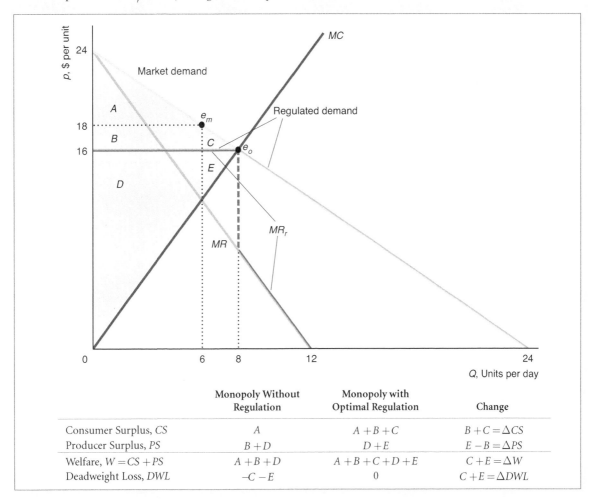

	Monopoly Without Regulation	Monopoly with Optimal Regulation	Change
Consumer Surplus, CS	A	A + B + C	B + C = ΔCS
Producer Surplus, PS	B + D	D + E	E − B = ΔPS
Welfare, W = CS + PS	A + B + D	A + B + C + D + E	C + E = ΔW
Deadweight Loss, DWL	−C − E	0	C + E = ΔDWL

not charge more than $16 per unit, the monopoly's regulated demand curve is horizontal at $16 (up to 8 units) and is the same as the market demand curve at lower prices. The marginal revenue curve corresponding to the regulated demand curve, MR_r, is horizontal where the regulated demand curve is horizontal (up to 8 units) and equals the marginal revenue curve, MR, corresponding to the market demand curve at larger quantities.

The regulated monopoly sets its output at 8 units, where MR_r equals its marginal cost, MC, and charges the maximum permitted price of $16. The regulated firm still makes a profit because its average cost is less than $16 at 8 units. The optimally regulated monopoly optimum, e_o, is the same as the competitive equilibrium, where marginal cost (supply) equals the market demand curve.[18] Thus, setting a price ceiling where the MC curve and market demand curve intersect eliminates the deadweight loss of monopoly.

How do we know that this regulation is optimal? The answer is that this regulated outcome is the same as would occur if this market were competitive, where welfare is maximized (Chapter 9). As the table accompanying Figure 11.8 shows, the deadweight loss of monopoly, $C + E$, is eliminated by this optimal regulation.

Nonoptimal Price Regulation. If the government sets the price ceiling at any point other than the optimal level, there is deadweight loss. Suppose that the government sets the regulated price below the optimal level, which is $16 in Figure 11.8. If it sets the price below the firm's minimum average cost, the firm shuts down, so the deadweight loss equals the sum of the consumer plus producer surplus under optimal regulation, $A + B + C + D + E$.

If the government sets the price ceiling below the optimally regulated price but high enough that the firm does not shut down, consumers who are lucky enough to buy the good benefit because they can buy it at a lower price than they could with optimal regulation. As we show in the following solved problem, there is a deadweight loss because less output is sold than with optimal regulation.

SOLVED PROBLEM 11.5

Suppose that the government sets a price, p_2, that is below the socially optimal level, p_1, but above the monopoly's minimum average cost. How do the price, quantity sold, quantity demanded, and welfare under this regulation compare to those under optimal regulation?

Answer

1. *Describe the optimally regulated outcome.* With optimal regulation, e_1, the price is set at p_1, where the market demand curve intersects the monopoly's marginal cost curve on the accompanying graph. The optimally regulated monopoly sells Q_1 units.

2. *Describe the outcome when the government regulates the price at p_2.* Where the market demand is above p_2, the regulated demand curve for the monopoly is horizontal at p_2 (up to Q_d). The corresponding marginal revenue curve, MR_r, is horizontal where the regulated demand curve is horizontal and equals the marginal revenue curve corresponding to the market demand curve, MR, where the regulated demand curve is downward sloping. The monopoly maximizes its profit by selling Q_2 units at p_2. The new regulated monopoly optimum is e_2, where MR_r intersects MC. The firm does not shut down when regulated as long as its average variable cost at Q_2 is less than p_2.

3. *Compare the outcomes.* The quantity that the monopoly sells falls from Q_1 to Q_2 when the government lowers its price ceiling from p_1 to p_2. At that lower price, consumers want to buy Q_d, so there is excess demand equal to $Q_d - Q_2$. Compared to optimal regulation, welfare is lower by at least $B + D$.

Comment: The welfare loss is greater if unlucky consumers waste time trying to buy the good unsuccessfully or if goods are not allocated optimally among consumers. A consumer who values the good at only p_2 may be lucky enough

---

[18]The monopoly produces at e_o only if the regulated price is greater than its average variable cost. Here, the regulated price, $16, exceeds the average variable cost at 8 units of $8. Indeed, the firm makes a profit because the average cost at 8 units is $9.50.

to buy it, while a consumer who values the good at p_1 or more may not be able to obtain it (Chapter 9).

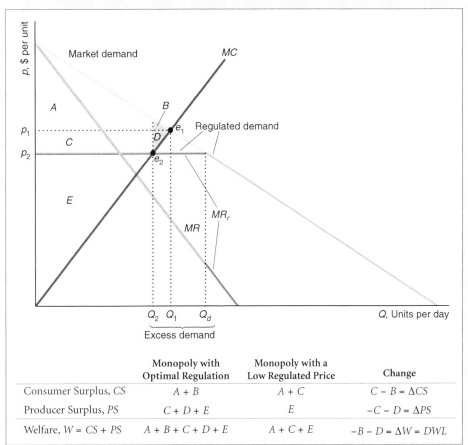

	Monopoly with Optimal Regulation	Monopoly with a Low Regulated Price	Change
Consumer Surplus, CS	A + B	A + C	$C - B = \Delta CS$
Producer Surplus, PS	C + D + E	E	$-C - D = \Delta PS$
Welfare, W = CS + PS	A + B + C + D + E	A + C + E	$-B - D = \Delta W = DWL$

Problems in Regulating. Governments often fail to regulate monopolies optimally for at least three reasons. First, due to limited information about the demand and marginal cost curves, governments may set a price ceiling above or below the competitive level.

Second, regulation may be ineffective when regulators are *captured*: influenced by the firms they regulate. Typically, this influence is more subtle than an outright bribe. Many American regulators worked in the industry before they became regulators and hence are sympathetic to those firms. For many other regulators, the reverse is true: They aspire to obtain good jobs in the industry eventually, so they do not want to offend potential employers. And some regulators, relying on industry experts for their information, may be misled or at least heavily influenced by the industry. For example, the California Public Utilities Commission urged telephone and cable companies to negotiate among themselves about how they wanted to open local phone markets to competition. Arguing that these influences are inherent, some economists contend that price and other types of regulation are unlikely to result in efficiency.

Third, because regulators generally cannot subsidize the monopoly, they may be unable to set the price as low as they want because the firm may shut down. In a natural monopoly where the average cost curve is strictly above the marginal cost curve, if the regulator sets the price equal to the marginal cost so as to eliminate deadweight loss, the firm cannot afford to operate. If the regulators cannot subsidize the firm, they must raise the price to a level where the firm at least breaks even.

APPLICATION

Natural Gas Regulation

Because U.S. natural gas monopolies are natural monopolies and regulators generally cannot subsidize them, the regulated price is set above marginal cost, so there is deadweight loss. The figure is based on the estimates of Davis and Muehlegger (2009).[19] If unregulated, this monopoly would sell 12.1 trillion cubic feet of natural gas per year, which is determined by the intersection of its marginal revenue and marginal cost curves. It would charge the corresponding price on the demand curve at point a. Its profit would equal the rectangle A, with a length equal to the quantity, 12.1 trillion cubic feet, and a height equal to the difference between the price at a and the corresponding average cost.

To eliminate deadweight loss, the government should set the price ceiling equal to the marginal cost of $5.78 per thousand cubic feet of natural gas so that the monopoly behaves like a price taker. The price ceiling or marginal cost curve hits

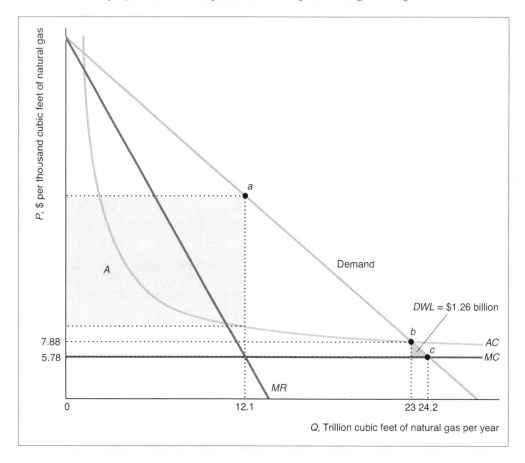

---

[19]We use their most conservative estimate, the one that produces the smallest deadweight loss. We approximate their demand curve with a linear one that has the same price elasticity of demand of -0.2 at point b. This figure represents the aggregation of state-level monopolies to the national level.

the demand curve at *c* where the quantity is 24.2 billion cubic feet per year—double the unregulated quantity. At that quantity, the regulated utility would lose money. The regulated price, $5.78, is less than the average cost at that quantity of $7.78, so it would lose $2 on each thousand cubic feet it sells, or $48.2 billion in total. Thus, it will be willing to sell this quantity at this price only if the government subsidizes it.

Typically, it is politically infeasible for a government regulatory agency to subsidize a monopoly. On average, the natural gas regulatory agencies set the price at $7.88 per thousand cubic feet, where the demand curve intersects the average cost curve and the monopoly breaks even, point *b*. The monopoly sells 23 trillion cubic feet per year. The corresponding price, $7.88, is 36% above marginal cost, $5.78. Consequently, there is deadweight loss of $1.26 billion annually, which is the gray triangle in the figure. This deadweight loss is much smaller than it would be if the monopoly were unregulated.

Increasing Competition

Encouraging competition is an alternative to regulation as a means of reducing the harms of monopoly. When a government has created a monopoly by preventing entry, it can quickly reduce the monopoly's market power by allowing other firms to enter. As new firms enter the market, the former monopoly must lower its price to compete, so welfare rises. Many governments are actively encouraging entry into telephone, electricity, and other utility markets that were formerly monopolized.

Similarly, a government may end a ban on imports so that a domestic monopoly faces competition from foreign firms. If costs for the domestic firm are the same as costs for the foreign firms and there are many foreign firms, the former monopoly becomes just one of many competitive firms. As the market becomes competitive, consumers pay the competitive price, and the deadweight loss of monopoly is eliminated.

Globally, governments are increasing competition in previously monopolized markets. For example, many U.S. and European governments are forcing former telephone and energy monopolies to compete.[20]

Similarly, under pressure from the World Trade Organization, many countries are reducing or eliminating barriers that protected domestic monopolies. The entry of foreign competitive firms into a market can create a new, more competitive market structure.[21]

11.8 Monopoly Decisions over Time and Behavioral Economics

We have examined how a monopoly behaves in the current period, ignoring the future. For many markets, this kind of analysis is appropriate. However, in some markets, today's decisions affect demand or cost in the future. In such markets, the monopoly may maximize its long-run profit by making a decision today that does

---

[20]See "Ending the Monopoly in Telephone Service" and "Deregulating Energy" in **MyEconLab**'s textbook resources for Chapter 11.

[21]See "Dominant Firm and Competitive Fringe" and "Creating anad Destroying an Auto Monopoly" in **MyEconLab**'s textbook resources for Chapter 11.

not maximize its short-run profit. For example, frequently a firm introduces a product—such as a new candy bar—by initially charging a low price or by giving away free samples so that customers learn about its quality and provide word-of-mouth advertising. We now consider an important reason why consumers' demand in the future may depend on a monopoly's actions in the present.

Network Externalities

The number of customers a firm has today may affect the demand curve it faces in the future. A good has a **network externality** if one person's demand depends on the consumption of a good by others.[22] If a good has a *positive* network externality, its value to a consumer grows as the number of units sold increases.

The telephone provides a classic example of a positive network externality. When the phone was introduced, potential adopters had no reason to get phone service unless their family and friends did. Why buy a phone if there's no one to call? For Bell's phone network to succeed, it had to achieve a *critical mass* of users—enough adopters that others wanted to join. Had it failed to achieve this critical mass, demand would have withered and the network would have died. Similarly, the market for fax machines grew very slowly until a critical mass was achieved when many end users owned them.

Direct Size Effect. Many industries exhibit positive network externalities where the customer gets a *direct* benefit from a larger network. The larger an ATM network (such as the Plus network), the greater the odds that you will find an ATM when you want one, so the more likely it is that you will want to use that network. The more people who use a particular computer operating system, the more attractive it is to someone who wants to exchange files or programs with other users.

Behavioral Economics. These examples of the direct effect of network externalities depend on the size of the network because customers want to interact with each other. However, sometimes consumer behavior depends on beliefs or tastes that can be explained by psychological and sociological theories. These explanations are the focus of a subfield of economics called *behavioral economics.*

One alternative explanation for a direct network externality effect is based on tastes. Harvey Liebenstein (1950) suggested that consumers sometimes want a good because "everyone else has it." A fad or other popularity-based explanation for a positive network externality is called a **bandwagon effect**: A person places greater value on a good as more and more people possess it.[23] The success of the iPod may be partially due to its early popularity. UGG boots may be another example of a bandwagon effect.

The opposite of the bandwagon effect (positive network externality), is a negative network externality called a **snob effect**: A person places greater value on a good as fewer and fewer people possess it. Some people prefer an original painting by an unknown artist to a lithograph by a star because no one else can possess that painting. (As Yogi Berra said, "Nobody goes there anymore; it's too crowded.")

---

[22]In Chapter 16, we discuss the more general case of an externality, which occurs when a person's well-being or a firm's production capability is directly affected by the actions of other consumers or firms rather than indirectly through changes in prices. The following discussion on network externalities is based on Liebenstein (1950), Rohlfs (1974), Katz and Shapiro (1994), Economides (1996), Shapiro and Varian (1999), and Rohlfs (2001).

[23]*Jargon alert*: Some economists use *bandwagon effect* to mean any positive network externality—not just those that are based on popularity.

Indirect Effect. In some markets, positive network externalities are indirect and stem from complementary goods that are offered when a product has a critical mass of users. Why buy a particular computer if software programs for it are not available? The more extra devices and software that work with a particular computer, the more people want to buy that computer; but these extra devices are available only if a critical mass of customers buys the computer. Similarly, the more people who drive diesel-powered cars, the more likely it is that gas stations will sell diesel fuel; and the more stations that sell the fuel, the more likely it is that someone will want to drive a diesel car. As a final example, once a critical mass of customers has broadband Internet service, more services will provide downloadable music and movies, and more high-definition Web pages will become available; and once those killer apps appear, more people will sign up for broadband service.

Network Externalities as an Explanation for Monopolies. Because of the need for a critical mass of customers in a market with a positive network externality, we frequently see only one large firm surviving. Visa's ad campaign tells consumers that Visa cards are accepted "everywhere you want to be," including places that "don't take American Express." One could view its ad campaign as an attempt to convince consumers that its card has a critical mass and therefore that everyone should switch to it.

The Windows operating system largely dominates the market—not because it is technically superior to Apple's operating system or Linux—but because it has a critical mass of users. Consequently, a developer can earn more producing software that works with Windows than with other operating systems; and the larger number of software programs makes Windows increasingly attractive to users.

But having obtained a monopoly, a firm does not necessarily keep it. History is filled with examples where one product knocks off another: "The king is dead; long live the king." Google replaced Yahoo! as the predominant search engine. Explorer displaced Netscape as the big-dog browser (and Firefox, Opera, and others lurk in the wings). Levi Strauss is no longer the fashion leader among the jeans set.

APPLICATION
Critical Mass and eBay

In recent years, many people have argued that natural monopolies emerge after brief periods of Internet competition. A typical Web business requires a large up-front fixed cost—primarily for development and promotion—but has a relatively low marginal cost. Thus, Internet start-ups typically have downward sloping average cost per user curves. Which of the actual or potential firms with decreasing average costs will dominate and become a natural monopoly?[24]

In the early years, eBay's online auction site, which started in 1995, faced competition from a variety of other Internet sites including one that the then mighty Yahoo! created in 1998. At the time, many commentators correctly predicted that whichever auction site first achieved a critical mass of users would drive the other sites out of business. Indeed, most of these alternative sites died or faded into obscurity. For example Yahoo! Auctions closed its U.S. and Canada sections of the site in 2007, and its Singapore section in 2008 (although its Hong Kong, Taiwan, and Japanese sites continue to operate in 2010).

---

[24]If Internet sites provide differentiated products (see Chapter 14), then several sites may coexist even though average costs are strictly decreasing. In 2007, commentators were predicting the emergence of natural monopolies in social networks such as MySpace. However, whether a single social network can dominate for long is debatable as the sites are differentiated. Even if MySpace or Facebook temporarily dominates other similar sites, it may eventually lose ground to Web businesses with new models, such as Twitter.

Apparently the convenience of having one site where virtually all buyers and sellers congregate—which lowers buyers' search cost—and creating valuable reputations by having a feedback system (Brown and Morgan, 2006), more than compensates sellers for the lack of competition in sellers' fees. Brown and Morgan (2009) found that, prior to the demise of the Yahoo! auction site, the same type of items attracted an average of two additional bidders on eBay and, consequently, the prices on eBay were consistently 20% to 70% percent higher than Yahoo! prices.

A Two-Period Monopoly Model

A monopoly may be able to solve the chicken-and-egg problem of getting a critical mass for its product by initially selling the product at a low introductory price. By doing so, the firm maximizes its long-run profit but not its short-run profit.

Suppose that a monopoly sells its good—say, root-beer-scented jeans—for only two periods (after that, the demand goes to zero as a new craze hits the market). If the monopoly sells less than a critical quantity of output, Q, in the first period, its second-period demand curve lies close to the price axis. However, if the good is a success in the first period—selling at least Q units—the second-period demand curve shifts substantially to the right.

If the monopoly maximizes its short-run profit in the first period, it charges p^* and sells Q^* units, which is fewer than Q. To sell Q units, it would have to lower its first-period price to $\underline{p} < p^*$, which would reduce its first-period profit from π^* to $\underline{\pi}$.

In the second period, the monopoly maximizes its profit given its second-period demand curve. If the monopoly sold only Q^* units in the first period, it earns a relatively low second-period profit of π_l. However, if it sold Q units in the first period, it makes a relatively high second-period profit, π_h.

Should the monopoly charge a low introductory price in the first period? Its objective is to maximize its long-run profit: the sum of its profit in the two periods.[25] It maximizes its long-run profit by charging a low introductory price in the first period if the extra profit in the second period, $\pi_h - \pi_l$, from achieving a critical mass in the first period is greater than its forgone profit in the first period, $\pi^* - \underline{\pi}$. This policy must be profitable for some firms: A Google search found 8.9 million Web pages touting introductory prices.

SUMMARY

1. **Monopoly Profit Maximization.** Like any firm, a monopoly—a single seller—maximizes its profit by setting its output so that its marginal revenue equals its marginal cost. The monopoly makes a positive profit if its average cost is less than the price at the profit-maximizing output. Because a monopoly does not have a supply curve, the effect of a shift in demand on a monopoly's output depends on the shapes of both its marginal cost curve and its demand curve. As a monopoly's demand curve shifts, price and output may change in the same direction or in different directions.

2. **Market Power.** Market power is the ability of a firm to charge a price above marginal cost and earn a positive profit. The more elastic the demand the monopoly faces at the quantity at which it maximizes its profit, the closer its price to its marginal cost and the closer the Lerner Index or price markup, $(p - MC)/p$, is to zero, which is the competitive level.

3. **Welfare Effects of Monopoly.** Because a monopoly's price is above its marginal cost, too little output is produced, and society suffers a deadweight loss. The monopoly makes higher profit than it would if it

---

[25]In Chapter 15, we discuss why firms place lower value on profit in the future than on profit today and how a firm can compare profit in the future to profit today. For now, we assume that the monopoly places equal value on profit in both periods.

acted as a price taker. Consumers are worse off, buying less output at a higher price.

4. **Taxes and Monopoly.** A specific or an ad valorem tax exacerbates the deadweight loss of a monopoly by further reducing sales and driving up the price to consumers. Unlike in a competitive market, the tax incidence on consumers can exceed 100% in a monopoly market. In a monopoly, the welfare losses from an ad valorem tax are less than from a specific tax that reduces output by the same amount (unlike in a competitive market where both taxes reduce welfare by the same amount).

5. **Cost Advantages That Create Monopolies.** A firm may be a monopoly if it controls a key input, has superior knowledge about producing or distributing a good, or has substantial economies of scale. In markets with substantial economies of scale, the single seller is called a natural monopoly because total production costs would rise if more than one firm produced.

6. **Government Actions That Create Monopolies.** Governments may establish government-owned-and-operated monopolies. They may also create private monopolies by establishing barriers to entry that prevent other firms from competing. Governments grant patents, which give inventors monopoly rights for a limited time.

7. **Government Actions That Reduce Market Power.** A government can eliminate the welfare harm of a monopoly by forcing the firm to set its price at the competitive level. If the government sets the price at a different level or otherwise regulates nonoptimally, welfare at the regulated monopoly optimum is lower than in the competitive equilibrium. A government can eliminate or reduce the harms of monopoly by allowing or facilitating entry.

8. **Monopoly Decisions over Time and Behavioral Economics.** If a good has a positive network externality so that its value to a consumer grows as the number of units sold increases, then current sales affect a monopoly's future demand curve. A monopoly may maximize its long-run profit—its profit over time—by setting a low introductory price in the first period that it sells the good and then later raising its price as its product's popularity ensures large future sales at a higher price. Consequently, the monopoly is not maximizing its short-run profit in the first period but is maximizing the sum of its profits over all periods.

QUESTIONS

■ = exercise is available on **MyEconLab**; * = answer appears at the back of this book; V = video answer by James Dearden is available online.

1. Show that after a shift in the demand curve, a monopoly's price may remain constant but its output may rise.

2. What is the effect of a franchise (lump-sum) tax on a monopoly? (*Hint*: Consider the possibility that the firm may shut down.)

3. When is a monopoly unlikely to be profitable? (*Hint*: Discuss the relationship between market demand and average cost.)

4. A monopoly has a constant marginal cost of production of $1 per unit and a fixed cost of $10. Draw the firm's MC, AVC, and AC curves. Add a downward-sloping demand curve, and show the profit-maximizing quantity and price. Indicate the profit as an area on your diagram. Show the deadweight loss.

*5. Can a firm be a natural monopoly if it has a U-shaped average cost curve? Why or why not?

6. Can a firm operating in the upward-sloping portion of its average cost curve be a natural monopoly? Explain.

7. Give as many examples as you can of government actions that created monopolies.

8. Show why a monopoly may operate in the upward- or downward-sloping section of its long-run average cost curve but a competitive firm will operate only in the upward-sloping section.

9. When will a monopoly set its price equal to its marginal cost?

10. Describe the effects on output and welfare if the government regulates a monopoly so that it may not charge a price above $\bar{p}$, which lies between the unregulated monopoly price and the optimally regulated price (determined by the intersection of the firm's marginal cost and the market demand curve).

11. Suppose that many similar price-taking consumers (such as Denise in Chapter 10) have a single good (candy bars). Jane has a monopoly in wood, so she can set prices. Assume that no production is possible. Using an Edgeworth box, illustrate the monopoly optimum and show that it does not lie on the contract curve (that is, it isn't Pareto efficient).

12. A monopoly drug company produces a lifesaving medicine at a constant cost of $10 per dose. The demand for this medicine is perfectly inelastic at prices less than or equal to the $100 (per day) income of the 100 patients who need to take this drug daily. At a higher price, nothing is bought. Show the equilibrium price and quantity and the consumer and producer surplus in a graph. Now the government

imposes a price ceiling of $30. Show how the equilibrium, consumer surplus, and producer surplus change. What is the deadweight loss, if any, from this price control?

13. The price of wholesale milk dropped by 30.3% in 1999 when the Pennsylvania Milk Marketing Board lowered the regulated price. The price to consumers fell by substantially less than 30.3%. Why? (*Hint*: Show that a monopoly will not necessarily lower its price by the same percentage as its constant marginal cost drops.)

14. Drug companies spend large sums to determine additional uses for their existing drugs. For example, GlaxoWellcome PLC, a pharmaceutical giant, learned that its drug bupropion hydrochloride is more effective than the nicotine patch for helping people quit smoking. That drug is now sold as Zyban, but it was introduced in 1997 as an antidepressant, Wellbutrin. Projected 1999 sales were $250 million for Zyban and $590 million for Wellbutrin. Using a graph, show the demand curves for Wellbutrin and Zyban and the aggregate demand for this drug, bupropion hydrochloride. On the graph, indicate the quantity of pills sold for each use and total use at the current price. Why did Glaxo, the monopoly producer, set the same price, $1.16 a pill, for both drugs?

15. Once the copyright runs out on a book or musical composition, the work can legally be put on the Internet for anyone to download. However, the U.S. Congress recently extended the copyright law to 95 years after the original publication. But in Australia and Europe, the copyright holds for only 50 years. Thus, an Australian Web site can post *Gone With the Wind*, a 1936 novel, or Elvis Presley's 1954 single "That's All Right," while a U.S. site cannot. Obviously, this legal nicety won't stop American fans from downloading from Australian or European sites. Discuss how limiting the length of a copyright would affect the pricing used by the publisher of a novel.

16. Are major-league baseball clubs profit-maximizing monopolies? Some observers of this market contend that baseball club owners want to maximize attendance or revenue. Alexander (2001) said that one test of whether a firm is a profit-maximizing monopoly is to check whether it is operating in the elastic portion of its demand curve, which, according to his analysis, is true. Why is that a relevant test? What would the elasticity be if a baseball club were maximizing revenue?

17. Hotels tend to charge high prices for phone calls made from guests' rooms. Cell phones endangered this nice little "monopoly" business to the point that average telephone profit per available room at hotels in the United States fell from $637 in 2000 to $152 in 2003 (Christopher Elliott, "Mystery of the Cellphone That Doesn't Work at the Hotel," *New York Times*, September 7, 2004, C6). But now many travelers complain that their cell phones don't work in hotels. Although hotels deny that they are doing anything as nefarious as blocking signals, Netline Communications Technologies in Tel Aviv says that it has sold hundreds of cell phone jammers to hotels around the world. A Federal Communications Commission rule prohibits these devices, but the rule is unenforced. By one estimate, a jammer that could block all cell phone transmissions would cost $25,000 for a small hotel and $35,000 to $50,000 for a big chain hotel. Assume that the blocker lasts for one year. Under what conditions (in terms of profit per room, number of rooms, and so forth) would it pay for a hotel to install a jammer, assuming the law permits it? Explain your answer.

18. Bleyer Industries Inc., the only U.S. manufacturer of plastic Easter eggs, once manufactured 250 million eggs each year. However, imports from China cut into its business. In 2005, Bleyer filed for bankruptcy because the Chinese firms could produce the eggs at much lower costs ("U.S. Plastic Egg Industry a Shell of Its Former Self," *San Francisco Chronicle*, January 14, 2005). Use graphs to show how a competitive import industry could drive a monopoly out of business.

19. Draw an example of a monopoly with a linear demand curve and a constant marginal cost curve.

   a. Show the profit-maximizing price and output, p^* and Q^*, and identify the areas of consumer surplus, producer surplus, and deadweight loss. Also show the quantity, Q_c, that would be produced if the monopoly were to act like a price taker.

   b. Now suppose that the demand curve is a smooth concave-to-the-origin curve (whose ends hit the axes) that is tangent to the original demand curve at the point (Q^*, p^*). Explain why this monopoly equilibrium is the same as with the linear demand curve. Show how much output the firm would produce if it acted like a price taker. Show how the welfare areas change.

   c. Repeat the exercises in part b if the demand curve is a smooth convex-to-the-origin curve (whose ends hit the axes) that is tangent to the original demand curve at the point (Q^*, p^*).

20. A country has a monopoly that is protected by a specific tariff, τ, on imported goods. The monopoly's profit-maximizing price is p^*. The world price of the good is p_w, which is less than p^*. Because the price of imported goods with the tariff is $p_w + \tau$, no foreign goods are imported. Under WTO pressure the government removes the tariff so that the supply of foreign goods to the country's consumers is horizontal at p_w. Show how much the former monopoly produces and what price it charges. Show who gains and who loses from removing the tariff. (*Hint*: Look at the effect of government price regulation on a monopoly's demand curve in Section 11.7.)

21. A monopoly chocolate manufacturer faces two types of consumers. The larger group, the hoi polloi, loves desserts and has a relatively flat, linear demand curve for chocolate. The smaller group, the snobs, is interested in buying chocolate only if the hoi polloi do not buy it. Given that the hoi polloi do not buy the chocolate, the snobs have a relatively steep, linear demand curve. Show the monopoly's possible outcomes—high price and low quantity, or low price and high quantity—and explain the condition under which the monopoly chooses to cater to the snobs rather than to the hoi polloi.

PROBLEMS

*22. Show that the elasticity of demand is unitary at the midpoint of a linear inverse demand function and hence that a monopoly will not operate to the right of this midpoint.

23. The inverse demand curve that a monopoly faces is
$$p = 100 - Q.$$
The firm's cost curve is $C(Q) = 10 + 5Q$. What is the profit-maximizing solution? How does your answer change if $C(Q) = 100 + 5Q$?

24. The inverse demand curve that a monopoly faces is
$$p = 10Q^{-0.5}.$$
The firm's cost curve is $C(Q) = 5Q$. What is the profit-maximizing solution?

25. If the inverse demand function facing a monopoly is $P(Q)$ and its cost function is $C(Q)$, show the effect of a specific tax, τ, on the monopoly's profit-maximizing output. How does imposing τ affect its profit?

26. In the "Botox Patent Monopoly" application, consumer surplus, area A, equals the deadweight loss, area C. Show that this equality is a result of the linear demand and constant marginal cost assumptions.

27. Based on the information in the "Botox Patent Monopoly" application, what would happen to the equilibrium price and quantity if the government had collected a specific tax of $75 per vial of Botox? What welfare effects would such a tax have?

28. Based on the information in the "Botox Patent Monopoly" application, what would happen to the equilibrium price and quantity if the government had set a price ceiling of $200 per vial of Botox? What welfare effects would such a tax have?

29. The Commonwealth of Pennsylvania is the monopoly retailer of wine in that state. Suppose that Quaker Cabernet has no close substitutes and that the statewide inverse demand function for this wine is $p = 5 - 0.001Q$. The state purchases the wine on the wholesale market for $2 per bottle, and the state-operated liquor stores incur no other expenses to sell this wine.

  a. What are the state's profit-maximizing price and quantity?

  b. Neighboring New Jersey permits private retailers to sell wine. They face the same statewide demand curve as in Pennsylvania. No interstate wine trade is permitted. Suppose the New Jersey market for Quaker Cabernet is perfectly competitive. What are the equilibrium price and quantity?

  c. New Jersey taxes wine sales. While the retailers pay the taxes on wine sales, they may pass on some or all of these taxes to consumers by raising prices. Identify the specific tax (tax per bottle sold) for which New Jersey's equilibrium market price and quantity equal the Pennsylvania monopoly price and quantity. Given the quantity tax, show that New Jersey's tax revenue equals Pennsylvania's profit. V

30. Suppose that all iPod owners consider only two options for downloading music to their MP3 players: purchasing songs from iTunes or copying songs from friends' CDs. With these two options, suppose the weekly inverse market demand for the Rolling Stones' song "Satisfaction" is $p = 1.98 - 0.00198Q$. The marginal cost to Apple Inc. of downloading a song is zero.

  a. What is Apple's optimal price of "Satisfaction"? How many downloads of "Satisfaction" does Apple sell each week?

  b. Now suppose that Apple sells a version of the iPod equipped with software in which songs played on the iPod must be downloaded from iTunes. For this iPod, the inverse market demand for "Satisfaction" is $p = 2.58 - 0.0129Q$. What is Apple's optimal price of downloads of

"Satisfaction" for this new player? How many downloads of "Satisfaction" does Apple sell each week? V

31. In addition to the hard-drive-based iPod, Apple produces a flash-based audio player. Its 512MB iPod Shuffle (which does not have a hard drive) sold for $99 in 2005. According to iSuppli, Apple's per-unit cost of manufacturing the Shuffle was $45.37. What was Apple's price/marginal cost ratio? What was its Lerner Index? If we assume (possibly incorrectly) that Apple acted like a short-run profit-maximizing monopoly in pricing its iPod Shuffle, what elasticity of demand did Apple believe it faced?

*32. In 1991, Humana hospitals charged very high prices relative to their marginal costs. For example, Humana's Suburban Hospital in Louisville, Kentucky, charged patients $44.90 for a container of saline solution (salt water) that cost the hospital 81¢ (Douglas Frantz, "Congress Probes Hospital Costs—$9 Tylenols, $118 Heat Pads," *San Francisco Chronicle*, October 18, 1991, A2). Calculate the hospital's price/marginal cost ratio, its Lerner Index, and the demand elasticity, ε, that it faced for saline solution (assuming that it maximizes its profit).

33. According to the California Nurses Association, Tenet Healthcare hospitals mark up drugs substantially. At Tenet's Sierra Vista Regional Medical Center, drug prices were 1,800% of the hospital's costs (Chuck Squatriglia and Tyche Hendricks, "Tenet Hiked Drug Prices, Study Finds More Than Double U.S. Average," *San Francisco Chronicle*, November 24, 2002, A1, A10). Assuming Tenet was maximizing its profit, what is the elasticity of demand that Tenet believes it faces? What is its Lerner Index for drugs?

34. According to one estimate, the parts for a Segway Human Transporter—which has 5 gyroscopes, 2 tilt sensors, dual redundant motors, and 10 microprocessors and can travel up to 12.5 mph—cost at least $1,500 (Eric A. Taub, "Segway Transporter Slow to Catch On," *San Francisco Chronicle*, August 11, 2003, E4). Suppose that a Segway's marginal cost is $2,000. Given that the Segway's price is $5,000, calculate the firm's price/marginal cost ratio, its Lerner Index, and the elasticity of demand it believes it faces (assuming that it is trying to maximize its short-run profit).

35. In 2005, Apple introduced the Mac mini G4, a miniature computer that weighs only 2.9 pounds but comes fully loaded with lots of memory and a large hard disk drive. According to one estimate, the cost of production was $258 (Toni Duboise, "Low-cost Apple Mini Packs Punch, but BYO Peripherals," www.eetimes.com), while its suggested price was $499. Although other firms produce computers, the Mac is viewed as a different product by aficionados. What is Apple's price/marginal cost ratio? What is its Lerner Index? If we assume that Apple is a profit-maximizing monopoly, what elasticity of demand does it believe it faces for this tiny computer?

36. The U.S. Postal Service (USPS) has a constitutionally guaranteed monopoly on first-class mail. It currently charges 44¢ for a stamp, which is probably not the profit-maximizing price, as the alleged USPS goal is to break even, not turn a profit. Following the postal services in Australia, Britain, Canada, Switzerland, and Ireland, the USPS allowed Stamps.com to sell a sheet of twenty 44¢ stamps with a photo of your dog, your mommy, or whatever for $18.99 (that's 94.95¢ per stamp, a 216% markup). Stamps.com keeps the extra profit beyond the 44¢ it pays the USPS. What is the firm's Lerner Index? If Stamps.com is a profit-maximizing monopoly, what elasticity of demand does it face for a customized stamp?

*37. Only Indian tribes can run casinos in California. These casinos are spread around the state so that each is a monopoly in its local community. California Governor Arnold Schwarzenegger negotiated with the state's tribes, getting them to agree to transfer a fraction of their profits to the state in exchange for concessions (Dan Morain and Evan Halper, "Casino Deals Said to Be Near," *Los Angeles Times*, June 16, 2004, 1). In 2004, he first proposed that the state get 25% of casino profits and then he dropped the level to 15%. He announced a deal with two tribes at 10% in 2005. How does a profit tax affect a monopoly's output and price? How would a monopoly change its behavior if the profit tax were 10% rather than 25%? (*Hint*: You may assume that the profit tax refers to the tribe's economic profit.)

38. In 1996, Florida voted on (and rejected) a 1¢-per-pound excise tax on refined cane sugar in the Florida Everglades Agricultural Area. Swinton and Thomas (2001) used linear supply and demand curves (based on elasticities estimated by Marks, 1993) to calculate the incidence from this tax given that the market is competitive. Their inverse demand curve was $p = 1.787 - 0.0004641Q$, and their inverse supply curve was $p = -0.4896 + 0.00020165Q$. Calculate the incidence of the tax that falls on consumers (Chapter 3) for a competitive market. If producers joined together to form a monopoly, and the supply curve is actually the monopoly's marginal cost curve, what is the incidence of the tax? (*Hint*: The incidence that falls on consumers is the difference between the

equilibrium price with and without the tax divided by the tax. You should find that the incidence is 70% in a competitive market and 41% in a monopoly.)

39. A monopoly manufactures its product in two factories with marginal cost functions $MC_1(Q_1)$ and $MC_2(Q_2)$, where Q_1 is the quantity produced in the first factory and Q_2 is the quantity manufactured in the second factory. The monopoly's total output is $Q = Q_1 + Q_2$. Use a graph (or math) to determine how much total output the monopoly produces and how much it produces at each factory. (*Hint*: Consider the cases where the factories have constant marginal costs—not necessarily equal costs—and where they have upward-sloping marginal cost curves.)

40. A monopoly sells music CDs. It has a constant marginal and average cost of $20. It faces two groups of potential customers: honest and dishonest people. The dishonest and the honest consumers' demand functions are the same: $p = 120 - Q$.
   a. If it is not possible for the dishonest customers to steal the music, what are the monopoly's profit-maximizing price and quantity? What is its profit? What are the consumer surplus, producer surplus, and welfare?
   b. Suppose that the dishonest customers can pirate the music. Answer the same questions as in part a.
   c. How do consumer surplus, producer surplus, and welfare change if piracy occurs?

*41. A monopoly produces a good with a network externality at a constant marginal and average cost of $2. In the first period, its inverse demand curve is $p = 10 - Q$. In the second period, its demand is $p = 10 - Q$ unless it sells at least $Q = 8$ units in the first period. If it meets or exceeds this target, then the demand curve rotates out by β (that is, it sells β times as many units for any given price), so that its inverse demand curve is $p = 10 - Q/\beta$. The monopoly knows that it can sell no output after the second period. The monopoly's objective is to maximize the sum of its profits over the two periods. In the first period, should the monopoly set the output that maximizes its profit in that period? How does your answer depend on β? (*Hint*: See the discussion of the two-period monopoly model in Section 11.8.)

42. A monopoly's production function is Cobb-Douglas, $Q = L^{0.5}K^{0.5}$, where L is labor and K is capital. The demand function is $p = 100 - Q$. The wage, w, is $1 per hour, and the rental cost of capital, r, is $4.
   a. What is the equation of the (long-run) expansion path? Illustrate in a graph.
   b. Derive the long-run total cost curve equation as a function of q.
   c. What quantity maximizes this firm's profit?
   d. Find the optimal input combination that produces the profit-maximizing quantity. Illustrate with a graph.

43. Suppose that the inverse demand function for a monopolist's product is $p = 9 - Q/20$. Its cost function is $C = 10 + 10Q - 4Q^2 + 2/3Q^3$.
   a. Draw marginal revenue and marginal cost curves. At what outputs does marginal revenue equal marginal cost?
   b. What is the profit-maximizing output? Check the second-order condition, $d^2\pi/dQ^2$, at the monopoly optimum. V

44. Suppose that the inverse demand for San Francisco cable car rides is $p = 10 - Q/1{,}000$, where p is the price per ride and Q is the number of rides per day.
   a. Suppose the objective of San Francisco's Municipal Authority (the cable car operator) is to maximize its revenues. What is the revenue-maximizing price?
   b. San Francisco calculates that the city's businesses benefit from tourists and residents riding on the city's cable cars at $4 per ride. Suppose the city's objective is to maximize the sum of the cable car revenues and the economic impact. What is the optimal price? V

12 Pricing and Advertising

Everything is worth what its purchaser will pay for it.
—Publilius Syrus (first century BC)

Why does Disneyworld Florida charge local residents $369 for an annual pass and out-of-towners $489? Why are airlines' fares substantially less if you book in advance? Why are some goods, including computers and software, bundled and sold at a single price? To answer these questions, we need to examine how monopolies and other noncompetitive firms set prices.

Often, these firms can use information about individual consumers' demand curves to increase their profits. Instead of setting a single price, they use **nonuniform pricing**: charging consumers different prices for the same product or charging a single customer a price that depends on the number of units purchased. By replacing a single price with nonuniform pricing, the firm raises its profit.

Why can a monopoly earn a higher profit from using a nonuniform pricing scheme than from setting a single price? A monopoly that uses nonuniform prices can capture some or all of the consumer surplus and deadweight loss that results if the monopoly sets a single price. As we saw in Chapter 11, a monopoly that sets a high single price sells only to the customers who value the good the most, and those customers retain some consumer surplus. The monopoly loses sales to other customers who value the good less than the single price. These lost sales are a *deadweight loss*: the value of these potential sales in excess of the cost of producing the good. But a monopoly that uses nonuniform pricing captures additional consumer surplus by raising the price for customers who value the good the most. By lowering the good's price for other customers, the monopoly sells more, thereby converting into profit what would otherwise be deadweight loss.

This chapter examines several types of nonuniform pricing, including price discrimination, two-part tariffs, and tie-in sales. A firm engages in **price discrimination** by charging consumers different prices for the same good based on individual characteristics, belonging to an identifiable sub-group of consumers, or the quantity purchased. For example, many magazine publishers price discriminate by charging college students less for subscriptions than they charge the general public. If a popular magazine were to charge a high price for everyone, many students—who are price sensitive (have relatively elastic demands)—would cancel their subscriptions. If, on the other hand, the magazine were to offer the student price to everyone, it would gain few additional subscriptions because most potential older adult subscribers are relatively price insensitive, and it would earn less from those older adults who are willing to pay the higher price. Thus, the magazine makes more profit by price discriminating.

Some noncompetitive firms that cannot practically price discriminate use other forms of nonuniform pricing to increase profits. One method is for a firm to charge a *two-part tariff*, where a customer pays one fee for the right to buy the good and another price for each unit purchased. For example, health club members pay an annual fee to join the club and then an additional fee each time they use the facilities.

In another type of nonuniform pricing, the *tie-in sale*, a customer may buy one good only if he or she agrees to buy another good or service. Vacation package deals, for example, may include airfare and a hotel room for a single price. Some restaurants offer a prix fixe menu, where a single price buys an appetizer, entrée, and dessert. A firm may sell copiers under the condition that customers agree to buy all future copier service and supplies from the firm.

A monopoly may also increase its profit by advertising. A monopoly (or another firm with market power) may advertise to shift its demand curve so as to raise its profit, taking into account the cost of advertising.

In this chapter, we examine seven main topics	1. **Why and How Firms Price Discriminate.** A firm can increase its profit by price discriminating if it has market power, can identify which customers are more price sensitive than others, and can prevent customers who pay low prices from reselling to those who pay high prices.

2. **Perfect Price Discrimination.** If a monopoly can charge the maximum that each customer is willing to pay for each unit of output, the monopoly captures all potential consumer surplus and sells the efficient (competitive) level of output.

3. **Quantity Discrimination.** Some firms profit by charging different prices for large purchases than they charge for small ones, which is a form of price discrimination.

4. **Multimarket Price Discrimination.** Firms that cannot perfectly price discriminate may charge a group of consumers with relatively elastic demands a lower price than they charge other groups.

5. **Two-Part Tariffs.** By charging consumers a fee for the right to buy any number of units and a price per unit, firms earn higher profits than they do by charging a single price per unit.

6. **Tie-In Sales.** By requiring customers to buy a second good or service along with the first, firms make higher profits than they do by selling the goods or services separately.

7. **Advertising.** A monopoly advertises to shift its demand curve and to increase its profit.

12.1 Why and How Firms Price Discriminate

Until now, we have examined how a monopoly sets its price if it charges all customers the same price. However, many noncompetitive firms increase their profits by charging *nonuniform prices*, which vary across customers. We start with the most common form of nonuniform pricing: price discrimination.

Why Price Discrimination Pays

For almost any good or service, some consumers are willing to pay more than others. A firm that sets a single price faces a trade-off between charging consumers who really want the good as much as they are willing to pay and charging a sufficiently low price that the firm does not lose sales to less enthusiastic customers. As a result, the firm usually sets an intermediate price. A price-discriminating firm that varies its prices across customers avoids this trade-off.

There are two reasons a firm earns a higher profit from price discrimination than from uniform pricing. First, a price-discriminating firm charges a higher price to customers who are willing to pay more than the uniform price, capturing some or all of their consumer surplus—the difference between what a good is worth to a consumer and what the consumer pays—under uniform pricing. Second, a price-discriminating firm sells to some people who are not willing to pay as much as the uniform price.

Who Can Price Discriminate

Not all firms can price discriminate. For a firm to price discriminate successfully, three conditions must be met.

First, a firm must have *market power*, otherwise it cannot charge any consumer more than the competitive price. A monopoly, an oligopoly firm, a monopolistically competitive firm, or a cartel may be able to price discriminate. A competitive firm cannot price discriminate.

Second, for a firm to profitably charge various consumers different prices, the **reservation price**—the maximum amount a person is willing to pay for a unit of output—must *vary* across consumers, and a firm must be able to *identify* which consumers are willing to pay relatively more. A movie theater manager may know that senior citizens have a lower reservation price for admission than do other adults. Theater employees can identify senior citizens by observation or using driver's licenses. Even if all customers are identical, a firm may be able to price discriminate over the number of units each purchases. If a firm knows how each individual's reservation price varies with the number of units, it can charge each customer a higher price for the first unit of a good than it charges for subsequent units.

Third, a firm must be able to *prevent or limit resales* from customers that the firm charges a relatively low price to those whom the firm wants to charge a relatively high price. Price discrimination is ineffective if resales are easy, because ease of reselling would inhibit the firm's ability to make higher-price sales. A movie theater owner can charge senior citizens a lower price than other adults because as soon as the seniors buy their tickets they enter the theater and don't have time to resell them.

Except for competitive firms, most firms have some market power, and many of those firms can identify which groups of customers have a relatively high reservation price. Usually, the biggest obstacle to price discrimination is a firm's inability to prevent resales. However in some markets, resales are inherently difficult or impossible, firms can take actions that prevent resales, or government actions or laws prevent resales.

APPLICATION

Disneyland Pricing

Disneyland, in southern California, is a well-run operation that rarely misses a trick when it comes to increasing its profit. (Indeed, Disneyland mints money: When you enter the park, you can exchange U.S. currency for Disney dollars, which can be spent only in the park.)

In 2010, Disneyland charges most out-of-state adults $299 for an annual pass to Disneyland and Disney's California Adventure park but charges southern Californians $219. This policy of charging locals a discounted price makes sense if visitors are willing to pay more than locals and if Disneyland can prevent locals from selling discounted tickets to nonlocals. Imagine a Midwesterner who's never been to Disneyland and wants to visit. Travel accounts for most of the trip's cost, so an extra few dollars for entrance to the park makes little percentage difference in the total cost of the visit and hence does not greatly affect that person's decision whether to go. In contrast, for a local who has been to Disneyland many times and for whom the entrance price is a larger share of the total cost, a slightly higher entrance fee might prevent a visit.

Charging both groups the same price is not in Disney's best interest. If Disney were to charge the higher price to everyone, many locals wouldn't visit the park. If Disney were to use the lower price for everyone, it would be charging nonresidents much less than they are willing to pay.[1]

Preventing Resales

Resales are difficult or impossible for most *services* and when *transaction costs are high*. If Joe the plumber charges you less than he charges your neighbor for clearing a pipe, you cannot make a deal with your neighbor to resell this service. The higher the transaction costs a consumer must incur to resell a good, the less likely are resales. Suppose that you are able to buy a jar of pickles for $1 less than the usual price. Could you practically buy and sell this jar to someone, or would the transaction costs be prohibitive? The more valuable a product or the more widely consumed it is, the more likely it is that transaction costs are low enough that resales occur.

Some firms act to raise transaction costs or otherwise make resales difficult. Disneyland prevents resales by checking a purchaser's driver's license and requiring that the ticket be used for same-day entrance. If your college requires that someone with a student ticket shows a student ID card before being admitted to a sporting event, it would be difficult to resell your low-price tickets to nonstudents, whom your college charges a higher price. When students at some universities buy computers at lower-than-usual prices, they must sign a contract that forbids them to resell the computer.

Similarly, a firm can prevent resales by *vertically integrating*: participating in more than one successive stage of the production and distribution chain for a good or service. Alcoa, the former aluminum monopoly, wanted to sell aluminum ingots to producers of aluminum wire at a lower price than it set for producers of aluminum aircraft parts. If Alcoa did so, however, the wire producers could easily resell their ingots. By starting its own wire production firm, Alcoa prevented such resales and was able to charge high prices to firms that manufactured aircraft parts (Perry, 1980).

Governments frequently establish policies to promote price discrimination and to bar resales. For example, U.S. federal and some state governments require that milk

---

[1]According to www.babycenter.com, it costs $411,214 to raise a child from cradle through college. Parents can cut that total in half, however: They don't *have* to take their kids to Disneyland.

producers, under penalty of law, price discriminate by selling milk at a higher price for fresh use than for processing (cheese, ice cream), and forbid resales. Government *tariffs* (taxes on imports) limit resales by making it expensive to buy goods in a low-price country and resell them in a high-price country. In some cases, laws prevent such reselling explicitly. Under U.S. trade laws, certain brand-name perfumes may not be sold in the United States except by their manufacturers.

APPLICATION	
Preventing Resale of Designer Bags	During the holiday season, stores often limit how many of the hottest items—such as Wii game consoles—a customer can buy. But it may surprise you that Web sites of luxury-goods retailers such as Saks Fifth Avenue, Neiman Marcus, and Bergdorf Goodman limit how many designer handbags one can buy: "Due to popular demand, a customer may order no more than three units of this item every 30 days." These limits are even more surprising given that luxury-goods sales in 2009 were off by at least 12% in the United States, 10% in Japan, and 8% in Europe compared to the previous year.

Why wouldn't manufacturers and stores want to sell as many units as possible? How many customers can even afford more than three Prada Visone Hobo handbags at $4,950 each? The simple explanation is that the restriction has nothing to do with "popular demand." It's designed to prevent resales so as to enable manufacturers to price discriminate internationally. Manufacturers pressure the U.S. retailers to limit sales so as to prevent anyone from buying large numbers of bags and reselling them in Europe or Asia where the same items in Prada and Gucci stores often cost 20% to 40% more. For example, the Prada Nappa Antique Tote sells for $1,280 at Saks Fifth Avenue in New York City, but it sells for $1,570 on Prada's Swiss Web site. The weakening U.S. dollar makes such international resales even more attractive, which explains why Prada's online site allows shipments to selected countries, expressly forbids resales, and limits purchases.

Not All Price Differences Are Price Discrimination

Not every seller who charges consumers different prices is price discriminating. Hotels charge newlyweds more for bridal suites. Is that price discrimination? Some hotel managers say no. They contend that honeymooners, more than other guests, steal mementos, so the price differential reflects an actual cost differential.

The price of a year's worth of *Entertainment Weekly* magazines is $192.50 at the newsstand, $38.95 with a standard subscription, and $34.95 with a college student subscription. The difference between the newsstand cost and the standard subscription cost reflects, at least in part, the higher cost of selling the magazine at a newsstand rather than mailing it directly to customers, so this price difference does not reflect pure price discrimination. But the price difference between the standard subscription rate and the college student rate reflects pure price discrimination because the two subscriptions are identical in every respect except the price.

Types of Price Discrimination

There are three main types of price discrimination. With **perfect price discrimination**—also called *first-degree price discrimination*—the firm sells each unit at the maximum amount each customer is willing to pay, so prices differ across customers, and a given customer may pay more for some units than for others. With **quantity discrimination** (*second-degree price discrimination*), the firm charges a different price for large quantities than for small quantities, but all customers who buy a given quantity pay the same price. With **multimarket price discrimination** (*third-degree price discrimination*), the firm charges different groups of customers different prices but charges a given customer the same price for every unit sold. Typically, not all customers pay different prices—the firm sets different prices only for a few groups of customers. Because this type of discrimination is the most common, the term *price discrimination* is often used to mean *multimarket price discrimination*.

In addition to price discriminating, many firms use other, more complicated types of nonuniform pricing. Later in this chapter, we examine two other frequently used nonuniform pricing methods—two-part tariffs and tie-in sales—that are similar to quantity discrimination.

12.2 Perfect Price Discrimination

If a firm with market power knows exactly how much each customer is willing to pay for each unit of its good and it can prevent resales, the firm charges each person his or her *reservation price*. Such an all-knowing firm *perfectly price discriminates*. By selling each unit of its output to the customer who values it the most at the maximum price that person is willing to pay, the perfectly price-discriminating monopoly captures all possible consumer surplus. For example, the managers of the Suez Canal set tolls individually, considering many factors such as weather and each ship's alternative routes.

First, we analyze how a firm uses its information about consumers to perfectly price discriminate. Next, we compare the perfectly price-discriminating monopoly to competition and single-price monopoly. By showing that the same quantity is produced as would be produced by a competitive market and that the last unit of output sells for the marginal cost, we demonstrate that perfect price discrimination is efficient. Then, we illustrate how the perfect price discrimination equilibrium differs from a single-price monopoly by using the Botox application from Chapter 11. Finally, we discuss how firms obtain the information they need to perfectly price discriminate.

How a Firm Perfectly Price Discriminates

Suppose that a monopoly has market power, can prevent resales, and has enough information to perfectly price discriminate. The monopoly sells each unit at its reservation price, which is the height of the demand curve: the maximum price consumers will pay for a given amount of output.

Graphical Analysis. Figure 12.1 illustrates how a perfectly price-discriminating firm maximizes its profit. The figure shows that the first customer is willing to pay $6 for a unit, the next customer is willing to pay $5, and so forth. This perfectly price-discriminating firm sells its first unit of output for $6. Having sold the first unit, the firm can get, at most $5 for the second unit. The firm must drop its price by $1 for each successive unit it sells.

A perfectly price-discriminating monopoly's marginal revenue is the same as its price. As the figure shows, the firm's marginal revenue is $MR_1 = \$6$ on the first unit, $MR_2 = \$5$ on the second unit, and $MR_3 = \$4$ on the third unit. As a result, *the firm's marginal revenue curve is its demand curve*.

This firm has a constant marginal cost of $4 per unit. It pays for the firm to produce the first unit because the firm sells that unit for $6, so its marginal revenue exceeds its marginal cost by $2. Similarly, the firm certainly wants to sell the second unit for $5, which also exceeds its marginal cost. The firm breaks even when it sells the third unit for $4. The firm is unwilling to sell more than three units because its

Figure 12.1 Perfect Price Discrimination

The monopoly can charge $6 for the first unit, $5 for the second, and $4 for the third, as the demand curve shows. Its marginal revenue is $MR_1 = \$6$ for the first unit, $MR_2 = \$5$ for the second, and $MR_3 = \$4$ for the third. Thus, the demand curve is also the marginal revenue curve. Because the firm's marginal and average cost is $4 per unit, it is unwilling to sell at a price below $4, so it sells three units, point e, and breaks even on the last unit.

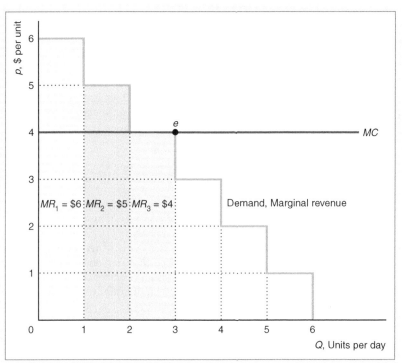

marginal cost would exceed its marginal revenue on successive units. Thus, like any profit-maximizing firm, a perfectly price-discriminating firm produces at point e, where its marginal revenue curve intersects its marginal cost curve. (If you find it upsetting that the firm is indifferent between producing two and three units, assume that the firm's marginal cost is $3.99, so it definitely wants to produce three units.)

This perfectly price-discriminating firm earns revenues of $MR_1 + MR_2 + MR_3 = \$6 + \$5 + \$4 = \$15$, which is the area under its marginal revenue curve up to the number of units it sells, three. If the firm has no fixed cost, its cost of producing three units is $\$12 = \$4 \times 3$, so its profit is $3.

The same type of analysis can be used with the usual, smooth demand curve. In Figure 12.2, a perfectly price-discriminating monopoly sells each unit at its reservation price, which is the height of the demand curve. As a result, the firm's marginal revenue curve, MR_d, is the same as its demand curve. The firm sells the first unit for p_1 to the consumer who will pay the most for the good. The firm's marginal cost for that unit is MC_1, so it makes $p_1 - MC_1$ on that unit. The firm receives a lower price and has a higher marginal cost for each successive unit. It sells Q_d units, where its marginal revenue curve, MR_d, intersects the marginal cost curve, MC. The last unit sells for p_c, so the monopoly just covers its marginal cost on the last unit. The firm is unwilling to sell additional units because its marginal revenue would be less than the marginal cost of producing them.

The perfectly price-discriminating monopoly's total producer surplus on the Q_d units it sells is the area below its demand curve and above its marginal cost curve, $A + B + C + D + E$. Its profit is the producer surplus minus its fixed cost, if any.

Calculus Analysis. A perfectly price-discriminating monopoly charges each customer the reservation price $p = D(Q)$, where $D(Q)$ is the inverse demand function

Figure 12.2 Competitive, Single-Price, and Perfect Discrimination Equilibria

In the competitive market equilibrium, e_c, price is p_c, quantity is Q_c, consumer surplus is $A + B + C$, producer surplus is $D + E$, and there is no deadweight loss. In the single-price monopoly equilibrium, e_s, price is p_s, quantity is Q_s, consumer surplus falls to A, producer surplus is $B + D$, and deadweight loss is $C + E$. In the perfect discrimination equilibrium, the monopoly sells each unit at the customer's reservation price on the demand curve. It sells Q_d ($= Q_c$) units, where the last unit is sold at its marginal cost. Customers have no consumer surplus, but there is no deadweight loss.

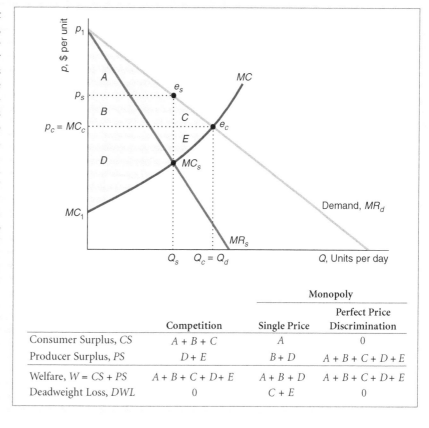

	Competition	Monopoly Single Price	Monopoly Perfect Price Discrimination
Consumer Surplus, CS	$A + B + C$	A	0
Producer Surplus, PS	$D + E$	$B + D$	$A + B + C + D + E$
Welfare, $W = CS + PS$	$A + B + C + D + E$	$A + B + D$	$A + B + C + D + E$
Deadweight Loss, DWL	0	$C + E$	0

and Q is total output. The discriminating monopoly's revenue, R, is the area under the demand curve up to the quantity, Q, it sells,

$$R = \int_0^Q D(z)\,dz,$$

where z is a placeholder for quantity. Its objective is to maximize its profit through its choice of Q:

$$\max_Q \pi = \int_0^Q D(z)\,dz - C(Q). \tag{12.1}$$

Its first-order condition for a maximum is found by differentiating Equation 12.1 (using Leibniz's rule, Chapter 9, footnote 19) to obtain

$$\frac{d\pi}{dQ} = D(Q) - \frac{dC(Q)}{dQ} = 0. \tag{12.2}$$

According to Equation 12.2, the discriminating monopoly sells units up to the quantity, Q, where the reservation price for the last unit, $D(Q)$, equals its marginal cost, $dC(Q)/dQ$. (This quantity is Q_d in Figure 12.2.)

For this solution to maximize profits, the second-order condition must hold:

$$\frac{d^2\pi}{dQ^2} = \frac{dD(Q)}{dQ} - \frac{d^2C(Q)}{dQ^2} < 0.$$

Given that the demand curve has a negative slope, the second-order condition holds if the marginal cost curve is upper sloping, $d^2C(Q)/dQ^2 > 0$, or if the demand curve has a greater (absolute) slope than the marginal cost curve.

The perfectly price-discriminating monopoly's profit is

$$\pi = \int_0^Q D(z)dz - C(Q).$$

For example, if $D(Q) = a - bQ$,

$$\pi = \int_0^Q (a - bz)dz - C(Q) = aQ - \frac{b}{2}Q^2 - C(Q). \tag{12.3}$$

The monopoly finds the output that maximizes the profit by setting the derivative of the profit in Equation 12.3 equal to zero:

$$a - bQ - \frac{dC(Q)}{dQ} = 0.$$

By rearranging terms, we find that $D(Q) = a - bQ = dC(Q)/dQ = MC$, as in Equation 12.2. Thus, the monopoly produces the quantity at which the demand curve hits the marginal cost curve.

APPLICATION

Google Uses Bidding for Ads to Price Discriminate

When you query Google, paid advertising appears next to your search results. The ads that appear vary with your search term. By making searches for unusual topics easy and fast, Google helps firms reach difficult-to-find potential customers with targeted ads. For example, a lawyer specializing in toxic mold lawsuits can place an ad that is seen only by people who search for "toxic mold lawyer." Such focused advertising has higher payoff per view than traditional print and broadcast ads that reach much larger, nontargeted groups ("wasted eyeballs") and avoids the problem of finding addresses for direct mailing.

Google uses auctions to price these ads. Advertisers are willing to bid higher to be listed first on Google's page. Goldfarb and Tucker (2008) found that how much lawyers will pay for context-based ads depends on the difficulty of making a match. Lawyers will pay more to advertise when there are fewer self-identified potential customers—fewer people searching for a particular phrase.

They also found that lawyers bid more when there are fewer customers, and hence the need to target ads is greater. Some states have anti-ambulance-chaser regulations, which prohibit personal injury lawyers from directly contacting potential clients by snail mail, phone, or e-mail for a few months after an accident. In those states, the extra amount bid for ads linked to personal injury keywords rather than for other keywords such as "tax lawyer" is $1.01 (11%) more than in unregulated states. We're talking big bucks here: Trial lawyers earned $40 billion in 2004, which is 50% more than Microsoft or Intel and twice that of Coca-Cola.

By taking advantage of advertisers' desire to reach small, difficult-to-find segments of the population and varying the price according to advertisers' willingness to pay, Google is essentially perfectly price discriminating.

Perfect Price Discrimination: Efficient but Harmful to Consumers

A perfect price discrimination equilibrium is efficient and maximizes total welfare, where welfare is defined as the sum of consumer surplus and producer surplus. As such, this equilibrium has more in common with a competitive equilibrium than with a single-price-monopoly equilibrium.

If the market in Figure 12.2 is competitive, the intersection of the demand curve and the marginal cost curve, MC, determines the competitive equilibrium at e_c, where price is p_c and quantity is Q_c. Consumer surplus is $A + B + C$, producer surplus is $D + E$, and there is no deadweight loss. The market is efficient because the price, p_c, equals the marginal cost, MC_c.

With a single-price monopoly (which charges all customers the same price because it cannot distinguish among them), the intersection of the MC curve and the single-price monopoly's marginal revenue curve, MC_s, determines the output, Q_s. The monopoly operates at e_s, where it charges p_s. The deadweight loss from monopoly is $C + E$. This efficiency loss is due to the monopoly's charging a price, p_s, that is above its marginal cost, MC_s, so less is sold than in a competitive market.

Again, the perfectly price-discriminating monopoly's total producer surplus on the Q_d units it sells is the area below its demand curve and above its marginal cost curve, $A + B + C + D + E$. Consumers receive no consumer surplus because each consumer pays his or her reservation price. The perfectly price-discriminating monopoly's equilibrium has *no deadweight loss* because the last unit is sold at a price, p_c, that equals the marginal cost, MC_c, as in a competitive market. Thus, both a perfect price discrimination equilibrium and a competitive equilibrium are efficient.

The perfect price discrimination equilibrium differs from the competitive equilibrium in two ways. First, in the competitive equilibrium, everyone is charged a price equal to the equilibrium marginal cost, $p_c = MC_c$; however, in the perfect price discrimination equilibrium, only the last unit is sold at that price. The other units are sold at customers' reservation prices, which are greater than p_c. Second, consumers receive some welfare (consumer surplus, $A + B + C$) in a competitive market, whereas a perfectly price-discriminating monopoly captures all the welfare. Thus, perfect price discrimination does not reduce efficiency—the output and total welfare are the same as under competition—but it does redistribute income away from consumers: Consumers are much better off under competition.

Is a single-price or perfectly price-discriminating monopoly better for consumers? The perfect price discrimination equilibrium is more efficient than the single-price monopoly equilibrium because more output is produced. A single-price monopoly, however, takes less consumer surplus from consumers than a perfectly price-discriminating monopoly. Consumers who put a very high value on the good are better off with a single-price monopoly, where they have consumer surplus, than with perfect price discrimination, where they have none. Consumers with lower reservation prices who purchase from the perfectly price-discriminating monopoly but not from the single-price monopoly have no consumer surplus in either case. All the social gain from the extra output goes to the perfectly price-discriminating firm. Consumer surplus is greatest with competition, lower with single-price monopoly, and eliminated by perfect price discrimination.

| APPLICATION Botox Revisited | We illustrate how perfect price discrimination differs from competition and single-price monopoly using the Application "Botox Patent Monopoly" in Chapter 11. The graph shows a linear demand curve for Botox and a constant marginal cost (and average variable cost) of \$25 per vial. If the market had been competitive (that is, the price equaled marginal cost at e_c), consumer surplus would have been area $A + B + C = \$750$ million per year, and there would have been no producer surplus or deadweight loss. In the single-price monopoly equilibrium, e_s, the Botox vials sell for \$400, and 1 million vials are sold. The corresponding con- |

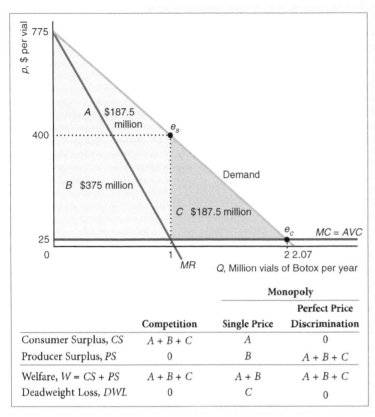

sumer surplus is triangle $A = \$187.5$ million per year, producer surplus is rectangle $B = \$375$ million, and the deadweight loss is triangle $C = \$187.5$ million.

If Allergan, the manufacturer of Botox, could perfectly price discriminate, its producer surplus would double to $A + B + C = \$750$ million per year, and consumers would obtain no consumer surplus. The marginal consumer would pay the marginal cost of $25, the same as in a competitive market.

Allergan's inability to perfectly price discriminate costs the company and society dearly. The profit of the single-price monopoly, $B = \$375$ million per day, is lower than that of a perfectly price-discriminating monopoly by $A + C = \$375$ million per year. Similarly, society's welfare under the single-price monopoly is lower than from perfect price discrimination by the deadweight loss, C, of $\$187.5$ million per year.

Transaction Costs and Perfect Price Discrimination

Although some firms come close to perfect price discrimination, many more set a single price or use another nonuniform pricing method. Transaction costs are a major reason these firms do not perfectly price discriminate: It is too difficult or costly to gather information about each customer's price sensitivity. Recent advances in computer technologies, however, have lowered these costs, allowing hotels, car- and truck-rental companies, cruise lines, and airlines to price discriminate more often.

Private colleges request and receive financial information from students, which allows the schools to nearly perfectly price discriminate. The schools give partial scholarships as a means of reducing tuition to relatively poor students.

Many auto dealerships try to increase their profit by perfectly price discriminating, charging each customer the maximum the customer is willing to pay. These firms hire salespeople to ascertain potential customers' willingness to pay and to bargain with them.

Many other firms believe that, taking the transaction costs into account, it pays to use quantity discrimination, multimarket price discrimination, or other nonuniform pricing methods rather than try to perfectly price discriminate. We now turn to these alternative approaches.

SOLVED PROBLEM 12.1

Competitive firms are the customers of a union, which is the monopoly supplier of labor services. Show the union's "producer surplus" if it perfectly price discriminates. Then suppose that the union makes the firms a take-it-or-leave-it offer: Firms must guarantee to hire a minimum of H^* hours of work at a wage of w^*, or they can hire no one. Show that by setting w^* and H^* appropriately, the union can achieve the same outcome as if it could perfectly price discriminate.

Answer

1. *Show the outcome and welfare areas if the union can perfectly price discriminate.* The figure shows the labor supply curve if the market were competitive. The union views this curve as its marginal cost curve. For each successive hour of labor service, the union sets the wage equal to the height of the demand curve and sells H^* total hours of labor services (see the discussion of Figure 12.2). Its producer surplus equals the total welfare: $A + B$.

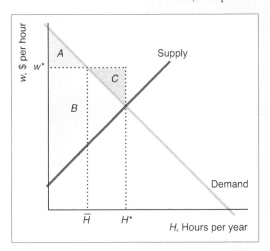

2. *Show that the firms will agree to hire H^* at w^*, and that the union will capture all of the surplus.* If the union gives the firms a take-it-or-leave-it offer of hiring H^* hours at w^* or of hiring no one, the firms will accept the offer because area C is the same size as area A in the figure. At a wage of w^*, the firms have "consumer surplus" (the amount they are willing to pay above the wage for a given amount of labor services) of A for the first $\overline{H}$ hours of work, but they have negative consumer surplus of C for the remaining $H^* - \overline{H}$ hours of work. Thus, they have no consumer surplus overall, so they are indifferent between hiring the workers or not. The union's producer surplus is $B + C$, which equals its surplus if it perfectly price discriminated: $A + B$. Similarly, the number of hours of labor service provided, H^*, is the same under both pricing schemes.

APPLICATION

Unions That Set Wages and Hours

Most unions act as a single-price monopoly of labor services. They set a wage and allow their customers to determine how many units of labor services to purchase. However, a few unions set both wages and a minimum number of work hours that employers must provide. Such contracts are common only in the transportation industry (excluding railroads and airplanes).

The International Longshore and Warehouse Union (ILWU) negotiates with companies represented by the Pacific Maritime Association. In 2008, a general longshoreman earned $125,461 on average. The union contract in effect through 2014 guarantees a weekly income for each worker because it effectively sets the minimum number of hours, but actual earnings depend on the amount of work available. It also guarantees an annual pension of $80,000 as of 2014.

The number of dockworkers has shrunk over the years as firms have automated to become more efficient. Consequently, the union has insisted that the lost positions be replaced with new clerical positions (whose average earnings were $139,862 in 2008). However, with a 20% reduction of hours during the 2009 recession and the threat of further reductions when the Panama Canal is enlarged in 2014, the union is currently more willing to accept automation and some loss of hours.

12.3 Quantity Discrimination

Many firms are unable to determine which customers have the highest reservation prices. However, firms may know that most customers are willing to pay more for the first unit than for successive units—in other words, that the typical customer's demand curve is downward sloping. Such firms can price discriminate by letting the price that each customer pays vary with the number of units purchased. Here, the price varies only with quantity: All customers pay the same price for a given quantity.

Not all quantity discounts are a form of price discrimination. Some reflect the reduction in a firm's cost with large-quantity sales. For example, the cost per ounce of selling soft drinks in large cups is less than that of selling it in small cups; the cost of cups varies little with size, and the cost of pouring and serving is the same. A restaurant offering quantity discounts on drinks may be passing on actual cost savings to larger purchasers rather than price discriminating. However, if the quantity discount is not due to cost differences, the firm is engaging in quantity discrimination. Moreover, a firm may quantity discriminate by charging customers who make large purchases more per unit than those who make small purchases.

Many utilities use *block-pricing* schedules, by which they charge one price for the first few units (a *block*) of usage and a different price for subsequent blocks. Both declining-block and increasing-block pricing are common.

The utility monopoly in Figure 12.3 faces a linear demand curve for each (identical) customer. The demand curve hits the vertical axis at $90 and the horizontal axis at 90 units. The monopoly has a constant marginal and average cost of $m = \$30$. Panel a shows how this monopoly maximizes its profit if it can quantity discriminate by setting two prices. The firm uses declining-block prices to maximize its profit.

The utility monopoly faces an inverse demand curve $p = 90 - Q$, and its marginal and average cost is $m = 30$. Consequently, the quantity-discounting utility's profit is

$$\pi = p(Q_1)Q_1 + p(Q_2)(Q_2 - Q_1) - mQ_2$$
$$= (90 - Q_1)Q_1 + (90 - Q_2)(Q_2 - Q_1) - 30Q_2,$$

where Q_1 is the largest quantity for which the first-block rate, $p_1 = 90 - Q_1$, is charged and Q_2 is the total quantity that a consumer purchases. The utility chooses Q_1 and Q_2 to maximize its profit. It sets the derivative of profit with respect to Q_1 equal to zero, $d\pi/dQ_1 = Q_2 - 2Q_1 = 0$, and the derivative of profit with respect to Q_2 equal to zero, $d\pi/dQ_2 = Q_1 - 2Q_2 + 60 = 0$. By solving these two equations simultaneously, the utility determines its profit-maximizing quantities, $Q_1 = 20$ and $Q_2 = 40$. The corresponding block prices are $p_1 = 90 - 20 = 70$ and $p_2 = 50$. That is, the monopoly charges a price of $70 on any quantity between 1 and 20—the first block—and $50 on any units beyond the first 20—the second block. (The point that determines the first block, $70 and 20 units, lies on the demand curve.) Given each consumer's demand curve, a consumer who decides to buy 40 units pays $1,400 (= 70×20) for the first block and $1,000 (= 50×20) for the second block.

If the monopoly can set only a single price (panel b), it produces where its marginal revenue equals its marginal cost, selling 30 units at $60 per unit. Thus, by quantity discriminating instead of using a single price, the utility sells more units, 40 instead of 30, and makes a higher profit, $B = \$1,200$ instead of $F = \$900$. With quantity discounting, consumer surplus is lower, $A + C = \$400$ instead of $E = \$450$; welfare (consumer surplus plus producer surplus) is higher, $A + B + C = \$1,600$ instead of $E + F = \$1,350$; and deadweight loss is lower, $D = \$200$ instead of $G = \$450$. Thus, in this example, the firm and society are better off with quantity discounting, but consumers as a group suffer.

Figure 12.3 Quantity Discrimination

If this monopoly engages in quantity discounting, it makes a larger profit (producer surplus) than it does if it sets a single price, and welfare is greater. (a) With quantity discounting, profit is $B = \$1{,}200$ and welfare is $A + B + C = \$1{,}600$. (b) If it sets a single price (so that its marginal revenue equals its marginal cost), the monopoly's profit is $F = \$900$, and welfare is $E + F = \$1{,}350$.

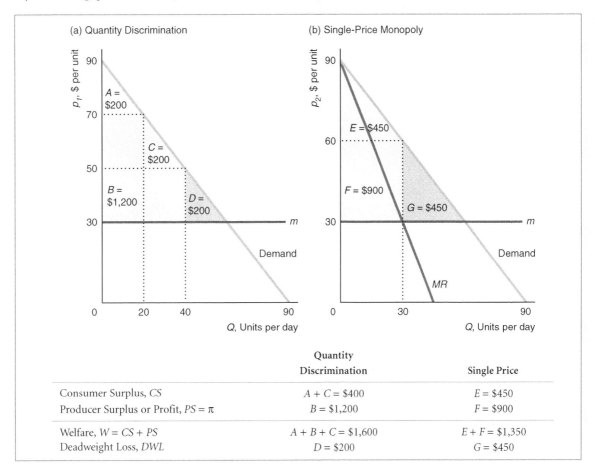

	Quantity Discrimination	Single Price
Consumer Surplus, CS	$A + C = \$400$	$E = \$450$
Producer Surplus or Profit, $PS = \pi$	$B = \$1{,}200$	$F = \$900$
Welfare, $W = CS + PS$	$A + B + C = \$1{,}600$	$E + F = \$1{,}350$
Deadweight Loss, DWL	$D = \$200$	$G = \$450$

The more block prices that the monopoly can set, the closer the monopoly can get to perfect price discrimination. A deadweight loss results from the monopoly's setting a price above marginal cost so that too few units are sold. The more prices the monopoly sets, the lower the last price and hence the closer it is to marginal cost.

12.4 Multimarket Price Discrimination

Typically, a firm does not know the reservation price for each of its customers. But the firm may know which groups of customers are likely to have higher reservation prices than others. The most common method of multimarket price discrimination is to divide potential customers into two or more groups and to set a different price for each group. All units of the good sold to customers within a group are sold at a single price. As with perfect price discrimination, to engage in multimarket price discrimination, a firm must have market power, be able to identify groups with different demands, and prevent resales.

For example, first-run movie theaters with market power charge seniors a lower ticket price than they charge younger adults because typically the elderly are not willing to pay as much to see a movie. By admitting seniors as soon as they prove their age and buy tickets, the theater prevents resales.

Multimarket Price Discrimination with Two Groups

Suppose that a monopoly can divide its customers into two (or more) groups—for example, consumers in two countries. It sells Q_1 to the first group and earns revenues of $R_1(Q_1)$, and it sells Q_2 units to the second group and earns $R_2(Q_2)$. Its cost of producing total output $Q = Q_1 + Q_2$ units is $C(Q)$. The monopoly can maximize its profit through its choice of prices or quantities to each group. We examine its problem when it chooses quantities:

$$\max_{Q_1, Q_2} \pi = R_1(Q_1) + R_2(Q_2) - C(Q_1 + Q_2). \tag{12.4}$$

The first-order conditions corresponding to Equation 12.4 are obtained by differentiating with respect to Q_1 and Q_2 and setting the partial derivative equal to zero:

$$\frac{\partial \pi}{\partial Q_1} = \frac{dR_1(Q_1)}{dQ_1} - \frac{dC(Q)}{dQ} \frac{\partial Q}{\partial Q_1} = 0, \tag{12.5}$$

$$\frac{\partial \pi}{\partial Q_2} = \frac{dR_2(Q_2)}{dQ_2} - \frac{dC(Q)}{dQ} \frac{\partial Q}{\partial Q_2} = 0. \tag{12.6}$$

Equation 12.5 says that the marginal revenue from sales to the first group, $MR^1 = dR_1(Q_1)/dQ_1$, should equal the marginal cost of producing the last unit of total output, $MC = dC(Q)/dQ$, because $\partial Q/\partial Q_1 = 1$. Similarly, Equation 12.6 shows that the marginal revenue from the second group, MR^2, should also equal the marginal cost. By combining Equations 12.5 and 12.6, we find that the two marginal revenues are equal where the monopoly is profit maximizing:

$$MR^1 = MC = MR^2. \tag{12.7}$$

A recent example illustrates the basic idea. A copyright gives Universal Studios the legal monopoly to produce and sell the *Mamma Mia!* DVD. Universal engaged in multimarket price discrimination by charging different prices in various countries because it believed that the elasticities of demand differ. The DVD sells for $20 in the United States, $36 (£22) in the United Kingdom, and $21 (C$23) in Canada.[2] Presumably, the cost to consumers of reselling across countries is high enough that Universal can ignore the problem of resales.[3]

---

[2] Sources of information and data for this section include Amazon Web sites for each country, www.ukfilmcouncil.org.uk, www.the-numbers.com/movies/2008/MAMIA-DVD.php, and www.leesmovieinfo.com. We assume that the demand curves in each country are linear.

[3] Why don't customers in higher-price countries order the DVDs from low-price countries using Amazon or other Internet vendors? Explanations include consumers' lack of an Internet connection, ignorance, higher shipping costs (although the price differentials slightly exceed this cost), language differences in the DVDs, region encoding (fear of incompatibilities), desire for quick delivery, and legal restrictions.

For simplicity, we consider how Universal sets its U.S. and U.K. prices. Universal charges its American consumers p_A for Q_A units, so its revenue is $p_A Q_A$. If Universal has the same constant marginal and average cost, m, in both countries, its profit (ignoring any sunk development cost and other fixed costs) from selling the DVD is $\pi_A = p_A Q_A - m Q_A$, where $m Q_A$ is its cost of producing Q_A units. Universal wants to maximize its combined profit, π, which is the sum of its American and British profits, π_A and π_B:

$$\pi = \pi_A + \pi_B = (p_A Q_A - m Q_A) + (p_B Q_B - m Q_B).$$

How should Universal set its prices p_A and p_B—or, equivalently, Q_A and Q_B—so that it maximizes its combined profit? Because its marginal cost is the same to both sets of customers, we can use our understanding of a single-price monopoly's behavior to answer this question. A multimarket-price-discriminating monopoly with a constant marginal cost maximizes its total profit by maximizing its profit from each group separately. Universal sets its quantities so that the marginal revenue for each group equals the common marginal cost, m, which is about $1 per unit.

The majority of Universal's sales for the *Mamma Mia!* DVD occurred in 2008 and 2009. The company sold about 6.33 million copies in the United States, and 5 million copies in the United Kingdom (where it was the UK all-time best-selling DVD). Figure 12.4 shows sales data through the end of that year. In panel a, Universal equates its marginal revenue to its marginal cost, $MR^A = m = \$1$, at Q_A

Figure 12.4 Multimarket Pricing of the *Mamma Mia!* DVD

Universal Studios, the monopoly producer of the *Mamma Mia!* DVD, charges more in the United Kingdom, $p_B = \$36$, than in the United States, $p_A = \$20$, because the elasticity of demand is greater in the United States. Universal sets the quantity independently in each country where its relevant marginal revenue equals its common, constant marginal cost, $m = \$1$. As a result, it maximizes its profit by equating the two marginal revenues: $MR^A = 1 = MR^B$.

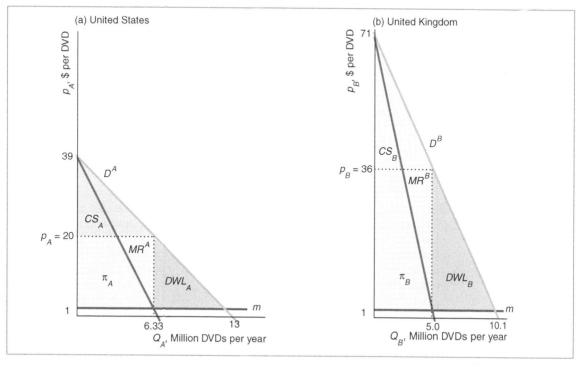

= 6.33 million DVDs. The resulting price is $p_A = \$20$ per DVD. In panel b, $MR^B = m = \$1$ at $Q_B = 5.0$ DVDs and the price is $p_B = \$36$.

This price-setting rule must be profit maximizing if the firm does not want to change its price for either group. Would the monopoly want to lower its price and sell more output in the United States? If it did, its marginal revenue would be below its marginal cost, so this change would reduce its profit. Similarly, if the monopoly sold less output in the United States, its marginal revenue would be above its marginal cost, which would reduce its profit. The same arguments can be made about its pricing in Britain. Thus, the price-discriminating monopoly maximizes its profit by operating where its marginal revenue for each country equals its common marginal cost.

Because the monopoly equates the marginal revenue for each group to its common marginal cost, $MC = m$, the marginal revenues for the two countries are equal, $MR^A = m = MR^B$, as in Equation 12.7. We can use this equation to determine how the prices for the two groups vary with the price elasticities of demand at the profit-maximizing outputs. Each marginal revenue is a function of the corresponding price and the price elasticity of demand: $MR^A = p_A(1 + 1/\varepsilon_A)$, where ε_A is the price elasticity of demand for U.S. consumers, and $MR^B = p_B(1 + 1/\varepsilon_B)$, where ε_B is the price elasticity of demand for U.K. consumers. Rewriting the equation using these expressions for marginal revenue, we find that

$$MR^A = p_A\left(1 + \frac{1}{\varepsilon_A}\right) = m = p_B\left(1 + \frac{1}{\varepsilon_B}\right) = MR^B. \qquad (12.8)$$

Given that $m = \$1$, $p_A = \$20$, and $p_B = \$36$ in Equation 12.8, Universal must believe that $\varepsilon_A = p_A/[m - p_A] = -20/19 \approx -1.05$ and $\varepsilon_B = p_B/[m - p_B] = -36/35 \approx -1.03$.[4]

By rearranging Equation 12.8, we learn that the ratio of prices in the two countries depends only on demand elasticities in those countries:

$$\frac{p_B}{p_A} = \frac{1 + 1/\varepsilon_A}{1 + 1/\varepsilon_B}. \qquad (12.9)$$

Substituting the prices and the demand elasticities into Equation 12.9, we determine that

$$\frac{p_B}{p_A} = \frac{\$36}{\$20} = 1.8 = \frac{1 + 1/(-20/19)}{1 + 1/(-36/35)} = \frac{1 + 1/\varepsilon_A}{1 + 1/\varepsilon_B}.$$

Thus, because Universal believes that the British demand curve is less elastic at its profit-maximizing prices, it charges British consumers 80% more than U.S. customers.

APPLICATION

Smuggling Prescription Drugs into the United States

Federal law forbids U.S. citizens from importing pharmaceuticals from Canada and other countries, but some people, city governments, and state governments openly flout this law. U.S. senior citizens have taken well-publicized bus trips across the Canadian and Mexican borders to buy their drugs at lower prices; and many Canadian, Mexican, and other Internet sites offer to ship drugs to U.S. customers.

A U.S. citizen's incentive to import is great, as the prices of many popular drugs are substantially lower in virtually every other country. The antidepression

---

[4]We obtain the expression that $\varepsilon_i = p_i/(m - p_i)$ by rearranging the expression in Equation 12.8: $p_i(1 + 1/\varepsilon_i) = m$.

drug Zoloft sells for one-third the U.S. price in Mexico and about one-half in Luxembourg and Austria. Citizens in the United States pay 75% more than residents of Canada, which sets its prices at the median level of the countries it surveys. In 2008, European prescription drug prices averaged just 61% and Japanese 67% of U.S. prices.

However, most U.S. citizens do not buy drugs from outside the country. According to Espicom, Canadian drug Internet imports were only $1.2 billion in 2004 compared to U.S. expenditures on pharmaceuticals of $270 billion. A 2008 poll found that only 11% of Americans reported ever having purchased pharmaceuticals outside of the United States. Thus, the ban appears to be relatively effective.

The Bush administration opposed changing the importation law. A 2008 poll found that 80% of Americans favored permitting importation of drugs, as European countries do. Congress debated the Pharmaceutical Market Access and Drug Safety Act of 2009 but did not vote on it that year. If it is enacted into law, Americans would be able to import prescription drugs from Canada and other nations legally.

Not surprisingly, U.S. pharmaceutical companies oppose imports. They fear the possibility of resales, by which the drugs they sell at lower prices in other countries will then be shipped to the United States. Resales would drive down the drug firms' U.S. prices. The lower prices in other countries may reflect price discrimination by pharmaceutical firms, more competition due to differences in patent laws, price regulation by governments, or other reasons.

GlaxoSmithKline, Pfizer, and other drug companies have tried to reduce imports by cutting off Canadian pharmacies that ship south of the border. Wyeth and AstraZeneca watch Canadian pharmacies and wholesale customers for spikes in sales volume that could indicate exports, and then restrict supplies to those pharmacies.

The most interesting question is not why many pharmaceutical companies oppose and U.S. citizens favor permitting such imports, but whether Canadians should oppose them. The following solved problem addresses this question.

SOLVED PROBLEM 12.2

A monopoly drug producer with a constant marginal cost of $m = 1$ sells in only two countries and faces a linear demand curve of $Q_1 = 12 - 2p_1$ in Country 1 and $Q_2 = 9 - p_2$ in Country 2. What price does the monopoly charge in each country? What quantity does it sell in each? What profit does it earn in each country with and without a ban against shipments between the countries?

Answer

If resales across borders are banned so that price discrimination is possible:

1. *Determine the profit-maximizing price that the monopoly sets in each country by setting the relevant marginal revenue equal to the marginal cost.* If the monopoly can price discriminate, it sets a monopoly price independently in each country (as in Section 11.1). By rearranging the demand function for Country 1, we find that the inverse demand function is $p_1 = 6 - 1/2Q_1$ for quantities less than 6, and 0 otherwise, as panel a in the figure shows. Because revenue is $R^1 = 6Q_1 - 1/2(Q_1)^2$, the marginal revenue curve is twice as steeply sloped as the linear inverse demand curve: $MR^1 = dR^1/dQ_1 = 6 - Q_1$. The monopoly maximizes its profit where its marginal revenue equals its marginal cost,

$$MR^1 = 6 - Q_1 = 1 = m.$$

Solving, we find that its profit-maximizing output is $Q_1 = 5$. Substituting this expression into the monopoly's inverse demand curve, we learn that its profit-maximizing price is $p_1 = 3.50$—see panel a. In Country 2, the inverse demand curve is $p_2 = 9 - Q_2$, so the monopoly chooses Q_2 such that $MR^2 = 9 - 2Q_2 = 1 = m$. Thus, it maximizes its profit in Country 2 where $Q_2 = 4$ and $p_2 = 5$, as panel b shows.

2. *Calculate the profits.* The monopoly's profit in each country is the output times the difference between the price and its constant average cost, 1. The monopoly's profit in Country 1 is $\pi_1 = (3.50 - 1)5 = 12.50$. Its profit in Country 2 is $\pi_2 = (5 - 1)4 = 16$. Thus, its total profit is $\pi = \pi_1 + \pi_2 = 12.50 + 16 = 28.50$.

If imports are permitted so that price discrimination is impossible:

3. *Derive the total demand curve.* If the monopoly cannot price discriminate, it charges the same price, p, in both countries. We can determine the aggregate demand curve it faces by horizontally summing the demand curves in each country at a given price (see Chapter 2). The total demand curve, D, in panel c is the horizontal sum of the demand curves for each of the two countries in panels a and b. Because no drugs are sold in Country 1 at prices above $p = 6$, the total demand curve equals Country 2's demand curve (panel b) at prices above 6. The total demand curve is the horizontal sum of the two countries' demand curves (panels a and b) at lower prices: $Q = (12 - 2p) + (9 - p) = 21 - 3p$, where $Q = q_1 + q_2$ is the total quantity that the monopoly sells. Thus, the total demand curve has a kink where $p = 6$ and $Q = 3$.

4. *Determine the marginal revenue curve corresponding to the total demand curve.* Because the total demand curve has a kink at $Q = 3$, the corresponding marginal revenue curve has two sections at either side of $Q = 3$. At quantities smaller than 3, the marginal revenue curve is the same as that of Country 2. At larger quantities, where the total demand curve is the horizontal sum of the two countries' demand curves, the inverse demand function is $p = 7 - \frac{1}{3}Q$, so the revenue function is $R = 7 - \frac{1}{3}Q^2$, and the marginal revenue function is $MR = dR/dQ = 7 - \frac{2}{3}Q$. Panel c shows that the marginal revenue curve "jumps" (is discontinuous) at $Q = 3$.

5. *Solve for the single-price monopoly solution.* The monopoly maximizes its profit where its marginal revenue equals its marginal cost. In panel c, the intersection of the marginal revenue and marginal cost curves occurs in the section where both countries are buying the good: $MR = 7 - \frac{2}{3}Q = 1 = m$. Thus, the profit-maximizing output is $Q = 9$. Substituting that quantity into the inverse total demand function indicates that the monopoly charges $p = 4$.

6. *Calculate the profit.* The monopoly's profits are $\pi_1 = (4 - 1)4 = 12$, $\pi_2 = (4 - 1)5 = 15$, and $\pi = 12 + 15 = 27$.

Comments: The monopoly's profit falls from 28.50 to 27 if it loses the ability to price discriminate. The price of the nondiscriminating monopoly, 4, lies between the two prices that it would charge if it could price discriminate: $3.50 < 4 < 5$. The nondiscriminating monopoly charges a single price that, effectively, is the average of the prices it would charge in the two countries if it could price discriminate. Consequently, if a monopoly wants to charge a relatively high price in the United States, and the U.S. market is large relative to the market in the other country, the single (average) price will be close to the price the monopoly would charge in the United States if it could price discriminate. U.S. consumers would benefit (slightly) and consumers in the other country would suffer. Hence, it is understandable why a low-price country might ban pharmaceutical exports, as Canadian officials announced in 2005 they were considering doing (though they haven't by early 2010).

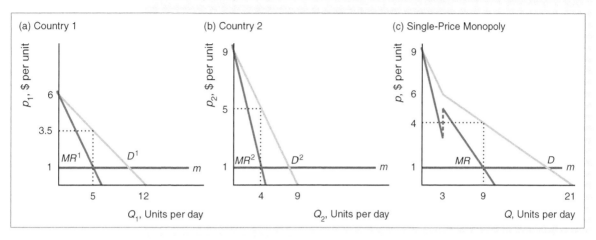

Identifying Groups

Firms use two approaches to divide customers into groups. One method is to divide buyers into groups based on *observable characteristics* of consumers that the firm believes are associated with relatively high or relatively low price elasticities. For example, movie theaters price discriminate using the age of customers. Similarly, some firms charge customers in one country higher prices than those in another country.[5] At the end of 2009, Windows 7 Ultimate Edition sold for $319.99 in the United States, £229.99 ($376.68) in Britain, ¥40,740 ($449.81) in Japan, and C$350.99 ($325.69) in Canada. These differences are much greater than can be explained by shipping costs and reflect multimarket price discrimination.

Another approach is to identify and divide consumers on the basis of their *actions*. The firm allows consumers to self-select the group to which they belong. For example, customers may be identified by their willingness to spend time to buy a good at a lower price. Firms price discriminate by taking advantage of the differing values that customers place on their time. For example, in the case of customers who are willing to spend time to obtain a bargain price, store owners might use queues (making people wait in line) and other time-intensive methods of selling goods. For high-wage people who are unwilling to "waste their time shopping," store managers may run sales at which consumers who visit the store and pick up the good themselves get a low price, while consumers who order by phone or over the Internet pay a higher price. This type of price discrimination increases profit if people who put a high value on their time also have less elastic demands for the good.

---

[5]A firm can charge a higher price for customers in one country than in another if the price differential is too small for many resales between the two countries to occur or if governments enforce import or export restrictions to prevent resales between countries. See "Gray Markets" in **MyEconLab**'s textbook resources for Chapter 12.

APPLICATION

Buying Discounts

Firms use various approaches to induce consumers to indicate whether they have relatively high or low elasticities of demand. For each of these methods, consumers must incur some cost, such as their time, to receive a discount. Otherwise, all consumers would get the discount. By spending extra time to obtain a discount, price-sensitive consumers are able to differentiate themselves.

Coupons. Many firms use discount coupons to multimarket price discriminate. Through this device, firms divide customers into two groups, charging coupon clippers less than nonclippers. Offering coupons makes sense if the people who do not clip coupons are less price sensitive on average than those who do. People who are willing to spend their time clipping coupons buy cereals and other goods at lower prices than those who value their time more. A 2009 study by the Promotion Marketing Association Coupon Council found that consumers who spend 20 minutes per week clipping and organizing coupons could save up to $1,000 on an average annual grocery bill of $5,000 or more. More than three-quarters of U.S. consumers redeem coupons. According to Inmar, a coupon-processing company, redemptions peaked in 1992 with 7.9 billion coupons redeemed. Redemptions fell to 2.6 billion, and stayed roughly at that level for a couple of years. However, due to the recession, coupon redemptions jumped 10% in the fourth quarter of 2008 and another 28% in the first half of 2009.

The introduction of digital (for example, **EverSave.com**) and cell phone (for example, **cellfire.com, getyowza.com, zavers.com**) coupons has made it easier for firms to target appropriate groups, but has lowered consumers' costs of using coupons, which means that a larger share of people use them. In the first half of 2009, customers redeemed nearly 10 million digital coupons, 25% more than in the same period in 2008. Digital coupons are more likely to be redeemed (15–20%) than are paper coupons (less than 1%).

Airline Tickets. By completing a user profile, airline customers indicate whether they are likely to be business travelers or vacationers. Airlines give customers a choice between high-price tickets with no strings attached and low-price fares that must be purchased long in advance.

Airlines know that many business travelers have little advance warning before they book a flight. These business travelers have relatively inelastic demand curves: They must travel at a specific time even if the price is relatively high. In contrast, vacation travelers can usually plan in advance. Because vacation travelers can drive, ride trains or buses, and postpone trips, they have relatively high elasticities of demand for air travel. The choice that airlines give customers ensures that vacationers with relatively elastic demands can purchase cheap seats while most business travelers with relatively inelastic demands buy high-price tickets (often more than four times higher than the plan-ahead rate). The average difference between the high and low price for passengers on the same U.S. route is 36% of an airline's average ticket price.

Reverse Auctions. Priceline.com and other online merchants use a name-your-own-price or "reverse" auction to identify price-sensitive customers. A customer enters a relatively low-price bid for a good or service, such as an airline ticket. Merchants decide whether or not to accept that bid. To prevent their less price-sensitive customers from using these methods, airlines force successful Priceline bidders to be flexible: to fly at off hours, to make one or more connections, and to accept any type of aircraft. Similarly, when bidding on groceries, a customer must list "one or two brands you like." As Jay Walker, Priceline's founder explained, "The manufacturers would rather not give you a discount, of course, but if you prove that you're willing to switch brands, they're willing to pay to keep you."

Rebates. Why do many firms offer a rebate of, say $5 instead of reducing the price on their product by $5? The reason is that a consumer must incur an extra, time-consuming step to receive the rebate. Thus, only those consumers who are very price sensitive and place a low-value on their time will actually apply for the rebate. According to a 2009 *Consumer Reports* survey, 47% of customers always or often apply for a rebate, 23% sometimes apply, 25% never apply, and 5% responded that the question was not applicable to them. The most common reasons given by those who didn't apply for a rebate were that doing so required "too many steps" or the "amount was too small."

SOLVED PROBLEM 12.3

A monopoly producer with a constant marginal cost of $m = 20$ sells in two countries and can prevent reselling between the two countries. The inverse linear demand curve is $p_1 = 100 - Q_1$ in Country 1 and $p_2 = 100 - 2Q_2$ in Country 2. What price does the monopoly charge in each country? What quantity does it sell in each country? Does it price discriminate? Why or why not?

Answer

1. *Determine the profit-maximizing price and quantity that the monopoly sets in each country by setting the relevant marginal revenue equal to the marginal cost.* In Country 1, the inverse demand curve is $p_1 = 100 - Q_1$, so the revenue function is $R^1 = 100Q_1 - (Q_1)^2$, and hence the marginal revenue function is $MR^1 = dR^1/dQ_1 = 100 - 2Q_1$. It equates its marginal revenue to its marginal cost to determine its profit-maximizing quantity: $100 - 2Q_1 = 20$. Solving, the monopoly sets $Q_1 = 40$. Substituting this quantity into its inverse demand function, we learn that the monopoly's price is $p_1 = 100 - 40 = 60$. Similarly, in Country 2, the inverse demand curve is $p_2 = 100 - 2Q_2$, so the revenue function is $R^2 = 100Q_2 - 2(Q_2)^2$, and hence the marginal revenue function is $MR^2 = dR^2/dQ_2 = 100 - 4Q_2$. Equating marginal revenue and marginal cost, $100 - 4Q_2 = 20$, and solving, the monopoly sets $Q_2 = 20$ in Country 2. Its price is $p_2 = 100 - (2 \times 20) = 60$. Thus, the monopoly sells twice as much in Country 1 as in Country 2 but charges the same price in both countries.

2. *Explain, by solving for a general linear inverse demand function, why the monopoly does not price discriminate.* Although the firm has market power, can prevent reselling, and faces consumers in the two countries with different demand functions, it does not pay for the monopoly to price discriminate. Consider the monopoly's problem with a general linear inverse demand function: $p = a - bQ$. Here, revenue is $R = aQ - bQ^2$, so $MR = dR/dQ = a - 2bQ$. Equating marginal revenue and marginal cost, $a - 2bQ = m$, and solving for Q, we find that $Q = (a - m)/(2b)$. Consequently, the price is $p = a - b(a - m)/(2b) = (a - m)/2$. Thus, the price depends only on the inverse demand function's intercept on the vertical axis, a, and not on its slope, b. Because both inverse demand functions in this example have the same vertical intercept—they differ only in their slopes—the monopoly sets the same equilibrium price in both countries. In equilibrium, the elasticity of demand is the same in both countries (Problem 38 asks you to show this result). Thus, while the monopoly could price discriminate, it chooses not to do so.

Welfare Effects of Multimarket Price Discrimination

Multimarket price discrimination results in inefficient production and consumption. As a result, welfare under multimarket price discrimination is lower than it is under competition or perfect price discrimination. Welfare may be lower or higher with multimarket price discrimination than with a single-price monopoly, however.

Multimarket Price Discrimination Versus Competition. Consumer surplus is greater and more output is produced with competition (or perfect price discrimination) than with multimarket price discrimination. In Figure 12.4, consumer surplus with multimarket price discrimination is CS_A (for American consumers in panel a) and CS_B (for British consumers in panel b). Under competition, consumer surplus is the area below the demand curve and above the marginal cost curve: $CS_A + \pi_A + DWL_A$ in panel a and $CS_B + \pi_B + DWL_B$ in panel b.

Thus, multimarket price discrimination transfers some of the competitive consumer surplus, π_1 and π_2, to the monopoly as additional profit and causes the deadweight loss, DWL_1 and DWL_2, of some of the rest of the competitive consumer surplus. The deadweight loss is due to the multimarket-price-discriminating monopoly's charging prices above marginal cost, which results in reduced production from the optimal competitive level.

Multimarket Price Discrimination Versus Single-Price Monopoly. From theory alone, it is impossible to tell whether welfare is higher if the monopoly uses multimarket price discrimination or if it sets a single price. Both types of monopolies set price above marginal cost, so too little is produced relative to competition. Output may rise as the firm starts discriminating if groups that did not buy when the firm charged a single price start buying.

The closer the multimarket-price-discriminating monopoly comes to perfect price discrimination (say, by dividing its customers into many groups rather than just two), the more output it produces, the less deadweight loss. However, unless a multimarket-price-discriminating monopoly sells significantly more output than it would if it had to set a single price, welfare is likely to be lower with discrimination because of consumption inefficiency and time wasted shopping. These two inefficiencies do not occur with a monopoly that charges all consumers the same price. As a result, consumers place the same marginal value (the single sales price) on the good, so they have no incentive to trade with each other. Similarly, if everyone pays the same price, consumers have no incentive to search for lower prices.

12.5 Two-Part Tariffs

We now turn to two other forms of second-degree price discrimination: *two-part tariffs* in this section and *tie-in sales* in the next section. Both are similar to the type of second-degree price discrimination we examined earlier because the average price per unit varies with the number of units that consumers buy.

With a **two-part tariff**, the firm charges a consumer a lump-sum fee (the first tariff) for the right to buy as many units of the good as the consumer wants at a specified price (the second tariff). Because of the lump-sum fee, consumers pay more per unit if they buy a small number of goods than if they buy a large number.

To get telephone service, you may pay a monthly connection fee and a price per minute of use. Some car rental firms charge a daily fee and a price per mile driven. The Dallas Cowboys football team sells *seat options* (most other teams call them *personal seat licenses*)—which give fans the right to buy season tickets each year for

30 years—at a cost between $16,000 and $150,000, where most season tickets range from $590 to $1,250.

To profit from two-part tariffs, a firm must have market power, know how demand differs across customers or with the quantity that a single customer buys, and successfully prevent resales. We now examine two results. First, we consider how a firm uses a two-part tariff to extract consumer surplus (as in our previous price discrimination examples). Second, we see how, if the firm cannot vary its two-part tariff across its customers, its profit is greater the more similar the demand curves of its customers are.

We illustrate these two points for a monopoly that knows its customers' demand curves. We start by examining the monopoly's two-part tariff where all its customers have identical demand curves, and then we look at one where its customers' demand curves differ.

A Two-Part Tariff with Identical Consumers

If all the monopoly's customers are identical, a monopoly that knows its customers' demand curve can set a two-part tariff that has the same two properties as the perfect price discrimination equilibrium. First, the efficient quantity, Q_1, is sold because the price of the last unit equals marginal cost. Second, all consumer surplus is transferred from consumers to the firm.

Suppose that the monopoly has a constant marginal and average cost of $m = \$10$ (no fixed cost) and that every consumer has the demand curve D^1 in panel a of Figure 12.5. To maximize its profit, the monopoly charges a price, p, equal to the

Figure 12.5 Two-Part Tariff

If all consumers have the demand curve in panel a, a monopoly can capture all the consumer surplus with a two-part tariff by which it charges a price, p, equal to the marginal cost, $m = \$10$, for each item and a lump-sum membership fee of $\mathcal{L} = A_1 + B_1 + C_1 = \$2,450$. Now suppose that the monopoly has two customers, Consumer 1 in panel a and Consumer 2 in panel b. If the monopoly can treat its customers differently, it maximizes its profit by setting $p = m = \$10$ and charging Consumer 1 a fee equal to its potential consumer surplus, $A_1 + B_1 + C_1 = \$2,450$, and Consumer 2 a fee of $A_2 + B_2 + C_2 = \$4,050$, for a total profit of $\$6,500$. If the monopoly must charge all customers the same price, it maximizes its profit at $\$5,000$ by setting $p = \$20$ and charging both customers a lump-sum fee equal to the potential consumer surplus of Consumer 1, $\mathcal{L} = A_1 = \$1,800$.

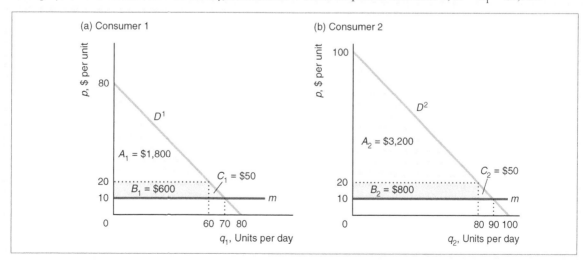

constant marginal and average cost, $m = \$10$, and just breaks even on each unit sold. By setting price equal to marginal cost, it maximizes the *potential consumer surplus*: the consumer surplus if no lump-sum fee is charged. It charges the largest possible lump-sum fee, $\mathscr{L}$, which is the potential consumer surplus $A_1 + B_1 + C_1 = \$2,450$. Thus, its profit is $\$2,450$ times the number of customers.

If the firm charged a higher per-unit price, it would sell fewer units and hence make a smaller profit. For example, if the monopoly charges $p = \$20$, it sells 60 units, making a profit from its unit sales of $B_1 = (\$20 - \$10)60 = \$600$. It must lower its fee to equal the new potential consumer surplus of $A_1 = \$1,800$, so its total profit per customer is only $\$2,400$. It loses area $C_1 = \$50$ by charging the higher price. Similarly, if the monopoly charged a lower per-unit price, its profit would be lower: It would sell too many units and make a loss on each unit because its price would be below its marginal cost.

Because the monopoly knows the demand curve, it could instead perfectly price discriminate by charging each customer a different price for each unit purchased: the price along the demand curve. Thus, this knowledgeable monopoly can capture all potential consumer surplus either by perfectly price discriminating or by setting its optimal two-part tariff.

If the monopoly does not know its customers' demand curve, it must guess how high a lump-sum fee to set. This fee will almost certainly be less than the potential consumer surplus. If the firm sets its fee above the potential consumer surplus, it loses all its customers.

A Two-Part Tariff with Nonidentical Consumers

Now suppose that there are two customers, Consumer 1 and Consumer 2, with demand curves D^1 and D^2 in panels a and b of Figure 12.5. If the monopoly knows each customer's demand curve and can prevent resales, it can capture the entire (single-price) consumer surplus by varying its two-part tariffs across customers. However, if the monopoly is unable to distinguish among the types of customers or cannot charge consumers different prices, efficiency and profitability fall.

Suppose that the monopoly knows its customers' demand curves. By charging each customer $p = m = \$10$ per unit, the monopoly makes no profit per unit but sells the number of units that maximizes the potential consumer surplus. The monopoly then captures all this potential consumer surplus by charging Consumer 1 a lump-sum fee of $\mathscr{L}_1 = A_1 + B_1 + C_1 = \$2,450$ and Consumer 2 a fee of $\mathscr{L}_2 = A_2 + B_2 + C_2 = \$4,050$. The monopoly's total profit is $\mathscr{L}_1 + \mathscr{L}_2 = \$6,500$. By doing so, the monopoly maximizes its total profit by capturing the maximum potential consumer surplus from both customers.

Now suppose that the monopoly has to charge each consumer the same lump-sum fee, $\mathscr{L}$, and the same per-unit price, p. For example, because of legal restrictions, a telephone company charges all residential customers the same monthly fee and the same fee per call, even though the company knows that consumers' demands vary. As with multimarket price discrimination, the monopoly does not capture the entire consumer surplus.

The monopoly charges a lump-sum fee, $\mathscr{L}$, equal to either the potential consumer surplus of Consumer 1, CS_1, or of Consumer 2, CS_2. Because CS_2 is greater than CS_1, both customers buy if the monopoly charges $\mathscr{L} = CS_1$, whereas only Consumer 2 buys if the monopoly charges $\mathscr{L} = CS_2$. The monopoly sets the lower or higher lump-sum fee depending on which produces the greater profit.

Any other lump-sum fee would lower its profit. The monopoly has no customers if it charges more than $\mathscr{L} = CS_2$. If it charges between CS_1 and CS_2, it loses money on Consumer 2 compared to what it could earn by charging CS_2, and it still does not sell to Consumer 1. By charging less than $\mathscr{L} = CS_1$, it earns less per customer and does not gain any additional customers.

In our example in Figure 12.5, the demand curves for Consumers 1 and 2 are $q_1 = 80 - p$ and $q_2 = 100 - p$. The consumer surplus for Consumer 1 is $CS_1 = \frac{1}{2}(80 - p)q_1 = \frac{1}{2}(80 - p)^2$. Similarly, $CS_2 = \frac{1}{2}(100 - p)^2$. If the monopoly charges the lower fee, $\mathscr{L} = CS_1$, it sells to both consumers and its profit is

$$\pi = 2\mathscr{L} + (p - m)(q_1 + q_2) = (80 - p)^2 + (p - 10)(180 - 2p).$$

Setting the derivative of π with respect to p equal to zero, we find that the profit-maximizing price is $p = 20$. The monopoly charges a fee of $\mathscr{L} = CS_1 = \$1,800$ and makes a profit of \$5,000. If the monopoly charges the higher fee, $\mathscr{L} = CS_2$, it sells only to Consumer 2, and its profit is

$$\pi = \mathscr{L} + (p - m)q_2 = \tfrac{1}{2}(100 - p)^2 + (p - 10)(100 - p).$$

The monopoly's profit-maximizing price is $p = 10$, and its profit is $\mathscr{L} = CS_2 = \$4,050$. The monopoly hence makes more by setting $\mathscr{L} = CS_1$ and selling to both customers.

Thus, the monopoly maximizes its profit by setting the lower lump-sum fee and charging a price $p = \$20$, which is above marginal cost. Consumer 1 buys 60 units, and Consumer 2 buys 80 units. The monopoly makes $(p - m) = (\$20 - \$10) = \$10$ on each unit, so it earns $B_1 + B_2 = \$600 + \$800 = \$1,400$ from the units it sells. In addition, it gets a fee from both consumers equal to the consumer surplus of Consumer 1, $A_1 = \$1,800$. Thus, its total profit is $2 \times \$1,800 + \$1,400 = \$5,000$, which is \$1,500 less than if it could set different lump-sum fees for each customer. Consumer 1 has no consumer surplus, but Consumer 2 enjoys a consumer surplus of \$1,400 (= \$3,200 − \$1,800).

Why does the monopoly charge a price above marginal cost when using a two-part tariff? By raising its price, the monopoly earns more per unit from both types of customers but lowers its customers' potential consumer surplus. Thus, if the monopoly can capture each customer's potential surplus by charging different lump-sum fees, it sets its price equal to marginal cost. However, if the monopoly cannot capture all the potential consumer surplus because it must charge everyone the same lump-sum fee, the increase in profit from Customer 2 due to the higher price more than offsets the reduction in the lump-sum fee (the potential consumer surplus of Customer 1).[6]

12.6 Tie-In Sales

Another type of nonuniform pricing is a **tie-in sale**, in which customers can buy one product only if they agree to purchase another product as well. There are two forms of tie-in sales.

---

[6]If the monopoly lowers its price from \$20 to the marginal cost of \$10, it loses B_1 from Customer 1, but it can raise its lump-sum fee from A_1 to $A_1 + B_1 + C_1$, so its total profit from Customer 1 increases by $C_1 = \$50$. The lump-sum fee it collects from Customer 2 also rises by $B_1 + C_1 = \$650$, but its profit from unit sales falls by $B_2 = \$800$, so its total profit decreases by \$150. The loss from Customer 2, −\$150, more than offsets the gain from Customer 1, \$50. Thus, the monopoly makes \$100 more by charging a price of \$20 rather than \$10. For another application, see "Warehouse Stores" in **MyEconLab**'s textbook resources for Chapter 12.

The first type is a **requirement tie-in sale**, in which customers who buy one product from a firm are required to make all their purchases of another product from that firm. Some firms sell durable machines such as copiers under the condition that customers buy copier services and supplies from them in the future. Because the amount of services and supplies that each customer buys differs, the per-unit price of copiers varies across customers.

The second type of tie-in sale is **bundling** (or a *package tie-in sale*), in which two goods are combined so that customers cannot buy either good separately. For example, a Whirlpool refrigerator is sold with shelves, and a Hewlett-Packard inkjet printer comes with black and color printer cartridges.

Most tie-in sales increase efficiency by lowering transaction costs. Indeed, tie-ins for efficiency purposes are so common that we hardly think about them. Presumably, no one would want to buy a shirt without buttons attached, so selling shirts with buttons lowers transaction costs. Because virtually everyone wants certain basic software, most companies sell computers with that software installed. Firms also often use tie-in sales to increase profits, as we now consider.

Requirement Tie-In Sales

Frequently, a firm cannot tell which customers are going to use its product the most and hence are willing to pay the most for it. These firms may be able to use a requirement tie-in sale to identify heavy users of the product and charge them more.

APPLICATION

IBM

In the 1930s, IBM increased its profit by using a requirement tie-in. IBM produced card punch machines, sorters, and tabulating machines (precursors of modern computers) that computed by using punched cards. Rather than selling its card punch machines, IBM leased them under the condition that the lease would terminate if any card not manufactured by IBM were used. (By leasing the equipment, IBM avoided resale problems and forced customers to buy tabulating cards from it.) IBM charged customers more per card than other firms would have charged. If we think of the extra payment per card as part of the cost of using the machine, this requirement tie-in resulted in heavy users' paying more for the machines than others did. This tie-in was profitable because heavy users were willing to pay more.[7]

Bundling

Firms that sell two or more goods may use bundling to raise profits. Bundling allows firms that cannot directly price discriminate to charge customers different prices. Whether bundling is profitable depends on customers' tastes and a firm's ability to prevent resales.

Imagine that you are in charge of selling season tickets for the local football team. Your stadium can hold all your potential customers, so the marginal cost of selling one more ticket is zero.

---

[7]The U.S. Supreme Court held that IBM's actions violated antitrust laws because they lessened competition in the (potential) market for tabulating cards. IBM's defense was that its requirement was designed to protect its reputation. IBM claimed that inferior tabulating cards might cause its machines to malfunction and that consumers would falsely blame IBM's equipment. The Court did not accept IBM's argument. The Court apparently did not understand—or at least care about—the price discrimination aspect of IBM's actions.

Should you bundle tickets for preseason (exhibition) and regular-season games, or should you sell books of tickets for the preseason and the regular season separately?[8] To answer this question, you have to determine how the fans differ in their desires to see preseason and regular-season games.

For simplicity, suppose that there are two customers (or types of customers). Both of these football fans are so fanatical that they are willing to pay to see preseason exhibition games: There's no accounting for tastes!

Whether you should bundle depends on your customers' tastes. It does not pay to bundle in panel a of Table 12.1, in which Fan 1 is willing to pay more for both regular-season and preseason tickets than Fan 2 is. Bundling does pay in panel b, in which Fan 1 is willing to pay more for regular-season but less for exhibition tickets than Fan 2 is.

To determine whether it pays to bundle, we have to calculate the profit-maximizing unbundled and bundled prices. We start by calculating the profit-maximizing unbundled prices in panel a. If you charge $2,000 for the regular-season tickets, you earn only $2,000 because Fan 2 won't buy tickets. It is more profitable to charge $1,400, sell tickets to both customers, and earn $2,800 for the regular season. By similar reasoning, the profit-maximizing price for the exhibition tickets is $500, at which you sell only to Fan 1 and earn $500. As a result, you earn $3,300 (= $2,800 + $500) if you do not bundle.

If you bundle and charge $2,500, you sell to only Fan 1. Your better option if you bundle is to set a bundle price of $1,500 and sell to both fans, earning $3,000. Nonetheless, you earn $300 more if you sell the tickets separately than if you bundle.

In this first example, in which it does not pay to bundle, the customer who values the regular-season tickets the most also values the preseason tickets the most. In contrast, in panel b, the fan who values the regular-season tickets more values the exhibition season tickets less than the other fan does. Here, your profit is higher if you bundle. If you sell the tickets separately, you charge $1,500 for regular-season tickets, earning $3,000 from the two customers, and $300 for preseason tickets, earning $600, for a total of $3,600. By selling a bundle of tickets for all games at $2,000 each, you earn $4,000. Thus, you earn $400 more by bundling than by selling the tickets separately.

Table 12.1 Bundling of Tickets to Football Games

(a) *Unprofitable Bundle*	Regular Season	Preseason	Bundle
Fan 1	$2,000	$500	$2,500
Fan 2	$1,400	$100	$1,500
Profit-maximizing price	$1,400	$500	$1,500
(b) *Profitable Bundle*	Regular Season	Preseason	Bundle
Fan 1	$1,700	$300	$2,000
Fan 2	$1,500	$500	$2,000
Profit-maximizing price	$1,500	$300	$2,000

---

[8]We assume that you don't want to sell tickets to each game separately. One reason for selling only season tickets is to reduce transaction costs. A second explanation is the same type of bundling argument that we discuss in this section.

By bundling, you can charge the fans different prices for the two components of the bundle. Fan 1 is paying $1,700 for regular-season tickets and $300 for exhibition tickets, while Fan 2 is paying $1,500 and $500, respectively.[9] If you could perfectly price discriminate, you would charge each consumer his or her reservation price for the preseason and regular-season tickets and would make the same amount as you do by bundling.

These examples illustrate that bundling a pair of goods pays if their demands are *negatively correlated*: Customers who are willing to pay relatively more for regular-season tickets are not willing to pay as much as others for preseason tickets, and vice versa. When a good or service is sold to different people, the price is determined by the purchaser with the *lowest* reservation price. If reservation prices differ substantially across consumers, a monopoly has to charge a relatively low price to make many sales. By bundling when demands are negatively correlated, the monopoly reduces the dispersion in reservation prices, so that it can charge more and still sell to a large number of customers.

APPLICATION

Available for a Song

Apple's iTunes Music store, the giant of music downloading, sold 2 billion songs at 99¢ each in 2008. However, many of its competitors did not use uniform pricing. Amazon's music downloading service uses song-specific or "variable" pricing. Nokia uses bundling, with unlimited song downloads on phones sold with a "Comes with Music" surcharge.

Starting in 2007, some record labels told Apple that they would not renew their contracts if Apple continued to use uniform pricing. Apparently responding to this pressure and the success of some of its competitors, Apple switched in 2009 to selling each song at one of three prices.

Did Apple's one-price-for-all-songs policy cost it substantial potential profit? How do consumer surplus and deadweight vary with pricing methods such as a single price, song-specific prices, bundling, and a two-part tariff? To answer these types of questions, Shiller and Waldfogel (2009) surveyed nearly 1,000 students and determined each person's willingness to pay for each of 50 popular songs. Then they used this information to calculate a firm's optimal pricing under various pricing schemes.

They considered a number of pricing methods. Under uniform pricing, a single profit-maximizing price is charged for each song (as in a single panel in Figure 12.4). Component pricing, where each song sells at its individual profit-maximizing price, is a type of multimarket price discrimination, as in Figure 12.4 where we have a separate panel for two groups of consumers. Here, we would have 50 separate panels—one for each individual song. Under bundling, a consumer pays a single price for the right to download any or all of the songs. Under the two-part tariff, a consumer pays for the right to buy any song, and then pays a single price for each song the consumer wants (as in either panel of Figure 12.5).

If we know the demand curve and the constant marginal cost, we can determine the consumer surplus, the producer surplus or profit, and the deadweight loss from a uniform price as in Figure 12.4. If we divide each of these areas by the total welfare under competition—the shaded area under the demand curve and above the marginal cost curve—we can determine the shares of *CS*, *PS*, and *DWL*. The table shows Shiller and Waldfogel's estimates of the percentage shares of *CS*, *PS*, and *DWL* under each of the four pricing methods.

---

[9]As with price discrimination, you have to prevent resales for bundling to increase your profit. Someone could make a $198 profit by purchasing the bundle for $2,000, selling Fan 1 the regular-season tickets for $1,699, and selling Fan 2 the preseason tickets for $499. Each fan would prefer attending only one type of game at those prices to paying $2,000 for the bundle.

	Share (%)		
	PS	CS	DWL
Uniform	8.4	42.4	29.2
Component	29.2	44.7	26.1
Bundling	36.5	40.3	23.2
Two-part tariff	36.9	43.1	20.0

If these students have tastes similar to those of the general market, then a music firm can increase its profit by switching from uniform pricing to any of the other pricing methods. Deadweight loss decreases under any of these alternative pricing methods, and consumers are better off with component pricing or a two-part tariff than with uniform pricing.

12.7 Advertising

In addition to setting its price or quantity, a monopoly has to make other decisions, one of the most important of which is how much to advertise. Advertising is only one way to promote a product. Other promotional activities include providing free samples and using sales agents. Some promotional tactics are subtle. For example, grocery stores place sugary breakfast cereals on lower shelves so they are at a child's eye level. According to a survey of 27 supermarkets nationwide by the Center for Science in the Public Interest, the average position of 10 child-appealing brands (44% sugar) was on the next-to-bottom shelf, while the average position of 10 adult brands (10% sugar) was on the next-to-top shelf.

A successful promotional campaign shifts the monopoly's demand curve by changing consumers' tastes or informing consumers about new products. The monopoly may be able to change the tastes of some consumers by telling them that a famous athlete or performer uses the product. Children and teenagers are frequently the targets of such advertising.[10] If the advertising convinces some consumers that they can't live without the product, the monopoly's demand curve may shift outward and become less elastic at the new equilibrium, at which the firm charges a higher price for its product. If the firm informs potential consumers about a new use for the product—for example, "Vaseline petroleum jelly protects lips from chapping"—demand at each price increases.

The Decision Whether to Advertise

Even if advertising succeeds in shifting the demand curve, it may not pay for the firm to advertise. If advertising shifts the demand curve outward or makes it less elastic, the firm's *gross profit*, which ignores the cost of advertising, must rise. However, the firm undertakes this advertising campaign only if it expects its *net profit* (gross profit minus the cost of advertising) to increase.

To illustrate a monopoly's decision making, in Figure 12.6 we examine Coke's analysis of how much to advertise. For simplicity, we model Coke as a monopoly (by ignoring Pepsi and other brands). We use the estimated demand curve for Coke, which takes into account its advertising, from Gasmi, Laffont, and Vuong (1992). If Coke does not advertise, it faces the demand curve D^1. If Coke advertises at its current level, its demand curve shifts from D^1 to D^2.

Coke's marginal cost, MC, is constant and equals its average cost, AC, at $5 per unit (10 cases). Before advertising, Coke chooses its output, $Q_1 = 24$ million units, where its marginal cost equals its marginal revenue, MR^1, based on its demand curve, D^1. The profit-maximizing equilibrium is e_1, and the monopoly charges a price of $p_1 = \$11$. The monopoly's profit, π_1, is a box whose height is the difference

---
[10]See "Smoking Gun Evidence?" in **MyEconLab**'s textbook resources for Chapter 12 for a discussion of cigarette advertising aimed at youths.

Figure 12.6 Advertising

Suppose that Coke were a monopoly. If it does not advertise, its demand curve is D^1. At its actual level of advertising, its demand curve is D^2. Advertising increases Coke's gross profit (ignoring the cost of advertising) from π_1 to $\pi_2 = \pi_1 + B$. Thus, if the cost of advertising is less than the benefits from advertising, B, Coke's net profit (gross profit minus the cost of advertising) rises.

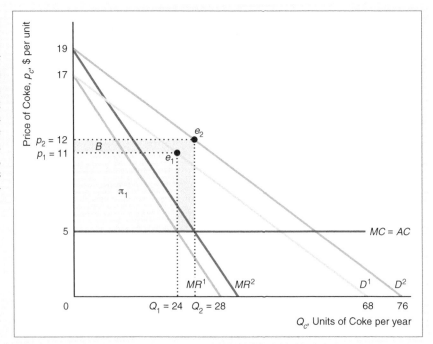

between the price and the average cost, $6 (= \$11 - \$5)$ per unit, and whose length is the quantity, 24 units (tens of millions of cases of 12-ounce cans).

After its advertising campaign (involving dancing polar bears or whatever) shifts its demand curve to D^2, Coke chooses a higher quantity, $Q_2 = 28$, where the MR^2 and MC curves intersect. In this new equilibrium, e_2, Coke charges $p_2 = \$12$. Despite this higher price, Coke sells more Coke after advertising because of the outward shift of its demand curve.

As a consequence, Coke's gross profit rises more than 36%. Coke's new gross profit is the rectangle $\pi_1 + B$, where the height of the rectangle is the new price minus the average cost, $7, and the length is the quantity, 28. Thus, the benefit, B, to Coke from advertising at this level is the increase in its gross profit. If its cost of advertising is less than B, its net profit rises, and it pays for Coke to advertise at this level rather than not to advertise at all.

How Much to Advertise

In general, how much should a monopoly advertise to maximize its net profit? To answer this question, we consider what happens if the monopoly raises or lowers its advertising expenditures by $1, which is its marginal cost of an additional unit of advertising. If a monopoly spends an additional $1 on advertising and its gross profit rises by more than $1, its net profit rises, so the extra advertising pays. In contrast, the monopoly should reduce its advertising if the last dollar of advertising raises its gross profit by less than $1, causing its net profit to fall. Thus, the monopoly's level of advertising maximizes its net profit if the last dollar of advertising increases its gross profit by $1. In short, the rule for setting the profit-maximizing amount of advertising is the same as that for setting the profit-maximizing amount of output: Set advertising or quantity where the marginal benefit (the extra gross profit from one more unit of advertising or the marginal revenue from one more unit of output) equals its marginal cost.

Formally, to maximize its profit, a monopoly sets its quantity, Q, and level of advertising, A, to maximize its profit. Again, for simplicity, we assume that advertising affects only current sales, so the demand function the monopoly faces is

$$p = p(Q, A).$$

As a result, the firm's revenue is

$$R = p(Q, A)Q = R(Q, A).$$

The firm's cost of production is the function $C(Q) + A$, where $C(Q)$ is the cost of manufacturing Q units and A is the cost of advertising because each unit of advertising costs \$1 (by choosing the units of measure appropriately).

The monopoly maximizes its profit through its choice of quantity and advertising:

$$\max_{Q, A} \pi = R(Q, A) - C(Q) - A. \tag{12.10}$$

Its necessary (first-order) conditions are found by differentiating the profit function in Equation 12.10 with respect to Q and A in turn:

$$\frac{\partial \pi(Q, A)}{\partial Q} = \frac{\partial R(Q, A)}{\partial Q} - \frac{dC(Q)}{dQ} = 0, \tag{12.11}$$

$$\frac{\partial \pi(Q, A)}{\partial A} = \frac{\partial R(Q, A)}{\partial A} - 1 = 0. \tag{12.12}$$

The profit-maximizing output and advertising levels are the Q^* and A^* that simultaneously satisfy Equations 12.11 and 12.12. Equation 12.11 says that output should be chosen so that the marginal revenue from one more unit of output, $\partial R/\partial Q$, equals the marginal cost, dC/dQ. According to Equation 12.12, the monopoly advertises to the point where its marginal revenue or marginal benefit from the last unit of advertising, $\partial R/\partial A$, equals the marginal cost of the last unit of advertising, \$1.

APPLICATION

Advertising Subsidizes Subscriptions

Virtually all magazines carry ads. All else the same, the larger a magazine's circulation, the more advertisers pay per ad. Consequently, a magazine may drop its subscription price to boost its circulation and, in turn, to increase its advertising revenue. Adjusting subscription prices is the key to increasing sales for most magazines.

Kaiser and Wright (2006) examined the market for magazine readership and advertising in Germany. They found that advertising "subsidizes" the cost to readers, and that magazines make most of their money from advertisers. Moreover, they found that increased demand by magazine readers raises advertising rates, but that higher demand by advertisers decreases cover prices.

In the second half of the twentieth century, total U.S. magazine circulation grew substantially until the mid-1990s. The total number of magazines sold remained relatively constant at 360 million copies between 1994 and 2008.

The share of ad revenue to total magazine revenue also rose substantially over time, reaching 59% in 2007. Ad revenue rose from \$15.5 billion in 1999 to \$25.5 billion in 2007. A combination of a long-term trend away from print media toward electronic media and the recession that started in 2008 has hammered the magazine industry, cutting the number of subscriptions and

SOLVED PROBLEM 12.4

A dog costume magazine, *Canine Haute Couture*, has a monopoly: It has no close substitutes. The magazine's price for an ad is aQ, where a is the price per unit of circulation and Q is the number of subscriptions. The n firms that produce dog costumes are each willing to place one ad per issue as long as the magazine charges no more than aQ. That is, a is determined by the advertising market. The magazine's inverse demand curve for subscriptions is $p(Q)$, where p is the price of a subscription. The magazine's marginal cost per subscription is constant at m (primarily printing, paper, and mailing), and its fixed cost is F (office space and salaries for editorial staff, authors, and photographers). Use a figure and calculus to show how the magazine determines its profit-maximizing quantity.

Answer

1. *Write the monopoly's profit.* The magazine's profit is

$$\pi = p(Q)Q + naQ - mQ - F,$$

where $p(Q)Q$ is the revenue the magazine receives from its subscribers, naQ is the advertising revenue, and mQ is its variable cost.

2. *Graphically show how the advertising shifts the demand curve.* We can think of the advertising revenue, naQ, as being much like a specific (per-unit) subsidy or negative tax, where na is the specific subsidy per subscription. Thus, the advertising revenue shifts up the demand curve as a subsidy would. In the figure, the curves D^1 and MR^1 are the demand curve for magazines and the corresponding marginal revenue curve if no ads were sold. The curves D^2 and MR^2 are the corresponding curves including advertising. Demand curve D^2 lies na units above D^1.

3. *Derive the monopoly's first-order condition.* The monopoly maximizes its profit by setting the optimal quantity (the only variable within its control). It sets the derivative of the profit function with respect to Q equal to zero:

$$\pi_Q = p(Q^*) + p_Q(Q^*)Q^* + na - m = 0.$$

The magazine's marginal revenue in the absence of advertising is $p(Q) + p_Q(Q)Q$, and its advertising revenue from the marginal subscription is na, so $p(Q) + p_Q(Q)Q + na$ is its marginal revenue, MR. The magazine equates this marginal revenue to its marginal cost, m, to determine its profit-maximizing output, Q^*.

4. *Use a graph to illustrate the role of advertising in determining the optimal output level.* As the figure shows, in the absence of advertising, the monopoly's optimum is determined by where its marginal revenue curve MR_1 (which corresponds to D^1) hits its marginal cost curve at m. It sells Q_1 subscriptions at a subscription price of p_1. With advertising, the monopoly operates where MR_2 (which corresponds to D^2) intersects its marginal cost curve. It provides Q_2 (= Q^* in our calculus solution) subscriptions at a price of p_2, which is the height of D^1 (the no-advertising demand curve) at that quantity. The firm receives $p^* = p_2 + na$ per subscription.

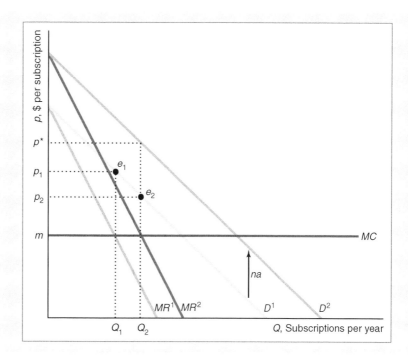

SUMMARY

1. **Why and How Firms Price Discriminate.** A firm can price discriminate if it has market power, knows which customers will pay more for each unit of output, and can prevent customers who pay low prices from reselling to those who pay high prices. A firm earns a higher profit from price discrimination than from uniform pricing because (a) the firm captures some or all of the consumer surplus of customers who are willing to pay more than the uniform price and (b) the firm sells to some people who would not buy at the uniform price.

2. **Perfect Price Discrimination.** To perfectly price discriminate, a firm must know the maximum amount each customer is willing to pay for each unit of output. If a firm charges customers the maximum that each is willing to pay for each unit of output, the monopoly captures all potential consumer surplus and sells the efficient (competitive) level of output. Compared to competition, total welfare is the same, consumers are worse off, and firms are better off under perfect price discrimination.

3. **Quantity Discrimination.** Some firms charge customers different prices depending on how many units they purchase. If consumers who want more water have less elastic demands, a water utility can increase its profit by using declining-block pricing, in which the price for the first few gallons of water is higher than that for additional gallons.

4. **Multimarket Price Discrimination.** A firm that does not have enough information to perfectly price discriminate may know the relative elasticities of demand of groups of its customers. Such a profit-maximizing firm charges groups of consumers prices in proportion to their elasticities of demand, the group of consumers with the least elastic demand paying the highest price. Welfare is less under multimarket price discrimination than under competition or perfect price discrimination but may be greater or less than that under single-price monopoly.

5. **Two-Part Tariffs.** By charging consumers one fee for the right to buy and a separate price per unit, firms may earn higher profits than if they charge only for each unit sold. If a firm knows its customers' demand curves, it can use two-part tariffs (instead of perfect price discrimination) to capture the entire consumer surplus. Even if the firm does not know each customer's demand curve or cannot vary the two-part tariffs across customers, it can use a two-part tariff to

make a larger profit than it could get if it set a single price.

6. **Tie-In Sales.** A firm may increase its profit by using a tie-in sale that allows customers to buy one product only if they also purchase another product. In a requirement tie-in sale, customers who buy one good must make all of their purchases of another good or service from that firm. With bundling (a package tie-in sale), a firm sells only a bundle of two goods together. Prices differ across customers under both types of tie-in sales.

7. **Advertising.** A monopoly advertises or engages in other promotional activities to shift its demand curve to the right or to make it less elastic so as to raise its profit (taking account of its advertising expenses).

QUESTIONS

■ = exercise is available on **MyEconLab**; * = answer appears at the back of this book; V = video answer by James Dearden is available online.

1. Alexx's monopoly currently sells its product at a single price. What conditions must be met so that he can profitably price discriminate?

*2. Spenser's Superior Stoves advertises a one-day sale on electric stoves. The ad specifies that no phone orders will be accepted and that the purchaser must transport the stove. Why does the firm include these restrictions?

*3. Many colleges provide students from low-income families with scholarships, subsidized loans, and other programs so that they pay lower tuitions than students from high-income families. Explain why universities behave this way.

4. In 2002, seven pharmaceutical companies announced a plan to provide low-income elderly people with a card guaranteeing them discounts of 20% or more on dozens of prescription medicines. Why did the firms institute this program?

5. Disneyland price discriminates by charging lower entry fees for children than for adults and for local residents than for other visitors. Why does it not have a resales problem?

6. The 2002 production run of 25,000 new Thunderbirds included only 2,000 cars for Canada. Yet potential buyers besieged Canadian Ford dealers. Many hoped to make a quick profit by reselling the cars in the United States. Reselling was relatively easy, and shipping costs were comparatively low. When the Thunderbird with the optional hardtop first became available at the end of 2001, Canadians paid C$56,550 for the vehicle, while U.S. customers spent up to C$73,000 in the United States. Why? Why would a Canadian want to ship a T-Bird south? Why did Ford require Canadian dealers to sign an agreement that prohibited moving vehicles to the United States?

7. As discussed in the "Google Advertising" application, advertisers on Google's Web site bid for the right for their ads to be posted when people search for certain phrases. Google's "Traffic Estimator Tool" provides potential advertisers with a guide to the auction prices they would expect to pay for different keywords in different locations. The traffic estimator provides a range of prices that other advertisers have recently paid for an ad to be ranked in the first three positions in a certain city and the search volume associated with that price range. Should a firm that provides local services (such as plumbing or pest control) expect to pay more or less for an ad in a small town or a large city? Why?

8. On August 2, 2005, Hertz charged $141.06 a day to rent a Taurus in New York City but only $66.68 a day in Miami. Is this price discrimination? Why or why not?

9. College students once could buy a computer at a substantial discount at a campus store. The discounts largely disappeared in the late 1990s, when PC companies dropped their prices. "The industry's margins just got too thin to allow for those [college discounts]," said the president of Educause, a group that promotes and surveys using technology on campus (David LaGesse, "A PC Choice: Dorm or Quad?" *U.S. News & World Report*, May 5, 2003, 64). Using the concepts and terminology discussed in this chapter, explain why shrinking profit margins are associated with the reduction or elimination of student discounts.

10. Ticketmaster Corp. used an Internet auction to sell tickets for a Sting concert (Leslie Walker, "Auctions Could Set Ticket Prices for Future Events," *San Francisco Chronicle*, October 13, 2003, E5).

   a. The floor seats were auctioned in a uniform price format where all winning bidders paid the same amount: the lowest bid ($90) at which all the seats were sold. Is this price discrimination? If so, what type?

   b. Suppose, instead, that each ticket was sold at the bid price to the highest bidder. Is this price discrimination? If so, what type?

11. Using the information in the "Botox Revisited" application, determine how much Allergan loses by being a single-price monopoly rather than a perfectly price-discriminating monopoly. Explain.

12. Consider a third pricing scheme that the union in Solved Problem 12.1 might use: It sets a wage, w^*, and lets the firms hire as many workers as they want (that is, the union does not set a minimum number of hours), but requires a lump-sum contribution to each worker's retirement fund. What is such a pricing scheme called? Can the union achieve the same outcome as it would if it perfectly price discriminated? (*Hint*: It could set the wage where the supply curve hits the demand curve.) Does your answer depend on whether the union workers are identical?

13. A firm is a natural monopoly (see Chapter 11). Its marginal cost curve is flat, and its average cost curve is downward sloping (because it has a fixed cost). The firm can perfectly price discriminate.
    a. In a graph, show how much the monopoly produces, Q^*. Will it produce to where price equals its marginal cost?
    b. Show graphically (and explain) what its profit is.

14. Are all the customers of the quantity-discriminating monopoly in panel a of Figure 12.3 worse off than they would be if the firm set a single price (panel b)? Why or why not?

15. A monopoly has a marginal cost of zero and faces two groups of consumers. At first, the monopoly could not prevent resales, so it maximized its profit by charging everyone the same price, $p = \$5$. No one from the first group chose to purchase. Now the monopoly can prevent resales, so it decides to price discriminate. Will total output expand? Why or why not? What happens to profit and consumer surplus?

16. Each week, a department store places a different item of clothing on sale. Give an explanation based on price discrimination for why the store conducts such regular sales.

17. Does a monopoly's ability to price discriminate between two groups of consumers depend on its marginal cost curve? Why or why not? [Consider two cases: (a) the marginal cost is so high that the monopoly is uninterested in selling to one group; (b) the marginal cost is low enough that the monopoly wants to sell to both groups.]

18. A monopoly sells two products, of which consumers want only one. Assuming that it can prevent resales, can the monopoly increase its profit by bundling them, forcing consumers to buy both goods? Explain.

19. How would the analysis in Solved Problem 12.2 change if $m = 7$ or if $m = 4$? (*Hint*: Where $m = 4$, the marginal cost curve crosses the *MR* curve three times—if we include the vertical section. The single-price monopoly will choose one of these three points where its profit is maximized.)

20. Abbott Laboratories, the patent holder of the anti-AIDS drug Norvir, raised the price from $1.71 to $8.57 per day in 2003 (Lauran Neergaard, "No Price Rollback on Costly AIDS Drug," *San Francisco Chronicle*, August 5, 2004, A4). In the United States, the price increase occurs only when low doses of Norvir are used to boost the effects of other anti-HIV medicines—not in Abbott's own Kaletra, a medicine that includes Norvir. Why did Abbott raise one price but not others?

21. In the spring of 2005, General Motors shifted its auto discounting policy to regionally targeted rebates, in which GM offers varying discounts to different parts of the United States. Suppose that GM dealers offer all consumers in a given region the same posted price for a specific model (which is GM's pricing policy for its Saturn automobiles). Assume that it is unprofitable for a consumer to purchase an automobile in a low-price area and then to resell it in a high-price area.
    a. What form of price discrimination is GM's new policy?
    b. What is the relationship between a region's price and its price elasticity of demand?
    c. GM also eliminated a high-profile discount program "in an apparent effort to damp consumer expectation of big price cuts" (Lee Hawkins Jr., "GM Alters U.S. Discount Program with a Region-Specific Strategy," *Wall Street Journal*, March 7, 2005, A2). How do expected future prices of an automobile affect the current demand? Is a national discount program that is targeted to reduce slumping sales a form of price discrimination? Explain. V

22. In the 2003 Major League Baseball season, the New York Mets charged fans up to twice as much to attend games against the Yankees and other popular teams than less popular or less competitive teams. Other professional teams have adopted the same pricing strategy. While the Yankees increased the prices of popular games, they dropped the price of upper-deck seats for some weekday games against weak opponents.
    a. A Mets-Yankees game is more popular than a Mets-Marlins game. Is the policy of charging fans more to see the Mets play the Yankees than the

Marlins a form of price discrimination? If so, which type?

b. What is the effect on the quantity of tickets demanded for a Mets-Yankees game if the Mets drop the price of the cheap seats for unpopular games? How do the Mets take this effect into account when setting ticket prices? In answering the question, assume that the Mets choose two ticket prices—one for a Mets-Yankees game and one for a Mets-Marlins game—to maximize the sum of revenues of the two games. V

23. Grocery store chains often set consumer-specific prices by issuing frequent-buyer cards to willing customers and collecting information about their purchases. Grocery chains can use that data to offer customized discount coupons to individuals.

a. Which type of price discrimination—first-degree, second-degree, or third-degree—are these personalized discounts?

b. How should a grocery store use past-purchase data to set individualized prices to maximize its profit? (*Hint*: Refer to a customer's price elasticity of demand.) V

24. The publisher Reed Elsevier uses what economists call a mixed-bundling pricing strategy. The publisher sells a university access to a bundle of 930 of its journals for $1.7 million for one year. It also offers the journals separately at individual prices. Because Elsevier offers the journals online (with password access), universities can track how often their students and faculty access journals and then cancel those journals that are seldom read. Suppose that a publisher offers a university only three journals—A, B, and C—at the unbundled, individual annual subscription prices of $p_A = \$1,600$, $p_B = \$800$, and $p_C = \$1,500$. Suppose a university's willingness to pay for each of the journals is $v_A = \$2,000$, $v_B = \$1,100$, and $v_C = \$1,400$.

a. If the publisher offers the journals only at the individual subscription prices, to which journals does the university subscribe?

b. Given these individual prices, what is the highest price that the university is willing to pay for the three journals bundled together?

c. Now suppose that the publisher offers the same deal to a second university with willingness to pay $v_A = \$1,800$, $v_B = \$100$, and $v_C = \$2,100$. With the two universities, calculate the revenue-maximizing individual and bundle prices. V

25. To promote her platinum-selling CD *Feels Like Home* in 2005, singer Norah Jones toured the country giving live performances. However, she sold an average of only two-thirds of the tickets available for each show, T^* (Robert Levine, "The Trick of Making a Hot Ticket Pay," *New York Times*, June 6, 2005, C1, C4).

a. Suppose that the local promoter is the monopoly provider of each concert. Each concert hall has a fixed number of seats. Assume that the promoter's cost is independent of the number of people who attend the concert (Ms. Jones received a guaranteed payment). Graph the promoter's marginal cost curve for the concert hall, where the number of tickets sold is on the horizontal axis. Be sure to show T^*.

b. If the monopoly can charge a single market price, does the concert's failure to sell out prove that the monopoly set too high a price? Explain.

c. Would your answer in part b be the same if the monopoly can perfectly price discriminate? Use a graph to explain.

26. According to a report from the Foundation for Taxpayer and Consumer Rights, gasoline costs twice as much in Europe than in the United States because taxes are higher in Europe. However, the amount per gallon net of taxes that U.S. consumers pay is higher than that paid by Europeans (24¢ per gallon net of taxes). The report concludes that "U.S. motorists are essentially subsidizing European drivers, who pay more for taxes but substantially less into oil company profits" (Tom Doggett, "US Drivers Subsidize European Pump Prices," *Reuters*, August 31, 2006). Given that oil companies have market power and can price discriminate across countries, is it reasonable to conclude that U.S. consumers are subsidizing Europeans? Explain your answer.

27. It costs the *San Francisco Chronicle* $10 to produce and deliver the Sunday edition, yet it charges only $2 (Ward Bushee, "S.F. Chronicle Turns the Page into a New Era," *San Francisco Chronicle*, February 1, 2009). Until recently, advertising more than covered the difference. As advertising dollars shrink, how is the *Chronicle* likely to change its pricing? Why?

PROBLEMS

*28. Suppose that the union in Solved Problem 12.1 faces a demand curve of $H = 100 - w$ and that the labor supply curve is $\underline{H} = w - 20$ (for $w \geq 20$). Solve for w^*, H^*, and $\overline{H}$.

29. In panel b of Figure 12.3, the single-price monopoly faces a demand curve of $p = 90 - Q$ and a constant marginal (and average) cost of $m = \$30$. Find the profit-maximizing quantity (or price) using math (Chapter 11). Determine the profit, consumer surplus, welfare, and deadweight loss.

30. Suppose that the quantity-discriminating monopoly in panel a of Figure 12.3 can set three prices, depending on the quantity a consumer purchases. The firm's profit is
$$\pi = p_1 Q_1 + p_2(Q_2 - Q_1) + p_3(Q_3 - Q_2) - mQ_3,$$
where p_1 is the high price charged on the first Q_1 units (first block), p_2 is a lower price charged on the next $Q_2 - Q_1$ units, p_3 is the lowest price charged on the $Q_3 - Q_2$ remaining units, Q_3 is the total number of units actually purchased, and $m = \$30$ is the firm's constant marginal and average cost. Use calculus to determine the profit-maximizing p_1, p_2, and p_3.

31. In the quantity-discrimination analysis in panel a of Figure 12.3, suppose that the monopoly can make consumers a take-it-or-leave-it offer (similar to the union offer in Solved Problem 12.1).

    a. Suppose the monopoly sets a price, p^*, and a minimum quantity, Q^*, that a consumer must pay to be able to purchase any units at all. What price and minimum quantity should it set to achieve the same outcome as it would if it perfectly price discriminated?

    b. Now suppose that the monopoly charges a price of $90 for the first 30 units and a price of $30 for subsequent units, but requires that a consumer buy at least 30 units to be allowed to buy any units. Compare this outcome to the one in part a and to the perfectly price-discriminating outcome.

*32. A patent gave Sony a legal monopoly to produce a robot dog called Aibo ("eye-BO"). The Chihuahua-sized robot can sit, beg, chase balls, dance, and play an electronic tune. When Sony started selling the toy in July 1999, it announced that it would sell 3,000 Aibo robots in Japan for about $2,000 each and a limited litter of 2,000 in the United States for about $2,500 each. Suppose that Sony's marginal cost of producing Aibos is $500. Its inverse demand curve is $p_J = 3,500 - \frac{1}{2} Q_J$ in Japan and $p_A = 4,500 - Q_A$ in the United States. Solve for the equilibrium prices and quantities (assuming that U.S. customers cannot buy robots from Japan). Show how the profit-maximizing price ratio depends on the elasticities of demand in the two countries. What are the deadweight losses in each country, and in which is the loss from monopoly pricing greater?

*33. A monopoly sells its good in the U.S. and Japanese markets. The American inverse demand function is $p_A = 100 - Q_A$, and the Japanese inverse demand function is $p_J = 80 - 2Q_J$, where both prices, p_A and p_J, are measured in dollars. The firm's marginal cost of production is $m = 20$ in both countries. If the firm can prevent resales, what price will it charge in both markets? [*Hint*: The monopoly determines its optimal (monopoly) price in each country separately because customers cannot resell the good.]

34. Universal Studios sold the *Mamma Mia!* DVD around the world. Universal charged $21.40 in Canada and $32 in Japan—more than the $20 it charged in the United States. Using the information about Universal's marginal cost and U.S. sales in Section 12.4, determine what the elasticities of demand must be in Canada and in Japan if Universal is profit maximizing.

*35. Warner Home Entertainment sold the *Harry Potter and the Prisoner of Azkaban* two-DVD movie set in China for about $3, which was only one-fifth the U.S. price, and sold about 100,000 units. The price was extremely low in China because Chinese consumers are less wealthy and because (lower-quality) pirated versions were available in China for 72¢–$1.20, compared to the roughly $3 required to purchase the legal version (Jin Baicheng, "Powerful Ally Joins Government in War on Piracy," *China Daily*, March 11, 2005, 13). Assuming a marginal cost of $1, what is the Chinese elasticity of demand? Derive the demand function for China and illustrate Warner's policy in China using a figure similar to panel a in Figure 12.4.

36. A monopoly sells its good in the United States, where the elasticity of demand is −2, and in Japan, where the elasticity of demand is −5. Its marginal cost is $10. At what price does the monopoly sell its good in each country if resales are impossible?

37. A monopoly sells in two countries, and resales between the countries are impossible. The demand curves in the two countries are
$$p_1 = 100 - Q_1,$$
$$p_2 = 120 - 2Q_2.$$
The monopoly's marginal cost is $m = 30$. Solve for the equilibrium price in each country.

38. Show that the equilibrium elasticities in the two countries must be equal in Solved Problem 12.3.

39. Using math, show why a two-part tariff causes customers who purchase few units to pay more per unit than customers who buy more units.

40. Show how a change in the advertising rate a affects the optimal number of subscriptions in Solved Problem 12.4.

41. Canada subsidizes Canadian magazines to offset the invasion of foreign (primarily U.S.) magazines, which take 90% of the country's sales. The Canada Magazine Fund provides a lump-sum subsidy to various magazines to "maintain a Canadian presence against the overwhelming presence of foreign magazines." Eligibility is based on high levels of investment in Canadian editorial content and reliance on advertising revenues. What effect does a lump-sum subsidy have on the number of subscriptions sold?

42. Show how a monopoly would solve for its optimal price and advertising level if it sets price instead of quantity.

43. The demand a monopoly faces is
$$p = 100 - Q + A^{0.5},$$
where Q is its quantity, p is its price, and A is its level of advertising. Its marginal cost of production is 10, and its cost of a unit of advertising is 1. What is the firm's profit equation? Solve for the firm's profit-maximizing price, quantity, and level of advertising.

44. What is the monopoly's profit-maximizing output, Q, and level of advertising, A, if it faces a demand curve of $p = a - bQ + cA^\alpha$, its constant marginal cost of producing output is m, and the cost of a unit of advertising is \$1?

45. For every dollar spent on advertising pharmaceuticals, revenue increases by about \$4.20 (CNN, December 17, 2004). If this number is accurate and the firms are operating rationally, what (if anything) can we infer about marginal production and distribution costs?

46. Knoebels Amusement Park in Elysburg, Pennsylvania, charges a lump-sum fee, $\mathcal{L}$, to enter its Crystal Pool. It also charges p per trip down the pool's water slides. Suppose that 400 teenagers visit the park, each of whom has a demand function of $q_1 = 5 - p$, and that 400 seniors also visit, each of whom has a demand function of $q_2 = 4 - p$. Knoebels's objective is to set $\mathcal{L}$ and p so as to maximize its profit given that it has no (non-sunk) cost and must charge both groups the same prices. What are the optimal $\mathcal{L}$ and p? V

47. Hershey Park sells tickets at the gate and at local municipal offices. There are two groups of people. Suppose that the demand function for people who purchase tickets at the gate is $Q_G = 10,000 - 100p_G$ and that the demand function for people who purchase tickets at municipal offices is $Q_G = 9,000 - 100p_G$. The marginal cost of each patron is 5.

   a. Suppose that Hershey Park cannot successfully segment the two markets. What are the profit-maximizing price and quantity? What is its maximum possible profit?

   b. Suppose that the people who purchase tickets at one location would never consider purchasing them at the other and that Hershey Park can successfully price discriminate. What are the profit-maximizing price and quantity? What is its maximum possible profit? V

14 Oligopoly

Anyone can win unless there happens to be a second entry. —George Ade

Three firms, Nintendo, Microsoft, and Sony, dominate the U.S. video game market. Each firm's profit depends on the actions it takes and on those of its rivals. In 2006, when Nintendo introduced the innovative wireless Wii game console at a relatively low price, its market share grew substantially until Nintendo was the dominant firm. However, in 2009, its game sales fell from 47% to 40% of the market, in part because its graphics have failed to keep up with those of its competitors. In 2009, after a major price cut, Sony's PlayStation PS3 game sales increased from 15% to 19% of the market. Stealing from Nintendo's playbook, Microsoft has differentiated its Xbox by adding functions that allow users to stream TV shows or connect to a social networking site, while still catering to hardcore gamers.[1] Thus, these manufacturers are constantly jockeying for an advantage by differentiating their products or undercutting the price of their competitors.

Video game producers are an **oligopoly**: a small group of firms in a market with substantial barriers to entry. Because relatively few firms compete in such a market, each can influence the price, and hence its actions affect rival firms. The need to consider the behavior of rival firms makes an oligopoly firm's profit maximization decision more difficult than that of a monopoly or competitive firm. A monopoly has no rivals, and a competitive firm ignores the behavior of individual rivals—it considers only the market price and its own costs in choosing its profit-maximizing output.

An oligopoly firm that ignores or inaccurately predicts its rivals' behavior is likely to suffer a loss of profit. For example, as its rivals produce more cars, the price that Ford can get for its cars falls. If Ford underestimates how many cars Toyota and Honda will produce, Ford may produce too many automobiles and lose money.

Oligopolistic firms may act independently or coordinate their actions. If firms coordinate setting their prices or quantities, the firms are said to **collude**. A group of firms that collude is called a **cartel**. If all the firms in a market collude and behave like a monopoly, the members of a cartel collectively earn the monopoly profit—the maximum possible profit. Generally, collusion is illegal in most developed countries.

If oligopolistic firms do not collude, they collectively earn less than the monopoly profit. Yet because there are relatively few firms in the market, oligopolistic firms that act independently may earn positive economic profits in the long run, unlike competitive firms.

---

[1]Millard, Elizabeth, "Nintendo Wii Outsells Xbox 360 and PlayStation 3," *Sci-Tech Today*, March 16, 2007; and Sarkar, Pia, "Low Price, Unique Controller Make Nintendo Most Popular," *San Francisco Chronicle*, March 17, 2007; **games.venturebeat.com/2009/12/11/sonys-playstation-3-is-looking-better-on-both-cost** (December 11, 2009); McCormick, Andrew, "Xbox Strikes Back," *Revolution Magazine*, December 21, 2009.

In an oligopolistic market, one or more barriers to entry keep the number of firms small. In a market with no barriers to entry, firms enter the market until profits are driven to zero. In perfectly competitive markets, enough entry occurs that firms face a horizontal demand curve and are price takers. However, in other markets, even after entry has driven profits to zero, each firm faces a downward-sloping demand curve. Because of this slope, the firm can charge a price above its marginal cost, creating a *market failure*: inefficient (too little) consumption (Chapter 9). **Monopolistic competition** is a market structure in which firms have market power (the ability to raise price profitably above marginal cost) but no additional firm can enter and earn a positive profit.

In this chapter, we examine cartelized, oligopolistic, and monopolistically competitive markets in which firms set quantities or prices. As we saw in Chapter 11, the monopoly equilibrium is the same whether a monopoly sets price or quantity. In contrast, the oligopolistic and monopolistically competitive equilibria differ if firms set prices instead of quantities.

In this chapter, we examine eight main topics

1. **Market Structures.** The number of firms, price, profits, and other properties of markets vary depending on whether the market is monopolistic, oligopolistic, monopolistically competitive, or competitive.

2. **Cartels.** If firms successfully coordinate their actions, they can collectively behave like a monopoly.

3. **Noncooperative Oligopoly.** There are many different models of oligopoly in which firms act without colluding, in which the equilibrium price and quantity range between competition at one extreme and monopoly at the other.

4. **Cournot Oligopoly Model.** In a Cournot model, in which firms simultaneously set their output levels without colluding, market output and firms' profits lie between the competitive and monopoly levels.

5. **Stackelberg Oligopoly Model.** In a Stackelberg model, in which a *leader* firm chooses its output level before follower rival firms choose their output levels, market output is greater than if all firms choose their output simultaneously, and the leader makes a higher profit than the other firms.

6. **Comparison of Collusive, Cournot, Stackelberg, and Competitive Equilibria.** Total market output declines from the competitive level to the Stackelberg level to the Cournot level and reaches a minimum with monopoly or collusion.

7. **Bertrand Oligopoly Model.** In a Bertrand model, in which firms simultaneously set their prices without colluding, the equilibrium depends critically on the degree of product differentiation.

8. **Monopolistic Competition.** When firms can freely enter the market but face downward-sloping demand curves in equilibrium, firms charge prices above marginal cost but make no profit.

14.1 Market Structures

Markets differ according to the number of firms in the market, the ease with which firms may enter and leave the market, and the ability of firms in a market to differentiate their products from those of their rivals. Table 14.1 lists the characteristics and properties of monopoly, oligopoly, monopolistic competition, and competition.

Table 14.1 Properties of Monopoly, Oligopoly, Monopolistic Competition, and Competition

	Monopoly	Oligopoly	Monopolistic Competition	Competition
1. Ability to set price	Price setter	Price setter	Price setter	Price taker
2. Price level	very high	high	high	low
3. Market power	$p > MC$	$p > MC$	$p > MC$	$p = MC$
4. Entry conditions	No entry	Limited entry	Free entry	Free entry
5. Number of firms	1	Few	Few or many	Many
6. Long-run profit	≥ 0	≥ 0	0	0
7. Strategy dependent on individual rival firms' behavior	No (has no rivals)	Yes	Yes	No (cares about market price only)
8. Products	Single product	May be differentiated	May be differentiated	Undifferentiated
9. Example	Local natural gas utility	Automobile manufacturers	Plumbers in a small town	Apple farmers

For each of these market structures, we assume that the firms face many price-taking buyers.

Competitive firms are price takers because they face horizontal demand curves; whereas monopolies, oligopolies, and monopolistically competitive firms are price setters because they face downward-sloping demand curves (row 1 of Table 14.1). All else the same, a monopoly sets a very high price, oligopolistic and monopolistically competitive firms set high prices, and competitive firms receive a low price equal to the marginal cost of production (row 2). That is, except in competitive markets, price is above marginal cost (row 3), which creates market failures (too little output is sold).

A monopoly or an oligopoly does not fear entry (row 4) because of insurmountable barriers to entry such as government licenses and patents. In both competitive and monopolistically competitive markets, entry occurs until no new firm can profitably enter (so the marginal firm earns zero profit). These impediments to entry restrict the number of firms so that there is only one firm (*mono*) in a monopoly, and, usually, only a few (*oligo*) firms in an oligopoly, while there are a few or many firms in monopolistically competitive markets and many in competitive markets (row 5). Monopolistically competitive markets have fewer firms than perfectly competitive markets do. Because they have relatively few rivals and hence are large relative to the market, each monopolistically competitive firm faces a downward-sloping demand curve.

Oligopolistic and monopolistically competitive firms pay attention to rival firms' behavior, in contrast to monopolistic or competitive firms (row 7). A monopoly has no rivals. A competitive firm ignores the behavior of individual rivals in choosing its output because the market price tells the firm everything it needs to know about its competitors.

Oligopolistic and monopolistically competitive firms may produce differentiated products (row 8). For example, Camry and Taurus automobiles differ in size, weight, appearance, and other characteristics. In contrast, competitive apple farmers sell undifferentiated (homogeneous) products.

14.2 Cartels

People of the same trade seldom meet together, even for merriment and diversion, but the conversation ends in a conspiracy against the public, or some contrivance to raise prices. —Adam Smith, 1776

Oligopolistic firms have an incentive to collude so as to increase their profits. However, because firms can make even more money by cheating on the cartel, firms do not always collude successfully.

Why Cartels Succeed or Fail

A thing worth having is a thing worth cheating for. —W. C. Fields

As Adam Smith noted two centuries ago, firms have an incentive to form a cartel in which each firm reduces its output, which leads to higher prices and higher profits for individual firms and the firms collectively. Luckily for consumers' pocketbooks, cartels often fail because a government forbids them and because each firm in a cartel has an incentive to cheat on the cartel agreement by producing extra output. We now consider why cartels form, what laws prohibit cartels, why cartel members have an incentive to deviate from the cartel agreement, and why some cartels succeed whereas others fail.

Why Cartels Form. A cartel forms if members of the cartel believe that they can raise their profits by coordinating their actions. Although cartels usually involve oligopolies, cartels may form in a market that would otherwise be competitive.

If a competitive firm is maximizing its profit, why should joining a cartel increase its profit? The answer involves a subtle argument. When a competitive firm chooses its profit-maximizing output level, it considers how varying its output affects its profit only. The firm ignores the effect that changing its output level has on other firms' profits. A cartel, by contrast, takes into account how changes in any one firm's output affect the profits of all members of the cartel.

If a competitive firm lowers its output, it raises the market price very slightly—so slightly that the firm ignores the effect not only on other firms' profits but also on its own. If all the identical competitive firms in an industry lower their output by this same amount, however, the market price will change noticeably. Recognizing this effect of collective action, a cartel chooses to produce a smaller market output than is produced by a competitive market.

Figure 14.1 illustrates this difference between a competitive market and a cartel. There are n firms in this market, and no further entry is possible. Panel a shows the marginal and average cost curves of a typical firm. If all firms are price takers, the market supply curve, S, is the horizontal sum of the individual marginal cost curves above minimum average cost, as shown in panel b. At the competitive price, p_c, each price-taking firm produces q_c units of output (where MC intersects the line at p_c in panel a). The market output is $Q_c = nq_c$ (where S intersects the market demand curve in panel b).

Now suppose that the firms form a cartel. Should they reduce their output? At the competitive output, the cartel's marginal cost (which is the competitive industry supply curve, S in panel b) is greater than its marginal revenue, so the cartel's profit rises if it reduces output. The cartel's collective profit rises until output is reduced by enough that its marginal revenue equals its marginal cost at Q_m, the monopoly

Figure 14.1 Competition Versus Cartel

(a) The marginal cost and average cost of one of the n firms in the market are shown. A competitive firm produces q_c units of output, whereas a cartel member produces $q_m < q_c$. At the cartel price, p_m, each cartel member has an incentive to increase its output from q_m to q^* (where the dotted line at p_m intersects the MC curve). (b) The competitive equilibrium, e_c, has more output and a lower price than the cartel equilibrium, e_m.

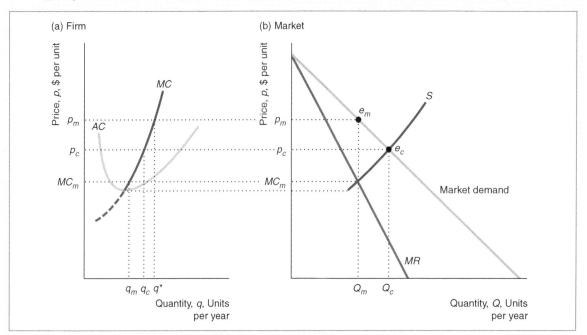

output. If the profit of the cartel increases, the profit of each of the n members of the cartel also increases. To achieve the cartel output level, each firm must reduce its output to $q_m = Q_m/n$, as panel a shows.

Why must the firms form a cartel to achieve these higher profits? A competitive firm produces q_c, where its marginal cost equals the market price. If only one firm reduces its output, it loses profit because it sells fewer units at essentially the same price. By getting all the firms to lower their output collectively, the cartel raises the market price and hence individual firms' profits. The less elastic the market demand curve faced by the potential cartel, all else the same, the higher the price the cartel sets (Chapter 11) and the greater the benefit from cartelizing. If the penalty for forming an illegal cartel is relatively low, some unscrupulous businesspeople may succumb to the lure of extra profits and join.

Laws Against Cartels. In the late nineteenth century, cartels (or, as they were called then, *trusts*) were legal and common in the United States. Oil, railroad, sugar, and tobacco trusts raised prices substantially above competitive levels.[2] In response to the trusts' high prices, the U.S. Congress passed the Sherman Antitrust Act in 1890 and the Federal Trade Commission Act of 1914, which prohibit firms from *explicitly* agreeing to take actions that reduce competition. In particular, cartels that

---

[2]Nineteenth-century and early twentieth-century robber barons who made fortunes due to these cartels include John Jacob Astor (real estate, fur), Andrew Carnegie (railroads, steel), Henry Clay Frick (steel), Jay Gould (finance, railroads), Mark Hopkins (railroads), J. P. Morgan (banking), John D. Rockefeller (oil), Leland Stanford (railroads), and Cornelius Vanderbilt (railroads, shipping).

are formed for the purpose of jointly setting price are strictly prohibited. By imposing penalties on firms caught colluding, these antitrust laws reduce the probability that cartels form.

Virtually all industrialized nations have *antitrust laws*—or, as they are known in other countries, *competition policies*—that limit or forbid some or all cartels. Canada's Competition Act, a federal law that governs most business conduct, contains both criminal and civil provisions aimed at preventing anticompetitive practices. The EU has a competition policy, which, under the Treaty of the European Community (EC Treaty or Treaty of Rome) in 1957, gives it substantial powers to prevent actions that hinder competition. The first provision is Article 81 EC, which prohibits "...all agreements between undertakings, decisions by associations of undertakings and concerted practices which may affect trade between Member States and which have as their object or effect the prevention, restriction or distortion of competition within the common market..."

Recently, the U.S. Department of Justice, quoting the Supreme Court that collusion is the "supreme evil of antitrust," stated that prosecuting cartels was its "top enforcement priority." However despite these laws, cartels persist for three reasons. First, international cartels and cartels within certain countries operate legally. Second, some illegal cartels operate believing that they can avoid detection or that if caught the punishment will be insignificant. Third, some firms are able to coordinate their activities without explicitly colluding and thereby avoid violating competition laws.

Some international cartels that are organized by countries rather than by firms are legal. The Organization of Petroleum Exporting Countries (OPEC) is an international cartel that was formed in 1960 by five major oil-exporting countries: Iran, Iraq, Kuwait, Saudi Arabia, and Venezuela. In 1971, OPEC members agreed to take an active role in setting oil prices.

Many illegal cartels flout the competition laws in major industrial countries, believing that they are unlikely to get caught or that the punishments they face are so negligible that it pays to collude. Small fines fail to discourage cartel behavior. In a cartel case involving the $9 billion American carpet industry, a firm with $150 million in annual sales agreed with the U.S. Justice Department to plead guilty and pay a fine of $150,000. It is hard to imagine that a fine of one-tenth of 1% of annual sales significantly deters cartel behavior.

Even larger fines fail to discourage repeated collusion. In 1996, Archer Daniels Midland (ADM) paid to settle three civil price-fixing-related cases: $35 million in a case involving citric acid (used in many consumer products), $30 million to shareholders as compensation for lost stock value after the citric acid price-fixing scandal became public, and $25 million in a lysine (used in animal feed and elsewhere) case. ADM paid a $100 million fine in a federal criminal case for fixing the price of lysine and citric acid in 1996 and settled a fructose corn syrup price-fixing case for $400 million in 2004.

To determine guilt, American antitrust laws use evidence of conspiracy (such as explicit agreements) rather than the economic effect of monopoly. Charging monopoly-level prices is not necessarily illegal—only the "bad behavior" of explicitly agreeing to raise prices is against the law. As a result, some groups of firms charge monopoly-level prices without violating the competition laws. These firms may *tacitly collude* without meeting by signaling to each other through their actions. Although the firms' actions may not be illegal, they behave much like cartels. For example, MacAvoy (1995) concluded that the major U.S. long-distance telephone companies tacitly colluded; as a result, each firm's Lerner Index (Chapter 11), $(p - MC)/p$, exceeded 60%, which is well above the competitive level, 0%.[3]

---

[3]See "Tacit Collusion in Long-Distance Service" in **MyEconLab**'s textbook resources for Chapter 14.

In the last couple of decades, the European Commission has been pursuing antitrust (competition) cases under laws that are similar to U.S. statutes. Recently, the European Commission, the DOJ, and the FTC have become increasingly aggressive, prosecuting many more cases. Following the lead of the United States, which imposes both civil and criminal penalties, the British government introduced legislation in 2002 to criminalize certain cartel-related conduct. The European Union uses only civil penalties, but its fines have increased dramatically, as have U.S. fines.

In 1993, the DOJ introduced the Corporate Leniency Program, guaranteeing that cartel whistle-blowers will receive immunity from federal prosecution. As a consequence, the DOJ has caught, prosecuted, and fined several gigantic cartels.[4] In 2002, the European Commission adopted a similar policy.[5] In 2004, Japan started pursuing antitrust cases more aggressively.

APPLICATION
Catwalk Cartel

Being thin, rich, and beautiful doesn't make you immune to exploitation. Some of the world's most successful models charged 10 of New York's top modeling agencies—including Wilhelmina, Ford, Next, IMG, and Elite—with operating a sleazy cartel that cut their commissions by millions of dollars.

Carolyn Fears—a 5'11" redheaded former model who had earned up to $200,000 a year—initiated the private antitrust suit when she learned that her agency not only charged her a 20% commission every time she was booked, but also extracted a 20% commission from her employers (mostly magazines). Her class-action lawsuit alleged that the agencies collectively fixed commissions for Claudia Schiffer, Heidi Klum, Gisele Bundchen, and thousands of other models over many years.

The agencies had formed an industry group, International Model Managers Association, Inc. (IMMA), which held repeated meetings. Monique Pillard, an executive at Elite Model Management, fired off a memo concerning one IMMA meeting, in which she "made a point ... that we are all committing suicide, if we do not stick together. Pauline's agreed with me but as usual, Bill Weinberg [of Wilhelmina] cautioned me about price fixing.... Ha! Ha! Ha! ... the usual (expletive)." As the trial judge, Harold Baer, Jr., observed, while "Wilhelmina objects to the outward discussion of price fixing, it is plausible from Pillard's reaction that Wilhelmina's objection was to the dissemination of information, not to the underlying price-fixing agreement."

The models argued that the association was little more than a front for helping agency heads monitor each other's pricing policies. Documents show that, shortly after association meetings, the agencies uniformly raised their commission rates from 10% to 15% and then to 20%. For example, at a meeting before the last increase, an Elite executive gave his competitors a heads-up—but had not informed his clients—that Elite planned to raise its commissions to 20%. He said that at Elite, "we were also favorable to letting everyone know as much as possible about our pricing policies."

The trial started in 2004. Most of the parties settled in 2005, and a final decision (after appeals) was handed down in 2007. IMG alone paid the models $11 million.

---

[4]See "Vitamin Price Fixing" in **MyEconLab**'s textbook resources for Chapter 14. Canadian and EU authorities also prosecuted and fined the international vitamin cartel participants.

[5]In 2008, the EU fined importers Dole and Del Monte for colluding with Chiquita. Chiquita was not fined because it blew the whistle on the illegal price fixing in northern European nations.

Why Cartels Fail. Many cartels fail even without legal intervention. *Cartels fail if noncartel members can supply consumers with large quantities of goods.* For example, copper producers formed an international cartel that controlled only about a third of the noncommunist world's copper production and faced additional competition from firms that recycle copper from scrap materials. Because of this competition from noncartel members, the cartel was not successful in raising and keeping copper prices high.

In addition, *each member of a cartel has an incentive to cheat on the cartel agreement.* The owner of a firm may reason, "I joined the cartel to encourage others to reduce their output and increase profits for everyone. I can make more money, however, if I cheat on the cartel agreement by producing extra output. I can get away with cheating if the other firms can't tell who's producing the extra output because I'm just one of many firms and because I'll hardly affect the market price." By this reasoning, it is in each firm's best interest for all *other* firms to honor the cartel agreement—thus driving up the market price—while it ignores the agreement and makes extra profitable sales at the high price.

Figure 14.1 illustrates why firms want to cheat. At the cartel output, q_m in panel a, each cartel member's marginal cost is MC_m. The marginal revenue of a firm that violates the agreement is p_m because it is acting like a price taker with respect to the market price. Because the firm's marginal revenue (price) is above its marginal cost, the firm wants to increase its output. If the firm decides to violate the cartel agreement, it maximizes its profit by increasing its output to q^*, where its marginal cost equals p_m. As more and more firms leave the cartel, the cartel price falls. Eventually, if enough firms quit, the cartel collapses.

Maintaining Cartels

To keep firms from violating the cartel agreement, the cartel must be able to detect cheating and punish violators. Further, members of a cartel must keep their illegal behavior hidden from customers and government agencies.

Detection and Enforcement. Cartels use various techniques to detect cheating. Some cartels, for example, give members the right to inspect each other's books. Some rely on governments to report bids on government contracts so that cartel firms can learn if a member bids below the agreed-on price. Cartels may also divide the market by region or by customers, making it more likely that a firm that steals another firm's customers is detected, as in the case of a two-country mercury cartel (1928–1972) that allocated the Americas to Spain and Europe to Italy. Another option is for a cartel to turn to industry organizations that collect data on market share by firm. A cheating cartel's market share would rise, tipping off the other firms that it cheated.

You perhaps have seen "low price" ads in which local retail stores guarantee to meet or beat the prices of competitors. These ads may in fact be a way for the firm to induce its customers to report cheating on a cartel agreement by other firms (Salop, 1986).

Various methods are used to enforce cartel agreements. For example, GE and Westinghouse, the two major sellers of large steam-turbine generators, included "most-favored-nation clauses" (more accurately, most-favored-customer clauses) in their contracts. A with a buyer contract stated that the seller would not offer a lower price to any other current or future buyer without offering the same price decrease to that buyer. This type of rebate clause creates a penalty for cheating on the cartel:

If either company cheats by cutting prices, it has to lower prices to all previous buyers as well. Threats of violence are another means of enforcing a cartel agreement.[6]

Government Support. Sometimes governments help create and enforce cartels, exempting them from antitrust laws. For example, U.S., European, and other governments signed an agreement in 1944 to establish a cartel to fix prices for international airline flights and prevent competition.[7]

Professional baseball teams have been exempted from some U.S. antitrust laws since 1922. As a result, they can use the courts to help enforce certain aspects of their cartel agreement. Major-league clubs are able to avoid competing for young athletes by means of a draft and contracts, limited geographic competition between teams, joint negotiations for television and other rights, and other collective actions.

Barriers to Entry. Barriers to entry that limit the number of firms help the cartel detect and punish cheating. The fewer the firms in a market, the more likely it is that other firms will know if a given firm cheats and the easier it is to impose penalties. Cartels with a large number of firms are relatively rare, except those involving professional associations. Hay and Kelley (1974) examined Department of Justice price-fixing cases from 1963 to 1972 and found that only 6.5% involved 50 or more conspirators, the average number of firms was 7.25, and 48% involved six or fewer firms.

When new firms enter their market, cartels frequently fail. For example, when only Italy and Spain sold mercury, they were able to establish and maintain a stable cartel. When a larger group of countries joined them, their attempts to cartelize the world mercury market repeatedly failed (MacKie-Mason and Pindyck, 1986).

Mergers. If antitrust or competition laws prevent firms from colluding, firms may try to merge instead. Recognizing this potential problem, U.S. laws restrict the ability of firms to merge if the effect would be anticompetitive. Whether the Department of Justice or the Federal Trade Commission challenges a proposed merger turns on a large number of issues. Similarly, for the last 12 years, the European Commission has been actively reviewing and blocking mergers. With only one exception (in 2002), none of the Commission's decisions has been rejected by the courts. One reason governments limit mergers is that all the firms in a market could combine and form a monopoly.

Would it be a good idea to ban all mergers? No, because some mergers result in more efficient production. Formerly separate firms may become more efficient because of greater scale, the sharing of trade secrets, or the closure of duplicative retail outlets. For example, when Chase and Chemical banks merged, they closed or combined seven Manhattan branches that were located within two blocks of other branches. Thus, whether a merger raises or lowers welfare depends on which of its two offsetting effects—reducing competition and increasing efficiency—is larger.

APPLICATION

Hospital Mergers: Market Power Versus Efficiency

Since the 1990s, the hospital market has consolidated substantially through mergers, with an average of nearly 60 mergers per year in major metropolitan areas. When two hospitals merge, there may be substantial efficiency gains from lack of duplication of functions, which may result in lower prices; however, the merger may result in less competition, which may lead to higher prices. Which

---

[6]See "Bad Bakers" in **MyEconLab**'s textbook resources for Chapter 14.

[7]The European Court of Justice struck down the central provisions of aviation treaties among the United States and eight other countries in 2002. The European Commission plans to try to negotiate new treaties.

effect dominates is an empirical question. Dafny (2009) finds that local hospital prices rise by about 40% after a merger, with the (apparently large) cost savings going to the hospitals rather than to the patients.

14.3 Noncooperative Oligopoly

How do oligopolistic firms behave if they do not collude? Although there is only one model of competition and only one model of monopoly, there are many models of noncooperative oligopolistic behavior that have many possible equilibrium prices and quantities.

Which model is appropriate depends on the characteristics of the market, such as the type of *actions* firms take—such as set quantity or price—and whether firms act simultaneously or sequentially. We examine the three best-known oligopoly models in turn. In the *Cournot model*, firms simultaneously choose quantities without colluding. In the *Stackelberg model*, a leader firm chooses its quantity and then the follower firms independently choose their quantities. In the *Bertrand model*, firms simultaneously and independently choose prices.

To illustrate these models as simply and as clearly as possible, we start by making three restrictive assumptions, which we will later relax. First, we initially assume that all firms are identical in the sense that they have the same cost functions and produce identical, *undifferentiated* products. We show how the market outcomes change if costs differ or if consumers believe that the products differ across firms.

Second, we initially illustrate each of these oligopoly models for a **duopoly**: an oligopoly with two (*duo*) firms. Each of these models can be applied to markets with many firms. The Cournot and Stackelberg outcomes vary, whereas the Bertrand market outcome with undifferentiated goods does not vary, as the number of firms increases.

Third, we assume that the market lasts for only one period. Consequently, each firm chooses its quantity or price only once.

To compare market outcomes under the various models, we need to be able to characterize the oligopoly equilibrium. Because oligopolistic firms may take many possible actions (such as setting price or quantity or choosing a level of advertising), the oligopoly equilibrium rule needs to refer to firms' behavior more generally than just setting output. Thus, we use the Nash equilibrium concept that we introduced in Chapter 13: a set of strategies is a *Nash equilibrium* if, when all other players use these strategies, no player can obtain a higher payoff by choosing a different strategy. In most models in this chapter, we use a special case of that definition that is appropriate for the single-period oligopoly models in which the only action that a firm can take is to set either its quantity or its price: A set of actions that the firms take is a *Nash equilibrium* if, holding the actions of all other firms constant, no firm can obtain a higher profit by choosing a different action.

14.4 Cournot Oligopoly Model

The French economist and mathematician Antoine-Augustin Cournot introduced the first formal model of oligopoly in 1838. Cournot explained how oligopoly firms behave if they simultaneously choose how much they produce. The firms act independently and have imperfect information about their rivals, so each firm must choose its output level before knowing what the other firms will choose. The quantity that one firm produces directly affects the profits of the other firms because the market price depends on total output. Thus in choosing its strategy to maximize its profit, each firm takes into account its beliefs about the output its rivals will sell. Cournot introduced an equilibrium concept that is the same as the Nash definition in which the action that firms take is to choose quantities.

We look at equilibrium in a market that lasts for only one period. Initially, we make four assumptions:

1. There are two firms and no other firms can enter the market.
2. The firms have identical costs.
3. The firms sell identical products.
4. The firms set their quantities simultaneously.

Later we relax each of these assumptions in turn and examine how the equilibrium changes.

Cournot Model of an Airline Market

To illustrate the basic idea of the Cournot model, we again examine the actual market where American Airlines and United Airlines compete for customers on flights between Chicago and Los Angeles, as we did in Chapter 13.[8] In our normal-form game example in Chapter 13, we assumed that the firms chose between only two output levels. Here, we generalize that analysis by allowing the firms to pick any output level they want. The total number of passengers flown by these two firms, Q, is the sum of the number of passengers flown on American, q_A, and those flown on United, q_U. No other companies can enter this market because they cannot obtain landing rights at both airports.[9]

How many passengers does each airline firm choose to carry? To answer this question, we determine the Nash equilibrium for this model. This Nash equilibrium, in which firms choose quantities, is also called a **Cournot equilibrium** or **Nash-Cournot equilibrium** or **Nash-in-quantities equilibrium**: a set of quantities chosen by firms such that, holding the quantities of all other firms constant, no firm can obtain a higher profit by choosing a different quantity.

The analysis in Chapter 13 of a special case of this airline problem where the two firms could choose from only two possible output levels illustrates a Nash-Cournot equilibrium. Here, we first generalize the analysis so that the firms can consider using any possible output level, and then we generalize the model to allow for a larger number of players, n. We determine the *best-response* (Chapter 13)—the strategy that maximizes a player's payoff given its beliefs about its rivals' strategies—of each firm and use that information to solve for the Nash-Cournot equilibrium.[10]

---

[8]This example is based on Brander and Zhang (1990). They reported data for economy and discount passengers taking direct flights between the two cities in the third quarter of 1985. In calculating the profits, we assume that Brander and Zhang's estimate of the firms' constant marginal cost is the same as the firms' relevant long-run average cost.

[9]Existing airline firms have the right to buy, sell, or rent landing slots. However, by controlling landing slots, existing firms can make entry difficult.

[10]As in Chapter 13, we could analyze this problem using a normal-form game with n players (firms), a choice of strategies (any real-number, nonnegative quantity), and a payoff (profit) function that is common knowledge (that is, each firm knows the profit function of all firms). It is possible to obtain that Nash equilibrium in a duopoly Cournot model with a linear demand curve and constant marginal cost by iterative elimination of strictly dominated strategies. With three or more firms, iterative elimination provides only the imprecise observation that each firm's quantity will not exceed the monopoly quantity (Gibbons, 1992). Thus, here we obtain the Nash-Cournot equilibrium using best-response functions, an approach that works with any number of firms and with nonlinear demand and marginal cost.

To determine the Cournot equilibrium, we need to establish how each firm chooses its quantity. We start by using the total demand curve for the Chicago–Los Angeles route and a firm's belief about how much its rival will sell to determine its *residual demand curve*: the market demand that is not met by other sellers at any given price (Chapter 8). Next, we examine how a firm uses its residual demand curve to determine its best response: the output level that maximizes its profit given its belief about how much its rival will produce. Finally, we use the information contained in the firms' best-response functions to determine the Nash-Cournot equilibrium quantities.

The quantity that each firm chooses depends on the residual demand curve it faces and its marginal cost. American Airlines' profit-maximizing output depends on how many passengers it believes United will fly.

Our estimated airline market demand function is linear,

$$Q = 339 - p, \tag{14.1}$$

where price, p, is the dollar cost of a one-way flight, and the total quantity of the two airlines combined, Q, is measured in thousands of passengers flying one way per quarter. Panels a and b of Figure 14.2 show that this market demand curve, D, is a straight line that hits the price axis at \$339 and the quantity axis at 339 units (thousands of passengers) per quarter. Each airline has a constant marginal cost, MC, and an average cost, AC, of \$147 per passenger per flight. Using only this information and our economic model, we can determine the Nash-Cournot equilibrium quantities for the two airlines.

Figure 14.2 illustrates two possibilities. If American Airlines were a monopoly, it wouldn't have to worry about United Airlines' actions. American's demand would

Figure 14.2 American Airlines' Profit-Maximizing Output

(a) If American is a monopoly, it picks its profit-maximizing output, $q_A = 96$ units (thousand passengers) per quarter, so that its marginal revenue, MR, equals its marginal cost, MC. (b) If American believes that United will fly $q_U = 64$ units per quarter, its residual demand curve, D^r, is the market demand curve, D, minus q_U. American maximizes its profit at $q_A = 64$, where its marginal revenue, MR^r, equals MC.

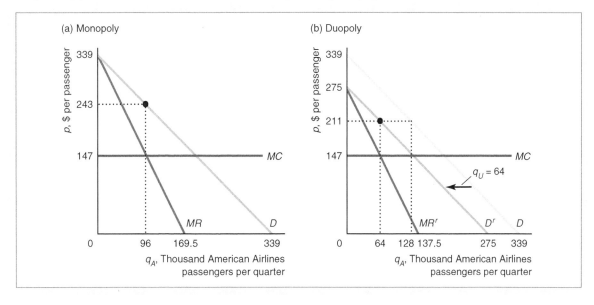

be the market demand curve, D in panel a. To maximize its profit, American would set its output so that its marginal revenue curve, MR, intersected its marginal cost curve, MC, which is constant at $147 per passenger. Panel a shows that the monopoly output is 96 units (thousands of passengers) per quarter and that the monopoly price is $243 per passenger (one way).

But because American competes with United, American must consider United's behavior when choosing its profit-maximizing output. American's demand is not the entire market demand. Rather, American is concerned with its residual demand curve. In general, if the market demand function is $D(p)$, and the supply of other firms is $S^o(p)$, then the residual demand function, $D^r(p)$, is

$$D^r(p) = D(p) - S^o(p).$$

Thus, if United flies q_U passengers regardless of the price, American transports only the residual demand, $Q = D(p) = 339 - p$ (Equation 14.1), minus the q_U passengers, so $q_A = Q - q_U$. The residual demand that American faces is

$$q_A = Q(p) - q_U = (339 - p) - q_U. \tag{14.2}$$

In panel b, American believes that United will fly $q_U = 64$, so American's residual demand curve, D^r, is the market demand curve, D, moved to the left by $q_U = 64$. For example, if the price is $211, the total number of passengers who want to fly is $Q = 128$. If United transports $q_U = 64$, American flies $Q - q_U = 128 - 64 = 64 = q_A$.

What is American's best-response, profit-maximizing output if its managers believe that United will fly q_U passengers? *American can think of itself as having a monopoly with respect to the people who don't fly on United.* That is, American can think of itself as having a monopoly with respect to its residual demand curve, D^r. We will use our analysis based on the residual demand curve to derive American's *best-response function*, $q_A = B_A(q_U)$, which shows American's best-response or profit-maximizing output, q_A, as a function of United's output, q_U.[11]

To maximize its profit, American sets its output so that its marginal revenue corresponding to this residual demand, MR^r, equals its marginal cost. Thus, our first step is to determine American's marginal revenue. Rearranging the terms in Equation 14.2 shows that American's residual inverse demand function is

$$p = 339 - q_A - q_U. \tag{14.3}$$

Consequently, its revenue function based on its residual demand function is

$$R^r(q_A) = pq_A = (339 - q_A - q_U)q_A = 339q_A - (q_A)^2 - q_U q_A.$$

American views its revenue as a function solely of its own output, $R^r(q_A)$, because American treats United's quantity as a constant. Thus, American's marginal revenue with respect to its residual demand function is

$$MR^r = \frac{dR^r(q_A)}{dq_A} = 339 - 2q_A - q_U. \tag{14.4}$$

Equating its marginal revenue with its marginal cost, $147, American derives its best-response function, $MR^r = 339 - 2q_A - q_U = 147 = MC$, or

$$q_A = 96 - \frac{1}{2}q_U = B_A(q_U). \tag{14.5}$$

---

[11]*Jargon alert*: Many economists refer to the best-response function as the reaction function.

Figure 14.3 plots American Airlines' best-response function, Equation 14.5, which shows how many tickets American sells for each possible q_U. As the best-response curve shows, American sells the monopoly number of tickets, 96, if American thinks United will fly no passengers, $q_U = 0$. The negative slope of the best-response curve shows that American sells fewer tickets the more people American thinks that United will fly. American sells $q_A = 64$ if it thinks q_U will be 64. American shuts down, $q_A = 0$, if it thinks q_U will be 192 or more, because operating wouldn't be profitable.

We can derive United's best-response function, $q_U = B_U(q_A)$, similarly. Given that the two firms have identical marginal costs and face the same market demand function, United's best-response function is the same as American's with the quantity subscripts reversed:

$$q_U = 96 - \frac{1}{2}q_A = B_U(q_A). \tag{14.6}$$

We obtain the Nash-Cournot equilibrium quantities by solving Equations 14.5 and 14.6 simultaneously for q_A and q_U.[12] This solution is the point where the firms' best-response curves intersect at $q_A = q_U = 64$. In a Nash-Cournot equilibrium, neither firm wants to change its output level given that the other firm is producing the equilibrium quantity. If American expects United to sell $q_U = 64$, American wants to sell $q_A = 64$. Because this point is on its best-response curve, American doesn't want to change its output from 64. Similarly, if United expects American to sell $q_A = 64$, United doesn't want to change q_U from 64. Thus, this pair of outputs is a Nash equilibrium: Given its correct belief about its rival's output, each firm is maximizing its profit, and neither firm wants to change its output.

Figure 14.3 **American's and United's Best-Response Curves**

The best-response curves show the output that each firm picks to maximize its profit, given its belief about its rival's output. The Cournot equilibrium occurs at the intersection of the best-response curves.

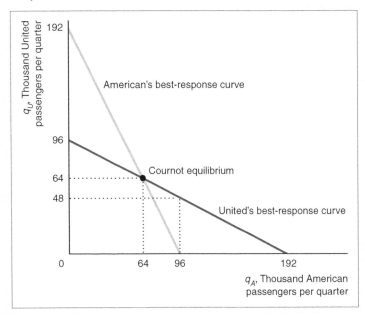

---

[12]For example, we can substitute for q_U in Equation 14.5 using Equation 14.6 to obtain an equation in only q_A. Then we can substitute that value of q_A in Equation 14.6 to obtain q_U. Alternatively, because the firms are identical, $q_A = q_U = q$, so we can replace both q_A and q_U with q in either best-response function and solve for q.

Any pair of quantities other than the pair at an intersection of the best-response functions is *not* a Nash-Cournot equilibrium. If either firm is not on its best-response curve, it wants to change its output to increase its profit. For example, the output pair $q_A = 96$ and $q_U = 0$ is not a Nash-Cournot equilibrium. American is perfectly happy producing the monopoly output if United doesn't operate at all: American is on its best-response curve. United, however, would not be happy with this outcome because it is not on United's best-response curve. As its best-response curve shows, if it knows that American will sell $q_A = 96$, United maximizes its profit by selling $q_U = 48$. Only if $q_A = q_U = 64$ does neither firm want to change its action. Based on statistical tests, Brander and Zhang (1990) reported that they could not reject the hypothesis that the Cournot model is consistent with American's and United's behavior.[13]

The Cournot Equilibrium with Two or More Firms

We've seen that the price to consumers is lower if two firms set output independently than if there is one firm or the firms collude. The price to consumers is even lower if there are more than two firms acting independently in the market. We now examine how the Nash-Cournot equilibrium varies with the number of firms. First, we solve the problem for general demand and marginal cost functions for n firms. Then, we solve using a linear inverse demand function and a constant marginal cost and apply that analysis to our airline example.

General Case. If output is homogeneous, the market inverse demand function is $p(Q)$, where Q, the total market output, is the sum of the output of each of the n firms: $Q = q_1 + q_2 + \cdots + q_n$. Each of the n identical firms has the same cost function, $C(q_i)$. To analyze a Cournot market of identical firms, we first examine the behavior of a representative firm. Firm 1 wants to maximize its profit through its choice of q_1:

$$\max_{q_1} \pi_1(q_1, q_2, \ldots, q_n) = q_1 p(q_1 + q_2 + \cdots + q_n) - C(q_1) = q_1 p(Q) - C(q_1). \quad (14.7)$$

Firm 1 views the outputs of the other firms as fixed, so $q_2, q_3, \ldots, q_n$ are constants. Firm 1's first-order condition is the partial derivative of its profit with respect to q_1 set equal to zero:[14]

$$\frac{\partial \pi}{\partial q_1} = p(Q) + q_1 \frac{dp(Q)}{dQ} \frac{\partial Q}{\partial q_1} - \frac{dC(q_1)}{dq_1} = 0. \quad (14.8)$$

Given that the other firms' outputs are constants, $dQ/dq_1 = d(q_1 + q_2 + \cdots + q_n)/dq_1 = dq_1/dq_1 = 1$. Making this substitution and rearranging terms, we see that the firm's first-order condition implies that Firm 1 equates is marginal revenue and its marginal cost:

$$MR = p(Q) + q_1 \frac{dp(Q)}{dQ} = \frac{dC(q_1)}{dq_1} = MC. \quad (14.9)$$

---

[13]Because the model described here is a simplified version of the Brander and Zhang (1990) model, the predicted output levels, $q_A = q_U = 64$, differ slightly from theirs. Nonetheless, our predictions are very close to the actual observed outcome, $q_A = 65.9$ and $q_U = 62.7$.

[14]We use a partial derivative to show that we are changing only q_1 and not the other outputs, $q_2, \ldots, q_n$. However, given that Firm 1 views those other outputs as constants so that the only variable in its profit function is q_1, we could use a derivative instead of a partial derivative.

Equation 14.9 gives the firm's best-response function, allowing the firm to calculate its optimal q_1 for any given set of outputs of other firms. We can write Firm 1's best-response function as an implicit function of the other firm's output levels: $p(q_1 + q_2 + \cdots + q_n) + q_1(dp/dQ) - dC(q_1)/dq_1 = 0$. Thus, for any given set of $q_2,\ldots, q_n$, the firm can solve for the profit-maximizing q_1 using this expression.

Solving the best-response functions for all the firms simultaneously, we obtain the Nash-Cournot equilibrium quantities $q_1, q_2,\ldots, q_n$. Because all the firms are identical, in equilibrium $q_1 = q_2 = \ldots = q_n = q$.

The marginal revenue expression can be rewritten as $p[1 + (q/p)(dp/dQ)]$. Multiplying and dividing the last term by n, noting that $Q = nq$ (given that all firms are identical), and observing that the market elasticity of demand, ε, is defined as $(dQ/dp)(p/Q)$, we can rewrite the first-order conditions, such as Equation 14.9, as

$$MR = p\left(1 + \frac{1}{n\varepsilon}\right) = \frac{dC(q)}{dq} = MC. \tag{14.10}$$

In Equation 14.10, the firm's marginal revenue is expressed in terms of the elasticity of demand of its residual demand curve, $n\varepsilon$, which is the number of firms, n, times the market demand elasticity, ε. For example, if $n = 2$, the elasticity of demand of either firm's residual demand curve is twice as elastic as the market demand curve at the equilibrium.

We can rearrange Equation 14.10 to determine the Nash-Cournot equilibrium price:

$$p = \frac{MC}{\left(1 + \dfrac{1}{n\varepsilon}\right)}. \tag{14.11}$$

That is, the Nash-Cournot equilibrium price is above the MC by $1/(1 + [n\varepsilon]) > 1$.[15] Holding ε constant, the more firms there are, the more elastic is the residual demand curve, which causes the price to fall. For example, if the market elasticity ε is constant at -1, then $p = MC/(1 - \frac{1}{2}) = 2MC$ if $n = 2$, $p = MC/(1 - \frac{1}{3}) = 1.5MC$ if $n = 3$, and $p = MC/(1 - \frac{1}{4}) \approx 1.33MC$ if $n = 4$. As n grows without bound, the price approaches MC.

By further rearranging Equation 14.11, we obtain an expression for the Lerner Index, $(p - MC)/p$, in terms of the market demand elasticity and the number of firms:

$$\frac{p - MC}{p} = -\frac{1}{n\varepsilon}. \tag{14.12}$$

The larger the Lerner Index, the greater the firm's market power. As Equation 14.12 shows, if we hold the market elasticity constant and increase the number of firms, the Lerner Index falls. As n approaches ∞, the elasticity facing any one firm approaches $-\infty$, so the Lerner Index approaches 0 and the market is competitive.

We can use what we have just learned to examine the incidence of a tax on consumers—the change in the consumers' price divided by the change in the tax (Chapter 2)—in an oligopolistic market. We already know that the incidence of a tax on consumers does not exceed 100% in a competitive market (Chapter 2), but can exceed 100% in a monopoly market (Chapter 11). The next Solved Problem shows that the incidence can exceed 100% in an oligopolistic market.

---

[15]From the Law of Demand, we know that $\varepsilon < 0$, so $1/[n\varepsilon] < 0$. Given that each firm is operating in the elastic portion of its residual demand curve (using the same argument as we did in Chapter 11 to show that a monopoly would not operate in the inelastic portions of its demand curve), $n\varepsilon < -1$, so $1 > -1/[n\varepsilon]$. Thus, $1/(1 + [n\varepsilon]) > 1$.

SOLVED PROBLEM 14.1

A market has n quantity-setting oligopolistic firms that produce a homogenous product and face a constant-elasticity market demand curve (Chapter 2) with an elasticity of ε. Each firm must pay a specific tax τ per unit and has a before-tax constant marginal cost of m, so its after-tax marginal cost is $m + \tau$. How much does the consumer price increase if the government increases the specific tax? Does the incidence of the tax on consumers exceed 100%?

Answer

1. *Solve for the after-tax Nash-Cournot equilibrium price.* By using Equation 14.11, we know that the after-tax Nash-Cournot equilibrium price is $p = (m + \tau)/(1 + 1/[n\varepsilon])$, where $m + \tau$ is the after-tax marginal cost and $n\varepsilon$ is the elasticity of the residual demand curve facing each firm.

2. *Differentiate the equilibrium price function to show how the price changes as τ increases.* By differentiating the Nash-Cournot equilibrium price equation with respect to τ, we learn that an increase in the specific tax changes the consumer price by $dp/d\tau = d[(m + \tau)/(1 + 1/[n\varepsilon])]/d\tau = 1/(1 + 1/[n\varepsilon])$.

3. *Show that the incidence of the tax exceeds 100%.* We know that the incidence of the tax on consumers is $dp/d\tau = 1/(1 + 1/[n\varepsilon])$, which exceeds $1 = 100\%$ by the discussion following Equation 14.11.

APPLICATION

Incidence of a Cigarette Tax

Solved Problem 14.1 shows that a specific tax on an oligopolistic market could have a consumer incidence greater than 100%. However, that result is based on a Cournot model with a particular demand and cost structure and does not hold for all oligopolistic markets.[16] Is the tax incidence greater than 100% in actual oligopolistic markets?

The U.S. cigarette market is oligopolistic, with the three largest cigarette firms controlling 90% of the market. In 2008, Wisconsin increased its specific tax on cigarettes by $1 per pack. Hanson and Sullivan (2009) estimate that the tax raised the price that consumers paid by between $1.08 and $1.17 per pack. That is, the incidence of the tax on consumers in this oligopolistic market exceeded 100% of the tax.

Delipalla and O'Donnell (2001) found that specific cigarette tax incidences on consumers exceeded 100% in France, but not in the other European countries with a state-owned producer of cigarettes (Italy, Portugal, and Spain). They estimated that consumer incidences exceeded 100% in Greece, Ireland, Luxembourg, and the United Kingdom, but not in other European countries with oligopolistic cigarette markets (Denmark, Germany, Ireland, and the Netherlands).

Linear Case. We cannot explicitly solve for a firm's best-response function or the Nash-Cournot equilibrium given general functional forms, but we can for specific particular functions, as we now show for the linear case. Suppose that the inverse market demand function is linear,

$$p = a - bQ,$$

and that each firm's marginal cost is m, a constant, and it has no fixed cost.

---

[16] Problem 24 asks you to show that the consumer incidence is less than 100% if the market demand curve is linear.

For this linear model, we can rewrite Firm 1's objective, Equation 14.7, as

$$\max_{q_1} \pi_1(q_1) = q_1[a - b(q_1 + q_2 + \cdots + q_n)] - mq_1. \quad (14.13)$$

Firm 1's first-order condition, Equation 14.9, to maximize its profit is

$$MR = a - b(2q_1 + q_2 + \cdots + q_n) = m = MC. \quad (14.14)$$

Because all firms have the same cost function, $q_2 = q_3 = \ldots = q_n \equiv q$ in equilibrium. Substituting these equalities into Equation 14.14, we find that the first firm's best-response function, B_1, is

$$q_1 = B_1(q_2, q_3, \ldots, q_n) = \frac{a - m}{2b} - \frac{n-1}{2}q. \quad (14.15)$$

The right-hand sides of the other firms' best-response functions are identical.

All these best-response functions must hold simultaneously. The intersection of the best-response functions determines the Nash-Cournot equilibrium. Given that all the firms are identical, all choose the same output level in equilibrium. Thus, we can solve for the equilibrium by setting $q_1 = q$ in Equation 14.15 and rearranging terms to obtain

$$q = \frac{a-m}{(n+1)b}. \quad (14.16)$$

Total market output, $Q = nq$, equals $n(a-m)/[(n+1)b]$. The corresponding price is obtained by substituting this expression for market output into the demand function:

$$p = \frac{a + nm}{n+1}. \quad (14.17)$$

Setting $n = 1$ in Equations 14.16 and 14.17 yields the monopoly quantity and price. As n becomes large, each firm's quantity approaches zero, total output approaches $(a - m)/b$, and price approaches m, which are the competitive levels.[17] The Lerner Index is

$$\frac{p - MC}{p} = \frac{a - m}{a + nm}. \quad (14.18)$$

As n grows large, the denominator in Equation 14.18 goes to infinity (∞), so the Lerner Index goes to 0 and there is no market power.

Airline Example. We can illustrate these results using our airline example, where $a = 339$, $b = 1$, $m = 147$, and $n = 2$. Suppose that additional airlines with an identical marginal cost of $m = \$147$ were to fly between Chicago and Los Angeles. Table 14.2 shows how the Cournot equilibrium price and the Lerner Index vary with the number of firms. Using the equations for the general linear model, we know that each firm's Nash-Cournot equilibrium quantity is $q = (339 - 147)/(n + 1) = 192/(n + 1)$ and the Nash-Cournot equilibrium price is $p = (339 + 147n)/(n + 1)$.

As we already know, if there were only one firm, it would produce the monopoly quantity, 96, at the monopoly price, $243. We also know that each duopoly firm's output is 64, so market output is 128 and price is $211. The duopoly market elasticity is $\varepsilon = -1.65$, so the residual demand elasticity that each duopoly firm faces is twice as large as the market elasticity, $2\varepsilon = -3.3$.

---

[17] As the number of firms goes to infinity, the Nash-Cournot equilibrium goes to perfect competition only if average cost is nondecreasing (Ruffin, 1971).

Table 14.2 Cournot Equilibrium Varies with the Number of Firms

Number of Firms, n	Firm Output, q	Market Output, Q	Price, p	Market Elasticity, ε	Residual Demand Elasticity, $n\varepsilon$	Lerner Index, $(p-m)/p = -1/(n\varepsilon)$
1	96	96	243	−2.53	−2.53	0.40
2	64	128	211	−1.65	−3.30	0.30
3	48	144	195	−1.35	−4.06	0.25
4	38.4	154	185.40	−1.21	−4.83	0.21
5	32	160	179	−1.12	−5.59	0.18
10	17.5	175	164.45	−0.94	−9.42	0.11
50	3.8	188	150.76	−0.80	−40.05	0.02
100	1.9	190	148.90	−0.78	−78.33	0.01
200	1.0	191	147.96	−0.77	−154.89	0.01

As the number of firms increases, each firm's output falls toward zero, but total output approaches 192, the quantity on the market demand curve where price equals the marginal cost of $147. Although the market elasticity of demand falls as the number of firms grows, the residual demand curve for each firm becomes increasingly horizontal (perfectly elastic). As a result, the price approaches the marginal cost, $147. Similarly, as the number of firms increases, the Lerner Index approaches the price-taking level of zero.

The table shows that having extra firms in the market benefits consumers. When the number of firms rises from 1 to 4, the price falls by a quarter and the Lerner Index is cut nearly in half. At 10 firms, the price is one-third less than the monopoly level, and the Lerner Index is a quarter of the monopoly level.

The Cournot Model with Nonidentical Firms

For simplicity, we initially assumed that the firms were essentially identical: All firms had identical costs and produced identical products. However, costs often vary across firms, and firms often differentiate the products they produce from those of their rivals.

Unequal Costs. In the Cournot model, the firm sets its output so as to equate its marginal revenue to its marginal cost, as specified by its first-order condition. If firms' marginal costs vary, then so will the firms' first-order conditions and hence their best-response functions. In the resulting Nash-Cournot equilibrium, the relatively low-cost firm produces more, as Solved Problem 14.2 illustrates. However, as long as the products are not differentiated, the firms charge the same price.

SOLVED PROBLEM 14.2

If the inverse market demand function facing a duopoly is $p = a - bQ$, what are the Nash-Cournot equilibrium quantities if the marginal cost of Firm 1 is m and that of Firm 2 is $m + x$, where $x > 0$? Which firm produces more and which has the higher profit?

Answer

1. *Determine each firm's best-response function.* Firm 1's profit is the same as in Equation 14.13 where $n = 2$: $\pi_1 = [a - b(q_1 + q_2)]q_1 - mq_1$. Consequently, its best-response function is the same as Equation 14.15,

$$q_1 = \frac{a - m - bq_2}{2b}. \tag{14.19}$$

Firm 2's profit is the same as in Equation 14.13 except that m is replaced by $m + x$. That is, $\pi_2 = q_2[a - b(q_1 + q_2)] - (m + x)q_2$. Setting the derivative of Firm 2's profit with respect to q_2 (holding q_1 fixed) equal to zero, and rearranging terms, we find that the first-order condition for Firm 1 to maximize its profit is $MR_2 = a - b(2q_2 + q_1) = m + x = MC_2$. Rearranging this expression shows that Firm 2's best-response function is

$$q_2 = \frac{a - (m + x) - bq_1}{2b}. \tag{14.20}$$

2. *Use the best-response functions to solve for the Nash-Cournot equilibrium.* To determine the equilibrium, we solve Equations 14.19 and 14.20 simultaneously for q_1 and q_2:[18]

$$q_1 = \frac{a - m + x}{3b}, \tag{14.21}$$

$$q_2 = \frac{a - m - 2x}{3b}. \tag{14.22}$$

3. *Use the Nash-Cournot equilibrium quantity equations to determine which firm produces more.* By inspection, $q_1 = [a - m + x]/[3b] > q_2 = [a - m - 2x]/[3b]$. As x increases, q_1 increases by $dq_1/dx = 1/[3b]$ and q_2 falls by $dq_2/dx = -2/[3b]$.

4. *Substitute the Nash-Cournot equilibrium quantity equations into the profit functions to determine which firm has a higher profit.* The low-cost firm has the higher profit. Using Equations 14.21 and 14.22, $q_1 + q_2 = (2a - 2m - x)/(3b)$. Substituting this expression and the expression for q_1 from Equation 14.21 into the profit function for Firm 1, we find that

$$\pi_1 = [a - m - b(q_1 + q_2)]q_1 = [a - m - (2a - 2m - x)/3](a - m + x)/(3b)$$
$$= (a - m + x)^2/[9b]$$

and, by similar reasoning, $\pi_2 = (a - m - 2x)^2/[9b]$. Thus,

$$\pi_1 = \frac{(a - m + x)^2}{9b} > \frac{(a - m - 2x)^2}{9b} = \pi_2.$$

---

[18] By substituting the expression for q_1 from Equation 14.19 into Equation 14.20, we obtain

$$q_2 = \left[a - m - x - b\left(\frac{a - m - bq_2}{2b}\right)\right]/(2b).$$

Solving for q_2, we derive Equation 14.22. Substituting that expression into Equation 14.19 and simplifying, we get Equation 14.21.

APPLICATION

Air Ticket Prices and Rivalry

Because costs vary across competing airlines and consumers often prefer one airline to another, airlines have unequal market shares. The markup of price over marginal cost is much greater on routes in which one airline carries most of the passengers than it is on other routes. Unfortunately for consumers, a single firm is the only carrier or the dominant carrier on 58% of all U.S. domestic routes (Weiher et al., 2002).

The first column of the table identifies the market structure for U.S. air routes. The last column shows the share of routes. A single firm (monopoly) serves 18% of all routes. Duopolies control 19% of the routes, three-firm markets are 16%, four-firm markets are 13%, and five or more firms fly on 35% of the routes.

Although nearly two-thirds of all routes have three or more carriers, one or two firms dominate virtually all routes. We call a carrier a *dominant firm* if it has at least 60% of ticket sales by value but is not a monopoly. We call two carriers a *dominant pair* if they collectively have at least 60% of the market but neither firm is a dominant firm and three or more firms fly this route. All but 0.1% of routes have a monopoly (18%), a dominant firm (40%), or a dominant pair (42%).

The first row of the table shows that the price is slightly more than double (2.1 times) marginal cost on average across all U.S. routes and market structures. (This average price includes "free" frequent-flier tickets and other below-cost tickets.) The price is 3.3 times marginal cost for monopolies and 3.1 times marginal cost for dominant firms. In contrast, over the sample period, the average price is only 1.2 times marginal cost for dominant pairs.

The markup of price over marginal cost depends much more on whether there is a dominant firm or dominant pair than on the total number of firms in the market. If there is a dominant pair, whether there are four or five firms, the price is between 1.3 times marginal cost for a four-firm route and 1.4 times marginal cost for a route with five or more firms. If there is a dominant firm, price is 2.3 times marginal cost on duopoly routes, 1.9 times on three-firm routes, 2.2 times on four-firm routes, and 3.5 times on routes with five or more firms.

Type of Market	Lerner Index, $(p - MC)/p$	Share of All Routes (%)
All market types	0.52	100
Dominant firm	0.68	40
Dominant pair	0.17	42
One firm (monopoly)	0.70	18
Two firms (duopoly)	0.55	19
Dominant firm	0.57	14
No dominant firm	0.33	5
Three firms	0.44	16
Dominant firm	0.47	9
No dominant firm	0.23	7
Four firms	0.44	13
Dominant firm	0.55	6
Dominant pair	0.23	7
No dominant firm or pair	0.52	~0
Five or more firms	0.23	35
Dominant firm	0.71	11
Dominant pair	0.29	23
No dominant firm or pair	0.09	0.1

14.4 Cournot Oligopoly Model

Thus, preventing a single firm from dominating a route may substantially lower prices. Even if two firms dominate the market, the markup of price over marginal cost is substantially lower than if a single firm dominates.

Differentiated Products Firms differentiate their products to increase their profits. A firm can charge a higher price if differentiation causes its residual demand curve to become less elastic. Whether the differentiation is related to a nonslip handle or a sneaker pump, if a firm can convince some customers that its branded product is superior, it can charge a higher price than it could if it sold plain or generic products.

For example, after Heinz introduced funny-color ketchup—Blastin' Green, Funky Purple, and Stellar Blue—its share of all ketchup rose substantially, from 50% in 1999 to more than 60% by 2005. (Contrary to my wife's views, my purchases did not contribute significantly to this increase.) However, its Kool Blue French fries were less successful.[19]

When Similac Organic infant formula was introduced, many parents switched from regular formula to what they believed was the healthier organic version, even though organic Similac sells for 30% more than regular Similac. (Babies may prefer the organic product because it is substantially sweeter than other formulas because of the added cane sugar. However, the EU banned such sweeteners in baby formula as of 2010.)

Even if the products are physically identical, if consumers think products differ, the Nash-Cournot quantities and prices will differ across firms. Each firm faces a different inverse demand function and hence charges a different price. For example, suppose that Firm 1's inverse demand function is $p_1 = a - b_1 q_1 - b_2 q_2$, where $b_1 > b_2$ if consumers believe that Good 1 is different from Good 2, and $b_1 = b_2 = b$ if the goods are identical. Given that consumers view the products as differentiated and Firm 2 faces a similar inverse demand function, we replace the single market demand with these individual demand functions in the Cournot model. The following solved problem shows how to solve for the Nash-Cournot equilibrium in an actual market.

SOLVED PROBLEM 14.3

Intel and Advanced Micro Devices (AMD) are the only firms that produce central processing units (CPUs), which are the brains of personal computers. Both because the products differ physically and because Intel's "Intel Inside" advertising campaign has convinced some consumers of its superiority, customers view the CPUs as imperfect substitutes. Consequently, the two firms' inverse demand functions differ:

$$p_A = 197 - 15.1 q_A - 0.3 q_I, \tag{14.23}$$

$$p_I = 490 - 10 q_I - 6 q_A, \tag{14.24}$$

---

[19]The Cow Protection Department of the Rashtriya Swayamsevak Sangh (RSS), India's largest and oldest Hindu nationalist group announced that it was introducing a new, highly differentiated soft drink called gau jal, or "cow water," made from cow urine—a truly differentiated product. (Page, Jeremy, "India to Launch Cow Urine as Soft Drink," *Times Online*, February 11, 2009, www.timesonline.co.uk/tol/life_and_style/food_and_drink/article5707554.ece).

where price is dollars per CPU, quantity is in millions of CPUs, the subscript I indicates Intel, and the subscript A represents AMD.[20] Each firm faces a constant marginal cost of $m = \$40$ per unit. (We can ignore the firms' fixed costs because we know that the firms operate and the fixed costs do not affect the marginal costs.) Solve for the Nash-Cournot equilibrium quantities and prices.

Answer

1. *Determine each firm's best-response function.* Substituting the inverse demand equations 14.23 and 14.24 into the definition of profit, we learn that the firms' profit functions are

$$\pi_A = (p_A - m)q_A = (157 - 15.1q_A - 0.3q_I)q_A, \quad (14.25)$$

$$\pi_I = (p_I - m)q_I = (450 - 10q_I - 6q_A)q_I. \quad (14.26)$$

The first-order conditions are $\partial \pi_A / \partial q_A = 157 - 30.2q_A - 0.3q_I$ and $\partial \pi_I / \partial q_I = 450 - 20q_I - 6q_A$. Rearranging these expressions, we obtain the best-response functions:

$$q_A = \frac{157 - 0.3q_I}{30.2}, \quad (14.27)$$

$$q_I = \frac{450 - 6q_A}{20}. \quad (14.28)$$

2. *Use the best-response functions to solve for the Nash-Cournot equilibrium.* Solving the system of best-response functions 14.27 and 14.28, we find that the Nash-Cournot equilibrium quantities are $q_A = 15{,}025/3{,}011 \approx 5$ million CPUs, and $q_I = 63{,}240/3{,}011 \approx 21$ million CPUs. Substituting these values into the inverse demand functions, we obtain the corresponding prices: $p_A = \$115.20$ and $p_I = \$250$ per CPU.

APPLICATION

Bottled Water

Bottled water is the most dramatic recent example of *spurious product differentiation*, where the products do not significantly differ physically. Firms convince consumers that their products differ through marketing.

According to a poll of U.S. consumers' top environmental fears reported in *The World's Water 2008–2009*, the single greatest fear, held by 53% of respondents, was that our drinking water isn't safe. Perhaps that helps to explain why the typical American consumed more than 25 gallons of bottled water in 2008. If safety is their reason to buy bottled water, these consumers are being foolish. Not only does the U.S. Environmental Protection Agency set a stricter standard for tap water than the standard set by the Federal Drug Administration on bottled water, but a quarter of all bottled water is tap water according to the Natural Resources Defense Council.

PepsiCo's top-selling bottled water, Aquafina, has a colorful blue label and a logo showing the sun rising over the mountains. From that logo, consumers may guess that the water comes from some bubbling spring high in an unspoiled wilderness. If so, they're wrong. Pepsi finally admitted that its best-selling bottled water comes from

---

[20] I thank Hugo Salgado for estimating these inverse demand functions and providing evidence that this market is well described by a Nash-Cournot equilibrium.

the same place as tap water: public-water sources. However, Pepsi insists that it filters the water using a state-of-the-art "HydRO-7 purification system," implying that such filtering (which removes natural minerals) is desirable. Coca-Cola has also admitted that its Dasani bottled water comes from public water sources.

14.5 Stackelberg Oligopoly Model

In the Cournot model, both firms announce their output decisions simultaneously. In contrast, suppose that one of the firms, called the *leader*, can set its output before its rival, the *follower*, does. This type of situation where one firm acts before the other arises naturally if one firm enters a market before the other.

Would the firm that acts first have an advantage? The German economist Heinrich von Stackelberg showed how to modify the Cournot model to answer this question.

Unlike in the Cournot model where both firms choose output at the same time, the Stackelberg leader, Firm 1, sets its output before the follower, Firm 2, chooses a quantity. How does the leader decide to set its output? We examined this question in Chapter 13 in the airline example where the firms could choose among only three possible output levels. Here, we consider the more general problem where the firms are free to choose any output level they want.

The leader realizes that once it sets its output, the rival firm will use its Cournot best-response curve to select a best-response output. Thus, the leader predicts what the follower will do before the follower acts. Using this knowledge, the leader chooses its output level to "manipulate" the follower, thereby benefiting at the follower's expense.

Calculus Solution

We start by deriving the Stackelberg equilibrium for a general, linear model, and then we apply that analysis to the airlines example. We can use calculus to derive the Stackelberg equilibrium for a general linear inverse demand function, $p = a - bQ$, where two firms have identical marginal costs, m. Because Firm 1, the Stackelberg leader, chooses its output first, it knows that Firm 2, the follower, will choose its output using its best-response function. Setting the number of firms $n = 2$ in Equation 14.15, we know that Firm 2's best-response function, B_2, is

$$q_2 = B_2(q_1) = \frac{a-m}{2b} - \frac{1}{2}q_1. \tag{14.29}$$

The market price depends on the output of both firms, $p(q_1 + q_2)$. Consequently, the Stackelberg leader's profit is a function of its own and the follower's output: $\pi_1(q_1 + q_2) = p(q_1 + q_2)q_1 - mq_1$. By replacing the follower's output with the follower's best-response function so that the leader's profit depends only on its own output, we can write the leader's profit function as

$$\begin{aligned}\pi_1(q_1 + B_2(q_1)) &= \left[p(q_1 + B_2(q_1)) - m\right]q_1 \\ &= \left[a - b(q_1 + B_2(q_1)) - m\right]q_1 \\ &= \left[a - b\left(q_1 + \frac{a-m}{2b} - \frac{1}{2}q_1\right) - m\right]q_1,\end{aligned} \tag{14.30}$$

where we have used Equation 14.29 to obtain the last line.

The Stackelberg leader's objective is to choose q_1 so as to maximize its profit in Equation 14.30. The leader's first-order condition is derived by setting the derivative of its profit with respect to q_1 equal to zero: $a - 2bq_1 - (a - m)/2 + bq_1 - m = 0$. Solving this expression for q_1, we find that the profit-maximizing output of the leader is

$$q_1 = \frac{a-m}{2b}. \tag{14.31}$$

Substituting the expression for q_1 in Equation 14.31 into the follower's best-response function 14.29 gives the equilibrium output of the follower:

$$q_2 = \frac{a-m}{4b}.$$

Thus, with a linear demand curve and constant marginal cost, the leader produces twice as much as the follower.[21]

We can use this analysis to ask what would happen in our airline example if American Airlines can act before United Airlines, so that American is a Stackelberg leader and United is a Stackelberg follower. Replacing the parameters in our linear analysis with the specific values for the airlines, $a = 339$, $b = 1$, $m = 147$, and $n = 2$, we find that American's output is $q_1 = (339 - 147)/2 = 96$, and United's output is $q_2 = (339 - 147)/4 = 48$.

Graphical Solution

We can illustrate this airline analysis with graphs. American, the Stackelberg leader, uses its residual demand curve to determine its profit-maximizing output. American knows that when it sets q_A, United will use its Cournot best-response function to pick its best-response q_U. Thus, American believes it faces a residual demand curve, D^r (panel a of Figure 14.4), that is the market demand curve, D (panel a), minus the output United will produce as summarized by United's best-response curve (panel b). For example, if American sets $q_A = 192$, United's best response is $q_U = 0$ (as United's best-response curve in panel b shows). As a result, the residual demand curve and the market demand curve are identical at $q_A = 192$ (panel a).

Similarly, if American set $q_A = 0$, United would choose $q_U = 96$, so the residual demand at $q_A = 0$ is 96 less than demand. The residual demand curve hits the vertical axis, where $q_A = 0$, at $p = \$243$, which is 96 units to the left of demand at that price. When $q_A = 96$, $q_U = 48$, so the residual demand at $q_A = 96$ is 48 units to the left of the demand.

American chooses its profit-maximizing output, $q_A = 96$, where its marginal revenue curve that corresponds to the residual demand curve, MR^r, equals its marginal cost, \$147. At $q_A = 96$, the price, which is the height of the residual demand curve, is \$195. Total demand at \$195 is $Q = 144$. At that price, United produces $q_U = Q - q_A = 48$, its best response to American's output of $q_A = 96$. Thus, as Figure 14.4 shows, the Stackelberg leader produces twice as much as the follower.

Why Moving Sequentially Is Essential

Why don't we get the Stackelberg equilibrium when both firms move simultaneously? Why doesn't American announce that it will produce the Stackelberg leader's

---

[21]Here, the leader produces the same quantity as a monopoly would, and the follower produces the same quantity as it would in the cartel equilibrium. These relationships are due to the linear demand curve and the constant marginal cost—they do not hold more generally.

output to induce United to produce the Stackelberg follower's output level? The answer is that when the firms move simultaneously, United doesn't view American's warning that it will produce a large quantity as a *credible threat*.

Figure 14.4 Stackelberg Equilibrium

(a) The residual demand that the Stackelberg leader faces is the market demand minus the quantity produced by the follower, q_U, given the leader's quantity, q_A. The leader chooses $q_A = 96$ so that its marginal revenue, MR^r, equals its marginal cost. The total output, $Q = 144$, is the sum of the output of the two firms. (b) The quantity that the follower produces is its best response to the leader's output, as given by its Cournot best-response curve.

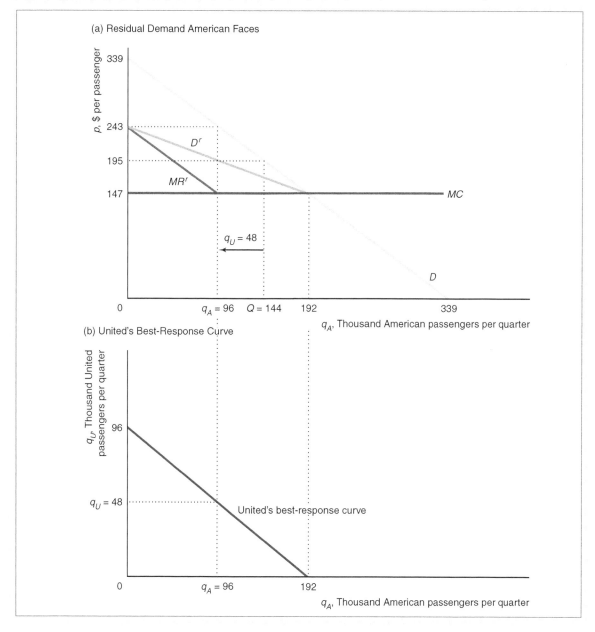

If United believed that threat, it would indeed produce the Stackelberg follower's output level. But United doesn't believe the threat because it is not in American's best interest to produce that large a quantity of output. If American produced the leader's level of output and United produced the Cournot level, American's profit would be lower than if it too produced the Cournot level. Because American cannot be sure that United will believe its threat and reduce its output, American will produce the Cournot output level.

Indeed, each firm may make the same threat and announce that it wants to be the leader. Because neither firm can be sure that the other will be intimidated and produce the smaller quantity, both produce the Cournot output level. In contrast, when one firm moves first, its threat to produce a large quantity is credible because it has already *committed* to producing the larger quantity, thereby carrying out its threat.

Strategic Trade Policy: An Application of the Stackelberg Model

Suppose that two identical firms in two different countries compete in a world market. Both firms act simultaneously, so neither firm can make itself the Stackelberg leader. However, a government may intervene to make its firm a Stackelberg leader. For example, the Japanese and French governments often help their domestic firms compete with international rivals; occasionally, so do U.S., British, Canadian, and many other governments. If only one government intervenes, it can make its domestic firm's threat to produce a large quantity of output credible, causing foreign rivals to produce the Stackelberg follower's level of output (Spencer and Brander, 1983).

We have already conducted a similar analysis in Solved Problem 14.2, where we showed that a firm with a lower marginal cost would produce more than its higher cost rival in a Nash-Cournot equilibrium. Thus, a government can subsidize its domestic firm to make it a more fearsome rival to the unsubsidized firm.

Government Subsidy for an Airline. We now modify our airline example to illustrate how one country's government can aid its firm. Suppose that United Airlines were based in one country and American Airlines in another. Initially, United and American are in a Nash-Cournot equilibrium. Each firm has a marginal cost of $147 and flies 64 thousand passengers (64 units) per quarter at a price of $211.

Now suppose that United's government gives United a $48-per-passenger subsidy but the other government doesn't help American. As a result, American's marginal cost remains at $147, but United's marginal cost after the subsidy is only $99.

The firms continue to act as in the Cournot model, but the playing field is no longer level.[22] How does the Nash-Cournot equilibrium change? Your intuition probably tells you that United's output increases relative to that of American, as we now show.

United still acts at the same time as American does, so United behaves like any Cournot firm and determines its best-response curve. United's best response to any given American output is the output at which its marginal revenue corresponding to its residual demand, MR^r, equals its marginal cost. The subsidy does not affect United's MR^r curve, but it lowers its MC curve, so United produces more output for any given American output after the cost falls.

Panel a of Figure 14.5 illustrates this reasoning. United's residual demand, D^r, lies 64 units to the left of the market demand, D, if American produces 64. The MR^r

---

[22]Don't you think that anyone who uses the phrase "level playing field" should have to pay a fine?

Figure 14.5 Effect of a Government Subsidy on a Cournot Equilibrium

(a) A government subsidy that lowers United's marginal cost from $MC^1 = \$147$ to $MC^2 = \$99$ causes United's best-response output to American's $q_A = 64$ to rise from $q_U = 64$ to 88. (b) If both airlines' marginal costs are $147, the Cournot equilibrium is e_1. If United's marginal cost falls to $99, its best-response function shifts outward. It now sells more tickets in response to any given American output than previously. At the new Cournot equilibrium, e_2, United sells $q_U = 96$, while American sells only $q_A = 48$.

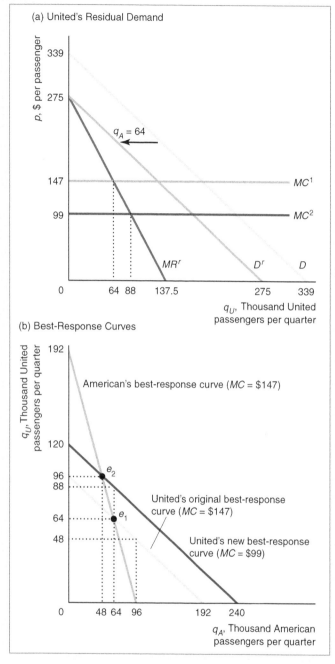

curve intersects the original marginal cost, $MC^1 = \$147$, at 64 and the new marginal cost, $MC^2 = \$99$, at 88. Thus if we hold American's output constant at 64, United produces more as its marginal cost falls.

Because this reasoning applies for any level of output American chooses, United's best-response curve in panel b shifts outward as its after-subsidy marginal cost falls.

United sets the marginal revenue that corresponds to its residual demand curve, MR_U, equal to its new, lower marginal cost, MC:

$$MR_U = 339 - 2q_U - q_A = 99 = MC.$$

Thus, United's best-response function is

$$q_U = 120 - \frac{1}{2}q_A.$$

This best-response function calls for United to provide more output for any given q_A than in the original best-response function, Equation 14.6, where $q_U = 96 - \frac{1}{2}q_A$.

As a result, the Nash-Cournot equilibrium shifts from the original e_1, at which both firms sold 64, to e_2, at which United sells 96 and American sells 48. Thus, the $48 subsidy to United causes it to sell the Stackelberg leader quantity and American to sell the Stackelberg follower quantity. The subsidy works by convincing American that United will produce large quantities of output.

Using the market demand curve, Equation 14.1, we find that the market price drops from $211 to $195, benefiting consumers. United's profit increases from $4.1 million to $9.2 million, while American's profit falls to $2.3 million. Consequently, United Airlines and consumers gain and American Airlines and taxpayers lose from the drop in United's marginal cost.

This example illustrates that a government subsidy to one firm *can* lead to the same outcome as in a Stackelberg equilibrium. Would a government *want* to give the subsidy that leads to the Stackelberg outcome?

The answer depends on the government's objective. Suppose that the government is interested in maximizing its domestic firm's profit net of (not including) the government's subsidy. The subsidy is a transfer from some citizens (taxpayers) to others (the owners of United). We assume that the government does not care about consumers—as is certainly true if they live in another country. Given this objective, the government maximizes its objective by setting the subsidy so as to achieve the Stackelberg equilibrium.

Table 14.3 shows the effects of various subsidies and a tax (a negative subsidy). If the subsidy is zero, we have the usual Cournot equilibrium. A $48-per-passenger subsidy leads to the same outcome as in the Stackelberg equilibrium and maximizes the government's welfare measure. At a larger subsidy, such as $60, United's profit rises, but by less than the cost of the subsidy to the government. Similarly, at smaller subsidies or taxes, welfare is also lower.

Table 14.3 Effects of a Subsidy Given to United Airlines

Subsidy, s	United			American	
	q_U	π_U	Welfare, $\pi_U - sq_U$	q_A	π_A
60	104	$10.8	$4.58	44	$1.9
48	96	$9.2	$4.61	48	$2.3
30	84	$7.1	$4.50	54	$2.9
0	64	$4.1	$4.10	64	$4.1
−30	44	$1.9	$3.30	74	$5.5

Notes: The subsidy is in dollars per passenger (and is a tax if negative). Output units are in thousands of passengers per quarter. Profits and welfare (defined as United's profits minus the subsidy) are in millions of dollars per quarter.

Problems with Government Intervention. Thus, in theory, a government may want to subsidize its domestic firm to make it produce the same output as it would if it were a Stackelberg leader. If such subsidies are to work as desired, however, four conditions must hold.

1. The government must be able to set its subsidy before the firms choose their output levels. The idea behind this intervention is that one firm cannot act before the other, but its government can act first.

2. The other government must not retaliate. If both governments intervene, both countries may lose, as Solved Problem 14.4 illustrates.

3. The government's actions must be credible. If the foreign firm's country doesn't believe that the government actually will subsidize its domestic firm, the foreign firm produces the Cournot level. Countries have difficulty in committing to long-term policies. For example, during the 1996 Republican presidential primaries, many candidates said that, if elected, they would reverse President Clinton's trade policies. The 2004 Democratic presidential candidates promised to change President George W. Bush's trade policies. Similarly, the major Democratic presidential candidates in the 2008 election had conflicting views on optimal trade policies.

4. The government must know enough about how the firms behave to intervene appropriately. If it doesn't know the demand function and the costs of all firms or whether they are engaged in a Cournot game, the government may intervene inappropriately.

Many economists who analyze strategic trade policies strongly oppose them because they are difficult to implement and mean-spirited, "beggar thy neighbor" policies. If only one government intervenes, another country's firm is harmed. If both governments intervene, both countries may suffer. For these reasons, the World Trade Organization (WTO) has forbidden the use of virtually all explicit export subsidies.

APPLICATION

Government Aircraft Subsidies

Governments consistently intervene in aircraft manufacturing markets. France, Germany, Spain, and the United Kingdom own and heavily subsidize Airbus, which competes in the wide-body aircraft market with the U.S. firm Boeing. The U.S. government decries the European subsidies to Airbus while directing lucrative military contracts to Boeing that the Europeans view as implicit subsidies. In 1992, the governments signed a U.S.–EU agreement on trade in civil aircraft that limits government subsidies (including a maximum direct subsidy limit of 33% of development costs and various limits on variable costs).

Irwin and Pavcnik (2004) found that aircraft prices increased by about 3.7% after the 1992 agreement. This price hike is consistent with a 5% increase in firms' marginal costs after the subsidy cuts.

Since then, Washington and the European Union have continued to trade counter-complaints in front of the WTO. Each repeatedly charged the other with illegally subsidizing its aircraft manufacturer. In 2010, the World Trade Organization ruled that Airbus received improper subsidies for its A380 superjumbo jet and several other airplanes, hurting Boeing, as the United States charged in 2005. And the cycle of subsidies, charges, agreements, and new subsidies continues.

SOLVED PROBLEM 14.4

In our duopoly, linear demand, constant marginal cost example, what happens to each firm's best-response function and the Nash-Cournot equilibrium quantities if each firm's home government gives it a specific subsidy of s (> 0) per unit of output and both firms' output is sold in a third country? Illustrate your result with a figure showing how the best-response curves shift.

Answer

1. *Modify the original Cournot best-response functions and equilibrium conditions to allow for the possibility that the firms receive a per-unit subsidy.* A per-unit subsidy reduces a firm's after-subsidy marginal cost. Thus, we can use the same equations we derived for the Cournot model for $n = 2$ where we replace the original marginal cost m by $m - s$. The subsidy changes the best-response function for Firm i (for $i = 1$ or 2) from Equation 14.15 to

$$q_i = \frac{a - m + s}{2b} - \frac{1}{2}q. \tag{14.32}$$

Similarly, the equilibrium output expression, formerly Equation 14.16, becomes

$$q = \frac{a - m + s}{3b}. \tag{14.33}$$

If $s = 0$, Equations 14.32 and 14.33 are the original, before-subsidy best-response function and equilibrium quantity function, respectively.

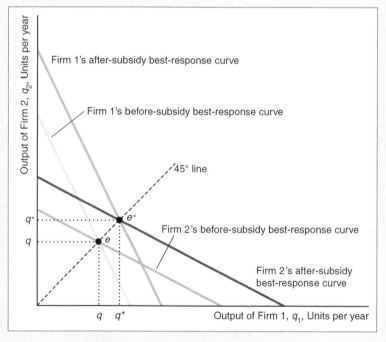

2. *Show how the best-response curves shift in response to the subsidy by differentiating the best-response function with respect to the subsidy.* Differentiating Equation 14.32 with respect to s, we find that $dq_i/ds = 1/(2b) > 0$. That is, if the other firm were to continue to produce q units of output, Firm i's best-response quantity would increase by $1/(2b)$. (In the airline example, where

$b = 1$, a \$1 subsidy would cause Firm i to increase its best-response output by $\frac{1}{2}$ unit, or 500 passengers per quarter.) Consequently, each firm's new best-response curve is parallel to the original curve and lies $1/(2b)$ units farther from the origin, as the figure shows.

3. *By differentiating the equilibrium conditions, show how the Nash-Cournot equilibrium changes as the subsidy increases.* Differentiating Equation 14.33 with respect to s, we find that $dq/ds = 1/(3b) > 0$. That is, if both firms receive the subsidy, equilibrium output for both firms rises by $1/(3b)$. In the figure, the equilibrium without the subsidy is e, where each firm produces $q = (a - m)/(3b)$, and the equilibrium with the subsidy is e^*, where each firm produces $q^* = (a - m + s)/(3b)$. (In the airline example, a \$1 subsidy would cause the equilibrium output to rise by a third of a unit, or about 333 passengers per quarter.)

Comment: In the subsidized equilibrium, the firms produce more than in the Cournot equilibrium, so both firms earn less. Thus, the subsidies hurt both countries.

14.6 Comparison of Collusive, Cournot, Stackelberg, and Competitive Equilibria

In Table 14.4, we compare the Cournot and Stackelberg equilibria to the collusive and competitive equilibria for the airline example. The table demonstrates that the Cournot and Stackelberg equilibrium quantities, prices, and profits lie between those for the competitive and collusive equilibria.

How would American and United behave if they colluded? They would maximize joint profits by producing the monopoly output, 96 units, at the monopoly price, \$243 per passenger (panel a of Figure 14.2). If the airlines colluded, they could split the monopoly quantity in many ways. American could act as a monopoly and serve all the passengers, $q_A = 96$ and $q_U = 0$, and possibly give United some of the

Table 14.4 Comparison of Airline Market Structures

	Monopoly	Cartel	Cournot	Stackelberg	Price Taking
q_A	96	48	64	96	96
q_U	0	48	64	48	96
$Q = q_A + q_U$	96	96	128	144	192
p	\$243	\$243	\$211	\$195	\$147
π_A	\$9.2	\$4.6	\$4.1	\$4.6	\$0
π_U	\$0	\$4.6	\$4.1	\$2.3	\$0
Total profit = $\Pi = \pi_A + \pi_U$	\$9.2	\$9.2	\$8.2	\$6.9	\$0
Consumer surplus, CS	\$4.6	\$4.6	\$8.2	\$10.4	\$18.4
Welfare, $W = CS + \Pi$	\$13.8	\$13.8	\$16.4	\$17.3	\$18.4
Deadweight loss, DWL	\$4.6	\$4.6	\$2.0	\$1.2	\$0

Notes: Passengers are in thousands per quarter. Price is in dollars per passenger. Profits, consumer surplus, welfare, and deadweight loss are in millions of dollars per quarter.

profits. Or they could reverse roles so that United served everyone: $q_A = 0$ and $q_U = 96$. Or the airlines could share the passengers in any combination such that the sum of the airlines' passengers equals the monopoly quantity:

$$q_A + q_U = 96. \tag{14.34}$$

Panel a of Figure 14.6 shows the possible collusive output combinations in Equation 14.34 as a line labeled "Contract curve." Collusive firms could write a contract in which they agree to produce at any of the points along this curve. In the figure, we assume that the collusive firms split the market equally so that $q_A = q_U = 48$.

If the firms were to act as price takers, they would each produce where their residual demand curve intersects their marginal cost curve, so price would equal marginal cost of \$147. The price-taking equilibrium is $q_A = q_U = 96$.

The cartel profits are the highest-possible level of profits that the firms can earn. The contract curve shows how the firms split the total monopoly-level profit. Panel b of Figure 14.6 shows the profit possibility frontier, which corresponds to the contract curve. At the upper left of the profit possibility frontier, United is a monopoly and earns the entire monopoly profit of approximately \$9.2 million per quarter.[23] At the lower right, American earns the entire monopoly profit. At points in between, they split the profit. Where they split the profit equally, each earns approximately \$4.6 million.

In contrast, if the firms act independently, each earns the Cournot profit of approximately \$4.1 million. Because the Cournot price, \$211, is lower than the cartel price, \$243, consumers are better off if the firms act independently than if they collude. The Stackelberg leader earns \$4.6 million, which is more than it could earn in a Cournot outcome, \$4.1 million. Total Stackelberg profit, \$6.9 million, is less than total Cournot profit, \$8.2 million, because the Stackelberg follower, earning \$2.3 million, is much worse off than in the Cournot equilibrium.

Table 14.4 also shows how welfare measures vary with market structure. As we did in Chapter 9, we define welfare as consumer surplus plus producer surplus, which is the sum of the two firms' profits in our example.

At one extreme, if one firm has a monopoly or if the two firms form a cartel and split the market equally, total output is relatively low, price is high, consumer surplus and welfare are low, and deadweight loss is high. At the other extreme, if American and United act as price takers, output is relatively high, price is low, consumer surplus and welfare are high, and society does not suffer a deadweight loss.

The duopoly Cournot and Stackelberg equilibria (in the table, American is the leader) lie between the extreme cases of monopoly or cartel and price taking. The Stackelberg equilibrium is closer to the price-taking equilibrium than the Cournot equilibrium in terms of total output, price, consumer surplus, welfare, and deadweight loss.

We showed that the Cournot equilibrium approaches the price-taking equilibrium as the number of firms grows. Similarly, we can show that the Stackelberg equilibrium approaches the price-taking equilibrium as the number of Stackelberg followers grows. As a result, the differences between the Cournot, Stackelberg, and price-taking market structures shrink as the number of firms grows.

---

[23]Each firm's profit per passenger is price minus average cost, $p - AC$, so the firm's profit is $\pi = (p - AC)q$, where q is the number of passengers the firm flies. The monopoly price is \$243 and the average cost is \$147, so the monopoly profit is $\pi = (243 - 147) \times 96$ units per quarter = \$9.216 million per quarter.

Figure 14.6 Duopoly Equilibria

(a) The intersection of the best-response curves determines the Cournot equilibrium. The possible cartel equilibria lie on the contract curve. If the firms act as price takers, each firm produces where its residual demand equals its marginal cost. (b) The highest possible profit for the two firms combined is given by the profit possibility frontier. It reflects all the possible collusive equilibria, including the one indicated where the firms split the market equally. All equilibria except collusive ones lie within the profit possibility frontier.

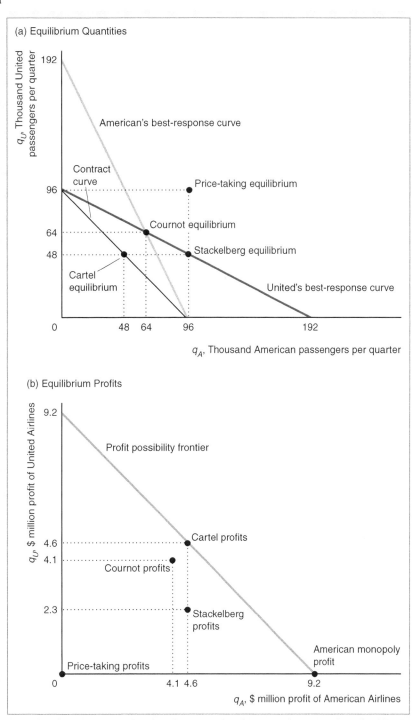

APPLICATION

Deadweight Losses in the Food and Tobacco Industries

Bhuyan and Lopez (1998) and Bhuyan (2000) estimated the deadweight loss for various U.S. food and tobacco manufacturing oligopolies and monopolistically competitive markets. Most of these industries have deadweight losses that are a relatively small percentage of sales because their prices and quantities are close to competitive levels. However, a few industries, such as cereal and flour and grain mills, have deadweight losses that are a relatively large share of sales, as the last column of the table shows.

Industry	Loss, $ millions	Share of Sales, %
Cereal	2,192	33
Flour and grain mills	541	26
Poultry and eggs	1,183	8
Roasted coffee	440	7
Cigarettes	1,032	6
All food manufacturing	14,947	5

14.7 Bertrand Oligopoly Model

We have examined how oligopolistic firms set quantities to try to maximize their profits. However, many such firms set prices instead of quantities and allow consumers to decide how much to buy. The market equilibrium is different if firms set prices rather than quantities.

In monopolistic and competitive markets, the issue of whether firms set quantities or prices does not arise. Competitive firms have no choice: They cannot affect price and hence can choose only quantity (Chapter 8). The monopoly equilibrium is the same whether the monopoly sets price or quantity (Chapter 11).

In 1883, the French mathematician Joseph Bertrand argued that oligopolies set prices and then consumers decide how many units to buy. The resulting Nash equilibrium is called a **Bertrand equilibrium** or **Nash-Bertrand equilibrium** or **Nash-in-prices equilibrium**: a set of prices such that no firm can obtain a higher profit by choosing a different price if the other firms continue to charge these prices.

Our analysis in this section shows that the price and quantity in a Nash-Bertrand equilibrium are different from those in a Cournot equilibrium. In addition, the properties of the Nash-Bertrand equilibrium depend on whether firms are producing identical or differentiated products.

Bertrand Equilibrium with Identical Products

We start by examining a price-setting oligopoly in which firms have identical costs and produce identical goods. The resulting Nash-Bertrand equilibrium price equals the marginal cost, as in the price-taking equilibrium. To show this result, we use best-response curves to determine the Nash-Bertrand equilibrium, as we did in the Nash-Cournot model.

Best-Response Curves. Suppose that each of the two price-setting oligopoly firms in a market produces an identical product and faces a constant marginal and average cost of $5 per unit. What is Firm 1's best response—what price should it set—if Firm 2 sets a price of $p_2 = \$10$? If Firm 1 charges more than $10, it makes no sales because consumers will buy from Firm 2. Firm 1 makes a profit of $5 on each unit it sells if it also charges $10 per unit. If the market demand is 200 units and both firms charge the same price, we would expect Firm 1 to make half the sales, so its profit is $500.

Suppose, however, that Firm 1 slightly undercuts its rival's price by charging $9.99. Because the products are identical, Firm 1 captures the entire market. Firm 1 makes a profit of $4.99 per unit and a total profit of $998. Thus, Firm 1's profit is higher if it slightly undercuts its rival's price. By similar reasoning, if Firm 2 charges $8, Firm 1 also charges slightly less than Firm 2.

Figure 14.7 shows that, if Firm 2 sets its price above $5, Firm 1's best response is to undercut Firm 2's price slightly so its best-response curve is above the 45° line by the smallest amount possible. (The distance of the best-response curve from the 45° line is exaggerated in the figure for clarity.)

Now imagine that Firm 2 charges $p_2 = \$5$. If Firm 1 charges more than $5, it makes no sales. The firms split the market and make zero profit if Firm 1 charges $5. If Firm 1 undercuts its rival, it captures the entire market, but it suffers a loss on each unit. Thus, Firm 1 will undercut only if its rival's price is higher than Firm 1's marginal and average cost of $5. By similar reasoning, if Firm 2 charges less than $5, Firm 1 chooses not to produce. The two best-response functions intersect only at e, where each firm charges $5. If its rival were to charge less than $5, a firm would choose not to produce.

It does not pay for either firm to change its price as long as the other charges $5, so e is a Nash-Bertrand equilibrium. In this equilibrium, each firm makes zero profit. Thus, *the Nash-Bertrand equilibrium when firms produce identical products*

Figure 14.7 Bertrand Equilibrium with Identical Products

With identical products and constant marginal and average costs of $5, Firm 1's best-response curve starts at $5 and then lies slightly above the 45° line. That is, Firm 1 undercuts its rival's price as long as its price remains above $5. The best-response curves intersect at e, the Bertrand or Nash equilibrium, where both firms charge $5.

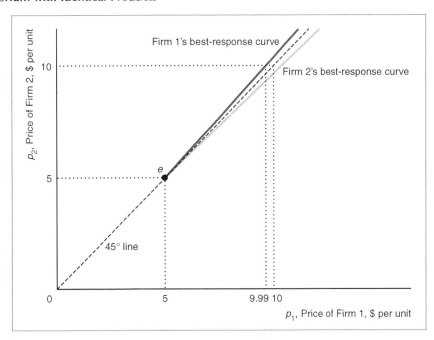

is the same as the price-taking, competitive equilibrium.[24] This result remains the same for larger numbers of firms.

Bertrand Versus Cournot. This Nash-Bertrand equilibrium differs substantially from the Nash-Cournot equilibrium. We can calculate the Nash-Cournot equilibrium price for firms with constant marginal costs of $5 per unit using Equation 14.11:

$$p = \frac{MC}{1 + 1/(n\varepsilon)} = \frac{\$5}{1 + 1/(n\varepsilon)}, \qquad (14.35)$$

where n is the number of firms and ε is the market demand elasticity. For example, if the market demand elasticity is $\varepsilon = -1$ and $n = 2$, the Nash-Cournot equilibrium price is $\$5/(1 - \frac{1}{2}) = \$10$, which is double the Nash-Bertrand equilibrium price.

When firms produce identical products and have a constant marginal cost, the Nash-Cournot model is more plausible than the Nash-Bertrand model. The Nash-Bertrand model—unlike the Nash-Cournot model—appears inconsistent with real oligopoly markets in at least two ways.

First, the Nash-Bertrand model's "competitive" equilibrium price is implausible. In a market with few firms, why would the firms compete so vigorously that they would make no profit, as in the Nash-Bertrand equilibrium? In contrast, the Nash-Cournot equilibrium price with a small number of firms lies between the competitive price and the monopoly price. Because oligopolies typically charge a higher price than competitive firms, the Nash-Cournot equilibrium is more plausible.

Second, the Nash-Bertrand equilibrium price, which depends only on cost, is insensitive to demand conditions and the number of firms. In contrast, the Nash-Cournot equilibrium price, Equation 14.11, depends on demand conditions and the number of firms as well as on costs. In our last example, if the number of firms rises from two to three, the Cournot price falls from $10 to $5/(1 - $\frac{1}{3}$) = $7.50, but the Nash-Bertrand equilibrium price remains constant at $5. Again, the Cournot model is more plausible because we usually observe market price changing with the number of firms and demand conditions, not just with changes in costs. Thus, for both of these reasons, economists are much more likely to use the Cournot model than the Bertrand model to study markets in which firms produce identical goods.

Nash-Bertrand Equilibrium with Differentiated Products

Why don't they make mouse-flavored cat food? —Steven Wright

If most markets were characterized by firms producing homogeneous goods, the Bertrand model would probably have been forgotten. However, markets with differentiated goods—such as those for automobiles, stereos, computers, toothpaste, and spaghetti sauce—are extremely common, as is price setting by firms. In such markets, the Nash-Bertrand equilibrium is plausible, and the two "problems" of the homogeneous-goods model disappear. That is, firms set prices above marginal cost, and prices are sensitive to demand conditions.

Indeed, many economists believe that price-setting models are more plausible than quantity-setting models when goods are differentiated. If products are differentiated and firms set prices, then consumers determine quantities. In contrast, if

---

[24] This result depends heavily on the firms' facing a constant marginal cost. If firms face a binding capacity constraint so that the marginal cost eventually becomes large (infinite), the Nash-Bertrand equilibrium may be the same as the Nash-Cournot equilibrium (Kreps and Scheinkman, 1983).

firms set quantities, it is not clear how the prices of the differentiated goods are determined in the market.

The main reason the differentiated-goods Bertrand model differs from the undifferentiated-goods version is that one firm can charge more than another for a differentiated product without losing all its sales. For example, Coke and Pepsi produce similar but not identical products; many consumers prefer one to the other.[25] If the price of Pepsi were to fall slightly relative to that of Coke, most consumers who prefer Coke to Pepsi would not switch. Thus, neither firm has to match its rival's price cut exactly to continue to sell cola.

Product differentiation allows a firm to charge a higher price because the differentiation causes its residual demand curve to become less elastic. That is, a given decrease in the price charged by a rival lowers the demand for this firm's product by *less*, the less substitutable the two goods. In contrast, if consumers view the goods as perfect substitutes, a small drop in the rival's price causes this firm to lose all its sales. For this reason, differentiation leads to higher equilibrium prices and profits in both the Bertrand and the Cournot models. As a result, a firm aggressively differentiates its products so as to raise its profit.[26]

General Demand Functions. We can use calculus to determine the Nash-Bertrand equilibrium for a duopoly. We derive equilibrium for general demand functions, and then we present the solution for the cola market. In both analyses, we first determine the best-response functions for each firm and then solve these best-response functions simultaneously for the equilibrium prices for the two firms.

Each firm's demand function depends on its own price and the other firm's price. The demand function for Firm 1 is $q_1 = q_1(p_1, p_2)$ and that of Firm 2 is $q_2 = q_2(p_1, p_2)$. For simplicity, we assume that marginal cost for both firms is constant, m, and neither has a fixed cost.

Firm 1's objective is to set its price so as to maximize its profit,

$$\max_{p_1} \pi_1(p_1, p_2) = (p_1 - m)q_1(p_1, p_2), \tag{14.36}$$

where $(p_1 - m)$ is the profit per unit. Firm 1 views p_2 as a constant. Firm 1's first-order condition is the derivative of its profit with respect to p_1 set equal to zero:

$$\frac{\partial \pi_1}{\partial p_1} = q_1(p_1, p_2) + (p_1 - m)\frac{\partial q_1(p_1, p_2)}{\partial p_1} = 0. \tag{14.37}$$

Equation 14.37 contains the information in Firm 1's best-response function: $p_1 = B_1(p_2)$.

Similarly, we can derive Firm 2's best-response function. Solving the best-response functions, Equations 14.36 and 14.37, simultaneously, we obtain the Nash-Bertrand equilibrium prices: p_1 and p_2. We illustrate this procedure for Coke and Pepsi.

---

[25]The critical issue is whether consumers believe products differ rather than whether the products physically differ because the consumers' beliefs affect their buying behavior. Although few consumers can reliably distinguish Coke from Pepsi in blind taste tests, many consumers strongly prefer buying one product over the other. I have run blind taste tests in my classes over the years involving literally thousands of students. Given a choice between Coke, Pepsi, and a generic cola, a very small fraction can consistently identify the products. However, people who do not regularly drink these products generally admit that they can't tell the difference. Indeed, relatively few of the regular cola drinks can clearly distinguish among the brands.

[26]Chance that a British baby's first word is a brand name: 1 in 4.—*Harper's Index 2004*.

Cola Market. Because many consumers view Coke and Pepsi as imperfect substitutes, the demand for each good depends on both firms' prices. Gasmi, Laffont, and Vuong (1992) estimated the demand curve of Coke:[27]

$$q_C = 58 - 4p_C + 2p_P, \qquad (14.38)$$

where q_C is the quantity of Coke demanded in tens of millions of cases (a case is 24 twelve-ounce cans) per quarter, p_C is the price of 10 cases of Coke, and p_P is the price of 10 cases of Pepsi. Partially differentiating Equation 14.38 with respect to p_C (that is, holding the price of Pepsi constant), we find that the change in quantity for every dollar change in price is $\partial q_C/\partial p_C = -4$, so a $1-per-unit increase in the price of Coke causes the quantity of Coke demanded to fall by 4 units. Similarly, the demand for Coke rises by 2 units if the price of Pepsi rises by $1, while the price of Coke remains constant: $\partial q_C/\partial p_P = 2$.

If Coke faces a constant marginal and average cost of m per unit, its profit is

$$\pi_C(p_C) = (p_C - m)q_C = (p_C - m)(58 - 4p_C + 2p_P). \qquad (14.39)$$

To determine Coke's profit-maximizing price given that Pepsi's price is held constant, we set the partial derivative of the profit function, Equation 14.39, with respect to the price of Coke equal to zero,

$$\frac{\partial \pi_C}{\partial p_C} = q_C + (p_C - m)\frac{\partial q_C}{\partial p_C} = q_C - 4(p_C - m) = 0, \qquad (14.40)$$

and solve for p_C as a function of p_P and m to find Coke's best-response function:

$$p_C = 7.25 + 0.25p_P + 0.5m. \qquad (14.41)$$

Coke's best-response function tells us the price Coke charges that maximizes its profit as a function of the price Pepsi charges. Equation 14.41 shows that Coke's best-response price is 25¢ higher for every extra dollar that Pepsi charges and 50¢ higher for every extra dollar of Coke's marginal cost. Figure 14.8 plots Coke's best-response curve given that Coke's average and marginal cost of production is $5 per unit, so its best-response function is

$$p_C = 9.75 + 0.25p_P. \qquad (14.42)$$

If $p_P = \$13$, then Coke's best response is to set p_C at $13.

Pepsi's demand curve is

$$q_P = 63.2 - 4p_P + 1.6p_C. \qquad (14.43)$$

Using the same approach as we used for Coke, we find that Pepsi's best-response function (for $m = \$5$) is

$$p_P = 10.4 + 0.2p_C. \qquad (14.44)$$

Thus, neither firm's best-response curve in Figure 14.8 lies along a 45° line through the origin. The Bertrand best-response curves have different slopes than the Cournot best-response curves in Figure 14.3. The Cournot best-response curves—which plot relationships between quantities—slope downward, showing that a firm produces less the more it expects its rival to produce (as Figure 14.3 illustrates for identical goods, and Solved Problem 14.3 shows for differentiated goods). In Figure

---

[27]Their estimated model allows the firms to set both prices and advertising. We assume that the firms' advertising is held constant. The Coke equation is Gasmi, Laffont, and Vuong's estimates (with slight rounding). The Pepsi demand equation reported below is their estimate rescaled so that the equilibrium prices of Coke and Pepsi are equal. Prices (to retailers) and costs are in real 1982 dollars per 10 cases.

14.7 Bertrand Oligopoly Model

Figure 14.8 Bertrand Equilibrium with Differentiated Products

If both firms have a constant marginal cost of $5, the best-response curves of Coke and Pepsi intersect at e_1, where each sets a price of $13 per unit. If Coke's marginal cost rises to $14.50, its best-response function shifts upward. In the new equilibrium, e_2, Coke charges a higher price, $18, than Pepsi, $14.

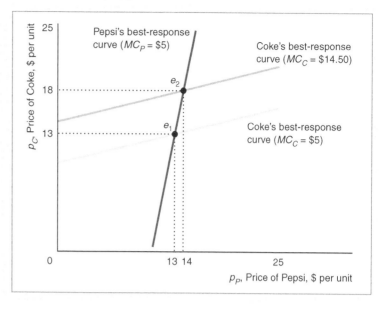

14.8, the Bertrand best-response curves—which plot relationships between prices—slope upward, indicating that a firm charges a higher price the higher the price the firm expects its rival to charge.

The intersection of Coke's and Pepsi's best-response functions, Equations 14.42 and 14.44, determines the Nash equilibrium. By substituting Pepsi's best-response function, Equation 14.44, for p_P in Coke's best-response function, Equation 14.42, we find that

$$p_C = 9.75 + 0.25(10.4 + 0.2p_C).$$

The solution to this equation is that p_C—the equilibrium price of Coke—is $13. Substituting $p_C = \$13$ into Equation 14.44, we discover that the equilibrium price of Pepsi is also $13, as Figure 14.8 illustrates.

In this Nash-Bertrand equilibrium, each firm sets its best-response price *given the price the other firm is charging*. Neither firm wants to change its price because neither firm can increase its profit by doing so.

Product Differentiation and Welfare. We've just seen that prices are likely to be higher when products are differentiated than when they are identical, all else the same. We also know that welfare falls as the gap between price and marginal cost rises. Does it follow that differentiating products lowers welfare? Not necessarily. Although differentiation leads to higher prices, which harm consumers, differentiation is desirable in its own right. Consumers value having a choice, and some may greatly prefer a new brand to existing ones.

One way to illustrate the importance of this second effect is to consider the value of introducing a new, differentiated product. This value reflects how much extra income consumers would require to be as well off without the good as with it.

APPLICATION

Welfare Gain from Greater Toilet Paper Variety

An article in the *Economist* asked, "Why does it cost more to wipe your bottom in Britain than in any other country in the European Union?" The answer given was that British consumers are "extremely fussy" in demanding a soft, luxurious texture—in contrast to barbarians elsewhere. As a consequence, they pay twice as much for toilet paper as the Germans and French, and nearly 2.5 times as much as Americans. (Indeed, British supermarkets reported that the share of luxury toilet paper sales spiked around Christmas 2009. Apparently during a major recession, Brits view luxury toilet paper as an appropriate present.)

Probably completely uninfluenced by this important cross-country research, Hausman and Leonard (2002) used U.S. data to measure the price effect and the extra consumer surplus from greater variety resulting from Kimberly-Clark's introduction of Kleenex Bath Tissue (KBT). Bath tissue products are divided into premium, economy, and private labels, with premium receiving more than 70% of revenue. Before KBT's entry, the major premium brands were Angel Soft, Charmin, Cottonelle, and Northern. ScotTissue was the leading economy brand.

Firms incur a sizable fixed cost from capital investments. The marginal cost depends primarily on the price of wood pulp, which varies cyclically. Because KBT was rolled out in various cities at different times, Hausman and Leonard could compare the effects of entry at various times and control for variations in cost and other factors.

The prices of all rival brands fell after KBT entered; the price of the leading brand, Charmin, dropped by 3.5%, while Cottonelle's price plummeted 8.2%. In contrast, the price of ScotTissue, an economy brand, decreased by only 0.6%.

Hausman and Leonard calculated that the additional consumer surplus due to extra variety was $33.4 million, or 3.5% of sales. When they included the gains due to lower prices, the total consumer surplus increase was $69.2 million, or 7.3% of sales. Thus, the gains to consumers were roughly equally divided between the price effect and the benefit from extra variety.

14.8 Monopolistic Competition

So far, we've concentrated on oligopolistic markets where the number of firms is fixed because of barriers to entry. We've seen that these firms in an oligopoly (such as the airlines in our example) may earn positive economic profits. We now consider firms in monopolistically competitive markets in which there are no barriers to entry, so firms enter the market until no more firms can enter profitably.

If both competitive and monopolistically competitive firms make zero economic profits, what distinguishes these two market structures? Competitive firms face horizontal residual demand curves and charge prices equal to marginal cost. In contrast, monopolistically competitive firms face downward-sloping residual demand curves and thus charge prices above marginal cost. Monopolistically competitive firms face downward-sloping residual demand because (unlike competitive firms) they have relatively few rivals or sell differentiated products.

The fewer monopolistically competitive firms, the less elastic the residual demand curve each firm faces. As we saw, the elasticity of demand for an individual Cournot firm is $n\varepsilon$, where n is the number of firms and ε is the market elasticity. Thus, the fewer the firms in a market, the less elastic the residual demand curve.

When monopolistically competitive firms benefit from economies of scale at high levels of output (the average cost curve is downward sloping), so that each firm is relatively large in comparison to market demand, there is room in the market for only a few firms. In the short run, if fixed costs are large and marginal costs are constant or diminishing, firms have economies of scale (Chapter 7) at all output levels, so there are relatively few firms in the market. In an extreme case with substantial enough economies of scale, the market may have room for only one firm: a natural monopoly (Chapter 11). The number of firms in equilibrium is smaller the greater the economies of scale and the farther to the left the market demand curve.

Monopolistically competitive firms also face downward-sloping residual demand curves if each firm differentiates its product so that at least some consumers believe that product is superior to other brands. If some consumers believe that Tide laundry detergent is better than Cheer and other brands, Tide won't lose all its sales even if Tide charges a slightly higher price than does Cheer. Thus, Tide faces a downward-sloping demand curve—not a horizontal one.

Monopolistically Competitive Equilibrium

In a monopolistically competitive market, each firm tries to maximize its profit, but each makes zero economic profit due to entry. Two conditions hold in a monopolistically competitive equilibrium: *marginal revenue equals marginal cost* because firms set output to maximize profit, and *price equals average cost* because firms enter until no further profitable entry is possible.

Figure 14.9 shows a monopolistically competitive market equilibrium. A typical monopolistically competitive firm faces a residual demand curve D^r. To maximize its profit, the firm sets its output, q, where its marginal revenue curve corresponding to the residual demand curve intersects its marginal cost curve: $MR^r = MC$. At that quantity, the firm's average cost curve, AC, is tangent to its residual demand curve. Because the height of the residual demand curve is the price, at the tangency point price equals average cost, $p = AC$, and the firm makes zero profit.

Figure 14.9 Monopolistically Competitive Equilibrium

A monopolistically competitive firm, facing residual demand curve D^r, sets its output where its marginal revenue equals its marginal cost: $MR^r = MC$. Because firms can enter this market, the profit of the firm is driven to zero, so price equals the firm's average cost: $p = AC$.

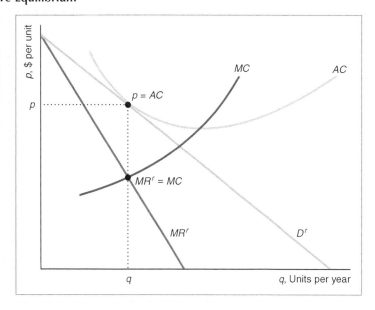

If the average cost were less than price at that quantity, firms would make positive profits and entrants would be attracted. If average cost were above price, firms would lose money, so firms would exit until the marginal firm was breaking even.

The smallest quantity at which the average cost curve reaches its minimum is referred to as *full capacity* or **minimum efficient scale**. The firm's full capacity or minimum efficient scale is the quantity at which the firm no longer benefits from economies of scale. Because a monopolistically competitive equilibrium occurs in the downward-sloping section of the average cost curve (where the average cost curve is tangent to the downward-sloping demand curve), a monopolistically competitive firm operates at less than full capacity in the long run.

Fixed Costs and the Number of Firms

The number of firms in a monopolistically competitive equilibrium depends on firms' costs. The larger each firm's fixed cost, the smaller the number of monopolistically competitive firms in the market equilibrium.

Although entry is free, if the fixed costs are high, few firms may enter. In the automobile industry, just to develop a new fender costs $8 to $10 million.[28] Developing a new pharmaceutical drug could cost more than $350 million.

We can illustrate this relationship using the airline example, where we now modify our assumptions about entry and fixed costs. Recall that American and United are the only airlines providing service on the Chicago–Los Angeles route. Until now, we have assumed that a barrier to entry—such as an inability to obtain landing rights at both airports—prevented entry and that the firms had no fixed costs. If fixed cost is zero and marginal cost is constant at $147 per passenger, average cost is also constant at $147 per passenger. As we showed earlier, each firm in this oligopolistic market flies $q = 64$ thousand passengers per quarter at a price of $p = \$211$ and makes a profit of $4.1 million per quarter.

Now suppose that there are no barriers to entry and each airline incurs a fixed cost, F, due to airport fees, capital expenditure, or other factors.[29] Each firm's marginal cost remains $147 per passenger, but its average cost,

$$AC = 147 + \frac{F}{q},$$

falls as the number of passengers rises, as panels a and b of Figure 14.10 illustrate for $F = \$2.3$ million.

If there are only two firms in a monopolistically competitive market, what must the fixed costs be so that the two firms earn zero profit? We know that these firms each receive a profit of $4.1 million in the absence of fixed costs. As a result, the fixed cost must be $4.1 million per firm for the firms to earn zero profit. With this fixed cost, the monopolistically competitive price and quantity are the same as they are in the oligopolistic equilibrium, $q = 64$ and $p = \$211$, and the number of firms is the same, but now each firm's profit is zero.

If the fixed cost is only $2.3 million and there are only two firms in the market, each firm makes a profit, as panel a shows. Each duopoly firm faces a residual

---

[28]James B. Treece ("Sometimes, You Gotta Have Size," *Business Week*, Enterprise 1993:200–1) illustrates the importance of fixed costs on entry in the following anecdote: "In 1946, steel magnate Henry J. Kaiser boasted to a Detroit dinner gathering that two recent stock offerings had raised a huge $50 million to invest in his budding car company. Suddenly, a voice from the back of the room shot out: 'Give that man one white chip.'"

[29]See "Virgin America's Fixed Costs" in **MyEconLab**'s textbook resources for Chapter 19.

Figure 14.10 Monopolistic Competition Among Airlines

(a) If each identical airline has a fixed cost of $2.3 million and there are two firms in the market, each firm flies $q = 64$ units (thousands of passengers) per quarter at a price of $p = \$211$ per passenger and makes a profit of $1.8 million. This profit attracts entry. (b) After a third firm enters, the residual demand curve shifts, so each firm flies $q = 48$ units at $p = \$195$ and makes zero profit, which is the monopolistically competitive equilibrium.

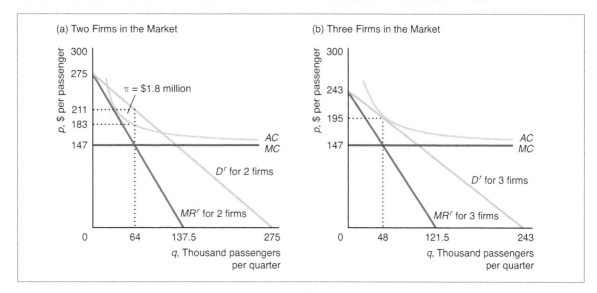

demand curve (labeled "D^r for 2 firms"), which is the market demand minus its rival's Cournot equilibrium quantity, $q = 64$. Given this residual demand, each firm produces $q = 64$, which equates its marginal revenue, MR^r, and its marginal cost, MC. At $q = 64$, the firm's average cost is $AC = \$147 + (\$2.3 \text{ million})/(64 \text{ units}) \approx \$183$, so each firm makes a profit of $\pi = (p - AC)q \approx (\$211 - \$183) \times 64$ units per quarter $\approx \$1.8$ million per quarter.

This substantial economic profit attracts an entrant. The entry of a third firm causes the residual demand for any one firm to shift to the left in panel b. In the new equilibrium, each firm sets $q = 48$ and charges $p = \$195$. At this quantity, each firm's average cost is $195, so the firms break even. No other firms enter because if one did, the residual demand curve would shift even farther to the left and all the firms would lose money. Thus, if the fixed cost is $2.3 million, there are three firms in the monopolistically competitive equilibrium. This example illustrates a general result: *The lower the fixed costs, the more firms there are in the monopolistically competitive equilibrium.*

SOLVED PROBLEM 14.5

What is the monopolistically competitive airline equilibrium if each firm has a fixed cost of $3 million?

Answer

1. *Determine the number of firms.* We already know that the monopolistically competitive equilibrium has two firms if the fixed cost is $4.1 million and three firms if the fixed cost is $2.3 million. With a fixed cost of $3 million, if there are only two firms in the market, each makes a profit of $1.1 (= \$4.1 - 3$) million. If another firm enters, though, each firm's loss is $-\$0.7 (= \$2.3 - 3)$

million. Thus, the monopolistically competitive equilibrium has two firms, each of which earns a positive profit that is too small to attract another firm. This outcome is a monopolistically competitive equilibrium because no other firm wants to enter.

2. *Determine the equilibrium quantities and prices.* We already know that each duopoly firm produces $q = 64$, so $Q = 128$ and $p = \$211$.

APPLICATION

Zoning Laws as a Barrier to Entry by Hotel Chains

U.S. local governments restrict land use through zoning. The difficulty of getting permission (generally from many agencies) to build a new commercial structure is a barrier to entry. Suzuki (2009) examines the effect on Texas municipalities' zoning laws on chain hotels (such as Best Western, Holiday Inn, Quality Inn, Comfort Inn, La Quinta Inn, and Ramada).

According to his estimates, construction costs are large even in the absence of zoning regulations: construction costs are $2.4 million for a new Best Western hotel and $4.5 million for a new La Quinta hotel. Going from a lenient to a stringent zoning policy increases a hotel's variable cost by 21% and its sunk entry cost by 19%. The average number of hotels in a small market falls from 2.3 under a lenient policy to 1.9 with a stringent policy due to the higher entry cost. As a consequence, there are 15% fewer rooms under a stringent policy, which increases the revenue per room by 7%. The change from the most lenient policy to the stringent policy decreases producer surplus by $1.5 million and consumer surplus by $1 million. Thus, more stringent zoning laws raise entry costs and thereby reduce the number of hotels and rooms, which causes the price to rise and lowers welfare.

SUMMARY

1. **Market Structures.** Prices, profits, and quantities in a market equilibrium depend on the market's structure. Because profit-maximizing firms set marginal revenue equal to marginal cost, price is above marginal revenue—and hence marginal cost—only if firms face downward-sloping demand curves. In monopoly, oligopoly, and monopolistically competitive markets, firms face downward-sloping demand curves, in contrast to firms in a competitive market. Firms can earn positive profits when entry is blocked with a monopoly or an oligopoly, in contrast to the zero profits that competitive or monopolistically competitive firms earn with free entry. Noncooperative oligopoly and monopolistically competitive firms, in contrast to competitive and monopoly firms, must pay attention to their rivals.

2. **Cartels.** If firms successfully collude, they produce the monopoly output and collectively earn the monopoly level of profit. Although their collective profits rise if all firms collude, each individual firm has an incentive to cheat on the cartel arrangement so as to raise its own profit even higher. For cartel prices to remain high, cartel members must be able to detect and prevent cheating, and noncartel firms must be unable to supply very much output. When antitrust laws or competition policies prevent firms from colluding, firms may try to merge if permitted by law.

3. **Noncooperative Oligopoly.** If oligopoly firms act independently, equilibrium output, price, and total firm profit lie between those of competition and cartel (monopoly). The market outcome depends on the characteristics of the market such as the number of firms, whether the firms produce differentiated products, and whether the firms act simultaneously or sequentially.

4. **Cournot Oligopoly Model.** If oligopoly firms act independently, market output and firms' profits lie

between the competitive and monopoly levels. In a Cournot model, each oligopoly firm sets its output simultaneously. In the Cournot (Nash) equilibrium, each firm produces its best-response output—the output that maximizes its profit—given the output its rival produces. As the number of Cournot firms increases, the Cournot equilibrium price, quantity, and profits approach the price-taking levels.

5. **Stackelberg Oligopoly Model.** If one firm, the Stackelberg leader, chooses its output before its rivals, the Stackelberg followers, the leader produces more and earns a higher profit than each identical-cost follower firm. A government may subsidize a domestic oligopoly firm so that the firm produces the Stackelberg leader quantity, which it sells in an international market. For a given number of firms, the Stackelberg equilibrium output is less than the efficient (competitive market) level but exceeds that of the Cournot equilibrium, which exceeds that of the collusive equilibrium (which is the same as a monopoly produces). Correspondingly, the Stackelberg price is more than marginal cost but less than the Cournot price, which is less than the collusive or monopoly price.

6. **Comparison of Collusive, Cournot, Stackelberg, and Competitive Equilibria.** Total market output is maximized and price is minimized under competition. For a given number of firms, the Stackelberg equilibrium output exceeds that of the Cournot equilibrium, which is greater than that of the collusive or monopoly equilibrium. Correspondingly, the Stackelberg price is less than the Cournot price, which is less than the collusive or monopoly price.

7. **Bertrand Oligopoly Model.** In many oligopolistic or monopolistically competitive markets, firms set prices instead of quantities. If the product is homogeneous and firms set prices, the Bertrand equilibrium price equals marginal cost (which is lower than the Cournot quantity-setting equilibrium price). If the products are differentiated, the Bertrand equilibrium price is above marginal cost. Typically, the markup of price over marginal cost is greater the more the goods are differentiated.

8. **Monopolistic Competition.** In monopolistically competitive markets after all profitable entry occurs, there are few enough firms such that each firm faces a downward-sloping demand curve. Consequently, the firms charge prices above marginal cost. These markets are not perfectly competitive because there are relatively few firms—possibly because of high fixed costs or economies of scale that are large relative to market demand—or because the firms sell differentiated products.

QUESTIONS

■ = exercise is available on **MyEconLab**; * = answer appears at the back of this book; V = video answer by James Dearden is available online.

1. At each Organization of Petroleum Exporting Countries (OPEC) meeting, Saudi Arabia, the largest oil producer, argues that the cartel should cut production. The Saudis complain that most OPEC countries, including Saudi Arabia (but not Indonesia or Venezuela), produce more oil than they are allotted under their cartel agreement (Romero, Simon, "Saudis Push Plan for Cut in Production by OPEC," *New York Times*, March 31, 2004). Use a graph and words to explain why cartel members would produce more than the allotted amount given that they know that overproduction will drive down the price of their product.

*2. Your college is considering renting space in the student union to one or two commercial textbook stores. The rent the college can charge per square foot of space depends on the profit (before rent) of the firms and hence on whether there is a monopoly or a duopoly. Which number of stores is better for the college in terms of rent? Which is better for students? Why?

3. Connecticut sets a maximum fee that bail-bond businesses can charge for posting a given-size bond (Ayres and Waldfogel, 1994). The bail-bond fee is set at virtually the maximum amount allowed by law in cities with only one active firm (Plainville, 99%; Stamford, 99%; and Wallingford, 99%). The price is as high in cities with a duopoly (Ansonia, 99.6%; Meriden, 98%; and New London, 98%). In cities with three or more firms, however, the price falls well below the maximum permitted price. The fees are only 54% of the maximum in Norwalk (3 firms), 64% in New Haven (8 firms), and 78% in Bridgeport (10 firms). Give possible explanations for this pattern.

4. The application "Deadweight Losses in the Food and Tobacco Industries" shows that the deadweight loss as a fraction of sales varies substantially across industries. One possible explanation is that the number of firms (degree of competition) varies across industries. Using Table 14.2, show how the deadweight loss varies in the airline market as the number of firms increases from one to three.

5. Southwest Airlines' cost to fly one seat 1 mile is 7.38¢ compared to 15.20¢ for USAir (*New York Times*, August 20, 2002, C4). Assuming that Southwest and USAir compete on a route, use a graph to show that their equilibrium quantities differ. (*Hint*: See Solved Problem 14.2.)

6. In 2005, the prices for 36 prescription painkillers shot up as much as 15% after Merck yanked its once-popular arthritis drug Vioxx from the market due to fears that it caused heart problems ("Prices Climb as Much as 15% for Some Painkillers," *Los Angeles Times*, June 3, 2005, C3). Can this product's exit be the cause of the price increases if the prices reflect a Cournot equilibrium? Explain.

7. Plot the best-response curve of the second firm in Solved Problem 14.2 if its marginal cost is m and if it is $m + x$. Add the first firm's best-response curve and show how the Nash-Cournot equilibrium changes as its marginal cost increases.

8. What is the effect of a government subsidy that reduces the fixed cost of each firm in an industry in a Cournot monopolistic competition equilibrium?

9. In the monopolistically competitive airlines model, what is the equilibrium if firms face no fixed costs?

10. In a monopolistically competitive market, the government applies a specific tax of $1 per unit of output. What happens to the profit of a typical firm in this market? Does the number of firms in the market change? Why?

11. Does an oligopoly or a monopolistically competitive firm have a supply curve? Why or why not? (*Hint*: See the discussion in Chapter 11 of whether a monopoly has a supply curve.)

12. In the Coke and Pepsi example, what is the effect of a specific tax, τ, on the equilibrium prices? (*Hint*: What does the tax do to the firm's marginal cost? You do not have to use math to answer this problem.)

13. In 1998, California became the first state to adopt rules requiring many SUVs, pickups, and minivans to meet the same pollution standards as other cars, effective in 2004. As the deadline drew near, a business group (which may have an incentive to exaggerate) estimated that using the new technology to reduce pollution would increase vehicle prices by as much as $7,000. A spokesperson for the California Air Resources Board, which imposed the mandate, said that the additional materials cost is only about $70 to $270 per vehicle. Suppose that the two major producers are Toyota and Ford, and these oligopolistic firms set prices on their differentiated products. Show the effect of the new regulation. Is it possible that the price for these vehicles would rise by substantially more than the marginal cost would? Explain your answer.

14. In 2008, cruise ship lines announced they were increasing prices from $7 to $9 per person per day because of increased fuel costs. According to one analyst, fuel costs for Carnival Corporation's 84-ship fleet jumped $900 million to $2 billion in 2008 and its cost per passenger per day jumped from $10 to $33. Assuming that these firms are oligopolistic and the outcome is a Cournot equilibrium, why did prices rise less than in proportion to per-passenger-per-day cost?

15. What happens to the homogeneous-good Bertrand equilibrium price if the number of firms increases? Why?

*16. Will price be lower if duopoly firms set price or if they set quantity? Under what conditions can you give a definitive answer to this question?

*17. Why does differentiating its product allow an oligopoly to charge a higher price?

18. In the initial Bertrand equilibrium, two firms with differentiated products charge the same equilibrium prices. A consumer testing agency praises the product of one firm, causing its demand curve to shift to the right as new customers start buying the product. (The demand curve of the other product is not substantially affected.) Use a graph to illustrate how this new information affects the Bertrand equilibrium. What happens to the equilibrium prices of the two firms?

PROBLEMS

19. How would the Cournot equilibrium change in the airline example if United's marginal cost were $100 and American's were $200?

20. In the initial Cournot oligopoly equilibrium, both firms have constant marginal costs, m, and no fixed costs, and there is a barrier to entry. Use calculus to show what happens to the best-response function of firms if both firms now face a fixed cost of F.

21. A duopoly faces a market demand of $p = 120 - Q$. Firm 1 has a constant marginal cost of $MC^1 = 20$. Firm 2's constant marginal cost is $MC^2 = 40$. Calculate the output of each firm, market output, and price if there is (a) a collusive equilibrium or (b) a Cournot equilibrium.

*22. What is the duopoly Cournot equilibrium if the market demand function is $Q = 1{,}000 - 1{,}000p$ and each firm's marginal cost is 28¢ per unit?

23. What is the equilibrium in this chapter's airline example if both American and United receive a subsidy of $48 per passenger?

*24. Consider a Cournot equilibrium where each of the n firms faces a constant marginal cost m, the market demand curve is $p = a - bQ$, and the government assesses a specific tax of τ per unit. What is the incidence of this tax on consumers?

*25. The demand that duopoly quantity-setting firms face is $p = 90 - 2q_1 - 2q_2$. Firm 1 has no marginal cost of production, but Firm 2 has a marginal cost of $30. How much does each firm produce if they move simultaneously? What is the equilibrium price?

26. According to Robert Guy Matthews, "Fixed Costs Chafe at Steel Mills," *Wall Street Journal*, June 10, 2009, stainless steel manufacturers are increasing prices even though the market demand curve had shifted to the left. In a letter to its customers, one of these companies announced that "Unlike mill increases announced in recent years, this is obviously not driven by increasing global demand, but rather by fixed costs being proportioned across significantly lower demand." If the firms are oligopolistic, produce a homogenous good, face a linear market demand curve and have linear costs, and the market outcome is a Nash-Cournot equilibrium, does the firm's explanation as to why the market equilibrium price is rising make sense? What is a better explanation?

27. Determine the Stackelberg equilibrium with one leader firm and two follower firms if the market demand curve is linear and each firm faces a constant marginal cost, m, and no fixed cost.

*28. Suppose that identical duopoly firms have constant marginal costs of $10 per unit. Firm 1 faces a demand function of $q_1 = 100 - 2p_1 + p_2$, where q_1 is Firm 1's output, p_1 is Firm 1's price, and p_2 is Firm 2's price. Similarly, the demand Firm 2 faces is $q_2 = 100 - 2p_2 + p_1$. Solve for the Bertrand equilibrium.

29. Solve for the Bertrand equilibrium for the firms described in Problem 28 if both firms have a marginal cost of $0 per unit.

30. Solve for the Bertrand equilibrium for the firms described in Problem 28 if Firm 1's marginal cost is $30 per unit and Firm 2's marginal cost is $10 per unit.

*31. The viatical settlement industry enables terminally ill consumers, typically HIV patients, to borrow against equity in their existing life insurance contracts to finance their consumption and medical expenses. The introduction and dissemination of effective anti-HIV medication in 1996 reduced AIDS mortality, extending patients' lives and hence delaying when the viatical settlement industry would receive the insurance payments. However, viatical settlement payments (what patients can borrow) fell more than can be explained by greater life expectancy. The number of viatical settlement firms dropped from 44 in 1995 to 24 in 2001. Sood et al. (2005) found that an increase in market power of viatical settlement firms reduced the value of life insurance holdings of HIV-positive persons by about $1 billion. When marginal cost rises and the number of firms falls, what happens to the Cournot equilibrium price? Use graphs or math to illustrate your answer. (*Hint*: If you use math, it may be helpful to assume that the market demand curve has a constant elasticity throughout.)

32. Firms in some industries with a small number of competitors earn normal economic profit. The *Wall Street Journal* (Gomes, Lee, "Competition Lives On in Just One PC Sector," March 17, 2003, B1) reports that the computer graphics chips industry is one such market. Two chip manufacturers, nVidia and ATI, "both face the prospect of razor-thin profits, largely on account of the other's existence."

   a. Consider the Bertrand model in which each firm has a positive fixed and sunk cost and a zero marginal cost. What are the Nash equilibrium prices? What are the Nash equilibrium profits?

   b. Does this "razor-thin" profit result imply that the two manufacturers necessarily produce chips that are nearly perfect substitutes? Explain.

   c. Assume that nVidia and ATI produce differentiated products and are Bertrand competitors. The demand for nVidia's chip is $q_V = \alpha - \beta p_V + \gamma p_A$; the demand for ATI's chip is $q_A = \alpha - \beta p_A + \gamma p_V$, where p_V is nVidia's price, p_A is ATI's price, and α, β, and γ are coefficients of the demand function. Suppose each manufacturer's marginal cost is a constant, m. What are the values of α, β, and γ for which the equilibrium profit of each chip manufacturer is zero? In answering this question, show that despite differentiated products, duopolists may earn zero economic profit. V

33. At a busy intersection on Route 309 in Quakertown, Pennsylvania, the convenience store and gasoline station, Wawa, competes with the service and gasoline station, Fred's Sunoco. In the Bertrand equilibrium with product differentiation competition for gasoline sales, the demand for Wawa's gas is $q_W = 680 - 500p_W + 400p_S$, and the demand for Fred's gas is $q_W = 680 - 500p_S + 400p_W$. Assume that the marginal cost of each gallon of gasoline is $m = \$2$. The gasoline retailers simultaneously set their prices.

   a. What is the Nash equilibrium?

   b. Suppose that for each gallon of gasoline sold, Wawa earns a profit of 25¢ from its sale of salty snacks to its gasoline customers. Fred sells no products that are related to the consumption of his gasoline. What is the Nash equilibrium? V

34. On an early Saturday morning in mid-July, each of three farmers–Abel, Bess, and Charles–decides how many sweet peppers to bring to the Perkasie, Pennsylvania, farmers' market. Each farmer has exactly 50 pounds of peppers to sell at either the farmers' market or at each farmer's home roadside stand. Each farmer's roadside stand is in a remote area of Bucks County, Pennsylvania, and, accordingly, is a monopoly. The inverse demand to Farmer i, $i = A$, B, or C, of selling q_{ih} peppers at his or her home roadside stand is $R_i = (5 - q_{ih}/10)q_{ih}$. In the market, the farmers are Cournot competitors. The inverse demand for peppers at the farmers' market is $10 - 0.1(q_{Am} + q_{Bm} + q_{Cm})$, where q_{im} is the amount each Farmer i sells at the market. What are the Nash-Cournot equilibrium quantities? What are the market and roadside stand prices? V

35. Acura and Volvo offer warranties on their automobiles, where w_A is the number of years of an Acura warranty and w_V is the number of years of a Volvo warranty. The revenue for Firm i, $i = A$ for Acura and V for Volvo, is $R_i = 32{,}000 w_i/(w_A + w_V)$. Its cost of providing the warranty is $C_i = 2{,}000 w_i$. Acura and Volvo simultaneously set warranties.

   a. What is the profit function for each firm?
   b. What are the Nash equilibrium warranties?
   c. Suppose that Acura and Volvo collude in setting warranties. What warranties do they set? V

36. In October 2002, the European Union fined Sotheby's auction house more than €20 million for operating (along with rival auction house Christie's) a price-fixing cartel (see "The Art of Price Fixing" in **MyEconLab**'s textbook resources for Chapter 14). The two auction houses were jointly setting the commission rates sellers must pay. Let r denote the jointly set auction commission rate, $D_i(r)$ represent the demand for auction house i's services by sellers of auctioned items, p denote the average price of auctioned items, F represent an auction house's fixed cost, and v denote its average variable cost of auctioning an object. At the agreed-upon commission rate r, the profit of an auction house i is $\pi_i = rpD_i(r) - [F + vD_i(r)]$.

   a. What is the sum of the profits of auction houses i and j?
   b. Characterize the commission rate that maximizes the sum of profits. That is, show that the commission rate that maximizes the sum of profits satisfies an equation that looks something like the monopoly's Lerner Index profit-maximizing condition, Equation 11.11.
   c. Do the auction houses have an incentive to cheat on their agreement? If Christie's does so while Sotheby's continues to charge r, what will happen to their individual and collective profits? V

37. In February 2005, the U.S. Federal Trade Commission (FTC) went to court to undo the January 2000 takeover of Highland Park Hospital by Evanston Northwestern Healthcare Corp. The FTC accused Evanston Northwestern of antitrust violations by using its post-merger market power in the Evanston hospital market to impose 40% to 60% price increases (Bernard Wysocki, Jr., "FTC Targets Hospital Merger in Antitrust Case," *Wall Street Journal*, January 17, 2005, A1). Hospitals, even within the same community, are geographically differentiated as well as possibly quality differentiated. The demand for an appendectomy at Highland Park Hospital is a function of the price of the procedure at Highland Park and Evanston Northwestern Hospital: $q_H = 50 - 0.01p_H + 0.005p_N$. The comparable demand function at Evanston Northwestern is $q_N = 500 - 0.01p_N + 0.005p_H$. At each hospital, the fixed cost of the procedure is $20,000 and the marginal cost is $2,000.

   a. Use the product-differentiated Bertrand model to analyze the prices the hospitals set before the merger. Find the Nash equilibrium prices of the procedure at the two hospitals.
   b. After the merger, find the profit-maximizing monopoly prices of the procedure at each hospital. Include the effect of each hospital's price on the profit of the other hospital.
   c. Does the merger result in increased prices? Explain.

*38. To examine the trade-off between efficiency and market power from a merger, consider a market with two firms that sell identical products. Firm 1 has a constant marginal cost of 1, and Firm 2 has a constant marginal cost of 2. The market demand is $Q = 15 - p$.

   a. Solve for the Cournot equilibrium price, quantities, profits, consumer surplus, and deadweight loss.
   b. If the firms merge and produce at the lower marginal cost, how do the equilibrium values change?

c. Discuss the change in efficiency (average cost of producing the output) and welfare—consumer surplus, producer surplus (or profit), and deadweight loss.

*39. Duopoly quantity-setting firms face the market demand
$$p = 150 - q_1 - q_2.$$
Each firm has a marginal cost of $60 per unit.
  a. What is the Cournot equilibrium?
  b. What is the Stackelberg equilibrium when Firm 1 moves first?

*40. An incumbent firm, Firm 1, faces a potential entrant, Firm 2, that has a lower marginal cost. The market demand curve is $p = 120 - q_1 - q_2$. Firm 1 has a constant marginal cost of $20, while Firm 2's is $10.
  a. What are the Cournot equilibrium price, quantities, and profits if there is no government intervention?
  b. To block entry, the incumbent appeals to the government to require that the entrant incur extra costs. What happens to the Cournot equilibrium if the legal requirement causes the marginal cost of the second firm to rise to that of the first firm, $20?
  c. Now suppose that the barrier leaves the marginal cost alone but imposes a fixed cost. What is the minimal fixed cost that will prevent entry?

41. Two firms, each in a different country, sell homogeneous output in a third country. Government 1 subsidizes its domestic firm by s per unit. The other government does not react. In the absence of government intervention, the market has a Cournot equilibrium. Suppose demand is linear, $p = 1 - q_1 - q_2$, and each firm's marginal and average costs of production are constant at m. Government 1 maximizes net national income (it does not care about transfers between the government and the firm, so it maximizes the firm's profit net of the transfers). Show that Government 1's optimal s results in its firm producing the Stackelberg leader quantity and the other firm producing the Stackelberg follower quantity in equilibrium.

42. Show the effect of a subsidy on Firm 1's best-response function in Solved Problem 14.4 if the firm faces a general demand function $p(Q)$.

43. Consider the Cournot model with n firms. The inverse linear market demand function is $p = a - bQ$. Each of the n identical firms has the same cost function $C(q_i) = \beta q_i + (\gamma/2)q_i^2$, where $a > \beta$. In terms of n, what is each firm's Nash equilibrium output and profit and the equilibrium price? As n gets very large (approaches infinity), does each firm's equilibrium profit approach zero? Why? V

Calculus Appendix

In mathematics you don't understand things. You just get used to them.
—John von Neumann

This appendix reviews the basic tools from calculus and mathematics that we use throughout this book.[1] It emphasizes unconstrained and constrained maximization.

A.1 Functions

A *function* associates each member of a set with a single member of another set. In this section, we first examine *functions of a single variable* and then discuss *functions of several variables*.

Functions of a Single Variable

Suppose that we are interested in a variable x that is a member or an element of a set X. For example, the set X may be the nonnegative real numbers. A function f associates elements of the set X with elements of a set Y, which may be the same set as X. The function f is a *mapping* from X to Y, which we denote by $f: X \to Y$. The set X is the *domain* of the function f, while Y is the *range* of the function. In applying the mapping from an element of X to Y, we write $y = f(x)$.

We concentrate on real-number functions. Frequently, these functions map from the set of real numbers ($X = \mathbb{R}$) into the same set of real numbers ($Y = \mathbb{R}$). However, sometimes we consider functions with a domain that is an *interval* within the real numbers. For example, we might study a function that maps the numbers between zero and one. Such intervals are written as [0, 1] if the interval includes zero and one, or as (0, 1) if the endpoints of the interval are not included in the set. One can also use a parenthesis and a bracket, writing (0, 1] for the interval of real numbers that are strictly greater than zero but less than or equal to one. By writing that $x \in (0, 1]$, we mean that the variable x can take on only a value that is greater than zero and less than or equal to one.

---

[1] Ethan Ligon is the co-author of this appendix. Two additional, advanced topics are available on **MyEconLab**.

Some examples of functions of a single variable include the

- *Identity function*: $f(x) = x$ for all $x \in X$.
- *Zero function*: $f(x) = 0$ for all $x \in X$.
- *Square root function*: $f(x) = \sqrt{x}$ for all $x \geq 0$.
- *Hyperbolic function*: $f(x) = 1/x$, which is not defined when $x = 0$.

These examples are called *explicit* functions because we can write them in the form $y = f(x)$. Some functions are *implicit* mappings between X and Y and are written in the form $g(x, y) = 0$. For example, $x^2 + y^2 - 1 = 0$ implicitly defines y in terms of x. We can always express an explicit function f in implicit form by defining $g(x, y) = y - f(x)$. However, it is not possible to express every implicit function explicitly. For example, the implicit function $g(x, y) = ay^5 + by^4 + cy^3 + dy^2 + ey + x = 0$ cannot generally be rewritten so that y is a closed-form expression of the variable x and the parameters a, b, c, d, and e.

Functions of Several Variables

A function may depend on more than one variable. An example of such a function is $y = f(x_1, x_2)$, where $x \in X_1$ and $x_2 \in X_2$. Then the domain of the function is written as $X = X_1 \times X_2$, where the symbol $\times$ when applied to sets means to take all possible combinations of elements of the two sets. For example, the set $X = [0, 1] \times [0, 1]$ contains all the pairs of real numbers between zero and one, inclusive. The function f associates elements of the domain, the set $X = X_1 \times X_2$, with elements of the range, the set Y. That is, f is a mapping from X to Y, which may be denoted either by $f: X \to Y$ or by $f: X_1 \times X_2 \to Y$.

An example of mapping from a pair of variables to a single variable is the well-known measure of physical fitness, the *body mass index* (BMI), which is a function of weight (in kilograms) and height (in meters):

$$\text{BMI} = \frac{\text{weight}}{(\text{height})^2}.$$

If we let the variable z measure the BMI, w reflect the weight, and h denote the height, we can write this function more compactly as

$$z = f(w, h) = \frac{w}{h^2}.$$

Other examples of functions of two or more variables are the

- *Cobb-Douglas function with two variables*: $y = f(K, L) = 3L^{0.33}K^{0.66}$.
- *Cobb-Douglas function with two variables and two parameters*: $y = f(K, L) = AL^\alpha K^{1-\alpha}$, where A and α are parameters rather than variables—they represent unknown numbers rather than quantities that can change. The previous example is a special case, where $A = 3$ and $\alpha = \frac{1}{3}$.
- *Cobb-Douglas function with n variables*:
  $y = f(x_1, x_2, x_3, \ldots, x_n) = Ax_1^{\alpha_1} x_2^{\alpha_2} \ldots x_n^{\alpha_n}$.

A.2 Properties of Functions

We make extensive use of several key properties that functions may possess. In this section, we start by discussing the main properties that we use, which are *monotonicity* (the graph of a function always goes up or always goes down), *continuity* (there are no breaks in the graph of the function), *concavity* and *convexity* (the function consistently curves upward or downward), and *homogeneity* (the function "scales" up or down consistently). After reviewing these properties, we list three properties of the logarithmic function that we use repeatedly.

Monotonicity

A monotonic function is one that is either always *increasing* or always *decreasing*. For example, the identity function, $f(x) = x$, is monotonically increasing. That is, as x increases, so does the value of the function $f(x)$. Some functions are monotonic only under certain conditions. For example, the function $f(x) = 1/x$ is monotonically decreasing when x is positive. The function $f(x) = x^2$ isn't monotonic; it is decreasing when x is negative and increasing when x is positive.

Continuity

A function exhibits the property of *continuity* if a graph of the function has no jumps or breaks. A function can be continuous *at a point* if there are no jumps or breaks very near the point; if the function is continuous at all points, we say that the function is continuous. A sufficient condition for a function to be continuous at a point a is

$$\lim_{x \to a} f(x) = f(a),$$

which indicates that the limit of the function $f(x)$ as x approaches a is $f(a)$.[2]

Concavity and Convexity

Economists make extensive use of the properties of concavity and convexity. We say that the function f is *concave* over a region A if the graph of the function $f(x)$ never goes below the line drawn between *any* pair of points in A. For example, in panel a of Figure A.1, we evaluate a function f with a domain X. Within this domain, we choose a subset A, and we evaluate f at two points x and x' within this subset A. This procedure gives us two points in the range of f, $f(x)$ and $f(x')$. The line connecting the points $(x, f(x))$ and $(x', f(x'))$ is below $f(x)$ for all x between x and x'.

This "never below the line" test reflects the intuition of concavity for functions of a single variable. But for functions of multiple variables and for testing the concavity of a function that we cannot easily draw, we have a better test. To illustrate this approach, we examine the concavity of a function of a pair of variables (x, y) that maps $f: X \times Y \to Z$. Again, let A be a subset of the domain of f, $X \times Y$, and choose two points from the domain, (x, y) and (x', y'). The function f is concave over A if, for any value of θ such that $0 < \theta < 1$ and for any pair (x, y) and (x', y') in A,

$$f(\theta x + [1-\theta]x', \theta y + [1-\theta]y') \geq \theta f(x, y) + [1-\theta]f(x', y'). \tag{A.1}$$

---

[2] If an infinite sequence tends toward some particular value as we progress through that sequence, that value is the limit of the sequence. For example, in the sequence $\{1, \frac{1}{2}, \frac{1}{3}, \frac{1}{4}, \ldots\}$ the nth element in the sequence equals $1/n$, where n is a positive whole number. As n gets larger, the value of $1/n$ tends to zero, so the limit of this sequence is zero (even though zero is not an element of the sequence).

Figure A.1 Concave and Convex Functions

Some functions are convex, some concave, and some neither. (a) This function is convex because a straight line drawn between any two points never goes above the curve. (b) This function is concave because a straight line drawn between two points never goes below the curve. (c) This function violates both of these conditions and thus is neither convex nor concave.

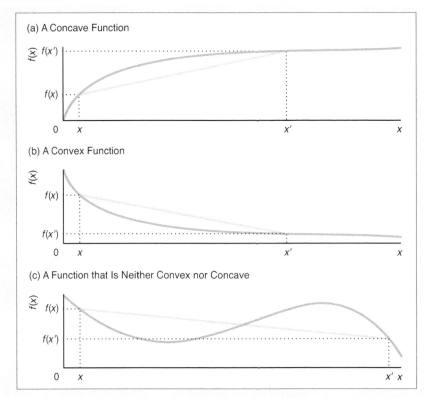

Equation A.1 is an extension of our "never below the line" test. If we let θ vary between zero and one, we can trace out all the values of the function f evaluated at points in A on the left-hand side of the inequality, while varying θ on the right-hand side of the expression traces out a line segment connecting the function f evaluated at (x, y) and at (x', y'). Thus, this expression says that the function lies above the connecting line.

Sometimes a distinction is drawn between a function that is *weakly concave* or *strictly concave*. A *weakly concave* function f satisfies the requirement in Equation A.1, while a *strictly concave* function satisfies a replacement condition:

$$f(\theta x + [1 - \theta]x', \theta y + [1 - \theta]y') > \theta f(x, y) + [1 - \theta]f(x', y').$$

A function is *convex* over a region A if the opposite of the concavity condition holds. That is, the function never goes *above* a line connecting points on the function, as panel b of Figure A.1 illustrates. The mathematical requirement is the same as the requirement for concavity with the inequality reversed: The function f is *weakly convex* over A if, for any value of θ such that $0 < \theta < 1$ and for any (x, y) and (x', y') in A,

$$f(\theta x + [1 - \theta]x', \theta y + [1 - \theta]y') \leq \theta f(x, y) + [1 - \theta]f(x', y').$$

The function is *strictly convex* if this expression holds with a strict inequality.

The function $f(x) = x^2$ is strictly convex. To demonstrate this convexity, we pick any two points on the real line x and x', and check that

$$f(\theta x + [1 - \theta]x') < \theta f(x) + [1 - \theta]f(x')$$

holds for this function. We substitute the actual function into this expression:

$$(\theta x + [1-\theta]x')^2 < \theta x^2 + [1-\theta](x')^2, \text{ or}$$

$$\theta^2 x^2 + [1-\theta]^2(x')^2 + 2\theta[1-\theta]xx' < \theta x^2 + [1-\theta](x')^2.$$

Rearranging terms,

$$\theta[1-\theta]x^2 + \theta[1-\theta](x')^2 - 2\theta[1-\theta]xx' > 0, \text{ or}$$

$$x^2 + (x')^2 - 2xx' = (x-x')^2 > 0.$$

Thus, this function is strictly convex.

In panel c of Figure A.1, the function x^3 is not concave or convex over the domain of real numbers: It is concave over the negative real numbers and convex over the positive real numbers. Finally, the Cobb-Douglas function $f(K, L) = AL^\alpha K^\beta$, where L and K are nonnegative real numbers, is concave if $\alpha + \beta \leq 1$.

Homogeneous Functions

A function $f(x_1, x_2, \ldots, x_n)$ is said to be *homogeneous* of degree γ if

$$f(ax_1, ax_2, \ldots, ax_n) = a^\gamma f(x_1, x_2, \ldots, x_n)$$

for any constant $a > 0$. For example, suppose that f is a production function and the set $\{x_i\}$ consists of inputs to production. Given a particular set of inputs $(x_1, x_2, \ldots, x_n)$, the production function tells us how much output, $q = f(x_1, x_2, \ldots, x_n)$, the firm can produce. What happens to q if we double all the inputs so that $a = 2$? If for any set of inputs, output always doubles, then the production function is homogeneous of degree one. If output does not change at all, then it is homogeneous of degree zero. If it always quadruples, it is homogeneous of degree two, and so on. Some other examples are

- The function $f(x) = 1$ is homogeneous of degree zero because doubling x leaves $f(x)$ unchanged.
- The square root function $f(x_1, x_2) = \sqrt{x_1 + x_2}$ is homogeneous of degree one-half because doubling x_1 and x_2 causes the function to change to $\sqrt{2x_1 + 2x_2} = \sqrt{2}\sqrt{x_1 + x_2} = 2^{0.5}\sqrt{x_1 + x_2}$.
- The function $f(x_1, x_2) = \sqrt{x_1 x_2}$ is homogeneous of degree one because $\sqrt{(2x_1)(2x_2)} = 2\sqrt{x_1 x_2}$.
- The Cobb-Douglas function $f(L, K) = AL^\alpha K^\beta$ is homogeneous of degree $\alpha + \beta$ because $A(2L)^\alpha(2K)^\beta = 2^{\alpha+\beta}AL^\alpha K^\beta$.
- The functions $f(x) = x + 1$ and $f(x_1, x_2) = x_1 + \sqrt{x_2}$ are not homogeneous of any degree.

Special Properties of Logarithmic Functions

Logarithms are wonderful, logarithms are fine.
Once you learn the rules of logs, you'll think they are sublime.

We use the logarithmic function repeatedly in this textbook because it has a number of desirable properties. For example, we can convert some multiplication problems into addition problems by using the logarithmic function. We always use the natural logarithm (or natural log) function of x, which we write as $\ln(x)$, where $x = e^{\ln(x)}$ for $x > 0$.

The key properties of logarithms that we use are

- The log of a product is equal to a sum of logs: $\ln(xz) = \ln(x) + \ln(z)$.
- The log of a number to a power is equal to the power times the log of the number: $\ln(x^b) = b \ln(x)$.
- It follows from this previous rule that the log of the reciprocal of x equals the negative of the log of x: $\ln(1/x) = \ln(x^{-1}) = -\ln(x)$.

A.3 Derivatives

We want a way to summarize how a function changes as its argument changes. One such measure is the slope. However, we generally use an alternative measure, the *derivative*, which is essentially the slope at a particular point. We illustrate the distinction between these two measures using a function of a single variable, $f\colon \mathbb{R} \to \mathbb{R}$.

The usual definition of a *slope* is "rise over run"—that is, the change in the value of a function when moving from point x_1 to another point x_2:

$$\text{Slope} = \frac{\text{rise}}{\text{run}} = \frac{f(x_2) - f(x_1)}{x_2 - x_1}.$$

This definition of a slope depends on comparing the function at *two* different points, x_1 and x_2. However, typically we want the slope of f at a point.

To determine the slope at a point, we first implicitly define the difference, h, between these points as $x_2 = x_1 + h$. Substituting this expression into our formula for the slope gives us

$$\frac{f(x_2) - f(x_1)}{x_2 - x_1} = \frac{f(x_1 + h) - f + (x_1)}{h}.$$

The derivative of a real-value function $f\colon \mathbb{R} \to \mathbb{R}$ at a point x in $\mathbb{R}$ is

$$\frac{\mathrm{d}f(x)}{\mathrm{d}x} = \lim_{h \to 0} \frac{f(x+h) - f(x)}{h}. \tag{A.2}$$

In the text of this book, we use two different notational conventions to denote the derivative of a function. Here and in most places in the text, we write the derivative using the notation $\mathrm{d}f(x)/\mathrm{d}x$. Sometimes for notational simplicity, we omit explicit reference to the argument of f, writing the derivative of f at x as $\mathrm{d}f/\mathrm{d}x$ where no ambiguity results.

The derivative has a graphical interpretation. The slope of a function between two points is equal to the slope of a straight line connecting those two points. The slope of such a straight line can be computed using the rise-over-run formula. In Figure A.2, the slope of a function between x_1 and x_2 is equal to the slope of a straight line connecting the two points $b = (x_1, f(x_1))$ and $(x_2, f(x_2))$. Now fix one of the points, b, and move the other point ever closer so that the run ($h = x_2 - x_1$) gets smaller and smaller. If the derivative exists, the rise, $f(x_2) - f(x_1) = f(x_1 + h) - f(x_1)$, will eventually get smaller and smaller as well, but typically at a different rate than the run. The limiting value of the ratio of the rise to the run will be the slope of an infinitesimally short line—the slope of the function at a point. The limiting value of this slope is the derivative, which equals the slope of a line tangent to the function at b.

Figure A.2 Derivative and Slope

The slope of a function between x_1 and x_2 is equal to the slope (= rise over run) of a straight line connecting the two points $b = (x_1, f(x_1))$ and $(x_2, f(x_2))$. If we fix one of the points, b, and move the other point closer, then the run ($h = x_2 - x_1$) grows smaller and smaller. If the derivative exists, the rise, $f(x_2) - f(x_1) = f(x_1 + h) - f(x_1)$, will eventually get smaller as well, but typically at a different rate than the run. The limiting value of this slope is the derivative, which equals the slope of a line tangent to the function at b.

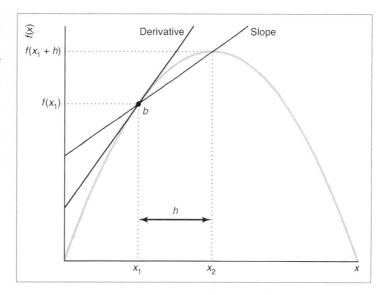

If $df(x)/dx$ is positive, the function is *increasing* at x. That is, as x increases slightly, the function evaluated at x also increases. Similarly, if $df(x)/dx$ is negative, the function is *decreasing* at x.

One problem with using derivatives instead of slopes is that in some circumstances, the derivative of a function may not be defined because the limit given in Equation A.2 does not exist. Discontinuous functions do not have derivatives at any point of discontinuity. For example, the derivative of the function $1/x$ does not exist at $x = 0$. The derivative also fails to exist for a continuous function at a kink, such as at $x = 0$ for the function $|x|$.

Rules for Calculating Derivatives

This book repeatedly uses a few rules for calculating the derivatives of functions.

- *The addition rule*: If a function $f: \mathbb{R} \to \mathbb{R}$ can be written as the sum of two other functions, so that $f(x) = g(x) + h(x)$, then

$$\frac{df(x)}{dx} = \frac{dg(x)}{dx} + \frac{dh(x)}{dx}.$$

In words, this expression says that the derivative of the sum is equal to the sum of the derivatives.

- *The product rule*: If a function $f: \mathbb{R} \to \mathbb{R}$ can be written as the product of two other functions, so that $f(x) = g(x)h(x)$ where g and h are both differentiable at x, then

$$\frac{df(x)}{dx} = \frac{dg(x)}{dx}h(x) + g(x)\frac{dh(x)}{dx}.$$

An important special case occurs when $g(x)$ is a constant, say, b. Then $dg(x)/dx = 0$, so the product rule yields the result that $dbh(x)/dx = bdh(x)/dx$.

- *The power rule*: If $f(x) = ax^b$, then the derivative of f at x, provided that the derivative exists, is
$$\frac{df(x)}{dx} = abx^{b-1}.$$
For example, using the power rule, we can show that $d(bx^2)/dx = 2bx$. Applying this result and the product rule, we can determine the derivative $d(bx^3)/dx$:
$$\frac{dbx^3}{dx} = x\frac{dbx^2}{dx} + \frac{dx}{dx}bx^2 = x(2bx) + bx^2 = 3bx^2.$$
Continuing in this vein using the product rule repeatedly, we learn that in general, $dbx^n/dx = nbx^{n-1}$.

- *The polynomial rule*: A polynomial function is a function that takes the form
$$f(x) = b_0 + b_1 x + b_2 x^2 + \cdots + b_n x^n,$$
where n is a nonnegative whole number. The *order* of the polynomial is the largest exponent, n. Using the power rule repeatedly (as we just showed), the derivative of the polynomial $f(x)$ is
$$\frac{df(x)}{dx} = b_1 + 2b_2 x + \cdots + nb_n x^{n-1}.$$

- *The reciprocal rule*: Using the power rule and the product rule, we can show that the derivative of the reciprocal of a function, $1/f(x)$, is
$$\frac{d[1/f(x)]}{dx} = -\frac{\frac{df(x)}{dx}}{[f(x)]^2}.$$

- *The quotient rule*: Using the reciprocal rule and the product rule, we can show that if $f(x) = g(x)/h(x)$, then
$$\frac{d[g(x)/h(x)]}{dx} = \frac{h(x)\frac{dg(x)}{dx} - g(x)\frac{dh(x)}{dx}}{[h(x)]^2}.$$

- *The chain rule*: We can compute the derivatives of functions such as $f(x) = g(h(x))$ by using all the previous rules,
$$\frac{df(x)}{dx} = \frac{dg(h(x))}{dx} = \frac{dg(h(x))}{dh(x)}\frac{dh(x)}{dx},$$
provided that h is differentiable at x and that g is differentiable at $h(x)$. As an example, let $h(x) = x^2$, and $g(z) = 2 + z^2$ so that $f(x) = g(h(x)) = 2 + x^4$. By direct differentiation, we know that $df(x)/dx = 4x^3$. We can derive the same result using the chain rule. First, we use the power rule to show that $dg(z)/dz = 2z$ and that $dh(x)/dx = 2x$. Second, we substitute $h(x)$ for z in the expression for $dg(z)/dz$, which gives us $dg(h(x))/dh(x)$, and apply the chain rule to obtain
$$\frac{dg(h(x))}{dx} = \frac{d[2 + h(x)]}{dh(x)}\frac{dh(x)}{dx} = (2x^2) \times (2x) = 4x^3.$$

- *The exponential rule*: For any differentiable function $g(x)$,
$$\frac{de^{g(x)}}{dx} = \frac{dg(x)}{dx}e^{g(x)}.$$

An important special case of this rule is that
$$\frac{\mathrm{d}ae^{bx}}{\mathrm{d}x} = abe^{bx}.$$

- *The exponent rule*: An exponential function is one that can be written in the form $f(x) = a^x$, where a number a is raised to the power x. One can use the properties of logarithms together with the exponential rule and the chain rule to show that
$$\frac{\mathrm{d}a^x}{\mathrm{d}x} = \frac{\mathrm{d}e^{\ln(a)x}}{\mathrm{d}x} = \ln(a)a^x.$$

- *The logarithm rule*: The derivative of the function $\ln(x)$ is
$$\frac{\mathrm{d}\ln(x)}{\mathrm{d}x} = \frac{1}{x}.$$

Higher-Order Derivatives

If the derivative exists everywhere in the domain, we say that the function is *continuously differentiable*. For example, the function $f(x) = 1/x$ on the domain $(0, 1]$ is a continuously differentiable function. We can use the power rule to show that the ordinary derivative is
$$\frac{\mathrm{d}[1/x]}{\mathrm{d}x} = \frac{\mathrm{d}[x^{-1}]}{\mathrm{d}x} = -\frac{1}{x^2}.$$

This derivative is itself continuously differentiable on $(0, 1]$. Accordingly, we can use the power rule to differentiate this derivative a second time:
$$\frac{\mathrm{d}[-1/x^2]}{\mathrm{d}x} = \frac{\mathrm{d}[-x^{-2}]}{\mathrm{d}x} = \frac{2}{x^3}.$$

Rather than referring to this result as the "derivative of the derivative of $f(x)$," we call it the *second derivative of $f(x)$*, which we write as $\mathrm{d}^2 f(x)/\mathrm{d}x^2$.

Higher-order derivatives are defined similarly. The derivative of the derivative of the derivative of $f(x)$, called the third derivative of $f(x)$, is written $\mathrm{d}^3 f(x)/\mathrm{d}x^3$. In general, the nth order derivative of $f(x)$ is $\mathrm{d}^n f(x)/\mathrm{d}x^n$.

Partial Derivatives

When using a function of more than one variable, we want to know how the value of the function varies as we change one variable while holding the others constant. Consider a function of two real variables, $f: \mathbb{R}^2 \to \mathbb{R}$. The slope of this function at a point is a little more complicated to define than the slope of a function with a single argument, because the slope of the function at a point now depends on direction. For example, let
$$f(N, E) = N^2 - E^2 + 1.$$

The variable names are chosen to evoke a map, where N reflects the latitude and E denotes the longitude. The value of the function f evaluated at a point on this map can then be thought of as corresponding to the altitude (height). Figure A.3 shows the surface and contour lines of this function.

This function takes the value of zero at the origin but changes in quite different ways as one moves away from the origin, depending on the direction of the move. If one were to move directly to the northeast, then N and E would increase at the

Figure A.3 Illustration of Partial Derivatives

The figure shows the surface and contour lines of the function $f(N, E) = N^2 - E^2 + 1$. If we move only in the N direction, the elevation rises at an increasing rate, whereas if we move only in the E direction, the elevation falls at the same increasing rate. The curves in the (N, E) plane are contour lines of the surface above the plane. The curves show that if E increases at the same rate as N, the elevation remains constant.

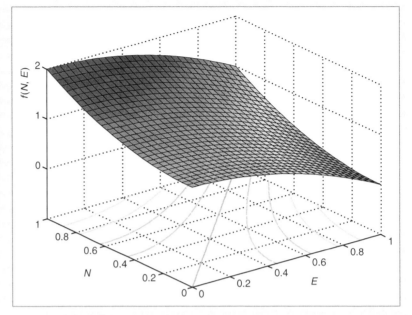

same rate (hence their squares do, too). Thus, if one moves directly to the northeast (or southwest), the altitude does not change. In the figure, the curves in the (N, E) plane are contour lines of the surface above the plane. The curves show that if E increases at the same rate as N, the elevation remains constant.

However, if one begins at the origin and heads directly north, then N increases while E remains fixed. One's altitude increases in this direction. If, on the other hand, one heads directly east, E increases while N remains fixed, and one heads downhill (after traveling E units, one attains an altitude of $1 - E^2$).

Going *just* north or *just* east gets at the idea behind the *partial derivative*: The idea is to vary the value of one variable while holding all the other variables fixed. This procedure also gives us an easy algorithm for computing the partial derivative of f with respect to, say, N: Just pretend that E is a constant, and compute the *ordinary* derivative. Thus, we have the partial derivative of f with respect to N,

$$\frac{\partial f(N, E)}{\partial N} = \frac{\partial (N^2 - E^2)}{\partial N} = \frac{\partial N^2}{\partial N} = 2N,$$

and the partial derivative of f with respect to E,

$$\frac{\partial f(N, E)}{\partial E} = \frac{\partial (N^2 - E^2)}{\partial E} = -\frac{\partial E^2}{\partial E} = -2E.$$

In the special case in which f is a function of only a single variable, the partial derivative is exactly the same as the ordinary derivative:

$$\frac{\partial f(x)}{\partial x} = \frac{df(x)}{dx}.$$

In the general case in which the function $f: \mathbb{R}^m \to \mathbb{R}$ depends on several variables, one can think of the partial derivative of f with respect to, say, the first variable as measuring the *direct* effect of a change in the first variable on the value of the function, while neglecting the effects that a change in this variable might have on *other* variables that might influence the value of $f(x)$. Just as the ordinary derivative of an ordinary derivative is called a second (ordinary) derivative, there are also higher-order partial derivatives. For example, the partial derivative of $g(x_1, x_2)$ with respect to x_1 is written as $\partial g(x_1, x_2)/\partial x_1$; the *second* partial derivative of $g(x_1, x_2)$ with respect to x_1 is written as $\partial^2 g(x_1, x_2)/\partial x_1^2$, while the second partial derivative of $g(x_1, x_2)$ with respect to x_2 is written as $\partial^2 g(x_1, x_2)/\partial x_2^2$.

We can derive second-order (or higher-order) derivatives that involve the repeated differentiation of the function with respect to more than one variable. For example, if we differentiate the partial derivative of our function $g(x_1, x_2)$ with respect to x_1, $\partial g(x_1, x_2)/\partial x_1$, with respect to x_2, we obtain the cross-partial derivative, $\partial^2 g(x_1, x_2)/(\partial x_1 \partial x_2)$. The order of differentiation doesn't matter for the functions we usually study. According to Young's Theorem, $\partial^2 f/(\partial x_1 \partial x_2) = \partial^2 f/(\partial x_2 \partial x_1)$ if the cross-partial derivatives $\partial^2 f/(\partial x_1 \partial x_2)$ and $\partial^2 f/(\partial x_2 \partial x_1)$ exist and are continuous. Similarly, $\partial^5 g(x_1, x_2)/\partial x_1^2 \partial x_2^3$ indicates partial differentiation of g with respect to x_1 twice and with respect to x_2 thrice, thus yielding a fifth-order partial derivative.

Euler's Homogeneous Function Theorem

A function $f: \mathbb{R}^n \to \mathbb{R}$ is *homogeneous* of degree γ if

$$f(tx_1, tx_2, \ldots, tx_n) = t^\gamma f(x_1, \ldots, x_n)$$

holds for all possible values of $x_1, x_2, \ldots, x_n$ and constant scalar t. That is, multiplying each of the arguments of the function by t increases the value of the function by t^γ. The degree need not be an integer. For example, the Cobb-Douglas function $A x_1^{\alpha_1} x_2^{\alpha_2} \ldots x_n^{\alpha_n}$ is homogeneous of degree $\alpha_1 + \alpha_2 + \cdots + \alpha_n$, where each α_i may be a fraction. Such a function satisfies Euler's homogeneous function theorem

$$\sum_{i=1}^n x_i \frac{\partial f(x_1, \ldots, x_n)}{\partial x_i} = \gamma f(x_1, \ldots, x_n).$$

A.4 Maximum and Minimum

Most microeconomic analysis concerns finding the maximum or minimum of a function. For example, a consumer chooses a bundle of goods to maximize utility, or a firm chooses inputs to minimize cost.

The problems of finding a maximum and finding a minimum may sound as though they are very different, but they are similar mathematically. We think of the problems of finding either *maxima* or *minima* as special cases of the more general problem of finding *extrema*.

Local Extrema

Mathematicians and economists are sometimes interested in the *local* properties of a function, or, equivalently, the properties of a function within the *neighborhood* of a point x. A local property is one that holds within a neighborhood of x—that is, within some positive (but possibly very small) distance $\varepsilon > 0$ from the point x. For example, a function has a local maximum at x^* if there exists an $\varepsilon > 0$ such that $f(x^*) \geq f(x)$ for all $x \in (x^* - \varepsilon, x^* + \varepsilon)$—that is, in the neighborhood of x^*.

A *local* extremum of a function $f(x)$ is either a local minimum or a local maximum of the function f. If we move from the local extremum at x by an amount less than ε, the value of the function becomes less extreme. Figure A.4 graphs the function $f(x) = x \sin(6\pi x)$, which has many peaks and troughs. All the local extrema are indicated with bullets. Points a, b, and c are local maxima, while points d, e, and f are local minima. All these local maxima and local minima together compose the set of local extrema. Point a is a local maximum because if we either increase or decrease x just a little, the value of $f(x)$ decreases. Similarly, d is a local minimum because if we either increase or decrease x slightly, the value of $f(x)$ increases.

Global Extrema

The *global maximum* (usually called the *maximum*) is the largest local maximum, and the *global minimum* (or *minimum*) is the smallest local minimum. In Figure A.4, the global maximum is point c and the global minimum is point f. If there are two local maxima that are both equally large and larger than all other points, we would say that there are *two* global maxima.

Existence of Extrema

In economics, we often want to know if a function has a maximum or a minimum in the relevant domain. For example, we might examine whether there is a minimum for a function $f: [0, 1] \to \mathbb{R}$; that is, f takes values from the interval between zero and one (inclusive) and maps them into the real line.

Not all such functions have a maximum or a minimum. Continuity of a function is a *sufficient* condition for the existence of both a maximum and a minimum. This result is a consequence of the *Extreme Value Theorem*: If the function f is continuous and defined on the closed interval $[a, b]$, there is at least one c in $[a, b]$ such that $f(c) \geq f(x)$ for all x in $[a, b]$, and there is at least one d in $[a, b]$ such that $f(d) \leq f(x)$

Figure A.4 Illustration of Local and Global Extrema

The bullets indicate the local extrema. Point c is the global maximum, and point f is the global minimum.

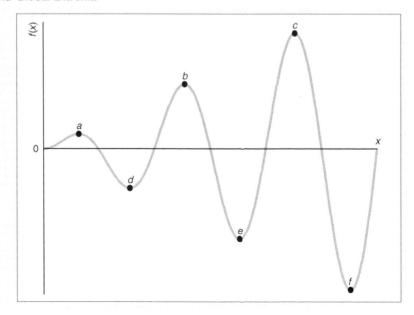

for all x in $[a, b]$. Functions that are not continuous *might* have minima and maxima—but there's no guarantee.

Figure A.5 illustrates several possibilities. Panel a shows a continuous function, $y = f(x) = 24x - 75x^2 + 50x^3$, with a single minimum and a single (local and global) maximum in $[0, 1]$. In panel b, the continuous function $y = f(x) = 1$ has an infinite number of maxima and minima in $[0, 1]$. In panel c, the discontinuity in the function

$$y = \begin{cases} 24x - 75x^2 + 50x^3, & x < 0.8 \\ 24x - 75x^2 + 50x^3, & x > 0.8 \end{cases}$$

is shown as a hollow circle. Because of this missing point, there is a unique maximum, but there isn't a global minimum within $[0, 1]$. Finally, the discontinuous function plotted in panel d,

$$y = \begin{cases} 0, & x < 0.8 \\ 1, & x \geq 0.8, \end{cases}$$

has an infinite number of maxima and minima in $[0, 1]$.

Figure A.5 Illustration of the Extreme Value Theorem

According to the Extreme Value Theorem, if a function is continuous and defined on the closed interval, it contains at least one minimum and at least one maximum. (a) This continuous function has a maximum at point a and a minimum at point b. (b) This continuous function has an infinite number of maxima and minima that equal one. (c) This function is discontinuous at the point marked with a hollow point, so the theorem cannot be used to draw inferences about the existence of minima and maxima. For the domain $(0, 1]$, the function has a maximum, but no minimum. (d) This discontinuous function has infinite maxima and minima.

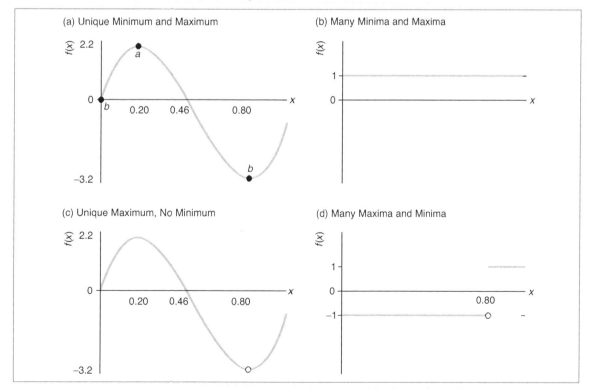

Uniqueness of Extrema

As panels b and d of Figure A.5 illustrate, even when a function has global maxima or global minima, there may be more than one maximum or minimum. We want to determine when the function will have a unique solution. There is a unique global maximum if the function f is strictly concave, and a unique global minimum if f is strictly convex. For example, in panel a of Figure A.5, when x is less than about 0.46, where the curve hits the horizontal axis, the function is concave, so there is a single global maximum. However, to the right of this point, the function is convex and has a single global minimum.

Interior Extrema

Often in the text, we care whether the maximum or minimum is located in the interior of the range of x or at one of the end points. To illustrate this distinction, we consider the function $f(x) = -(x - \frac{1}{2})^2/2$, where x lies within $[0, 1]$, as panel a of Figure A.6 shows. This function has a maximum at point a where $x^* = 0.5$, which we call an *interior* maximum because $x^* \in (0, 1)$ and it is not on the edge of the domain $[0, 1]$. That is, x^* is not zero or one. In contrast, in panel b, because the maximum of the function $g(x) = -x^2/2$ is zero at point a, which is on the edge or *corner* of the domain $[0, 1]$, the maximum of this function is *not* interior.

A.5 Finding the Extrema of a Function

Because it is not always practical to plot functions and look for extrema, we use calculus to find local extrema. The key insight is that for functions that are continuously differentiable, the *slope* of the function at any interior minimum or maximum

Figure A.6 Interior Extrema

In panel a, the maximum, point a, occurs at $x = 0.5$, which lies in the interior of the interval $[0, 1]$. In panel b, the maximum at a is at the corner—not in the interior of the domain.

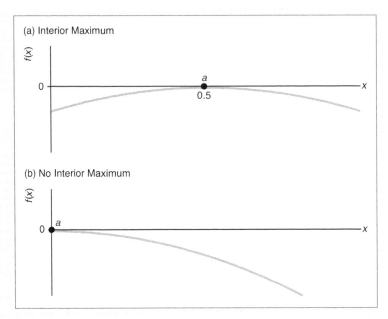

is zero. Figure A.7 illustrates that the slope of the graph at every interior local minimum or maximum is zero.

Because derivatives can be thought of as the slope of a function, one way to find all the interior local extrema of a continuously differentiable function is to find where the partial derivatives of the function equal zero. Let's begin with a problem that has only a single independent variable and $f: [0, 1] \to \mathbb{R}$, where f is assumed to be continuously differentiable and strictly concave. What is the importance of these assumptions?

Figure A.7 Extrema and the First-Order Condition (F.O.C.)

If a function is continuously differentiable and concave, it must have a unique maximum. Further, if the F.O.C. has a solution (that is, the function has a point where its slope is zero), the F.O.C. characterizes the unique maximum. (a) This function is continuously differentiable and concave, so the F.O.C. identifies a unique maximum (at point *a*). (b) The function is continuously differentiable, so it has at least one maximum, but the function is not concave, so the maximum may not be unique (indeed, there are two maxima at the end points). The function is convex, so the F.O.C. characterizes a minimum. (c) The function is continuously differentiable, so it possesses a maximum in the interval [0, 1]. However, at point *a* where the F.O.C. holds, the function is neither concave nor convex, so *a* is neither a minimum nor a maximum—it is a saddle point. (d) The function is concave, so this maximum will be unique. However, the F.O.C. does not have a solution in the interval [0, 1]—there is no place where the function has a slope equal to zero—so the unique maximum is not characterized by the F.O.C.

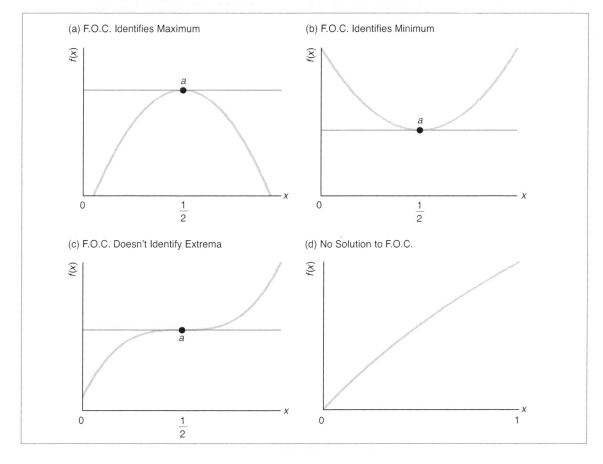

There are two important consequences of our assumption that f is continuously differentiable. First, because f is continuously differentiable, it must also be continuous, so we know that it has a maximum. Second, because it is continuously differentiable, we know that its derivative exists, and hence we can use this derivative to determine the local extrema.

Because f is assumed to be strictly concave, we know that it has a unique global maximum. Thus, if we find a point x where $df(x)/dx = 0$, it follows that this point x is the unique global maximum of the function f over the interval $[0, 1]$.

The usual way to write the problem of finding a maximum of a function $f(x)$ is

$$\max_{x} f(x),$$

where *max* is called the *max operator*, the variable x that appears below the max operator is the *choice variable*, and f is the function to be maximized and is called the *objective function*.

Any x^* in $[0, 1]$ that solves $df(x^*)/dx = 0$ is a point at which the function $f(x)$ has a local maximum. The equation $df(x)/dx = 0$, in which we set the first-order derivative equal to zero, is called the *first-order condition*. The x^* that solves this equation, $df(x^*)/dx$, is called a *critical value*. Given our assumptions that f is continuously differentiable and concave, we know that x^* is a unique global maximum.

So far, we've assumed that f is concave, as in panel a of Figure A.7. In practice, we need to check whether the function is concave. For example, if we falsely assume that the function is concave and it is convex, we may find a minimum rather than a maximum, as in panel b.

If $f(x^*)$ is at least twice-differentiable in a neighborhood of x^*, we can use the *second-order condition* to determine whether the function is concave in that neighborhood. The second-order condition for concavity is that the second derivative of $f(x^*)$ is negative, $d^2f(x^*)/dx^2 < 0$. If this condition holds, we know that the x^* that the first-order condition identified is a unique maximum in this neighborhood of x^*. In contrast, if the second derivative is positive, we know that the function is convex in this neighborhood and that we have found a minimum.

Examples

We can illustrate this approach using several examples where $f: [0, 1] \to \mathbb{R}$. Our first maximization problem is

$$\max_{x} -\tfrac{1}{2}\left(x - \tfrac{1}{2}\right)^2.$$

The first-order condition is $df(x)/dx = \tfrac{1}{2} - x = 0$, so $x^* = \tfrac{1}{2}$, as panel a of Figure A.7 shows. The second-order condition is $d^2f(x^*)/dx^2 = -1 < 0$, so $\tfrac{1}{2}$ is a maximum. One can demonstrate that this function f is continuously differentiable and concave throughout the domain, so $f(\tfrac{1}{2}) = 0$, point a, is the global maximum of this function.

Now consider the maximization problem

$$\max_{x} \tfrac{1}{2}\left(x - \tfrac{1}{2}\right)^2.$$

The first-order condition is $df(x)/dx = x - \tfrac{1}{2} = 0$, so this problem has the same critical value, $x = \tfrac{1}{2}$, as in the previous example. Because f is continuously differentiable, we know that it has a maximum and a minimum on $[0, 1]$. The second-order condition is $d^2f(\tfrac{1}{2})/dx^2 = 1 > 0$ so $x^* = \tfrac{1}{2}$ is a minimum, as panel b of Figure A.7 shows. There are two global maxima, which are not interior, at $x = 0$ and $x = 1$.

The maximization problem

$$\max_x \tfrac{1}{3}\left(x - \tfrac{1}{2}\right)^3$$

has a first-order condition $df(x)/dx = (x - \tfrac{1}{2})^2 = 0$, so the critical value is again at $x = \tfrac{1}{2}$. Because f is continuously differentiable, we know it has a maximum on $[0, 1]$, but as in the previous example, the maximum is not interior; instead, it occurs at $x = 1$. This function is neither concave nor convex at $x = \tfrac{1}{2}$, so $x^* = \tfrac{1}{2}$ is neither a minimum nor a maximum of f, as panel c of Figure A.7 illustrates. It is called a *saddle point*. We have a saddle point when the second-order condition is zero, as in this case: $d^2f(\tfrac{1}{2})/dx^2 = 2(x - \tfrac{1}{2}) = 2(\tfrac{1}{2} - \tfrac{1}{2}) = 0$. The sign of the second derivative changes from one side to the other of the saddle point.

Finally, the maximization problem

$$\max_x \ln(x + 1)$$

yields the first-order condition $1/(x + 1) = 0$. Here, f is continuously differentiable and strictly concave, so we know that a unique global maximum exists. However, there is no value of x in the $[0, 1]$ interval that solves the first-order condition. Consequently, we know that the unique global maximum is *not* interior (in this case, it occurs at the end point where $x = 1$), as panel d of Figure A.7 illustrates.

More generally, we may want to find the maximum of a function of several variables, and hence several choice variables appear under the max operator. To use calculus to solve such a maximization problem, we compute the partial derivatives of the objective function with respect to each of the choice variables and then set these equal to zero. These equations, in which the first-order partial derivatives are set equal to zero, are called the *first-order conditions*.

For example, let $g: [0, 1] \times [0, 1] \to \mathbb{R}$, and assume that g is continuously differentiable and strictly concave. Then we know, as we did for f, that g has a unique global maximum. Accordingly, we can write the problem as

$$\max_{x_1, x_2} g(x_1, x_2),$$

which yields the pair of first-order conditions

$$\frac{\partial g(x_1, x_2)}{\partial x_1} = 0, \tag{A.3}$$

$$\frac{\partial g(x_1, x_2)}{\partial x_2} = 0. \tag{A.4}$$

The solution to Equations A.3 and A.4 determines where the global maximum of g is located, if a solution exists. If a solution to these equations does not exist, then the maximum must lie on the boundary of the choice set $[0, 1] \times [0, 1]$, so either x_1 or x_2 (or both) must be equal to either zero or one at the maximum.

Indirect Objective Functions and the Envelope Theorem

Economic problems generally involve choice variables that are under the control of a person or a firm, such as how much of a good to buy or produce. Economic problems may also depend on *exogenous* parameters that influence the decision maker's behavior but are not under the decision maker's direct control, such as the price at which the good can be bought or sold. We can add these exogenous parameters to the formulation of a maximization problem.

To illustrate this approach, we examine a function g: $[0, 1] \times [0, 1] \times \mathbb{R} \to \mathbb{R}$. We write this function and its arguments as $g(x_1, x_2, z)$, where the variables x_1 and x_2 are choice variables and z is an exogenous parameter. We assume that g is continuously differentiable in all three of its arguments and is strictly concave in the first two (the choice variables). Consequently, g has a unique global maximum (even if g is not concave in the exogenous parameters).

The decision maker's problem of choosing x_1 and x_2 to maximize g given z is written as

$$\max_{x_1, x_2} g(x_1, x_2, z).$$

The first-order conditions are

$$\frac{\partial g(x_1, x_2, z)}{\partial x_1} = 0,$$

$$\frac{\partial g(x_1, x_2, z)}{\partial x_2} = 0,$$

so the optimal choice of x_1 and x_2 typically depends on the value of z. Accordingly, the values of x_1 and x_2 that solve the optimization problem for a given z may be written as $x_1^*(z)$ and $x_2^*(z)$.

Given a solution to the maximization problem, the value of g at the maximum is $g(x_1^*(z), x_2^*(z), z)$ Given some value z, the act of maximization determines the optimal values of x_1^* and x_2^* Accordingly, we may sometimes write the maximum as

$$V(z) = g(x_1^*(z), x_2^*(z), z) = \max_{x_1, x_2} g(x_1, x_2, z).$$

The function $V(z)$ is called the *value function* because it tells us what the value of z is to the decision maker. It is also called the *indirect objective function*, in contrast to $g(x_1, x_2, z)$, which is the *direct objective function*.

A natural question to ask is how the value function changes when z changes. At first glance, this problem is very complicated because (as we have seen) a change in z has a direct effect on the value of $g(x_1, x_2, z)$ and it *also* causes the decision maker to change x_1 and x_2 in ways that may be complicated. However, at least for *small* changes in z, an important shortcut to solving this problem exists. The *Envelope Theorem* tells us that the direct effect of small changes in z matter but that the indirect effects do not. That is, according to the Envelope Theorem, the solution to our particular problem is

$$\frac{\partial V(z)}{\partial z} = \frac{\partial g(x_1, x_2, z)}{\partial z}. \tag{A.5}$$

We offer another, more general statement of this theorem below when we discuss the solutions to constrained maximization problems, and offer a constructive proof.

Comparative Statics. Not only do we want to know how a change in the exogenous parameter affects the value function, but we also want to know how this change in the exogenous parameter, z, affects the choice variables, x_1 and x_2. We can use our first-order conditions to answer this question because the first-order conditions show how the optimal choice of x_1 and x_2 depends on z. In our example, the first-order conditions are

$$\frac{\partial g(x_1^*(z), x_2^*(z), z)}{\partial x_1(z)} = 0,$$

$$\frac{\partial g(x_1^*(z), x_2^*(z), z)}{\partial x_2(z)} = 0.$$

Provided that the function g is twice continuously differentiable, we can then compute the derivatives of each of these first-order conditions with respect to the exogenous parameter:

$$\frac{\partial^2 g}{\partial x_1^2}\frac{dx_1^*(z)}{dz} + \frac{\partial^2 g}{\partial x_1 \partial x_2}\frac{dx_2^*(z)}{dz} + \frac{\partial g}{\partial z} = 0, \qquad (A.6)$$

$$\frac{\partial^2 g}{\partial x_1 \partial x_2}\frac{dx_1^*(z)}{dz} + \frac{\partial^2 g}{\partial x_2^2}\frac{dx_2^*(z)}{dz} + \frac{\partial g}{\partial z} = 0, \qquad (A.7)$$

where we omit the arguments to the function g for notational simplicity.

By treating the derivatives $dx_1^*(z)/dz$ and $dx_2^*(z)/dz$ as variables in the pair of linear Equations A.6 and A.7 and the partial derivatives of g as coefficients, we can solve this system of equations to determine how the maximizing choice of x_1 and x_2 changes for small changes in z. That is, we can solve for $dx_1^*(z)/dz$ and $dx_2^*(z)/dz$.

A.6 Maximizing with Equality Constraints

Most questions in microeconomics involve maximizing or minimizing an objective function subject to one or more *constraints*. For example, consumers maximize their well-being subject to a budget constraint. A firm chooses the cost-minimizing bundle of inputs subject to a feasibility constraint that summarizes which combinations of inputs can produce a given amount of output.

There are two commonly used approaches to solving problems with equality constraints mathematically: the substitution method and Lagrange's method. To illustrate these two approaches, we consider the problem of maximizing the function $g(x_1, x_2)$ subject to the constraint that $h(x_1, x_2) = z$, where z is an exogenous parameter. We write the constraint in implicit function form as $z - h(x_1, x_2) = 0$. This *constrained* maximization problem is written

$$\max_{x_1, x_2} g(x_1, x_2)$$
$$\text{s.t. } z - h(x_1, x_2) = 0. \qquad (A.8)$$

Conceptually, we need to find the set of all those x_1 and x_2 that satisfy the constraint $z - h(x_1, x_2) = 0$, and from only this set, we need to choose those values of x_1 and x_2 that maximize $g(x_1, x_2)$.

Substitution Method

Sometimes we can solve a constrained maximization problem by substituting the constraint into the objective so that the problem becomes an unconstrained problem. We can rewrite the constraint as $x_1 = r(x_2, z)$. Because this solution for x_1 as a function of x_2 contains the information in the constraint, we can substitute it into our objective function and rewrite the problem as an unconstrained maximum:

$$\max_{x_2} g(r(x_2, z), x_2).$$

Because we wrote x_1 as a function of x_2, the unconstrained maximization problem has only one choice variable, x_2.

As with any unconstrained maximum problem, we use the first-order condition,

$$\frac{\partial g(r(x_2, z), x_2)}{\partial x_1} \frac{\partial r(x_2, z)}{\partial x_2} + \frac{\partial g(r(x_2, z), x_2)}{\partial x_2} = 0, \quad (A.9)$$

to find the critical value of the choice variable x_2. We solve the first-order equation, Equation A.9, for x_2^*, substitute this solution for x_2 into $x_1 = r(x_2, z)$ to obtain $x_1^* = r(x_2^*, z)$, and then substitute x_1^* and x_2^* into the objective function to determine the maximum.

The following example illustrates this approach, where the objective function is $g(x_1, x_2) = x_1 x_2$ and the constraint is $z - h(x_1, x_2) = z - x_1 - x_2$, so the constrained maximization problem is

$$\max_{x_1, x_2} \ln(x_1 x_2)$$

$$\text{s.t. } z - x_1 - x_2 = 0. \quad (A.10)$$

Using the constraint to solve for x_1 in terms of x_2, we find that $x_1 = r(x_2, z) = z - x_2$. Substituting this function into the objective function, we obtain the corresponding unconstrained maximization problem:

$$\max_{x_2} \ln((z - x_2)x_2) = \ln(z - x_2) + \ln(x_2).$$

Because the first-order condition is $-1/(z - x_2) + 1/x_2 = 0$, the solution of the first-order condition is $x_2^* = 0.5z$. Substituting this expression into the formula for x_1, we find that $x_1^* = z - 0.5z = 0.5z$. Evaluating the objective function at the maximizing values x_1^* and x_2^*, we find that $g(x_1^*, x_2^*) = \ln(0.25z^2)$.

The problem with using this method is that writing x_1 as a function of x_2 and z may be very difficult. If we have many constraints, this approach will usually be infeasible or impractical.

Lagrange's Method

Joseph Louis Lagrange developed an alternative method to solving a constrained maximization problem that works for a wider variety of problems than the substitution method does. As with the substitution method, Lagrange's method (or the Lagrangian method) converts a constrained maximization problem into an unconstrained maximization problem.

Solving a General Problem. The first step of Lagrange's method is to write the *Lagrangian function*, which is the sum of the original objective function, $g(x_1, x_2)$, and the left-hand side of the constraint, $z - h(x_1, x_2) = 0$, multiplied by a constant, λ, called the Lagrangian *multiplier*:

$$\mathcal{L}(x_1, x_2, \lambda; z) = g(x_1, x_2) + \lambda[z - h(x_1, x_2)]. \quad (A.11)$$

If $\lambda = 0$ or the constraint holds, the Lagrangian function is identical to the original objective function.

The second step is to find the critical values of the (unconstrained) Lagrangian function, Equation A.11, where the choice variables are the original ones and λ:

$$\max_{x_1, x_2, \lambda} \mathcal{L}(x_1, x_2, \lambda; z) = g(x_1, x_2) + \lambda\big[z - h(x_1, x_2)\big]. \tag{A.12}$$

To do so, we use the first-order conditions:

$$\frac{\partial \mathcal{L}(x_1, x_2, \lambda; z)}{\partial x_1} = \frac{\partial g(x_1, x_2)}{\partial x_1} - \lambda \frac{\partial h(x_1, x_2)}{\partial x_1} = 0, \tag{A.13}$$

$$\frac{\partial \mathcal{L}(x_1, x_2, \lambda; z)}{\partial x_2} = \frac{\partial g(x_1, x_2)}{\partial x_2} - \lambda \frac{\partial h(x_1, x_2)}{\partial x_2} = 0, \tag{A.14}$$

$$\frac{\partial \mathcal{L}(x_1, x_2, \lambda; z)}{\lambda} = z - h(x_1, x_2) = 0. \tag{A.15}$$

We simultaneously solve the first-order conditions, Equations A.13, A.14, and A.15, for the critical values of $x_1^*(z)$, $x_2^*(z)$ and $\lambda^*(z)$. Then, we substitute $x_1^*(z)$ and $x_2^*(z)$ into the original objective function to determine the maximum value, $g(x_1^*(z), x_2^*(z))$.

The key result of Lagrange's method is that the solution to this unconstrained problem, Equation A.12, also satisfies the original constrained problem, Equation A.8. Lagrange's method can be generalized to handle problems with more choice variables and more constraints. For each constraint, we need an additional Lagrange multiplier.

An Example. To illustrate this method, we return to the problem A.10, where $g(x_1, x_2) = \ln(x_1 x_2)$ and the constraint is $z - h(x_1, x_2) = z - x_1 - x_2$. The Lagrangian problem is

$$\max_{x_1, x_2, \lambda} \mathcal{L}(x_1, x_2, z, \lambda) = \ln(x_1 x_2) + \lambda(z - x_1 - x_2).$$

The first-order conditions are

$$1/x_2 = \lambda,$$
$$1/x_1 = \lambda,$$
$$z - x_1 - x_2 = 0.$$

Solving these first-order conditions simultaneously, we find that

$$x_1^*(z) = 0.5z, \quad x_2^*(z) = 0.5z, \quad \text{and} \quad \lambda^*(z) = 2/z.$$

Because this solution is the same as the one we obtained using the substitution method, the maximum value of our original objective function is also the same: $g(x_1^*(z), x_2^*(z)) = \ln(0.25 z^2)$.

Interpreting the Lagrange Multiplier. The Lagrange multiplier not only helps us convert a constrained maximization problem to an unconstrained problem but also provides additional information that is often valuable in economic problems. The value of λ that solves the first-order conditions can be interpreted as the (marginal) cost of the constraint.

The change in the original objective function with respect to a change in z is

$$\frac{dg(x_1^*, x_2^*)}{dz} = \frac{\partial g}{\partial x_1}\frac{dx_1^*}{dz} + \frac{\partial g}{\partial x_2}\frac{dx_2^*}{dz}.$$

By substituting the first-order conditions for the original choice variables, Equations A.13 and A.14, into this expression, we obtain

$$\frac{dg(x_1^*, x_2^*)}{dz} = \lambda^* \frac{\partial h}{\partial x_1} \frac{dx_1^*}{dz} + \lambda^* \frac{\partial h}{\partial x_2} \frac{dx_2^*}{dz}. \qquad (A.16)$$

Differentiating the first-order condition for the Lagrange multiplier, Equation A.15, we have the additional result that

$$\frac{\partial h}{\partial x_1} \frac{dx_1^*}{dz} + \frac{\partial h}{\partial x_2} \frac{dx_2^*}{dz} = 1. \qquad (A.17)$$

Substituting Equation A.17 into Equation A.16, we find that

$$\frac{dg(x_1^*, x_2^*)}{dz} = \lambda^*. \qquad (A.18)$$

Equation A.18 shows that the critical value of the Lagrange multiplier reflects the sensitivity of the original objective function to a change in the exogenous parameter, z. In our last example, a small increase in z changes the value of the objective function by a factor of $\lambda = 2/z$. The Lagrange multiplier shows the value of relaxing the constraint slightly.

On **MyEconLab**, there are two more sections of this appendix. The first, Section A.7, addresses how to use a method similar to Lagrange's to maximize subject to inequality constraints. The second, Section A.8, shows that there is a close connection between constrained maxima and minima problems, which is called *duality*.

Definitions

I hate definitions. —Benjamin Disraeli

action: a move that a player makes at a specified stage of a game, such as how much output a firm produces in the current period. (13)*

adverse selection: opportunism characterized by an informed person's benefiting from trading or otherwise contracting with a less-informed person who does not know about an *unobserved characteristic* of the informed person. (18)

asymmetric information: the situation in which one party to a transaction knows a material fact that the other party does not. (18)

auction: a sale in which a good or service is sold to the highest bidder. (13)

average cost (*AC*): the total cost divided by the units of output produced: $AC = C/q$. (7)

average fixed cost (*AFC*): the fixed cost divided by the units of output produced: $AFC = F/q$. (7)

average product of labor (AP_L): the ratio of output, q, to the number of workers, L, used to produce that output: $AP_L = q/L$. (6)

average variable cost (*AVC*): the variable cost divided by the units of output produced: $AVC = VC/q$. (7)

backward induction: a process in which we first determine the best response by the last player to move, next determine the best response for the player who made the next-to-last move, and then repeat the process until we reach the move at the beginning of the game. (13)

bad: something for which less is preferred to more, such as pollution. (3)

bandwagon effect: the situation in which a person places greater value on a good as more and more other people possess it. (11)

barrier to entry: an explicit restriction or a cost that applies only to potential new firms—existing firms are not subject to the restriction or do not bear the cost. (9)

behavioral economics: adds insights from psychology and empirical research on human cognition and emotional biases to the rational economic model to better predict economic decision making. (3)

Bertrand equilibrium (*Nash-Bertrand equilibrium* or *Nash-in-prices equilibrium*): a set of prices such that no firm can obtain a higher profit by choosing a different price if the other firms continue to charge these prices. (14)

best response: the strategy that maximizes a player's payoff given its beliefs about its rivals' strategies. (13)

bounded rationality: people's limited capacity to anticipate, solve complex problems, and enumerate all options. (3)

budget line (*budget constraint*): the bundles of goods that can be bought if a consumer's entire budget is spent on those goods at given prices. (3)

bundling (*package tie-in sale*): a type of tie-in sale in which two goods are combined so that customers cannot buy either good separately. (12)

cartel: a group of firms that explicitly agree (collude) to coordinate their activities. (14)

certification: a report that a particular product meets or exceeds a given standard. (18)

cheap talk: unsubstantiated claims or statements. (18)

collude: coordinate actions such as setting prices or quantities among firms. (14)

common knowledge: information that all players have about the rules of the game and the understanding that each player's payoff depends on actions taken by all players, all players want to maximize their payoffs, all players know that all players know the payoffs and that their opponents are payoff maximizing, and so on. (13)

common property: a resource that is available to anyone. (16)

comparative advantage: the ability to produce a good at a lower opportunity cost than someone else. (10)

comparative statics: the method economists use to analyze how variables controlled by consumers and firms

---

*Numbers refer to the chapter where the term is defined.

react to a change in *environmental variables* (also called *exogenous variables*) that they do not control. (2)

compensating variation (*CV*): the amount of money one would have to give a consumer to offset completely the harm from a price increase. (5)

complete information: the situation where the payoff function is common knowledge among all players. (13)

constant returns to scale (*CRS*): the property of a production function whereby when all inputs are increased by a certain percentage, output increases by that same percentage. (6)

consumer surplus (*CS*): the monetary difference between the maximum amount that a consumer is willing to pay for the quantity of the good purchased and what the good actually costs. (5)

contingent fee: a payment to a lawyer that is a share of the award in a court case (usually after legal expenses are deducted) if the client wins and nothing if the client loses. (19)

contract curve: the set of all Pareto-efficient bundles. (10)

cost (*total cost*, C): the sum of a firm's variable cost and fixed cost: $C = VC + F$. (7)

Cournot equilibrium (*Nash-Cournot equilibrium* or *Nash-in-quantities equilibrium*): a set of quantities chosen by firms such that, holding the quantities of all other firms constant, no firm can obtain a higher profit by choosing a different quantity. (14)

credible threat: an announcement that a firm will use a strategy harmful to its rivals that the rivals believe is rational in the sense that it is in the firm's best interest to use it. (13)

cross-price elasticity of demand: the percentage change in the quantity demanded in response to a given percentage change in the price of another good. (2)

deadweight loss (*DWL*): the net reduction in welfare from a loss of surplus by one group that is not offset by a gain to another group. (9)

decreasing returns to scale (*DRS*): the property of a production function whereby output rises less than in proportion to an equal percentage increase in all inputs. (6)

demand curve: a plot of the demand function that shows the quantity demanded at each possible price, holding constant the other factors that influence purchases. (2)

demand function: the correspondence between the quantity demanded, price, and other factors that influence purchases. (2)

discount rate: a rate reflecting the relative value an individual places on future consumption compared to current consumption. (15)

diseconomies of scale: the property of a cost function whereby the average cost of production rises when output increases. (7)

dominant strategy: a strategy that produces a higher payoff than any other strategy the player can use for every possible combination of its rivals' strategies. (13)

duopoly: an oligopoly with two (*duo*) firms. (14)

durable good: a product that is usable for a long period, typically for many years. (7)

dynamic game: a game in which players move either sequentially or repeatedly. (13)

economic cost (*opportunity cost*): the value of the best alternative use of a resource. (7)

economic profit: revenue minus opportunity (economic) cost. (8)

economically efficient: minimizing the cost of producing a specified amount of output. (7)

economies of scale: the property of a cost function whereby the average cost of production falls as output expands. (7)

economies of scope: a situation in which it is less expensive to produce goods jointly than separately. (7)

efficiency in production: a situation in which the principal's and the agent's combined value (profits, payoffs) is maximized. (19)

efficiency in risk bearing: a situation in which risk sharing is optimal in that the person who least minds facing risk—the risk-neutral or less-risk-averse person—bears more of the risk. (19)

efficiency wage: an unusually high wage that a firm pays workers as an incentive to avoid shirking. (19)

efficient contract: an agreement with provisions that ensure that no party can be made better off without harming the other party. (19)

efficient production (*technological efficiency*): a situation in which the current level of output cannot be produced with fewer inputs, given existing knowledge about technology and how to organize production. (6)

elasticity: the percentage change in one variable in response to a given percentage change in another variable, holding other relevant variables constant. (2)

elasticity of substitution (σ): the percentage change in the capital-labor ratio divided by the percentage change in the *MRTS*. (6)

endowment: an initial allocation of goods. (10)

endowment effect: the condition that occurs when people place a higher value on a good if they own it than they do if they are considering buying it. (3)

Engel curve: the relationship between the quantity demanded of a single good and income, holding prices constant. (4)

equilibrium: a situation in which no participant wants to change its behavior. (2)

equivalent variation (*EV*): the amount of money one would have to take from a consumer to harm the consumer by as much as the price increase. (5)

essential facility: a scarce resource that rivals need to use to survive. (11)

excess demand: the amount by which the quantity demanded exceeds the quantity supplied at a specified price. (2)

excess supply: the amount by which the quantity supplied is greater than the quantity demanded at a specified price. (2)

exhaustible resources: nonrenewable natural assets that cannot be increased, only depleted. (15)

expansion path: the cost-minimizing combination of labor and capital for each output level. (7)

expenditure function: the relationship showing the minimal expenditures necessary to achieve a specific utility level for a given set of prices. (3)

extensive form: a representation of a game that specifies the n players, the sequence in which they make their moves, the actions they can take at each move, the information that each player has about players' previous moves, and the payoff function over all possible strategies. (13)

externality: an event in which a person's well-being or a firm's production capability is directly affected by the actions of other consumers or firms rather than indirectly through changes in prices. (16)

fair bet: a wager with an expected value of zero. (17)

fair insurance: a bet between an insurer and a policyholder in which the value of the bet to the policyholder is zero. (17)

firm: an organization that converts *inputs* such as labor, materials, and capital into *outputs*, the goods and services that it sells. (6)

fixed cost (F): a production expense that does not vary with the level of output. (7)

fixed input: a factor of production that cannot be varied practically in the short run. (6)

flow: a quantity or value that is measured per unit of time. (15)

free ride: to benefit from the actions of others without paying. (16)

game: a competition between players (such as individuals or firms) in which strategic behavior plays a major role. (13)

game theory: a set of tools that economists, political scientists, military analysts, and others use to analyze players' strategic decision making. (13)

general-equilibrium analysis: the study of how equilibrium is determined in all markets simultaneously. (10)

Giffen good: a commodity for which a decrease in its price causes the quantity demanded to fall. (4)

good: a commodity for which more is preferred to less, at least at some levels of consumption. (3)

incentive compatible: a condition in which a contract provides inducements such that the agent wants to perform the assigned task rather than engage in opportunistic behavior. (19)

incidence of a tax on consumers: the share of the tax that falls on consumers. (2)

income effect: the change in the quantity of a good a consumer demands because of a change in income, holding prices constant. (4)

income elasticity of demand (*income elasticity*): the percentage change in the quantity demanded in response to a given percentage change in income. (2)

increasing returns to scale (*IRS*): the property of a production function whereby output rises more than in proportion to an equal increase in all inputs. (6)

indifference curve: the set of all bundles of goods that a consumer views as being equally desirable. (3)

indifference map (*preference map*): a complete set of indifference curves that summarize a consumer's tastes. (3)

inferior good: a commodity of which less is demanded as income rises. (4)

interest rate: the percentage more that must be repaid to borrow money for a fixed period of time. (15)

internal rate of return (*irr*): the discount rate such that the net present value of an investment is zero. (15)

internalize the externality: to bear the cost of the harm that one inflicts on others (or to capture the benefit that one provides to others). (16)

isocost line: a plot of all the combinations of inputs that require the same (*iso*) total expenditure (*cost*). (7)

isoquant: a curve that shows the efficient combinations of labor and capital that can produce a single (*iso*) level of output (*quant*ity). (6)

Law of Demand: consumers demand more of a good the lower its price, holding constant tastes, the prices of other goods, and other factors that influence the amount they consume. (2)

learning by doing: the productive skills and knowledge of better ways to produce that workers and managers gain from experience. (7)

learning curve: the relationship between average costs and cumulative output. (7)

Lerner Index (*price markup*): the ratio of the difference between price and marginal cost to the price: $(p - MC)/p$. (11)

limited liability: a condition whereby the personal assets of corporate owners cannot be taken to pay a corporation's debts even if it goes into bankruptcy. (6)

long run: a long enough period of time that all inputs can be varied. (6)

marginal cost (MC): the amount by which a firm's cost changes if it produces one more unit of output: $MC = \Delta C/\Delta q$. (6)

marginal product of labor (MP_L): the change in total output resulting from using an extra unit of labor, holding other factors (capital) constant. (6)

marginal profit: the change in the profit a firm gets from selling one more unit of output. (8)

marginal rate of substitution (MRS): the maximum amount of one good that a consumer will sacrifice (trade) to obtain one more unit of another good. (3)

marginal rate of technical substitution ($MRTS$): how many units of capital a firm can replace with an extra unit of labor while holding output constant. (6)

marginal rate of transformation (MRT): the trade-off the market imposes on the consumer in terms of the amount of one good the consumer must give up to obtain more of the other good. (3)

marginal revenue (*MR*): the change in revenue a firm gets from selling one more unit of output. (8)

marginal revenue product of labor (*MRP$_L$*): the additional revenue from the last unit of labor. (15)

marginal utility: the extra utility that a consumer gets from consuming the last unit of a good. (3)

market: an exchange mechanism that allows buyers to trade with sellers. (1)

market failure: inefficient production or consumption, often because a price exceeds marginal cost. (9)

market power: the ability of a firm to charge a price above marginal cost and earn a positive profit. (11)

market structure: the number of firms in the market, the ease with which firms can enter and leave the market, and the ability of firms to differentiate their products from those of their rivals. (8)

microeconomics: the study of how individuals and firms make themselves as well off as possible in a world of scarcity, and the consequences of those individual decisions for markets and the entire economy. (1)

minimum efficient scale (*full capacity*): the smallest quantity at which the average cost curve reaches its minimum. (14)

mixed strategy: a strategy in which the player chooses among possible actions according to probabilities the player assigns. (13)

model: a description of the relationship between two or more economic variables. (1)

monopolistic competition: a market structure in which firms have market power but no additional firm can enter and earn a positive profit. (14)

monopoly: the only supplier of a good for which there is no close substitute. (11)

monopsony: the only buyer of a good in a market. (15)

moral hazard: opportunism characterized by an informed person's taking advantage of a less-informed person through an *unobserved action*. (18)

multimarket price discrimination (*third-degree price discrimination*): a situation in which a firm charges different groups of customers different prices but charges a given customer the same price for every unit sold. (12)

Nash equilibrium: a set of strategies such that, when all other players use these strategies, no player can obtain a higher payoff by choosing a different strategy. (13)

Nash-Bertrand equilibrium (*Bertrand equilibrium* or *Nash-in-prices equilibrium*): a set of prices chosen by firms such that no firm can obtain a higher profit by choosing a different price if the other firms continue to charge these prices. (14)

Nash-Cournot equilibrium (*Cournot equilibrium* or *Nash-in-quantities equilibrium*): a set of quantities chosen by firms such that, holding the quantities of all other firms constant, no firm can obtain a higher profit by choosing a different quantity. (14)

natural monopoly: a situation in which one firm can produce the total output of the market at lower cost than several firms could. (11)

network externality: the situation where one person's demand for a good depends on the consumption of the good by others. (11)

nonuniform pricing: the practice of charging consumers different prices for the same product or charging a single customer a price that depends on the number of units purchased. (12)

normal form: a representation of a static game of complete information, which specifies the players in the game, their possible strategies, and the payoff function that specifies the players' payoffs for each combination of strategies. (13)

normal good: a commodity of which more is demanded as income rises. (4)

normative statement: a conclusion as to whether something is good or bad. (1)

oligopoly: a small group of firms in a market with substantial barriers to entry. (14)

open-access common property: resources to which everyone has free access and an equal right to exploit. (16)

opportunistic behavior: taking advantage of someone when circumstances permit. (18)

opportunity cost (*economic cost*): the value of the best alternative use of a resource. (7)

opportunity set: all the bundles a consumer can buy, including all the bundles inside the budget constraint and on the budget constraint. (3)

Pareto efficient: describing an allocation of goods or services such that any possible reallocation would harm at least one person. (10)

partial-equilibrium analysis: an examination of equilibrium and changes in equilibrium in one market in isolation. (10)

patent: an exclusive right granted to the inventor to sell a new and useful product, process, substance, or design for a fixed time. (11)

payoffs (of a game): players' valuations of the outcome of the game, such as profits for firms or utilities for individuals. (13)

perfect competition: a market structure in which buyers and sellers are price takers. (8)

perfect complements: goods that a consumer is interested in consuming only in fixed proportions. (3)

perfect information: the situation where the player who is about to move knows the full history of the play of the game to this point, and that information is updated with each subsequent action. (13)

perfect price discrimination (*first-degree price discrimination*): the situation in which a firm sells each unit at the maximum amount each customer is willing to pay, so prices differ across customers, and a given customer may pay more for some units than for others. (12)

perfect substitutes: goods that a consumer is completely indifferent as to which to consume. (3)

pooling equilibrium: an equilibrium in which dissimilar people are treated (paid) alike or behave alike. (18)

positive statement: a testable hypothesis about cause and effect. (1)

price discrimination: the practice in which a firm charges consumers different prices for the same good based on individual characteristics, belonging to an identifiable sub-group of consumers, or the quantity purchased. (12)

price elasticity of demand (*demand elasticity* or *elasticity of demand*): the percentage change in the quantity demanded in response to a given percentage change in the price at a particular point on the demand curve. (2)

price elasticity of supply (*supply elasticity*): the percentage change in the quantity supplied in response to a given percentage change in the price. (2)

prisoners' dilemma: a game in which all players have dominant strategies that lead to a profit (or another payoff) that is inferior to what they could achieve if they cooperated and pursued alternative strategies. (13)

private cost: the cost of production only, not including externalities. (16)

producer surplus (*PS*): the difference between the amount for which a good sells and the minimum amount necessary for the seller to be willing to produce the good. (9)

production function: the relationship between the quantities of inputs used and the *maximum* quantity of output that can be produced, given current knowledge about technology and organization. (6)

production possibility frontier: the maximum amount of outputs that can be produced from a fixed amount of input. (7)

profit (π): the difference between a firm's revenue, R, which is what it earns from selling a good, and its cost, C, which is what it pays for labor, materials, and other inputs: $\pi = R - C$. (6)

property right: an exclusive privilege to use an asset. (16)

public good: a commodity or service whose consumption by one person does not preclude others from also consuming it. (16)

pure strategy: strategy in which each player chooses a single action. (13)

quantity demanded: the amount of a good that consumers are willing to buy at a given price during a specified time period (such as a day or a year), holding constant the other factors that influence purchases. (2)

quantity discrimination (*second-degree price discrimination*): the situation in which a firm charges a different price for large quantities than for small quantities, but all customers who buy a given quantity pay the same price. (12)

quantity supplied: the amount of a good that firms *want* to sell during a given time period at a given price, holding constant other factors that influence firms' supply decisions, such as costs and government actions. (2)

quota: a limit that a government sets on the quantity of a foreign-produced good that may be imported. (2)

rent seeking: efforts and expenditures to gain a rent or a profit from government actions. (9)

rent: a payment to the owner of an input beyond the minimum necessary for the factor to be supplied. (9)

requirement tie-in sale: a type of nonuniform pricing in which customers who buy one product from a firm are required to make all their purchases of another product from that firm. (12)

reservation price: the maximum amount a person is willing to pay for a unit of output. (12)

residual demand curve: the market demand that is not met by other sellers at any given price. (8)

residual supply curve: the quantity that the market supplies that is not consumed by other demanders at any given price. (8)

risk: the situation in which the likelihood of each possible outcome is known or can be estimated, and no single possible outcome is certain to occur. (17)

risk averse: unwilling to make a fair bet. (17)

risk neutral: indifferent about making a fair bet. (17)

risk preferring: willing to make a fair bet. (17)

risk premium: the amount that a risk-averse person would pay to avoid taking a risk. (17)

rules of the game: regulations that determine the *timing* of players' moves and the *actions* that players can make at each move. (13)

screening: an action taken by an uninformed person to determine the information possessed by informed people. (18)

separating equilibrium: an equilibrium in which one type of people takes actions (such as sending a signal) that allows them to be differentiated from other types of people. (18)

shirking: a moral hazard in which agents do not provide all the services they are paid to provide. (19)

short run: a period of time so brief that at least one factor of production cannot be varied practically. (6)

shortage: a persistent excess demand. (2)

signaling: an action taken by an informed person to send information to a less-informed person. (18)

snob effect: the situation in which a person places greater value on a good as fewer and fewer people possess it. (11)

social cost: the private cost plus the cost of the harms from externalities. (16)

standard: a metric or scale for evaluating the quality of a particular product. (18)

static game: a game in which each player acts only once and the players act simultaneously (or, at least, each player acts without knowing rivals' actions). (13)

stock: a quantity or value that is measured independently of time. (15)

strategic behavior: a set of actions a player takes to increase the player's payoff, taking into account the possible actions of other players. (13)

strategic interdependence: a situation in which a player's optimal strategy depends on the actions of others. (13)

strategy: a battle plan that specifies the action that a player will make conditional on the information available at each move and for any possible contingency. (13)

subgame perfect Nash equilibrium: the situation in which players' strategies are a Nash equilibrium in every subgame. (13)

substitution effect: the change in the quantity of a good that a consumer demands when the good's price rises, holding other prices and the consumer's utility constant. (4)

sunk cost: a past expenditure that cannot be recovered. (7)

supply curve: the quantity supplied at each possible price, holding constant the other factors that influence firms' supply decisions. (2)

supply function: the correspondence between the quantity supplied, price, and other factors that influence the number of units offered for sale. (2)

tariff (*duty*): a tax only on imported goods. (9)

technical progress: an advance in knowledge that allows more output to be produced with the same level of inputs. (6)

technological efficiency (*efficient production*): property of a production function such that the current level of output cannot be produced with fewer inputs, given existing knowledge about technology and how to organize production. (6)

tie-in sale: a type of nonuniform pricing in which customers can buy one product only if they agree to purchase another product as well. (12)

total cost (C): the sum of a firm's variable cost and fixed cost: $C = VC + F$. (7)

total product of labor: the amount of output (or *total product*) that a given amount of labor can produce holding the quantity of other inputs fixed. (6)

transaction costs: the expenses, over and above the price of the product, of finding a trading partner and making a trade for the product. (2)

two-part tariff: a pricing system in which the firm charges a consumer a lump-sum fee (the first tariff) for the right to buy as many units of the good as the consumer wants at a specified price (the second tariff). (12)

utility: a set of numerical values that reflect the relative rankings of various bundles of goods. (3)

utility function: the relationship between utility measures and every possible bundle of goods. (3)

variable cost (VC): a production expense that changes with the quantity of output produced. (7)

variable input: a factor of production whose quantity the firm can change readily during the relevant time period. (6)

winner's curse: auction winner's bid exceeds the common-value item's value. (13)

Index

401(k) plans, 91

abilities, 650–653
abundance of exhaustible resources, 558
accidents, 574–575
Acid Rain Program, 582
actions
  customer, 417
  in game theory, 439
  that create monopolies, 380–384
  that reduce market power, 384–389
  unobserved, 634
ad valorem tariffs, 312
ad valorem taxes
  defined, 38–39
  effect on consumers, 43–44
  effect on monopolies, 376–377
  similar of effects of specific and, 44
addition rule, A:7
adult transitivity, 89–90
adverse selection
  defined, 633–634
  ignorance of quality drives out high-quality goods, 636–643
  lemons market, 639–640
  reduction by equalizing information, 635–636
  responses to, 634–636
advertising
  cooperation and, 450–453
  investing with, 622
  price and, 427–431, 646
after-the-fact monitoring, 681–684
agents
  defined, 659–660
  principal-agent problem, 660–663
agriculture
  contracts and productivity, 669–670
  welfare effects of subsidies, 304–307
air pollution regulations, 571–575
airline market
  Cournot oligopoly model, 484–488
  government subsidization, 500–505
  Nash-Cournot equilibrium with two or more firms, 491–492
airline tickets
  multimarket price discrimination, 418
  rivalry and prices, 494–495
alcohol market, 147
aligners, 188

Allais effect, 624
allocations
  efficiency in, 346–348
  efficiency vs. equity, 352–353
  of equity, 348–352
  property right, 578–582
  scarce resource, 1–3
allocative costs, 307, 309
alternative price support, 305–306
amortize, 208
antitrust laws
  defined, 479
  support for cartels, 482
ANWR (Arctic National Wildlife Refuge), 36–38
Apple, 369–371
applications of competitive model. *See* competitive model
Arctic National Wildlife Refuge (ANWR), 36–38
Arrow-Pratt measure of risk aversion, 610–612
Arrow's Impossibility Theorem, 350
ascending-bid auctions, 463
assets, 541
assumptions
  about consumer preferences, 59–60
  defined, 4–5
  finding function extrema, A:15–A:16
asymmetric information
  cheap talk, 648–649
  education as signal of ability, 649–653
  efficiency and moral hazards, 662–663
  ignorance of quality drives out high-quality goods, 636–643
  information about employment risks, 646–647
  market power from price ignorance, 643–646
  overview, 632–633
  problems, 657–658
  problems due to, 633–634
  production efficiency with, 667–670
  questions, 656
  responses to adverse selection, 634–636
  screening in hiring, 654–655
  summary, 655–656
attainment, 573
attitudes toward risk

  defined, 604–610
  investing and, 619
auctions
  game theory of, 462–466
  monopoly right, 381
Australian water quotas, 150–151
automobiles
  economies of scope, 238
  internalizing externalities, 574–575
  leased, 682
  lemons market, 636–643
average costs
  curves, 212–213
  effect of taxes on, 216–217
  finding short-run curves, 215–216
  long-run as envelope for short-run, 231–233
  long run curve shapes, 229–230
  in monopolistic competition, 515
  shape of curve, 214–215
average fixed costs
  defined, 211
  finding short-run curves, 216
average product of labor
  graph interpretation, 180–181
  in short-run production, 178–179
average revenue, 360–361
average variable costs
  curves, 212–213
  defined, 211
  finding short-run curves, 215–216
  shape of curve, 214–215
aversion, loss, 626–627
aversion, risk. *See* risk aversion
avoidable costs
  defined, 210
  in long run, 218
  shutdown rule and, 252–253
avoiding risk, 612–619

backward induction, 455
ban on imports
  defined, 309
  vs. free trade, 310–312
bandwagon effect, 390
bargaining ability, 334
barriers to entry
  creating monopolies, 380–381
  defined, 300–301

I-1

maintaining cartels, 482
zoning laws as, 518
Beef Promotion and Research Act, 590
behavior, opportunistic. *See* opportunistic behavior
behavioral economics
in consumer choice, 89–92
monopolies and, 389–392
strategic, 439
time-varying discounting, 551
of uncertainty, 622–627
Belgium, 449
Bentham, Jeremy, 351
Bertrand equilibrium, 508
Bertrand, Joseph, 508
Bertrand oligopoly model, 483, 508–514
best response
of Bertrand model with differentiated products, 510–514
of Bertrand model with identical products, 508–510
of Cournot model, 484–488
of Cournot model with nonidentical firms, 492–497
of Cournot model with two or more firms, 488–492
given government subsidization of airline, 504–505
Nash equilibrium and, 444–446
of Stackelberg model, 497–498
bidders' curse, 466
bidding
as price discrimination, 406
strategies in private-value auctions, 464–466
Black Death, 533–534
black market, 47
block-pricing schedules, 410
BLS (Bureau of Labor Statistics), 127
BMI (body mass index), A:2
body mass index (BMI), A:2
bonds
efficiency wages as, 681
monitoring with, 678–680
Borenstein, Severin, 36
Borlaug, Norman, 183
borrowing, subprime, 683–685
Botox, 381–383, 407–408
bottled water, 496–497
bounded rationality, 92
boutique fuels, 275
branches of game tree, 454
Britain
Black Death, 533–534
toilet paper variety, 514
bubonic plague, 533–534
budget constraints
child care, 154–156
comparing three welfare measures, 144
in consumer choice, 74–75
with food stamps, 152
income tax rate effect on, 164
increasing income shifts demand curve, 103–106
minimizing expenditure, 87–89
bundles
defined, 59
determining inflation, 120–122

endowment effect, 90–91
optimal, 76–81
ordinal preferences, 65–66
preference maps, 61–62
revealed preference, 128–129
bundling, 424–427
Bureau of Labor Statistics (BLS), 127
business profit
in competitive model, 286
defined, 249
buyers, 245

cable cars, 365
calculation cost, 92
calculus
derivatives, A:6–A:11
finding function extrema, A:14–A:19
functions. *See also* functions, A:1–A:2
maximizing with equality constraints, A:19–A:22
maximum and minimum of functions, A:11–A:14
minimizing costs with, 222–223
perfect price discrimination, 404–406
properties of functions, A:2–A:6
Stackelberg model solution, 497–498
using to find utility maximization, 81–86
Canadian oil sands, 259
Canine Haute Couture, 430–431
cap-and-trade system, 581–582
capital costs, 207–209
capital markets
discount rates, 542
durability, 547–548
human capital, 548–551
interest rates, 541–542
investing, 544–547
overview, 540–541
stream of payments, 542–544
time-varying discounting, 551–552
capital services
diminishing marginal rate of technical substitution, 190–191
estimating cost curves, 230–231
on isocost line, 218–220
production inputs, 176
returns to scale in, 193–196
in short-run production, 177–179
substitution in long run production, 189–190
captured regulators, 387
carbon dioxide regulations, 571–575
cardinal measure, 65
cartels
comparison of Cournot, Stackelberg, competitive equilibria and, 505–508
defined, 440, 474
overview, 477–483
cash vs. food stamps, 151–153
Cashflow 101, 466
catwalk cartel, 480
ceilings, price, 45–48, 307–309
central processing units (CPUs)
Cournot model with nonidentical firms, 495–496
learning by doing, 235
certainty effect, 624–625

certification, 641–642
CES (constant-elasticity-of-substitution) functions
deriving demand curves with, 98–99
production, 191–192
utility, 83–84
chain rule, A:8
chance node, 620
cheap talk, 648–649
cheating, cartel
enforcement, 481–482
incentives for, 481
Cher, 288
chicken, playing, 449
child care subsidies, 154–156
children's transitivity, 89–90
Chinese monopolies, 378
choice variable, A:16
choices
consumer. *See* consumer choices
contract, 685–686
framing, 624–625
Christmas trees, 249–250
cigarette advertising, 452–453
Clean Air Act, 571
client-lawyer contracts, 671–673
clothing
consumer surplus in, 147
indifference curve, 73
club goods, 585
Coase Theorem, 578–581
Cobb-Douglas functions, A:2
Cobb-Douglas production functions
defined, 184
determining long-run cost, 228
factor demand, 530
finding elasticity of substitution, 192
finding short-run cost curves, 215–216
returns to scale, 194
Cobb-Douglas utility functions
defined, 69
deriving compensated demand function, 117
deriving demand curves with, 99
expenditure function, 88–89
finding utility maximization, 85–86
labor supply curve, 159
cola
advertising, 453
Bertrand oligopoly model, 512–513
COLAs (cost-of-living adjustments), 120–127
college
education as signal of ability, 649–653
investing in, 549–551
collusion
cartels, 477–483
comparison of Cournot, Stackelberg, competitive equilibria and, 505–508
defined, 474
commitments
credible threat and, 456–457
sequential movement in Stackelberg model and, 499–500
common knowledge, 440
common property
defined, 564
open-access, 582–584

common value, 464
company towns, 538–539
comparative advantage, 338–341
comparative statics
   defined, 22–27
   effect of specific tax on monopoly, 373–374
   of indirect objective functions, A:18–A:19
comparisons
   collusive, Cournot, Stackelberg and competitive equilibria, 505–508
   prospect and expected utility theories, 625–626
   short and long-run labor demand curves, 530–531
   trade policies, 309–317
   welfare measures, 142–145
compensated change in price, 113
compensated demand curves
   consumer welfare and, 140
   with CPI adjustments, 122–125
   defined, 114–116
   deriving with Slutsky equation, 116–119
compensating variation
   comparing welfare measures, 142–145
   defined, 140
   indifference curve analysis of, 141–142
competition
   competitive exchange, 334–338
   in exhaustible resources, 553–558
   increasing to regulate monopolies, 389
   inefficiency with externalities, 566–569
   long-run. See long-run competition
   market structure, 475–476
   monopolistic, 514–518
   monopoly vs. welfare with externalities, 577–578
   overview, 243
   perfect, 244–248
   policies, 479
   problems, 283–284
   profit maximization, 248–253
   questions, 280–283
   relative productivity and, 197
   short-run. See short-run competition
   summary, 279–280
   tourist-trap model, 644–645
   vs. cartel, 477–478
   vs. multimarket price discrimination, 420
competitive equilibrium
   comparison of collusive, Cournot, Stackelberg equilibria and, 505–508
   factor market, 532–534
   monopoly externalities and, 575–577
   in two interrelated markets, 324–326
competitive factor markets
   demand, 531–532
   equilibrium, 532–534
   firm's long-run demand, 529–531
   firm's short-run demand, 525–529
competitive model
   comparing policies: trade, 309–317
   maximizing welfare, 293–296
   overview, 285–286

policies that create wedge between supply and demand curves, 301–309
policies that shift supply curves, 297–301
problems, 321
producer welfare, 289–292
questions, 318–321
summary, 317–318
zero long-run profit, 286–289
complements
   defined, 10
   perfect, 71
complete information, 440
completeness property
   defined, 59
   indifference curves, 62–64
   preference maps, 60–62
compounded interest, 542
compulsion, 590
concavity
   defined, A:3–A:5
   indifference curve, 70
conditions
   first-order condition, A:15–A:16
   for monopoly profit maximization, 359–360
   for natural monopoly, 378
confidence interval, B:3
constant-cost market, 272
constant-elasticity demand curves, 30–32
constant-elasticity-of-substitution (CES) functions
   deriving demand curves with, 98–99
   production, 191–192
   utility, 83–84
constant-elasticity supply curves, 34–35
constant marginal mining costs, 553–557
constant returns to scale, 193–196
constraints
   budget. See budget constraints
   in consumer choice. See consumer choices
   effect of government on consumer welfare, 149–156
   maximizing with equality, A:19–A:22
   in modeling, 5–6
consumer choices
   behavioral economics, 89–92
   budget constraints, 74–75
   constraint on maximizing utility, 81–86
   consumer's optimal bundle, 76–81
   indifference curves curvature, 70–73
   labor-leisure, 156–159
   minimizing expenditure, 87–89
   ordinal preferences, 65–66
   overview, 57–58
   preferences, 58–64
   problems, 95–96
   questions, 93–94
   summary, 92–93
   utility and indifference curves, 66–67
   utility function, 64–65
   willingness to substitute, 67–69
consumer durables, 4
Consumer Price Index (CPI)
   adjustment to demand, 122–124
   demand and inflation, 120–122
   size of substitution bias, 126–127

Consumer Reports, 613, 641
consumer surplus
   comparing welfare measures, 142–145
   loss from higher price, 146
   markets in which losses are large, 146–149
   maximizing welfare, 293–296
   measuring, 135–139
   producer surplus and, 285
   of television, 142
consumer welfare
   deriving labor supply curves. See labor supply curves
   effect of perfect price discrimination on, 406–408
   effect of trade policies on, 309–317
   effects of government policies on, 149–156
   expenditure function and, 140–145
   market consumer surplus, 146–149
   overview, 134–139
consumers
   demands and weather, 613
   effect of specific tax on, 40–42
   effect of specific tax on monopoly, 374–376
   income elasticities and, 106–111
   information. See information
   optimum, 77
   same equilibrium no matter who is taxed, 43–44
consumption
   distortion loss, 314
   efficiency, 342–343
   exhaustible resources, 553–558
   inefficient, 305
   public goods and, 585
contingency contracts
   with asymmetric information, 669
   contract choice, 685–686
   defined, 662
   efficiency of, 672–673
   with full information, 666–667
   rewards linked to firm's success, 677
continuity, A:3
continuously differentiable functions
   defined, A:9
   finding extrema, A:14–A:16
   maximum and minimum of, A:12–A:13
contract curves, 332, 333–334
contracts and moral hazards
   contract choice, 685–686
   monitoring, 677–685
   overview, 659–660
   payments linked to production or profit, 676–677
   principal-agent problem, 660–663
   problems, 688–689
   production efficiency, 663–670
   questions, 687–688
   summary, 686–687
   trade-offs between efficiency in production and risk-bearing, 670–675
control variables, 82
controls, price, 45–49
convex indifference curves, 72, 80–81
convexity, A:3–A:5

cooperation in game theory, 450–453
corn market, 325–326
corner solution, 77–80
corporations, 174
correlation, 613–614
cost-benefit analysis of pollution, 569, 570
cost curves
  estimating vs. introspection, 230–231
  long-run, 229–230
  production functions and shape of, 213–216
  short-run, 212–213
cost-of-living adjustments (COLAs), 120–127
costs
  advantages that create monopolies, 377–380
  durability and, 547–548
  increase effect on short-run firm supply curve, 261–262
  long-run. *See* long-run costs
  long-run market supply with varying, 271–273
  lower costs in long run, 231–236
  measuring, 206–209
  minimizing, 87–89
  overview, 205–206
  problems, 241–242
  producing multiple goods, 237–238
  profit maximization, 248
  questions, 239–241
  raising entry and exit, 300–301
  short-run. *See* short-run costs
  summary, 238–239
  unequal in Cournot model, 492–495
cotton, 271
coupons, 418
Cournot, Antoine-Augustin, 483–484
Cournot equilibrium. *See also* Nash-Cournot equilibrium, 484
Cournot oligopoly model
  airline market, 484–488
  comparison of collusive, Stackelberg and competitive equilibria, 505–508
  effect of government subsidy on, 500–501
  equilibrium with two or more firms, 488–492
  with nonidentical firms, 492–497
  overview, 483–484
CPI (Consumer Price Index)
  adjustment to demand, 122–124
  demand and inflation, 120–122
  size of substitution bias, 126–127
CPUs (central processing units)
  Cournot model with nonidentical firms, 495–496
  learning by doing, 235
credible threat
  government subsidization of airline, 503
  in sequential games, 456–457
  sequential movement in Stackelberg model and, 499–500
critical mass, 390–392
critical value, A:16

cross-price elasticity of demand, 33
cumulative output, 235
current marginal benefits, 540
current marginal rental costs, 540
curves
  contract, 332, 333–334
  cost. *See* cost curves
  demand. *See* demand curves
  indifference. *See* indifference curves
  supply. *See* supply curves
  utility, 66–67
customers. *See also* consumers
  identifying groups for price discrimination, 417–419
  multimarket price discrimination, 412–415
  two-part tariff with identical, 421–422
  two-part tariff with nonidentical, 422–423

deadweight loss
  of Christmas presents, 296
  defined, 294
  effect of natural gas price ceiling, 309
  in food and tobacco industries, 508
  of monopolies, 372–373
  nonuniform pricing and, 398
  welfare effects of price ceilings, 307
decision-making, 603
  allocation of scarce resources, 2
  attitudes toward risk, 604–610
  degree of risk aversion, 610–612
  expected utility theory, 603
  over time, 389–392
  under uncertainty, 602–603
  uses of microeconomic models, 7–8
decision nodes
  defined, 454
  investing with risk, 620
decision trees
  investing with advertising, 622
  investing with risk, 620
  investing with uncertainty and discounting, 621
decreasing-cost market, 273
decreasing functions
  defined, A:3
  derivatives, A:7
decreasing returns to scale, 193–196
defaults on loans, 683
deferred payments, 680
deficiency payments, 305–306
degree of risk
  aversion, 610–612
  defined, 598–602
demand
  consumer theory and income elasticities, 106–111
  cost-of-living adjustment, 120–127
  defined, 10–16
  effects of price increase, 111
  elasticity, 28–33
  factor market, 531–532
  income and substitution effects with inferior good, 113–114
  income and substitution effects with normal good, 112–113

overview, 97–98
problems, 132–133
for public goods, 586
questions, 130–132
revealed preference, 128–129
Slutsky equation, 116–120
summary, 130
weather and, 613
demand curves
  compensated, 114–116
  defined, 12–15
  deriving, 98–103
  deriving competitive firm's, 246–248
  effect of shift of supply curve depending on shape, 27
  effect of shift on monopolies, 366–367
  elasticities along, 29–32
  factor market, 531–532
  finding market equilibrium with, 20–21
  income changes shifting, 103–106
  leisure, 157
  long-run factor demand, 529–531
  monopoly, 360–361
  monopoly market power and shape of, 367–368
  monopsony, 536
  perfect competition, 244–245
  in perfect price discrimination, 403–404
  policies that create wedge between supply curves and, 301–309
  shapes of, 27
  short-run factor demand, 525–529
demand elasticities
  low market power and, 371
  in monopolies, 362–363
  monopoly market power and, 368
  over time, 35–36
demand functions
  in Bertrand model, 511
  compensated, 114–116
  defined, 11–15
  finding market equilibrium with, 21
  inverse, 135–137
  summing, 15–16
  system of, 98–100
democracy, 348–352
derivatives, A:6–A:11
deriving
  competitive firm's demand curve, 246–248
  contract curves, 333–334
  demand curves, 98–103
descending-bid auctions, 463
designer bags, 402
detection, cartel, 481–482
deviations from perfect competition, 245–246
difference between actual and expected outcomes, 601–602
differentiated products
  in Bertrand model, 510–514
  in Cournot model, 495–497
diminishing marginal rate of substitution, 70

diminishing marginal rate of technical substitution, 190–191
diminishing marginal returns, 182–184
diminishing marginal returns to labor, 213–215
diminishing marginal utility of wealth, 604
direct objective functions, A:18
direct size effect, 390
discounts
    buying, 418–419
    investing with uncertainty and, 621
    rates in capital markets, 542
    time-varying, 551–552
discrete changes, 23–24
discrimination, price. See pricing
discrimination, statistical, 654–655
diseconomies of scale, 229
diseconomies of scope, 237–238
disequilibrium, 22
Disneyland pricing, 401
distribution of wealth, 344–346
distribution, probability, 599–600
diversification
    insurance only for risks, 618–619
    risk avoidance, 613–615
dollars, 135–139
domain, A:1–A:2
dominant firms, 494
dominant pairs, 494
dominant strategies, 442–443
drilling for oil, 235
drug smuggling, 414–417
dual minimization problem, 87
duality, A:22
duopoly, 483
durable goods
    capital costs, 207–209
    in capital markets, 547–548
Dutch auctions
    defined, 463
    equivalence of outcomes, 465–466
duties, 309
dynamic games
    defined, 440
    overview, 453
    repeated games, 461–462
    sequential games, 454–461

e-book readers, 458–460
early bird, 544
eBay
    adverse selection on, 643
    auction game theory, 463–464
    bidders' curse, 466
    critical mass and, 391–392
    willingness to pay, 137–138
economic costs. See also costs
    defined, 206–207
    profit maximization, 249
economic efficiency
    defined, 205
    input choices, 218–226
economic profit. See also profit
    defined, 249
    zero long-run in competitive model and, 286–289

economic relationships, B:1–B:3
economic welfare. See general equilibrium and economic welfare
economics, behavioral. See behavioral economics
economies of scale, 229
economies of scope, 237–238
Edgeworth boxes, 329–330
education
    investing in, 548–551
    as signal of ability, 649–653
efficiency
    in Coase Theorem, 579
    comparative advantage and production, 338–339
    of competition, 337
    in competitive exchange, 335
    defined, 346–348
    education as signal, 652–653
    gift-giving, 296
    hospital mergers, 482–483
    principal-agent problem, 662–663
    product mix, 342
    production, 175
    production and moral hazards, 663–670
    role of government in, 344–346
    symmetric information, 637–638
    Theory of the Second Best, 353–354
    trade-offs between production and risk-bearing, 670–675
    valuing public goods, 591
    vs. equity, 352–353
    wages, 680–681
efficient allocations
    in competitive exchange, 335
    obtaining using competition, 337–338
efficient contracts, 662, 663–664
effluent charges, 572
EIS (Energy Information Service), 36
elastic demand curves, 30
elastic supply curves, 34
elasticities
    CES and demand, 98–99
    consumer surplus and, 146–149
    consumer theory and income, 106–111
    demand, 28–33
    of demand in monopolies, 362–363
    dependence of specific tax effects on, 40–43
    deriving with Slutsky equation, 117–119
    long run vs. short run, 35–38
    monopoly market power and, 368
    monopsony, 536
    in noncompetitive factor markets, 534–535
    residual supply, 273–274
    salience and, 92
    substitution, 191–193
    supply, 34–35
electric generation efficiency
    economies of scope, 238
    monopolies, 198
emissions fees, 573–575
emissions standards, 572–575
employment. See also labor

cheap talk, 648–649
child care and, 154–156
in company towns, 538–539
education as signal of ability, 649–653
effect of lottery winnings on, 162–163
information about risks, 646–647
investing in human capital, 548–551
labor supply curves. See labor supply curves
minimum wage with incomplete coverage, 326–329
monitoring, 677–685
screening in hiring, 654–655
endangered species, 33
endowment effect, 90–91
endowments, 329–330
Energy Information Service (EIS), 36
enforcement, 481–482
Engel curves, 104–106
English auctions
    defined, 463
    strategies, 465
entry
    dynamic entry games, 457–458
    ease of market, 245
    long-run market supply curve, 268–270
    maintaining cartels, 482
    raising costs, 300–301
    zero long-run profit with free and limited, 286–289
Envelope Theorem, A:18
environment
    falling discount rates and, 552
    gas taxes and, 42–43
    pollution. See externalities
    variables, 23–26
Environmental Protection Agency (EPA), 582
equality constraints, A:19–A:22
equalizing information, 635–636
equations. See also functions
    Arrow-Pratt measure of risk aversion, 610–612
    average product of labor, 178
    budget constraint, 74–75
    compensated demand curve, 114–116
    constant-elasticity demand curve, 30–31
    contract curve, 333–334
    CPI substitution bias, 126
    cross-price elasticity of demand, 33
    economies of scope, 237
    elasticities, 28
    elasticity of substitution, 191–193
    expansion path, 227
    expected utility theory, 603
    expected value, 600
    finding short-run cost curves, 215–216
    income elasticity of demand, 32, 106
    inflation indexes, 121–122
    isocost line, 220
    isoquant, 185
    labor-leisure choice, 157–159
    marginal expenditure, 536
    marginal product of labor, 178

marginal rate of technical substitution, 189–190, 221
minimizing costs, 222–223
monopoly market power and demand elasticity, 368
perfect price discrimination, 405–406
price ceiling, 46
price elasticity of demand, 28–32
price elasticity of supply, 34
probability, 598
producer surplus, 291
profit, 175, 248
profit maximization, 251–252
residual demand curve, 246–248
residual supply, 273–274
revealed preference, 129
short-run production, 177
Slutsky equation, 116–120
system of demand, 98–100
total cost, marginal cost and average cost, 210–211
using to find utility maximization, 81–86
variance, 601
welfare, 293
equilibrium, market. See market equilibrium
equilibrium, Nash. See Nash equilibrium
equilibrium price, 20
equilibrium quantity, 20
equity
  defined, 348–352
  problems with asymmetric information, 638
  role of government in, 344–346
  Theory of the Second Best, 353–354
  vs. efficiency, 352–353
equivalent variation
  comparing welfare measures, 142–145
  defined, 140
  indifference curve analysis of, 141–142
  of quotas, 150
error term, B:1
essential facilities, 377–378
essential goods, 31
estimates
  cost curves vs. introspection, 230–231
  difficulty assessing probabilities, 622–624
  regression, B:1–B:3
Euler's homogeneous function theorem, A:11
event study, 288
excess demand, 22
excess production, 305
excess supply, 22
exchange economy
  competitive, 334–338
  defined, 329–334
excise taxes, 91
exclusion, 585
exercise price, 677
exhaustible resources, 553–558
exhaustive outcomes, 600
exit
  ease of market, 245

long-run market supply curve, 268–269
raising costs, 300–301
exogenous parameters, A:17–A:19
exogenous variables, 23
expansion paths
  defined, 226–227
  short-run and long-run, 233–234
expected net present value, 621
expected utility theory
  defined, 603
  prospect theory and, 625–626
expected value
  defined, 600–601
  variance and standard deviation from, 601–602
expenditure functions
  consumer welfare and, 140–145
  defined, 88–89
  deriving from Cobb-Douglas function, 117
expenditures. See costs
expenses, 208
experience
  in auction bidding, 465
  lowering costs, 234–236
explicit costs, 206
explicit functions, A:2
exponent rule, A:9
exponential discounting, 551
exponential rule, A:8–A:9
extensive-form diagram, 454–455
extensive-form games, 453
externalities
  allocating property rights to reduce, 578–582
  inefficiency of competition with, 566–569
  lemons market with variable quality, 639–640
  market structure and, 575–578
  open-access common property, 582–584
  overview, 563–566
  problems, 594–595
  public goods, 584–591
  questions, 593–594
  regulation, 569–575
  summary, 592
extrema
  finding function, A:14–A:19
  finding maximum and minimum, A:11–A:14
Extreme Value Theorem, A:12–A:13

factor markets
  capital. See capital markets
  competitive. See competitive factor markets
  exhaustible resources, 553–558
  monopsony, 535–540
  noncompetitive, 534–535
  overview, 524–525
  problems, 560–562
  questions, 559–560
  summary, 559

factor prices
  costs and changes in, 224–226
  short-run firm supply curve and, 261–262
fair bets, 604
fair insurance, 616–617
Fair Labor Standards Act of 1938, 48
falling discount rates, 552
falling exhaustible resource prices, 557–558
farming subsidies, 304–307
Federal Trade Commission Act of 1914, 478
financial assets, 541
firms
  competition. See competition
  Cournot oligopoly model with non-identical, 492–497
  Cournot oligopoly with two or more, 488–492
  deriving competitive demand curve, 246–248
  long-run factor demand, 529–531
  long-run market supply with different, 270–271
  long-run market supply with identical, 269–270
  long-run supply curve, 267
  number of in monopolistic competition, 516–518
  overview, 172–173
  ownership and management, 173–176
  perfect price discrimination, 403–406
  policies that restrict, 297–300
  price discrimination, 399–403
  production. See production
  rewards linked to success, 677
  short-run factor demand, 525–529
  short-run market supply curve with different, 262–263
  short-run market supply curve with identical, 262–263
  short-run supply curve, 260–262
  signaling by, 642–643
  zero long-run profit in competitive model, 286–289
first-best equilibrium, 353
first-degree price discrimination, 402
first-mover advantages and disadvantages, 460–461
first-order condition, A:15–A:17
first-price auctions, 463, 465–466
First Theorem of Welfare Economics, 337
Fisher index, 127
fixed costs
  curves, 212–213
  defined, 210
  long-run, 218
  measuring producer surplus, 291
  in monopolistic competition, 516–518
fixed-fee contracts
  with asymmetric information, 668
  defined, 661
  efficiency of, 671
  with full information, 665
fixed inputs
  defined, 177

Green Revolution and, 182–184
in short-run production, 177
fixed payments, 671–672
fixed-proportion production functions
  defined, 186
  finding elasticity of substitution, 192
fixed quality, 636–639
flight insurance, 617–618
floors, price
  defined, 48–49
  welfare effect of, 303–307
flows
  defined, 540–541
  stream of payments, 542–544
flu vaccine shortage, 2
followers, 497
food industry
  deadweight loss in, 508
  indifference curve, 73
  rent *seek*ing in, 317
Food Stamp Program, 151–153
food stamps, 151–156
for-profit firms, 174
Ford, Henry, 199
formats, auction, 463
formulas. *See* equations
fossil fuel taxes, 42–43
framing choices, 624–625
free entry
  long-run market supply with, 269–270
  perfect competition and, 245
  zero long-run profit with, 286
free riding
  defined, 588–589
  reducing, 590
free trade. *See also* trade
  defined, 309
  Theory of the Second Best and, 353–354
  vs. ban on imports, 310–312
  vs. quota, 315–316
  vs. tariffs, 312–315
frequency and risk, 598
Friedman-Savage utility, 609–610
full capacity, 516
full information
  defined, 644
  production efficiency with, 665–667
full insurance, 616–617
functions
  CES utility, 83–84
  Cobb-Douglas production. *See* Cobb-Douglas production functions
  Cobb-Douglas utility. *See* Cobb-Douglas utility functions
  compensated demand curve, 114–116
  demand, 11–15
  derivatives, A:6–A:11
  expenditure, 88–89
  finding extrema, A:14–A:19
  finding market equilibrium with, 21
  indifference curves and utility, 66–67
  inverse demand function, 135–137
  long-run cost, 227–228
  marginal revenue product of labor, 534
  maximum and minimum of, A:11–A:14

monopoly profit, 359–360
overview, A:1–A:2
production, 176
production and shape of cost curves, 213–216
profit, 250
properties of, A:2–A:6
prospect theory, 626–627
quasilinear utility, 72–73
residual demand, 246
residual supply, 273
short-run labor demand, 526–527
social welfare and equity, 348–352
supply, 16–18
utility, 64–65
future payments, 543
future value, 542

gambler's fallacy, 623
gambling
  Arrow-Pratt measure of risk aversion and, 611
  prospect theory, 625–627
  risk in, 608–610
game theory
  auctions, 462–466
  cooperation, 450–453
  dynamic games, 453
  multiple Nash equilibria and mixed strategies, 446–450
  normal-form games, 441–442
  overview, 437–440
  predicting game outcome, 442–446
  problems, 471–473
  questions, 467–471
  repeated games, 461–462
  sequential games, 454–461
  summary, 467
game tree, 454–455
games, 439
games of change, 608–610
gasoline
  price ceiling, 45–47
  prices, 78–79
  supply curves, 275–276
  taxes, 42–43
general-equilibrium analysis, 324
general equilibrium and economic welfare
  competitive exchange, 334–338
  defined, 323–329
  efficiency, 346–348
  efficiency vs. equity, 352–353
  equity, 348–352
  exchange economy, 329–334
  overview, 322–323
  problems, 356–357
  production and trading, 338–344
  questions, 355–356
  role of government, 344–346
  summary, 355
  Theory of the Second Best, 353–354
general partnerships, 174
Ghirardelli Chocolate Company, 172
Giffen goods
  defined, 114
  determining, 116–119
gift-giving, 296

Gillette, King C., 199
global extrema, A:12
golden handcuffs, 677
goods
  determining allocations, 3
  durability in capital markets, 547–548
  durable, 207–209
  ignorance of quality driving out high-quality, 636–643
  inflation indexes, 120–122
  policies that shift supply curves, 297
  public, 584–591
  shipping fees and, 120
  substitution. *See* substitution
  trade-offs, 2
Google, 406
government
  actions that create monopolies, 380–384
  actions that reduce market power, 384–389
  allocation of scarce resources, 2
  demand considerations, 11
  effects of sales tax, 38–44
  externality regulation, 569–575
  import policies effect on supply curves, 19–20
  laws against cartels, 478–480
  obtaining efficient allocation using competition, 337–338
  policies that create wedge between supply and demand curves, 301–309
  policies that shift supply curves, 297–301
  policy effects on consumer welfare, 149–156
  price ceiling, 45–48
  price floors, 48–49
  promoting price discrimination, 401–402
  role in efficiency and equity, 344–346
  supply considerations, 16
  support for cartels, 482
  taxing externalities in noncompetitive markets, 578
  uses of microeconomic models, 7–8
Gramm, Phil, 303
grants of monopoly rights, 380
graphs
  concavity and convexity, A:3–A:5
  deriving demand curves with, 100–103
  game tree, 454–455
  indifference maps, 62–63
  perfect price discrimination, 403–404
  preference maps, 60–62
  short-run production, 180–181
  Stackelberg model solution, 498
Green Revolution, 182–184
gross profit, 427–429
gross substitutes, 33
gunk, 566–569

happiness, 60
Hicks, John, 114
Hicksian demand curves, 114
high-output strategy, 442
high-quality goods, 636–643

higher-order derivatives, A:9
hill of happiness, 66
hire contracts
  with asymmetric information, 668–669
  defined, 662
  with full information, 665–666
  piece rate, 676–677
hiring
  cheap talk, 648–649
  education as signal of ability, 649–653
  information about employment risks, 646–647
  screening in, 654–655
hit-and-run entry, 268
hold percentages, 609
homogeneous functions
  defined, A:5
  Euler's theorem, A:11
homogeneous outputs
  Bertrand model with, 508–510
  Cournot equilibrium with two or more firms, 488–490
horizontal demand curves
  elasticities along, 31
  perfect competition, 244–245
horizontal supply curves, 34
hospital mergers, 482–483
hostage for good behavior, 678
hourly rate
  defined, 662
  efficiency of, 671, 672
housing market, 147
human capital, 548–551
Hurricane Katrina, 619
hyperbolic functions, A:2
hypothesis testing, 5

identical consumers, 421–422
identical firms
  long-run market supply with, 269–270
  short-run market supply curve with, 262–263
identical products, 244–245
identity, 25
identity functions, A:2
ignorance
  in consumer choice, 91–92
  market power from price, 643–646
  of quality drives out high-quality goods, 636–643
ILWU (International Longshore and Warehouse Union), 409
imperfect information
  in game theory, 440
  in normal-form game, 442
imperfect substitutes, 71
implicit costs, 206
implicit functions, A:2
import policies
  effect on supply curves, 19–20
  free trade vs. ban on, 310–312
  free trade vs. quota, 315–316
  free trade vs. tariff, 312–315
  overview, 309–310
  rent *seeking*, 316–317
  smuggling prescription drugs, 414–417
Impossibility Theorem, 350

In Rainbows, 589
incentives
  compatibility, 663
  efficiency wages, 680–681
  linked to firm's success, 677
incidence of tax, 43–44
incidence of tax on consumers
  defined, 41
  specific tax on monopoly, 374–376
incidence of tax on firms, 41
income
  budget constraints, 74–75
  buying happiness, 60
  changes shift demand curve, 103–106
  consumer theory and elasticities, 106–111
  demand considerations, 11
  distribution of wealth, 345
  elasticity of demand, 32–33
income-consumption curves
  defined, 104–106
  income elasticities and, 107–108
income effects
  comparing three welfare measures, 144–145
  in compensated demand curve, 114–116
  deriving with Slutsky equation, 116–119
  with inferior good, 113–114
  on labor supply curves, 159–161
  with normal good, 112–113
  price increases and, 111
income elasticity of demand, 144
income taxes
  distribution of wealth, 345
  effect on labor supply curves, 163–167
income threshold model, 4
incomplete information, 440
increasing cost markets, 271–272
increasing functions
  defined, 66
  derivatives, A:7
  monotonicity of, A:3
increasing prices. *See* price increases
increasing returns to scale, 193–196
independent outcomes, 614
indifference, 59
indifference curves
  curvature, 70–73
  defined, 66–67
  examining CV and EV effects with, 141–142
  finding optimal bundle, 76–81
  finding optimal bundles on, 76–81
  marginal rate of substitution, 67–69
  in mutually beneficial trades, 331–332
indirect effects, 391
indirect objective functions, A:17–A:19
individual uses of microeconomic models, 7–8
inefficiency in consumption, 305
inefficiency of competition with externalities, 566–569
inelastic supply curves, 34
inferior goods
  comparing welfare measures for, 142

defined, 107
income and substitution effects with, 113–114
normal goods and, 108–109
shipping fees and, 120
inflation, 122–127
inflation indexes, 120–122
information
  asymmetric. *See* asymmetric information
  avoiding risk with, 613
  demand considerations, 10
  in game theory, 440
  perfect competition, 245
  production efficiency with full, 665–667
  salience, 91–92
inkjet printers, 233
innovations
  alternatives to patents, 383–384
  economies of scale and, 230
  patents, 381–383
  productivity and, 198–200
inputs
  choice in long-run costs, 218–226
  defined, 173
  law of diminishing marginal returns, 182–184
  long-run factor demand, 529
  long-run market supply with varying prices, 271–273
  production, 176
  production time and variability of, 177
  returns to scale, 193–196
  short-run cost, 209–210
  substituting long-run production, 189–190
  zero long-run profit and scarce, 287–288
insurance
  avoiding risk with, 615–619
  choosing contracts, 674–675
  controlling opportunism with universal coverage, 634
integrated circuits, 187–188
interdependence, 331–332
interest rates
  in capital markets, 541–542
  exhaustible resource, 555
  subprime borrowing, 683
interior extrema, A:14
interior solutions, 77
internal rate of return
  defined, 545
  investment methods, 546–547
internalizing externalities, 573–575
international cartels, 479
International Longshore and Warehouse Union (ILWU), 409
intervals, A:1
interviews, job, 654
introspection vs. estimating cost curves, 230–231
inverse demand functions
  measuring consumer surplus, 135–137
  of monopolies, 360–361

investing
    in capital markets, 544–547
    in human capital, 548–551
    in safety, 647
    under uncertainty, 619–622
invisible hand, 21
iPod, 369–371
isocost line, 218–220
isoquants
    defined, 184–188
    variation of marginal rate of technical substitution along, 190
iterated elimination of strictly dominated strategies
    defined, 443–444
    Nash equilibrium and, 444–445
iTunes price discrimination, 426–427

Jaws, 623
job interviews, 654
Jordan, Michael, 565–566

Kennedy tax cuts, 164
Kleenex Bath Tissue (KBT), 514
knowledge. *See* information

labor
    costs and changes in, 224–226
    diminishing marginal rate of technical substitution, 190–191
    diminishing marginal returns, 213
    estimating cost curves, 230–231
    factor market demand, 531–532
    on isocost line, 218–220
    long-run factor demand, 529–531
    marginal revenue product of, 534
    monopsony expenditures, 536–540
    perfect price discrimination in unions, 409
    production inputs, 176
    returns to scale in, 193–196
    short-run factor demand, 525–529
    in short-run production, 177–184
    substitution in long run production, 189–190
labor saving innovations, 199
labor supply curves
    income and substitution effects, 159–161
    income tax rates and, 163–167
    labor-leisure choice, 156–159
    shape, 161–163
Lagrangian method
    constrained maximization with, A:20–A:22
    finding utility maximization, 84–86
    maximizing outputs, 223–224
    minimizing costs with, 222–223
laser printers, 233
Laspeyres index, 127
last-dollar rule, 220–222
late bloomer, 544
Law of Demand
    defined, 13
    Giffen goods and, 114

law of diminishing marginal returns, 182–184
laws. *See also* policies
    against cartels, 478–480
    preventing opportunism, 640
    zoning as barrier to entry, 518
leader, 497
learning by doing, 234–236
leased cars, 682
leisure
    labor-leisure choice, 156–159
    on labor supply curve, 161–163
length of patents, 381
Lerner Index, 369–371, 491–492
licensing
    creating monopolies, 380
    occupational, 24
    taxicabs, 299–300
limited entry
    long-run market supply with, 270
    zero long-run profit with, 286–289
limited information, 644
limited liability, 174
limiting lemons, 640–643
linear case, 490–491
linear demand curves, 29–30
linear production functions
    defined, 186
    finding elasticity of substitution, 192
live music, 69, 86
loans, subprime, 683–685
local extrema, A:11–A:12
logarithm rule, A:9
logarithms, A:5–A:6
long run, 177
long-run competition
    equilibrium, 276–279
    firm supply curve, 267
    market supply curve, 268–276
    profit maximization, 266
    zero profit in, 286–289
long-run costs
    estimating cost curves vs. introspection, 230–231
    function, 227–228
    input choice, 218–226
    lowering, 231–236
    overview, 218
    shape of curves, 229–230
    variation with output, 226–228
long-run elasticities, 35–38
long-run factor demand, 529–531
long-run production
    diminishing marginal rates of technical substitution, 190–191
    isoquants, 184–188
    overview, 184
    substituting inputs, 189–190
    substitution elasticity, 191–193
losses
    aversion, 626–627
    consumption distortion, 314
    deadweight. *See* deadweight loss
lottery
    risk aversion and, 609
    working after winning, 162–163
low-output strategy, 442

low-probability gambles, 624
lowest-isocost rule, 220–222
luxury goods, 107

Malthus, Thomas, 182–184
Mamma Mia!, 412–415
management
    firm, 175
    relative productivity, 197
manufacturing. *See* production
maps
    function, A:1–A:2
    indifference, 62–63
    preference, 60–62
marginal costs
    curves, 212–213
    defined, 210
    effect of taxes on, 216–217
    externalities and, 567
    measuring producer surplus, 290–291
    in monopolistic competition, 515
    monopoly market power and elasticity of, 368
    shape of curve, 214
    telephone pole, 547–548
marginal expenditure, 536
marginal firms, 269
marginal product of labor
    graph interpretation, 180–181
    law of diminishing marginal returns, 182–184
    in short-run production, 178–179
marginal profits, 251
marginal rate of substitution
    competition and comparative advantage, 342–343
    defined, 67–69
    diminishing, 70
    efficient product mix, 342
marginal rate of technical substitution
    defined, 189–190
    diminishing, 190–191
    minimizing costs, 221
marginal rate of transformation
    comparative advantage and, 339–340
    competition and comparative advantage, 342–343
    defined, 75
    number of producers and, 341
marginal returns, law of diminishing, 182–184
marginal revenue
    defined, 252
    in monopolistic competition, 515
    in perfect price discrimination, 403–404
marginal revenue curves
    of monopolies, 360–361
    price elasticity of demand and, 362–363
marginal revenue product of labor
    defined, 526
    function, 534
marginal tax rates, 163–167
marginal utility
    defined, 68
    in mutually beneficial trades, 331–332

marginal utility of wealth
    risk aversion, 604
    risk neutrality, 607
    risk preference, 608
marginal value, 135
marginal willingness to pay, 135–139
market basket, 59
market clearing price, 22
market consumer surplus, 146–149
market equilibrium
    comparison of collusive, Cournot, Stackelberg and competitive equilibria, 505–508
    competitive factor, 532–534
    economic welfare and. *See* general equilibrium and economic welfare
    effect of specific tax, 39–40
    effect of trade policies on, 309–317
    long-run competition, 276–279
    of monopolistic competition, 515–516, 517–518
    of monopsony, 536
    of perfect price discrimination, 405
    policies that create wedge between supply and demand curves, 301–309
    policies that shift supply curves, 297–301
    price floors and, 49
    shocking, 22–27
    short-run competition, 264–266
    with shortages, 46
    in supply-and-demand model, 20–22
    who is taxed and, 43–44
market failure
    defined, 296
    due to asymmetric information, 632
    externalities and, 567–568
    monopolistic competition, 475
market power
    exhaustible resources and, 558
    government actions that reduce, 384–389
    hospital mergers, 482–483
    of monopolies, 367–371
    price discrimination and, 400
    from price ignorance, 643–646
market structures
    defined, 243
    externalities and, 575–578
    oligopoly, 475–476
markets
    capital. *See* capital markets
    competition. *See* competition
    competitive equilibrium in two interrelated, 324–326
    factor. *See* factor markets
    first-mover advantages and disadvantages, 460–461
    lemons, 636–643
    long-run supply curve, 268–276
    pollution, 581–582
    prices determining allocations, 3
    for public goods, 585–588
    short-run supply curve, 262–264
Marshall, Alfred, 114
Marshallian demand curves, 114
materials, 176

max operators, A:16
maximization
    with equality constraints, A:19–A:22
    example, A:16–A:17
    output, 223–224
    profit. *See* profit maximization
    utility, 331–332
    welfare, 293–296
maximizing behavior
    constraint on utility, 81–86
    income tax revenue, 166–167
    in modeling, 5–6
    in production function, 176
maximum of functions, A:11–A:14
McDonald's, 371
measures
    Arrow-Pratt of risk aversion, 610–612
    comparing welfare, 142–145
    consumer surplus, 135–139
    cost, 206–209
    producer surplus, 289–291
    short-run costs, 210–211
medallion systems, 299–300
median voters, 591
medical market, 147
mergers
    maintaining cartels, 482–483
    reducing free riding with, 590
metal monopolies, 378
methods
    Lagrangian, A:20–A:22
    substitution, A:19–A:20
microeconomics
    defined, 1–3
    models, 3–7
    summary, 8
    uses of models, 7–8
minimizing costs
    in consumer choice, 87–89
    with input choices, 220–223
    isocost line, 219
minimum efficient scale, 516
minimum of functions, A:11–A:14
minimum wage
    with incomplete coverage, 326–329
    in monopsonies, 539–540
    as price floor, 48–49
MIRS (modular integrated robotized system), 230
mixed strategies and multiple Nash equilibria, 446–450
modeling agency cartel, 480
models
    Bertrand oligopoly, 508–514
    competitive properties and applications. *See* competitive model
    Cournot oligopoly. *See* Cournot oligopoly model
    microeconomic, 3–7
    principal-agent problem, 661
    Stackelberg oligopoly. *See* Stackelberg oligopoly model
    two-period monopoly, 392
    uses of microeconomic, 7–8
modular integrated robotized system (MIRS), 230

monitoring contracts and moral hazards, 677–685
monopolies
    cost advantages that create, 377–380
    decisions over time and behavioral economics, 389–392
    defined, 50
    electric generation, 198
    externalities and, 575–577
    government actions that create, 380–384
    government actions that reduce market power, 384–389
    market power, 367–371
    market structure, 475–476
    overview, 358–359
    perfect price discrimination, 403–406
    price, 645–646
    problems, 395–397
    profit maximization, 359–367
    quantity discrimination, 410–411
    questions, 393–395
    single-price vs. multimarket price discrimination, 420
    summary, 392–393
    taxes and, 373–377
    two-period monopoly model, 392
    vs. competitive welfare with externalities, 577–578
    welfare effects of, 372–373
monopolistic competition
    defined, 475
    market structure, 475–476
    of oligopolies, 514–518
monopsony
    defined, 524
    factor markets, 535–540
monopsony power, 537
monotonicity, 60, A:3
moral hazards. *See also* contracts and moral hazards, 634
more-is-better property
    defined, 60
    finding optimal bundle, 80–81
    indifference curves, 62–64
    preference maps, 60–62
Morgenstern, Oskar, 603
movements along demand curves
    comparative statics, 24
    defined, 13–14
movements along indifference curves, 112–113
movements along supply curves, 17–18
Mugabe, Robert G., 47
multimarket analysis
    in corn and soybean markets, 325–326
    defined, 324–325
multimarket price discrimination
    defined, 403
    identifying groups, 417–419
    overview, 411–412
    with two groups, 412–417
    welfare effects of, 420
multiple Nash equilibria and mixed strategies, 446–450
multiple regression, B:3
multiplier, Lagrange, A:20–A:22

music
  contracts, 673–674
  price discrimination in, 426–427
  substitution between recorded and live, 69
mutual funds, 615
mutually beneficial trades, 331–333
mutually exclusive outcomes, 599–600

Nano, 200
Nash-Bertrand equilibrium
  with differentiated products, 510–514
  with identical products, 508–510
Nash-Cournot equilibrium
  comparison of collusive, Cournot, Stackelberg, competitive equilibria and, 505–508
  effect of government subsidy on, 500–502
  given government subsidization of airline, 504–505
  with nonidentical firms, 492–497
  of oligopoly, 484–488
  with two or more firms, 488–492
  vs. Nash-Bertrand equilibrium, 510
Nash equilibrium
  best response and, 444–446
  cooperation and, 450–452
  in dynamic entry games, 457–458
  in dynamic games, 459–460
  employment risks, 647
  free riding, 588
  multiple and mixed strategies, 446–450
  in noncooperative oligopolies, 483
  subgame perfect, 455–456
Nash-in-prices equilibrium, 508
Nash-in-quantities equilibrium, 484
Nash, John, 444
natural disaster insurance, 619
natural gas
  effect of price ceiling, 309
  regulation, 388–389
natural ingredients, 452
natural monopolies
  defined, 378–380
  eBay as, 391–392
necessities, 107
needs vs. wants, 7
negative correlation
  defined, 426
  diversification and, 614
negative externalities, 565
negotiation, 334
neighborhood, A:11
net present value, 621
  investing with uncertainty, 621
  investment methods, 545–546
net profit. *See also* profit, 427–429
network externalities, 390–392
neutral technical changes, 198
neutrality, risk. *See* risk neutrality
"never below the line" test, A:3–A:4
New York Stock Exchange Composite Index, 615
New York Stock Exchange (NYSE), 615
Newsom, Gavin, 365
no economies of scale, 229

nominal prices, 120
non-neutral technical changes, 199
nonattainment, 573
noncompetitive factor markets, 534–535
noncompetitive markets, 578
noncooperation
  in normal-form game, 442
  in oligopolies, 483
nondiversifiable risks, 618–619
nondurable services, 524
nonidentical consumers, 422–423
nonidentical firms, 492–497
nonoptimal price regulation, 386–387
nonprofit firms, 173–174
nonsatiation
  defined, 60
  in mutually beneficial trades, 331–332
nonuniform pricing. *See also* pricing, 398
normal-form games, 441–442
normal goods
  comparing welfare measures for, 142
  defined, 107
  income and substitution effects with, 112–113
  necessity of, 108–109
  shipping fees and, 120
normative statements, 6–7
not-for-profit sector, 173–174
number of units in auctions, 463
NYSE (New York Stock Exchange), 615

objective experts, 640
objective functions, A:16
observable characteristics, 417
occupational licensing, 24
OECD (Organization for Economic Cooperation and Development), 164
oil drilling
  learning by doing, 235
  taxing, 36–38
oil sands, 259
oil shale, 259
oligopolies
  Bertrand model, 508–514
  cartels, 477–483
  comparison of collusive, Cournot, Stackelberg and competitive equilibria, 505–508
  defined, 50
  game theory and, 437
  market structures, 475–476
  monopolistic competition, 514–518
  noncooperative, 483
  overview, 474–475
  problems, 520–523
  questions, 519–520
  summary, 518–519
oligopsony, 535
OPEC (Organization of Petroleum Exporting Countries), 479
open-access common property, 582–584
opportunistic behavior
  avoiding with contract choice, 685–686
  controlling with universal coverage, 634
  defined, 632

  due to asymmetric information, 633–634
  laws preventing, 640
  monitoring, 677–685
opportunity costs
  capital costs and, 207–209
  deadweight loss, 294
  defined, 206–207
  profit maximization, 249
opportunity set
  cash vs. food stamps, 151–152
  defined, 75
opt in vs. opt out programs, 91
optimal bundle, 76–81
optimal price regulation, 384–386
optimal product mixes, 341
optimal provision of public goods, 586–588
ordinal preferences, 65–66
Organization for Economic Cooperation and Development (OECD), 164
Organization of Petroleum Exporting Countries (OPEC), 479
organizational innovations, 199–200
outcomes, 597
output decisions
  in long-run competition, 266
  rules for maximizing profits, 250–252
  in short-run competition, 253–257
outputs
  choosing price vs. quantity in monopolies, 366
  cost of producing multiple goods, 237–238
  cumulative, 235
  defined, 173
  forming cartels, 477–478
  isoquants, 184–188
  law of diminishing marginal returns, 182–184
  long-run cost variation with, 226–228
  long-run market supply with varying prices, 271–273
  maximizing, 223–224
  monopoly profit maximization, 363–365
  production, 176
  short-run cost measures and, 210
  short-run production, 177–184
  why less than competitive lowers welfare, 293–294
  why more than competitive lowers welfare, 295–296
overbidding, 465, 466
overcompensation, 122–125
overconfidence, 623
overhead, 210
overpopulation, 182–184
overuse of common property, 583–584
ownership
  endowment effect, 90–91
  firm, 173–176

Paasche index, 127
Pacific Gas & Electric (PG&E), 547–548
package tie-in sales, 424
paper mill pollution

cost-benefit analysis, 569
regulations, 572–573
supply-and-demand analysis, 566–568
parallel markets, 47
Pareto efficient
competition and comparative advantage, 344
competitive equilibrium as, 337
defined, 322
free trade as, 329, 332–333
obtaining efficient allocation using competition, 337–338
Pareto principle
defined, 322
government use of, 346–348
for optimal provision of public goods, 587
partial derivatives, A:9–A:11
partial-equilibrium analysis
in corn and soybean markets, 325–326
defined, 323
partnerships, 174
patents
creating monopolies, 381–383
defined, 358
payoff functions
cooperation and, 450–453
defined, 439
payoff matrix, 441
perfect competition
defined, 243
overview, 244–248
perfect complements, 71–72
perfect information
in game theory, 440
in repeated games, 461
perfect Nash equilibrium, subgame, 455–456
perfect negative correlation, 614
perfect positive correlation, 614
perfect price discrimination, 402, 403–409
perfect substitutes
defined, 70–71
deriving demand curves with, 99–100
perfectly competitive markets, 49–50
perfectly elastic demand curves, 30
perfectly elastic supply curves, 34
perfectly inelastic demand curves
defined, 29
effect of specific tax on, 41–42
perfectly inelastic supply curves, 34
permits, 297–300
personal budget constraints, 74–75
Personal Responsibility and Work Opportunity Reconciliation Act (PRWORA), 155
personal seat licenses, 420
PG&E (Pacific Gas & Electric), 547–548
Philadelphia, 329
philosophy, utilitarian, 351–352
piece rate, 662, 676–677
piracy, 383–384
policies
comparing trade, 309–317
effects on consumer welfare, 149–156
externality regulation, 569–575

government subsidization of airline, 500–505
laws against cartels, 478–480
price controls, 45–49
strategic trade with Stackelberg model, 500–505
tax salience and, 92
that create wedge between supply and demand curves, 301–309
that shift supply curves, 297–301
using Pareto principle in, 346–348
pollution externalities. *See* externalities
polynomial rule, A:8
pooling equilibrium, 650–652
positive correlation, 614
positive externalities, 565–566
positive monotonic transformation, 66
positive network externalities, 390
positive statements, 6–7
possible Nash equilibrium, 448–449
power rule, A:8
prediction
game outcome, 442–446
with modeling, 3–7
uses of microeconomic models, 7–8
preference relations, 59
preferences
allocating equity through voting, 348–352
in consumer choice, 58–64
ordinal, 65–66
present bias, 551
risk, 604, 608
valuing public goods, 592
prescription drugs, 414–417
present bias, 551, 552
present value
defined, 542
investing with uncertainty, 621
preventing resales, 400–402
price
advertising and, 646
airline ticket and rivalry, 494–495
allocation of scarce resources, 3
choosing in monopolies, 366
comparative statics, 22–27
costs and changes in factor, 224–226
demand considerations, 10
in demand function, 11–15
driving market equilibrium, 21–22
equilibrium, 20
exhaustible resource, 553–558
inflation indexes, 120–122
of leisure, 157–159
long-run competitive equilibrium, 276–279
long-run market supply with varying, 271–273
market power from ignorance, 643–646
in monopolistic competition, 515
monopoly market power and elasticity of, 367–368
profit maximization and, 260–262
regulating monopoly, 384–389
short-run competitive equilibrium, 264–266

in supply function, 16–18
theory, 1
tourist-trap model, 644–645
price ceilings
defined, 45–48
welfare effects of, 307–309
price-consumption curves, 101–102
price elasticity of demand
defined, 28–32
in monopolies, 362–363
price elasticity of supply, 34–35
price-fixing, 477–483
price floors
defined, 48–49
welfare effect of, 303–307
price increases
comparing three welfare measures, 142–145
compensated demand curves, 114–116
effect on consumer surplus, 138–139
effects on demand, 111
exhaustible resource, 556–557
income and substitution effects with inferior good, 113–114
income and substitution effects with normal good, 112–113
indifference curve analysis of, 141–142
loss of market consumer surplus, 146
policies that shift supply curves, 297–300
Slutsky equation, 116–120
welfare effect of sales tax, 301–303
price markup, 369
price setters
defined, 50
monopolies as, 358
price takers
defined, 49–50
perfect competition, 244
Priceline.com, 418–419
pricing
advertising, 427–431
multimarket discrimination. *See* multimarket price discrimination
overview, 398–399
perfect discrimination, 403–409
price fixing in cartels, 477–483
problems, 434–436
quantity discrimination, 410–411
questions, 432–434
summary, 431–432
tie-in sales, 423–427
two-part tariffs, 420–423
why and how firms discriminate, 399–403
Prince, 35
principal-agent problem, 660–663
principals, 659–660
priorité de droite, 449
prisoners' dilemma
cooperation and, 450–452
defined, 443
private costs, 566
private firms, 173–174
private marginal costs, 567
private producer surplus, 567
private sector, 173–174

private value
  bidding in private-value auctions, 464–466
  defined, 464
probabilities
  degree of risk, 598–600
  difficulty in assessing, 622–624
  investing with altered, 621–622
  low-probability gambles, 624
  in mixed strategies, 447–448
producer surplus
  defined, 285
  externalities and, 567
  maximizing welfare, 293–296
  measuring with supply curve, 289–291
  using, 291–292
producer welfare, 289–292
producers
  comparative advantage and number of, 341
  incidence of tax on, 43–44
product liability laws, 640
product rule, A:7
production
  costs of multiple good, 237–238
  efficiency and moral hazards, 663–670
  efficiency in, 662
  excess, 305
  firms and, 172–173
  long-run. *See* long-run production
  overview, 176–177
  payments linked to, 676–677
  prices determining allocations, 3
  problems, 203–204
  questions, 201–203
  returns to scale, 193–196
  short-run. *See* short-run production
  summary, 200–201
  supply considerations, 16
  technical change and productivity, 196–200
  trade and, 338–344
  trade-offs, 2
  trade-offs between efficiency and risk-bearing, 670–675
  why less output lowers welfare, 293–294
  why more output lowers welfare, 295–296
production functions
  Cobb-Douglas. *See* Cobb-Douglas production functions
  defined, 176
  shape of cost curves and, 213–216
production possibility frontier
  comparative advantage and, 338–341
  defined, 237–238
  efficient product mix, 342
profit
  defined, 248–250
  payments linked to, 676–677
  producer surplus and, 291
  zero long-run in competitive model, 286–289
profit matrix
  for dominant strategy, 441
  for iterated dominance, 443

profit maximization
  with asymmetric information, 667–670
  comparison of collusive, Cournot, Stackelberg, competitive equilibria and, 505–508
  competition, 248–253
  in competitive model, 289
  cooperation and, 450–452
  in Cournot model, 484–488
  with efficient contract, 663–664
  firm management, 175–176
  forming cartels, 477–478
  with full information, 665–667
  long-run competition, 266
  long-run factor demand, 529
  monopoly, 359–367
  monopsony, 536–540
  with price discrimination, 399–403
  short-run competition, 253–259
  short-run factor demand, 525–529
profit-sharing contracts
  with asymmetric information, 669
  defined, 667
progress, technical, 198–200
properties
  competitive model. *See* competitive model
  consumer preference, 59–60
  function, A:2–A:6
  isoquant, 185–186
  market structures, 476
  open-access common property, 582–584
  prospect theory, 626–627
property rights
  allocating to reduce externalities, 578–582
  externalities and, 564
  open-access common property, 582–584
  piracy and, 383–384
prospect theory, 625–627
protectionary policies
  rent seeking, 316–317
  tariffs, 314
PRWORA (Personal Responsibility and Work Opportunity Reconciliation Act), 155
public firms, 173–174
public goods, 564, 584–591
public sector, 173–174
public utilities, 379
punishment for opportunism, 682
purchasing considerations, 10–11
pure strategy, 446–447

quadratic short-run cost functions, 363
quality, 636–643
quantity
  choosing in monopolies, 366
  comparative statics, 22–27
  demand, 10
  demand for with income increases, 106–111
  in demand function, 11–15
  discrimination, 402, 410–411

equality between supply and demand, 44–49
  equilibrium, 20
  stocks and flows, 540–541
  supply, 16
quantity-setting game, 441–442
quasilinear utility functions
  comparing three welfare measures, 145
  defined, 72–73
  deriving demand curves with, 100
quitting smoking, 103
quotas
  effect on consumer welfare, 149–151
  in international trade, 309
  vs. free trade, 315–316
quotient rule, A:8

Radiohead, 589
railroads, 238
range of function, A:1–A:2
Rank, Mark, 151
rank ordering, 65–66
ranked voting, 350–351
rare earth element monopolies, 378
rates
  defined, 75
  discount, 542
  interest, 541–542
  of return, 544–547
rational preferences, 60
rationing, 149–151
Rawls, John, 352
Rawlsian welfare functions, 352
Reagan tax cuts, 164
real prices, 120
rebates, 419
reciprocal rule, A:8
record companies, 673–674
recorded music
  finding utility maximization, 86
  marginal rate of substitution, 69
recovering preferences, 128–129
redistribution of wealth, 344–346
Redwood trees, 556–557
reflection effect, 625
regression, B:1–B:3
regulations. *See also* policies
  demand considerations, 11
  externality, 569–575
  monopoly, 384–389
  supply considerations, 16
  taxicab, 297–300
relative productivity, 197–198
relocating workers, 126
rent seeking, 316–317
rents
  capital markets and investing, 540
  exhaustible resource, 555–556
  fixed-fee with asymmetric information, 668
  fixed-fee with full information, 665
  zero long-run profit and, 287–289
repeated games, 461–462
reputation, 640–641
requirement tie-in sales, 424

resales
    preventing, 400–402
    price discrimination and, 400
research stimulation, 381
reservation price
    defined, 403
    lemons market, 637
residual demand curves
    of Cournot model, 485
    defined, 246–248
residual profit, 661
residual supply curves, 273–274
resources
    creating monopolies, 377–378
    exhaustible, 553–558
    microeconomics of, 1–3
restructuring, 198
retirement savings, 543–544
returns to scale
    long run curve shapes, 229
    in production, 193–196
returns to specialization, 196
revealed preference, 128–129
revenue
    income tax rates and labor supply curve, 163–167
    marginal revenue product of labor function, 534
    profit maximization, 248
    short-run factor demand, 525–526
    shutdown rule, 253
    tax and rent seeking, 316
revenue-sharing contracts
    with asymmetric information, 669
    with full information, 666–667
reverse auctions, 418–419
right angle indifference curves, 71–72
rights
    grants/auctions of monopoly, 380–381
    patent, 381–383
risk
    of adverse selection, 635
    attitudes toward, 604–610
    avoidance, 612–619
    defined, 597
    degree of, 598–602
    information about employment, 646–647
    trade-offs between efficiency in production and risk-bearing, 670–675
risk aversion
    defined, 603
    degree of, 610–612
    expected utility and, 604–607
    gambling and, 608–610
    investing and, 620–621
risk-bearing, 662
risk neutrality
    defined, 604
    expected utility and, 607–608
    investing and, 620
risk pooling, 613–615
risk preference
    defined, 604
    expected utility and, 608
risk premium, 605–606

rivalry
    air ticket price, 494–495
    public goods and, 584–585
rules for calculating derivatives, A:7–A:9
rules of game, 439

S&P 500 (Standard & Poor's Composite Index of 500 Stocks), 615
saddle point, A:17
safety, 646–647
sales tax
    effects on supply-and-demand model, 38–44
    welfare effect of, 301–303
salience, 91–92
San Francisco, 365
satiation, 60
saving for retirement, 543–544
scale
    economies of, 229
    returns in production, 193–196
scarce inputs, 286–288
scarce resources
    allocation of, 1–3
    factor markets of exhaustible, 553–557
    that create monopolies, 377–378
scope, economies of, 237–238
Scott, Dr. Alan, 381–382
screening
    consumer, 640–641
    controlling opportunism with, 635
    in hiring, 654–655
sealed-bid auctions
    defined, 463
    equivalence of outcomes, 465–466
seat options, 420
second-degree price discrimination, 402
second derivatives, A:9
second-order conditions, A:16
second-price auctions
    consumer surplus, 137–138
    defined, 463
    strategies in, 464–465
Second Theorem of Welfare Economics, 338
secret ingredients, 452
seeking rents, 316–317
selection, adverse. See adverse selection
self-control, 552
selling
    exhaustible resources, 553
    perfect competition, 245
semiconductors, 187–188, 225–226
separating equilibrium, 650–652
sequential games, 454–461
sequential movement, 498–500
services
    preventing resales, 400
    prices determining allocations, 3
    trade-offs, 2
setting prices. See pricing
several variable functions, A:2
shading bid, 466
shapes
    importance of supply and demand curve, 27
    isoquant, 186

labor supply curve, 161–163
    of long-run cost curves, 229–230
    monopoly market power and demand curve, 367–368
    production functions and cost curve, 213–216
shareholders, 174
sharing contracts, 662
shark attacks, 623
Sherman Antitrust Act in 1809, 478
shift of demand curves
    defined, 14–15
    due to income changes, 103–106
    effect in monopolies, 366–367
shift of supply curves
    comparative statics, 24
    effect depending on demand curve shape, 27
    policies that create, 297–301
shipping fees, 120
shirking
    defined, 634
    monitoring, 677–685
    preventing with contract choice, 685–686
shocks to equilibrium
    defined, 22–27
    using consumer surplus to study, 146
    using producer surplus to study, 291
short run, 177
short-run competition
    equilibrium, 264–266
    firm supply curve, 260–262
    market supply curve, 262–264
    profit maximization, 253–259
short-run costs
    curves, 212–213
    effect of taxes on, 216–217
    expansion paths, 233–234
    long-run costs as envelope for, 231–233
    measures, 210–211
    overview, 209–210
    production functions and shape of cost curves, 213–216
    summary, 217
short-run factor demand, 525–529
short-run labor demand
    comparing to long-run labor demand, 530–531
    defined, 526–529
short-run production
    interpretation of graphs, 180–181
    law of diminishing marginal returns, 182–184
    overview, 177–179
short-run vs. long-run elasticities, 35–38
shortages, 46
shutdown rule
    defined, 252–253
    in long-run competition, 266
    in monopolies, 365–366
    in short-run competition, 257–259
signaling
    controlling opportunism with, 635–636
    defined, 461–462

education as signal of ability, 649–653
limiting lemons with, 642–643
simplification by assumption, 4–5
single price monopolies, 420
single variable functions, A:1–A:2
size, returns to, 193–196
slope
derivatives, A:6–A:11
finding function extrema, A:14–A:15
Law of Demand, 13–14
supply curves, 18
Slutsky equation
comparing three welfare measures, 144
defined, 116–120
smoking, 103
smuggling prescription drugs, 414–417
sniping, 138
snob effect, 390
social costs
defined, 566
open-access common property, 583
social marginal costs, 567–568
social pressures, 590
social welfare functions, 348–352
society's welfare, 293–296
sole proprietorships, 174
soybean market
partial-equilibrium vs. multimarket analysis of, 325–326
subsidies, 304–306
specialization, returns to, 196
specific tariffs, 312
specific taxes
defined, 39
dependence of effects on elasticities, 40–43
effect on monopolies, 373–376
effect on monopolies vs. ad valorem tax, 376–377
effect on oligopolistic markets, 490
equilibrium effects of, 39–40
same equilibrium no matter who is taxed, 43–44
welfare effect of, 301–303
spillover effects, 324
splitting contracts, 662
sport-utility vehicles (SUVs)
finding optimal bundle, 78–79
negative externality, 565
spurious product differentiation, 496–497
square root functions, A:2
Stackelberg, Heinrich von, 497
Stackelberg oligopoly model
calculus solution, 497–498
comparison with collusive, Cournot and competitive equilibria, 505–508
defined, 483
essential sequential movement, 498–500
graphical solution, 498
strategic trade policy, 500–505
Standard & Poor's Composite Index of 500 Stocks (S&P 500), 615
standard deviation in degree of risk, 601–602
standard errors, B:3
standards, limiting lemons, 641–642

state-run insurance pools, 619
states of nature
defined, 597
expected value, 600
principal-agent problem, 661
static games
cooperation, 450–453
defined, 440
multiple Nash equilibria and mixed strategies, 446–450
normal-form games, 441–442
predicting game outcome, 442–446
statics, comparative. See comparative statics
statistical discrimination, 654–655
steppers, 188
stocks
defined, 540
mutual funds, 615
storage opportunities, 35–36
straight indifference curves, 70–71
strategic advertising, 452–453
strategic behavior, 439
strategic interdependence, 439
strategic trade policy, 500–505
strategies
bidding in private-value auctions, 464–466
in game theory, 439
multiple Nash equilibria and mixed, 446–450
for normal-form game, 441–442
predicting game outcome, 442–446
sequential game, 454–461
stream of payments, 542–544
strict concavity, A:4
strict convexity, A:4–A:5
strict preferences, 59
subgame perfect Nash equilibrium, 455–456
subgames, 454–455
subjective probabilities
of risk, 598–599
risk aversion and, 606–607
subprime borrowing, 683–685
subscription, 429–430
subsidies
child care, 154–156
food stamps, 151–153
government airline, 500–505
monopoly regulation and, 387–389
subscription by advertising, 429–430
Theory of the Second Best, 353–354
welfare effect of price floor, 303–307
substitution
budget constraints, 75
CES and demand, 98–99
constrained maximization with, A:19–A:20
CPI bias, 126–127
curvature of indifference curves, 70–73
demand considerations, 10
demand elasticities over time, 35–36
deriving demand curves with perfect, 100
diminishing marginal rates of technical substitution, 190–191

finding utility maximization, 82–84
input, 187–188
isoquant, 186
long-run production inputs, 189–190
market power and, 371
saving endangered species, 33
willingness and utility, 67–69
substitution effects
in compensated demand curve, 114–116
deriving with Slutsky equation, 114–116
effects with inferior good and income, 113–114
on labor supply curves, 159–161
with normal good, 112–113
price increases and, 111
revealed preference, 129
substitution elasticity
deriving with Slutsky equation, 117–118
in long-run production, 191–193
summary statistics, 28
summing
demand functions, 15–16
supply functions, 18–19
sunk costs
defined, 209
shutdown rule, 252–253
supervision, 677–685
supply, 16–20
supply-and-demand model
comparative statics, 22–27
demand, 10–16
demand elasticity, 28–33
effects of sales tax, 38–44
long run vs. short run elasticities, 35–38
market equilibrium, 20–22
overview, 9–10
problems, 54–56
quantity equality between, 44–49
questions, 51–54
summary, 51
supply, 16–20
supply elasticity, 34–35
when to use, 49–50
supply curves
defined, 17–18
finding market equilibrium with, 20–21
firm long-run competition, 267
firm short-run competition, 260–262
import policies affect on, 19–20
labor. See labor supply curves
lack of in monopolies, 366
market long-run competition, 268–276
market short-run competition, 262–264
measuring producer surplus with, 289–291
monopsony, 536
policies that create wedge between demand curves and, 301–309
policies that shift, 297–301
shapes of, 27

I-16 Index

supply elasticities
  defined, 34–35
  over time, 36–38
supply functions
  finding market equilibrium with, 21
  summing, 18–19
supply shock, 27
surgeons, 642
surplus, consumer. *See* consumer surplus
surplus, producer. *See* producer surplus
SUVs (sport-utility vehicles)
  finding optimal bundle, 78–79
  negative externality, 565
Swarthmore college, 208–209
symmetric information, 637–638

tacit collusion, 479
talk is cheap, 648–649
tangency rule, 220–222
tariffs
  defined, 309
  limiting resales with, 402
  two-part, 420–423
  vs. free trade, 312–315
Tata Motors, 200
Tax Act of 2003, 79
taxes
  cigarette, 103
  to control pollution, 573–575
  distribution of wealth, 345
  effect of income tax on labor supply curves, 163–167
  effect on long-run competitive equilibrium, 278–279
  effect on oligopolistic markets, 490
  effect on short-run costs, 216–217
  effect on short-run equilibrium, 265–266
  effect on short-run labor demand, 528–529
  effects of sales, 38–44
  externality in noncompetitive markets, 578
  markets in which consumer surplus losses are large, 146
  monopolies and, 373–377
  salience, 91–92
  wage, 329
taxicab regulations, 297–300
technological efficiency
  defined, 175
  determining, 205
  input choices, 218–226
technology
  change and productivity, 190–191
  diminishing marginal rates of technical substitution, 190–191
  economies of scale and innovation, 230
  exhaustible resources and, 558
  marginal rate of technical substitution, 189–190
telephone poles, 547–548
television, 142
testing
  hires, 654
  theories, 5
  transitivity property, 89–90

theories
  Arrow's Impossibility Theorem, 350
  Coase Theorem, 578–581
  Envelope Theorem, A:18
  Euler's homogeneous function theorem, A:11
  expected utility, 603, 625–626
  Extreme Value Theorem, A:12–A:13
  First Theorem of Welfare Economics, 337
  game. *See* game theory
  prospect, 625–627
  revealed preference, 128–129
  Second Theorem of Welfare Economics, 338
  testing, 5
Theory of the Second Best, 353–354
third-party comparisons, 641
thread mill
  comparing short and long-run labor demand curves, 531
  short-run labor demand, 526–527
threatening to punish, 461–462
tie-in sales
  defined, 399
  price and, 423–427
time
  consistency, 551
  discounts that vary, 551–552
  in game theory, 439
  monopolies and decisions over, 389–392
  production and variability of inputs, 177
  stocks and flows, 540–541
tobacco industry
  consumer surplus in, 147
  consumption and income, 103
  deadweight loss in, 508
  rent seeking, 317
  returns to scale in, 194–196
toilet paper variety, 514
torts, 672
total cost curves, 212–213
total costs, 210
total effect, 112–113
total product of labor, 177–178
tourist-trap model, 644–646
trade
  comparative advantage and benefits of, 340
  comparing policies, 309–317
  exchange economy, 329–334
  long-run market supply curve with, 273–276
  market in pollution, 581–582
  production and, 338–344
  strategic policies with Stackelberg model, 500–505
  Theory of the Second Best, 353–354
trade-offs
  defined, 2
  between efficiency and risk-bearing, 670–675
traffic accidents, 574–575
transaction costs
  defined, 50

  lowering with tie-in sales, 424
  perfect competition, 245
  perfect price discrimination and, 408–409
  preventing resales, 400–401
transformation, 75
transitivity property
  defined, 59–60
  indifference curves, 62–64
  preference maps, 60–62
  tests of, 89–90
transportation market
  consumer surplus in, 147
  economies of scope, 238
true cost-of-living adjustments, 124–125
Twinkie tax, 3
two-part tariffs
  defined, 399
  price and, 420–423
two-period monopoly model, 392
two-stage game, 454–461

unbiased estimates, B:2
uncertainty
  attitudes toward risk, 604–610
  avoiding risk, 612–619
  behavioral economics, 622–627
  decision-making under, 602–603
  degree of risk, 598–602
  degree of risk aversion, 610–612
  expected utility theory, 603
  investing under, 619–622
  overview, 597–598
  problems, 629–631
  questions, 628–629
  summary, 627–628
uncompensated demand curves
  defined, 114–115
  effect of price increase on consumer surplus, 138–139
uncorrelated outcomes, 614
unearned income
  income and substitution effects on labor supply curves, 159–161
  labor-leisure choice, 157–159
  shape of labor supply curves, 161–163
unemployment, 48–49
unions, 409
unique equilibrium, 651–652
unique extrema, A:14
unit taxes, 39
unitary elasticity, 29
United States distribution of wealth, 344–346
United States electric generation efficiency, 198
United States Food Stamp Plan, 151
United States Postal Service (USPS), 371
United States Statistical Abstract, 174
universal coverage, 634
unobserved actions
  defined, 634
  principal-agent problem, 660–663
unobserved characteristics, 633
U.S. distribution of wealth, 344–346
U.S. electric generation efficiency, 198
U.S. Food Stamp Plan, 151

U.S. Postal Service (USPS), 371
U.S. Statistical Abstract, 174
uses of microeconomic models, 7–8
uses of supply-and-demand model, 49–50
utilitarian philosophy, 351–352
utilities market
   consumer surplus in, 147
   electric generation efficiency, 198
   public as natural monopoly, 379
   quantity discrimination, 410–411
utility
   cash vs. food stamps, 151–153
   constraint on maximizing, 81–86
   expected utility theory, 603
   indifference curves curvature, 70–73
   minimizing expenditure while maximizing, 87–89
   in mutually beneficial trades, 331–332
   willingness to substitute, 67–69
utility curves
   defined, 66–67
   indifference curves and, 66–67
utility functions
   CES, 83–84
   Cobb-Douglas. *See* Cobb-Douglas utility functions
   in consumer choice, 64–65
   consumer welfare, 135
   deriving demand curves with, 98–100
   indifference curves and, 66–67
   quasilinear, 72–73
utility possibility frontier, 348
utils, 64

value
   auctioned good, 464
   critical, A:16
   expected, 600–601
   investing with uncertainty, 621
   marginal, 135
   net present, 545–546
   prospect theory function, 626–627
   of public goods, 590–592
   stocks and flows, 540–541
   variance and standard deviation from expected, 601–602
value functions, A:18
value judgments
   food stamps, 153
   positive vs. normative statements, 6–7

variable costs
   defined, 210
   measuring producer surplus, 290–291
   shape of curve, 214–215
variable inputs
   defined, 177
   in short-run production, 179
variable quality, 639–640
variables
   environmental, 23–26
   exogenous, 23
   function, A:1–A:2
variance in degree of risk, 601–602
varying scale economies, 197
vertical demand curves, 31
vertical integration, 401
vertical supply curves
   elasticities along, 34
   of labor, 162
Viagra, 33
von Neumann, John, 603
voting
   allocating equity through, 349–351
   valuing public goods, 591–592

wages
   in company towns, 538–539
   costs and changes in, 224–226
   effect of plague on, 533–534
   effect on short-run labor demand, 527–528
   efficiency, 680–681
   in hire contracts, 662
   income and substitution effects on labor supply curves, 159–161
   income tax rate effect on, 163–167
   labor-leisure choice, 157–159
   minimum with incomplete coverage, 326–329
   set by unions, 409
wants vs. needs, 7
water, bottled, 496–497
water quotas, 150–151
weak concavity, A:4
weak convexity, A:4
weak domination, 464
weak preferences, 59
wealth, distribution of, 344–346
weather, 613
wedge, 44

weighted income elasticities, 110–111
welfare
   in competitive model, 289–292
   consumer. *See* consumer welfare
   defined, 285
   effect of government airline subsidy on, 502
   effect of trade policies on, 309–317
   effects of monopolies, 372–373
   effects of monopsony, 540, 541
   effects of multimarket price discrimination, 420
   effects of taxes on monopolies, 376–377
   externalities that affect. *See* externalities
   general equilibrium and economic. *See* general equilibrium and economic welfare
   maximizing with competition, 293–296
   policies that create wedge between supply and demand curves, 301–310
   policies that shift supply curves, 297–301
   product differentiation and, 513–514
welfare economics, 285
willingness to accept, 296
willingness to pay
   deadweight loss of Christmas presents, 296
   measuring consumer welfare, 135–139
   for public goods, 586
Wilshire 5000 Index Portfolio, 615
winner's curse, 466
Wolff, Lewis, 546
Woods, Tiger, 288–289
wool subsidy, 303
worker relocation, 126
The World's Water 2008–2009, 496

Xerox, 371

zero functions, A:2
zero long-run profit, 286–289
Zimbabwe, 47–48
zoning laws, 518